KU-620-605

PRINCIPLES OF ADMINISTRATIVE LAW

LEGAL
REGULATION
OF
GOVERNANCE

LIVERPOOL JMU LIBRARY

3 1111 01415 3058

WITHDRAWN

PRINCIPLES OF ADMINISTRATIVE LAW

LEGAL
REGULATION
OF
GOVERNANCE

SECOND
EDITION

PETER CANE • LEIGHTON MCDONALD

OXFORD
UNIVERSITY PRESS
AUSTRALIA & NEW ZEALAND

OXFORD
UNIVERSITY PRESS

Oxford University Press is a department of the University of Oxford.

It furthers the University's objective of excellence in research, scholarship, and education by publishing worldwide. Oxford is a registered trademark of Oxford University Press in the UK and in certain other countries.

Published in Australia by
Oxford University Press
253 Normanby Road, South Melbourne, Victoria 3205, Australia

© Peter Cane and Leighton McDonald 2012

The moral rights of the authors have been asserted.

First published 2008
Second edition published 2012

All rights reserved. No part of this publication may be reproduced, stored in a retrieval system, or transmitted, in any form or by any means, without the prior permission in writing of Oxford University Press, or as expressly permitted by law, by licence, or under terms agreed with the appropriate reprographics rights organisation. Enquiries concerning reproduction outside the scope of the above should be sent to the Rights Department, Oxford University Press, at the address above.

You must not circulate this work in any other form and you must impose this same condition on any acquirer.

National Library of Australia Cataloguing-in-Publication entry

Author: Cane, Peter, 1950–
Title: Principles of administrative law: legal regulation of governance / Peter Cane, Leighton McDonald.

Edition: 2nd ed.

ISBN: 9780195576092 (pbk.)

Notes: Includes index.
Subjects: Administrative law—Australia.

Other Authors/Contributors: McDonald, Leighton.

Dewey Number: 342.9406

Reproduction and communication for educational purposes

The Australian *Copyright Act 1968* (the Act) allows a maximum of one chapter or 10% of the pages of this work, whichever is the greater, to be reproduced and/or communicated by any educational institution for its educational purposes provided that the educational institution (or the body that administers it) has given a remuneration notice to Copyright Agency Limited (CAL) under the Act.

For details of the CAL licence for educational institutions contact:

Copyright Agency Limited
Level 15, 233 Castlereagh Street
Sydney NSW 2000
Telephone: (02) 9394 7600
Facsimile: (02) 9394 7601
Email: info@copyright.com.au

Edited by Joy Window
Typeset by diacriTech
Proofread by Roz Edmond
Indexed by Julie King
Printed by Sheck Wah Tong Printing Press Ltd.

Links to third party websites are provided by Oxford in good faith and for information only. Oxford disclaims any responsibility for the materials contained in any third party website referenced in this work.

Contents

Table of Cases

Preface

We acknowledge and celebrate the First Australians on whose traditional lands we live and work and whose cultures are among the oldest continuing cultures in the world.

Law books come in various shapes and sizes. The traditional textbook is very long and sets out to deal comprehensively with an area of law. A book with 'introduction' in its title may be a sort of short textbook that aims to provide the student with rudimentary rather than detailed coverage of the subject. A monograph typically has a narrower focus than either a short or a long text, dealing in depth with one topic or a small set of related topics within an area of law. Unlike the typical textbook, a monograph will often contain an overarching 'thesis' or 'argument' that the author wants to explore or defend.

This book does not fall neatly into any of these categories. It is shorter than the typical textbook but longer than the typical introduction. While we provide no single or unitary explanation of or argument about administrative law, throughout the book we develop a number of themes to help the reader find in administrative law a whole that is more than the sum of its various and often confusing parts. By introducing insights from legal history, comparative law, legal theory and empirical legal research, our aim has been to offer a set of ideas, and to suggest ways of thinking about administrative law that will provide a path through a dense and confusing mass of detail. In short, we have tried not just to provide a statement of the law but also to interpret and make some sense of it. This objective has necessarily required us to leave out a lot of the detail to be found in longer books. However, we have tried to avoid the trap, into which short books sometimes fall, of making the law seem more straightforward and clear than it actually is. Not everyone will approve of our presentation and interpretations of the law or agree with all our arguments; but that is inevitable and, indeed, desirable. More important by far than simply learning the law is learning to think critically about the law.

We hope this book will be of interest to readers who already have some knowledge of the subject in addition to serving its primary objective of facilitating the learning of those coming to the subject for the first time. To assist with the book's primary purpose, it is supplemented by a companion volume of cases and materials. Such volumes were originally introduced (in the USA in the late nineteenth century) to facilitate an interactive, 'Socratic' form of teaching; but more often now they merely provide a sort of portable library of relevant (and, often, much abridged) readings. Some cases and materials volumes include significant amounts of connecting 'text' as well as questions and comments on the extracts; and such a volume can be thought of as a sort of 'illustrated textbook'. Once again, our volume of cases and materials does not fit this mould. It contains fewer extracts than is typical and those extracts are generally longer than is usual. You can read more about how best to use the cases and materials volume in its preface.

In the context of the delivery of university-level administrative law courses, we are hopeful that the use of this book will free up more class time than might otherwise be available for intellectually rewarding explorations of the complexities and uncertainties of the law. By setting out the key principles and essential technical details of the subject, the book is intended to enable teachers and students to use class time to engage with our interpretations and arguments, to consider practical applications of the principles we discuss, and to allow space for critical analysis based on particular cases and other readings that may also be prescribed. This sort of engagement with administrative law will, we believe, enable students to understand better the limits and promise of administrative law in appropriately mediating the relationship between the 'governors' and the 'governed' in our society.

There have been various significant changes in the law since we wrote the first edition. The most obvious difference between this edition and the first is the addition of a new chapter on freedom of information (FOI). Our decision to expand the treatment of FOI was partly a result of feedback from users of the first edition but also partly of major changes, in 2009 and 2010, to the federal FOI regime, which make it one of the most innovative in the world. Further, numerous important cases have been woven into the judicial review chapters. The chapters on the Scope of Judicial Review and Restricting Judicial Review have been restructured and rewritten in light of cases such as *Kirk, Plaintiff M61*, and *Futuris*. More generally, the whole text has been updated to take account of recent developments. In this respect, we note that although the High Court's decision in *Williams v Commonwealth* [2012] HCA 23 was handed down after the manuscript had been delivered, we were able to incorporate some preliminary discussion of this important decision in Chapters 3 and 11. Similarly, reference has been made to the decision in *Public Service Association of South Australia Inc v Industrial Relations Commission of South Australia* [2012] HCA 25. On the other hand, *Plaintiff S10/2011 v Minister for Immigration and Citizenship* [2012] HCA 31 was handed down too late in the production process for it to be considered. This case is relevant to the principles concerning the implication of procedural fairness obligations (see 5.2.2.1), though the plurality framed the issue as whether the relevant legislative provisions excluded any such obligations (see 5.2.2.2). The approach of the plurality in *Plaintiff S10/2011* demonstrates that procedural fairness obligations may be impliedly excluded by the statute, notwithstanding that in many contexts the presumption that procedural fairness should apply remains extremely difficult to dislodge.

Like the first edition, this second edition has been a collaborative effort. Peter Cane has taken prime responsibility for Chapters 1, 2 and 8–12, and Leighton McDonald for Chapters 3–7. We gratefully thank all the members of the production team at OUP for their efficiency and support. In addition we would like to thank Kiri McEwan and Cameron Winnett for their able research assistance and Oscar Roos for helpful comments on the first edition of this book.

Peter thanks Daniel Stewart for very helpful and perceptive comments on a draft of Chapter 10. Peter completed the bulk of the work on this edition while visiting the Law Faculty of the University of Cambridge as (joint) Arthur L Goodhart Professor of Legal Science. He sincerely thanks the Faculty for their warm hospitality and for the privilege and pleasure of spending time with them.

Leighton thanks Will Bateman, Christos Mantziaris, James Stellios, and Daniel Stewart for sharing their knowledge of and insights into Australian public law. Daniel and Will read drafts of the judicial review chapters and made very valuable criticisms and suggestions. Thanks, also, to Anika and Joe.

Peter Cane and Leighton McDonald
Canberra
21 September 2012

1

Getting Our Bearings

The purposes of this introductory chapter are first to give a general idea of what we mean by 'administrative law' and to raise some basic and recurring issues about this area of law; and, second, to provide an outline of the contents of the book. In fulfilling the first aim, three main points will be made. One concerns the 'scope' of administrative law—that is, when the rules of administrative law apply. A distinction will be drawn between two different approaches to this issue, which we will call 'institutional' and 'functional'. The functional approach alerts us to an important distinction between public law (which includes administrative law) and private law. A second point concerns the meaning of the word 'law' in the phrase 'administrative law'. We will suggest that it is best to give this word a broader rather than a narrower meaning. The last point concerns the aims and purposes of administrative law. Here a distinction will be drawn between two different approaches, which we will call 'legal' and 'regulatory'.

1.1 The scope of administrative law

As a provisional starting point, we can think of administrative law as the area of law that focuses on the executive branch of government (the 'administration'). Administrative law is one of the core subjects in the law school curriculum. Dividing the law up into areas such as tort, contract, constitutional law and so on dates from the nineteenth century, when legal scholars started writing textbooks. It is a rather artificial approach, of course, because life does not fit neatly into lawyers' boxes; and in recent years courts and academics have become more interested in how the boxes intersect and form larger units. For example, you will now find books and law school courses entitled 'The Law of Obligations'—an amalgam of tort, contract, equity and restitution. Administrative lawyers have been rather slow on the uptake, but there are now some books entitled *Public Law*, and it has even been suggested that the 'unity of public law' will be found in the combination of constitutional, administrative and international law.[1]

A different way of packaging the law—perhaps more relevant in practice—is into boxes with labels such as 'immigration law', 'planning law', 'social security law' and so on. In one way, the focus of this book is narrower than any of these legal topics, but in another way broader. It is broader because the legal rules and mechanisms we will examine are potentially relevant to all the various interactions between 'governors' and 'the governed', whatever their particular subject matter. It is narrower because our primary concern is with the role of law in constraining and controlling the conduct of governors in their

---

1   D Dyzenhaus (ed), *The Unity of Public Law* (Oxford: Hart Publishing, 2004).

dealings with the governed, whereas 'immigration law', for instance, covers a diversity of issues relating to the legal regulation of the international movement of people. This book is mainly about just one aspect of the multifarious interactions between governors and governed. That aspect may be encapsulated in the term 'legal accountability'.[2] Legal accountability may be contrasted with various other forms of accountability such as political accountability (9.4), bureaucratic accountability and market-based (or 'competitive') accountability (11.3; 12.1.3.2).

The word 'administrative' in the phrase 'administrative law' makes reference to the idea of separation of powers. We will discuss this concept in greater detail later. Here we need only note its core, which can be found in two propositions. The first is that we should not allow too much power to be concentrated in the hands of any one individual or institution. This is why there are three broadly distinguished branches of government—the legislature, the executive and the judiciary—with broadly distinctive functions. The other proposition is that those who exercise power should be subject to some form of external check. Administrative law, as traditionally understood, is primarily concerned with providing an external check on the exercise of power by the executive branch of government. Legal control of the legislature—in the form of judicial review of legislation, for instance—is typically thought of as part of constitutional law, not administrative law. Ironically, perhaps, the judicial branch of government is more or less immune from external control, partly because of the high value attached to 'independence of the judiciary' as a protection for the rights and interests of the governed against excessive interference by governors.

The concept of 'the executive branch of government' is more complex than it may at first appear. The paradigmatic executive body is the government department headed by a popularly elected minister of state and staffed by public servants, who are appointed rather than elected. But in Australia there is a long history of the use of statutory corporations to perform functions which, in certain other countries, might be performed by departments of state. Furthermore, in the past 25 years or so, various functions that were previously performed by government departments or government-owned businesses have been transferred to non-governmental bodies through the use of techniques such as privatisation of public assets and contracting-out (or 'outsourcing') of functions—particularly the provision of 'public services'—to the private sector. For instance, Australia's largest telecommunications company, Telstra—once wholly owned by the federal government—is now entirely owned by private investors; and private law firms now provide many legal services to the federal government that would once have been delivered 'in-house' by legally trained public servants. So-called 'public–private partnerships' have become increasingly popular vehicles for the provision of new infrastructure such as roads and hospitals.

In England, such developments have had a dramatic impact on administrative law.[3] Whereas the subject matter of administrative law used predominantly to be understood 'institutionally' in terms of legal control of exercises of power by the executive branch of government, it is now understood primarily in 'functional' terms, as concerned with legal control of the exercise of *public functions*, whether by government or non-government entities. Diffusion of public functions and power has not so far had a large impact on Australian administrative law, which is still quite institutionally focused. Nevertheless, it is important not to take an unduly narrow approach to administrative law by thinking of it as concerned only with controlling the exercise of power by governmental officials, because it embodies principles and promotes values—concerned with procedural fairness, for instance—that may well be thought relevant

---

2   Common alternative expressions of the idea of holding decision-makers to account include 'checking', 'controlling', 'scrutinising' and 'overseeing' decision-makers and decision-making.

3   See P Cane, *Administrative Law*, 5th edn (Oxford: Oxford University Press, 2011), 266–72. The European Convention on Human Rights has also had a significant impact: ibid, 103–6.

to certain exercises of power by non-governmental entities.[4] This issue of the 'scope' of administrative law—whether it is and should be defined institutionally or functionally, or in some other way—is one of the most difficult and pervasive legal questions addressed in this book.

A significant result of the 'functional turn' in English administrative law has been the articulation of a much sharper distinction between public law and private law than had traditionally been recognised. In crude terms, private law is concerned with relations between citizens, whereas public law is concerned with relations between governors and governed. The traditional English approach to thinking about legal control of government was formulated by the highly influential Victorian[5] jurist, A V Dicey in his *Introduction to the Study of the Law of the Constitution*, first published in 1885. In his view, the best way of controlling government power was to subject public officials to the 'ordinary law' applicable to citizens generally, administered and enforced by an independent judiciary: equality before the law. By 'the ordinary law', Dicey meant 'private law', as we would now call it—tort and contract law in particular. A prime example of the application of 'ordinary law' to the activities of public officials is the use of the tort of trespass to provide remedies for wrongful arrest and search of persons, and wrongful search and seizure of property, by the police. Dicey can be read as denying that there was (or, perhaps, that there should be) any public/private distinction in English law. In adopting this position, Dicey was reacting against the French system. In the late eighteenth century the revolutionary government in France passed a law prohibiting courts from hearing complaints against the government. Instead, Napoleon established a body, called the Conseil d'Etat, to hear claims against the state. This body was part of the executive, not the judicial, branch of government. Dicey's view was that 'special' laws applicable only to the government in its dealings with citizens ('public law'), administered by special 'tribunals' rather than the ordinary 'courts', were a formula for government privilege and lawlessness.

Dicey's 'equality principle' did not accurately describe the law of his day. Many of the basic principles of administrative law—concerned with interactions between citizens and government—had been developed by the late nineteenth century and were distinct from principles of private law. Moreover, at the time Dicey was writing, 'the Crown' (as opposed to individual public officials and other organs of government) was immune from liability in tort. Nor did Dicey's preference for the ordinary courts hinder the establishment in the twentieth century, in both England and Australia, of numerous 'tribunals' (as distinct from courts) to adjudicate disputes (in relation to taxation, for instance) between citizens and the state. But his views profoundly influenced the way judges and scholars thought about the law. For English lawyers, private law was the paradigm of judge-made ('common') law. Administrative law existed, but assumed no very strong identity in judicial and scholarly minds. Although the first major textbooks of English private law (tort, contract and so on) were written in the nineteenth century, books on administrative law did not appear in England until the 1950s. The 1960s witnessed a dramatic flexing of English judicial muscles in leading administrative law cases[6] in which the House of Lords[7] displayed a renewed willingness to exercise control over executive decision-making. It is to this period that the development of modern English administrative law is usually traced.

---

4   For instance, it has long been recognised that principles of procedural fairness (5.2) are applicable to 'domestic tribunals' such as sporting licensing and disciplinary bodies. See generally J R S Forbes, *Justice in Tribunals*, 2nd edn (Sydney: Federation Press, 2006).

5   That is, belonging to the age of Queen Victoria.

6   Such as *Conway v Rimmer* [1968] AC 910; *Anisminic Ltd v Foreign Compensation Commission* [1969] 2 AC 147 and *Padfield v Minister of Agriculture, Fisheries and Food* [1968] AC 997.

7   Then the UK's final court of appeal, which has now been transformed into the UK Supreme Court.

The first Australian administrative law text was published in 1950.[8] The birth of modern Australian administrative law can probably be fixed at the publication of the Kerr Committee Report in 1971.[9] This report was influenced by the English case law developments of the 1960s, and it set in train a course of events that eventually led to what is sometimes called 'the new administrative law': codification of the grounds of judicial review of administrative action in the *Administrative Decisions (Judicial Review) Act 1977* (Cth) (*ADJR Act*), establishment of the Administrative Appeals Tribunal (AAT) and the office of the Commonwealth Ombudsman, the enactment of the *Freedom of Information Act 1982* (Cth), and the emergence of the Federal Court as the leading administrative law forum in Australia.

Despite the coming of age of Australian administrative law in the past 40 years, the distinction between public law and private law is still less boldly drawn in Australia than in some other legal systems. This is, in part, a result of the fact (noted earlier) that—for complex reasons[10]—Australian administrative law has not taken as sharp a functional turn as English law. Also, although there are tribunals in Australia that adjudicate only disputes between governors and governed, there is no distinction within the Australian court system between public law courts and private law courts. Australian courts—whether federal or state—that have administrative law jurisdiction can also adjudicate disputes between citizen and citizen.[11] By contrast, one of the main reasons why French law (for instance) distinguishes strongly between public and private law is that there are two sets of courts—public law courts and private law courts. Similarly, the development of the distinction between public law and private law in England in the last 35 years has gone hand in hand with institutional changes that led to the establishment of the Administrative Court in 2001.[12]

To summarise so far: there are two contrasting ways of defining the scope of administrative law—institutional and functional. Although neither system adopts either approach in a pure form to the total exclusion of the other, in the past 25 years or so English law has taken a much sharper functional turn than Australian law. The functional turn has brought in its wake a finely drawn distinction between private law and public law.

The significance of the term 'governance' in the book's subtitle and of the terms 'governors' and 'the governed' used in this chapter can be explained in terms of this distinction between institutional and functional approaches to the scope of administrative law. The functions which, according to the functional approach, define the scope of administrative law, may be thought of as 'governmental' in the sense that these are functions that would appropriately be performed by organs of government even if they are in fact performed by non-governmental entities. The word 'governance' is apt to capture the idea that government, as well as being a set of institutions, is also a set of activities. Pursuing this line of thinking, we might say that administrative law is about control of governance (certain activities or functions) rather than about the control of government (certain institutions).

We have already noted that in England the scope of administrative law is defined not in terms of 'governance' or 'governmental functions', but in terms of the related but slightly different concept of 'public functions'. A possible advantage of the concept of 'public function' over that of 'governmental

---

8   W Friedmann, *Principles of Australian Administrative Law* (Melbourne: Melbourne University Press, 1950)—a slim volume of 112 pages written, perhaps significantly, by a European emigré.

9   See further 8.1.

10   Related to the way the scope of administrative law is defined, for instance, in s 75 of the Constitution and in statutes such as the *ADJR Act* and the *Administrative Appeals Tribunal Act* ('*AAT Act*'): see generally Chs 2 and 3.

11   The same is true of some tribunals in the states and territories.

12   The Administrative Court is part of the Queen's Bench Division of the High Court.

function' is that the latter might seem to be restricted to functions and activities that have in the past been performed by government, or are currently being performed by government, or are likely to be performed by government in the future. By contrast, public functions can be understood—without any reference to the institutions of government—as those that we consider ought to be performed in the interests of the public as a whole and not in order to further the partisan interests of any individual or group. Instead of speaking of 'governors' and 'the governed' we might substitute (somewhat clumsily) terms such as 'public functionaries' and 'recipients of public services'. Extending this line of thinking, we could understand administrative law as being a branch of public law and, as such, concerned with ensuring that public functions and activities are performed and conducted in the interests of the public at large, rather than in the partisan interests of any particular individual or group. Whereas private law allows individuals to exercise (private) power to further their own interests or those of other individuals or groups, public law is designed to ensure that (public) power is exercised in the public interest. There is obviously much room for disagreement about whether particular functions and activities should be classified as public or private in this sense, but some such distinction is needed in order to define the scope of the application of administrative law in functional terms.

Whether we adopt the language of publicness or the language of governance, the distinction—to which both allude—between different types of functions and activities raises two fundamental issues about the scope of administrative law. One is whether the rules and principles of administrative law should apply to certain functions and activities regardless of whether they are performed and conducted by governmental or non-governmental entities. Conversely, the other is whether there are certain functions and activities to which the rules and principles of administrative law should not apply, regardless of whether they are performed and conducted by governmental or non-governmental entities. The first case in which the High Court gave serious and direct consideration to such issues was decided only in 2003.[13]

So the reason for including the word 'governance' in the book's subtitle, for using the terms 'governors' and 'the governed', and for discussing the functional approach in this chapter, is not to describe the current state of Australian administrative law, but rather to alert you to the relevance of phenomena such as privatisation, corporatisation and outsourcing, and of the distinction between institutional and functional approaches, to the scope and purposes of administrative law. Australian courts are yet adequately to come to grips with such issues—as we will see particularly in Chapters 2 and 3 in relation to judicial review, and more generally throughout the book—even though they are unavoidable in one form or another because they mark the boundaries of application of the rules and principles of administrative law.

1.2 Law

The second point to be made in this chapter concerns the word 'law' in the phrase 'administrative law'.

This book is primarily about the use of 'law' to control the exercise of power by governors over the governed. Statutes (such as the *ADJR Act*) and decisions of appellate courts (such as the Federal Court and the High Court) are the two main sources of relevant rules and principles that qualify as (administrative) 'law' in the fullest sense. But it is best not to interpret the word 'law' too narrowly.

---

13   *NEAT Domestic Trading Pty Ltd v AWB Ltd* (2003) 216 CLR 277; see further 3.5.1.4.2.

This is because the exercise of governmental power is framed, influenced, structured, guided and controlled by a plethora of rules and principles that are not 'legal' in the strict sense. For instance, although ombudsmen (9.3) cannot make 'law' that binds the entities subject to their jurisdiction to exercise their powers in certain ways and not others, they can and do develop informal principles of 'good administration' that such entities would ignore at their peril. Even more important, perhaps, are rules and principles generated within and by decision-making bodies themselves to bring order and consistency to the exercise of their powers. These go by various names, such as 'policy', 'administrative rules', 'tertiary rules', 'informal rules', 'codes of practice', 'guidelines', 'quasi-legislation', 'soft law' and so on. Many such rules are indistinguishable in form and content from rules that have the full status of law, and their practical, if not their formal, significance and force may be equivalent to those of legal rules in the strict sense. As we will see in due course, the courts have developed principles governing the use by decision-makers of informal rules to structure the exercise of power and the relationship of such rules to the formal law.[14]

1.3 Two approaches to administrative law

The third point we want to make in this chapter concerns two different ways of understanding the nature and purposes of administrative law, which we will call 'legal' and 'regulatory'. Among scholars, the term 'regulation' has no universally agreed meaning. For our purposes, however, we can adopt a common understanding of regulation as the deliberate attempt to influence human behaviour. In this sense, regulation is one of the major functions of governments. For instance, governments regulate the movement of persons in and out of their countries. They regulate their nations' economies by controlling competition and by protecting consumers against abuse of market power. Governments regulate the safety of workplaces; the operations of the gambling industry; the quality of the food we eat, the air we breathe and the water we drink; and so on.

The book's subtitle ('legal regulation of governance') is designed to suggest the possibility of thinking about administrative law as a form of regulation. The regulatory perspective can be contrasted with a 'legal' perspective.[15] The basic difference between these two approaches is one of focus. As you would expect, the sharp focus of the regulatory approach is on the future—on influencing human behaviour and its outcomes. Law may appear in this picture in softer focus as a regulatory 'tool', but so may various other techniques of regulation. By contrast, the sharp focus of the legal approach is on law and legal institutions, with regulation in softer focus as one, but only one, of their possible purposes or aims.

What might be involved in taking a regulatory approach to administrative law? In the abstract, we can think about regulation in terms of a system. A regulatory system—we might say—has three components: a set of standards that announce how people ought to behave; a mechanism for monitoring compliance with those standards; and a mechanism for promoting future compliance. This understanding of regulation makes it relatively easy to see how we might interpret administrative law as a regulatory system.[16] Administrative law consists of a set of rules and principles about how decisions

---

14   See 5.3.3. See also 8.6.3, 8.8.2.

15   The terms 'legal' and 'regulatory' have been chosen purely for convenience. Both terms can be used in various ways, and we are using them in the sense explained here.

16   For more detailed discussion see P Cane, 'Administrative Law as Regulation' in C Parker et al. (eds), *Regulating Law* (Oxford: Oxford University Press, 2004).

ought to be made. For instance, the rules of procedural fairness tell decision-makers that they must adopt fair procedures (5.2); there are rules requiring decision-makers to act consistently with relevant legal requirements (5.3); to make their decisions only on the basis of properly established 'jurisdictional' facts (5.4.3.1); and so on. Understood as regulatory standards, the purpose of these rules and principles is to influence the way that decision-makers exercise their functions. Although there is no formal body that has responsibility for monitoring compliance with rules and principles of administrative law, interested and affected individuals and groups are given an incentive to monitor compliance by the availability of mechanisms, such as judicial review and merits review, for complaining about breaches of administrative law norms. Rules of 'standing' (Chapter 6) specify which individuals and groups are allowed to activate such mechanisms. Courts, tribunals, ombudsmen and so on 'enforce' administrative law by providing qualified complainants with various forms of redress for breaches of its rules and principles, and in this way provide decision-makers with incentives to comply in future with the requirements of administrative law.

From the regulatory point of view, the main purpose of administrative law is to influence the way decision-makers exercise their powers. It follows that the success of administrative law as a regulatory tool should be judged primarily by its effects on bureaucratic behaviour. The impact of administrative law is an empirical or factual question that can—in principle, at least—be investigated by research aimed at assessing the relationship between administrative law and the behaviour of administrators. The regulatory approach to administrative law is quite a new development, and it is only in recent decades that scholars have seriously begun to investigate the impact of administrative law on bureaucratic behaviour (see 12.2).

The regulatory approach to administrative law is significantly different from the legal approach. The emphasis in the regulatory approach is on the future. The regulatory goal of administrative law is to influence the way decision-makers behave in the future rather than to deal with the way they have behaved in the past. From the regulatory perspective, there is little point 'crying over spilt milk'. Better to take steps to prevent further spills—perhaps by making the person responsible clean it up, or perhaps in some other way. By contrast, the legal approach presents administrative law as being primarily concerned with providing complainants with redress for past breaches of administrative law, and society with a means by which decision-makers can be held accountable for such breaches.[17] Many lawyers would also view administrative law as performing what might be called the 'expressive' role of embodying and thereby promoting certain values, such as legality, rationality, procedural fairness, and so on.[18] Administrative law can perform this role by its very existence, independently of its effects on bureaucratic behaviour, or even of whether individual grievances are redressed. This is certainly not to say that lawyers do not attribute to administrative law a goal of improving standards for future decision-making.[19] Indeed, there is no reason to think that administrative law might not, at least in some cases and to some extent, promote regulatory, accountability-related and expressive goals simultaneously (although in other cases, the goals might conflict). However, from the legal perspective, the regulatory goal is subsidiary to the law's expressive

---

17 In terms of the distinction between criminal law and civil (i.e. non-criminal) law, administrative law is commonly treated as a branch of civil law. However, providing remedies and redress for grievances is not the only mode of accountability. Punishments and penalties are also important. We do not consider them in this book (except briefly in 9.4.4.5), partly for reasons of space and partly because they are not included in the typical administrative law syllabus.

18 P Cane, 'Theory and Values in Public Law' in P P Craig and R Rawlings (eds), *Law and Administration in Europe: Essays in Honour of Carol Harlow* (Oxford: Oxford University Press, 2003).

19 See especially the discussion in 8.8.1.

and accountability-related purposes. Viewed from a legal rather than a regulatory perspective, the value and success of administrative law will primarily be judged not by its effects on bureaucratic behaviour, but in terms of the acceptability of the values it embodies and expresses and its ability to provide redress to those adversely affected by unlawful decisions.

The goal that the regulatory understanding attributes to administrative law is quite limited in regulatory terms. Regulatory schemes typically have social goals, such as protecting the environment, or strengthening the economy, or improving the quality of education, or the health of workers. The ultimate goal of regulatory schemes is typically to make society better in some social or economic respect. By contrast, the primary regulatory goal of administrative law is to promote what might be called 'process values', such as fair procedure and compliance by decision-makers with legal limitations on their powers. Such process values are not unimportant, but in a significant sense, they are subsidiary or incidental to—and may hinder—the achievement of the social goals for which regulatory schemes are typically established. This is not to say that good decision-making process has no independent value of its own. For example, following fair procedures is often said to be important, not only for the sake of reaching good decisions, but also because doing so respects the individuality and worth of those affected by decisions (see 5.2.1). On the other hand, fair procedure is of no significance except in the context of making decisions that promote some goal other than merely following the procedure. This explains why lawyers traditionally understand administrative law negatively in terms of constraints and limitations imposed on the achievement of regulatory and other social goals, rather than positively in terms of the promotion of such social goals.[20] This in turn explains why the regulatory account may seem to be somewhat at odds with the legal account of administrative law and its goals. Of course, it would be possible to define the regulatory purpose of administrative law in terms of the type of broad regulatory goals mentioned at the beginning of this paragraph. But if that were done, administrative law would go into even softer focus as the number and variety of available tools for promoting those wider goals increased.

A noteworthy feature of the regulatory approach is that it understands law as one, but by no means the only, technique or tool for influencing human behaviour. For instance, law plays a significant role in promoting safety on the roads and in the workplace. But other factors, such as education, may also significantly influence the way people behave, and changes in social attitudes (to drink-driving, for instance) can have significant effects on human conduct. A major preoccupation of the regulatory approach is to compare and contrast law with other tools and techniques of regulation. By getting law into perspective in this way, the regulatory approach pays a valuable dividend that can equally enrich the legal approach to administrative law.

For instance, we noted earlier that judicial review is only one mode of legal accountability, which can usefully be compared and contrasted with investigations by ombudsmen and by parliamentary committees, proceedings before tribunals, internal review and so on, in terms of their desirability and efficiency as techniques for holding decision-makers accountable to those adversely affected by their decisions and actions (see further Chapter 9).[21] Adopting the regulatory approach also encourages us to ask questions about the relative importance of these various accountability mechanisms in terms, for instance, of the volume and types of complaints they handle and the degree of satisfaction that they

---

20   'Lawyers are often criticised because their work is not constructive. It is not their business to contribute to constructive activities of the community, but to keep the foundations and framework steady': Sir Owen Dixon, *Swearing in as Chief Justice of the High Court* (1952) 85 CLR xi.

21   C Scott, 'Accountability in the Regulatory State' (2000) 27 *Journal of Law and Society* 38.

provide to complainants. Legal accountability can also be compared and contrasted, for instance, with market-based accountability through competitive pressure. Indeed, one of the motivations for measures such as privatisation and contracting-out is precisely to subject functions and activities to 'the discipline of the market'. We will explore this theme in some detail in 11.3.2.

By encouraging us to compare and contrast accountability techniques, the regulatory approach may also lead us to ask important questions such as whether judicial review is a good or bad thing; whether courts are well or ill-equipped to exercise control over bureaucratic decision-making; and whether, as many lawyers tend to assume, more judicial review is necessarily better than less. This last question is relevant to consideration of what are called privative clauses, among other things. Privative clauses (Chapter 7) are statutory provisions designed to prevent certain decisions being questioned by the courts. In Australia in recent years they have, for instance, been much used to shield immigration decisions from judicial scrutiny. Lawyers tend to think that privative clauses are generally undesirable simply because they limit the scope of judicial review. Less often do they consider the possibility that alternative accountability mechanisms may—in some contexts at least—be just as desirable and effective as judicial review, or even more so.

A helpful way of summarising this aspect of the regulatory approach is to say that it encourages us to think about accountability in terms of issues of 'institutional design' and the (horizontal) relationships and interactions between various organs and modes of accountability. By contrast, the legal approach focuses more on accountability in terms of the (vertical) relationship between governors and the governed. In traditional constitutional terms, we might say that the legal approach is rooted in the concept of the rule of law, whereas the regulatory approach draws our attention to the sorts of issues addressed by the concept of separation of powers. This difference is reflected in reactions to phenomena such as privatisation and contracting out. Whereas 'legalists' tend to worry that such developments undermine the rule of law by weakening the accountability of the governors to the governed, 'regulationists' focus more on comparing and contrasting the patterns and techniques of accountability characteristic of the various modes of service provision and how they distribute accountability tasks among various agents of accountability. So understood, the two approaches can provide complementary perspectives on accountability even though, according to the regulatory approach, accountability is not the (prime) purpose of administrative law.

As indicated at the beginning of this chapter, our approach to administrative law is framed by the concept of accountability, and this book does not offer a consistently regulatory account of administrative law. It is not, for instance, organised around the three components of a regulatory system described earlier. One reason for not adopting the regulatory approach more rigorously is that in our opinion an accountability-based analysis is broadly more faithful to the historical development of administrative law and to the way it is currently viewed by Australian courts and legislatures. Thus, it provides a more accurate picture of the current law. However, at various points, we do seek to address the kinds of issues that the regulatory approach encourages us to think about; this is done to enrich our understanding of the law, and also because the regulatory approach is an increasingly popular way of thinking about law, especially among academics. For instance, the distinction between the legal and regulatory approaches underpins the discussion of 'non-justiciability' in 3.6.2; the consideration in 8.8 of the 'normative function' of merits review; and the discussion in 9.1 of the distinction between grievance handling and system monitoring. It also resonates with our analysis of standing in Chapter 6, and it informs the approach we take in Chapter 11. In short, we incorporate important insights of the regulatory approach into an account that understands administrative law primarily as an accountability mechanism.

1.4 The book's geography

The presence of the word 'principles' in the title of the book tells you that our aim is to provide a large-scale rather than a fine-grained map of the terrain of administrative law. A good grasp of the big picture makes it easier to fill in the details by reading statutes and cases, and consulting larger texts[22] and reference books. The book is divided into 12 chapters. Chapter 2 surveys the institutional structure of the Australian administrative law system, the sources and development of Australian administrative law, and the political and constitutional framework within which it operates. Chapters 3–8 on the one hand, and Chapter 9 on the other, reflect a distinction between two modes of reviewing decisions and holding decision-makers accountable, which may be called 'adjudicative' and 'non-adjudicative' respectively. The classic account of adjudication is that of the influential American jurist Lon Fuller.[23] Fuller identified various modes of dispute resolution of which adjudication was one. Mediation and conciliation are others. Each mode has characteristic strengths and weaknesses. According to Fuller, adjudication involves presentation by disputing parties of 'arguments and proofs' to an impartial third person designated (by the parties or the state) to resolve the dispute on the basis of the evidence presented and the arguments made. Adjudication is a relatively 'closed' mode of decision-making involving only three parties: two disputants and the neutral adjudicator.

A distinction is sometimes drawn between two forms of adjudication: adversarial and inquisitorial. The difference between these two forms of adjudication—which is only a matter of degree—resides in the respective role of the adjudicator in each. In an adversarial system, the adjudicator is a more or less passive target of presentations by the parties of their competing arguments and versions of events. By contrast, in an inquisitorial system, the adjudicator plays a more active part in investigating relevant facts and in assisting the parties to develop their arguments and proofs. The Australian judicial system is essentially adversarial, but in some adjudicative bodies—notably tribunals and, to a lesser extent, inferior courts—the adjudicator may take a more active (inquisitorial) part in the proceedings than is traditionally the case in courts.

Chapters 3–8 deal with the two main forms of adjudicative review of decision-making: judicial review and merits review. As its name implies, judicial review is review by courts. By contrast, merits review is typically a job of 'tribunals'. The word 'tribunal' is sometimes used in a broad sense to refer to any adjudicative body. But here it is being used in a narrower sense to mean 'an adjudicative body other than a court'. In the older literature on tribunals, the term is sometimes used to refer not only to adjudicative bodies, but also to what we would now call 'regulatory agencies'—entities (such as the Australian Competition and Consumer Commission (ACCC)) responsible for administering schemes designed to regulate economic and social activity. The explanation for this usage lies in a distinction between two modes of regulation: rule-making and individual decision-making.

For example, a regulatory agency that has power to control industrial emissions into waterways may be permitted to exercise this power by making general rules that specify acceptable levels of emission and that apply to all members of the regulated group, or it may alternatively be permitted to exercise the power by setting emission levels for each individual member of the regulated group on the basis of the particular circumstances in which each individual operates. Moreover, a regulatory agency that exercises

---

22   M Aronson, B Dyer and M Groves, *Judicial Review of Administrative Action*, 4th edn (Pyrmont, NSW: Lawbook Co, 2009) provides the best, detailed account of judicial review.

23   L L Fuller, 'The Forms and Limits of Adjudication' (1978) *Harvard Law Review* 353.

a power to make rules may also be empowered to entertain applications by individuals for exemption from the rules based on their individual circumstances, or for modification of the rules as they apply to their particular operations.

Application of the term 'tribunal' to regulatory agencies recognised the individual decision-making power that regulatory agencies may possess. It led some writers to distinguish further between 'policy-oriented' and 'court-substitute' tribunals. Policy-oriented tribunals were bodies responsible for administering a regulatory scheme by making decisions about the application of the scheme to individual members of the regulated group. Court-substitute tribunals, by contrast, were understood as being 'independent' bodies, whose sole function was to determine disputes between governors and governed. So, for example, a tribunal might be established to hear appeals against decisions made by a regulatory agency about the application of a regulatory scheme to an individual member of the regulated population. Many aspects of administrative law apply to tribunals in both senses of the word, but in the discussion of merits review in Chapter 8, we are concerned only with court-substitute tribunals.

As we will see (3.2.2; 8.6), the distinction between judicial review (by courts) and merits review (by tribunals) is complex and difficult. It is related to another tricky distinction between 'review' and 'appeal' (despite its name, merits review is effectively a form of appeal). Both distinctions reflect ideas about the appropriate relationship between various organs of government, traditionally framed in terms of a 'doctrine' of 'separation of powers'. As we saw in 1.1, 'separation of powers' stands for two basic ideas: first, that we should avoid allowing power to become too concentrated in the hands of any one individual or institution; and, second, that exercise of power should be subject to control by some person or institution independent of and external to the power-holder. However, these two ideas are in some tension with one another because the greater the power of one body (such as a court) to check or control exercise of power by another body (such as a government agency), the greater the risk that the controller may end up exercising the very power it is meant to be checking. Managing this tension requires a system in which the various branches of government can check and balance exercises of power by the other branches without appearing to usurp the others' functions. The distinctions between judicial review and merits review, and between review and appeal, are designed to achieve such a resolution. Thus it is said (for instance) that in reviewing administrative decisions and actions, courts should concern themselves only with the 'legality' of the decision or action under review and not with its 'merits' (3.2.2); and that there is a fundamental difference between reviewing an administrative decision and entertaining a 'general' appeal[24] against that decision (3.2.1). Whereas it is thought appropriate for one court to hear a general appeal against the decision of another court because both belong to the same branch of government, it is not appropriate for a court to hear a general appeal from a decision of an administrative body that belongs to a different branch of government. One way of expressing this general idea is in terms of some concept of 'deference'. For instance, we might say that by refraining from reviewing the merits of a decision, a court shows deference to a decision-maker.[25]

The significance of the so-called 'doctrine' of separation of powers varies between the administrative law systems of the Australian states[26] and the federal administrative law system. This is partly because of the way the constitutions of the states and the Commonwealth respectively are drafted, and partly

---

24 As opposed to an appeal on a point of law.

25 It should be noted, however, that the High Court rejects this characterisation: *Corporation of the City of Enfield v Development Assessment Commission* (2000) 199 CLR 135, 153.

26 In the book, the term 'states' refers collectively to the states and territories unless otherwise indicated.

because of the way the High Court has interpreted the Commonwealth Constitution. The first three chapters of the Australian Constitution reflect the traditional tripartite division (or 'separation') of governmental institutions and functions—legislative, executive and judicial—and deal respectively with the powers of each branch. By contrast, although the governmental systems of the states are structured around this traditional tripartite division, it is not explicitly embodied in the terms of their constitutions. In this respect, the constitutions of the states reflect the British heritage of the Australian legal system (2.1), whereas the Commonwealth Constitution reflects an American heritage (2.2) (the first three articles of the US Constitution correspond to the first three chapters of the Australian Constitution).

The High Court has interpreted this feature of the drafting of the Australian Constitution as requiring a sharp distinction to be drawn between judicial and non-judicial power. In terms of this distinction, while judicial review obviously belongs to the courts, merits review is classified as a non-judicial function. As such, it cannot be exercised by federal courts but must be exercised by non-judicial bodies, called 'tribunals', which are more closely identified with the executive branch. As a result, in federal administrative law the distinction between judicial review and merits review is tightly drawn because it has constitutional and institutional significance. At the same time, as we will see (3.2.2), the distinction also operates more loosely to limit the control that courts may exercise over decision-making by non-judicial bodies. In state administrative law, the distinction lacks the constitutional significance it has in federal law, but nevertheless operates to limit the scope of judicial review. Because of this difference between federal and state law, the discussion of merits review in Chapter 8 will focus primarily on federal law.

Chapter 9 deals with non-adjudicative review. Here it is useful to distinguish between internal and external modes of review. Internal review is review conducted within the decision-making body itself. For most people who make complaints against government, some form of internal review is the first and last port of call. The most significant forms of external, non-adjudicative review are those conducted by legislatures and ombudsmen. An important distinction between internal reviews and reviews by ombudsmen on the one hand, and parliamentary review on the other, is that the former normally deal with complaints by individuals, whereas the latter is more typically concerned with matters of policy affecting the public as a whole or some section of the public. Although judicial review and merits review are, in a sense, the core of administrative law, we can gain a fuller understanding of their role as accountability mechanisms by comparing and contrasting them with other accountability institutions that form part of what might be called 'the administrative law system'. This is one of the lessons we learn from the regulatory approach.

In terms of the public/private distinction, we can say that Chapters 3–9 are concerned with public accountability mechanisms. In Chapter 10 we examine a precondition of effective accountability for the exercise of public power—freedom of information (FOI). Without knowledge of what government is doing, it may be difficult for members of the public to mobilise the various public accountability mechanisms discussed in this book. In practice, however, FOI appears to be little used to promote accountability. Besides access to public information about government, FOI legislation is also concerned with providing individuals with access to information about themselves, held by government. This function of FOI accounts for the majority of applications for access to government-held information.

Whereas Chapters 3–9 deal with public accountability mechanisms, by contrast Chapter 11 deals with the possibilities for using private law—tort and contract law in particular—to hold governors accountable to the governed. For present purposes, we might define private law as law developed to regulate relationships between citizens, as opposed to relationships between citizens and governors. We noted earlier that, in Dicey's opinion, the liability of public officials to be sued in the ordinary courts for breach of laws that applied equally to ordinary citizens was the most legitimate and desirable form of accountability. Certain uses of private law to control exercises of state power against citizens were well established in the nineteenth century. For example, the tort of trespass was commonly used to challenge the use of police powers to arrest individuals and to search people and premises. Such use of private law neatly fitted Dicey's paradigm of equality before the law because actions, for wrongful arrest and for trespass to land by the police, had to be brought against the individual officer who made the arrest or conducted the search. Nineteenth-century English cases also established that statutory corporations, for instance, could be sued for negligent performance of their statutory functions. However, English law had more difficulty with the idea that citizens might sue the government, as such, for breaches of private law. Indeed, traditionally the Crown—meaning central as opposed to local government—was immune from liability in tort, and could be sued in contract only with the consent of the Attorney-General.

As we will see (2.3.5), these rules protecting governments from being sued in private law were abolished much earlier in Australia than they were in England. But even so, it was not really until the 1970s that courts in England and Australia started seriously to develop the law governing the tort liability of public authorities. Perhaps the first important case was the decision of the UK House of Lords in *Home Office v Dorset Yacht Co Ltd*,[27] but since then, appeal courts in both England and Australia have dealt with many cases concerning the application of rules and principles of tort law to the activities of public authorities.

The significance of private law as a means of controlling exercises of power by public authorities rests partly on a deeply entrenched principle that damages are not available as a remedy for breaches of rules and principles of constitutional law and administrative law. By contrast, of course, damages are the main remedy for torts and breaches of contract. The fundamental issue arising out of the use of private law to obtain redress for harm caused by decisions and actions of public authorities concerns whether and in what way the rules and principles of private law ought to be qualified or modified when they are applied to decisions and activities of public authorities.

Also explored in Chapter 11 is the way in which the ideas of agreement, and mutual rights and obligations, that underpin the legal concept of contract have been used to provide a framework for creating structures for accountability and regulation within governmental organisations as an alternative to hierarchical modes of accountability and regulation.

Finally, in Chapter 12 you will find a discussion of views about what administrative law in general, and judicial review in particular, are for; and of what we know about their impact on the behaviour of decision-makers to whom they are addressed. This discussion takes us beyond legal 'doctrine' in two distinct, although complementary, directions—one theoretical and the other empirical. The aim is to see how our understanding of the law can be broadened and deepened, on the one hand by deeper reflection on the purposes of administrative law and judicial review, and on the other by empirical research into their effects on human behaviour. The two questions addressed in Chapter 12 reflect (but cut across) the distinction between the legal and regulatory approaches discussed in 1.3. In this way, the conclusion to the book brings us back full circle to its beginning.

---

27   [1970] AC 1004.

2

Historical and Constitutional Contexts

The aim of this chapter is to provide some background needed for a rounded understanding of contemporary Australian administrative law. Australia has a complex system of government and public administration, the product of a rich heritage that can usefully be thought of as having three distinct strands. For convenience, we may call these the British,[1] the American and the colonial. We will consider each in turn. We will then trace how the three strands were woven together in the course of the twentieth century.

There are two important reasons for paying careful attention to the development of Australian administrative law. One is that knowing something about the law's past helps us better to appreciate its present and possible future(s). Law is a dynamic phenomenon, and many of its features can only be fully understood historically. Second, a developmental approach provides a good introduction to the relationship between constitutional and administrative law—or, in other words, to the constitutional context of administrative law. It is very difficult to acquire a sound grasp of administrative law without having a lively appreciation of this relationship and context. Even if the significance of some of the matters discussed in the chapter is not immediately obvious, their relevance will become increasingly clear in the remainder of this chapter and in later chapters. In terms of the distinction between the legal and regulatory approaches to administrative law (see 1.3), the underlying framework of this chapter is inevitably provided by the former because the latter is a very recent development and is, anyway, largely a creation of academics and is not reflected in the thinking of those responsible for making and developing the law.

Before proceeding, we should first note that Australian administrative law (like Australian law more generally) has no Indigenous heritage. In legal terms, the British who colonised Australia in the decades following 1788 treated the Indigenous population effectively as fauna, and the land as theirs for the taking. As far as the newcomers were concerned (but contrary to the fact, of course), the Indigenous peoples had no social customs or norms deserving of the description 'law'.[2] It was not until late in the

---

1   Although, technically, Australian (administrative) law derives from English (administrative) law—which means the (administrative) law of England and Wales; there is no such thing as British law—we use the word 'British' in the non-technical sense it bears in phrases such as 'the British Empire' and 'the British Commonwealth' because of its more complex governance-related and historical resonances. Where technical precision is required on matters of law, we use the word 'English'.

2   A Castles, *An Australian Legal History* (Sydney: Law Book Co, 1982), 515, 526–9, 540–1; see also A C Castles and M C Harris, *Lawmakers and Wayward Whigs: Government and Law in South Australia* (Adelaide: Wakefield Press, 1987), Ch 1.

twentieth century that non-Indigenous Australians made any serious attempt to establish and recognise the relationships of Indigenous Australians to their land.[3]

2.1 The British heritage

2.1.1 English law in Australia

The British treated the colonisation of Australia as a process of 'peaceful settlement of an empty land rather than … conquest or cession[4] by the original occupiers'.[5] This meant that, in theory, there was no local law to accept or reject. The settlers had to bring their law with them. This was no simple matter, however. The relationship between Australian and English law was from the start, and remains to this day, a complex one. The new colony was a frontier society, lacking the institutions required for straightforward adoption and implementation of a highly developed set of laws, many of which were, anyway, more or less inappropriate to the circumstances in which the settlers found themselves. So far as statute law is concerned, the basic principle was that local legislation could be struck down as invalid if it was 'repugnant' to (that is, in conflict with) English statutes applicable in Australia. In relation to state legislatures, this principle survived in theory, though not in practice, until 1986 (with the passage of the *Australia Acts* (see 2.4.2.1)). Unsurprisingly, adoption of English models for local legislation was common (although nothing like universal) practice in the nineteenth century; there are plenty of examples from the twentieth century as well. In more recent times, Australian legislatures have become increasingly self-reliant, but also more eclectic in their borrowings from abroad.

It was in 1986, too, that the remaining rights of appeal from state courts to the Privy Council were abolished, thus freeing all Australian courts of any obligation to follow decisions of a non-Australian judicial body. In fact, the narrow obligation to follow Privy Council decisions was of little significance compared with the inclination of many Australian judges, well into the twentieth century, to treat English case law as the foundation on which Australian common law was built. As the amount and sophistication of Australian common law has increased, reference and deference to English judicial pronouncements has become less necessary and less common. Even so, the basic conceptual structure of Australian law is the same as that of English law, and this will guarantee the latter's significance in Australia for the foreseeable future, even if only as a force to react against.

Over the past two centuries, then, the approach of Australian courts and legislatures to the British heritage has displayed a complex mixture of imitation, adaptation, reaction and innovation. It is impossible to understand Australian administrative law fully without appreciating its British antecedents. On the other hand, a rounded understanding equally requires acknowledgment of the distinctive political, social, economic and cultural environments in which English law has been adopted and adapted in Australia.

---

3   H Reynolds, *The Law of the Land*, 3rd edn (Camberwell: Penguin Books, 2003).

4   That is, 'handing over'.

5   B Kercher, *An Unruly Child: A History of Law in Australia* (St Leonards: Allen and Unwin, 1995), 4.

2.1.2 Responsible government

In institutional terms, the most important aspect of the British heritage is the system of 'responsible government' as it is called. Responsible government developed in Britain in the late eighteenth and early nineteenth centuries. In his famous work entitled *The English Constitution*, which was first published in book form in 1867,[6] the English political journalist Walter Bagehot described a system in which the executive government (the 'Cabinet') relied for its initial and continuing existence on the support of an elected legislature—the House of Commons. In a 'presidential' system of government, such as that of the USA, both the legislature and the executive are effectively elected by popular vote, whereas under the 'parliamentary' system described by Bagehot, the executive was effectively elected by the legislature, which was itself elected by the voters to perform this function. In other words, while there is a separation of executive and legislature under a presidential system, under a parliamentary system the power of the legislature to 'hire and fire' the executive integrates the legislative and executive branches of government. The mechanism of integration was the principle of 'collective ministerial responsibility' (CMR). As its name implies, this principle dictated that individual members of the government—the ministers of state—would stand or fall as a group depending on whether they retained or lost the confidence of the Commons.[7]

Bagehot was writing before the rise of political parties as we know them today. In the system he described, members of parliament were free to vote as individuals, and between 1832 and 1867, 'no fewer than 10 governments were brought to an end by adverse votes in the Commons'.[8] For Bagehot, the 'efficient secret' of the English constitution was the control exercised over the government by the elected representatives of the body of enfranchised citizens. By contrast, in a two-party parliamentary system such as exists today in both Britain and Australia, the making of governments is the result of electoral success, and governments typically give up office voluntarily and only when an election is due, or earlier if government strategists detect good prospects of electoral success. Because party discipline is very much stronger now than it was in Bagehot's day, members of parliament belonging to the party in government rarely vote against the party line, and certainly not on a matter of confidence affecting the survival of the executive.

In such a system, the effective mechanism of integration of the executive and the legislature is the principle of individual ministerial responsibility (IMR) rather than that of CMR. Nowadays, CMR demands the loyalty of members of the government to its policies, and dictates the confidentiality of cabinet deliberations and the inner workings of the government machine, but it makes little or no contribution to the making and breaking of governments. IMR (as we will see in more detail later: 9.4.1) requires members of the government to provide the legislature with information about and explanations for their conduct and that of their public servants; to take remedial steps when things go wrong; and in extreme cases of personal failure or misconduct, to resign. IMR allows the legislature to exercise a measure of control over the executive without threatening its existence.

In terms of administrative law, IMR is of more significance than CMR. A persistent underlying theme of administrative law theory is a distinction between legal and political responsibility (or

---

6   A standard modern edition is that of R H S Crossman (Fontana/Collins, 1963).

7   The other feature of responsible government is that most of the powers of the head of state (Monarch, Governor-General, Governor)—except the power to appoint the government—must be exercised on the advice of the government of the day.

8   A H Birch, *Representative and Responsible Government* (Toronto: University of Toronto Press, 1964), 135.

'accountability'). This distinction signals that the role of legal institutions is to enforce accountability in the name of law, not policy. The distinction between law and policy (like the related distinctions between legality and merits, and between procedure and substance) is deployed to set limits on judicial control of the executive and other public decision-makers. IMR is one important mechanism of political accountability and a significant feature of the environment in which judicial review is conducted. On the other hand, there is a common view that because of the strength of party discipline, IMR is a relatively weak accountability mechanism.[9] This view has found expression in recent times in the establishment of merits review tribunals (Chapter 8) and ombudsmen (9.3), and an increasing emphasis on and use of formalised 'internal' review and complaint-handling procedures (9.2).

2.1.3 Supremacy of parliament and the rule of law

Perhaps even more than other areas of the common law, administrative law is characterised by abstract concepts and general principles: unreasonableness (5.4.4), jurisdiction (4.4.1, 5.4.1), error of law (5.4.2), fair hearing (5.2.2), irrelevant considerations (5.3.1), legitimate expectation (5.2.2.1; 5.2.2.4), and so on. This is partly explained by the fact that administrative law is concerned with a very large and diverse set of activities and functions: immigration, social security, land management, taxation, and so on. It is only by the application of abstract concepts and general principles to the conduct of particular activities and functions that more concrete and specific rules are generated. Another explanation for the open texture of administrative law's concepts and principles is that it deals with large issues of institutional and constitutional design. Two of the most abstract ideas relevant to such issues are the supremacy of parliament and the rule of law. So far as Anglo-Australian administrative law is concerned, by far the most influential exposition of these two ideas was that of the nineteenth-century English jurist A V Dicey, whose *Introduction to the Study of the Law of the Constitution* was first published in 1885.[10] There are at least three different ways of reading Dicey's book: as a description of the British constitution of his day; as a prescriptive statement of the way he thought the constitution should operate; and as a discussion of basic issues of constitutional design. As description, Dicey's analysis—especially his exposition of the concept of the rule of law—has been extensively criticised, as have many of his normative views. We will adopt the third approach to his work.

2.1.3.1 Supremacy of parliament

As Dicey understood it, the supremacy of parliament had four major implications: first, that in the case of conflict between statute law and common law, statute law would prevail; second, that parliament was free to enact whatever laws it chose; third, that no Act of Parliament could be challenged in the courts on grounds of invalidity or unconstitutionality; and, fourth, that no parliament could bind its successors. From this last proposition it followed that any and every statute could, in theory at least, be repealed by parliament following its ordinary procedures (express repeal); and that in any conflict between an earlier and a later Act, the later would prevail and the earlier would be repealed to the extent of the conflict (implied repeal).

---

9   *R v Toohey; Ex parte Northern Land Council* (1981) 151 CLR 170.

10   The standard modern edition of this work is A V Dicey, *An Introduction to the Law of the Constitution*, 10th edn (E C S Wade, ed) (London: Macmillan, 1959).

In the UK the supremacy of the Westminster parliament has been qualified in two significant respects. First, UK courts now have power to invalidate statutes that conflict with European Community law.[11] Second, although a statutory provision that infringes a right under the European Convention on Human Rights is not, for that reason, invalid, under s 4 of the *Human Rights Act 1998* (UK) it can be declared to be incompatible with the Convention.[12] Such a declaration effectively obliges the government either to amend the provision to remove the incompatibility or pass legislation that expressly excludes the operation of the Convention in the relevant respect. The classic operation of parliamentary supremacy has also been modified by Scottish devolution and the creation of the Scottish Parliament. Although Acts of the Scottish Parliament are invalid to the extent of any inconsistency with Acts of the UK Parliament at Westminster, and although the UK Parliament has power to legislate for Scotland on matters over which the Scottish Parliament has legislative power, it seems that Acts of the Scottish Parliament enjoy a legal status higher than that of delegated legislation made by a minister of the UK government or by a local government authority (and higher than that of legislation made by the Welsh Assembly) while, nevertheless, being subject to judicial review.[13]

2.1.3.2 Rule of law

In his famous exposition of the rule of law, Dicey praised the British constitution on four grounds: first, that under it the exercise of power by government over citizens was constrained by clear rules of law; second, that those laws were applied and enforced by 'ordinary' courts rather than by 'special' tribunals; third, that the rules that constrained the exercise of power by government were the same rules as regulated the conduct of citizens; and, fourth, that the rights of citizens were protected by the ordinary law rather than by a 'higher law' (or 'constitutional') bill of rights.[14]

The first of these points addresses a persistent theme in administrative law, namely the (appropriate) balance between rules and discretion. Discretion implies choice, while rules imply (enforceable) restriction of choice. It is unrealistic to imagine that any human activity, whether governmental or not, could be entirely regulated by (enforceable) rules, even assuming that this would be desirable if possible. Dicey is often criticised for adopting some such view, but it seems more likely that what he opposed was not discretion but unconstrained ('arbitrary') discretion. In this light, Dicey's problem was how to reconcile his views about parliamentary supremacy, and the unconstrained discretion of the legislature, with his account of the rule of law. His solution was to argue, in effect, that the power of parliament was subject to political and social constraints that made legal limitations unnecessary. This argument may seem to some not only inconsistent but also dangerously complacent. But as we will see, the implication that law is not the only effective or desirable way of controlling power underpins much modern thinking about accountability and the role of administrative law.

---

11   *R v Secretary of State for Transport, ex parte Factortame Ltd (No 2)* [1991] 1 AC 603.

12   There is a similar provision in the *Human Rights Act 2004* (ACT) and in the *Charter Rights and Responsibilities Act 2006* (Vic). In *Momcilovic v R* [2011] HCA 34 it was unsuccessfully argued that the power to make a declaration of incompatibility is unconstitutional on the ground that making such a declaration is a non-judicial function incompatible with the exercise of judicial power.

13   *AXA General Insurance Ltd v Lord Advocate* [2011] UKSC 46; [2012] 1 AC 868.

14   According to Tamanaha, Dicey's was 'the first prominent modern formulation and analysis of the rule of law in a liberal democratic system': B Z Tamanaha, *On the Rule of Law: History, Politics, Theory* (Cambridge: Cambridge University Press, 2004), 63. Since then, the literature has blossomed. Chapters 7 and 8 of Tamanaha's book provide a very accessible introduction to and summary of modern debates. See further 12.1.3.1.

Turning to the second aspect of Dicey's account of the rule of law, ordinary courts have two relevant distinguishing characteristics: they are protected from external influence and control by a strong principle of judicial independence; and they typically have jurisdiction to hear a very wide range of disputes between citizen and citizen as well as between citizen and government. By contrast, the independence of members of administrative tribunals tends to be less protected than that of judges (for instance, they are typically appointed for relatively short, fixed periods rather than until a specified retirement age); and, historically, individual administrative tribunals (in England, at least) typically had 'specialist' jurisdiction over a relatively narrow set of disputes between citizen and government (for instance, in the area of social security or immigration). In England, in recent years, steps have been taken to strengthen the independence of tribunals from the executive; and in both England and Australia there are now tribunals with broad 'general' jurisdiction alongside more specialist bodies.

In 1.1 we noted that Dicey's preference for the ordinary courts did not hinder the development of administrative tribunals in the twentieth century. Instead, the issue of 'ordinary' versus 'administrative' courts underlay a debate about whether tribunals should be identified with the judicial or the executive branch of government. In the first half of the twentieth century, tribunals in Britain were identified with the executive branch of government. However, the Franks Committee on administrative tribunals, which reported in 1957, recommended that tribunals be treated as part of the judicial branch of government. More recently, the Leggatt Review, *Tribunals for Users* (2001), recommended that the rather chaotic tribunal system should be rationalised and integrated more fully with the court system.[15] The continuing influence of Diceyan ideas is obvious in these proposals.

Related to Dicey's preference for ordinary courts was his championing of the 'equality principle'. This is discussed in 1.1, 2.3.5 and 11.1.

Dicey's aversion to Bills of Rights grew out of a view that the most important protection for the individual against government was to be found not in statements of rights but in remedies, such as habeas corpus and damages in tort. This argument taps into one of the most important characteristics of classic English administrative law, namely its remedial orientation, to which we now turn.

2.1.4 The prerogative writs

In medieval England the writ was a tool of governance, a document containing orders or instructions sent by one government official to another. Writs were routinely used by central government—both the executive and the courts—to communicate with local functionaries. There were many types of writ, with names that referred to the order or instruction contained in the writ. Perhaps the most famous type of writ was habeas corpus, which instructed a gaoler to release a prisoner who was being unlawfully detained. For our purposes, the most important writs were certiorari, prohibition and mandamus. A writ of prohibition ordered its addressee not to make some (unlawful) decision or perform some (unlawful) action. A writ of mandamus ordered its addressee to make some decision or perform some action required by law. A writ of certiorari ordered its addressee to deliver to the court the official record of some decision made by the addressee so that the decision could be 'quashed'—deprived of legal effect.

In the Middle Ages, these three types of writ were used for administrative purposes. In the course of the seventeenth century the Court of King's/Queen's Bench began to use them as a technique for

---

15 The general thrust of the review's recommendations has been implemented in the *Tribunals, Courts and Enforcement Act 2001*. See P Cane, *Administrative Tribunals and Adjudication* (Oxford: Hart Publishing, 2010), 46–8.

LIVERPOOL JOHN MOORES UNIVERSITY
LEARNING SERVICES

controlling unlawful conduct by officials such as justices of the peace (who, in addition to judicial functions, performed various administrative functions such as issuing licences), agencies such as the Sewer Commissioners (who had extensive powers to organise the provision of drainage facilities) and 'boards'. They gradually replaced actions for damages in tort as the prime technique by which 'common law courts' (primarily the Court of King's/Queen's Bench) provided remedies for government lawlessness. They came to be called 'prerogative' writs, because they were understood as tools for the exercise of royal control (by the King's/Queen's courts) over the machinery of government. One of the catalysts for the development of these writs by the Court of King's/Queen's Bench was the abolition of the conciliar courts (the most notorious of which was the Court of Star Chamber), through which the monarch had exercised direct personal control over government officials.

Each type of writ followed a standard formula to which were added the details of the circumstances that had caused the writ to be issued. An important result of the formulaic nature of the writs was that the applicant for a writ had to show that the various elements of the formula were present in the circumstances of the complaint. For instance, certiorari might issue only if the challenged decision was made in exercise of a judicial function. As this example suggests, although the preconditions for the issue of the various writs included what we would now call 'grounds of judicial review' (such as error of law and procedural unfairness), they were not all necessarily related to whether the applicant had a legitimate cause for complaint. An applicant with a 'good case on the merits' might fail if some other precondition for the issue of the requested writ was not satisfied. This potential gap between 'the merits' and success in court was a general feature of what is called the 'formulary system' of pleading, which was characteristic of English law until the nineteenth century. In the course of the 1800s, culminating in the *Judicature Acts* of 1875–77, the formulary system was replaced by a system under which the claimant had to convince the court that the facts of the claim revealed a good 'cause of action', not that it satisfied certain specified preconditions for actionability. Importantly for our purposes, the prerogative writs escaped these reforms and retained their formulaic character well into the twentieth century.

In nineteenth-century England many of the functions that had formerly been performed at local level (by justices of the peace and local agencies) came under central control in government departments and other national agencies. As a result, the prerogative writs were applied to the activities of central government, although not until the 1960s was it finally settled that they were available to challenge decisions made personally by ministers of state.[16] By the middle of the twentieth century the formulary nature of the prerogative writs (by this time renamed prerogative 'orders') became a cause of serious dissatisfaction. It no longer seemed acceptable that a 'good claim' might fail because some condition for the issue of a prerogative order, unrelated to the 'merits' of the claim, was not satisfied. At first, English courts sought to evade the restrictions on the availability of the prerogative orders by developing the 'equitable remedies' of injunction and declaration.[17] These remedies were originally used in 'private law' (contract, tort and so on); but now they provided a useful means of escaping the technicalities of the public law remedies of certiorari, prohibition and mandamus that were the result of their formulary inheritance.

In 1977 in England, the procedures for applying for the prerogative orders and equitable remedies in public law matters were streamlined. This led to the development of a distinction between public law claims and private law claims and, most recently, to the replacement of the prerogative orders by remedies called quashing orders, prohibiting orders and mandatory orders. The upshot is that the formulary

---

16   *Padfield v Minister of Agriculture, Fisheries and Food* [1968] AC 997.

17   The declaration was first awarded against a public official in *Dyson v Attorney-General* [1911] 1 KB 410.

system has, by a rather unexpected route, been replaced by one in which the claimant pleads a breach of public law and requests a suitable remedy. In other words, the exclusion of public law from the reforms of the nineteenth century has now been made good. There has been a fundamental shift of the centre of gravity of the English law of judicial review of administrative action away from remedies (is there an appropriate 'form of action'?) to the grounds of review (does the claimant have a good cause of action for which a remedy should be provided?). As we will see later (4.1–4.3), the older and the newer models of the relationship between remedies and grounds of review exist side by side in Australian law, creating an extremely complex picture.

2.2 The American heritage

A milestone in the history of Australian administrative law was the coming together of the six Australian colonies into the federated Commonwealth of Australia in 1901. The most important model for the Australian Constitution was the US Constitution. Like its US counterpart, the Australian Constitution embodies a separation of powers in its first three chapters, devoted respectively to the legislature, the executive and the judiciary. Section 1 vests the legislative power of the Commonwealth in the federal parliament; s 61 vests the executive power of the Commonwealth in the Queen; and s 71 vests the judicial power of the Commonwealth in the High Court of Australia and such other federal courts as the parliament creates.

This arrangement does not require that each of the branches of government exercise only the type of governmental power primarily allocated to that branch: legislative to the legislature, administrative to the executive, and judicial to the courts. For instance, the power of the houses of parliament to deal with contempt of their proceedings involves exercise of judicial power; the extensive powers of the executive to make regulations involve the exercise of legislative power; and law-making is necessarily incidental to the adjudication of disputes by the judiciary. In Australia, the most significant aspect of separation of powers is that relating to the position of the federal judiciary in the governmental system (further explored in 2.4.1.4).

Although the modern idea of separation of powers is often traced back to Montesquieu's eighteenth-century discussion of the British constitution in *Esprit des Lois*, Dicey considered that analysis to be based on a misunderstanding of the British system. Dicey spent only two pages on separation of powers in his 500-page *Introduction to the Study of the Law of the Constitution*. The main point of that brief passage was to criticise the French version of separation of powers, on which was based the system of special administrative courts, which were associated with the executive branch of government rather than the judicial branch.[18] For Dicey, the rule of law (which he championed) and separation of powers (as manifested in the French system) were inimical to one another; and the whole point of the independence of the judiciary (which is usually seen as a basic implication of separation of powers, and which Dicey considered to be compromised in the French system of administrative courts) was to enable the judiciary to protect the rights of the individual citizen from unlawful encroachment by the government. Despite the US influence on the Australian Constitution, this 'protection of the individual', 'rule of law' ideology permeates Australian administrative law in both its federal and state manifestations.

---

18   See further 1.1.

2.3 The colonial heritage

The aim of this section is to explore the development of Australian administrative law in the period before federation in 1901. Among the factors that played an important role in the development of Australian law in the nineteenth century are that the British settled Australia in order to expand the capacity of their prison system; that the settlers more or less ignored the legal customs of the Indigenous people and adopted English law; that Australia was a very large, undeveloped country a long way from London; and that it had (and still has) a small population for its size, gathered in widely scattered centres.

2.3.1 Supremacy of parliament

In the period before 1823, governors were presented with a 'practical opportunity for the rejection of English legal principles'.[19] But no Australian legislature has ever enjoyed supremacy in the full Diceyan sense.[20] In that year, the New South Wales Act established the Legislative Council. Before a law was laid before the council, the Chief Justice had to certify that it was consistent with English law so far as the circumstances of the colony permitted—a form of judicial review of legislation. With the establishment of responsible government in the 1850s, the *Colonial Laws Validity Act 1865* (Imp) effectively removed the consistency requirement and substituted royal assent for judicial review 'as the main imperial control over colonial legislation in the second half of the nineteenth century'.[21] The colonial legislatures were given very wide power to legislate for the 'peace, order and good government' of their respective territories. Even so, they could not pass laws with extra-territorial operation, or that conflicted with statutes of the Westminster parliament the operation of which extended to the colonies (that had 'paramount force'). Moreover, in making laws about its 'constitution, powers and procedure', a colonial legislature had to comply with any applicable procedural ('manner and form') requirements, including requirements imposed by the legislature itself.[22]

But in one very significant respect, the colonial legislatures, like their successors in the Australian states today, enjoyed the sort of freedom that Dicey celebrated. With the exception of the Australian Capital Territory and Victoria, no Australian legislature has so far enacted a bill of rights, and in neither jurisdiction does any court have power to strike down legislation for incompatibility with a protected right. Nor does the Australian Constitution contain a bill of rights, although in recent years the High Court has implied certain fundamental rights into the Constitution, and commentators vary in their assessment of the resources available in the Constitution for the further protection of individual rights.[23] The relative lack in Australia of formal protection of human rights arguably reflects a view that the role of judges and courts in controlling the other branches of government should be quite limited: one important effect of a judicially enforced bill of rights is to increase the power of the judiciary vis-à-vis the executive and the legislature.

---

19   Kercher, *An Unruly Child*, 202; see also Castles, *Australian Legal History*, 383.

20   See 2.1.3.1.

21   Kercher, *An Unruly Child*, 124.

22   *Colonial Laws Validity Act 1865* (Imp), s 5. For detailed discussion see R D Lumb, *The Constitutions of the Australian States* (St Lucia: University of Queensland Press, 1977), 98–115; and see 5th edn (1991) and 2.4.2.1 for discussion of the present position.

23   G Williams, *Human Rights under the Australian Constitution* (Melbourne: Oxford University Press, 1999).

2.3.2 Rule of law

Prisons are not law-free zones, but they *are* characterised by strong internal regulatory and disciplinary systems that leave considerable scope for official discretion within a more or less permissive legal framework. The early settlement at Sydney Cove was no ordinary prison, and in the first few decades of British occupation the operative balance between law and discretion left ample room for official freedom and gubernatorial prerogative. In David Neal's account of the first 50 years of New South Wales,[24]

> ... the rule of law—a set of concepts encompassing legal rules, institutions, processes of reasoning and powerful symbols—played a prime role in changing New South Wales from a penal colony to a free society. The colonists used the imported rule of law ideology to settle the terms on which authority would be exercised in the colony and to force the colonial power to grant its penal colony the institutions and conditions of a free society.

We know relatively little about judicial review of executive action in colonial Australia. Section 2 of the *New South Wales Act* (Imp) of 1823 conferred on the new Supreme Courts of New South Wales and Tasmania wide jurisdiction, including that to issue prerogative writs. Various colonial legislative provisions also created statutory remedies in the nature of the prerogative writs. The first recorded (and successful) application for a prerogative writ (of mandamus) was made in 1824.[25] Certiorari was, apparently, much used in Victoria, but rarely in New South Wales and Queensland, mandamus proving the most popular writ in those colonies.[26] The prerogative writs were frequently used to control the activities of judicial officers—justices of the peace and magistrates—but also against ministers of state, and administrative and regulatory boards and agencies. It seems that on the whole, the local judges stuck reasonably close to English authority when granting or refusing applications for public law remedies. Certainly, colonial courts made no attempt to alter fundamentally the formulary nature of prerogative writs; and, as in England, Australian equivalents of the *Judicature Acts*, passed towards the end of the nineteenth century, left the writs untouched.[27]

2.3.3 Responsible government

New South Wales was the first colony to be granted responsible government—by the *New South Wales Constitution Act 1855* (Imp). This Act put in place a constitution that provided for a bicameral legislature consisting of an appointed upper house (Legislative Council) and an elected lower house (Legislative Assembly). Some of the existing limitations on the law-making powers of the New South Wales legislature were removed, but others remained. The critical section (s 37) of the 1855 Act drew a distinction between two categories of public officials, one consisting of those 'liable to retire from office on political grounds' and the other of those not in the first class. Power to appoint officials in the latter category was given to the Governor acting on the advice of the Executive Council (the political executive), while power to appoint officials in the former category (in effect, the members of the Executive Council) was given to the Governor alone. Section 18 exempted political officials from the rule disqualifying members

---

24 D Neal, *The Rule of Law in a Penal Colony: Law and Power in Early New South Wales* (Cambridge: Cambridge University Press, 1991), xii.

25 Castles, *Australian Legal History*, 185–6.

26 P Finn, *Law and Government in Colonial Australia* (Melbourne: Oxford University Press, 1987), 75–8, 112–3, 139–40.

27 Castles, *Australian Legal History*, 362–3. In NSW the *Judicature Act* reforms were not adopted until 1970.

of the Legislative Assembly from holding public office. It was these provisions that were taken to have introduced responsible government, replacing a system in which members of the executive government held permanent posts by appointment. A central plank of responsible government is the principle that the non-political head of state normally acts on the advice of the government. But this principle was nowhere written down, and the scope of its operation was a cause of considerable disagreement and debate in the late nineteenth century.[28]

The main outlines of responsible government as it was established in the nineteenth century remain in place in the states. Queensland and the two territories have unicameral legislatures, while all the other states have bicameral legislatures. All the upper houses are now elected. As a generalisation, the upper houses of the Australian states are more powerful than the UK upper house—the House of Lords—in terms of the consequences of refusal by the upper house to pass legislation already passed by the lower house—including appropriation ('supply') legislation required to fund government activity.[29] To this extent, responsible government has different connotations in Australia than in the UK.

In 2.1.2, we saw that the two main mechanisms of responsible government are individual and collective ministerial responsibility (IMR and CMR). In colonial Australia, CMR was more significant than IMR.[30] This was partly because political parties as we understand them today had not developed; and partly because the Governor-in-Council (the Governor acting on the advice of the Executive Council—the Cabinet) played a much different and more active role in day-to-day government than its UK equivalent, the Queen-in-Council.[31] Many powers and functions that in Britain might reside in a government department or government agency were conferred in Australia (and especially in Victoria) on the Governor-in-Council. (The significant consequences of this difference will be explored in 2.3.4.) This is not to say that individual ministers were not repositories of important powers and functions; and the distinction between legal and political accountability which, as we noted in 2.1.2, plays a foundational role in administrative law, and is built on the IMR principle, is to be found in the nineteenth-century case law.[32]

2.3.4 Prerogative writs

As noted in 2.3.2, we know relatively little about the history of administrative law and judicial review in the colonial period. One point of significance does emerge, however. As we have seen (2.1.4), in England the prerogative writs were established as the prime vehicle of judicial review of administrative action in the seventeenth century. The writs were 'prerogative' because they were closely associated with royal control of the machinery of government; hence the traditional title of applications for prerogative orders—*R v A; Ex parte B*, where *R* means 'the Crown', *B* stands for the applicant for the writ and *A* stands for the respondent. As royal power waned, and many of the governmental functions originally performed directly by or in the name of the monarch were effectively transferred to the executive, a distinction came to be drawn between the Crown and the monarch. In the British context, 'the Crown' came to refer collectively to the ministers of state and the government departments through

---

28   Lumb, *The Constitutions of the Australian States*, 5th edn, 66–8.

29   Lumb, *The Constitutions of the Australian States*, 5th edn, 51–60.

30   Finn, *Law and Government in Colonial Australia*, 11–12, 45–7, 51–2, 86–90, 123.

31   Finn, *Law and Government in Colonial Australia*, 12.

32   Finn, *Law and Government in Colonial Australia*, 55–6.

which their functions were performed.[33] In the seventeenth and eighteenth centuries, the prerogative orders were used primarily against local officials and agencies. In the nineteenth century, many of the functions formerly performed by local officials and bodies were transferred to central government departments and national agencies. The use of the prerogative orders against such national agencies was unproblematic, but their use against ministers and departments created the constitutionally unseemly spectre of the Crown controlling the Crown by applying for a royal writ from one of his or her Majesty's judges.

This problem of identification of the government with the monarchy was less acute in Australia for several reasons. One is that by the time Australia was colonised, royal power had already waned significantly. A second is that because of the great physical distance between Australia and the UK, colonial governments from the very earliest days enjoyed a significant degree of practical freedom and independence. Third, because of the large size of the country, its lack of economic and physical development, and its very small population, colonial governments in Australia provided many more services and performed many more functions than did the central government in Britain. Fourth (as we noted in 2.3.3), a major vehicle for such activity in the latter half of the nineteenth century was the Governor-in-Council. Fifth, and for similar reasons, whereas in nineteenth-century Britain local government authorities (which were never identified with the Crown, but were 'creatures of statute') came to play an increasingly significant role in delivering public services, local government was very slow to develop in Australia, and to this day plays a much smaller role than in Britain.[34] 'Central' government (in the guise of the colonial governments) played a correspondingly greater role.[35]

The result of all this seems to have been that colonial courts (especially in Victoria) were quite willing to subject the Governor-in-Council and colonial ministers to judicial review.[36] In the twentieth century, Australian courts became less assertive in relation to the Governor-in-Council, and it was not until the 1980s that the amenability of such bodies to judicial review, other than for exceeding statutory power, was re-established.[37] More recently, the High Court has held that the remedies of mandamus and prohibition available under s 75(v) of the Australian Constitution are 'constitutional', not 'prerogative', writs because their function is to enforce the *rule of law* (not the power of the monarch) against officers of the Commonwealth including, of course, ministers of state.[38] In England, the amenability of ministers to the prerogative writs was not settled until 1968;[39] and not until 1994 was it decided that an injunction (also available under s 75(v) of the Australian Constitution) could be awarded against a minister.[40] It is

---

33   *Town Investments Ltd v Department of Environment* [1978] AC 359.

34   J McNeill, 'Local Government in the Australian Federal System' in B Dollery and N Marshall (eds), *Australian Local Government: Reform and Renewal* (Melbourne: Macmillan, 1997), 18–20; L Pearson, *Local Government Law in New South Wales* (Sydney: Federation Press, 1994), 1–3; P May, 'Amalgamation and Virtual Local Government' in B Dollery, N Marshall and A Worthington (eds), *Reshaping Australian Local Government: Finance, Governance and Reform* (Sydney: University of NSW Press, 2003), 80–82.

35   In the UK in the 1980s and 1990s changes in the relationship between central and local government led some commentators to detect a transformation of local government from a form of local democracy into a mere service provider: P Cane, *Administrative Law*, 5th edn (Oxford: Oxford University Press, 2011), 29–33. Selway detects a similar change in the role of state governments in Australia: B Selway, 'Mr Egan, the Legislative Council and Responsible Government' in A Stone and G Williams (eds), *The High Court at the Crossroads* (Sydney: Federation Press, 2000), 63.

36   Finn, *Law and Government in Colonial Australia*, 91–5.

37   *R v Toohey; Ex parte Northern Land Council* (1981) 151 CLR 170; *FAI Insurances Ltd v Winneke* (1982) 151 CLR 342.

38   See further 2.4.1.2.

39   *Padfield v Minister of Agriculture, Fisheries and Food* [1968] AC 997.

40   *M v Home Office* [1994] 1 AC 377.

also worth noting that whereas (Her Majesty's) judges of superior English courts are not amenable to judicial review, judges of superior federal courts (except the High Court)[41] are.[42]

The summary point is that as a result of its colonial past, Australian administrative (and constitutional) law is much less weighed down with monarchical baggage than its English counterpart.

2.3.5 Claims against the government

This point is also illustrated by the Australian history of tort and contract claims against government. At the time responsible government was coming to Australia, the Crown in the UK (in the guise of central government) was immune from liability in tort, and could be sued in contract only with the permission ('fiat') of the Attorney-General. Dicey's equality principle (1.1; 2.1.3.2; 11.1) referred to the fact that individual officials could be sued in tort, and ignored the fact that the central government, as a collective entity, could not be held liable either 'personally' or vicariously. In most of the Australian colonies, these restrictions on the civil liability of the government were abolished in the nineteenth century,[43] although in England they remained in place until 1947. Now (as we will see in more detail in Chapter 11) the basic principle is that government is subject to the same liability rules as ordinary citizens, with only such modifications and exceptions as are considered necessary and justifiable to take account of its peculiar functions and responsibilities.

2.4 Federation and onwards

In exploring the development of Australian administrative law in the twentieth century, it is convenient to divide the period into two.

2.4.1 1901–1970

Federation was one of the most important milestones in the history of Australian administrative law. In 1900, England had a unitary legal system. There was a single, hierarchically organised set of judicial institutions (courts) with the House of Lords at its apex. The legislative and executive institutions were layered (central, local), but the legal authority of the local layer was derived from that of the central legislature (the Queen-in-Parliament), which was the highest legal authority in the system. Local government, in other words, was a 'creature of statute'. Although the superior courts were not creatures of statute and their authority was not derived from statute, according to the doctrine of the supremacy of parliament their status as law-makers was subordinate to, rather than coordinate with, that of the Queen-in-Parliament.

The internal structure of each of the colonial legal systems was essentially similar to that of the English system. Certainly, the powers of their legislatures were limited in certain respects, and these limitations were enforceable by courts. But colonial governments did not have the inferior legal status

---

41   *Federated Engine Drivers' and Firemen's Association of Australasia v The Colonial Sugar Refining Company* (1916) 22 CLR 103, 117 (Isaacs, Gavan Duffy and Rich JJ).

42   For example, *R v Commonwealth Court of Conciliation and Arbitration; Ex parte Whybrow & Co* (1910) 11 CLR 1.

43   Finn, *Law and Government in Colonial Australia*, Ch 6; 'Claims Against the Government Legislation' in P D Finn (ed), *Essays on Law and Government, Volume 2: The Citizen and the State in the Courts* (Sydney: LBC Information Services, 1996).

of local government in England. It is also true that litigants could appeal from colonial Supreme Courts to the Privy Council, but this did not make the Supreme Courts into inferior English courts. The Privy Council stood to the colonial judicial systems as the House of Lords stood to the English judicial system.

Federation transformed these constitutional arrangements by creating a new legal system and a complex set of relationships between it and the six existing colonial legal systems. Australia's judicial system now had two layers, one federal and the other state. Federal courts had jurisdiction in matters of federal law, and state courts had jurisdiction in matters of state law—including, in both cases, administrative law. However, the layers were connected in three ways: first, jurisdiction over matters of federal law could be conferred on state courts; second, the High Court had jurisdiction to hear appeals from decisions of state courts on matters of state law as well as federal law; and, third, the Privy Council retained jurisdiction to hear appeals, from both state Supreme Courts and the High Court, on certain matters of federal law as well as on matters of state law, thus binding all Australian courts to decisions of a single tribunal. As a result, although the common law on any particular issue might vary from state to state, the High Court and the Privy Council were in a position to lay down rules of common law that applied uniformly in all the states. Furthermore, on matters in which state law and federal law overlapped (such as the tort liability of public authorities), these courts could create a single Australian common law that applied uniformly at both federal and state levels. For most of the twentieth century the High Court was the only federal court of general jurisdiction, a situation made feasible in practice by what is obscurely known as the 'autochthonous expedient' of giving state courts jurisdiction over matters of federal law.

Federation also created a two-layered legislative and executive system. The federal parliament was given specific legislative powers listed in ss 51 and 52 of the Australian Constitution, and the state legislatures retained residual power, under their existing constitutions, to make laws for 'peace, order and good government'. State laws were subordinated to federal law in the sense that under s 109 of the Australian Constitution state laws would be invalid to the extent of any inconsistency with federal law. But ss 106–108 of the Australian Constitution expressly preserved the pre-existing constitutional position of the states, subject to the operation of the Constitution. Local government retained its pre-federation character as a creation of the state legislatures, and received no recognition in the Australian Constitution.[44]

Federation had other less obvious effects as well. Dicey perceptively observed that '[f]ederalism … means legalism—the predominance of the judiciary in the constitution—the prevalence of a spirit of the legality among the people'.[45] Because legislative, executive and judicial powers are divided between the various components of a federal system, a constitutional court, with a high degree of independence from the political process, is needed to police that division. Federalism necessarily 'legalises' issues about the allocation of power that, in a unitary system, either do not arise or can be resolved politically, without recourse to law. This partly explains why there is an explicit separation of powers in the Australian Constitution. At the same time, the fact that in Australia a federal system was laid on a foundation of responsible government, which had been developed in the context of a unitary system, gives Australian administrative (and constitutional) law a complex and dynamically hybrid nature.

---

44   C Aulich and R Pietsch, 'Left on the Shelf: Local Government and the Australian Constitution' (2002) 61 *Australian Journal of Public Administration* 14; N McGarrity and G Williams, 'Recognition of Local Government in the Commonwealth Constitution' (2010) 21 *Public Law Review* 164.

45   Dicey, *Introduction to the Law of the Constitution*, 175.

2.4.1.1 Supremacy of parliament

The legislative powers of the Commonwealth parliament are limited by the Constitution, and those limitations are enforceable by courts. In the early years of federation, the Imperial Parliament retained power to make laws that applied to Australia. This power was removed by the *Statute of Westminster 1931* (UK), but the Imperial Parliament's power to make laws affecting the states remained. Federation imposed a further limitation on the legislative powers of the states. Under s 109 of the Constitution any inconsistency between state and Commonwealth law is resolved in favour of the latter. Otherwise, the constitutional position of the state legislatures was unchanged by federation, and the general constitutional concept of the supremacy of parliament applied similarly to the federal legislature as to the legislatures of the states.

2.4.1.2 Rule of law

Section 75(iii) of the Australian Constitution confers on the High Court 'original jurisdiction' 'in all matters … in which the Commonwealth, or a person suing or being sued on behalf of the Commonwealth, is a party'. Section 75(v) confers on the court original jurisdiction 'in all matters … in which a writ of Mandamus or prohibition or an injunction is sought against an officer of the Commonwealth'. There is a view that s 75(iii) is broader in scope than s 75(v), and that s 75(v) was inserted merely to remove any risk that the more general provision might be interpreted as not conferring jurisdiction to award the remedies enumerated in the narrower provision. Be that as it may, the effect of s 75(v) (which, in practice, provides the prime basis for judicial review by the High Court) is to provide for a measure of judicial control of officers of the Commonwealth, which the legislature cannot remove. The classic statement of the purpose of s 75(v) is that of Dixon J in *Bank of New South Wales v Commonwealth* (the *Bank Nationalisation* case): 'to make it constitutionally certain that there would be a jurisdiction capable of restraining officers of the Commonwealth from exceeding federal law'.[46] This statement firmly established the rule of law (as understood by the High Court (12.1.3.1)) as the conceptual foundation of judicial review.

2.4.1.3 Responsible government

The framers of the Australian Constitution opted for a system of responsible government.[47] Opponents argued that responsible government was inconsistent with federalism because it implied that a government could continue in office so long as it enjoyed the confidence of the lower (popularly elected) house[48] and that the 'states' house'—the Senate[49]—would lack the power to force a government to resign.[50] As things have turned out, the operation of the party system has robbed the Senate of any meaningful role in protecting states' rights. On the other hand, the power of the Senate to block legislation and supply, and the fact that minor parties and independants may hold the balance of power

---

46   (1948) 76 CLR 1, 363.

47   See ss 62–4 of the Australian Constitution.

48   The 'house of government' as it is sometimes called.

49   Sometimes called the 'house of review'.

50   J Quick and R R Garran, *The Annotated Constitution of the Australian Commonwealth* (Sydney: Angus & Robertson, 1901), 706–7.

in the upper house, injects an element of CMR into the federal system of government which is lacking in unicameral systems (such as that in Queensland) and in bicameral systems in which the upper house has weaker powers than the Senate, or is typically under government control, or both. The Australian Senate may present the government with an unstable and potentially hostile source of opposition, which may force it to choose between compromise, or even acquiescence, and its own demise (by way of a double dissolution).

2.4.1.4 Separation of powers

Although the Australian Constitution devotes separate chapters to legislative, executive and judicial powers respectively, and allocates each to a different governmental institution, the precise implications of this arrangement are not spelled out. At the turn of the twentieth century, the English constitution was characterised not only by integration of legislature and executive in accordance with the principle of responsible government, but also by a loose attitude to judicial power. Most significantly, the Lord Chancellor simultaneously filled the roles of sitting judge and head of the judiciary, member and chair of the upper house of the legislature (the House of Lords) and minister of state. Because the framers of the Australian Constitution opted for a system of responsible government, it was inevitable that the textual separation of legislative and executive power would be read as being compatible with the integration of legislature and executive that characterises responsible government. The text was also held to be consistent with the statutory conferral of delegated legislative powers on the executive.[51] Less clear was what should be made of the separation of judicial power in Chapter III of the Constitution. Should it be interpreted to mean that the judicial power of the Commonwealth could be exercised *only* by federal courts established under Chapter III? Did it mean that *only* judicial power could be conferred on such courts? What was 'the judicial power of the Commonwealth', anyway?

Confronted with the equivalent issue under the US Constitution, the Supreme Court in 1856 drew a distinction between a private rights and public rights, holding that disputes about the former had to be adjudicated by Article III courts, but that disputes about the latter could be adjudicated by courts not established under Article III, or by court-substitute tribunals.[52] However, the Supreme Court has progressively departed from this approach, and the modern case law contains two separate strands of reasoning. According to one, judicial power may be conferred on adjudicators that are not Article III courts provided the exercise of that power is subject to a suitable measure of judicial review by an Article III court.[53] According to the other, judicial power may be conferred on adjudicators that are not Article III courts provided the conferral of such power in the particular case does not unduly undermine the purposes of separation of judicial power, namely to protect the rights of individuals and to prevent excessive concentration of power in the hands of other branches of government.[54]

The High Court's approach to this issue has most in common with the first of these three lines of reasoning.[55] As early as 1909, Griffith CJ enunciated the principle that parliament has no power to invest the judicial power of the Commonwealth 'in any hands' other than those of a Chapter III court.[56] Literally

---

51 *Victorian Stevedoring and General Contracting Co Pty Ltd v Dignan* (1941) 46 CLR 73.

52 *Murray's Lessee v Hoboken Land and Improvement Co* (1856) 18 How 272, 284.

53 E.g. *Crowell v Benson* (1932) 285 US 22.

54 E.g. *Commodity Futures Trading Commission v Schor* (1986) 478 US 833.

55 But for hints of the second see *Harris v Caladine* (1991) 172 CLR 84.

56 *Huddart Parker & Co Pty Ltd v Moorehead* (1909) 8 CLR 330, 355.

applied, this principle could have prevented the creation of administrative tribunals and the conferral of adjudicative functions on the executive with the result, in the opinion of Isaacs J, that 'administration [would be] hampered and either injustice suffered or litigation fostered'.[57] His (widely accepted) view was that efficient conduct of the complex business of government in the welfare and regulatory state required the creation of non-judicial adjudicative bodies. The High Court's technique for facilitating the creation of such bodies was to distinguish between adjudicative functions that are the sole preserve of the judicial branch ('exclusively' or 'inherently' judicial functions), and adjudicative functions that may be performed by either the judicial or the executive branch according to convenience ('innominate' or 'hybrid' functions). In 1956, Griffith CJ's principle was supplemented by the converse proposition that a non-judicial function may not be exercised by a Chapter III court unless it is incidental to judicial functions.[58] Thus was added to the catalogue of functions the category of 'exclusively non-judicial functions'—adjudicative functions that are not incidental to the exercise of the judicial power of the Commonwealth.

The High Court has recognised three exceptions to the principle that judicial power may not be conferred on bodies the members of which are not appointed under s 72 of the Constitution. It has held that military tribunals and courts martial, public service disciplinary tribunals and the houses of parliament exercising their privilege to punish contempts of parliament may exercise judicial power even though they are not Chapter III courts.[59] To the extent that separation of judicial power is designed to protect individual rights and to avoid (the appearance of) conflict of interest, these exceptions are contestable, except perhaps so far as the first relates to proceedings conducted in the actual course of hostilities.

The distinctions between exclusively judicial, innominate and exclusively non-judicial functions have generated an impenetrable thicket of case law that, fortunately, need not be surveyed in this book. But as we will see (in 2.4.2.4), these distinctions and the constitutional principles that produced them have had a profound impact on the development of the Australian administrative law system. As the jurisprudence of the US Supreme Court demonstrates, however, the High Court's interpretation of the separation of judicial power in the Australian Constitution is not the only one possible. There was nothing inevitable about the way the institutional structure of Australian administrative law was to develop in the latter part of the twentieth century.

2.4.1.5 Prerogative writs

As we have seen (2.4.1.2), s 75(v) of the Australian Constitution confers judicial review jurisdiction on the High Court in terms of power to issue injunctions and writs of mandamus and prohibition. It is not clear why s 75(v) does not confer jurisdiction to award a writ of certiorari or, conversely, why it confers jurisdiction to issue an injunction. The fact that the jurisdiction is 'original' means that the applicant for a s 75(v) remedy may apply in the first instance to the High Court and need not initially go to any other court which has power to award such remedies against officers of the Commonwealth. In practice, however, most applications for these remedies are made in the first instance to the Federal Magistrates Court or the Federal Court of Australia, on which the *Judiciary Act 1903* (Cth) confers jurisdiction equivalent to that of the High Court under s 75(v).

---

57   *Federal Commissioner of Taxation v Munro* (1926) 38 CLR 153, 178.

58   *R v Kirby; Ex parte Boilermakers' Society of Australia* (the *Boilermakers'* case) (1956) 94 CLR 254.

59   L Zines, *The High Court and the Constitution*, 5th edn (Annandale, NSW: Federation Press, 2008), 272–3.

Section 75(v) says nothing about the grounds on which the enumerated remedies can be awarded, and it is unclear to what extent any of the grounds of judicial review are constitutionally entrenched.[60] Given that the *Constitution* was drafted at the end of the nineteenth century, it is not surprising that it refers to remedies rather than grounds of review or (more generally) some concept of judicial review of government action. Nor is it surprising that it defines the scope of the jurisdiction institutionally in terms of the concept of 'officer of the Commonwealth' rather than in terms of some concept of reviewable functions. So, for instance, it seems clear that a government-owned corporation is not an officer of the Commonwealth, and so not amenable to the s 75(v) jurisdiction, even if it was established in order to perform some core governmental (or 'public') function (3.4.1.2).

The fact that s 75(v) does no more than confer jurisdiction to award the enumerated remedies alerts us to an issue that looms large in Australian administrative law, namely the importance to an applicant for judicial review of choosing the right court in which to make the application. The prominence of this 'jurisdictional' issue is a result of the fact that the powers of federal courts derive entirely from the Constitution or from statute. As a result, their scope is tied to the words of the text, and federal courts are less free to fill gaps in their jurisdiction than they would be if their judicial review jurisdiction, like that of the Court of Queen's Bench in England and of the Supreme Courts of the Australian states, were 'inherent'—invented and defined by the courts themselves.

During the period with which we are currently dealing, it was assumed that the grounds of judicial review under s 75(v) were to be found in the common law governing the availability of the enumerated remedies. (Recall that under the English formulary system, the grounds of judicial review took the form of preconditions for the issue of a writ rather than of causes of action in their own right.) This meant that the substantive law of judicial review under s 75(v), and the law of judicial review as it operated in the states, could develop in tandem. This was fortunate because the High Court was given a dual role in developing administrative law by virtue of having original jurisdiction under s 75(v), and also jurisdiction to hear appeals from state Supreme Courts from decisions on matters of state administrative law (subject, in this period, to the appellate jurisdiction of the Privy Council). It would have been at least inconvenient if the substantive law of judicial review under s 75(v) were to be different from its common law counterpart.

For most of this period, the High Court's judicial review caseload was dominated by matters arising out of the industrial conciliation and arbitration system and involving the exercise of judicial or quasi-judicial functions. As in the United Kingdom at that time, judicial review was relatively infrequently used to challenge administrative action by the executive, which meant that the High Court, like the colonial courts of the nineteenth century and the state courts in this period, made little or no contribution to the development of a distinctively Australian substantive law of judicial review.

2.4.2 1970 onwards

2.4.2.1 Supremacy of parliament

The major event of this period affecting the powers of Australian legislatures was the enactment of the *Australia Acts* in 1986. Section 2(1) of the Acts removed the limitation imposed by the *Colonial Laws Validity Act* preventing state legislatures from passing legislation with extra-territorial effect.

---

60   See 7.2.3.

The Acts also removed the power of the Westminster parliament to pass statutes affecting the states and, consequently, the requirement that state legislation should be consistent with such statutes. However, s 6 of the *Australia Acts* preserves the requirement that state legislation 'respecting the constitution, powers or procedure of the parliament of the state shall be of no force or effect unless it is made in such manner and form as may from time to time be required by a law made by that parliament'. It is unclear whether, independently of this provision, state parliaments may impose manner and form requirements in relation to (in other words, entrench) legislation respecting other topics.[61]

2.4.2.2 Rule of law

The rule of law remains the foundational justification for judicial review in Australian law. But in more recent years the principle has been interpreted as much in terms of constitutional design as in terms of protecting the individual from official power (see, for example, 6.1). In its modern guise, the rule of law is a constraint on the exercise not only of executive power, but also of judicial power. So understood, the rule of law counsels courts that their proper role is to enforce the *law*, not to judge the wisdom or propriety of government *policy*. This interpretation may be understood as a spin-off from the developments to be outlined in a moment (in 2.4.2.4). Dicey saw separation of powers as inimical to the rule of law, but the modern Australian view is that separation of powers secures the reign of law over the courts.

2.4.2.3 Responsible government

Responsible government in Australia is not a clearly defined legal doctrine based on a set of detailed legal rules. Rather, it is sustained by a combination of constitutional law, constitutional conventions and political practices. Courts play a role in developing and policing the system.[62] In *Egan v Willis*[63] a minister of the New South Wales government was suspended for contempt of the Legislative Council and physically removed from the chamber when he refused to table documents requested by the Council. The minister brought what was, in essence, a judicial review claim for a declaration that the suspension resolution was unlawful, and an action in trespass in respect of his removal from the chamber. The case raised delicate issues about the extent to which the courts should interfere with the internal workings of parliament. Its effect was to establish, as a matter of (judicially enforceable) common law as opposed to (unenforceable) constitutional convention, that the council had the power to suspend a minister who refuses to produce a document that is not subject to privilege. Selway argued that such legalisation of the political process is undesirable because it 'entrenches' a system of government that he considered to be highly unsatisfactory.[64]

In *Lange v Australian Broadcasting Commission*[65] the High Court took the view that in giving legal effect to ideas of responsible government in the federal context, it should stick closely to the words of the Australian Constitution itself. By contrast, in *Egan* it gave legal force to what had previously been

---

61   Lumb, *The Constitutions of the Australian States*, 5th edn, 127–31; A Twomey, 'Manner and Form Limitations on the Power to Amend State Constitutions' (2004) 15 *Public Law Review* 169; J Goldsworthy, 'Manner and Form Revisited: Reflections on *Marquet's* Case' in M Groves (ed), *Law and Government in Australia* (Sydney: Federation Press, 2005).

62   Selway, n 35 above.

63   (1998) 195 CLR 424.

64   Op cit, n 35 above, 55–6, 65.

65   (1997) 189 CLR 520.

unenforceable constitutional conventions that were neither expressed nor implied in the New South Wales Constitution. Evans prefers this latter approach.[66] But perhaps no choice need be made. The difference between the *Lange* and *Egan* approaches may be explicable on the basis, first, that *Lange* concerned the highly controversial issue of the extent to which fundamental rights can be read into the Australian Constitution; and, second, that the adoption of a system of responsible government in the context of framing a federal constitution was the result of conscious deliberation about the construction of a new governmental system, while its adoption in New South Wales was the result of the organic growth of an existing colonial system of government out of the British root-stock.

In the past 40 years, ideas about responsible government have provided the background for the establishment of a plethora of institutions designed to strengthen accountability in public affairs. Such institutions include merits review tribunals (Chapter 8), ombudsmen (9.3), human rights and privacy commissions, anti-corruption bodies, parliamentary committees (9.4.4.3), and 'internal' review and complaint mechanisms (9.2). Although they are often explained and justified in terms of the relative inability of parliaments to monitor and control governments, they are probably better understood not in terms of the relationship between the government and the legislature, but as products of a social and political climate in which those who exercise public power and authority are expected to be more directly responsive to the subjects of that authority and power.

2.4.2.4 Separation of powers

By the middle of the twentieth century, administrative law and what has come to be called 'the administrative justice system' were causing considerable dissatisfaction. One ground of criticism was the focus of the law on remedies at the expense of grounds of review, and another was the potential gap between the merits and the success of judicial review applications caused by various 'technical' preconditions for the issue of prerogative writs. We will examine these complaints in a moment (in 2.4.2.5). The patchy and disorganised nature of the 'system' of administrative tribunals was another source of unease.

In 1968 the Commonwealth government appointed an Administrative Review Committee to examine administrative law and the administrative justice system. A main recommendation of the Kerr Committee's 1971 Report[67] was the establishment of a tribunal, with jurisdiction covering a wide range of government activities, to review decisions of administrative officials and first-tier administrative tribunals. In support of this recommendation, the committee argued that inadequate provision was currently made for citizens to challenge administrative decisions 'on their merits'. It was the committee's view that most administrative decisions raise 'non-justiciable issues', and that reviewing the merits (as opposed to the legality) of such decisions is not a judicial function and therefore could not be committed to Chapter III courts. For this reason, the new tribunal was to be established not as a Chapter III court, but as a body exercising power under Chapter II of the Constitution. The Administrative Appeals Tribunal was established by the *Administrative Appeals Tribunal Act 1975* (Cth), and was charged with what is now called 'merits review' (Chapter 8).

The sharp distinction between merits review and judicial review, and the strict separation of judicial power on which it is based, are probably the most distinctive aspects of Australian administrative law.

---

66   S Evans, 'Commentary' in Stone and Williams (eds), *The High Court at the Crossroads*, 73.

67   Commonwealth Administrative Review Committee, *Commonwealth Administrative Review Committee Report,* Parliament of the Commonwealth of Australia Paper No 144 (1971).

Ostensibly, at least, they have produced a very different administrative justice system from that found in the UK, where administrative tribunals are firmly located within the judicial branch of government. The Australian system is also—on its face, anyway—different from that in the USA, where Article III courts and non-Article III tribunals are treated as species of the same genus.

2.4.2.5 Prerogative writs

The Kerr Committee's other main recommendations were establishment of a new federal court to exercise judicial review jurisdiction, and introduction of a simplified procedure of applying for judicial review. The former recommendation led to the creation of the Federal Court of Australia, which is now the prime forum for judicial review applications under the federal law. The latter recommendation was implemented by the enactment of the *Administrative Decisions (Judicial Review) Act 1977* (Cth) (*ADJR Act*). For present purposes, the main features of the *ADJR Act* were, first, replacement of the procedure of applying for one of the prerogative writs or for a declaration or injunction with a single procedure of applying for an order for review; second, a shift of the focus of judicial review law from remedies to grounds of review, by reconceptualising remedies in terms of 'the powers of the court in respect of an application for an order for review' (s 16); third, a detailed statement of the grounds of review (ss 5 and 6); and, fourth, an obligation, on request, to give reasons for decisions (s 13). The *ADJR Act* will be discussed in some detail in later chapters. Here, only a few general points need to be made.

First, although the *ADJR Act* created a new, simplified judicial review regime at the federal level, it did not purport to affect either the common law of judicial review applicable in the states or the law of judicial review under s 75(v) of the Constitution, both of which retained the prerogative writs. At the time of writing, only three state jurisdictions have adopted clones of the *ADJR Act*. As a result, there are three main avenues for judicial review applications in Australia, each distinct from the others: s 75(v) of the Constitution, the *ADJR Act*[68] and the common law regime. The result is a complex and crowded juridical landscape, littered with traps for the unwary. Second, although the grounds of review listed in the *ADJR Act* were essentially intended to restate the common law, they depart from and supplement it in various ways. The extent to which the grounds of judicial review under the *ADJR Act* and the common law (as it has developed since 1977) differ raises a number of complex issues.

Third, one aim—and the effect—of the establishment of the Federal Court and the enactment of the *ADJR Act* was greatly to reduce the High Court's caseload under s 75(v) of the Constitution. In the course of the 1980s, largely as a result of an upsurge in the international movement of persons and uncontrolled immigration into Australia, challenges under the *ADJR Act* to immigration decisions came to represent a very significant proportion of the Federal Court's judicial review caseload.[69] In the eyes of successive governments, the Federal Court adopted an unreasonably pro-immigrant stance in many cases. In order to counter this trend, various statutory provisions were enacted from 1989 onwards, designed to clip the wings of the Federal Court in immigration matters. The net result of these provisions and their interpretation by the High Court[70] was to give immigrants a strong incentive to invoke the court's constitutionally entrenched judicial review jurisdiction under s 75(v). As a result, the High

---

68   The state regimes modelled on the *ADJR Act* can be included in this category for present purposes.

69   For a more detailed account see S Gageler, 'The Impact of Migration Law on the Development of Australian Administrative Law' (2010) 17 *Australian Journal of Administrative Law* 92.

70   In *Abebe v Commonwealth* (1999) 197 CLR 510.

Court was swamped by a flood of immigration cases. In order to address the problem, legislative changes conferred on the Federal Court the same jurisdiction to issue injunctions and writs of prohibition and mandamus as the High Court has under s 75(v); and they were designed to subject immigration decisions to the constitutionally entrenched minimum of judicial review (which the legislature cannot remove) and no more.

As a result of the enactment of the *ADJR Act*, the development of s 75(v) jurisprudence had been more or less in abeyance since 1980 when, at the turn of the twenty-first century, as a result of the legislative developments just outlined, the High Court was confronted by the need to reinterpret s 75(v) in the light of developments in administrative law in the previous 20 years and in a context (immigration) in which it had relatively rarely been applied. To complicate matters even further, those developments had taken place in an environment dominated by the *ADJR Act*, by which the grip of the technicalities of the prerogative writs had been released. The result is a body of judicial review law that is distinct from the *ADJR Act* regime, and its relationship with the remedy-based common law that has developed in the states in uncertain in various respects.

The relationship between the s 75(v) constitutional regime of judicial review on the one hand, and the statutory and common law judicial review regimes on the other, has become even more complex as a result of the High Court's decision in *Kirk v Industrial Court of New South Wales*.[71] Section 75(v) of the Australian Constitution creates an entrenched minimum of judicial review that the federal parliament cannot remove. State constitutions contain no such provision. The effect of *Kirk*, however, is to impose an analogous limitation on the power of state parliaments. This development raises a host of issues, two of which deserve brief mention here. First, the s 75(v) minimum of judicial review is restricted to claims against 'officers of the Commonwealth'. Will the state analogue be similarly limited—say, to claims against 'officers of the State'? Second, what will be the impact of the law developed under s 75(v) on the common law of judicial review in the states to the extent that it exceeds the minimum provision required by *Kirk*?

It is no exaggeration to call the law of judicial review in Australia a mess and a quagmire. The reformers of the 1970s cherished the hope of simplifying the administrative justice system. But in less than 40 years, their efforts have produced only increased complexity and more traps for litigants.

Now that we have gained some sense of the historical development and constitutional context of Australian administrative law and the administrative justice system, we are in a better position to navigate the maze of its highways and byways.

---

71   (2010) 239 CLR 531.

3

The Scope of Judicial Review

3.1 General introduction to judicial review

This and the next four chapters are concerned with judicial review. In thinking about judicial review in particular (and administrative law more generally), it is important always to bear in mind that Australia is a federation, and not to identify Australian law exclusively with federal law. Although the Australian legal system has an integrated judicial system, it remains useful to distinguish between the judicial review jurisdiction exercised by federal courts—the High Court and the Federal Court in particular[1]—and that exercised by state courts. At the federal level, the High Court's 'original' judicial review jurisdiction derives from the Constitution. By statute, the Federal Court shares this 'constitutional' jurisdiction,[2] but also has further sources of jurisdiction under the *Administrative Decisions (Judicial Review) Act 1977* (Cth) and (separately) under the *Judiciary Act 1903* (Cth). By contrast, state courts have what is called 'inherent' or 'supervisory' judicial review jurisdiction. Until recently, the legal source of this jurisdiction was thought to be the common law. However, the High Court has controversially held, in *Kirk's* case (2010), that aspects of this jurisdiction are, like the High Court's 'original' jurisdiction, derived from and protected by the federal Constitution.[3] Although the constitutional basis for the Supreme Courts' entrenched judicial review jurisdiction is distinct from the High Court's jurisdiction to review decisions made by 'officers of the Commonwealth', we will see that the purpose and nature of the two jurisdictions have been conceptualised consistently. To make matters more complex, in some states, courts also have statutory sources of judicial review jurisdiction. In three of the four states where such statutes exist, the approach has been to a greater or lesser extent to clone the basic approach to judicial review adopted by the *ADJR Act* (3.5.3).

Understanding of the system of judicial review in Australia is further confounded by the fact that associated with these various sources of judicial review jurisdiction may be different bodies of law dealing with matters such as the scope and grounds of, and access to, judicial review, as well as the available remedies. Most obviously, the *ADJR Act* (like its state clones) not only confers judicial review jurisdiction, but also contains rules about the scope and grounds of, and access to, judicial review, and about remedies. While the effect of the *Kirk* decision will broadly be to 'bring into alignment' the law

---

1   On the jurisdiction of the Federal Magistrates Court see note 95 below.

2   *Judiciary Act 1903* (Cth), s 39B.

3   *Kirk v Industrial Court of New South Wales* (2010) 239 CLR 531. The basis for this conclusion is examined in 3.4.3 and 7.1.

associated with the supervisory jurisdiction of state courts on these matters with the law applicable in the constitutional judicial review jurisdiction of the High Court (and the statutory *Judiciary Act* jurisdiction of the Federal Court)[4] the extent of any differences remains unclear. In addition to its 'original' judicial review jurisdiction, the High Court has appellate jurisdiction in relation to the judicial review jurisdiction of other federal courts, both constitutional and statutory, and also in relation to the various sources of judicial review jurisdiction exercised by state courts.

Although a degree of technical detail is necessary in explaining the law, we have tried to avoid getting overly bogged down in the intricacies of this extremely complex system in order to provide a strategic overview. Important things to bear in mind when reading the judicial review chapters are:

- the distinction between federal law and state law;

- the distinction between judicial review and merits review; and

- the distinction between the various sources of judicial review jurisdiction—the Constitution, the *ADJR Act*, other federal statutes (notably the *Judiciary Act*), state statutes and the common law.

This is a big ask; but it is important not to lose sight of the forest by trying to count the trees.

To succeed in a judicial review application, an applicant must satisfy a number of distinct requirements: the court must have jurisdiction to judicially review the impugned act or decision and it must accept that the application raises 'justiciable' issues; the applicant must be an appropriate person to bring the application (that is, the applicant must have 'standing'); there must be a breach of an administrative law norm (that is, a 'ground of review' must be available); and the court must also have power to grant an appropriate remedy. Additionally, it must be the case that the legislature has not validly excluded or diminished the court's review jurisdiction. In practice, these issues may be interrelated in various ways. But it is helpful to deal with the issues separately so that their interrelations can be properly understood.

This raises the question of the order in which they are best discussed. There is no single, correct way of arranging an analysis of judicial review, and we have chosen to order the topics as follows: scope of judicial review, that is, issues connected with the courts' judicial review jurisdiction (Chapter 3); judicial review remedies (Chapter 4); grounds of judicial review (Chapter 5); access to judicial review, principally a discussion of 'standing' to seek review (Chapter 6); and, finally, statutory restriction of judicial review (Chapter 7).

Although at first sight it may appear odd to deal with the remedies which may be awarded if all other elements of a judicial review application are present before discussing those elements, it will be seen that a discussion of remedies equips us with a conceptual apparatus and the requisite language necessary for a clear understanding of issues relevant to the grounds of review, standing and the exclusion of review by statute.[5] For example, the need to establish that a ground of judicial review amounts to a 'jurisdictional error' depends upon the remedy sought and the source of the court's jurisdiction to engage in review; standing is remedy-specific; and the interpretation of statutes attempting to oust judicial review jurisdiction has been affected by concepts (including 'jurisdictional error') which developed in the context of the availability of particular remedies. Although these chapters may be read in any order,

---

4   J Spigelman, 'The Centrality of Jurisdictional Error' (2010) 21 *Public Law Review* 77, 91.

5   Historically, this can be explained by the fact that the law of judicial review developed through the medium of the prerogative writs: 2.1.4. In other words, administrative law was remedially oriented. For this reason some of the concepts necessary to understand the nature of the courts' review jurisdiction (i.e. the scope of review) are related to concepts which have their origin in the availability of judicial review's remedies.

we think that reading them in the order they are presented will provide an illuminating picture of the conceptual structure of the law of judicial review.

In this chapter we begin the examination of judicial review by considering how far the law of judicial review extends. We answer the question: what decisions or acts are subject to judicial review? It should be remembered, however, that it is difficult to understand the appropriate scope of judicial review in isolation from its substantive principles—the content of the legal norms with which decision-makers subject to judicial review must comply is obviously relevant to the question of whether particular decisions and decision-makers *should* be reviewed against those norms. Indeed, the question of the scope of judicial review (what or whose decisions are to be reviewable) is necessarily answered in the context of background ideas about its general nature and purposes. Thus, before examining the scope of the jurisdiction of Australian courts under the variety of federal and state judicial review regimes, we begin with an overview of the nature of this review jurisdiction.

3.2 The nature of the courts' review jurisdiction

Judicial review was originally a product of the common law. For this reason the courts' power (that is, jurisdiction) to undertake judicial review, in the absence of statutory or constitutional authorisation, is traditionally describes as being 'inherent'. Put simply, the courts claimed for themselves the power to review certain acts and decisions of government administration.[6] For the historically minded, the obvious question is: how did the judges get away with this institutional power grab? Part of the answer lies in the fact that the bodies and officers being reviewed at that time were typically thought to have a 'judicial' nature (and thus were appropriately reviewed by the superior courts).[7] It was also the case that the 'administration' over which the courts were asserting their jurisdiction was locally based rather than the 'Crown' (that is, the powerful central government).[8] Whatever the historical details, the continuing assertion of this review power is justified by reference to its *limited* nature. The courts have consistently (if not always persuasively) denied that the purpose of review is to usurp the powers given by statute or common law to government administrators. This denial introduces the notion that judicial review is part of a superior court's 'supervisory' jurisdiction. The purpose of review is not to *usurp* powers of administrators but merely to *supervise* their exercise. The meaning of this claim tends to be explored by reference to two fundamental distinctions: the contrasts between *appeal* and *review*, and *judicial* (or legality) review and *merits* review. The questions of whether these distinctions adequately reflect the role of judges undertaking review, and the extent to which judges should respect these distinctions, are subject to ongoing debates. But they can be adequately considered only after the substantive principles or grounds of review have been examined.

---

6   The decisive period for the assertion of this jurisdiction was the seventeenth century: L L Jaffe and E G Henderson, 'Judicial Review and the Rule of Law: Historical Origins' (1956) 72 *Law Quarterly Review* 345.

7   In the relevant period the justices of the peace (i.e. lay judicial officers) became the 'administrators of England': ibid, 363.

8   *Mayor and Aldermen of the City of London v Richard Henry Cox* (1867) LR 2 HL 239, 254.

3.2.1 The appeal/review distinction

The distinction between appeal and review focuses on the idea that, although appeal courts can typically substitute their own decision for that of the original decision-maker, a review court cannot. Even if a court undertaking judicial review decides that there is only one legally available outcome, the court will, in most circumstances, remit the decision to the original decision-maker to be made in accordance with the law.[9] Whereas judicial review was originally a creation of the common law, appeals are creatures of statute.[10] As such, appeals come with whatever powers and procedures are deemed appropriate by the legislature.[11] A general appeal—where the appellate body can consider all aspects of a decision (law, fact, and policy)—typically carries with it a remedial power to substitute a new decision. This remedial power stands in sharp contrast with the legal consequences attaching to judicial review's standard remedies which are connected with conclusions about the legality (validity), and not the correctness, of decisions.[12] (Note that appeals may be limited to points or questions of law and, if this is the case, the function of the court hearing an appeal is in essence the same as that performed by a judicial review.) The difficulty with this way of stating the distinction between review and appeal—which focuses on the more limited remedial powers of judicial review which typically do not enable the substitution of a new decision to replace that of the original decision-maker—is that it tells us very little about any substantive differences between appeal and review (whether they are decided on the basis of different principles). It merely restates the basic functions of judicial review remedies.

The court's limited remedial powers in judicial review applications are reflective of the traditional 'supervisory' rationale for judicial review under which the role of the courts, in upholding the 'rule of law', is to ensure those exercising powers conferred by parliament are kept within 'the limits of their jurisdiction';[13] that is, to ensure that they do not act beyond their powers (ultra vires).[14] Thus, although courts may ensure that decision-makers do not exceed their legal powers, judicial review is 'not intended to take away from [government] authorities the powers and discretions properly vested in them by law and to substitute the courts as the bodies making the decisions'.[15] Courts can supervise the boundaries of an administrator's legal powers, but should not exercise those powers. In this way, 'neither branch usurps or intrudes upon the functions proper to the other'.[16] Nevertheless the distinction between review and appeal in and of itself gives little away about the substantive nature of the supervision undertaken by judicial review courts.

---

9   *Minister for Immigration and Ethnic Affairs v Guo* (1997) 191 CLR 559, 598 ('*Guo*').

10   See *Fox v Percy* (2003) 214 CLR 118, 124.

11   *Kostas v HIA Insurance Services Pty Ltd* (2010) 241 CLR 390, 399–400 [27].

12   The traditional judicial review remedies (the prerogative writs) allow courts to quash decisions illegally or unlawfully made (certiorari), prohibit the commencement or continuation of illegal action (prohibition), or compel the performance of certain legal duties (mandamus). These remedies are explained in Chapter 4.

13   Jaffe and Henderson, n 6 above, 358.

14   On the distinction between jurisdictional and non-jurisdictional errors, and ultra vires and intra vires, see 4.4.1 and 4.4.2.

15   *Chief Constable of North Wales Police v Evans* [1982] 3 All ER 141, 145 ('*Evans*').

16   *Minister for Immigration and Ethnic Affairs v Guo* (1997) 191 CLR 559, 600.

3.2.2 Judicial review, merits review and the separation of powers

The distinction between judicial (or legality) review and merits review can be understood as an elaboration of the distinction between review and appeal, though the focus is less on the formal remedial powers available to the court and more on the notion that the grounds on which decisions may be reviewed must be restricted. That is, the distinction between judicial review and merits review emphasises that principles or norms of judicial review are distinct from, and more limited than, the full set of principles, norms and matters relevant to the correctness or wisdom of the original administrative decision. However, the notion that the legal boundaries patrolled by judicial review are not coextensive with the merits of a decision does not indicate how exactly those boundaries are to be ascertained.

Judicial review, it is sometimes said, involves 'a review of the manner in which the decision was made'.[17] But this way of drawing the distinction between review (which focuses on procedure) and the merits (which focuses on substance) is potentially misleading. Although some grounds of judicial review do focus on procedure, others clearly raise matters of substance.[18] The so-called *Wednesbury* unreasonableness ground of review is only the starkest example: a decision may be held illegal where it is so unreasonable that no reasonable decision-maker could have so decided (5.4.4). No matter how deferential judges are in applying this ground of review, it cannot be coherently characterised as raising only procedural questions. Much the same can be said about the 'error of law' ground of review (5.4.2, 5.4.3.3), which may allow judges to replace an administrator's conclusion about what the law requires in particular circumstances with their own conclusion, which again raises questions about the substantive correctness of the decision.[19]

In theory, where an administrator is exercising statutory powers, the idea that judicial review should patrol the boundaries of their powers appears straightforward. However, the reality is that the legal boundaries that circumscribe the decision-making powers of the executive government are, in any given situation, defined by a complex amalgam of statutory limitations and common law doctrine as applied to the particulars of an individual case (see 5.1.1).[20] Consequently, few commentators deny the *extensive* creative role played by modern judges in stating the legal boundaries of executive power, even where those powers derive from statute.[21] At least to some extent, then, it is possible for judges to allow themselves to be guided by principles which concern whether the decision was right or fair, by reference to general norms of 'good administration' or theories about the appropriate relationship between individuals and the state.[22] This is not to say that judges make everything up and are wholly unconstrained. But if they are limited by a clear distinction between legal issues and the merits, this remains to be satisfactorily articulated.

---

17   *Evans* [1982] 3 All ER 141, 155 (Lord Brightman).

18   In 5.3 we examine grounds which focus on errors related to the reasoning processes of decision-makers—a broader notion than procedure.

19   See, further, P Cane, 'Merits Review and Judicial Review: The AAT as Trojan Horse' (2000) 28 *Federal Law Review* 213, 222.

20   See T R S Allan, 'Legislative Supremacy and legislative Intent: A Reply to Professor Craig' (2004) 24 *Oxford Journal of Legal Studies* 563.

21   This is so even for those who believe that judicial review is an elaborate exercise in statutory interpretation, where judges are in theory doing the bidding of the legislature (5.1.3): see, e.g., M Elliot, *The Constitutional Foundations of Judicial Review* (Oxford: Hart Publishing, 2001).

22   Notwithstanding that judges often deny this: see 5.1.1.

What is clear is that the legality/merits divide reflects a deeply ingrained concern that judicial review should not, in the name of the 'rule of law', enable judges to unduly colonise public administration by reference to their own perceptions of what 'good administration' requires. Although the distinction has traditionally been seen as a corollary of the ultra vires or rule of law rationale for judicial review, it also reflects complex ideas about the separation of powers, according to which legal checks on the executive should not allow judges to arrogate to themselves functions which have been given to more appropriate (and, perhaps, more legitimate) decision-makers (3.6.2.1). For example, Brennan J has argued that courts are not equipped (that is, they lack the expertise and resources) to make decisions which require individual and community interests to be balanced and that adversarial processes are not well suited to decision-making which requires multiple interests to be considered and balanced.[23] In Australia, these functional reasons for restraint and the fact that the separation of judicial power from executive power is entrenched in the Commonwealth Constitution have led many to conclude that the separation of powers principle is the best available candidate to guide the judicial choices which mark out the limits of judicial review.[24] However, like most abstract constitutional principles, the separation of powers has received different interpretations in different times and places and it continues to be vigorously contested.[25] According to the 'pure' version, there are supposedly three distinct powers of government—legislative, executive and judicial—each of which is to be carried out by a distinct institution (which does not share personnel with the others). We have already seen that this version of the separation of powers is not a feature of Australian constitutional practice (2.4.1.4). Indeed, if applied rigorously, it would make all modern governments unrecognisable. Moreover, although this version of the separation of powers certainly attempts to disperse power—the 'accumulation of all powers … in the same hands' wrote Madison, 'is the very definition of tyranny'[26]—it arguably undermines one of the most effective means available to prevent the abuse of authority, namely that 'power should be a check to power'.[27]

In Australia, the High Court has held that Ch III of the Constitution subjects federal executive power to the law and, further, that it is the job of the judicature to declare and enforce the legal limits of the powers conferred upon administrative decision-makers (2.4.1.2; 3.4.1).[28] This is central to the court's understanding of how the rule of law is secured under Australia's constitutional arrangements, which, in turn, is part of the justification for the court's strict approach to the separation of federal judicial power (2.4.1.4). According to this strict approach to the separation of *judicial* power (at

---

23   *Attorney-General (NSW) v Quin* (1990) 170 CLR 1, 37. For further discussion, see Matthew Groves, 'Federal Constitutional Influences on State Judicial Review' (2011) 39 *Federal Law Review* 399, 400.

24   See, e.g., M Aronson, B Dyer and M Groves, *Judicial Review of Administrative Action*, 4th edn (Pyrmont, NSW: Lawbook Co, 2009), 169; B Selway, 'The Principle Behind Common Law Judicial Review of Administrative Action—The Search Continues' (2002) 30 *Federal Law Review* 217. The rule of law also has constitutional status, albeit the diminished status of a 'constitutional assumption': *Australian Communist Party v Commonwealth* (1951) 83 CLR 1. However, this principle is understood more as a corollary of the separation of judicial power than as a principle with independent and direct normative impact: *Re Minister for Immigration and Multicultural Affairs; ex parte Lam* (2003) 214 CLR 1, 23 (McHugh and Gummow JJ) ('*Lam*').

25   Compare E Barendt, 'Separation of Powers and Constitutional Government' [1995] *Public Law* 599; and A Tomkins, *Public Law* (Oxford: Oxford University Press, 2003), Ch 23.

26   J Cooke (ed), *The Federalist* (Middletown: Wesleyan University Press, 1961), 324 (James Madison).

27   C L Montesquieu *The Spirit of the Laws* (T Nugent trans, 1873) Bk XI, Ch IV, 172 [trans of: *De l'Esprit des Lois*]. This theme is a central feature of US constitutional design.

28   *Corporation of City of Enfield v Development Assessment Commission* (2000) 199 CLR 135, 153 ('*Enfield*').

the Commonwealth level), whatever the 'merits' of administrative decision-making involves, it is off limits to federal judges as it would involve the courts in the exercise of non-judicial functions (8.1; 8.2.1).

Again, however, this analysis (like the basic rule of law or ultra vires justification for judicial review) fails to illuminate the *specific criteria* by which the boundaries of legal powers are to be drawn. Although it is clear that 'the merits of administrative action, to the extent that they can be distinguished from legality, are for the repository of the relevant power and, subject to political control, for the repository alone',[29] it is difficult to give concrete content to the concept of 'the merits' of a decision in a non-circular way. As one judge concluded, the merits of a decision are to be found in 'that diminishing field left after permissible judicial review'.[30] That is, the legality/merits distinction is simply marked by whether or not a particular ground of judicial review is available in a given case; if it is not, then judges cannot interfere with the 'merits' of the decision. But the question we have been examining is whether the separation of powers principle can provide guidance on this very issue, that is, when courts can permissibly undertake judicial review.

It is, then, difficult to conclude that the separation of powers enables us to clarify the details of the boundary between merits and legality review. Nonetheless, it is important to acknowledge that the strict separation of judicial power in Australia plays a substantial role in heightening judicial sensibilities to the importance of leaving *some* latitude for administrators to get things 'wrong'.[31] In this way we can also understand the wariness of Australian judges about enforcing so-called 'substantive' versions of the 'rule of law', which explicitly invite judges to make value judgments on the fairness of outcomes.[32] There is, in short, a separation of powers sensibility which runs much deeper in the Australian judicial psyche (influenced by an entrenched constitutional separation of judicial power) than in the English.

> In Australia, the existence of a ... written federal constitution, with separation of the judicial power, necessarily presents a frame of reference which differs from both the English and other European systems ... An aspect of the rule of law under the *Constitution* is that the role or function of Ch III courts does not extend to the performance of the legislative function of translating policy into statutory form or the executive function of administration.[33]

The constitutional separation of powers influences, even if it does not determine, the development of specific doctrines associated with the grounds of judicial review. Admittedly, this is a vague conclusion. However, to the extent the constitutional context for judicial review contemplates both judicial values associated with legality and other values associated with administration, it may be, as one influential judge has suggested, that the search for 'conceptually definitive boundaries and precise tests' of the function of judicial review 'is doomed to fail'.[34] What can be concluded, however, is that legality/merits distinction is flexible enough for judges to pay considerable deference to decision-makers even if it is accepted that their decisions are subject to judicial review.

---

29   *Attorney-General (NSW) v Quin* (1990) 170 CLR 1, 36 (Brennan J).

30   *Greyhound Racing Authority (NSW) v Bragg* [2003] NSWCA 388, [46]. See Aronson, Dyer and Groves n 24 above, 171–2.

31   E.g. *Minister for Immigration and Citizenship v SZJSS* (2010) 243 CLR 164, 175–8.

32   *Lam* (2003) 214 CLR 1, 2 (McHugh and Gummow JJ).

33   Ibid, 24–5.

34   J Basten, 'The Supervisory Jurisdiction of the Supreme Courts' (2011) 85 *Australian Law Journal* 273, 294.

3.3 The shifting and complex boundaries of judicial review

Armed with this overview of the nature of judicial review and its basic rule of law and separation of powers rationales, it is unsurprising to discover that the most straightforward way to delineate the scope of judicial review is to say that the law focuses on the review of *government* power (in particular, review of the administrative or executive branch of government).[35] Though this is true as a broad-brush generalisation, the scope of judicial review in Australia is characterised by considerable complexity for a number of reasons.

First, even under the 'institutional approach' to the scope of judicial review (where its subject matter is delimited by reference to the institutions of the executive branch of government (1.1)), the common law never subjected *all* government decision-makers to judicial review. Historically, certain decision-makers (for example, Governors and the Governor-General) and categories of power (for example, prerogative powers) were immune from review (3.6.2.2). Moreover, although the law is increasingly hostile to immunities based on formal classifications of powers or categories of decision-makers, it continues to be the case that the nature of a particular power may take its exercise beyond review by the courts (because it is 'non-justiciable' (3.6.2) or an exercise of 'private' rather than 'public' power (3.6.1)), at least in relation to some of the substantive grounds of judicial review.

Second, attention must be paid to attempts by the legislature to oust or diminish the courts' powers of judicial review. Although there is an entrenched minimum provision of judicial review at the Commonwealth and state levels, legislatures can remove the availability of some of judicial review's remedies and, subject to unclear limits, it appears there are legislative techniques which may operate to diminish the practical efficacy of judicial review. These issues will be examined in Chapter 7. Although judicial review is certainly focused upon the control of government power, it has never applied uniformly to each and every exercise of power by the government.

The third reason why the law has not contented itself with general references to the amenability of 'government' decisions to review is, perhaps, logically prior to questions about whether particular government decisions should be subject to judicial review. Before asking whether certain decisions made by the 'government' should not be reviewable, we first need to know what 'government' is and which decision-makers are included within it. It turns out that this basic question has never been given a satisfactory answer. In part, this uncertainty reflects the historical development of administrative law, where the availability of the prerogative writs (particularly certiorari and prohibition) adapted slowly and haphazardly in response to the changing modes of public administration (2.1.4). In more recent times, the boundaries of the executive branch of government (and the applicability of judicial review to particular decisions) have been further complicated by the changing nature of governance (1.1). These developments have, particularly in England, squarely raised the question of the extent to which some 'private' decision-makers are or should be subject to judicial review, at least when undertaking 'public' or 'governmental' functions. Australian courts are only just beginning to think through these developments (3.4.1.2; 3.5.1.4.2; 3.6.1).

---

35   M Aronson, 'Is the ADJR Act Hampering the Development of Australian Administrative Law?' (2004) 15 *Public Law Review* 202, 209.

The final reason for complexity is that much depends on the source and terms of the jurisdiction of the court in which an application for review is brought. Some states have statutory regimes in addition to 'supervisory' common law jurisdiction (and part of the 'supervisory' review jurisdiction is now considered to be entrenched by operation of the Commonwealth Constitution). At the federal level, there are multiple statutory sources of jurisdiction in addition to the High Court's constitutionally entrenched judicial review jurisdiction. To an extent, this level of complexity is the price of federalism; it reflects the need to define, by constitutional[36] or statutory[37] provisions, the limits of federal judicial review jurisdiction (2.4.2.5). Thus, although the law relevant to determining the scope of judicial review in the various state and federal jurisdictions often raises broadly similar underlying issues, these issues are channelled through differently formulated constitutional, statutory and common law tests.

In reaching the conclusion, in *Kirk*, that aspects of state Supreme Courts' supervisory jurisdiction cannot be removed by legislation, the High Court emphasised the constitutionally mandated role that state Supreme Courts play in an *integrated* Australian judicature created by the Constitution. Consistent with this emphasis, our discussion of the law delimiting the scope of review in Australia will consider constitutional sources of review jurisdiction, statutory sources of jurisdiction, and then common law sources of judicial review jurisdiction. It is often helpful to think about the various sources of jurisdiction in terms of a basic divide between state and federal jurisdiction. However, the fact that a core part of the state courts' jurisdiction is now conceptualised as being derived from the Constitution and the acceptance of the role state Supreme Courts play in an integrated judicature supervised by the High Court[38] provide reasons for commencing our analysis with the constitutional sources of judicial review jurisdiction. Moreover, an understanding of the increasing influence of the Constitution on judicial review in federal and state jurisdictions is crucial to understanding the doctrinal trajectory of the law.

Before turning to the details of the law delimiting the scope of review under the various constitutional, statutory and common law sources of jurisdiction in Australia, it is worth emphasising that the question of the appropriate scope of review raises fundamental issues about what judicial review is for—in whatever jurisdictional context the question arises. If we scratch the surface of the often technical and complicated legal rules which determine the reach of the principles of judicial review, we are likely to uncover large questions: the nature of 'public' power; the competing mechanisms and justifications for checking its exercise; and at the highest level of abstraction, the relationship between individuals and the various institutions of the state. Despite the fact that it is difficult to fit all of the pieces of Australian law's jurisdictional jigsaw neatly together, the discussion in the remainder of this chapter indicates the emergence of three conceptually distinct bases for judicial review—constitutional review (deriving from s 75(v) of the Constitution, but also replicated in s 39B(1) of the *Judiciary Act*, in respect of the exercise of federal jurisdiction and, from s 73 of the Constitution, in respect to state Supreme Courts),[39] statutory review (typified by the Commonwealth *ADJR Act*, though some states have analogous judicial review statutes), and the continuance of 'common law' or supervisory review jurisdictions of the states, to the extent these go beyond the jurisdiction of state Supreme Courts which is guaranteed by the Constitution.[40]

---

36   Australian Constitution ss 75(v) and 75(iii): see 3.4.1, 3.4.2.

37   Principally, the *Administrative Decisions (Judicial Review) Act 1977* (Cth) ('*ADJR Act*') and ss 39B(1) and (1A)(c) of the *Judiciary Act 1903* (Cth): see 3.4.1, 3.5.1, 3.5.2.

38   *Kirk v Industrial Court of New South Wales* (2010) 239 CLR 531, 581.

39   The extent to which doctrinal differences which have existed between section 75(v) cases and judicial review cases arising in state jurisdictions will be minimised over time is an issue raised by the *Kirk* decision: see Spigelman, n 4 above, 81.

40   Where the alternative sources of jurisdiction conferred by s 75(iii) of the Constitution and s 39B(1A)(c) of the *Judiciary Act* fit into this picture is considered below.

3.4 Constitutional sources of judicial review jurisdiction

3.4.1 Section 75(v) of the Constitution and s 39B of the *Judiciary Act*

The High Court's constitutionally entrenched 'original' (as opposed to appellate) judicial review jurisdiction is conferred in terms of the availability of named remedies—mandamus, prohibition and injunction—against an 'officer of the Commonwealth' (see 2.4.1.2). This review jurisdiction has a high constitutional purpose: to ensure that the High Court has jurisdiction to determine the legality of Commonwealth government decisions. In recent years, it has been routinely cited as an important institutional protection for the maintenance of the 'rule of law' in Australia.[41] Although this lofty purpose has long been recognised, the importance of s 75(v) has, in recent years, been strongly reasserted (2.4.1.5; 2.4.2.5). In part, and to pre-empt some of our discussion of the *ADJR Act*, this was due to the way in which the federal statutory review regime attempted to reorient the law of judicial review—away from the prerogative writs to a focus on the grounds on which decisions could be reviewed. The *ADJR Act* was intended to simplify the law in a number of ways (see 3.5.1) by sweeping away technicalities associated with judicial review's remedies. We will see that although the *ADJR Act* was never intended to provide a jurisdictional basis for the review of all government decisions (that is, its scope was limited), the intention to provide a simplified form of review has been partially frustrated by narrow interpretations of the Act's jurisdictional requirements (3.5.1).

Indeed, soon after the commencement of the *ADJR Act* it was recognised that some decisions, which could not be reviewed under that Act, would fall within the High Court's s 75(v) jurisdiction. Thus in 1983, s 39B(1) was inserted into the *Judiciary Act* to confer an identical jurisdiction (subject to minor exceptions) upon the Federal Court. To avoid overburdening the High Court with a significant trial function, the *Judiciary Act* was also amended to allow cases commenced in its original jurisdiction to be remitted to the Federal Court.[42] Despite the fact that s 39B(1) duplicated the terms of s 75(v) of the Constitution, it is fair to say that the Federal Court initially developed the substantive law largely by reference to the common law[43] (subject to the 'officer of the Commonwealth' requirement, which is considered below). Until recently, review under s 39B(1) was often dubbed 'common law' review.

3.4.1.1 The emergence of the 'constitutional' remedies

The constitutional foundation of judicial review under s 75(v) (and by implication, s 39B(1))[44] is now a preoccupation of Australian law. In large part, this can be explained as a by-product of the legislature's successive attempts to curb the Federal Court's powers to review migration decisions. For a period in

---

41   For example, *Plaintiff S157/2002 v Commonwealth* (2003) 211 CLR 476. In Australia, the need for an impartial tribunal to maintain the federal division of legislative power is another recurrent justification for the judicial enforcement of the rule of law by the judicial branch: *R v Kirby; Ex parte Boilermakers' Society of Australia* (1956) 94 CLR 254, 276.

42   *Judiciary Act 1903* (Cth), s 44(2A).

43   See, e.g., *Minister for Arts, Heritage and Environment v Peko-Wallsend Ltd* (1987) 15 FCR 274.

44   *Deputy Commissioner of Taxation v Richard Walter Pty Ltd* (1995) 183 CLR 168, 181, 192–3, 212.

the 1990s, the legislature purported to withdraw the Federal Court's jurisdiction (under both the *ADJR Act* and the *Judiciary Act*). Review was limited to those grounds specifically listed in the *Migration Act 1958* (Cth), grounds which were narrower than those available under the *ADJR Act* and s 39B(1) of the *Judiciary Act*. (This was in part a response to a perception that some Federal Court judges were playing fast and loose with the legality/merits distinction.) As the High Court's entrenched jurisdiction under s 75(v) was necessarily left intact,[45] applicants flooded its lists[46] to avail themselves of what were (correctly) presumed to be more generous grounds of review than those available in the Federal Court (2.4.2.5). Although the *Migration Act* has since been amended—and the Federal Court's s 39B(1) jurisdiction restored—there is now a clear judicial consciousness that this jurisdiction should be developed in the shadow of the Constitution. The High Court has rebadged the s 75(v) remedies by replacing the language of 'prerogative writs' with that of the 'constitutional writs' and the 'constitutional injunction'.[47] This change in nomenclature prompted suggestions that the general principles of judicial review under s 75(v) do not necessarily coincide with those at common law—though post-*Kirk* it has been said that although care is advisable in applying s 75(v) to 'cases arising in State jurisdictions', not so much care is required as before that decision.[48] The extent to which judicial review principles under s 75(v) will continue to converge with review under the supervisory review jurisdiction of state Supreme Courts remains unclear (see 4.5.3). Further, the extent and significance of divergences between review under these regimes and that under the *ADJR Act* (and other statutory sources of review) is also uncertain.

The grounds of judicial review available under s 75(v) are tightly linked to the available remedies. (The availability of remedies is discussed in detail in Chapter 4.) Substantively, 'jurisdictional error' has become the conceptual lodestar of judicial review under s 75(v) and s 39B(1) of the *Judiciary Act*, as the constitutional writs are available *only* for excess or denial of jurisdiction. At common law, certiorari is available for both jurisdictional and non-jurisdictional errors of law (in the case of the latter, if they are apparent on the face of the record) (see 4.1). It is now accepted that certiorari (though not named in s 75(v)) is available as an 'ancillary' remedy, that is, where it is necessary for the 'effective' exercise of the remedies which are named in s 75(v).[49] However, if the errors complained of are *within* jurisdiction there 'is no remedy under s 75(v) to which certiorari might be appended'.[50] That is, even though certiorari has been granted in applications under s 75(v), it will *not* be granted for a non-jurisdictional error. The extent to which the 'constitutional injunction' may take s 75(v) review beyond the notion of jurisdictional error has been raised, but not resolved (4.5.3). These developments have raised many questions about the substantive principles applicable in an application for a constitutional remedy, including the question of the extent to which any of these grounds of judicial review are constitutionally entrenched (7.2.3). What is crystal clear is that the constitutional significance of the distinction between jurisdictional and non-jurisdictional error places it at the centre of contemporary administrative law in Australia. Although complaints about the coherence and usefulness of this distinction have a long history and continue to be

---

45   A constitutional challenge to this scheme, whereby the Federal Court was given lesser jurisdiction than the High Court, was rejected in *Abebe v Commonwealth* (1999) 197 CLR 510.

46   The High Court was appalled by this result. See, e.g., *Re Minister for Immigration and Multicultural Affairs; Ex parte Durairajasingham* (2000) 168 ALR 407 (McHugh J).

47   *Re Refugee Review Tribunal; Ex parte Aala* (2000) 204 CLR 82 ('*Aala*').

48   J Spigelman, n 4 above, 81.

49   *Aala* (2000) 204 CLR 82, 107; *Bodruddaza v Minister for Immigration and Multicultural Affairs* (2007) 228 CLR 651, 67.

50   *Re McBain; Ex parte Australian Catholic Bishops Conference* (2002) 209 CLR 372, 403 ('*Re McBain*').

voiced, the High Court would have to reconceive the basis of its jurisdiction under s 75(v) to bury the concept of jurisdictional error. This is unlikely given that in *Kirk* the constitutionally protected measure of state judicial review was also marked out by reference to this distinction (3.4.3; 7.1).

Although the scope of 'constitutional' judicial review is broader in some aspects than that of the *ADJR Act* (recall that s 39B(1) was enacted in recognition of this fact), it is subject to two important limitations, discussed below.

3.4.1.2 'Officer of the Commonwealth'

Applications for 'constitutional' remedies under s 75(v) are limited to claims where relief is sought 'against an officer of the Commonwealth'. Thus the High Court's constitutional jurisdiction clearly depends upon *some* sort of institutional nexus being established between the decision-maker and the government. On the other hand, the government can achieve policy outcomes through a number of different institutional structures and, increasingly, enlists or encourages the participation of private bodies. Clearly the interpretation of 'officer of the Commonwealth' involves significant choices to be made as to the nature and closeness of the required connection.

The High Court has emphasised that the constitutional purpose of review under s 75(v) counsels judicial vigilance against its possible evasion.[51] Yet the orthodox approach to defining 'officer of the Commonwealth' has raised the prospect that government *can* evade judicial scrutiny under s 75(v) (and s 39B(1)) by the expedient of adopting the corporate form. According to the orthodox approach to the definition, an officer of the Commonwealth is 'a person appointed by the Commonwealth to an identifiable office who is paid by the Commonwealth for the performance of their functions under the office and who is responsible to and removable by the Commonwealth concerning the office'.[52] Although this definition has been applied to encompass a long list of Commonwealth decision-makers—including public servants, the Commonwealth Director of Public Prosecutions and police, ministers, members of the AAT, and federal judges (excluding justices of the High Court)[53]—there have been some surprising exclusions. The assumptions underpinning most of the exclusions appear to be that a formal appointment to an 'office' is required and, thus, that the 'office' must be distinct from the entity who fills it.[54] The High Court is yet to rule authoritatively on this issue.

It is difficult to accept that these restrictive assumptions are demanded by the spare text of the Constitution, particularly given the acknowledged constitutional purpose served by s 75(v) and the ease with which the Commonwealth can transact its business by the expedient of adopting the

---

51   *Bank of New South Wales v Commonwealth* (1948) 76 CLR 1; *Deputy Commissioner of Taxation v Richard Walter Pty Ltd* (1995) 183 CLR 168.

52   *Broadbent v Medical Board of Queensland* [2011] FCA 980 [100]; a distillation of Isaacs J's influential approach in *R v Murray and Cormie; Ex parte The Commonwealth* (1916) 22 CLR 437, 452–3. In *R v Murray and Cormie*, the application of this approach led to the conclusion that a state judge exercising federal jurisdiction (s 77(iii) of the Constitution allows the parliament to confer federal jurisdiction on state courts) is not an officer of the Commonwealth. federal courts (and their judges) do qualify as officers of the Commonwealth (4.5.3).

53   For a more complete list of 'persons' held to be an officer of the Commonwealth, see Aronson, Dyer and Groves, n 24 above, 36–7.

54   See, e.g., *Vietnam Veterans' Affairs Association of Australian (NSW Branch Inc) v Cohen* (1996) 70 FCR 419, 432. The cases also indicate that officers or employees of corporate bodies are beyond the reach of s 75(v): see, e.g., *Post Office Agents Assn Ltd v Australian Postal Commission* (1988) 84 ALR 563, 575. For persuasive critique, see Aronson, Dyer and Groves, n 24 above, 38–39.

corporate form.[55] Some cases appear to justify the exclusion of corporate bodies or agencies from the reach of s 75(v) on the basis of their independence from government, though why this should be so has not been adequately explained.[56]

The limitation that a decision-maker be an 'officer of the Commonwealth' must mean that many decisions made by non-government bodies cannot be reviewed under s 75(v). But should the bare fact that a decision-maker is not formally part of the government necessarily leave its decisions beyond review? An example of this general question was vividly illustrated in *Plaintiff M61*.[57] The plaintiffs were being detained on Christmas Island (an 'excised offshore place'). They were unable to make an application under the *Migration Act* for a protection visa on the basis of their claimed refugee status— only 'onshore' applications were allowed—unless the minister gave permission for an application to be made. Having given such permission, the minister also had a power to grant a visa. Both powers were stated in highly discretionary terms, and the Act specifically provided that the minister was not even under a duty to consider whether or not to exercise them.[58] On the evidence, the High Court concluded that the minister had decided to consider whether to exercise his powers in *every* case where a person detained offshore asserted that they were owed protection as a refugee. This consideration involved two distinct administrative processes which the minister had put into place prior to any decision being made to issue a visa. First, there was a Refugee Status Assessment (RSA) undertaken by a departmental officer. The second process could be invoked by an applicant if the RSA was unfavourable: the RSA could be reviewed on its merits, through an Independent Merits Review (IMR). What is of present interest is that the IMR 'was undertaken by persons who were not officers of the Department, but had been engaged by a company with which the Department had contracted for the provision of such reviews'.[59] Given the prevalence of what is known variously as contracting-out or outsourcing, whereby governments contract with a private body to undertake a function on its behalf (1.1), the question of whether the High Court's supervisory jurisdiction covered the IMR process is one which may have general implications for the level of legal accountability available in relation to this mode of government decision-making and service delivery.[60]

The High Court did not, however, need to give a clear answer to this question of whether independent contractors may be covered by s 75(v) 'in circumstances where some aspects of the exercise of statutory or executive authority of the Commonwealth has been "contracted out"'[61] as it was able to rely on other sources of jurisdiction to grant the only appropriate remedy (a declaration, which is not one of the remedies named in s 75(v)).[62] Nevertheless, the clear assumption was that neither the contractor (a private corporation) nor the employees who conducted the IMRs would qualify as officers of the Commonwealth on the orthodox approach to the meaning of 'officer of the Commonwealth'.

---

55   Particularly given that decisions of statutory corporations will often not be 'made under an enactment' and not reviewable under the *ADJR Act*. Some of these decisions may, however, be reviewable under s 75(iii) or s 39B(1A)(c): 3.4.2 and 3.5.2.

56   As Aronson, Dyer and Groves, n 24 above, 39 note, it is hard to reconcile with the fact that federal judges (whose independence cannot be doubted) are amenable to the jurisdiction: see, e.g., *Re McBain; Ex parte Australian Catholic Bishops Conference* (2001) 209 CLR 372.

57   *Plaintiff M61/2010E v Commonwealth* (2010) 243 CLR 319.

58   'No-consideration' clauses are discussed at 7.2.4.2.

59   *Plaintiff M61/2010E v Commonwealth* (2010) 243 CLR 319, 333.

60   See M Groves, 'Outsourcing and s 75(v) of the Constitution' (2011) 22 *Public Law Review* 3.

61   *Plaintiff M61/2010E v Commonwealth* (2010) 243 CLR 319, 345.

62   This aspect of the case is discussed at 7.2.4.2.

There may not be a generally applicable answer to the question of whether independent contractors are amendable to s 75(v) review, as the answer may depend upon exactly which 'aspects of the exercise of statutory or executive authority of the Commonwealth' have been outsourced. But it is, at the very least, difficult to see why decision-makers exercising statutory powers formally delegated to them under statute should be excluded, merely because they are not in the direct employ of the government.[63]

The question of whether judicial review remedies may be granted against non-government bodies has also been raised in other jurisdictional contexts. For example, the *NEAT* case focused on whether a private corporation given a role in a scheme of public regulation, whereby it could protect its own statutory monopoly to export wheat by vetoing an application made to the government regulator to allow its competitors to export wheat, was amenable to review under the *ADJR Act* (see 3.5.1.4.2). More generally, the English case *Datafin* held that common law judicial review should be available wherever a decision-maker is exercising public functions, an approach which may apply in the context of the exercise of state Supreme Court's supervisory jurisdiction in Australia (see 3.6.1). In *NEAT* the statute very explicitly recognised that decisions of a private entity would have a pivotal role in the overall scheme of public regulation. In *Datafin*, the decision-maker was a self-regulatory body whose powers were arguably further removed from any statutory source of power—which may make it more difficult to conclude that the decision-maker was acting on the behalf or behest of the Commonwealth government than in circumstances akin to those in the *NEAT* case.

Section 75(v)'s rule of law purpose does justify 'a flexible and expansive approach' to the meaning of officer of the Commonwealth.[64] Nevertheless, although some non-government bodies may have a sufficiently close connection to the execution of statutory and executive powers to qualify as 'officer of the Commonwealth', the constitutional text is likely to make it difficult for the High Court to fully adopt the English public function test.[65]Although the High Court dodged these important questions in *Plaintiff M61*, it would be surprising if the opportunity to consider them does not arise again.[66]

3.4.1.3 The 'matter' concept

The Constitution confers jurisdiction, and allows for the parliament to make laws conferring jurisdiction, *only* in relation to specified 'matters'. In the canonical formulation, 'there can be no matter … unless there is some immediate right, duty or liability to be established by the determination of the

---

63   Cf *Plaintiff M61*, where the statutory powers in question were not delegated and could only be exercised by the minister personally.

64   As argued by Groves, n 60 above.

65   The High Court has emphasised that whereas the jurisdictional requirements of the *ADJR Act* focus on the (statutory) source of the power, s 75(v) refers to the identity of the decision-maker: *Griffith University v Tang* (2005) 221 CLR 89, 113. Groves, n 60 above, 9, concludes that it would be ironic if the supervisory jurisdiction of the Supreme Courts (which he assumes will adopt the *Datafin* principle) prove to be 'more flexible and adaptive than the High Court's own constitutionally entrenched review jurisdiction'. Given that the constitutional basis for the Supreme Court's jurisdiction is less explicit than the High Court's, this may indeed be ironic. But it would not be incoherent to the extent differences are thought justified by the text and structure of the Constitution. Further, as noted in 3.4.3, the High Court's most recent formulation of the entrenched supervisory review jurisdiction of the Supreme Courts, in *Public Service Association of South Australia Inc v Industrial Relations Commission of South Australia* [2012] HCA 25, [29], [55], gives emphasis to review being available for jurisdictional errors made by 'the executive government of the State, its Ministers or authorities'.

66   The same questions may arise under s 75(iii) (3.4.2). Section 75(iii) gives the court jurisdiction in cases where 'the Commonwealth' (or a person acting on 'behalf of the Commonwealth') is a party to the suit. Currently the term 'the Commonwealth' is understood such that government corporations can be reviewed in the s 75(iii) jurisdiction. The issue is governed by the factors set out in *Inglis v Commonwealth Trading Bank of Australia* (1969) 119 CLR 334, 337–41 (Kitto J); see also *Australian Securities and Investments Commission v Edensor Nominees Pty Ltd* (2001) 204 CLR 559, 608.

court' and no 'declaration of the law divorced from any attempt to administer that law'.[67] However, as the judicial review of administrative action rarely focuses on the determination of 'the underlying rights of the parties'—it is concerned with whether a decision was lawfully or validly made, not a person's legal entitlement to a particular decision[68]—it is doubtful whether the appropriate boundaries of judicial review are usefully determined by reference to the abstract and indeterminate concepts of 'rights' and 'obligations' or 'liabilities' alone (see further 3.5.1.4).[69]

It is clear that a 'matter' is present only where there is a justiciable controversy. The concept of 'non-justiciability' is also used at common law to determine whether a decision over which a superior court otherwise has jurisdiction is nonetheless unsuitable for judicial resolution. The common law idea of non-justiciability is particularly important in relation to the review of 'prerogative powers' and is discussed below in the context of common law limitations on the exercise of the supervisory review jurisdiction of state Supreme Courts (3.6.2). A particular focus of non-justiciability in the s 75(v) jurisdiction has been the exclusion of abstract or 'hypothetical' questions from the 'matter' concept.[70] It is for this reason that jurisdiction to issue 'advisory opinions' cannot be conferred on the High Court.[71] Relatedly, the requirement of a justiciable 'matter' intersects with the question of whether an applicant has sufficient interest ('standing') to bring the action.[72]

3.4.2 An alternative source of federal constitutional review jurisdiction: s 75(iii)

The High Court can also engage in judicial review under the original jurisdiction granted by s 75(iii) of the Constitution. This provision does not define jurisdiction in terms of remedies but through the requirement that one of the parties to a suit be 'the Commonwealth'.[73] It has been suggested that this jurisdiction may 'at least to a large extent' overlap with s 75(v).[74] Indeed some judges have suggested that s 75(v) 'may not add to the jurisdiction conferred by s 75(iii)'.[75] It is difficult to know what to make of these suggestions, which have not been fully explained. Nevertheless, a number of points can be made.

First, it is clear that the High Court can hear claims and grant remedies under s 75(iii) in situations where s 75(v) review is not available. Importantly, the court has read the phrase 'the Commonwealth' as capable of encompassing bodies corporate; thus statutory corporations are 'the Commonwealth' and

---

67   *In re Judiciary and Navigation Acts* (1921) 29 CLR 257, 265–6.

68   Cf *Re McBain* (2002) 209 CLR 372, 413 (McHugh J); *Minister for Immigration and Multicultural Affairs v Bhardwaj* (2002) 209 CLR 597, 618 (McHugh J).

69   For an excellent account of the High Court's approach to the concept of matter, see J Stellios, *The Federal Judicature: Chapter III of the Constitution* (Sydney: LexisNexis, 2010).

70   See *Mellifont v Attorney-General (Qld)* (1991) 173 CLR 289.

71   *In re Judiciary and Navigation Acts* (1921) 29 CLR 257. The reluctance of the courts to answer hypothetical questions is also relevant to the availability of declaratory relief (4.5.1.5).

72   *Croome v Tasmania* (1997) 191 CLR 119. However, the legislature can provide for open standing (i.e. allow any person to bring proceedings) and still confer a jurisdiction in relation to a 'matter': *Truth About Motorways v Macquarie* (2000) 200 CLR 591.

73   Section 75(iii) states that the High Court has jurisdiction in matters 'in which the Commonwealth, or a person suing or being sued on behalf of the Commonwealth, is a party'.

74   *Deputy Commissioner of Taxation v Richard Walter Pty Ltd* (1995) 183 CLR 168, 204.

75   *Aala* (2000) 204 CLR 82, 92.

government-owned corporations may also qualify as 'the Commonwealth'.[76] In *Plaintiff M61*, the court was able to assume that the private contractor and its employees were not officers of the Commonwealth because it had jurisdiction under s 75(iii). Although it was not asserted that the private decision-makers were themselves 'the Commonwealth', the court held that it was sufficient that the applicants also sought relief 'against the Minister and either a departmental officer or the Secretary of the Department—all officers of the Commonwealth'.[77] In exercising jurisdiction under s 75(iii) the court has been prepared to grant a remedy even where no jurisdictional error was shown.[78] *Plaintiff M61* again serves as an illustration. Although it was concluded that mandamus was not an appropriate remedy—because there was neither a duty to exercise the power or even to consider its exercise[79]—a declaration was granted. The declaration was made on the basis of two errors. One error involved a failure to observe the requirements of procedural fairness. It is well accepted that such an error amounts to a jurisdictional error. The second error was characterised as an error of law due to a failure on the part of the (private) IMR decision-maker to treat provisions of the *Migration Act* (as interpreted by Australian courts) as binding. Despite the importance of the distinction between jurisdictional error and non-jurisdictional error in the s 75(v) review context, the court appears to assume that a declaration could issue for a mere error of law; nowhere is an attempt made to categorise the identified errors as going to jurisdiction.

Our second point in relation to the s 75(iii) jurisdiction is that it appears to be a less secure foundation for review than s 75(v). Section 75(v) has been interpreted as linking the available writs (mandamus and prohibition) to the notion of 'jurisdictional error', and this has disabled the parliament from using 'privative clauses' (Chapter 7) to exclude the court's jurisdiction to grant these remedies for such jurisdictional errors (4.5.3; 7.1). In contrast, the orthodox view is that s 75(iii) does not constitutionally entrench the availability of particular remedies or the substantive law which is to be applied in cases involving the Commonwealth as a party. Thus, although s 75(iii) may give the High Court jurisdiction to award certiorari (and declarations) for non-jurisdictional errors of law, it is open to the parliament to legislate to prevent such relief being granted.[80]

Finally, it can be observed that, although it is possible that the judicial review jurisdiction under s 75(iii) will develop along a conceptual path distinct from that which the court has travelled under s 75(v) (see 2.4.2.5), it would make little sense for the substantive principles applicable to the s 75(iii) jurisdiction enabled either the parliament or parties to disputes to outflank the key elements of the scheme of s 75(v) review which has been progressively constructed by the High Court over the last 10–20 years. As a general matter, *Kirk* points toward a harmonisation of the law applicable to s 75(v) and supervisory review jurisdiction of state Supreme Courts. In this context it would be ironic if major differences in the substantive principles of review were to emerge in the development of the court's s 75(iii) review jurisdiction.[81]

---

76 See n 66.

77 *Plaintiff M61/2010E v Commonwealth* (2010) 243 CLR 319, 345. The court also speculated that jurisdiction under s 75(i) might be a source of jurisdiction, insofar as the proceedings could be characterised as a matter arising under a treaty (namely, the Refugees Convention and the Refugees Protocol).

78 *Project Blue Sky Inc v Australian Broadcasting Authority* (1998) 194 CLR 355. This case was initiated in the High Court's s 75(iii) jurisdiction but remitted to the Federal Court for trial: *Project Blue Sky Inc v Australian Broadcasting Authority* (1996) 68 FCR 455, 456. See further 4.3.

79 In these circumstances, the court also concluded that certiorari would have no utility. On the availability of these remedies, see 4.5.1.1 and 4.5.1.3.

80 *Plaintiff S157* (2003) 211 CLR 476, 507.

81 It should be noted that s 75(iii) is not limited to 'judicial review' cases. For example, s 75(iii) has a role in giving the High Court jurisdiction to hear common law actions in contract and tort against 'the Commonwealth': *Commonwealth v Mewett* (1997) 191 CLR 471.

3.4.3 A constitutional source for the state Supreme Courts' supervisory jurisdiction: s 73(ii)

The legal foundation for the state Supreme Courts' 'supervisory' judicial review jurisdiction has long been accepted to be the common law, a jurisdiction which was originally inherited from the 'superior' courts in England. Although this common law jurisdiction now finds expression in the statute books, it retains its common law nature (see 3.6).[82] However, as a result of the decision in *Kirk*, part of the state judicial review law has been constitutionalised, in the sense that a state legislature, like the Commonwealth parliament, is limited in the extent to which it can oust judicial review (see 7.1).[83]

A fuller examination of the constitutional argument offered in *Kirk* for this conclusion will be left to Chapter 7, as its primary purpose was to insulate state judicial review from statutory attempts to restrict it. Three features of the conclusion in *Kirk* should be emphasised for present purposes. First, the constitutional peg for the identification of the jurisdiction was s 73(ii), which gives the High Court jurisdiction to hear and determine appeals from state Supreme Courts. The Court concluded that this provision requires state legislatures to maintain a body which continues to meet the 'constitutional description' of a Supreme Court. The Court reasoned that one of the minimum characteristics of such a body was the power to 'confine inferior courts and tribunals within the limits of their authority to decide … on grounds of jurisdictional error'.[84]

Second, the conceptual basis for the entrenched provision of state courts' supervisory jurisdiction is the same as is applicable for s 75(v): 'power to grant relief on account of jurisdictional error' is the measure of review that is protected. In this way the court claimed to vindicate the 'continued need for, and utility of, the distinction between jurisdictional and non-jurisdictional error in the Australian constitutional context'.[85]

Third, the rule of law justification emphasised in the context of articulating the High Court's s 75(v) jurisdiction was thought equally applicable to the creation of an entrenched jurisdiction to determine the legality of state government decisions. Although the language of the 'rule of law' was not used, the concern to prevent 'islands of power immune from supervision and restraint' clearly serves this constitutional purpose.[86] As Justice Spigelman neatly concluded, 'the effect of *Kirk* is that there is, by force of s 73, an "entrenched minimum provision of judicial review" applicable to state decision-makers of a similar, probably of the same, character as the High Court determined in [*Plaintiff S157*] to exist in the case of Commonwealth decision-makers by force of s 75(v) of the *Constitution*'.[87]

Despite being underpinned by the same conceptual scheme and underlying rationale, there remain questions as to what, if any, doctrinal differences may exist between review pursuant to s 75(v) (or s 39B(1) of the *Judiciary Act*) and cases arising in state jurisdictions. We consider a number of examples of suggested differences between the availability of the 'constitutional writs' and the availability of prerogative writs in state jurisdiction in Chapter 4, which deals generally with the law of remedies.

---

82   See Aronson, Dyer and Groves, n 24 above, 20–3.

83   Thereby overturning the received wisdom that although the courts would interpret legislative attempts to restrict or oust judicial review, well drafted legislation could exclude the Supreme Court's judicial review: Spigelman, n 4 above, 81.

84   *Kirk v Industrial Court of New South Wales* (2010) 239 CLR 531, 566.

85   Ibid, 581.

86   Ibid, 581.

87   Spigelman, n 4 above, 81; *Chase Oyster Bar Pty Ltd v Hamo Industries Pty Ltd* (2010) 78 NSWLR 393, 402.

Here we make two points. First, existing doctrinal discrepancies should, by force of the logic of *Kirk*, diminish over time. Unless there are strong reasons for maintaining any differences, this will be a positive trend. Second, an obvious possible difference arises from the fact that the constitutionally entrenched jurisdiction of state Supreme Courts is not expressly limited by reference to language analogous to the 'officer of the Commonwealth' requirement. This difference may enable the courts to move further towards a functional understanding of the scope of review in relation to state judicial review than is possible in relation to the interpretation of s 75(v)'s 'officer of the Commonwealth' requirement. Certainly, if the logic of *Datafin's* public function principle is accepted as being applicable in state jurisdictions(see 3.6.1) then the minimum provision of review at state level may exceed that protected at the Commonwealth level. Alternatively, it is possible that the High Court could conceptualise the meaning and purpose of jurisdictional review (that is, including the entrenched element of the supervisory jurisdiction of state courts) as being limited to decision-making powers which are tethered in some way to statutory sources and, perhaps, to those executive powers which can be exercised only by government decision-makers.[88] In *Public Service Assoication of South Australia Inc v Industrial Relations Commission of South Australia*, the High Court framed the constitutional limits articulated in *Kirk* as follows: 'State legislative power does not extend to depriving a State Supreme Court of its supervisory jurisdiction in respect of jurisdictional error by the executive government of the State, its Ministers or authorities.'[89]

3.5 Statutory sources of judicial review jurisdiction

3.5.1 *Administrative Decisions (Judicial Review) Act 1977* (Cth)

When the *ADJR Act* was enacted in 1977 (on the back of the publication of two influential reports criticising the existing complexity of the remedially oriented law of judicial review),[90] the clear hope was that it would become the main vehicle for judicial review of decisions of the Commonwealth government. The *ADJR Act* included a number of modifications to the common law, not least the important entitlement to a statement of reasons in relation to reviewable decisions.[91] Substantively, the Act was 'substantially declaratory of the common law',[92] though the common law grounds of

---

88   See the discussion of 'prerogative powers' below, 3.6.2.2.

89   *Public Service Association of South Australia Inc v Industrial Relations Commission of South Australia* [2012] HCA 25, [29] (French CJ), [55] (Gummow Hayne, Crennan J, Kiefel Bell JJ); Heydon J made the same point at [84].

90   Commonwealth Administrative Review Committee, *Commonwealth Administrative Review Committee Report*, Parliament of the Commonwealth of Australia Paper No 144 (1971) ('Kerr Committee Report'); Commonwealth, *Prerogative Writ Procedures: Committee of Review*, Parliamentary Paper No 56 (1973) ('Ellicott Committee Report').

91   *Administrative Decisions (Judicial Review) Act 1977* (Cth), s 13. The common law denies the existence of a general duty to give reasons for administrative decisions: *Public Service Board of New South Wales v Osmond* (1986) 159 CLR 656 (see 5.2.4). Without access to reasons for decisions, many grounds of review relating to the decision-maker's reasoning can become very difficult to establish.

92   *Minister for Aboriginal Affairs v Peko-Wallsend Ltd* (1986) 162 CLR 24, 39 ('*Peko-Wallsend*'). There is an interesting debate over the effect of codification on the grounds of review (see 5.1.2).

review were broadened in a few instances.[93] The Act's most fundamental reform was to turn on its head the traditional approach to determining the availability of review. As we have seen, prior to the enactment of the *ADJR Act* the law was remedially oriented (2.1.4 and 2.4.1.5). The Act shifted attention away from the availability of particular remedies and towards whether or not a ground of review could be established, that is, whether a legal error could be shown (4.2). For reasons that soon will become apparent, the effort to reorient the law has not been as influential as might have been hoped because the *ADJR Act* has gaps—some such gaps were predictable, but others have surprised many observers.[94]

Applications under the *ADJR Act* may be made to either the Federal Court or the Federal Magistrates Court.[95] The drafters of the Act chose to confer a general jurisdiction on the court subject to a number of exceptions.[96] The key to understanding the scope of the *ADJR Act* is the phrase, 'decision to which this Act applies'. Applications for an order of review may be brought under the *ADJR Act* by 'aggrieved' persons in relation to (1) a 'decision to which this Act applies' (s 5); (2) proposed and actual conduct engaged in for the purpose of making a 'decision to which this Act applies' (s 6); and (3) a failure to make a 'decision to which this Act applies' (s 7). This key phrase—'decision to which this Act applies'—is defined in s 3(1) by reference to three elements. There must be:

1   a decision;
2   of an administrative character;
3   made under an enactment.[97]

Although the High Court has cautioned against treating these as discrete requirements,[98] the reality is that each element has generated a considerable amount of litigation which has not resulted in an integrated set of principles. Before turning to this surprisingly technical and complex jurisprudence, it is important to note the two types of decisions specifically exempted from the Act's coverage.

At the time the *ADJR Act* was enacted, it was widely assumed that vice-regal decisions were immune from review at common law. Hence decisions made by the Governor-General were excluded. This much-criticised exclusion is increasingly anachronistic,[99] especially as the common law has since

---

93   Most significantly 'errors of law' (s 5(1)(f)) need not appear on 'the face of the record'—this being legal code for saying that they need not be classified as 'jurisdictional errors' (see 4.1). See also 5.4.3.2.

94   The statistics reveal the contemporary reality to be 'that the ADJR Act is no longer the primary source used in judicial review applications in the Federal Court': Administrative Review Council, Judicial Review in Australia Consultation Paper (April 2011), 57. (The statistics are discussed, ibid, 53–6).

95   The Federal Magistrates Court began operation in 2000. It shares the Federal Court's administrative law jurisdiction under the *ADJR Act* (and that part of the s 39B *Judiciary Act* jurisdiction relating to migration matters). In the remainder of our discussion of the *ADJR Act*, references to the 'court' refer to both the Federal Court and the Federal Magistrates Court.

96   Contrast the jurisdiction of the Administrative Appeals Tribunal, under which a decision must be specifically identified as reviewable by the statute pursuant to which it is made (see 8.5.1.2).

97   The form of expression of this definition was complicated in 2000, when it was modified to provide for the review of the activities of Commonwealth authorities in the course of certain Commonwealth–state cooperative schemes, but the essential elements of the definition remain unaffected. State and territory legislation listed in Schedule 3 of the Act is included in the s 3(1) definition of 'enactment'. Decisions made under such enactments are reviewable where made by a 'Commonwealth authority or an officer of the Commonwealth'.

98   *Griffith University v Tang* (2005) 221 CLR 89.

99   Commonwealth, Administrative Review Council, *Review of the Administrative Decisions (Judicial Review) Act: The Ambit of the Act*, Report No 32 (1989), 45–9; M Groves, 'Should We Follow the Gospel of the *Administrative Decisions (Judicial Review) Act 1977* (Cth)?' (2010) 34 *Melbourne University Law Review* 736, 750–1.

moved on.[100] Moreover, the fact that decisions made by government ministers are reviewable exposes the immunity as one of form rather than substance (as vice-regal officers typically act on the advice of ministers).[101]

The second category of decisions excluded from review encompasses those decisions listed in Schedule 1 of the Act. Examples include certain decisions made in areas as diverse as tax assessments, criminal process, employment, migration, security and defence.[102]

3.5.1.1 'Decision' in *Bond*

The *ADJR Act's* definition of its core jurisdictional concept can be accused of tautology: one of the elements of a 'decision to which the Act applies' is a 'decision'. While the Act does attempt to give some further guidance, its inclusive list of 'decisions' catalogues some rather obvious examples before concluding that the notion also includes 'doing or refusing to do any other act or thing'.[103]

The High Court's first detailed consideration of the question of the meaning of 'decision' came in *Australian Broadcasting Tribunal v Bond*,[104] and resulted in a significant restriction of the scope of *ADJR Act* review. According to Mason CJ's leading judgment, the meaning of 'decision' entails two elements. First, reviewable decisions will, in general, be 'final or operative and determinative'. This 'finality' element is subject to an important, if sometimes overlooked, caveat. Where a statute specifically provides for the making of a decision which is a mere step along the way in the course of reaching an ultimate decision, this 'intermediate' decision can accurately be described as 'a decision made under an enactment', and is itself reviewable. Second, it is an 'essential quality' that decisions be 'substantive' determinations.[105] This understanding of 'decision' was, in part, adopted in order to clarify the meaning of 'conduct' in the statutory scheme. 'Conduct' was said to be an 'essentially procedural' concept which focused upon the actual conduct of proceedings and not on intermediate conclusions reached en route to final, substantive decisions.[106] 'It would be strange,' wrote the Chief Justice, 'if "conduct" were to extend

---

100   *R v Toohey; Ex parte Northern Land Council* (1981) 151 CLR 170 ('*Toohey*'). The High Court rejected an argument that the conventions of ministerial responsibility provided an adequate accountability mechanism for gubernatorial decisions (which are made on the advice of a responsible minister). The Court's approach accepts that the modern day strictures of party discipline have allowed the executive to effectively control the parliament.

101   M Aronson, 'Is the *ADJR Act* Hampering the Development of Australian Administrative Law?' (2004) 15 *Public Law Review* 202, 209.

102   Groves, n 99 above, 752, has noted a steady expansion in the list of exclusions and emphasised the existing role of the Senate Scrutiny of Bill Committee in drawing the attention of the Senate to the diminution of judicial review rights (see generally also 5.4.6; 9.4.4.3). Such a role falls within Standing Order 24 (1)(a)(iii) which enables the Committee to report on provisions which 'make rights, liberties or obligations unduly dependent upon non-reviewable decisions'.

103   *Administrative Decisions (Judicial Review) Act 1977* (Cth), s 3(2):
    (a)   'making, suspending, revoking or refusing to make an order, award or determination;
    (b)   giving, suspending, revoking or refusing to give a certificate, direction, approval, consent or permission;
    (c)   issuing, suspending, revoking or refusing to issue a licence, authority or other instrument;
    (d)   imposing a condition or restriction;
    (e)   making a declaration, demand or requirement;
    (f)   retaining, or refusing to deliver up, an article; or
    (g)   doing or refusing to do any other act or thing.'

104   (1990) 170 CLR 321 ('*Bond*').

105   Ibid.

106   Mason CJ noted that the two examples of conduct given in s 3(5) of the Act are 'the taking of evidence or the holding of an inquiry or investigation': ibid, 342.

generally to unreviewable decisions which are in themselves no more than steps in the deliberative or reasoning process.'[107]

This interpretive approach means that factual findings will often lack the element of finality required for there to be a 'decision'. (The question of whether or not a statute specifically provides for the making of preliminary findings of fact may reflect an accident of drafting rather than a principled judgment about the appropriateness of review.) Furthermore, findings of fact are 'substantive', not 'procedural', which means they will not qualify as reviewable 'conduct' either.

Why, it might be asked, was the High Court so concerned to read 'decision' restrictively, given the *ADJR Act*'s remedial purposes? Chief Justice Mason's most persuasive arguments related to two policy concerns.[108]

The first of these policy arguments resonates with our discussion of the limited nature of judicial review. Review of factual determinations, it was feared, could transform *ADJR Act* review into merits review. Were this intended, parliament would not, Mason CJ contended, have bothered also to provide a separate scheme of merits review.[109] Furthermore, an *ADJR Act* review was to be understood against the common law background which did not ordinarily 'extend [review] to findings of fact as such'. So to extend judicial review would bring 'about a radical change in the relationship between the executive and judicial branches of government'.[110]

It is true that judicial review remedies do not typically enable judges to substitute their own findings of fact for those of administrators.[111] But Mason CJ's fear relates mainly to the idea that the criteria for judicial review cannot allow judges to make overall evaluative judgments about the correctness of administrative decisions. If every factual error an administrator made constituted a legal error, it would be difficult to cling to the notion that judicial review is limited to ensuring that powers are exercised within power (intra vires or legally) rather than correctly. Yet it is difficult to accept that Mason CJ's brief reference to the legality/merits distinction in *Bond* adequately justifies the restrictive approach taken to jurisdiction under the *ADJR Act*. As explained above (3.2.2), the contours of the boundaries which circumscribe an administrator's legal powers are often contestable; it is not a matter of simply reading powers off a statute. Thus, although there is no legal error in simply making wrong findings of fact,[112] it is equally clear that the common law grounds of review do allow for determinations of fact to be reviewed in some cases (5.4.3.3). Further, not only does the *ADJR Act* explicitly contemplate review of facts in some instances,[113] but much of Mason CJ's own judgment in *Bond* discussed the circumstances in which particular grounds of judicial review do allow courts to review findings of fact at common law and under the *ADJR Act*.[114]

---

107   Ibid.

108   Mason CJ also relied on textual arguments but, as argued by Toohey and Gaudron JJ in their concurring opinion, the terms of the Act do not track a neat conceptual divide between process (conduct) and substance (decision): see ibid, 376. Cf *Griffith University v Tang* (2005) 221 CLR 89, 121–2 [60–61] ('*Tang*').

109   *Administrative Appeals Tribunal Act 1975* (Cth).

110   *Bond* (1990) 170 CLR 321, 341.

111   The jurisdictional fact doctrine is an important exception (see 5.4.3.1).

112   *Waterford v Commonwealth* (1987) 163 CLR 54, 77–8.

113   Section 5(3). Mason CJ also explains that the s 5(1)(f) error of law ground can also involve attacks on factual findings: *Bond* (1990) 170 CLR 321, 359, quoting with approval *Minister for Immigration, Local Government and Ethnic Affairs v Pashmforoosh* (1989) 18 ALD 77.

114   *Bond* (1990) 170 CLR 321, 355–9.

The second of *Bond's* policy concerns related to the risk which premature judicial review can pose to efficient administration.[115] Judicial review's capacity to fragment and delay administrative processes is well illustrated by the facts of *Bond*. The Australian Broadcasting Tribunal convened an inquiry into whether or not companies holding television licences in Queensland (and 'dominated' by the flamboyant businessman, Alan Bond) continued to be 'fit and proper persons to hold the licences'. The statute provided that it was a ground for the exercise of the power to revoke or vary the licences, that the licensees (in this case, the corporate entities controlled by Mr Bond, not Mr Bond himself) had been found not to be fit and proper persons.[116] In the course of very lengthy hearings the tribunal made a number of determinations, including a factual finding that Mr Bond was not a fit and proper person to hold a broadcasting licence. The tribunal had not yet determined whether or not the licences should be revoked or varied.

In this context, Mason CJ's worries about fragmentation of administrative processes and premature review applications are certainly understandable.[117] However, the requirement of finality or determinative effect does not mean 'that antecedent conclusions or findings which contribute to the ultimate or operative decisions are beyond reach'. This is because the review of a final decision 'will expose for consideration the reasons which are given for the making of the decision and the processes by which it is made'.[118] Thus, even though the court held that the finding about whether Mr Bond was himself a fit and proper person to hold a broadcasting licence was not reviewable, to the extent that this played a part in the decision that the licensee companies were no longer fit and proper persons (which was a reviewable decision because legislation specifically provided for its making), it might then have been exposed for judicial consideration. Judicial review of many preliminary determinations is not denied so much as delayed.

3.5.1.2 *Bond's* legacy

Prior to *Bond*, the Federal Court had indicated that 'decision' should be construed broadly, and that the problem of premature applications could be controlled through judicious exercise of the court's broad remedial discretion to refuse a remedy (s 16).[119] In contrast, *Bond* ushered in countless jurisdictional challenges and has generated a large,[120] highly technical[121] and sometimes

---

115   Ibid, 336.

116   Ibid, 330.

117   At common law, the requirement that certiorari not be granted unless there is a discernible legal effect can be understood as reflecting a similar concern as preliminary steps in an administrative inquiry or investigation often lack such an effect (see 4.5.1.1).

118   *Bond* (1990) 170 CLR 321, 338. The Federal Court has concluded that 'conduct overtaken by a subsequent decision is not independently reviewable but should be considered in the context of the review of the decision itself': *Minister for Immigration and Multicultural Affairs v Ozamanian* (1996) 71 FCR 1, 20.

119   *Lamb v Moss* (1983) 49 ALR 533.

120   Ironically, the attempt to limit the involvement of premature judicial intervention has proved fodder for many days of legal argument in court.

121   For example, the reviewability of reports and recommendations has caused problems. Section 3(3) of the *ADJR Act* states that reports are 'decisions' 'where provision is made by an enactment for the making of a report or recommendation before a decision is made'. The Federal Court has always read this provision narrowly and it applies only where the report or recommendation is a 'condition precedent to the making of a [reviewable] decision': *Edelsten v Health Insurance Commission* (1990) 27 FCR 56, 70; *Ross v Costigan* (1982) 41 ALR 319, 332. But where a report is not a legal precondition for a reviewable decision, the courts have, with some difficulty, applied the test set out in *Bond*: *Kelson v Forward* (1995) 60 FCR 39; cf *Electricity Supply Association of Australia Ltd v Australian Competition and Consumer Commission* (2001) 111 FCR 230.

absurd[122] jurisprudence. We do not propose to review the many cases dealing with the meaning of 'decision' and 'conduct' following *Bond*, partly because the cases have been reviewed elsewhere,[123] but also because the analysis too often 'leads nowhere'.[124]

Further, despite the legitimate policy objective of maintaining the integrity of administrative process and discouraging premature (often strategic) applications for review, the existence of alternative sources of jurisdiction for the Federal Court has rendered much of the *ADJR Act* jurisprudence futile. Section 39B(1) (which in effect gives the Federal Court the jurisdiction given by s 75(v) of the Constitution to the High Court—see 3.4.1) plugs many of the gaps which have emerged under the *ADJR Act*—because its scope is not restricted by the concepts of 'decision' or 'conduct' and because it is possible for applicants to plead both sources of jurisdiction.[125]

3.5.1.3 'Administrative' decisions

Review under the *ADJR Act* is limited to decisions 'of an administrative character'. The 'evident purpose' of this element of the Act's jurisdictional phrase 'is the exclusion of decisions of a "legislative" or "judicial" character'.[126] The courts have not been prepared to accept that decisions which might also legitimately fall within other general classifications—such as educational, commercial or employment—cannot also qualify as administrative decisions. By a process of elimination, decisions which are neither 'legislative' nor 'judicial' will be classified as administrative.[127]

Subordinate legislation is not directly reviewable under the *ADJR Act* as it is not a decision of an administrative character.[128] (Once a decision has been made under subordinate legislation it can be challenged under the *ADJR Act* on the basis that there was no legal authority for it, that is, because the subordinate legislation was itself not lawful.) It will, however, often be reviewable under s 39B(1) of the *Judiciary Act* (if made by an 'officer of the Commonwealth' (3.4.1.2))[129] or under s 39B(1A) (c) (see 3.5.2). Despite such alternative avenues of review, the terms of the *ADJR Act* have, in a number of cases, required the courts to struggle to draw a line between administrative and legislative decisions.

---

122   Here our example concerns so-called 'self-executing' provisions (i.e. statutory provisions which provide for consequences to flow automatically in particular circumstances). Some cases (e.g. *Century Yuasa Batteries Pty Ltd v Federal Commissioner of Taxation* (1997) 73 FCR 528) have held that actions based on such provisions do not involve reviewable decisions because official action based upon such provisions (e.g. demanding payment) are not a substantive determination of anything—the consequences being dictated by the legislative provision. For an alternative approach, see *Peverill v Meir* (1989) 95 ALR 401.

123   Aronson, Dyer and Groves, n 24 above, 62–8; R Creyke and G Hill, 'A Wavy Line in the Sand: Bond and Jurisdictional Issues in Judicial and Administrative Review' (1998) 26 *Federal Law Review* 15.

124   J McMillan, 'Recent Themes in Judicial Review of Federal Executive Action' (1996) 24 *Federal Law Review* 347, 367.

125   In 1997 the *Judiciary Act* was again amended to expand the Federal Court's jurisdiction. Section 39B(1A)(c) provides: 'The original jurisdiction of the Federal Court of Australia also includes jurisdiction in any matter … arising under any laws made by the Parliament': see below 3.5.2. The Federal Court's jurisdiction is further bolstered by the notions of 'associated' and 'accrued' jurisdiction: see Z Cowen and L Zines, *Cowen and Zines' Federal Jurisdiction in Australia*, 3rd edn (Annandale: Federation Press, 2002) 137–47, 148–50; Aronson, Dyer and Groves, n 24 above, 46–52.

126   *Griffith University v Tang* (2005) 221 CLR 89, 123 ('*Tang*').

127   *Burns v Australian National University* (1982) 40 ALR 707, 714.

128   As powers to make regulations are often formally reposed in the Governor-General, the exercise of these powers also falls under the express exclusion of such decisions: 3.5.1. The justification of both exclusions has been questioned by the Administrative Review Council Discussion Paper.

129   See, e.g., *Roche Products Pty Ltd v National Drugs and Poisons Schedule Committee* (2007) 163 FCR 451.

The High Court has contrasted the decisions in *Queensland Medical Laboratory v Blewett*[130] and *Federal Airports Corporation v Aerolineas Argentinas*,[131] to illustrate the 'instability of the distinctions' involved in drawing this line.[132] In the first case, it was held that a ministerial decision to substitute a new table of fees for an existing table, set out in a schedule to the relevant enactment, was of a legislative character.[133] Although Gummow J accepted that legislation normally involves the formulation of general rules (whereas administration applies the law or rule to a particular case) he did not think that all decisions of a legislative character must formulate a rule of general application.[134] Rather, emphasis was placed on how legislative decisions *change* the content of the law. As the decision to adopt a new table had the effect of replacing an existing law, it was classed as legislative. By contrast, in *Aerolineas Argentinas*, the Federal Court concluded that a determination by the Federal Airports Corporation to change the applicable landing charges which applied generally and clearly changed the law was, nonetheless, administrative in nature. The commercial nature of the decision-maker (the government corporation was required to act in a commercially sound manner) indicated that the decision to raise fees was 'in the execution or administration of the *Federal Airports Corporation Act*'.[135] Increasingly, the courts have relied upon considering a number of factors thought to constitute the indicia of legislative decisions, none of which can be considered determinative.[136] These factors include features of the decision (whether it has a general or rule-like quality, has binding legal effect, or raises broad questions of policy). They also include issues concerning supervision of the decision. Thus, whereas being subject to parliamentary oversight is a likely indicator of a legislative decision, the availability of merits review is associated with administrative decisions. Finally, issues concerning the production of the decision can be relevant. For example, requirements to consult and give public notification are said to indicate that a decision has a legislative character.

The 'instability' in these cases is probably inevitable.[137] What constitutes legislation or a legislative decision has more to do with its institutional mode of production (how it is produced) than with a conceptual understanding of the nature of making or changing the 'law'. For example, most legal theorists accept that common law judges make law, but this does not mean that courts thereby become functionally equivalent to legislatures—courts are constrained by different principles and processes of decision-making.[138] In light of these difficulties, it is little surprise that there have been calls for the 'administrative' part of the *ADJR Act*'s jurisdictional formula to be dropped.[139]

---

130   *(1988) 84 ALR 615 ('Blewett').*

131   (1997) 76 FCR 582 (*'Aerolineas Argentinas'*).

132   The Court declined to enter the fray of the controversy: *Tang* (2005) 221 CLR 89, 123.

133   Schedules to an Act form part of that statute: *Acts Interpretation Act 1901* (Cth), s 13(2).

134   Contrast *Minister for Industry and Commerce v Tooheys Ltd* (1982) 42 ALR 260.

135   *Aerolineas Argentinas* (1997) 76 FCR 582, 592.

136   See, e.g., *Queensland v Central Queensland Land Council Aboriginal Corporation* (2002) 125 FCR 89.

137   Some judges have suggested that the root cause of the problem is that the two categories—legislative and administrative— are not mutually exclusive and, therefore, that a single decision may accurately be described as falling into both. For a recent discussion of the point, see *Schwennesen v Minister for Environmental and Resource Management* (2010) 176 LGERA 1, 12–13.

138   See, e.g., P Cane, 'Taking Disagreement Seriously: Courts, Legislatures and the Reform of Tort Law' (2005) 25 *Oxford Journal of Legal Studies* 393.

139   Groves, n 99 above, 743; Aronson, n 35 above.

3.5.1.4 Decisions 'made ... under an enactment'[140]

There have been cases exploring the s 3(1) definition of 'enactment' which, among other things, includes 'an instrument (including rules, regulations or by-laws) made under' a Commonwealth Act.[141] Subordinate or delegated legislation (9.4.3) thus qualifies as an enactment. There are, however, many kinds of documents which can be made under legislation and which can, in a variety of ways, influence government decision-making. And the question of whether particular documents might qualify as an 'instrument' has caused some difficulties.

The courts' basic approach to this question has been to require that if an exercise of power is to qualify as an instrument it must, like a statute, have the capacity to affect the rights or obligations of individuals. Instruments, that is, must have a law-like ability unilaterally to affect rights or obligations. *Chittick v Ackland* held that a document setting out the terms and conditions of employment in a public agency was an instrument for three reasons: (1) it was itself made under an enactment (as required by the statutory definition);[142] (2) it allowed for the making of administrative decisions; and (3) it had the capacity to affect legal rights and obligations.[143] The third criterion has been further qualified by requiring that the decision-maker must have statutory power to effect unilateral (that is, non-consensual) alterations to the 'instrument' (so, for example, a contract will not qualify as an instrument). In *Australian National University v Lewins*, a university promotions policy did not enable the university unilaterally to alter employment contracts with staff, and therefore the policy could not qualify as an 'instrument'.[144]

It is sometimes suggested that decisions made which are not authorised by a statute (that is, they are based on a jurisdictional error) cannot be made 'under' an enactment for the purposes of *ADJR Act* review. The argument has been rejected (accepting it would surely defeat the purpose of enacting a statutory scheme of legality review).[145] Next, it is clear that the requirement that decisions be made *under* an enactment rules out review of non-statutory government powers. In particular, 'prerogative powers' and other forms of non-statutory executive powers are unreviewable. We discuss the meaning, and reviewability, of prerogative powers further below (3.6.2.2). It will become apparent that as a result of this limitation the reach of review under the *ADJR Act* is less than that of the common law (and 'constitutional') schemes of review. But although the exclusion of review of non-statutory powers is clear, the requirement that decisions be made *under* an enactment has generated a great deal of controversy. Although there were some early indications that an expansive approach would be taken,[146] the trend of the cases has been to read this requirement restrictively. Although rarely articulated, two policy considerations have structured judicial thinking on this issue.

---

140   Parts of this section draw on C Mantziaris and L McDonald, 'Federal Judicial Review Jurisdiction After *Griffith University v Tang*' (2006) 17 *Public Law Review* 22.

141   Certain Commonwealth enactments are excluded, and some state and territory Acts are included (by reference to Schedule 3).

142   In *Chapmans v Australian Stock Exchange Ltd* (1966) 67 FCR 402, 409 the 'Listing Requirements' of the stock exchange were operative as a matter of contract and, though referred to in the relevant statute, could not be said to be made under it.

143   *Chittick v Ackland* (1984) 1 FCR 254, 264.

144   *Australian National University v Lewins* (1996) 68 FCR 87, 103; Aronson, Dyer and Groves, n 24 above, 78.

145   *Ozmanian v Minister for Immigration, Local Government and Ethnic Affairs* (1996) 137 ALR 103, 125–7. Nevertheless, the argument appears to be the source of continuing confusion: see, e.g., *QGC Pty Ltd v Bygrave (No 2)* (2010) 189 FCR 412.

146   In *Minister for Immigration and Ethnic Affairs v Mayer* (1985) 157 CLR 290, the High Court accepted that the Minister's written determination of a claim for refugee status, although not expressly authorised by an enactment, was impliedly authorised and thus made *under* the enactment. The Act did expressly authorise a decision to grant a visa on the basis of the Minister's determination. See also *Aye v Minister for Immigration and Citizenship* (2010) 269 ALR 298, 308–10.

First, concerns similar to those expressed in *Bond's* case have arisen. In *Salerno*, the Full Federal Court stated:

> If a general authorisation in a statute for a decision by an organisation set up under that legislation is sufficient to make it a decision under the statute, and thus open to judicial review, every intra vires action of that organisation that has decisional effect and every kind of conduct engaged in by it for the purpose of making a decision will be examinable by the court. The potential for massive disruption of the organisation's activities that would be the consequence of such a conclusion is manifest.[147]

The suggestion is that some decisions, even if final or determinative, should nonetheless remain unreviewable because it would be too disruptive to allow review of the full range of decisions made by a statutory authority in the course of administering the statute under which it is established.

But the above passage can also be read as introducing a second, more fundamental, policy issue. Traditionally, many routine administrative decisions (such as decisions to enter into contracts) have not been subjected to judicial review on the basis that 'public' (that is, administrative) law principles are inappropriate, and 'private' decisions are better regulated by private law (such as the law of contract) (3.6.1).[148] The conclusion that decisions which are perceived to be exercises of 'private' powers are not 'made … under an enactment' can thus be influenced by an unarticulated value judgment that the jurisdictional phrase can, and should, be read in a way which does not extend the scope of judicial review beyond 'governmental' or 'public' decision-making. Interesting questions have arisen in relation to (1) statutory authorities making ostensibly 'private' decisions; and (2) non-government entities making decisions in a statutory regulatory scheme.

3.5.1.4.1 'Private' decisions of statutory authorities

A broad reading of the requirement that decisions be made *under* an enactment would potentially allow for the review of *all* decisions made by governmental authorities established by statute. The courts have understandably resisted this result. Further, and despite some early equivocations,[149] the Federal Court has also resisted the conclusion that all decisions made by a statutory corporation[150] or agency will necessarily be reviewable under the *ADJR Act*. Contractual decisions, which at common law have traditionally been thought of as 'private' and unreviewable, have been a particular focus of attention. On this question, the Federal Court concluded that neither decisions made to enter into new contracts (under broad statutory powers to enter into contracts or to exercise all the powers of a natural person) nor decisions made pursuant to the terms of an existing contract were reviewable under the *ADJR Act*.[151]

In *Griffith University v Tang*[152] the High Court stated a new test for the determination of whether a decision is made *under* an enactment. The decision must be (1) 'expressly or impliedly required or

---

147 *Salerno v National Crime Authority* (1997) 75 FCR 133, 143.

148 See Aronson, Dyer and Groves, n 24 above, 134–49.

149 See, e.g., *Australian Capital Territory Health Authority v Berkeley Cleaning Group Pty Ltd* (1985) 7 FCR 575.

150 A statutory corporation created by specific legislation is to be distinguished from a government corporation created under the general legislation which enables entities to incorporate (*Corporations Act 2001*).

151 See, e.g., *General Newspapers Pty Ltd v Telstra Corporation* (1993) 45 FCR 164, 170; *Australian National University v Burns* (1985) 43 ALR 25; *Hutchins v Deputy Commissioner of Taxation* (1996) 65 FCR 269.

152 (2005) 221 CLR 89. *Tang* arose under the *Judicial Review Act 1991* (Qld), which relevantly limits jurisdiction to decisions made 'under an enactment'. Section 16(1) of the Queensland *Judicial Review Act* ties its interpretation to that of the *ADJR Act*, in all relevant respects. Curiously, *Tang's* lawyers did not plead other potential sources of jurisdiction exercisable by the Queensland Supreme Court, namely its 'common law jurisdiction' and its jurisdiction under s 4(b) of the *Judicial Review Act* to review decisions made within a state-funded scheme or program.

authorised by the enactment'; and (2) 'the decision must itself confer, alter or otherwise affect legal rights or obligations'.[153] The rights or obligations affected may already be in existence (derived from the 'general law' or another statute), or they may be 'new' rights or obligations arising from decisions required or authorised by the enactment. In reference to the contract cases, the court concluded that legislative capacity to contract 'will not, without more, be sufficient to empower [a government] body unilaterally to affect the rights or liabilities of any other party'.[154] The message is that, in general, decisions taken pursuant to a contract or to enter into a contract affect rights and obligations through the operation of the contractual agreement and contract law.[155]

Tang's case was not, however, a contract case. The impugned decision, made by the university (a statutory body), was to exclude Tang from her PhD studies for academic misconduct. In the absence of any alternative source of legal capacity to make the decision (that is, a contract) or an alternative basis on which the decision was given legal effect (that is, contract law),[156] one would have assumed that the exclusion decision would, straightforwardly, be made under the enactment which, in a general sense, clearly authorised it. However, applying its newly declared test, the court held that, while the decision to expel Tang was in broad terms authorised by the *Griffith University Act 1998* (Qld) (what other source of power could there be?), the decision did not affect her legal rights and obligations. It was concluded that Tang 'enjoyed no relevant legal rights and the university had no obligations under' the legislation; the relationship was merely one of 'mutual consensus'.[157] The application of the new test thus withdrew a decision of a 'public' body[158] from judicial scrutiny under the *ADJR Act*.

The reasons in support of *Tang's* test are surprisingly thin. First, it was suggested that the requirement that a decision must also have an 'administrative character' casts 'light on the force to be given by the phrase "under an enactment"'. 'What is it [about a decision], in the course of administration', the majority asked, 'which has merited the legislative conferral of a right of judicial review'? The answer appears to be that only decisions which confer, alter or affect legal rights or obligations *merit* judicial review. This is a very unclear suggestion.[159] Moreover, it sits uneasily with

---

153   *Tang* (2005) 221 CLR 89, 130–1 (Gummow, Callinan and Heydon JJ). Gleeson CJ wrote a concurring opinion; Kirby J dissented.

154   Ibid, 129. Interestingly, the *ADJR Act* line of cases excluding contractual decisions from review (confirmed in *Tang*) has been used to reinforce the common law position that powers which find their legal source in a contract are not amenable to judicial review: *Khuu & Lee Pty Ltd v Corporation of the City of Adelaide* (2011) SASR 235, 239–40. On the common law position, see 3.6.1.

155   For a discussion of the extent to which this approach leaves open some scope for the judicial review of government tendering (procurement) decisions, see A E Cassimatis, 'Judicial Attitudes to Judicial Review: A Comparative Examination of Justifications Offered for Restricting the Scope of Judicial Review in Australia, Canada and England' (2010) 34 *Melbourne University Law Review* 1, 23–7. The case for judicial review of procurement decisions which fail to follow statutory procedures is stronger than that in relation to a decision which is contrary to non-statutory procedures.

156   Given the Federal Court jurisprudence on the reviewability of contract decisions, the High Court was clearly surprised about the parties' 'silence on the existence of a contract': *Tang* (2005) 221 CLR 89, 107–9; 120–1; 142–3, 154.

157   The *Griffith University Act* gave the university all the powers of an individual, including the power to do anything necessary or convenient in connection with its functions. Its function included the conferral of higher education awards. This was a function which separate legislation prohibited non-university educational providers from performing. Kirby J noted that the university (along with other institutions legislatively deemed to have university status) enjoyed something like 'monopoly powers', and rejected the characterisation of the relationship between the parties as 'voluntary' or 'consensual': ibid, 155–6.

158   Adopting the 'institutional' approach to administrative law (1.1), the university, having been established and constituted by statute, was a public body.

159   Especially given the court's refusal to enter the controversy over the meaning of 'administrative character': see 3.5.1.3. The joint judgment attempts to bolster this reasoning by reference to a 'line of authority' dealing with the meaning of 'instrument' under the *ADJR Act*. But the relevance of the cases cited is questionable: see Mantziaris and McDonald, n 140 above.

the extension of the law of procedural fairness, which now protects a wide variety of interests in addition to legal 'rights' (5.2.2.1). Similarly, the law of standing has moved past a focus on rights, and now allows aggrieved persons with a 'special interest' to commence judicial review (6.2).[160] It has helpfully been suggested that the rights and obligations test should be understood as a requirement that a decision has a 'legal effect' referable to a statutory scheme.[161] But even if one interprets the *Tang* test in this way, where a decision breaches 'soft law' requirements (i.e. those which derive from decision-maker's internal policies and manuals rather than a statute), it will fall beyond the reach of the *ADJR Act*.[162] The difficulty for Ms Tang was that the university code which she alleged had been breached did not have statutory force.

The joint judgment also cryptically connects the constitutional concept of 'matter' to the 'rights and obligations' test: 'The meaning of the constitutional term "matter", it is claimed, 'requires some immediate right, duty or liability to be established by the court dealing with an application for review under the *ADJR Act*.'[163] (Chapter III of the Constitution confers, and allows parliament to confer, federal jurisdiction only in relation to the 'matters' specified therein (3.4.1.3).) This connection (though added almost as an afterthought) potentially has far-reaching implications. As all sources of federal jurisdiction are restricted by the 'matter' concept, the restrictive 'rights and obligations' test may apply beyond the context of the *ADJR Act*. This would have the consequence that judicial review in federal jurisdiction could never proceed on the basis of 'breach' of soft law requirements (which confer no 'rights' nor impose any 'obligations),[164] even in relation to the operation of increasingly popular executive schemes which have no statutory basis.[165]

A uniform criterion for the determination of the availability of the judicial review of federal government decisions, across the various sources of federal jurisdiction, clearly has the virtue of promoting consistency in delimiting the scope of judicial review. However, we doubt whether the 'matter' concept, and the 'rights and obligations' test associated with it in *Tang*, are appropriate tools for that task. An analysis of such abstract concepts is not demanded by the text of the *ADJR Act* and is likely to conceal rather than reveal the policy considerations relevant to deciding which decisions made by public authorities *should* be subjected to administrative law norms.

One glaring problem in *Tang* (which the court did not confront) was that the decision to deny review of the university's decision resulted in an absence of *any* body of legal principles by which the relationship between the parties would be regulated and structured. This is quite different from the denial of judicial review of decisions based on 'private' contractual powers, which are regulated by contract law. (There is no general law—analogous to contract law—governing 'voluntary' or

---

160   See *Tang* (2005) 221 CLR 89, 117, 144 (Kirby J).

161   D Stewart, '*Griffith University v Tang*, "Under an Enactment" and Limiting Access to Judicial Review' (2005) 33 *Federal Law Review* 525, 545. If this is what the High Court intended, one wonders whether the test was well formulated: M Taggart, '"Australian Exceptionalism" in Judicial Review' (2008) 36 *Federal Law Review* 1, 19.

162   This will be so even accepting that the ultimate decision is (as was accepted in *Tang*) impliedly authorised by statute. See generally M Aronson, 'Private Bodies, Public Power and Soft Law in the High Court' (2007) 35 *Federal Law Review* 1.

163   *Tang* (2005) 221 CLR 89, 131.

164   Aronson, above n 162, 20–23. Post-*Tang*, the Federal Court has accepted that legitimate expectations that policy will be followed do not create 'substantive' rights: *White Industries Australia Ltd v Federal Commissioner of Taxation* (2007) 160 FCR 298; *Bilborough v Deputy Commissioner of Taxation* (2007) 162 FCR 160.

165   See generally Commonwealth Ombudsman, *Executive Schemes*, Report 12/2009 (2009). Such schemes are commonly used to deliver aid and relief and to provide incentives for industry. There are also compensation schemes such as the Scheme for Compensation for Detriment caused by Defective Administration (CDDA) which enables claims to be made in relation to defective administration.

'consensual' relationships.)[166] Perhaps the High Court was right that the relationship between Tang and the university should not be subject to administrative law's norms—despite the decision having been made by a body established by statute, and despite its significant impact on an individual's interests. But this issue deserved to be explicitly addressed, given the court was proceeding on the assumption that there was no contract between the Tang and the university. It is true that the statutory words limiting the courts' jurisdiction to decisions made 'under an enactment' must be given their due. It is more difficult, however, to see how the rights and obligations test flows directly from the text of the *ADJR Act*. In these circumstances, it is disappointing that the court's reasons in *Tang* shed so little light on the policy question of whether particular decisions are best left regulated by private law or should be subjected to administrative law norms.[167]

In dissent, Kirby J expressly recognised the centrality of the public/private distinction. He argued that 'the reality' was 'that the relevant "arrangement" between the university and [Tang] consisted *solely* in the exercise by the university of its statutory powers under the Higher Education Act [which prevented non-universities from conferring higher education awards] and University Act'.[168] For this reason, he concluded that the decision to terminate the relationship between the parties involved an exercise of public power, and should be reviewable under the Queensland equivalent of the *ADJR Act*.

Although there are a number of cases which have applied the *Tang* test, little has been clarified. Some cases have descended into unsatisfying discussions of, or conclusions about the distinction between rights and other sorts of interests (such as privileges).[169] Other cases appear to have taken a broader approach which focuses on whether a decision has statutory consequences.[170] The continuing confusion is illustrated by *Eastman v Besanko*.[171] A majority of the Federal Court held that a decision not to order an inquiry under s 424 of the *Crimes Act 1914* (Cth) into a murder conviction was not a decision under an enactment because there was no 'right to the order of an inquiry' and the statutory power authorising the decision 'did not create a duty to order an inquiry'.[172] Although he did not find it necessary to decide the point, Dowsett J concluded that this approach 'may reflect an unduly restrictive' application of *Tang*. Any decision to order an inquiry would enliven statutory duties, the performance of which could be enforced. It was, therefore, 'difficult, in general terms, to see how' the

---

166   See *Tang* (2005) 221 CLR 89, 111 (Gleeson CJ); 128, 131 (Gummow, Callinan and Heydon JJ). The only applicable legal principle is that which is not prohibited is allowed. This is the so-called 'closure' rule of private law. The 'closure' rule of public law is the converse: government cannot act without specific legal authority: see Charles Sampford, 'Law, Institutions and the Public Private Divide' (1991) 20 *Federal Law Review* 185, 204–5; J Raz, *The Authority of Law: Essays on Law and Morality* (Oxford: Oxford University Press, 1979) 72, 75–9. See also n 250 below.

167   Legal rights and obligations can be affected by decisions made by government under *both* private and public law powers.

168   *Tang* (2005) 221 CLR 89, 155.

169   *Palmer v The Chief Executive, Qld Corrective Services* [2010] QCA 316, a case which involved a refusal to exercise a discretionary power to allow property to be brought into a prison as per a prisoner's request. The court held that a decision to prevent a prisoner from holding several boxes of legal material was not made under an enactment because, *inter alia*, 'a prisoner has no right to his personal property, while in prison'; the prisoner had no more than a 'privilege' to access his property: ibid, [29]–[30]. (The court relied in part on the fact that there was no duty to exercise the power, but this has not prevented review in other contexts: see *Plaintiff M61/2010E v Commonwealth* (2010) 243 CLR 319.) In *Nona v Barnes* [2012] QSC 35 a coroner's decision not to provide information to the Department of Public Prosecutions did not affect legal rights or obligations despite the fact the applicants had a 'substantial' interest in the course which was taken (or not taken) by the coroner. In *Rawson Finances Pty Ltd v Deputy Commissioner of Taxation* (2010) 189 FCR 189 a decision by the ATO to commence legal action to recover a tax debt was said to create a 'circumstance', not a 'right'.

170   E.g., *Reynolds v Tasmanian Heritage Council* (2011) 246 FLR 454.

171   *Eastman v Besanko* (2010) 244 FLR 262.

172   Ibid, 307–8.

decision 'could be described as being other than a decision under an enactment'.[173] Other cases reveal difficulties in disentangling the underlying purpose of the *Tang* test with different principles limiting the availability of review, such as whether a decision is substantive in the *Bond* sense (3.5.1.1),[174] standing requirements (Chapter 6),[175] or whether a justiciable controversy arises (3.6.2).[176] As Groves has fairly concluded, '*Tang* arguably raised more questions about the jurisdictional formula of the *ADJR Act* than it settled.'[177]

3.5.1.4.2 Decisions by non-government entities under statutory schemes of regulation

Fewer cases have dealt with the question of whether the decisions of non-government bodies can be reviewable under the *ADJR Act*.[178] But this question is likely to be of growing importance. Scholars of regulation have observed that an increasing range of social and economic activity is regulated by non-governmental actors. Using a well-worn metaphor, the contemporary state is said to do less rowing and more steering than it once did. Although trends such as privatisation and contracting out (or outsourcing) have meant that governments have ceased to provide certain 'public' goods and services, they typically maintain a role in overseeing their provision by other 'private' actors.[179] Moreover, governments nowadays regulate in the knowledge that aspects of their 'steering' function have been 'outsourced' to, or claimed by, 'business organisations, NGOs (non-government organisations), and others'.[180] Schemes of 'self-regulation', under which non-governmental actors are simultaneously the providers and subjects of regulation, are common.[181] In other regulatory regimes, the regulatory function is shared between government and non-governmental actors and dependent upon cooperative action. These features of modern governance are the circumstances of what is sometimes called the 'new regulatory state'.[182]

    NEAT Domestic Trading Pty Ltd v AWB Ltd[183] involved the now-notorious company responsible for the marketing and export of Australian wheat.[184] AWB was owned by Australian wheat growers who sold their wheat into a common pool for export under the 'single desk' policy. The actual responsibility for marketing and selling the common pool was conferred on AWBI Ltd, a wholly owned subsidiary of AWB.

---

173   Ibid, 283.

174   *Rawson Finances Pty Ltd v Deputy Commissoner of Taxation* (2010) 189 FCR 189.

175   *Hu v Migrations Agents Registration Authority* [2010] FCA 674.

176   *Eastman v Australian Capital Territory* (2008) 2 ACTLR 180.

177   Groves, n 99 above, 745.

178   Although the university in the *Tang* case was not a government body it was publicly funded and set up by statute, which at least raises the question of whether it should be subject to public law norms.

179   It is often assumed that privatisation and deregulation go hand in hand, but privatisation is typically followed by re-regulation. For some empirical evidence, see I Ayres and J Braithwaite, *Responsive Regulation: Transcending the Deregulation Debate* (New York: Oxford University Press, 1992), 7–12.

180   C Parker and J Braithwaite, 'Regulation' in P Cane and M Tushnet (eds), *The Oxford Handbook of Legal Studies* (Oxford: Oxford University Press, 2003), 126.

181   For example, the regulation of advertising standards: see *Dorf Industries Pty Ltd v Toose* (1994) 127 ALR 654.

182   L McDonald, 'The Rule of Law in the "New Regulatory State"' (2004) 33 *Common Law World Review* 197, 199. This nomenclature marks a departure from the 'administrative' or 'welfare' state, thought to define the role of the state throughout much of the twentieth century.

183   (2003) 216 CLR 277 ('*NEAT*').

184   See *Report of the Inquiry into Certain Australian Companies in Relation to the UN Oil-for-Food Programme* (Commonwealth of Australia, 2006).

LIVERPOOL JOHN MOORES UNIVERSITY
LEARNING SERVICES

Both companies were incorporated under the *Corporations (Victoria) Act 1990* (Vic) and, like other private companies, were expected to maximise profits for their shareholders. However, unlike most private companies, AWBI played an important—even dominant—role in the regulation of Australian wheat exports. Under the 'single-desk' policy (which was reflected in the terms of the *Wheat Marketing Act 1989* (Cth)) only AWBI had the legal right to export wheat. And although the *Wheat Marketing Act* did allow the Wheat Export Authority (a government statutory corporation) to issue consent for others to export wheat, there was a catch: s 57(3B) of the *Wheat Marketing Act* prohibited the Wheat Export Authority from issuing consent unless it had received AWBI's 'prior approval in writing'. AWBI thus had the de facto power to protect its own export monopoly.[185]

In *NEAT*, a majority of the High Court concluded that the AWBI's decision to veto an application to export wheat was not reviewable under the *ADJR Act* and also that the common law remedies of prohibition, certiorari and mandamus were unavailable.[186] Given the significance of the 'functional turn' that judicial review has taken in England (1.1), *NEAT* was a disappointing decision insofar as it failed to engage with the underlying issues.[187] The reasoning was brief and the precise basis for the decision opaque. The majority gave three reasons for its conclusion that 'public law remedies' did not lie against AWBI's refusal to give its consent.[188]

The first reason clearly related to the applicability of the *ADJR Act*. The court argued that, although s 57(3B) of the *Wheat Marketing Act* gave statutory significance to the consent decision, 'that subsection did not … confer statutory authority on AWBI to make the decision'.[189] Rather, AWBI gained its power to give approval in writing from its status as a legal person: it, like any other private actor, had ample power to approve in writing an application to export wheat. In contrast, the Wheat Export Authority's decision to consent (or not) to any export was 'the operative and determinative decision which the [legislation] requires or authorises'.[190] For these reasons, the court concluded that it was 'neither necessary nor appropriate' to conclude that the AWBI's decision was 'made under' the *Wheat Marketing Act*.[191] It may be accepted that there is a distinction between (1) a decision which is a precondition to the making of a further decision; and (2) that further decision itself. And it may be conceded that this distinction may be of importance in determining whether it is 'appropriate' to conclude that a decision is 'made under an enactment' and thus reviewable. But simply stating the distinction does not explain its importance.[192]

Justice Kirby's dissent highlighted the artificiality of the conclusion that AWBI's refusal decision did not derive from the Act, but from its status as a legal entity. Although it is true that any legal person (including the AWBI) can issue approvals to the Wheat Export Authority (or any government authority), in the absence of statutory significance such approvals are legally meaningless. For this reason, AWBI's decision should be characterised as having been made under an enactment: it was provided for,

---

185   The *Wheat Marketing Act* was silent on the criteria by which the AWBI was to decide to issue or withhold consent.

186   The manner in which these questions arose for determination involved complex technical issues, but they do not require examination for present purposes.

187   C Mantziaris, 'A "Wrong Turn" on the Public/Private Distinction: *NEAT Domestic Trading Pty Ltd v AWB Ltd*' (2003) 14 *Public Law Review* 197; see further 3.5.1.

188   The court expressly declined to answer to the general 'question of whether public law remedies may be granted against private bodies': *NEAT* (2003) 216 CLR 277, 297.

189   Ibid, 298.

190   Ibid, 297.

191   Ibid, 298.

192   M Aronson, n 101 above, 1, 10.

required and given legal force by the statute. This conclusion was 'appropriate' because, as Gleeson CJ argued,[193] AWBI's export monopoly was created by legislation and reflects a legislative judgment that this arrangement was in the interest of wheat growers generally and indeed the 'national interest'.[194]

The court's second and third reasons for denying public law remedies emphasised the 'private' status of AWBI and asserted that its private (commercial) objectives (to maximise profits) could not sensibly be accommodated with any administrative law obligations. (Exactly why administrative law norms might not, at least partially, restrict its unbridled pursuit of profit was not explained.)[195] It is not entirely clear, however, whether these additional reasons should be taken as relevant for considering the applicability of the *ADJR Act*, as opposed to 'the grant of relief in the nature of prohibition, certiorari or mandamus' (which was also held to be unavailable).[196] In *Tang*, the court explained the inapplicability of the *ADJR Act* in *NEAT* by emphasising *only* the first of the reasons given—namely, that 'the statutory condition precedent was a decision made *dehors* [that is, not under] the federal statute, although, once made, it had a critical effect for the operation of the federal statute'.[197] Below (3.6.1) we return to this aspect of *NEAT* in our discussion of the reviewability at common law of 'public' decisions made by non-government decision-makers.[198]

Some light may be cast on the meaning, in this context, of 'under an enactment' by a case which raised the reviewability of a decision made by a state government officer under the *ADJR Act*. The phrase 'under an enactment' means 'under a Commonwealth enactment'. The case of *Glasson v Parkes Rural Distributions Pty Ltd*[199] concerned a decision of a state officer under a Commonwealth–state regulatory scheme which was funded and controlled by the Commonwealth.[200] The High Court denied review of the decision on the ground that because Commonwealth legislation was not the source of (1) the power to appoint the decision-maker; (2) the power to make the decision; or (3) the decision's legal effect, the decision was made 'under' state law. *Glasson* suggests that the question of whether a decision is made 'under an enactment' depends not only on the source of the power or capacity to make a decision (as suggested in *NEAT*), but also on the source of the decision's force and effect, that is, whether the legal consequences of a decision derive from the statute.[201]

In considering the reviewability of decisions undertaken by non-government (private) bodies under the *ADJR Act*, it must be conceded that the 'under an enactment' requirement does mean that

---

193   Gleeson CJ appeared to agree with Kirby J on the application of the *ADJR Act* (*NEAT* (2003) 216 CLR 277, 290–1) though he did not find it necessary to decide the point as he had decided that AWBI had not, in any event, breached any ground of judicial review.

194   Ibid, 290.

195   Gleeson CJ held that the AWBI could consider its own commercial interests, but must also consider other factors: ibid. There is no logical inconsistency in this position.

196   Ibid, 300. The court does not clearly separate these questions.

197   *Tang* (2005) 221 CLR 89, 130.

198   The reviewability of 'private' (non-government) decision-makers in the constitutional regime of judicial review is limited by the requirement that the challenge relates to 'an officer of the Commonwealth': see 3.4.1.2. In contrast to the emphasis given to the private status of the decision-maker in *NEAT*, it is clear that the company contracted to conduct the IMR in *Plaintiff M61* could not undertake its decision-making on the basis of private interests in the context of the statutory scheme which authorised its participation in the decision-making process (see above 3.4.1.2).

199   (1984) 155 CLR 234.

200   On the reviewability of a decision made by a Commonwealth officer under state law, see G Hill, 'Reviewing Decisions by Commonwealth Bodies Made Under State or Territory Legislation' (2006) 17 *Public Law Review* 112.

201   For a sophisticated attempt to reconcile these cases, see G Hill, 'The AD(JR) Act and Uunder an enactment": Can NEAT Domestic be reconciled with Glasson?' (2004) 11 *Australian Journal of Administrative Law* 135.

the courts are unable to fully embrace a functional approach to the scope of judicial review, under which performance of any and all 'public functions' (no matter the formal source of power) would be reviewable. By the same token, the Act's language surely does not preclude reference to functional criteria, insofar as its terms focus on whether a decision is made 'under an enactment', not on the institutional (government or non-government) status of the decision-maker. As the *NEAT* majority accepted, the answer to the question of whether or not a decision is made under an enactment may depend in part on whether or not it is 'appropriate' to read a capacity to make a decision as deriving from a statute.

3.5.1.5 Jurisdictional gaps under the *ADJR Act*

Despite the hopes of its sponsors, the straightforward conceptual structure of the *ADJR Act* has become mired in a jurisdictional swamp.[202] The difficulty is not so much that there are limits to the reach of judicial review under the Act, but that these limits have not been justified by reference to underlying principles concerning the appropriate scope of judicial review. Although the Federal Court will often have alternative sources of jurisdiction (3.5.2), the recent reliance on the 'matter' concept in *Tang* may make some of these gaps hard to plug as they will apply to all sources of federal jurisdiction.[203]

3.5.2 Jurisdiction under the *Judiciary Act*

We have already explained that s 39B(1) of the *Judiciary Act* confers jurisdiction on the Federal Court in the same terms used by s 75(v) of the Constitution (3.4.1). In 1997, s 39B(1A)(c) was inserted into the *Judiciary Act* to create a further source of federal judicial review jurisdiction. The Court's jurisdiction was extended to include all matters 'arising under any laws made by the parliament'.[204] This provision does not entirely plug jurisdictional gaps arising under the *ADJR Act* (for example, in relation to non-statutory executive powers), but it does significantly expand the court's judicial review jurisdiction. One important consequence of the amendment is that the Federal Court can review the legality of subordinate legislation (which is not reviewable under the *ADJR Act*, as it is not of an administrative character), regardless of whether the decision-maker is an 'officer of the Commonwealth'. It is necessary to identify a right, duty or defence which owes its existence to a law made by the parliament, but it is 'somewhat unclear' what this involves.[205] One Federal Court judge has suggested that s 39B(1A)(c) was 'intended to provide ample scope for judicial review jurisdiction',[206] and the Administrative Review Council has recently expressed puzzlement as to why the provision appears to be so little used by judicial

---

202   In this context it is worth noting that for some time decisions under the *Migration Act 1958* (Cth) were excluded from coverage by the *ADJR Act*. The *ADJR Act* is now available in relation to some migration decisions, though Schedule 1 excludes 'privative clause decisions'. *Plaintiff S157/2002 v Commonwealth* (2003) 211 CLR 476 ('*Plaintiff S157*') held that decisions which were affected by jurisdictional errors were not 'privative clause decisions'. This means that there is no practical reason to plead the *ADJR Act* (which does not normally require the demonstration of a 'jurisdictional error') in preference to s 39B(1) of the *Judiciary Act* (which does require a jurisdictional error). Amendments introduced in 2005 had the effect of requiring most first instance review applications to be lodged in the Federal Magistrates Court. The Federal Magistrates Court exercises the same original jurisdiction as would the High Court under s 75(v) of the Constitution: s 476 *Migration Act 1958* (Cth). See Aronson, Dyer and Groves, n 24 above, 41–2.

203   E.g. *Motor Trades Association of Australia Superannuation Fund Pty Ltd v Australian Prudential Regulation Authority* (2008) 169 FCR 483, 491–2.

204   Like s 39B(1), this jurisdiction is limited insofar as matters relating to criminal process are specifically excluded.

205   *McGowan v Migration Agents Registration Authority* (2003) 129 FCR 118, 127. See further A Robertson, 'The Administrative Law Jurisdiction of the Federal Court—Is the AD(JR) Act Still Important?' (2003) 24 *Australian Bar Review* 8.

206   *Saitta Pty Ltd v Commonwealth* (2000) 106 FCR 554, [89].

review applicants.[207] It is possible that limitations on the availability of the two main sources of federal review jurisdiction (the *ADJR Act* and the constitutional basis of review developed pursuant to s 75(v) and s 39B(1) of the *Judiciary Act*) will lead to greater attention being paid to the limits and conceptual basis of review under s 39B(1A)(c) (and, indeed, s 75(iii) of the Constitution) (see also 2.4.2.5).[208]

3.5.3 Statutory sources of judicial review jurisdiction in state courts

In addition to their supervisory or common law jurisdiction (see 3.6), some state Supreme Courts have statutory judicial review jurisdiction. The Australian Capital Territory, Queensland and Tasmania all have legislation which is, to a greater or lesser extent, modelled on the Commonwealth *ADJR Act*.[209] The large interpretive questions associated with these statutory regimes align with those under the Commonwealth Act, though there are some differences in detail. Perhaps the most interesting departure from the Commonwealth model appears in the Queensland Act. The *Judicial Review Act 1991* (Qld) extends the scope of statutory review beyond the basic jurisdictional requirements set out in the *ADJR Act* to include administrative decisions made by public officers or employees under a non-statutory 'scheme or program' which involves the use of funds appropriated by parliament or from a tax, charge, fee or levy authorised by an enactment.[210] Jurisdiction conferred on the Supreme Court of Victoria under the *Administrative Law Act 1978* (Vic) has a different conceptual basis.[211]

Although the Commonwealth parliament may invest state (by which, recall, we mean state and territory) courts with federal jurisdiction,[212] there is very little scope for state courts to exercise federal judicial review jurisdiction.[213]

3.6 The supervisory jurisdiction of state Supreme Courts

All state Supreme Courts have 'common law' or 'supervisory' judicial review jurisdiction, a jurisdiction originally inherited from the 'superior' courts in England (see 3.2).[214] As we have seen (3.4.3), *Kirk's* case recognised that aspects of state judicial review jurisdiction have constitutional significance.

---

207 *Judicial Review in Australian—Consultation Paper* (April 2011), 45–6.

208 It should be noted that these sources of jurisdiction are not limited to 'judicial review' cases. For example, s 75(iii) has a role in giving the High Court jurisdiction to hear common law actions in contract and tort against 'the Commonwealth': *Commonwealth v Mewett* (1997) 191 CLR 471.

209 See *Judicial Review Act 1991* (Qld); *Judicial Review Act 2000* (Tas); *Administrative Decisions (Judicial Review) Act 1989* (ACT). On possible options for the adoption of a statutory judicial review jurisdiction in New South Wales, see Discussion Paper, Reform of Judicial Review in NSW (NSW Department of Justice & Attorney General, March 2011).

210 *Judicial Review Act 1991* (Qld), subs 4(b). For discussion, see Groves, n 99 above, 753–6.

211 See Aronson, Dyer and Groves, n 24 above, 26–9; Groves, above n 99. Western Australia rejected a proposal to enact a judicial review statute modelled on the ADJR Act: see Law Reform Commission of Western Australia, *Report on Judicial Review of Administrative Decisions*, Project No 95 (2002).

212 Constitution, s 77(iii). To show their erudition, lawyers like to refer to this capacity as the 'autochthonous expedient'. (The Federal Court was not created until 1975.)

213 See Aronson, Dyer and Groves, n 24 above, 87–90; Leslie Zines, *Cowen and Zines' Federal Jurisdiction in Australia*, 3rd edn (Sydney: Federation Press, 2002), 196–7.

214 See Aronson, Dyer and Groves, n 24 above, 20–22.

Kirk held that a defining characteristic of a state Supreme Court is the power to review decisions made by state decision-makers on the basis of jurisdictional error. The jurisdiction of state Supreme Courts to engage in judicial review is, to this extent, entrenched by the Constitution and, in this sense, has its ultimate legal source in the Constitution. Note, however, that the argument which gave this jurisdiction a basis in the Constitution does not, analogously to the terms of s 75(v), explicity confine review to decisions made by 'officers of a State'.

In *Kirk*, the High Court recognised that this supervisory review jurisdiction is 'governed in fundamental respects by principles established as part of the common law of Australia'.[215] Moreover, the court accepted that some aspects of the relief which may be granted in exercise of this jurisdiction[216] are not entrenched by the Constitution (and thus may be excluded by the legislature). The line between when relief is entrenched by the Constitution and when it is not is marked out by the key distinction between non-jurisdictional and jurisdictional errors. This means that the approach to the availability of the 'constitutional writs' under s 75(v) also applies in relation to the availability of the prerogative writs (or orders in the nature of the writs) in matters of state law—subject to the exception that certiorari may issue for non-jurisdictional error on the face of the record if the parliament has not ousted its availability on this ground. Declarations and injunctions may also available in administrative law cases for non-jurisdictional legal errors (see 4.3).[217]

The scope of judicial review at common law is delineated in terms of two basic issues. First, there is the much discussed public/private distinction, raising the questions of whether some non-government bodies are potentially subject to judicial review and whether the 'private' decisions of government decision-makers are immune from review. The focal point of judicial review is undoubtedly the review of government decisions, in particular, the review of the decisions of the executive arm of government (not the legislature or the superior courts—although, as was apparent in *Kirk*—the decisions of 'inferior courts' are also subject to judicial review). However, a large preoccupation of administrative lawyers over the past 25 years has been whether judicial review may extend to 'private' decision-makers where they are exercising 'public' powers or functions. On the other side of the equation, there has been a long reluctance to subject decisions based on 'private' or 'common law' powers to judicial review. Although the details remain far from clear, the received wisdom is that powers deriving from contract alone are not reviewable.[218]

Second, the courts have developed the idea of 'non-justiciability' to limit the reach of review. Even if a decision is acknowledged to be 'public', jurisdiction to review that decision may be declined if it is concluded that the decision is not apt or suitable for review by judges and courts.

3.6.1 Review of 'public' decisions

In the early stages of the development of judicial review, the courts were not self-consciously concerned to mark out anything so abstract as its 'scope'. Rather, the question was the availability of one or other

---

215   *Kirk v Industrial Court of New South Wales* (2010) 239 CLR 531, 581.

216   Certiorari is available for non-jurisdictional error on the face of the record (see 4.1.1; 4.5.1.1).

217   As noted below in this section, the High Court has acknowledged that these remedies should be considered part of the framework of administrative law principles developed at common law, regardless of whether they have been sought using any special procedural regime specifically intended to apply to 'judicial review'.

218   *R v Criminal Injuries Compensation Board, ex p Lain* [1967] 2 QB 864, 882, though some principles of judicial review (such as procedural fairness obligations) may be implied contractual terms, and thus actionable in contract law.

of the prerogative writs (and later the remedies of declaration or injunction).[219] English administrative law has now reached the position where the scope of judicial review is no longer conceptualised in this 'remedy-oriented' way; rather, the territory is demarcated by reference to a broad distinction between public functions (which are reviewable) and private functions (which are not). A large question for common law judicial review in Australia is the extent to which these English developments will be embraced.

In the pivotal *Datafin* case, the English Court of Appeal held that the City Panel on Takeovers and Mergers was amenable to judicial review.[220] In many ways, the takeover panel was a typical regulatory body: it promulgated a code of practice to be followed, adjudicated possible breaches of the code, and exercised various powers to enforce the code. What was 'remarkable' about the panel, however, was that it existed without 'visible means of legal support'. It was not an institution of government—its powers could not be traced to statute or the 'prerogative powers' (3.6.2.2). Nor was its power based on a contract. Nonetheless, it exercised immense de facto power: a breach of the code could result in public censure and in other bodies exacting heavy penalties in the exercise of their statutory or contractual powers. Although the panel was characterised as a self-regulatory body,[221] the court also emphasised the role played by the government in encouraging its establishment and the broader regulatory context, which included statutory provisions related to its activities.[222] The court even speculated that if the panel did not exist, the government would have had to create something just like it.

The basic principle to be extracted from *Datafin* is that decisions which are made in the exercise of a 'public function' are subject to judicial review. The corollary of this principle is that 'private functions' or powers are not judicially reviewable (even if exercised by a government body).[223] All this prompts the important question: what is a 'public function' or a decision with 'public elements'? Stated at this level of abstraction this question is, perhaps, only answerable by normative stipulation: a public function is one which *should* be considered public and *should* be subject to judicial review. The English courts have, in essence, recognised that whether a function is 'public' may change over time and will inevitably depend upon the broader legal and political context. Thus, in determining the 'publicness' of a given function they have looked to contextual criteria, reducing emphasis on the abstract nature of particular functions. For example, it has been asked whether the government would be likely to exercise a function if it was not being performed by the 'private' actor. Emphasis has also been placed on the extent to which the function operates as a key plank of a regulatory structure which includes government

---

219   The history is intricate: see S A de Smith, 'Administrative Law: Wrongs and Remedies' (1952) 15 *Modern Law Review* 189; E G Henderson, *Foundations of English Administrative Law: Certiorari and Mandamus in the Seventeenth Century* (Cambridge, Mass: Harvard University Press, 1963).

220   *R v Panel on Take-overs and Mergers, Ex parte Datafin* [1987] QB 815 ('*Datafin*').

221   Connoting 'a system whereby a group of people, acting in concert, use their collective power to force themselves and others to comply with a code of conduct of their own devising': ibid, 826.

222   The regulatory scheme might have been more accurately conceptualised as 'co-regulation': I Ayres and J Braithwaite, *Responsive Regulation: Transcending the Deregulation Debate* (New York: Oxford University Press, 1992), 102.

223   In an earlier case, *R v Criminal Injuries Compensation Board, ex parte Lain* [1967] 2 QB 864, it was held that judicial review covers 'every case in which a body of persons of a public as opposed to a purely private or domestic character has to determine matters affecting subjects': at 882. That case, however, involved a decision-making body which was clearly an emanation of the government: namely, a board set up to compensate victims of crime. The question was whether the administration of this compensation scheme was reviewable, even though it lacked statutory backing, having been established by reference to 'prerogative' or common law powers (see 3.6.2.2). *Lain* rejected the theory that the *source* of a government decision-maker's power was *determinative* of its amenability to judicial review; *Datafin* extended this logic such that even non-government bodies may be subject to judicial review based upon the public *nature* of the powers (or functions) exercised.

decision-makers.[224] These contextual factors, however, have not (and could not have) removed the necessity for judges to make value judgments about the appropriate scope of judicial review.[225]

The question of whether a function is 'public' has also been partially answered by judicial acceptance that the exercise of contractual powers is (generally speaking) a 'private' function. To this extent, the legal source of a body's power can indicate the nature of the functions performed and thus be relevant to its amenability to review. In the *Aga Khan* case, the fact that a jockey club's enormous (monopoly) powers over the livelihood of its members derived from a contract indicated that the powers were 'in no sense governmental'; the only available remedies against the club were to be found in contract law.[226] On the other hand, there are cases where bodies empowered by contract (such as trade unions and sporting clubs) have been subject to obligations which are ostensibly very similar to those applicable in judicial review cases (especially, obligations of procedural fairness). The juridical basis of these decisions is, however, often difficult to identify with precision as 'administrative-law-like' obligations have often been implied into the terms of the contracts which constitute such entities.[227] The result is a rather confused body of case law on the susceptibility of contract-based entities to 'judicial review' (see also 4.5.1.1; 4.5.1.4). Part of the confusion arises as the remedies granted in such cases have been declarations or injunctions rather than the prerogative writs, and this has enabled judges to avoid directly deciding whether 'judicial review' extends to such bodies.[228]

It will be recalled that in *NEAT* (3.5.1.4.2), the High Court held that neither the *ADJR Act* nor the common law prerogative writs were available in relation to a decision by a private corporation, where that decision was a statutory prerequisite to the giving of permission to export wheat by a statutory authority.[229] Although the majority denied that it was answering the general question of 'whether public

---

224   For a longer list of factors drawn from the English cases, see E Kryrou, 'Judicial Review of Decisions of Non-Governmental Bodies Exercising Governmental Powers: Is *Datafin* Part of Australian Law?' (2012) 86 *Australian Law Journal* 20, 31–2.

225   See CD Campbell, 'The Nature of Power as Public in English Public Judicial Review' (2009) 68 *Cambridge Law Journal* 90. It is difficult to give a purely factual answer to the question: would the government exercise function if (counterfactually) the non-government body did not? Similarly, the integration of a function into an overall regulatory regime inevitably involves questions of judgment and degree. See P Cane, *Administrative Law*, 5th edn (Oxford: Clarendon Press, 2011), 271–2. The distinction between public and private functions has gained added significance in the United Kingdom since the enactment of the *Human Rights Act 1998* (UK) ('HRA'). The effect of ss 6(3)(b) and 6(5) is that the *HRA* applies not only to 'public authorities' but also to bodies 'certain of whose functions are of a public nature, save in respect of a particular act if the nature of that act is private': see *YL v Birmingham City Council* [2008] 1 AC 95, [3] ('YL'). In *YL* the House of Lords adopted a factor-based approach to the meaning of 'public function' for the purposes of the *HRA*. However, the House of Lords indicated that the fact that a private company is acting pursuant to private law contractual obligations (as opposed to a statutory duty or power) is a strong indication that the function exercised is not of a public nature. Although the approaches to the scope of common law judicial review and review under the *HRA* are similar in the United Kingdom, the House of Lords in *YL* emphasised that the applicable principles are not necessarily coextensive. See further Cane, ibid, 103–6.

226   *R v Disciplinary Committee of the Jockey Club, ex parte Aga Khan* [1993] 2 All ER 853. The possibility that an affected member of the public (who was not a party to the contract) might seek judicial review was not entirely foreclosed. See also *D'Souza v The Royal Australian and New Zealand College of Psychiatrists* (2005) 12 VR 42, 58 ('certiorari is not available in respect of a decision whose powers derive only from private contract'); *Khuu & Lee Pty Ltd v Corporation of the City of Adelaide* (2011) 110 SASR 235, 240, [19] (a decision sourced in a general statutory power to contract was not reviewable as it was 'an ordinary decision made in the course of a conventional commercial relationship'); *Forbes v New South Wales Trotting Club Ltd* (1979) 143 CLR 242 (declaratory relief granted against a sporting club).

227   This reasoning can be forced, particularly in relation to unincorporated associations (whose decisions have traditionally been reviewable only in very limited circumstances): see Aronson, Dyer and Groves, n 24 above, 151–5; 942–3.

228   See *Chase Oyster Bar Pty Ltd v Hamo Industries Pty Ltd* (2010) 78 NSWLR 393, 412, [79].

229   The Federal Court had no jurisdiction under s 39B(1) as AWBI was not an officer of the Commonwealth, but it had jurisdiction under the *Trade Practices Act* and also, no doubt, under s 39B(1A)(c). To the extent that general common law remedies were thus denied, it may be presumed that the principles would be those applicable in the common law jurisdictions of the states.

law remedies may be granted against private bodies', its conclusion that neither the *ADJR Act* nor the common law judicial review remedies could not apply to the AWBI (without so much as citing *Datafin*) has left Australian administrative lawyers guessing about the applicability of the *Datafin* principle in Australia. Given that the 'single desk policy' for the export of Australian wheat was (1) devised by the Commonwealth government; (2) depended heavily on the statutory scheme for its efficacy; and (3) gave AWBI an integral role in what was acknowledged to be a 'scheme of public regulation', there is a strong argument that English courts, applying the contextual criteria of 'publicness' (considered above), would have accepted jurisdiction. On the other hand, the fact that the majority accepted that the AWBI was entitled to act to protect its private interests distinguishes the decision-maker's role from the regulatory function performed by the panel in *Datafin* and may justify a different conclusion.[230]

In addition to the question of jurisdiction, the court in *Datafin* also commented on the relevance of the identity and characteristics of the decision-maker and of the power being exercised to the applicability of particular grounds of review, taking the view that this issue should be approached with sensitivity to context. A similar approach was adopted by Gleeson CJ in *NEAT*.[231] Under such an approach the 'private' nature of the decision-maker may lead to the conclusion that certain grounds of review should have no, or only a restricted, application. Where exercises of statutory powers are being reviewed, the grounds of review are applied in a manner which is sensitive to the statutory context. How the grounds are applied will routinely depend upon the identity and nature of the statutory decision-maker. To the extent the decisions of private decision-makers are reviewable, there is no reason to think that this principle would not be applicable. Although in *NEAT* Gleeson CJ accepted the *ADJR Act* was available, he argued that the ground of review requiring a decision-maker to consider the merits of each case (and not to inflexibly apply policy) must be applied in a way which was consistent with the statutory scheme, a scheme which recognised the legitimacy of the private corporation (AWBI) systematically preferring its own financial interests to those of others.[232]

There is now a considerable list of cases in state Supreme Courts which have considered or cited the *Datafin* principle.[233] Although it has been confirmed that the Supreme Courts' supervisory jurisdiction 'can be invoked with respect to exercises of statutory powers … whether or not the person to whom any orders equivalent to the prerogative writs are to be directed is a public officer',[234] no consensus has been reached as to whether the *Datafin* principle represents the common law of Australia. Given the High Court's reticence in *NEAT* to provide guidance the conflicting views about the status of *Datafin* within intermediate appellate courts is understandable and little is to be gained from a close analysis of the cases. The lack of clear Australian authority on the extent to which non-government bodies are potentially subject to review may, in part, reflect the accidents of litigation. It may be, however, that the *Datafin* approach is difficult to reconcile with the conceptual basis of the constitutionally entrenched

---

230   Cf *YL v Birmingham City Council* [2008] 1 AC 95; *Aston Cantlow Parochial Church Council v Wallbank* [2004] 1 AC 546, [7].

231   *NEAT* (2003) 216 CLR 277, 290.

232   Ibid, 290. Nevertheless, Gleeson CJ accepted that some grounds of review were consistent with AWBI's private interests.

233   The cases are usefully collected in Kryrou, n 223 above. In particular, contrast the acceptance of the *Datafin* as applicable in Victoria in *CECA Institute Pty Ltd v Australian Council for Private Education & Training* (2010) 245 FLR 86 and *Mickovski v Financial Ombudsman Service Ltd* [2011] VSC 257 with the conclusion of the New South Wales Court of Appeal that 'there is an absence of authority in Australia addressing the question of whether or not *Datafin* applies' and that the High Court's 'statements of general principle … might be thought to adopt a more limited scope for the operation of public law remedies': *Chase Oyster Bar Pty Ltd v Hamo Industries Pty Ltd* (2010) 78 NSWLR 393, 413. See also the equivocation in *Khuu & Lee Pty Ltd v Corporation of the City of Adelaide* (2011) 110 SASR 235.

234   *Chase Oyster Bar Pty Ltd v Hamo Industries Pty Ltd* (2010) 78 NSWLR 393, 398; see also 413 and 455; *Perinepod Pty Ltd v Georgiou Building Pty Ltd* [2011] WASCA 217, [96].

review jurisdiction of the High Court, which is available only in respect of jurisdictional error. Judicial review, on this approach, is available when a decision-maker acts outside the limits of its authority, the traditional ultra vires rationale for judicial review. But whereas the notion of jurisdictional error makes clear sense in the context of statutory powers (and possibly executive powers), it less obviously makes sense in relation to the decisions of private bodies which are not made pursuant to statutory authority.[235] This may provide a reason why the remedies of declaration and injunction (which are not tied to the concept of jurisdictional error) continue to be the preferred relief in seeking review of non-governmental decision-makers.

The reasons why it has been possible for the courts to largely side-step resolving the status of the *Datafin* principle in Australian law probably also include important procedural differences between judicial review in England and in the common law jurisdictions of the Australian states. In England, a series of important procedural reforms, begun in 1978, are credited with propelling judicial review further into the so-called 'functional turn'.[236] The essence of the reforms was to establish a procedural regime for 'judicial review' applications which did not depend on the remedy sought. The reformed English rules provided that orders akin to the old prerogative writs had to be sought by way of the judicial review procedure; declarations and injunctions could be sought under this procedure, but were also available through the general alternative procedures applicable to private law claims. This procedural regime for judicial review led the House of Lords, in *O'Reilly v Mackman*, to articulate the 'exclusivity principle'.[237]

Under this principle, where an application raised 'public law' issues it usually had to be brought under the procedural regime specifically intended to apply to judicial review (regardless of the remedy sought). The reason given for this rule was that it would be an 'abuse of process' to use 'private law' procedures for what was in essence a 'public law' case, because the judicial review procedural regime was more advantageous to defendants than that applicable in private law matters.[238] As interpreted, the procedural reforms required the English courts to clearly identify whether a claim was brought in public or private law.[239]

In Australia, most state jurisdictions have undertaken reforms aimed at simplifying the procedures associated with the prerogative writs.[240] These changes have not prevented courts making 'orders in the nature of the prerogative writs', but have focused, rather, on the introduction of simpler and more flexible

---

235   For a perceptive discussion which raises this possibility, see D Stewart, 'Who's responsible? Justiciability of private and political decisions' in J Farrell and K Rubenstein (eds), *Sanctions, Accountability and Governance in a Globalised World* (Cambridge, 2009). In *Stewart v Ronalds* (2009) 76 NSWLR 99, 128, Handley AJA expressed doubts about whether procedural fairness obligations could arise without any 'authority in statute, prerogative, or consensual compact and without any legally recognised power' where the decision-maker had been 'given the task of investigation and report' under a contractual relationship—thereby emphasising the lack of what can be thought of as jurisdictional limits deriving from the source of authority, rather than the private status of the decision-maker.

236   The story is more fully told in Cane, n 224 above, 248–72.

237   [1983] 2 AC 237.

238   For example, shorter time limits apply for judicial review applications and applicants are required to seek leave to proceed.

239   Judicial review procedure is now governed by Part 8 of the *Civil Procedure Rules 1998* as modified by Part 54. A 'claim for judicial review' is defined as 'a claim to review the lawfulness of (i) an enactment; or (ii) a decision, action or failure to act in relation to the exercise of a public function': *Civil Procedure Rules 1998* r 54.1(2)(a). See Cane, n 224 above, 250–1.

240   See, generally, Butterworths, *Halsbury's Laws of Australia*, vol 1(2) (at 1 September 2010) 10 Administrative Law, '4 Judicial Review', [10–1339], [10–1342]. The traditional two-stage writ procedure (whereby an ex parte application for an 'order nisi' precedes a hearing on the substance on which the order nisi is 'discharged' or made 'absolute') continues to apply in Western Australia, though there have been proposals for reform: Law Reform Commission of Western Australia, *Report on Judicial Review of Administrative Decisions: Options for Reform*, Project No 95 (2002). This procedure also applies in the High Court's s 75(v) jurisdiction, although the *High Court Rules 2004* now refer to the order nisi as an 'order to show cause': Pt 25 r 20.01.1.

procedures. The important point, for our purposes, is that the various procedural reforms have not led to anything like England's 'exclusivity principle'.

The High Court's response to a now-superseded procedural regime in South Australia, which had been closely modelled on the reforms which precipitated the judicial development of the exclusivity principle in England, is instructive. Rule 98 of the *Supreme Court Rules 1987* (SA)[241] provided for a procedure through which orders in the nature of the prerogative writs *must* be sought and also *allowed* for the grant of declarations and injunctions on a summons for judicial review where the court considers this 'just and convenient'. Similarly to the English procedure, r 98 conferred procedural advantages on judicial review defendants (for example, a requirement that an applicant must seek leave to proceed).[242] Despite these similarities, no rule requiring all 'public law' matters to be commenced through the 'judicial review' procedure developed in South Australia.[243] In *Enfield*, the plaintiffs sought declarations and injunctions in relation to the purportedly invalid (ultra vires) activities of a public authority *outside* the r 98 procedural regime for judicial review. The plaintiffs thereby evaded any advantages the defendant would have enjoyed had the action been commenced under r 98. Far from objecting to this procedural course, the High Court encouraged it—the 'cast' of the proceedings illustrated the positive role played by declaration and injunction 'in the shaping of modern administrative law'.[244]

If the question is litigated, there is no avoiding the need to determine whether a particular non-government body, such as the panel in *Datafin* or a private company like the AWBI, is subject to some or all of the obligations judicial review imposes upon government decision-makers and whether particular remedies are available. But the absence of an exclusive procedural regime for judicial review cases in Australian 'common law' jurisdictions has contributed to the maintenance of a remedially focused conceptual approach to delimiting the scope of judicial review, largely by reference to rules governing the availability of remedies.[245] (We examine this body of law in Chapter 4.) For example, it has been said that although (orders in the nature of) the prerogative writs do not issue against 'private' clubs, declarations and injunctions are available in relation to decisions of such bodies that are affected by errors which would constitute a ground of judicial review if the decision had been made by a government defendant.[246] The upshot is that the overall picture of the scope of judicial review in the common law jurisdictions of the states remains difficult to bring into sharp focus.

3.6.2 The meaning of 'non-justiciability'

'Justiciability' is said to refer 'to the aptness of a question for judicial solution'.[247] If a court concludes that a decision is non-justiciable, it will decline to exercise its jurisdiction to review it on the basis that judicial

---

241   This procedural regime was replaced in 2006 by the *Supreme Court Civil Rules*, rules 199–201.

242   Rule 200 of the *Supreme Court Civil Rules 2006* also requires permission to proceed.

243   'We do not have a general rule of procedural exclusivity in this country': *Jacobs v Onesteel Manufacturing Pty Ltd* (2006) 93 SASR 568, 592.

244   *Enfield* (2000) 199 CLR 135, 144.

245   For example, *D'Souza v The Royal Australian and New Zealand College of Psychiatrists* (2005) 12 VR 42. Daniel Stewart, 'Non-statutory Review of Private Decisions by Public Bodies' (2006) 47 *Australian Institute of Administrative Law Forum* 17 approaches the question of whether or not the decisions made by the university in *Tang* would have been subject to common law review in this way.

246   For example, *McClelland v Burning Palms Surf Life Saving Club* (2002) 191 ALR 759, 779–80.

247   Geoffrey Marshall, 'Justiciability' in A G Guest (ed), *Oxford Essays in Jurisprudence: First Series* (Oxford: Clarendon Press, 1961), 269.

involvement is not 'appropriate' or 'proper'—even assuming that judges should attempt to steer clear of the merits of the decision (as in theory they always should). Traditionally conceived, this conclusion is blunt: a finding of non-justiciability is a finding that a decision is not amenable to judicial review. We shall see, however, that the law appears to be moving away from this all-or-nothing approach to justiciability and that certain decisions or issues may be non-justiciable in relation to some grounds of review, but not others.

3.6.2.1 Separation of powers and institutional choice

To understand the uncertain state of the law on 'non-justiciability' it helps to place it in an institutional context. The primary justification for the separation of powers doctrine is sometimes thought to be the protection of liberty. The dispersion of power, particularly when the various sources of power operate to check and balance one another, reduces the threat of arbitrary exercises of power. However, the commitment to separating power can also be, and often is, justified by the importance of matching particular tasks (functions) to institutions (forms). According to Barber, the 'separation of powers is a vigorous contemporary doctrine that recognises the central importance of institutional choice' in constitutional analysis and design.[248] Viewed in this way, the distinction between the legality of a decision and its merits is not merely reflective of the importance of a strictly separated judicial branch to disperse power and to provide a 'rule of law' check on the executive branch. The separation of powers principle also ensures that courts do not meddle in matters which their institutional forms and capacities are *ill-suited* to resolve—such as high level policy or (in the US phrase) 'political questions'. This concern, that functions and institutions be appropriately matched, is reflected not only in the common law categories of review versus appeal and legalities versus merits, but also in the notion of 'non-justiciability'.

3.6.2.2 Review of prerogative powers

Executive power has traditionally been authorised by statute or the 'prerogative powers of the Crown', which are recognised by the common law. A brief excursion into the history of the judicial review of the prerogative powers also helps to place the modern law of non-justiciability in context.[249] There are two basic schools of thought about the nature of 'prerogative powers', and judicial usage varies. On the broadest interpretation, prerogative powers encompass *all* non-statutory powers of the executive arm of government,[250] including 'common law' powers held in common with other legal persons (for example,

---

248   Nicholas Barber, 'Prelude to the Separation of Powers' (2001) 60 *Cambridge Law Journal* 57.

249   The meaning of the 'Crown' is notoriously shrouded in mystery. The term is often used in the United Kingdom to simply refer to the central government: see *Town Investments v Department of Environment* [1978] AC 359 but cf *M v Home Office* [1994] AC 377. In Australia, the term is losing favour, and 'in most contexts its use appears to be unnecessary because the concept or idea to be conveyed can equally be conveyed without mention of the Crown': Nicholas Seddon, 'The Crown' (2000) 29 *Federal Law Review* 245, 246. For most purposes the term is used to refer to the executive government of a state or the Commonwealth. For present purposes, the key point to notice is that the so-called prerogative powers which were historically associated with the British Crown are now thought to be within the powers formally reposed in the Governor-General by s 61 of the Constitution, at least 'to the extent they are appropriate to the position of the Commonwealth under the Constitution and to the sphere of responsibility vested in it by the *Constitution*': *Barton v Commonwealth* (1974) 131 CLR 477, 498. Of course, these powers are exercisable only on the advice of the Commonwealth Government (formally speaking, the Executive Council). Some prerogative powers are held exclusively by the Commonwealth, others are shared with the states, and some are held only by the states. See *Federal Commissioner of Taxation v Official Liquidator of EO Farley Ltd* (1940) 63 CLR 278; L Zines, *The High Court and the Constitution*, 5th edn (Sydney: Federation Press, 2008), 346–7.

250   Dicey held this view: A V Dicey, *Introduction to the Study of the Law of the Constitution*, 10th edn, (Macmillan, 1959), 424–6.

the power to enter into contracts or to conduct non-coercive inquiries).[251] The narrower view is that prerogative powers are those non-statutory powers of the executive arm which are thought to be specific or unique to it (that is, which other legal persons do not have).[252] Important examples of prerogative powers include the powers to declare war, enter into treaties, conduct foreign diplomacy, award honours, grant pardons, and to appoint judges. On either interpretation, prerogative powers are creations of the common law. As such, they are capable of being modified or abolished by statute.[253]

Since the seventeenth century power struggles between the Crown and parliament in England (through which the principle of parliamentary sovereignty was forged (2.1.3.1)), courts have resisted attempts by the executive to add to its own prerogative powers. Indeed, a central purpose of the 1689 *Bill of Rights* was to disable the Crown from collecting taxes without statutory authorisation, and also from invoking prerogative powers to dispense with the application of the law. The courts from then on accepted that it was not open to them to broaden the prerogative, leaving the necessity for new executive powers to be determined by the legislature alone.[254]

Despite a general judicial reluctance (in Australia and England) to allow the scope of prerogative powers to expand, there have been recent suggestions by some Australian judges that the executive power of the Commonwealth (conferred by the sparse terms of s 61 of the Constitution) extends beyond the categories of prerogative powers recognised at common law and the express constitutional powers to 'execute' and 'maintain' the Constitution and the laws of the Commonwealth.[255] In the *Tampa Case*, it was held that s 61 includes powers which are 'appropriate' to the responsibilities of the Commonwealth, to be articulated 'by reference to Australia's status as a sovereign nation and by reference to the terms of the *Constitution* itself'.[256] Similarly, in *Pape*, French CJ suggested that the power conferred by s 61 is 'not limited to statutory powers and the prerogative'.[257] Such suggestions assume that any powers which are 'essential' to the existence of a sovereign nation must repose in the national *executive*.[258] If the extent of executive power is 'cut free' from established prerogative powers, then 'there is … no source of guidance

---

251   It has been suggested that the common law default rule for private law that 'everything is permitted except what is expressly forbidden' applies not only to private individuals, but also to government when it is exercising 'common law' powers: *Malone v Metropolitan Police Commissioner* [1979] Ch 344. This suggestion, at the very least, requires considerable qualification. In particular, non-statutory 'common law' executive powers cannot be used to raise taxes and appropriate public monies, or for coercive or punitive purposes: see R Creyke and J McMillan, *Control of Government Action: Text, Cases and Commentary*, 2nd edn (Sydney: LexisNexis, 2009), 495–6. Furthermore, *Malone* has suffered severe academic criticism and later English cases have accepted the opposite principle as correct: namely, 'that any action taken [by the government] must be justified by positive law': *R v Somerset County Council, ex parte Fewings* [1995] 1 All ER 513.

252   This was Blackstone's view: W Blackstone, *Commentaries on the Laws of England* (Clarendon Press, 1765) vol 1, 232.

253   *Attorney-General v De Keyser's Royal Hotel* [1920] AC 508; *Ruddock v Vardarlis* (2001) 110 FCR 491 ('*Tampa Case*').

254   *British Broadcasting Corporation v Johns* [1965] 1 Ch 32, 79. Cf *R v Secretary of State for the Home Department, Ex parte Northumbria Police Authority* [1989] 1 QB 26 where an existing prerogative was applied to novel circumstances, which arguably had the effect of broadening the scope of the power.

255   For a helpful account of executive power in the context of s 61 of the Constitution, see Anne Twomey, 'Pushing the Boundaries of Executive Power—*Pape*, the Prerogative and Nationhood Powers' (2010) 34 *Melbourne University Law Review* 313. The nature and limits on powers derived from s 61 are argued to be 'ill-defined and ill-confined'.

256   *Tampa Case* (2001) 110 FCR 491. For compelling criticism, see G Winterton, 'The Limits and Use of Executive Power by Government' (2003) 31 *Federal Law Review* 421, 429; Zines, 358–9.

257   Though it was noted that 'history and common law inform its content': *Pape v Commissioner of Taxation* (2009) 238 CLR 1, [127]. *Pape* appears to accept that national emergencies (including the vague concept of economic emergency) may justify expenditure unrelated to a head of Commonwealth legislative powers. See C Saunders, 'The Sources and Scope of Commonwealth Power to Spend' (2009) 20 *Public Law Review* 251.

258   Even if it is accepted that a sovereign nation must hold certain powers, this does not dictate which branch of government should hold those powers (or, in particular, that they be held by the executive branch): S Evans, 'The Rule of Law, Constitutionalism and the MV *Tampa*' (2002) 13 *Public Law Review* 94, 97.

as to the boundaries of executive power'.[259] To the extent that the boundaries of prerogative powers (or additional executive powers conferred by s 61 of the Constitution) are 'elastic and ill-defined', the notion that the government, like all others, is bound by the law can be undermined.[260]

The Australian law regarding non-statutory executive power has been significantly complicated by the High Court's decision in *William v Commonwealth*.[261] That case concerned a constitutional challenge to payments made directly by the Commonwealth to a private service provider to fund the delivery of 'chaplaincy services' into schools operated by the Queensland State Government. A majority of the Court ruled that the payments were unlawful on the ground that they exceeded the executive power of the Commonwealth under s 61 and no Commonwealth Act otherwise authorised the expenditure.[262] Notwithstanding the narrow basis upon which *Williams* was decided, at least three important propositions concerning Commonwealth executive power can be distilled from the judgment.

First, a majority of the Court held that s 61 does not confer the same powers or capacities on the Commonwealth executive as are conferred by the common law upon natural persons.[263] Second, a majority held that the scope of executive power in s 61 is not defined by the heads of Commonwealth legislative power contained in ss 51, 52 and 122.[264] Third, a majority of the Court held that considerations of the federal distribution of powers and responsible government limit the scope of Commonwealth executive power.[265]

We can now take up the story of the reviewability of prerogative powers. This story is different from that of the review of statutory powers,[266] though these differences are sometimes overdrawn. In the case of the Crown's prerogative powers, the courts historically limited themselves to asking 'whether the prerogative power exists' and its extent.[267] Most of the developing grounds of judicial review going to the *manner* of the exercise of discretionary powers (matters broadly concerned with reasoning processes) were only available in relation to statutory powers.[268] Prerogative powers were thus largely 'immune' from judicial review.

All this changed with the decision in *CCSU*,[269] which established that reviewability was to be determined by reference to the nature or subject matter of a power, rather than its source. (*CCSU* was

259   J Spigelman, 'Public Law and the Executive' (2010) 34 *Australian Bar Review* 10, 19.

260   See Tomkins, *Public Law*, n 25 above, 83.

261   [2012] HCA 23.

262   [2012] HCA 23, [4] (French CJ), [161] (Gummow and Bell JJ), [290] (Hayne J), [548] (Crennan J), [594]–[595] (Kiefel J). Justice Heydon dissented.

263   [2012] HCA 23, [37]–[39] (French CJ), [151]–[158] (Gummow and Bell JJ), [204], [215]–[216] (Hayne J), [516] (Crennan J), [595] (Kiefel J).

264   [2012] HCA 23, [27], [36] (French CJ), [134]–[136] (Gummow and Bell JJ), [544] (Crennan J).

265   [2012] HCA 23, [38], [58]–[60] (French CJ), [136], [144] (Gummow and Bell JJ), [251]–[252] (Hayne J), [497]–[517] (Crennan J), [581]–[595] (Kiefel J).

266   See further n 261.

267   See S A de Smith, H Woolf and J Jowell, *Judicial Review of Administrative Action*, 6th edn (London: Sweet and Maxwell, 2005), 188. For a recent example, see *Tampa Case* (2001) 110 FCR 491.

268   Such as the requirements to act for proper (authorised) purposes, to consider relevant consideration, not to consider irrelevant considerations, and *Wednesbury* unreasonableness: see Chapter 5. Prior to the decision in *Padfield v Minister of Agriculture, Fisheries and Food* [1968] AC 997, it was the case that the legislature could evade the application of such grounds by 'giving powers to ministers … in terms so broad that it becomes difficult for a court ever to hold that they have been exceeded': S A de Smith, *Judicial Review of Administrative Action* (London: Stevens & Sons, 1959), 240. *Padfield's* case established that all statutory powers, even when conferred in broad terms on politically accountable decision-makers, are subject to limitations which may be discerned from the scope, objects and purposes of the statute.

269   *CCSU v Minister for the Civil Service* [1985] AC 374 ('*CCSU*').

part of a more general movement in English law away from a focus on the institutional source of the power in determining its reviewability, to a focus on the nature of the power exercised (see 3.6.1).) This development was not expected to produce a major change in the law, as the content of many prerogative powers and the circumstances in which they were likely to be exercised would render review of the manner of their exercise inappropriate, that is, non-justiciable. In *CCSU*, for example, the decision under review reflected judgments concerning the requirements of national security and therefore raised 'a non-justiciable question'. Indeed, some judges have thought that many prerogative powers would typically (perhaps always) be unsuitable for review because of the nature of the subject matter of those powers.[270] On the other hand, the logic of *CCSU* opened up the possibility that some statutory powers may also prove to be non-justiciable (at least in terms of the manner of their exercise), given that their justiciability is to be determined by reference to the nature of the power, not its formal legal source.[271]

Although the High Court has not directly evaluated the *CCSU* approach to the review of prerogative powers (or executive powers deriving from s 61 of the Constitution), Australian commentary and judicial opinion is overwhelmingly supportive of its general thrust.[272]

3.6.2.3 Non-justiciability and the rule of law

The conclusion that some exercises of executive power raise non-justiciable questions arguably limits the reach of the rule of law (at least as enforced by the courts) over government actions. Courts and commentators tend to justify conclusions of 'non-justiciability' by reference to two related themes. The first has to do with the comparative expertise and institutional capacities of judges and courts; the second concerns their 'relative political responsibility'.[273]

In relation to the first theme, it is often argued that courts are ill-equipped to involve themselves in 'polycentric' problems—that is, disputes characterised by numerous, complex, interrelated issues and which potentially affect a large number of interests. The courts' adjudicative methodology (which relies on the presentation of arguments by two opposing parties) cannot, it is said, adequately respond to all implicated interests. Consequently, courts cannot accurately anticipate the 'complex repercussions of judicial intervention'.[274] They can neither judge the substance of the issues raised nor can they adequately

---

270   For example, ibid, 418.

271   This proposition was accepted in *Aye v Minister for Immigration and Citizenship* (2010) 269 ALR 298. See also *Church of Scientology v Woodward* (1980) 154 CLR 25.

272   See, e.g., *Victoria v Master Builders' Association of Victoria* [1995] 2 VR 121; *Minister for Local Government v South Sydney City Council* (2002) 55 NSWLR 381; F Wheeler, 'Judicial Review of Prerogative Power in Australia: Issues and Prospects' (1992) 14 *Sydney Law Review* 432, 443. The High Court's decision in *Toohey* (1981) 151 CLR 170 is consistent with the general approach of *CCSU*. In *Toohey* the court held that statutory decisions made by the Crown's representative were reviewable on the basis of the manner in which they were exercised (in particular, on the ground of acting for unauthorised purposes).

273   T Endicott, 'The Reason of the Law' (2003) 48 *American Journal of Jurisprudence* 83, 98. Alexander Bickel explained the analogous US 'political questions' doctrine as reflecting 'the court's sense of lack of capacity, compounded in unequal parts of (a) the strangeness of the issue and its intractability to principled resolution; (b) the sheer momentousness of it, which tends to unbalance judicial judgment; (c) the anxiety, not so much that the judicial judgment will be ignored, as that perhaps it should but will not be; (d) finally ('in a mature democracy'), the inner vulnerability, the self-doubt of an institution which is electorally irresponsible and has no earth to draw strength from': *The Least Dangerous Branch: the Supreme Court at the Bar of Politics* (New York: Bobbs-Merrill, 1962), 184.

274   J Allison, 'The Procedural Reason for Judicial Restraint' [1996] *Public Law* 452, 453–5 describing Lon Fuller's classic argument. Fuller evoked the image of a spider's web—'pull on one strand and the resulting tensions ... will rather create a different complicated pattern of tensions'.

understand the impact that judicial review (even on the traditional grounds) will have on the complex policy field in question. In short, courts face an information deficit which should caution against any intervention.

Minister for Arts, Heritage and Environment v Peko-Wallsend[275] provides a good example of this line of reasoning. The Commonwealth Cabinet had decided to nominate Stage 2 of the Kakadu National Park for inclusion on the World Heritage List, established under an international convention ratified by Australia.[276] The Federal Court was in no doubt that the mere fact that the power exercised was a 'prerogative power' was inconclusive of whether it should be subject to judicial review. In reaching the conclusion that the decision was nonetheless non-justiciable, Bowen CJ emphasised that 'the whole subject matter of the decision involved complex policy questions relating to the environment, the rights of Aborigines, mining and the impact on Australia's economic position of allowing or not allowing mining as well as matters affecting private interests'.[277] The fearsome complexity of the policy considerations and the multiplicity of those whose interests might be affected induced the court to vacate the field, leaving the questions to be resolved in 'the political arena'.[278]

There are a number of difficulties with the use of 'polycentricity' as a basis for immunising decisions from review. First, polycentricity is clearly a matter of degree. Many government decisions are characterised by policy complexity and it is often difficult for anyone (let alone judges) to confidently predict how particular interventions will work themselves out in practice.[279] Yet most such decisions are undoubtedly reviewable. Second, the assumption that adversarial processes are ill-suited to resolving complex policy disputes or that judges lack particular expertise in polycentric disputes implausibly assumes a static model of adjudication—the procedures of courts, like other institutions, can be changed to reflect the nature of the tasks they are set.

Third, and most fundamentally, it has been argued that the deployment of the concept of 'polycentricity' to deny the availability of judicial review fails to appreciate the limited nature of judicial review; in particular, that review is never supposed to be directed at the (polycentric) merits of a decision.[280] The legalities (the only issues the courts are supposed to consider) are, it is argued, *ex hypothesi* appropriate for judicial resolution. The strength of this argument depends on how much weight the law/merits distinction can bear. This can only be fully considered in light of an understanding of the nature and application of the substantive grounds of review. However, if it is concluded that the legality/merits distinction cannot always inoculate judges from considering issues connected with the correctness of decisions, non-justiciability may be conceptualised as a sort of constitutional safety valve, allowing judges to avoid damaging confrontations with the executive in highly sensitive contexts.

---

275   (1987) 15 FCR 274.

276   One issue in the case was whether cabinet decisions could ever be reviewable. Though it was not necessary to decide the question, two of the three judges thought not. See further *South Australia v O'Shea* (1987) 163 CLR 378; M Harris, 'The Courts and the Cabinet: "Unfastening the Buckle"' [1989] *Public Law* 251.

277   *Minister for Arts, Heritage and Environment v Peko-Wallsend* (1987) 15 FCR 274, 278–9.

278   Ibid, 279. See also *CCSU* [1985] AC 374, 411 (Lord Diplock).

279   For a critique of the notion that 'policy' can be clearly distinguished from administrative acts, see P Bayne, 'The Court, the Parliament and the Government: Reflections on the Scope of Judicial Review' (1991) 20 *Federal Law Review* 1, 7–12. The logic behind the conclusion that courts are ill-adapted to resolve polycentric problems also supports the conclusion that they are ill-placed to comprehend the repercussions of determinations based upon 'the scope of vague statutory formulas, general principles of review and the judicial discretion nevertheless to deny a remedy in particular circumstances' (i.e. factors involved in many routine judicial review applications): Allison, n 273 above, 460.

280   C Finn, 'The Justiciability of Administrative Decisions: A Redundant Concept?' (2002) 30 *Federal Law Review* 239.

The second major justification for the doctrine of non-justiciability raises the question of where political responsibility for certain executive decisions should properly rest. For instance, Wilcox J concluded in *Peko-Wallsend* that the decision to implement a treaty should be treated as non-justiciable because judicial involvement in the area of international relations was 'a course bristling with problems'. Similarly, the judges in *CCSU* concluded that judges should fear to tread into areas raising questions of national security, an area where 'those upon whom the responsibility rests [that is, the government], and not the courts of justice, must have the last word'.[281] The New South Wales Court of Appeal declined to review a decision of the Lieutenant-Governor (taken on the advice of the Premier) to withdraw the applicant's commission as a minister because 'the subject lay at the heart of the political process'.[282]

It would be surprising if the mere connection (no matter how remote) of a decision with politically sensitive subject matters was a sufficient reason to render it non-justiciable. Indeed, the trend in recent cases is away from a fixed set of prerogative powers or particular subject matters which are considered, *in all circumstances*, to be judicial no-go areas. An interesting example of this trend is the *Abbasi* case,[283] where the English Court of Appeal accepted that in some instances, certain grounds of judicial review could be sensibly applied to actions or decisions made in the conduct of international relations (a subject matter traditionally seen as off limits to judges). Feroz Ali Abbasi, a British national, was held at Guantanamo Bay in Cuba, having been captured by American forces in Afghanistan. At the time the case was heard, it was accepted that Abbasi had no avenue under US law to test the legality of his detention (the Court of Appeal famously concluded that he was in a 'legal black hole').[284] Abbasi's family wanted the British government to make representations on his behalf to the US government, which it refused to do.

The Court of Appeal held that the justiciability of this matter turned on the particular content of the decision being challenged. If Abbasi wanted to challenge a decision to refuse even to consider whether to render diplomatic assistance, then that decision *would* be justiciable. In reaching this conclusion the court held that the government's actions had given rise to a 'legitimate expectation' that requests would be duly considered (though not necessarily acted upon). Despite the sensitivities involved, the judicial imposition of an obligation to consider a request to engage in diplomacy 'would seem unlikely itself to impinge on any forbidden [non-justiciable] area [that is, foreign affairs]'.[285] That is, the court would not have to consider any non-justiciable issues. In Abbasi's circumstances, however, this was no help; his case had been considered. On the actual decision to refuse to render assistance the court was very clear: 'the Secretary of State must be free to give full weight to foreign policy considerations, which are not justiciable'.[286] This line of analysis opens up the possibility that some decisions affecting national security or international relations may be justiciable, but only if the application of the grounds of review will not raise non-justiciable issues.[287]

---

281   *CCSU* [1985] AC 374.

282   *Stewart v Ronalds* (2009) 76 NSWLR 99, 112.

283   *R (Abbasi) v Secretary of State for Foreign and Commonwealth Affairs, Ex parte Abbasi* [2003] UKHRR 76 CA ('*Abbasi*').

284   It was also accepted that Abassi's fundamental human rights were being violated 'as a result of the conduct of the authorities of a foreign state': ibid, [80].

285   Ibid, [108].

286   Ibid, [99].

287   Some grounds of review are arguably more likely to require judicial judgments about non-justiciable issues (such as national security of international relations) than others. As a general proposition it might be thought that review grounds which require judgments about which purposes are permissible, what considerations relevant, or whether a decision is irrational or unreasonable are more likely to require judgments about non-justiciable issues than those required to ensure a decision-maker has afforded affected persons procedural fairness. (In the case of procedural fairness, it may be, however, that the requirements of a fair hearing will be modified when it concerns politically sensitive issues (5.2.2.3).)

To the general argument that the final say in relation to some decisions (for example, national security and international relations) should be left with more politically responsible actors, it may again be responded that judges are *not* required to judge the substance of these questions but only the legalities; the 'starting point for all cases of judicial review is that the primary tasks have not been given to courts'.[288] In *Abbasi*, for example, the refusal to review the decision not to make diplomatic representations may be explained on the basis that the breadth of the discretion to refuse diplomatic assistance simply meant that no ground of review was capable of being made out. Yet it is unclear whether this response supports the conclusion that the notion of non-justiciability should be banished from the law, leaving us to get on with the hard slog of better articulating the nature and limits of the specific grounds of review by reference to the law/merits distinction.[289] Nevertheless, there appears to be a shrinking number of decisions which are likely to be considered non-justiciable in the strict sense of not being reviewable at all—without a close examination of the nature of the controversy.[290]

In the *Hicks* case, judicial review was sought in relation to a decision by the Minister for Immigration not to request David Hick's release from internment at Guantanamo Bay, Cuba, where he was being held on suspicion of terrorism offences (though no charges had been laid).[291] Tamberlin J refused to strike out the application on non-justiciability grounds (which were approached through a consideration of whether there was a 'matter' sufficient to ground federal jurisdiction (3.4.1.3)). The idea that there are 'forbidden areas', such as foreign policy, which are immune from judicial review was considered to be difficult to reconcile with the executive power of the Commonwealth being vested by and subject to the limits spelt out in s 61 of the Constitution. To the extent that limitations or obligations are placed upon administrative decision-makers by statute or the Constitution, these should be enforceable by the judiciary in the name of its constitutionally recognised function of protecting the rule of law (7.1).[292] This approach also indicates that the issue will be whether a particular ground of judicial review is available, and suggests that the reasons underpinning the development of the non-justiciability doctrine will resurface as considerations influencing the intensity of judicial review. An apparent counter-example to this way of thinking about non-justiciability is *Aye v Minister for Immigration and Citizenship*.[293] The exercise of a statutory power to decide that a person's 'continued presence in Australia was inimical to Australia's foreign policy interests' was held to be non-justiciable because it was a 'political matter'. This conclusion meant an exercise of statutory power which led inevitably to the cancellation of a person's visa could be taken without first affording that person any form of hearing. The Court did not attempt to explain why affording a hearing would necessarily involve it in the determination of non-justiciable matters.[294] As remarked in the *Hicks* case, the meaning of non-justiciability is 'far from settled black-letter law'.[295]

In assessing the trend away from the notion that there are some sorts of decisions which are not appropriately reviewed by judges, it may be asked whether the rule of law ideal really does require *every*

---

288   Aronson, Dyer and Groves, n 24 above, 128–9.

289   Cf Finn, n 279 above, 260–3.

290   See P Daly, 'Justiciability and the "Political Questions" Doctrine' [2010] *Public Law* 160.

291   *Hicks v Ruddock* (2007) 156 FCR 574.

292   See the obiter remarks of Perram J in *Habib v Commonwealth* (2010) 183 FCR 62, 72–3; and D Stewart, n 234 above, 325.

293   (2010) 187 FCR 449.

294   Lander J dissented on the justiciability point. His Honour emphasised the fact that the decision 'directly affects the appellant by depriving her of a right to continue to reside in Australia': ibid, 319.

295   *Hicks v Ruddock* (2007) 156 FCR 574, 600.

executive decision to be controlled by judges. If the nature of a particular decision indicates that the application of most or all of the grounds of judicial reviews are incapable of meaningfully constraining the decision-maker, then the inevitable conclusion will be that there is no illegality. It may be argued that findings of non-justiciability not only explain certain decisions more honestly, but also prevent governments from hiding behind the cloak of legality.[296] This consequence has the virtue of raising for consideration the potential need for strengthening non-judicial forms of accountability in these sensitive areas of executive decision-making.

The progressive rejection of immunities from judicial review based on formal criteria (notably, the legal source of the power or identity of the decision-maker) has clearly required judges to make normative (value-based) judgments about whether the substantive principles of judicial review *should* be applied to particular decisions, and whether judges are, comparatively speaking, well placed to supervise such decisions. These are intrinsically difficult questions and it is perhaps unsurprising to find that the courts have been unable to develop clear legal rules or principles.

In the case of non-justiciability it has been suggested that much depends 'on the experience and constitutional instinct' of the judges.[297] In this context it is undoubtedly true that classifying a decision as non-justiciable will come at a cost to the rule of law wherever it is clear that the decision is one which ought to be reviewed on at least some of the normal grounds of review.[298] In a period of extraordinary proliferation of 'anti-terrorism' legislation, there is no doubt that judicial review can contribute to the protection of the rights of individuals. It must also be remembered that unsubstantiated claims concerning the imperatives of national security can, all too easily, lead to an abdication of judicial responsibility.[299] (On this question, the historical record of judges should give real cause for concern.[300]) On the other hand, there are also clear dangers associated with easy assumptions that each and every executive decision (no matter how trivial or grave) must always be subject to meaningful judicial review standards. The possibility that the rule of law may, in at least some circumstances, be best pursued through non-judicial accountability mechanisms can too easily be overlooked.[301]

---

296   Endicott, n 272 above, 98.

297   D G T Williams, 'Justiciability and Discretionary Power' in M Taggart (ed), *Judicial Review of Administrative Action in the 1980s* (Auckland: Oxford University Press, 1986), 121.

298   E.g., L Sossin, 'The Rule of Law and the Justiciability of Prerogative Powers: A Comment on *Black v Crétien*' (2002) 47 *McGill Law Journal* 435.

299   See D Dyzenhaus, 'Humpty Dumpty Rules or the Rule of Law: Legal Theory and the Adjudication of National Security' (2003) 28 *Australian Journal of Legal Philosophy* 1.

300   See K Ewing, 'The Futility of the Human Rights Act' [2004] *Public Law* 829; A W B Simpson, *In the Highest Degree Odious: Detention Without Trial in War-time Britain* (Oxford: Oxford University Press, 1992).

301   It is worth remembering that the rule of law is not a project that can be sustained by the judges acting alone: L L Fuller, *The Morality of Law*, revised edn (New Haven: Yale University Press, 1969), 44.

4

Judicial Review Remedies

4.1 The common law remedial model

4.1.1 The basic scheme

Two general approaches to thinking about the availability of a judicial review remedy may be helpfully identified. The first and older model was developed by the common law. We have already seen that judicial review developed through the provision of certain remedies, in particular, the prerogative writs (2.1.4). The basic functions of these remedies were to 'quash' (or 'deprive of legal effect') invalid or unlawful administrative decisions (by certiorari), to prevent illegal administrative acts or decisions (by prohibition), and to require the performance of 'public duties' (by mandamus). A writ, however, was not something the court could issue merely on the basis that a breach of an administrative law norm was established. Rather, a writ was a sort of formula with various ingredients (2.1.4). In order to be awarded the remedy asked for in the writ, the applicant had to convince the court that all the ingredients of the formula were present in the facts of their case. Conduct falling within grounds of review (or 'breaches of administrative law norms')[1] was among the ingredients of the writs. In this chapter we use the term 'error' to refer to conduct which falls within (or 'constitutes' or 'establishes') one or more of the grounds of judicial review or which breaches some other legal requirement.

Certain errors appeared in the list of ingredients of all the writs. Simplifying a little, these were called 'jurisdictional errors'. In principle, any and all of the writs were available to remedy such errors. By contrast, with one exception, none of the writs was available to remedy what were called 'non-jurisdictional errors'.[2] In other words, non-jurisdictional errors were unremediable. The exception was that certiorari was available to remedy a non-jurisdictional error of law, but only if the error 'appeared on the face of the record' (4.5.1.1). In other words, error of law on the face of the record appeared in the list of ingredients of the writ of certiorari but not of mandamus or prohibition.

---

1   The language of 'grounds of review' is a litigation-focused way of identifying administrative law norms, i.e. those norms developed in the context of judicial review with which administrators must comply. Of course, 'administrative law' is more than the law of judicial review but our use of the phrase 'administrative law norms' in this context is intended to emphasise the fact that these norms are not only relevant in judicial review proceedings but also operate as normative principles to guide administrative behaviour.

2   The distinction between jurisdictional and non-jurisdictional errors is explained at 4.4.1, and returned to at 5.4.1.

Under the common law remedial model, therefore, there were three types of error: remediable jurisdictional, remediable non-jurisdictional and unremediable non-jurisdictional. Certiorari was the only remedy available to remedy non-jurisdictional error of law on the face of the record. There was an important difference between the effect of certiorari as a remedy for jurisdictional error and its effect as a remedy for non-jurisdictional error on the face of the record. In the former case it *retrospectively* invalidated or 'nullified' the decision, whereas in the latter it *prospectively* set it aside. This difference in remedial consequence was justified by an assumption that if an error is non-jurisdictional, then the decision-maker's jurisdiction (authority to decide) was unaffected and, therefore, a valid decision could still be made. On the other hand, classifying an error as jurisdictional identifies its consequence as invalidating the decision because the decision-maker lacked the authority to make it.[3] Thus, under the common law model an application for a writ in relation to a decision that has already been made might have one of three remedial outcomes: no remedy (if the applicant's case was missing an ingredient that appeared in the list of ingredients of all the writs—for instance, if the only error that could be shown was a non-jurisdictional error of law that did not appear on the face of the record); retrospective invalidation; and prospective quashing.[4] In this chapter we shall refer to a decision which could be retrospectively quashed as (retrospectively) 'invalid' and to a decision that could be prospectively quashed as (prospectively) 'unlawful'.

It is worth pausing to explain the distinction between retrospective quashing and prospective quashing in a little more detail. Retrospective quashing means that the decision is taken to have been invalid *from the time it was made*. Where certiorari has the remedial outcome or consequence of retrospective invalidity, the court, in effect, announces the invalidity or 'nullity' of the decision, it having been invalid *ab initio* (that is, from the beginning).[5] If a decision-maker has an obligation to make a decision, and their 'purported' decision is retrospectively invalidated, mandamus may also issue to require that the decision be remade (this time, according to law). Prospective quashing means that the decision is deprived of effect, but only *from the time of the court's order*. In such cases, the effect of certiorari is to deprive the decision of effect rather than to announce its invalidity. The challenged decision is therefore a valid exercise of power up until the time of the court's decision; but from then on, the court's decision functions to deprive it of any continuing legal effect. The effect of prospective quashing is the functional equivalent of reversal on appeal.[6] Where a decision is 'retrospectively invalidated', any acts purportedly based on that 'decision', whether before or after the act of invalidation, will

---

3   J Basten, 'The Supervisory Jurisdiction of Supreme Courts' (2011) 85 *Australian Law Journal* 273, 287.

4   See, e.g., *Hicks v Minister for Immigration and Multicultural and Indigenous Affairs* (2005) 146 FCR 427, 437, [38]. The writ used to achieve the effect of retrospective invalidation and prospective quashing is certiorari. Prohibition issues to prevent the making of a decision which, if made, would be in excess of jurisdiction and, thus, subject to retrospective invalidation. Mandamus requires the performance of a public duty when not to do so would amount to a failure to exercise jurisdiction. Mandamus may issue to require the remaking of a decision (which the decision-maker was under a duty to make) if the decision was affected by a jurisdictional error and thus retrospectively invalid. The original decision may not need to be first quashed (by certiorari) because that decision (which was made in excess of the decision-maker's jurisdiction) does not (in law) exist. See further 4.5.1.1, 4.5.1.2, and 4.5.1.3.

5   It is not, however, the case that decisions which would be retrospectively invalidated if appropriate proceedings were brought can have no legal effects or consequences whatsoever. The degree to which such decisions can have legal effect depends upon the context in which this question is asked: see 4.7.

6   As H W R Wade 'Administrative Tribunals and Administrative Justice' (1981) 55 *Australian Law Journal* 374 noted, the error or law ground was, in essence, rediscovered in the *Northumberland* case (see 4.5.1.1) to make up for the fact that there was no statutory right of appeal on a point of law from many tribunals.

lack legal justification.[7] Where a decision is prospectively quashed, acts based on the decision up until the time of the court order will be valid, but any acts based on the decision after the court has determined that it was unlawfully made will lack legal justification. Although it may have sometimes been assumed that certiorari operates retrospectively even where it issues for non-jurisdictional errors,[8] it is difficult to find instances of judges articulating the point with clarity. Cases cited for the proposition that certiorari operates retrospectively typically involve errors which would be classified as jurisdictional,[9] or where the timing from which an order will take effect was not raised as an issue of any practical importance.[10] In any event, the logic which underpins the idea of retrospective invalidity (that it is the decision-maker's lack of jurisdiction that justifies the remedial consequence of invalidity) is difficult to reconcile with the idea that retrospective invalidity may also be the consequence of non-jurisdictional errors.

Although the distinction between retrospective invalidity and prospective unlawfulness may have significant practical implications, in many cases nothing of importance will depend on ascertaining whether a decision is quashed with retrospective or prospective effect. Suppose, for example, that a condition imposed on a licence is invalidated. If the applicant has not, at the time of the court order, breached the condition she will not care whether the decision is retrospectively or prospectively quashed. In either case, she may safely ignore the condition in the future and, on these facts, she has no reason to worry about the past.

4.1.2 Making sense of unremediable error

Readers will by now be asking an obvious question: why, under the common law remedial model, did the law recognise a category of 'unremediable' errors? Surely, it may be thought, the whole point of judicial review is to uphold the rule of law, and this means that there should be remedies available when administrative decision-makers ('the governors') breach any legal requirement applicable to their acts and decisions. Part of the answer to this question is simply that the notion of an unremediable error was part and parcel of the logic of the formulary, writ-based system. However, more interesting answers, based on important constitutional principles, may be developed in support of the seemingly counter-intuitive notion of unremediable errors.

One possible justification for the conclusion that not all errors should result in either retrospective invalidity or prospective unlawfulness appeals to advantages routinely associated with the existence of administrative discretion. To confer a discretionary power on an administrator is to give that administrator a degree of freedom to choose if, when or how to exercise the power. That freedom may

---

7   This proposition holds true only if the legal powers to perform later acts are conditioned upon the validity of the initial decision. Not all acts which, as a practical matter, are based on a prior, invalid decision are necessarily invalid. For example, in *Ruddock v Taylor* (2005) 222 CLR 612 it was held, as a matter of statutory construction, that a decision to detain a person under s 189 of the *Migration Act 1958* (Cth) did not depend on the validity of an earlier decision to cancel that person's visa under s 501 of that Act, even though the cancellation of the visa was clearly the catalyst for the detention decision. This was because s 189 required an officer to detain not only where a person was known to be an unlawful non-citizen but also in cases where the officer 'reasonably suspects that a person has that status'. Cf *Park Oh Ho v Minister for Immigration and Ethnic Affairs* (1989) 167 CLR 637, 645 where the 'voidness [i.e. retrospective invalidity] of the deportation orders remove[d] the only lawful basis of the appellant's incarceration'. If an action by a decision-maker is not validly authorised, then it may be possible for an affected person to bring an action in tort (e.g. false imprisonment) in relation to that action.

8   Aronson, Dyer and Groves, 802 cite a passage in a single judgment in *Re McBain; Ex parte Australian Catholic Bishops Conference* (2002) 209 CLR 372, 424–5 as evidencing such an assumption.

9   E.g. *R v Muirhead and Bracegirdle; Ex parte Attorney-General* [1942] SASR 226, where the decision was quashed for fraud.

10   E.g. *R v Leeds Crown Court; Ex parte Bradford Chief Constable* [1975] QB 314.

be limited in various ways, and such limitations may be enforceable, for instance, by a court exercising judicial review jurisdiction. But if the administrator's discretionary freedom of choice is to have any substance at all, the power of the court to quash decisions of the administrator made in exercise of the discretion must itself be limited. If the court could quash any decision that it considered to be 'wrong' or an erroneous exercise of the power, the administrator's discretion would not be merely limited—it would be effectively removed (in principle at least). This point is sometimes made—somewhat confusingly—by saying that a discretion to decide must include freedom to make 'wrong' as well as 'right' decisions. This formulation is confusing because in it the word 'wrong' does not refer to a decision that is incorrect in any absolute sense, but rather to a decision that the reviewing court thinks falls outside the proper limits of the decision-maker's freedom of choice.

Discretionary power has a number of potential benefits. Most obviously it enables a flexible approach to decision-making. Flexibility may be at a premium in contexts where 'individualised justice' is desired,[11] where the considerations relevant to sound decision-making are subject to change,[12] or where there are advantages in 'responsive' decision-making or regulation.[13] On the other hand, rules—which eliminate discretion by imposing obligations on decision-makers—also have advantages. For example, rules can promote consistency, they can obviate the need to 'reinvent the wheel' each time a decision is made, and their use can also increase the legitimacy of decision-making (especially where those who make the rules have a better democratic pedigree than those who apply them).[14] In reality, decision-making is never purely 'discretionary', nor can it be entirely 'rule-bound': it is always a matter of there being more or less scope for choice. The trick is to strike the right balance between rules and discretion. However, the right balance 'must be determined for each discretionary power in each particular context'.[15] This means that generalisations about whether discretionary or rule-bound decision-making is 'better' are invariably misleading.

We can, however, conclude that the advantages of increasing the choices open to a particular decision-maker may outweigh any disadvantages. And this conclusion is sufficient to raise questions about the influential view that those committed to the 'rule of law' should be concerned to restrict the growth of discretionary powers wherever possible. It is true that administrative discretions can be abused, and there is a strong case that their exercise should be subject to various checks and balances. Indeed, the development of many of the grounds of judicial review has been influenced by a tacit acceptance of the need to 'confine and structure' discretionary powers (5.3). Yet it is going too far to claim that the very existence of discretion detracts from our commitment to the values (such as non-arbitrariness and individual autonomy) which underpin the rule of law. The rule of law ideal need not be thought of as requiring the 'rule of rules'.[16]

---

11 Calls for 'individualised justice' amount to a request that decision-makers closely consider the individual particulars of a case, an approach which the inflexible application of a rule may prevent. On some theories of justice, what individuals are due should be determined by the application of 'universal' rules. For a critique of this idea, see I M Young, *Justice and the Politics of Difference* (Princeton NJ: Princeton University Press, 1990), Ch 4.

12 For example, where the regulated field is subject to rapid technological development it may be better to deal with novel problems incrementally, rather than by trying to lay down comprehensive rules in advance.

13 Rules may be misunderstood, ignored or disobeyed if they are insufficiently responsive to the needs or expectations of those being regulated. For some examples, see J Braithwaite, 'Rules and Principles: A Theory of Legal Certainty' (2002) 27 *Australian Journal of Legal Philosophy* 47.

14 On the pluses and minuses of rules, see C Sunstein, 'Problems With Rules' (1995) 83 *California Law Review* 953.

15 K C Davis, *Discretionary Justice* (Urbana: University of Illinois Press, 1971), 221.

16 See L McDonald, 'The Rule of Law in the "New Regulatory State"' (2004) 33 *Common Law World Review* 197.

A second reason to accept the possibility of unremediable errors invokes the concept of separation of powers. Like the rule of law, the separation of powers ideal can be interpreted in various ways. On the one hand, the idea that power needs to be 'checked and balanced' by other sources of power justifies a level of judicial review of administrative action. On the other hand, the separation of powers recognises that each branch of government has a comparative advantage in the performance of particular functions. Administrative powers are given to particular decision-makers who possess the qualifications, experience and competence which are considered appropriate for the exercise of those powers. Indeed, the conferral of a power on an administrator may itself be taken to imply that judges have no warrant to usurp that power. Review which is too intrusive risks either 'judicialising' the administrative process or turning the courts into de facto administrators who lack the appropriate 'skill-set'.

We have seen that these aspects of separation of powers thinking are prominent in attempts to distinguish between legality and merit review (3.2.2), but they can also be invoked to justify the conclusion that some errors should be unremediable. Although judges do have general expertise in law and legal interpretation, the recognition that some errors should not attract a remedy is one technique by which courts can defer to administrators on the question of how the law should be applied in their particular area of expertise, experience and competence. To be sure, this is only one of a number of possible modes of judicial deference to administrative decision-makers. A second mode is the exercise of the courts' discretion to refuse judicial review remedies, which exists at common law and, as we will see, under the *ADJR Act* (4.2 and 4.6). A third general mode of deference works through defining the grounds of judicial review so as not to invite judges to trespass into the 'merits' of administrative decision-making.

4.2 The *ADJR Act* remedial model

After the writ-based 'common law' remedial model had reached maturity, courts began to award the remedies of declaration and injunction (which were initially used in private law disputes) in public law cases. Unlike the writ-based remedies, these remedies do not operate as formulae with grounds of review among their ingredients, but rather as free-standing remedial orders which, in appropriate cases, can be made in respect of breaches of any and every administrative law norm. The use of declarations and injunctions became more prominent from the mid-twentieth century, partly as a way of evading various technical limitations on the availability of the writs that resulted from their rigid formulary character. Although they did not significantly alter the basic remedial functions of judicial review,[17] their use did not fit neatly into the writ-based system, where the primary focus was on conditions for the availability of particular remedies rather than on breach of administrative law norms. The increasing use of declarations and injunctions thus destabilised the writ system and can be understood as part of a process that culminated in the introduction, in 1977, of a completely different remedial model under the *ADJR Act*.

Under the *ADJR Act* remedial model, the first question is not whether a particular remedy is available, but rather whether one of the specified grounds of review has been established. If so, the court may in its discretion make any or a combination of the 'orders' listed in s 16 of the Act. These orders perform the same basic functions as the common law remedies (4.5.2).However, under the *ADJR Act* remedial model there are no breaches of administrative law norms that are, in principle, unremediable. Nor does the *ADJR Act* recognise the distinction between jurisdictional and non-jurisdictional errors. This is

---

17   Injunctions can perform the same function as either prohibition or mandamus (4.5.1.4); declarations state the rights and
      obligations of the parties but can function to 'shadow' the effects of the other judicial review remedies (4.5.1.5).

seen most clearly in the case of review for 'error of law' which can attract a remedial order regardless of 'whether or not the error of law appears on the face of the record' (s 5(1)(f)).[18] Less obviously, there is an emerging consensus that s 5(1)(b) of the *ADJR Act*, which allows for review where 'procedures that were required by law to be observed in connection with the making of the decision were not observed', allows for review of procedural errors which would not amount to jurisdictional errors and therefore would not result in retrospective invalidity at common law.[19] The only question is whether or not procedures 'required by law … in connection with the making of the decision' have been observed.[20]

In principle, then, any of the remedial orders listed in s 16 can be made by a court to remedy breaches of any and all of the administrative law norms (that is, the grounds of review) listed in ss 5 and 6 of the *ADJR Act*. Like the common law remedies, however, all the *ADJR Act* remedial orders are discretionary (4.6). However, although the court may ultimately refuse to make a remedial order, the point to reiterate is that under the *ADJR Act* model there are no breaches of a ground of review which cannot, in principle, attract a remedial order.

The *ADJR Act*'s new remedial model was undoubtedly born of significant dissatisfaction with the common law model, in particular the perception that choosing the correct remedy approximated a game of remedial roulette.[21] Moreover, the success or failure of an application for common law judicial review was difficult to predict because it was notoriously difficult to draw the key distinction between jurisdictional and non-jurisdictional errors (5.4.1). As a reaction against the common law model, it can also be observed that the enactment of the *ADJR Act* was the culmination of an intellectual process which had involved self-conscious attempts by administrative lawyers to articulate and study the grounds of review independently from the availability of particular remedies.[22] This trend allowed them to conceptualise the 'grounds of review' more generally as reflecting norms which regulate the activities of 'the governors' rather than merely as conditions of the award of particular remedies.

---

18   See *Jadwan Pty Ltd v Secretary, Department of Health and Aged Care* (2003) 145 FCR 1, 17–8.

19   *Minister for Immigration and Multicultural Affairs v Yusuf* (2001) 206 CLR 323, 341, 371–2; *Muin v Refugee Review Tribunal* (2002) 190 ALR 601, [169]; *Re Minister for Immigration and Multicultural and Indigenous Affairs; Ex parte Applicants S134* (2003) 211 CLR 441, 460.

20   *Minister for Health and Family Services v Jadwan Pty Ltd* (1998) 89 FCR 478, 479. There have been cases which appear to proceed on the assumption that breach of statutory procedures will not be remediable under s 5(1)(b) if the consequence of that breach would not (under the *Project Blue Sky* analysis (see 4.3)) be 'invalidity': e.g. *Murray v Native Title Tribunal* (2002) 77 ALD 96, 111 [54]. This view is difficult to reconcile with the position that s 5(1)(b) of the *ADJR Act* enables review for breaches of procedures which are 'required by law' but which do not amount to jurisdictional errors. It may also be in tension with the proposition that '[t]he remedies that are available under the *ADJR Act* do not recognise any distinction between decisions involving jurisdictional error and decision made in error within jurisdiction': *Lansen v Minister for Environment and Heritage* (2008) 174 FCR 14, 44. The precise relationship between breaches of procedures 'required by law' and jurisdictional procedural errors remains murky. See, further, the discussion of the exercise of discretion to refuse an *ADJR Act* remedy, at 4.3.

21   Commonwealth Administrative Review Committee, *Commonwealth Administrative Review Committee Report*, Parliament of the Commonwealth of Australia Paper No 144 (1971), 20 ('Kerr Committee Report').

22   This trend is illustrated by the changing emphasis given to the grounds of review in key Australian texts. In the first Australian administrative law text book (published in 1950) there was no separate chapter devoted to the grounds of review: W Friedmann, *Principles of Australian Administrative Law* (Melbourne: Melbourne University Press, 1950). By the time this book reached its third edition in 1966, the new authors (David Benjafield and Harry Whitmore) attempted to place 'considerably more emphasis on the substantive principles of judicial review', and this was reflected in an entire chapter on the norms of natural justice and a further chapter dealing with ultra vires, jurisdictional error and error of law: D Benjafield and H Whitmore, *Principles of Australian Administrative Law* (Sydney: Law Book Co, 1966). H Whitmore and M Aronson, *Review of Administrative Action* (Sydney: Law Book Co, 1978) marked a new departure in Australian administrative law texts and clearly articulated the intellectual trend towards understanding the grounds of review and availability of remedies as discrete questions for study. Whereas '[i]n past days it could be claimed that the principles of review could only be understood in the context of the special remedies', the authors declared that it had become 'possible to discuss the principles of review independently of the remedies': 39. (Interestingly, Harry Whitmore was a member of the Kerr Committee, whose report, n 21 above, ultimately led to the enactment of the *ADJR Act*.)

4.3 The continuing significance of the common law remedial model

Although the *ADJR Act* has deeply influenced the way administrative lawyers think about judicial review, it has not supplanted the common law remedial model. The common law model remains significant in three ways. First, it survives in the context of the supervisory jurisdiction of state Supreme Courts (3.6). Under state law, orders in the nature of the prerogative writs[23] still exist and, with the exception of certiorari, their availability continues to be limited to cases where 'jurisdictional'—as opposed to 'non-jurisdictional'—error is shown. It is true that the category of jurisdictional errors has significantly expanded (5.4.1). This means that the common law game of remedial roulette is not as dangerous as it once was, because most errors (at least those made by administrative decision-makers as opposed to inferior courts) can be classified as 'jurisdictional'. But the link between the availability of the prerogative writs and the distinction between jurisdictional and non-jurisdictional errors remains of some significance in common law judicial review in state courts—indeed, in *Kirk* the distinction was used to align the constitutionally entrenched measure of judicial review jurisdiction exercised by state Supreme Courts with the High Court's jurisdiction under s 75(v) of the Constitution (3.4.3) (The *ADJR Act* remedial model is obviously adopted where review in state courts proceeds under state legislation modelled on the *ADJR Act* (3.5.3)).

Second, the scheme of 'constitutional' regime of judicial review entrenched by s 75(v) of the Constitution (3.4.1) follows the basic contours of the common law remedial model: an applicant must apply for one of the remedies specified in s 75(v) of the Constitution and the 'constitutional writs' of mandamus and prohibition are available only for 'jurisdictional errors' (3.4.1.1; 4.5.3). Common law review in the states and constitutional review under s 75(v) developed before the *ADJR Act* model was worked out. But the original writ-based version of the common law remedial model has been complicated by the availability (under s 75(v)) of the 'constitutional injunction' and (in the states) of declarations and injunctions. For example, as we will see below (4.5.3), it *may* be that the constitutional injunction can be issued for non-jurisdictional errors, though the position is far from clear. All we need conclude for the moment is that the availability of the various remedies of the constitutional review regime still depends in part on what sort of error has been committed.

In order to explain the third way in which the common law remedial model continues to be relevant, we need to examine in some detail the High Court's important decision in *Project Blue Sky Inc v Australian Broadcasting Authority*.[24] In this case the court deployed a core component of the common law remedial model in deciding whether declaratory and injunctive relief was available for breach of statutory requirements.[25] The court's analysis appears to assume the trichotomy of

---

23   In all state jurisdictions other than Western Australia, applicants now apply for 'orders in the nature of' the old prerogative writs under simplified procedures. The received wisdom, though it is coming under some pressure, is that these procedural changes have not altered the principles governing when these remedies will be available. See *Solution 6 Holdings Ltd v Industrial Relations Commission of NSW* (2004) 60 NSWLR 558, 591, 597, 601; *Chase Oyster Bar Pty Ltd v Hamo Industries Pty Ltd* (2010) 78 NSWLR 393, 447–9.

24   (1998) 194 CLR 355. The authors thank Graeme Hill for access to an unpublished manuscript which contains a suggestive analysis of *Project Blue Sky*.

25   The case was lodged in the High Court's s 75(iii) jurisdiction before being remitted to the Federal Court for trial: *Project Blue Sky Inc v Australian Broadcasting Authority* (1996) 68 FCR 455, 456. It is likely that the principles relevant to judicial review based on the High Court's s 75(iii) jurisdiction will develop along the similar lines to the common law, or (perhaps) to the principles applicable under s 75(v) (see 3.4.2).

remedial consequences—retrospective invalidity, prospective unlawfulness, or validity (that is, no remedy)—which, as explained above, was an important corollary of the three types of error recognised under the common law remedial model.[26]

Although the High Court used different terminology, it explicitly recognised the distinction between retrospective invalidity and prospective unlawfulness. The particular question in *Project Blue Sky* concerned the legal effect of a decision made in breach of a statutory provision.[27] The majority held that the breach did not render the decision 'invalid' (by which it meant retrospectively invalid) but that it was, nonetheless, 'unlawful'.[28] The Court awarded a declaration to this effect and indicated that 'in an appropriate case' an applicant with standing could 'obtain an injunction restraining' the decision-maker from 'taking any further action based on its unlawful action'.[29] This ruling meant that the decision-maker could not continue to rely on the unlawful decision. In short, the remedial solution arrived at by the court was the functional equivalent of unlawfulness under the common law model.

Project Blue Sky does not explicitly mention the third of the remedial outcomes contemplated by the traditional common law trichotomy of remedial consequences, namely no remedy. But the decision does seem to contemplate the possibility that a decision which breaches a statutory provision may be either prospectively unlawful or retrospectively invalid. Prior to *Project Blue Sky* it was well accepted that errors consisting of a breach of a 'directory' (as opposed to a 'mandatory') statutory provision would not attract *any* remedy. That is, breach of a 'directory' provision would not make a decision either (retrospectively) invalid or (prospectively) unlawful. In *Project Blue Sky*, the court argued that the distinction between directory and mandatory provisions is unhelpful because it simply 'records a result [about whether the decision is valid or not] which has been reached on other grounds'.[30] In determining the remedial consequence of a breach of a statutory provision, the 'better test' is 'to ask whether it was a purpose of the legislation that an act done in breach of the provision should be invalid'.[31]

However, the remedial conclusion reached in *Project Blue Sky*—that is, that the decision, though not invalid, was unlawful—suggests that the difficulties the court had with the directory/mandatory distinction went beyond its 'conclusory nature'.[32] Arguably, the real problem with the distinction is that it operates as an on/off switch for determining the availability of a remedy—either the decision which breaches a legal requirement is invalid and a remedy is available or it is valid and the court is powerless. The importance of the analysis in *Project Blue Sky* is that it suggests the existence of a third remedial option for breach of a legal requirement, namely 'prospective unlawfulness'.

If our interpretation is correct, *Project Blue Sky* recognises that the category of 'mandatory' statutory provisions in truth contains two subcategories: (1) statutory provisions, breach of which will result in retrospective invalidity; and (2) statutory provisions breach of which results only in prospective unlawfulness.[33] In working out which subcategory is involved, the court argued that one must look to

---

26   Namely, jurisdictional, remediable non-jurisdictional, and unremediable non-jurisdictional errors (4.1.1).

27   Acting within the limits of statutory authority or power is one of the most basic administrative law norms.

28   *Project Blue Sky Inc v Australian Broadcasting Authority* (1998) 194 CLR 355, 392–3.

29   Ibid, 393.

30   Ibid, 390.

31   Ibid.

32   M Aronson, B Dyer and M Groves, *Judicial Review of Administrative Action*, 4th edn (Pyrmont, NSW: Lawbook Co, 2009), 357–8.

33   In *Detala Pty Ltd v Byron Shire Council* (2002) 133 LGRA 1, [53] it was concluded that a provision was mandatory in the sense that failure to comply would 'result in invalidity or unlawfulness'. Although, in *Project Blue Sky*, the High Court concluded the mandatory/directory distinction is unhelpful, it continues to be invoked in many cases to record conclusions about whether breach of a requirement has the result of invalidity.

the 'purposes of the legislation', which is to say that the question must be answered by the methods of statutory interpretation. Consistent with this approach, a question may also arise about whether a breach of a statutory provision has the consequence of either prospective unlawfulness or retrospective invalidity, or alternatively has no effect on the decision so that no remedy for the error will be available. The court did not say anything explicitly about this question, but the logic of *Project Blue Sky* may suggest that its answer is also to be found in the 'purposes of the legislation'.[34] As the court noted, the statute typically will not say anything explicit on the question of what remedial consequences should flow from a particular error or a breach of one of its provisions. Reference must be made to 'the language of the statute, its subject matter and objects, and the consequences for the parties'.[35] It may be questioned whether the best way to approach the remedial consequences of a breach of an administrative law norm is via the concepts of jurisdictional error and invalidity associated with the common law remedial model. An alternative approach would be to more clearly articulate the range of factors relevant to remedial consequences as relevant to the courts' discretion to award judicial review remedies.

Perhaps the most significant aspect of *Project Blue Sky* is the recognition of a category of legal error which, although insufficient to result in retrospective invalidity, may result in prospective unlawfulness. One significant implication of the court's decision is now apparent: the category of errors for which prospective unlawfulness is the appropriate remedial consequence is no longer limited to 'error of law on the face of the record', as was the case under the original writ-based common law system, but now (post-*Project Blue Sky*) arguably includes all breaches of statute (or of non-statutory administrative law norms or legal requirements) of which it can be said that the 'purposes of the legislation' require the remedial consequence of prospective unlawfulness. Although it is accepted that *Project Blue Sky* rests on a distinction between decisions that may be unlawful despite being validly made,[36] it is fair to say that the general circumstances which may justify a declaration or injunction on the basis of an unlawful (but valid) exercises of power remain to be articulated.[37]

Finally, two comments can be made about how the distinctions underpinning the decision in *Project Blue Sky* relate to the *ADJR Act* remedial model—though the courts have not adequately addressed this issue. First, in order to preserve (under the *ADJR Act*) the legislature's ability to provide that a statutory provision or administrative law norm is 'directory' (that is, a provision or norm breach of which should not have any remedial consequence), it must be open to a court to conclude that breach of such a statutory provision or administrative law norm does not, in the circumstances, establish any of the grounds of review listed under ss 5 and 6 of the *ADJR Act*. This is because, under the scheme of the *ADJR Act*, breach of *any* ground justifies a remedial order (even though the court, in its discretion can refuse to make any such order). Once an error which amounts to a ground of review under the *ADJR Act* is established, the court then has a discretionary power to set aside the decision. In other words, under the *ADJR Act* remedial model, in contrast to the common law model, there are no unremediable errors. How a legislative intention that breach of a statutory (or other administrative law) requirement has no remedial consequence fits together with the *ADJR Act*'s assumption that there are no unremediable errors is not immediately apparent.

---

34   See *O'Halloran v Wood* [2004] FCA 544 (unreported, Selway J, 5 May 2004), [23].

35   *Project Blue Sky Inc v Australian Broadcasting Authority* (1998) 194 CLR 355, 388.

36   E.g. *Comcare v Eames* (2008) 101 ALD 90, 101.

37   Consider, for example, *Kutlu v Director of Professional Services Review* (2011) 280 ALR 428, 439 where the conclusion that unlawfulness (as distinct from invalidity) could attract no remedy in the statutory context was not explained.

The second comment to be made concerns the exercise of the discretion under the *ADJR Act* to refuse a remedy. Under the *ADJR Act any* breach of *any* of the grounds of review contained in ss 5 and 6 is a remediable error which can lead to the making of *any* of the orders specified in s 16. Interestingly, however, the power to quash or set aside a decision (s 16(1)(a)) specifies that the court may, in its discretion, specify the date from which its order is to operate. In deciding the date from which a decision is to be set aside it is 'for the court, having regard to all relevant circumstances, to select among the alternatives the date which will best do justice as between the parties and any other affected person.'[38] However, the common law assumption that the typical consequence of an error is retrospective invalidity has been given considerable weight in the exercise of the discretion to set an operative date for the court's order.[39] It may therefore be that the *Project Blue Sky* scheme of remedial consequences will become influential in the context of the *ADJR Act* by influencing how the court's remedial discretion is exercised.

4.4 Three troublesome distinctions

Armed with an understanding of the basic common law remedial model and the associated trichotomy of remedial consequences of error, we are now in a position to introduce some of administrative law's most troublesome distinctions. Clarifying the meaning of three distinctions—all of which are related to the notion of 'invalidity'—helps to explain the nature and availability of each of the remedies which may be awarded in judicial review proceedings.

4.4.1 Jurisdictional error/non-jurisdictional error

As we have seen, this distinction was originally developed by the common law and was used to determine the availability of the prerogative writs of certiorari, prohibition and mandamus. As a general rule, errors of law which 'go to jurisdiction' would justify the award of these remedies but non-jurisdictional errors (that is, errors made *within* a decision-maker's jurisdiction) would not. The distinction between jurisdictional and non-jurisdictional errors is notoriously difficult to draw, and this issue is discussed in detail later (5.4.1).

Under the common law scheme, a decision affected by jurisdictional error was retrospectively invalid, whereas a decision affected by non-jurisdictional error was either prospectively unlawful (if it was an error of law on the face of the record) or valid. As we have seen, the decision in *Project Blue Sky* apparently stands for the proposition that any breach of any statutory provision (and, perhaps, of any non-statutory administrative law norm or other legal requirement) may render a decision either retrospectively invalid or prospectively unlawful or have no effect on its validity, depending on the intention of the legislature expressed in a statute. Thus, the *Project Blue Sky* methodology for determining whether breach of a statutory requirement (or other administrative law norm) results in invalidity can also be used to determine whether that breach amounts to a jurisdictional error.[40]

---

38   *Wattmaster Alco Pty Ltd v Button* (1986) 13 FCR 253, 257.

39   Ibid, 258; see also *Lansen v Minister for Environment and Heritage* (2008) 174 FCR 14, 45.

40   For prominent examples, see *Commisioner of Taxation v Futuris* (2008) 237 CLR 146, 156, 161; *Minister for Immigration and Citizenship v SZIZO* (2009) 238 CLR 627, 637.

4.4.2 Ultra vires/intra vires decisions

The distinction between decisions made 'ultra vires' (beyond power) and those made 'intra vires' (within power) is based on the same idea as the distinction between jurisdictional errors and errors made within jurisdiction, namely that decision-makers must not act beyond the limits of their powers. If jurisdiction is taken to mean 'the power to decide', then exceeding jurisdiction amounts to the same thing as exceeding power. The best explanation for the existence of two distinctions for one idea is historical. To simplify the law's messy history, it can be said that, whereas the language of 'jurisdiction' was associated closely with the supervision of 'inferior courts' and other statutory tribunals, the language of 'ultra vires' and powers was associated with the supervision of other species of statutory decision-makers.[41] It was also under the rubric of 'ultra vires' that the courts developed grounds of review, concerned with *reasoning processes* associated with the exercise of discretionary powers, which take review beyond questions of jurisdiction or authority.[42] We will discover later (5.4.1) that the notion of jurisdictional error as a condition of the award of orders in the nature of the prerogative writs—at least when applied to administrative decision-makers—is wide, and that grounds of review which focus on the quality of the reasoning processes which precede the making of an administrative decision can qualify as jurisdictional errors.

Indeed, in the contemporary literature of administrative law, jurisdictional error and ultra vires are often used interchangeably. And just as a decision affected by jurisdictional error is retrospectively invalid, so also is an ultra vires decision. By contrast, an intra vires decision is valid.[43]

4.4.3 Void decisions/voidable decisions

A decision which is 'void' is treated in law as a 'nullity'. In theory, this means that the decision is treated as never having had any legal effect. In the context of judicial review, to conclude that a decision is void is equivalent to a conclusion that it is retrospectively invalid—that the decision was invalid *ab initio* ('from the beginning').

A court order establishing the retrospective invalidity of a void decision can be understood in two ways. One approach sees the courts' role as being to declare the fact that the decision never had any effect in law—its voidness is 'announced', not established. An alternative approach is that 'void' decisions

---

41   See S A de Smith, 'Administrative Law: Wrongs and Remedies' (1952) 15 *Modern Law Review* 189.

42   G Airo-Farulla, 'Rationality and Judicial Review of Administrative Action' (2000) 24 *Melbourne University Law Review* 543, 550–4. It was once common to distinguish between the 'narrow' and 'broad' grounds of ultra vires. The first related to legal limitations on powers specifically set out in the statute (statutory bodies can only do those things which are expressly or impliedly authorised by statute). The second category encompassed grounds of review concerned with the reasoning processes of a decision-maker who could abuse or misuse of discretionary power by, for example, taking account of an irrelevant matter, failing to consider relevant matters, acting for unauthorised purposes, acting so unreasonably that no reasonable decision-maker could have so exercised the power, or impermissibly fettering or transferring their discretion (see 5.3).

43   In the conceptual scheme underlying the ultra vires/intra vires distinction, there is no equivalent of prospective unlawfulness. Historically, the ultra vires/intra vires distinction was usually applied to administrative decision-makers other than 'judicial' type bodies such as inferior courts and some tribunals. This meant that questions about (non-jurisdictional) 'error of law on the face of the record' did not typically arise, because 'ordinary' administrative decision-makers do not produce a formal 'record' in the sense that term traditionally bears in the phrase 'error of law on the face of the record'. On the meaning of the 'record', see 4.5.1.1.

are 'presumed' valid until a court decides otherwise.[44] On this view, the court's order establishing the voidness of the decision has a *constitutive* (not simply a declaratory) effect on the legal status of the impugned decision by rebutting the presumption of validity.[45] The constitutive view of the court's role has the advantage of accounting for the fact that a void decision may, nonetheless, be legally effective for some purposes. For example, if a void decision is not challenged by a person with standing within the time limit for a judicial review application to be brought, then the decision cannot be impeached (at least in judicial review proceedings).[46] The constitutive approach also better accounts for the fact that judicial review remedies are discretionary (4.6)—if the court's order is merely declaratory, it is hard to make sense of the discretion to refuse a remedy.[47]

Finally, the constitutive view of the court's role when judicially reviewing a void decision reflects the practical reality that even a void decision 'bears no brand of invalidity upon its forehead'.[48] Unless appropriate proceedings are brought it may not be possible (for example, because the decision denies a benefit) or wise (for example, because legal uncertainty is destabilising) for an affected person to simply ignore a decision, even if, as a matter of legal theory, it is 'no decision at all'. The tension between factual and legal reality is illustrated by the comment that, although '[i]t is a fact that a flawed decision will usually have practical effect until the Court declares it to be a decision made in circumstances of jurisdictional error', this 'does not mean that the decision was ever a valid decision or ever had any legal foundation'.[49]

The term 'voidable' is confusingly used in at least two ways. Sometimes it expresses the idea that a void decision will be presumed valid until duly invalidated by a court.[50] By contrast, it is also used to identify decisions which, though not void (but 'unlawful' in our terminology), may be prospectively quashed.

Like the distinction between mandatory and directory requirements, the distinction between void and voidable decisions is losing popularity on the basis that it expresses a conclusion about the remedial consequences of establishing an error, rather than explaining how that conclusion has been reached.[51] Furthermore, the language is confusing not only in the way we have just described, but also because the conclusion that a decision is 'void' or a 'nullity' performs a number of functions in the law, in addition to describing the remedial consequence of retrospective invalidity (see 4.7).

---

44   See M Taggart, 'Rival theories of Invalidity in Administrative Law: Some Practical and Theoretical Consequences' in M Taggart (ed), *Judicial Review of Administrative Action in the 1980s* (Auckland: Oxford University Press in association with the Legal Research Foundation Inc, 1986) 70.

45   The concept of voidness or nullity has also played a role in the determination of the legal effectiveness of administrative decisions affected by error in contexts unrelated to the remedial consequences which flow from a successful judicial review application (see 4.7).

46   On the other hand, the capacity to invoke invalidity in a collateral challenge (4.7.2) has attracted some scholars to the void *ab initio* idea, see, e.g., C Forsyth, 'The Metaphysics of Nullity—Invalidity, Conceptual Reasoning and the Rule of Law' in C Forsyth and I Hare (eds), *The Golden Metwand and the Crooked Cord: Essays in Honour of Sir Willaim Wade QC* (Clarendon Press, Oxford, 1998), 141.

47   For a case which raises this problem, see *SZKUO v Minister for Immigration and Citizenship* (2009) 180 FCR 438.

48   *Smith v East Elloe Rural District Council* [1956] AC 736, 769.

49   *Lansen v Minister for Environment and Heritage* (2008) 174 FCR 14, 49.

50   See, e.g., *F Hoffmann-La Roche and CoAG v Secretary of State for Trade and Industry* [1975] AC 295 and *Forbes v New South Wales Trotting Club Ltd* (1979) 143 CLR 242, 277. In *Minister for Immigration and Multicultural Affairs v Bhardwaj* (2002) 209 CLR 597, 646, Hayne J observed that a presumption of regularity does not render all administrative decisions valid until they are set aside but may operate to 'identify and emphasise the need for proof of some invalidating feature before a conclusion of invalidity may be reached'.

51   *Minister for Immigration and Multicultural Affairs v Bhardwaj* (2002) 209 CLR 597, 613.

4.5 The judicial review remedies

It is convenient to begin with a brief overview of the nature and function of the common law remedies, before considering the position under constitutional sources of judicial review jurisdiction and the *ADJR Act*.

4.5.1 The common law remedies

At common law, two categories of remedies are available. First, there are orders in the nature of[52] the 'prerogative writs' of certiorari, prohibition and mandamus. Second, there are the remedies of declaration and injunction. Although judges sometimes refuse the title 'judicial review' to applications for these latter remedies,[53] this makes little sense where the remedies are used as a means to enforce compliance with administrative law norms and other legal requirements.

4.5.1.1 Certiorari

Certiorari is a 'quashing' order; it deprives a decision of legal effect. As we have seen, it is possible for a decision to be deprived of legal effect either retrospectively or prospectively, and which option is appropriate turns on the nature of the error identified. In particular, where the error is jurisdictional, the court may quash the decision with retrospective effect—and where the error is committed *within* jurisdiction (and is apparent on the face the record), the court may quash it with prospective effect.[54]

Often, the achievement of an applicant's practical objectives requires nothing more than a quashing order. If, for example, an applicant challenges a decision to cancel a benefit (for example, a licence), a remedy which deprives the decision of legal effect restores them to the position they enjoyed prior to the making of the adverse decision. However, a person who is denied a benefit or permission will wish for more than the restoration of the status quo. For this reason, certiorari is often combined with mandamus (4.5.1.3), which compels the decision-maker to remake the decision according to law.

The availability of certiorari is subject to a number of limitations. These limitations are not as numerous or onerous as they once were, but remain of some importance. For a period in its history, certiorari was limited to the decisions made by a body or person with a duty to act judicially.[55] This requirement led to a very complex and unsatisfactory body of case law. However, the New South Wales Court of Appeal recently concluded that the requirement reflects 'language of an earlier age' and has, at least by implication, been jettisoned.[56] The parallel idea that only decision-makers under a duty to act judicially are bound by the rules of procedural fairness has been completely discarded (5.2.2.1) and there is no doubt that certiorari's reach extends beyond tribunals and inferior courts to administrative officials.

---

52   See n 23.

53   *Corporation of the City of Enfield v Development Assessment Commission* (2000) 199 CLR 135, 144–5.

54   In *Re McBain; Ex parte Australian Catholic Bishops Conference* (2002) 209 CLR 372, a case concerning the operation of certiorari to control superior federal court judges (i.e. not the normal context of administrative law judicial review), some members of the High Court appeared to assume, without explanation, that the certiorari for non-jurisdictional error of law on the face of the record would quash with retrospective effect.

55   Reflecting the fact that, prior to the development of the modern administrative state, the prerogative writs were developed to supervise the activities of inferior courts and court-like tribunals: 2.1.4.

56   *Chase Oyster Bar Pty Ltd v Hamo Industries Pty Ltd* (2010) 78 NSWLR 393, 400.

It was once thought that the 'Crown' was immune from certiorari (and prohibition). Any immunity, however, does not extend to ministers of the Crown. Moreover, it is now accepted as anomalous that the remedy should be available in relation to decisions of ministers but not decisions made formally by the Crown's representative (that is, a state Governor or the Governor-General), who typically exercises the powers of the office on ministerial advice.[57]

A more important limitation on the availability of certiorari is the requirement that the impugned decision have some sort of legal effect. In the classic formulation, the decision must 'determine questions affecting the rights of subjects'.[58] According to a more modern statement, 'a discernible or apparent legal effect upon rights' is required.[59] The simple theory behind this limitation is that it is not logically possible to deprive a decision of legal effect if it has no legal effect. This theory does not require an effect upon 'rights' in a narrow sense, but only that an applicant's interests are affected in a legally significant way. For example, in *Ainsworth* it was held that a government report, the contents of which were clearly detrimental to the applicant's business reputation, could not be quashed because nothing of legal significance turned on the publication of the report.[60] Even though the High Court was prepared to conclude that the publication of the report had breached the rules of procedural fairness (and to make a declaration to that effect), it was not prepared to formally quash it.

The requirement that there be a discernible legal effect can also ground arguments that certiorari is not available to quash decisions made at a preliminary stage of the decision-making process, such as a recommendation.[61] This issue turns on whether there is a sufficient nexus between the recommendation or preliminary decision and an ultimate decision which does have a legal effect. In *Hot Holdings*, for example, a non-binding recommendation as to whether a mining exploration licence should be granted was subject to certiorari because the final determination could not be made before the recommendation was considered.[62] While the report in *Ainsworth* had no legal consequences (though it clearly had practical ones) the recommendation in *Hot Holdings* had a 'discernible legal effect' upon the exercise of the final determination.[63]

Certiorari applies only to bodies 'having legal authority'.[64] This means that certiorari extends to 'every case in which a body of persons of a public as opposed to a purely private or domestic character has to determine matters affecting subjects'.[65] This formulation clearly covers statutory authorities and government bodies exercising prerogative or non-statutory executive powers.[66] Certiorari is also available in relation to non-government bodies exercising statutory powers, though the question of whether the

---

57   See *R v Toohey; Ex parte Northern Land Council* (1981) 151 CLR 170.

58   *R v Electricity Commissioners; Ex parte London Electricity Joint Committee Co (1920) Ltd* [1924] 1 KB 171, 205.

59   *Hot Holdings Pty Ltd v Creasy* (1996) 185 CLR 149, 158.

60   *Ainsworth v Criminal Justice Commission* (1992) 175 CLR 564.

61   Cf the requirement under the *ADJR Act* that reviewable decisions be 'final or operative and determinative': 3.5.1.1. In *Byrne v Marles* [2008] VR 612, 631 it was concluded that the *ADJR Act* cases on this issue were suggestive of the conclusion that a decision to investigate a complaint 'is not sufficiently connected with a final decision affecting rights to be susceptible to certiorari'.

62   *Hot Holdings Pty Ltd v Creasy* (1996) 185 CLR 149.

63   *Hot Holdings Pty Ltd v Creasy* (1996) 185 CLR 149, 174. See also *Rodger v De Gelder* [2011] NSWCA 97.

64   *R v Electricity Commissioners; Ex parte London Electricity Joint Committee Co (1920) Ltd* [1924] 1 KB 171, 205.

65   *R v Criminal Injuries Compensation Board; Ex parte Lain* [1967] 2 QB 864, 882.

66   On the possibility that a restrictive reading of 'matter', which is relevant to the exercise of all sources of federal jurisdiction, may limit the availability of all judicial review remedies where an exercise of non-statutory public power is in breach of 'soft laws' (such as practice manuals, procedure pamphlets, guidelines), see M Aronson, 'Private Bodies, Public Power and Soft Law in the High Court' (2007) 35 *Federal Law Review* 1, 20–2.

exercise by non-government decision-makers of non-statutory 'public powers' remains uncertain.[67] Given that declarations and injunctions are available against non-government (that is, private) bodies, the uncertainty about the availability of certiorari may remain an untested question as applicants are likely to be advised to seek a private law remedy (that is, declaration or injunction—see also 3.6.1).

Unlike prohibition and mandamus, certiorari is available not only in relation to decisions affected by jurisdictional error, but also to decisions affected by (non-jurisdictional) error of law on the face of the record. We will discuss the distinction between jurisdictional and non-jurisdictional errors later (5.4.1). What does it mean to say that an error of law appears on the face of the record?

Historically, only certain decision-making bodies (notably, 'courts of record') generated a 'record' in the relevant sense. Moreover, normally only the document that initiated the proceedings, the pleadings (if any), and the formal decision were 'recorded' in the relevant sense. Error of law on the face of the record was an important ground of judicial review in the eighteenth century, but fell into disuse in the nineteenth century as the scope of judicial review was expanded to cover administrative organs of governance which did not generate records. It was revived in *R v Northumberland Compensation Appeal Tribunal; Ex parte Shaw*[68] in response to the fact that there were many tribunal decisions of which no right of appeal to a court was provided by statute. In the wake of this decision, English courts expanded the concept of the record to include 'both the reasons for decision and the complete transcript of proceedings' within the record.[69] Because errors of law are most likely to appear in the transcript and the reasons, this development had the potential (in the words of the High Court in *Craig's* case) to '[transform] certiorari into a discretionary general appeal for error of law'.[70] The court considered this problematic. Although legislatures often provide for appeals 'on questions of law' from tribunals and other decision-makers (for example, under s 44 of the *Administrative Appeals Tribunal Act*), the High Court emphasised that they sometimes have sound reasons for not making provision for such an appeal—for instance that providing a right of appeal might 'increase the financial hazards to which those involved in even minor litigation' are exposed,[71] or that the value of finality in decision-making undercuts any arguments in favour of conferring a right of appeal. For these reasons the court concluded that whether or not the traditional scope of the 'record' should be significantly expanded is properly a matter for the legislature. Although in *Kirk* the High Court raised the question of whether the importance of 'compelling inferior tribunals to observe the law' had been adequately balanced with the policy reasons underlying the decision in *Craig*,[72] it is fair to conclude that the court did not purport to 'qualify or alter' the present application of the approach to defining the record articulated in *Craig's* case.[73]

In relation to inferior courts, it was held in *Craig* that the record comprises no more than the documentation which initiates the proceedings, the pleadings (if any) and the formal order.[74] Reasons for

---

67   In *Forbes v New South Wales Trotting Club Ltd* (1979) 143 CLR 242 declaratory relief was sought against a non-government body exercising a 'public' function.

68   [1952] 1 KB 338.

69   *Craig v South Australia* (1995) 184 CLR 163, 180.

70   Ibid, 181.

71   Ibid, 181.

72   *Kirk v Industrial Relations Commission of NSW* (2010) 239 CLR 531, 577. The court also made the point that where a statutory appeal for error of law does exist, the concern about extending the scope of certiorari and, thus, the financial hazards to which parties are exposed is overstated: 578. Of course, where there is a statutory right of appeal on a question of law the practical importance of certiorari's availability is greatly diminished.

73   *Barrett v Coroner's Court* (SA) 108 SASR 568, 601, [144].

74   *Craig v South Australia* (1995) 184 CLR 163, 182.

decision can be 'incorporated' into the record to the extent that the tribunal chooses to do so. Such choice, however, must be deliberate and will not be inferred from vague or 'accidental' references prefacing an order, such as 'for the reasons given'. Moreover, the court said that where reasons (or other documents) are expressly incorporated by the terms of an order, they are included only to the extent that they are 'an integral part of that order'.[75] In some state jurisdictions, statute expressly provides that reasons for decision are part of the record for the purposes of certiorari.[76]

4.5.1.2 Prohibition

Prohibition is an order to a decision-maker to refrain from exceeding its jurisdiction. It is not available in relation to non-jurisdictional errors. Prohibition presupposes that the decision-maker has not completed its function. Once the legal effect of a decision has been finalised, it is too late to seek or award prohibition.

The historical development of prohibition and certiorari are deeply intertwined, and it is usually said that they are subject to the same general limitations. The caveat is that the requirement that a decision must have a discernible legal effect may not apply to prohibition with the same force as it does to certiorari.[77] If this conclusion can be justified, it would require acceptance of the proposition that, although it makes no logical sense to quash a decision which has no legal effect, it does make sense to prohibit the making of a decision even if it would have no discernible legal effect.

4.5.1.3 Mandamus

The function of mandamus is to enforce the performance of a public duty.[78] Mandamus is available in cases where there has been 'actual' or 'constructive' failure to perform the duty or exercise a jurisdiction.[79] A constructive failure to exercise jurisdiction occurs when the decision-maker attempts to fulfil their obligations or exercise their jurisdiction but makes a decision which is affected by a jurisdictional error. In theory, because the decision is 'void' (or a 'nullity') the duty remains unperformed or the jurisdiction remains unexercised, as the case may be. For this reason, mandamus can and sometimes does issue to require the decision to be remade without certiorari being issued to quash it. Where the error affecting the decision is non-jurisdictional, a court can issue mandamus only if it also issues certiorari to quash the initial decision—that decision being 'voidable', rather than 'void'.

In Chapter 3 we saw that, although the scope of common law judicial review has historically been limited to the supervision of public bodies, attention has increasingly been directed to the nature of the power exercised, rather than the formal legal source of that power. Despite this trend, the extent to

---

75   Ibid. See also *Seiffert v Prisoners Review Board* [2011] WASCA 148, [182–183].

76   *Supreme Court Act 1970* (NSW), s 69(4); *Administrative Law Act 1978* (Vic), s 10. Note, however, that expanding the definition of 'the record' to include reasons does not covert certiorari into a general appeal for error of law to the extent that certiorari 'does not invite a scouring of all the evidence before the inferior court': *Easwaralingam v Director of Public Prosecutions* (2010) 208 A Crim R 122, 128.

77   See *Ainsworth v Criminal Justice Commission* (1992) 175 CLR 564, 581.

78   In this section we consider only the prerogative writ of mandamus and orders in the nature of this writ. On the action for 'statutory mandamus' (e.g. *Supreme Court Act 1970* (NSW) s 65), see Aronson, Dyer and Groves, n 32 above, 854–860.

79   *R v War Pensions Entitlement Appeal Tribunal; Ex parte Bott* (1933) 50 CLR 228, 242–3. In some circumstances, a person who suffers damage as a result of a breach of statutory duty by a public official can bring an action in tort for damages or an injunction.

which certiorari and prohibition are available to supervise private, non-government decision-makers remains unclear (4.5.1.1). In the case of mandamus, the question of its availability is explicitly focused upon whether the unperformed duty is owed to the 'public'. Thus, to the extent that a 'private' body or person is under a 'public duty', mandamus may issue to compel its performance.[80] The flip-side of this proposition is that mandamus will not enforce a 'private' obligation even against a government (public) respondent.[81]

The most interesting issue about the availability of mandamus concerns the nature of the public duties performance of which it can compel. 'Duties' are often distinguished from 'discretions'.[82] Where a person or body is under a duty, they are compelled to act in a particular way: either they have fulfilled their duty or they have not. Where, on the other hand, a person or body has a discretionary power, they have some element of *choice* about if, when and how that power is to be exercised. This choice will not be an unlimited choice; indeed, many of the grounds of judicial review set limits on how discretionary powers may be exercised (5.3). But within these limits, it is for the decision-maker to decide what to do.

The basic distinction between discretions and duties is straightforward in theory but difficult to draw in practice. For example, where the legislature states that a decision-maker must perform some act, it may do so in highly specific terms or (in contrast) by reference to general aspirations. For example, legislation may impose a duty to 'afford the best primary education to all children'[83] or to provide a 'telephone service as efficiently and economically as practicable'.[84] At most, these duties set out general principles rather than hard and fast rules which prescribe how the duty-bearer must act in specific situations. Unless the courts are willing to develop detailed rules for the fulfilment of aspirational duties, such duties necessarily confer choices (that is, discretion) on the duty-bearer. This does not mean that performance of the duty is entirely beyond judicial supervision. Decisions made in performance of vague or aspirational duties may (in theory at least) be reviewed in much the same way as exercises of discretionary powers. But the courts are unlikely to compel the exercise of aspirational duties.[85] This is particularly so where the duties involve 'continuing actions which the courts are not in a position to supervise', or where the duty is one among a multiplicity of functions an administrative body with limited resources must perform.[86] The reluctance of courts to become actively involved reflects their general reluctance to usurp functions conferred on administrators, and also their concerns about the appropriateness of judicial involvement in 'polycentric' decision-making (3.6.2.3). Although this reluctance is understandable, a complete failure to perform even an aspirational duty may provoke the courts to act.[87]

---

80   The reason the High Court held mandamus was not appropriate in *NEAT Domestic Trading Pty Ltd v AWB Ltd* (2003) 216 CLR 277 was the conclusion that AWBI's commercial interests could not be sensibly accommodated with a 'public' duty (3.5.1.4.2; 3.6.1).

81   *John Fairfax & Sons Ltd v Australian Telecommunications Commission* [1977] 2 NSWLR 400.

82   This and the following paragraph draw on P Cane, *Administrative Law*, 4th edn (Oxford: Clarendon Press, 2004), 50–2.

83   *Ex parte Wilkes; Re Minister for Education* [1962] SR (NSW) 220.

84   See *Yamirr v Australian Telecommunications Corporation* (1990) 96 ALR 739.

85   Such duties have also been referred to as 'target' duties: *R v Inner London Education Authority; Ex parte Ali* (1990) 2 Admin LR 822, 878. Wade characterised them as 'political' duties: H W R Wade, *Administrative Law* (Oxford: Clarendon Press, 1961), 119.

86   E Campbell, 'Enforcement of Public Duties Which Are Impossible to Perform' (2003) 10 *Australian Journal of Administrative Law* 201, 202.

87   See the discussion in *Yamirr v Australian Telecommunications Corporation* (1990) 96 ALR 739, 749. Applicants wishing to have particular laws enforced by way of judicial review often struggle to establish they have standing to bring a judicial review application: Ch 6.

The distinction between duties and discretions does not mean that mandamus has no relevance to the exercise of discretionary powers. It may be relevant in two ways. First, mandamus can be used to order a decision-maker to exercise a discretionary power where the decision-maker has a duty to exercise that power.[88] It will not, however, normally issue to compel a decision-maker to exercise a discretionary power in a particular way. All the order can achieve is to ensure that the decision-maker selects one of the options open to them.[89] In rare cases, the courts have held that there are no legally permissible reasons which would enable a discretionary power to be exercised other than in a particular way, and thus that mandamus may command the administrator to act in the only way open to them.[90] In typical cases, however, to require that a discretionary power be exercised in a particular way would compromise the distinction between legality and the merits.

Second, although the matter will depend on statutory context it will often be the case that decision-makers have an obligation at least to consider whether or not to exercise their powers (including broad, discretionary powers), even if they are not required to exercise them.[91] The performance of such an obligation may also be required by mandamus. It is clear, however, that such an obligation can be negated by a contrary statutory intention.[92]

As with certiorari and prohibition (4.5.1.1), the Crown and its servants have historically been immune from mandamus. Prerogative writs were issued in the sovereign's name, and it was therefore considered a legal embarrassment for these writs to issue against the sovereign. Yet in the context of modern Australian government, more embarrassment is likely to result from exempting high-ranking government officials from the reach of judicial review's core remedies. Although the matter has not been clearly decided, most commentators believe that Crown immunity from the prerogative writs is no longer a viable proposition of the common law.[93]

4.5.1.4 Injunction

As already noted, the injunction and declaration developed in the context of private law disputes. The use of these 'equitable' remedies in Australian public law is of increasing importance and their availability is generously construed on the basis that they developed as a response to the 'technicalities hedging the prerogative remedies'.[94] Perhaps this is one reason for the assumption that if judicial review is to be extended over 'private' decision-making bodies in Australia, this is more likely to be achieved by use of equitable remedies than by the prerogative writs. Indeed, the introduction of the injunction into public law was in part a means to enforce principles very like the grounds of judicial review (principally the

---

88   In *Public Service Association of South Australia Inc v Industrial Relations Commission of South Australia* [2012] HCA 25, [91] Heydon J said, '[i]n the absence of statutory language to the contrary a grant of jurisdiction ordinarily carries with it a duty to exercise it'.

89   *R v Commonwealth Court of Conciliation and Arbitration; Ex parte Ozone Theatres (Aust) Ltd* (1949) 78 CLR 389.

90   For example, *Commissioner of State Revenue (Vic) v Royal Insurance Australia Ltd* (1994) 182 CLR 51; *Save our Suburbs (SOS) NSW Incorporated v Electoral Commissioner of New South Wales* (2002) 55 NSWLR 642, 656.

91   E.g. *Herrington Re Election for offices in Communications Division of the CEPU* (2005) 144 IR 143, 148 [31].

92   *Plaintiff M61/2010E v Commonwealth* (2010) 243 CLR 319, 335 made it clear that a no-consideration clause—which provides that there is no duty to consider whether to exercise a power—can be effective to prevent the issue of the prerogative/constitutional writs: '[b]ecause the Minister is not bound to consider exercising either of the relevant powers, mandamus will not issue to compel consideration, and certiorari would have no practical utility' (see 7.2.4.2).

93   Aronson, Dyer, and Groves, n 32 above, 836.

94   *Bateman's Bay Local Aboriginal Land Council v The Aboriginal Community Benefit Fund Pty Ltd* (1998) 194 CLR 247, 257.

rules of procedural fairness) against non-government (private) bodies, such as clubs and trade unions, that were not subject to the prerogative writs but which exercised regulatory functions that could have serious impacts on affected individuals.[95] In Australia, the juridical basis for the grant of injunctions to enforce such requirements on 'domestic' bodies or tribunals remains unclear, but is commonly justified on the basis of implied contractual terms.[96]

The increasing popularity of the public law injunction is not to be explained by its ability to achieve a distinct remedial outcome in judicial review proceedings: the injunction performs functions equivalent to prohibition and mandamus. An injunction may either prohibit a particular act (prohibitory injunction) or require that a particular act be done (mandatory injunction). However, unlike prohibition and mandamus, it seems that an injunction may be issued even in cases of non-jurisdictional error. As noted above (4.3), in *Project Blue Sky*, the High Court accepted that an injunction could be granted to prohibit an administrative authority from taking any action based on a (prospectively) unlawful, as opposed to a retrospectively invalid, decision. On the other hand, we also noted that a statute may provide that no remedy—not even a declaration or injunction—will be available for breach of a particular statutory requirement.

In Australia, the immunity of the Crown from the injunction has been either wholly or partially eroded by statute.[97] The immunity never applied to the 'constitutional injunction' (4.5.3).

4.5.1.5 Declaration

The declaration can be described as a remedy that 'shadows' other judicial review remedies. A court may declare that a decision is invalid (cf certiorari); that an as-yet unmade decision would exceed jurisdiction (cf prohibition and injunction); and that a public duty should be performed (cf mandamus and injunction). The key functional difference between declarations and the remedies they 'shadow' is that, technically speaking, declarations change nothing: they do not formally quash the decision under review, nor can they create legally enforceable rights and obligations. Declarations are not 'coercive' remedies, and non-compliance with the court's decision does not constitute contempt of court.[98] In addition to shadowing the functions of the other remedies, the declaration can also be used to give formal guidance about how discretionary powers should be exercised— for example, by stating what should or should not be considered for a power to be lawfully exercised.[99]

Despite the non-coercive nature of declarations, they have become a very popular remedy in administrative law. In part this popularity reflects the fact that declarations may be available even when the 'shadowed' remedy is not.[100] Another explanation is that the declaration is sometimes thought to be (appropriately) less aggressive than the alternatives, precisely because of its non-coercive nature. (This explains why declarations have long been available against the Crown.) With rare exceptions,

---

95   For example, by disciplining members for breaches of the club or association rules.

96   Aronson, Dyer and Groves, n 32 above, 943.

97   The *Crown Proceedings Act* in the Australian Capital Territory, the Northern Territory, Tasmania and South Australia does not allow mandatory injunctions against the Crown, though it seems that the Crown, in this context, is limited to state Governors (or equivalent positions in the territories). See Aronson, Dyer and Groves, n 32 above, 931.

98   A judicial declaration will, however, raise a *res judicata* between the parties: *Bass v Permanent Trustees Co Ltd* (1999) 198 CLR 334, 356.

99   For example, *Green v Daniels* (1977) 13 ALR 1, 15–16.

100   For example, *Ainsworth v Criminal Justice Commission* (1992) 175 CLR 564 (see 4.5.1.1); *Plaintiff M61/2010E v Commonwealth* (2010) 243 CLR 319, 359.

government decision-makers in Australia can be relied upon to respect an authoritative statement by a court about what the law requires.[101] Also, judicial review may sometimes form part of a wider political strategy to influence government policy, and in that case a declaration may be sufficient for an applicant's purposes.[102]

Declarations have been issued in a wide variety of contexts, and the High Court has resisted the establishment of rules limiting their availability. Although it is sometimes said that there are no limits to the courts' jurisdiction to grant declaratory relief, there are a number of general discretionary factors affecting its availability, which will be considered below. Moreover, when federal judicial power is exercised, the principle that declaratory orders should be directed to the determination of legal controversies, as opposed to 'abstract or hypothetical questions', is not merely a discretionary factor, but an aspect of the jurisdictional question of whether or not there is a 'matter' (3.4.1.3). However, it may not be easy to distinguish between an unobjectionable declaratory order and one which answers a hypothetical question or constitutes an 'advisory opinion'.[103] For instance, where a taxpayer was threatened with adverse consequences if he did not provide certain information demanded by a tax form, one can understand why the courts did not require the taxpayer to wait until he was prosecuted for not complying before allowing him to test the legality of the attempt to collect the information.[104] In England, courts have gone further and have issued declaratory relief in relation to non-statutory circulars or pamphlets issued by a public decision-maker which gave erroneous legal advice.[105] Because such documents strictly lack legal force, their legal accuracy might be thought not to raise a legal issue; and therefore that any decision by a court concerning their accuracy would be no more than advisory. Some commentators have suggested that Australian courts may interpret more strictly the requirement that declarations not stray into hypothetical questions or be purely advisory.[106] On the other hand, in *Plaintiff M61*[107] the High Court granted a declaration even in the absence of an obligation on the decision-maker to consider whether or not to exercise the power in question.[108]

It has been held that a declaration cannot be awarded that a decision is unlawful because affected by a non-jurisdictional error of law on the face of the record.[109] This is because (or so the argument goes) such a decision is not void. If it were void (that is, if it were a nullity from the beginning), a declaration would be sufficient to establish that. However, a decision affected by error of law on the face of the record is not a nullity from the beginning. It needs to be deprived of legal effect, and a declaration, which cannot create or alter legal rights and obligations, cannot do this. This line of reasoning may need to be reconsidered in the

---

101 Vindicating the judicial presumption that court declarations will be honored (e.g. *Davies v Minister for Urban Development and Planning* [2011] SASC 87, citing *Franklin v The Queen (No 2)* [1974] QB 208, 218).

102 The popularity of declarations is connected with the increasing amount of 'public interest' or 'interest group' litigation: 6.4.

103 *Electricity Supply Association of Australia v ACCC* (2001) 113 FCR 230, 265–6.

104 *Dyson v Attorney-General* [1911] 1 KB 410.

105 *Gillick v West Norfold and Weisbach Area Health Authority* [1986] AC 112.

106 N J Young, 'Declarations and Other Remedies in Administrative Law' (2004) 12 *Australian Journal of Administrative Law* 35, 46. See also M Aronson, ' Private Bodies, Public Power and Soft Law in the High Court' (2007) 35 *Federal Law Review* 1, 16, where it is suggested that the High Court's interpretation of 'matter' may limit the availability in federal jurisdiction of declarations in relation to 'soft law' norms because they do not affect rights or obligations (see also 3.5.1.4).

107 *Plaintiff M61/2010E v Commonwealth* (2010) 243 CLR 319, 359–60.

108 The question of whether this decision has liberalised the availability of declaratory relief is helpfully discussed in C Tran, 'The "Fatal Conundrum" of "No-Consideration" Clauses After *Plaintiff M61*' (2011) 39 *Federal Law Review* 303, 315–20. See also 7.2.4.2.

109 *Punton v Ministry of Pensions and National Insurance (No 2)* [1964] 1 All ER 448. Aronson, Dyer and Groves, n 32 above, 924–5, cite a number of cases where the reasoning in *Punton (No 2)* has been adopted in Australian courts.

light of the High Court's decision in *Project Blue Sky* (4.3). That case seems to establish that a declaration can be awarded in relation to a decision affected by breach of a statutory provision the effect of which is not to render the decision invalid but only unlawful. It would seem to follow that a declaration of unlawfulness could be awarded in relation to a decision affected by breach of a non-statutory administrative law norm (such as the norm of legality), even if the breach (being non-jurisdictional) did not make the decision void, but only unlawful. The High Court indicated that if the decision-maker ignored the declaration and treated the decision as valid despite its unlawfulness, the applicant could potentially return to court for an injunction to restrain further reliance on or execution of the decision.

4.5.2 *ADJR Act* remedies

Section 16(1) of the *ADJR Act* lists the orders which may, in the court's discretion, be made:

1   an order quashing or setting aside the decision, or a part of the decision, with effect from the date of the order or from such earlier or later date as the court specifies;
2   an order referring the matter to which the decision relates to the person who made the decision for further consideration, subject to such directions as the court thinks fit;
3   an order declaring the rights of the parties in respect of any matter to which the decision relates;
4   an order directing any of the parties to do, or to refrain from doing, any act or thing the doing, or the refraining from the doing, which the court considers necessary to do justice between the parties.

As explained above (4.2), the *ADJR Act* breaks the link forged under the common law model between grounds of review and the remedial consequence of establishing a ground of review, and also abandons the distinction between jurisdictional and non-jurisdictional errors.[110]

As at common law, remedial options under the *ADJR Act* include quashing (s 16(1)(a)), prohibiting (s 16(1)(d)), mandatory (s 16(1)(b)) and declaratory (s 16(1)(c)) orders. It is often claimed that the Act gave the courts greater remedial flexibility. For instance, s 16(1)(a) expressly enables the court to choose (in its discretion) the date from which a quashing order will operate, whereas certiorari for jurisdictional errors is assumed to operate retrospectively. However, it seems that at common law, declaratory relief may be issued with prospective effect in lieu of certiorari, where the court is concerned that retrospective quashing may have undesirable effects such as frustrating reasonable expectations.[111] Conversely, the fact that, at common law, quashing for jurisdictional error has retrospective effect has influenced the exercise of the court's discretion under the *ADJR Act* to choose the operative date of orders setting aside decisions.[112] Under the *ADJR Act*, if the court does not specify a date from which

---

110   See *Jadwan Pty Ltd v Secretary, Department of Health and Aged Care* (2003) 145 FCR 1, 17–8. Although the breach of an *ADJR Act* ground will often amount to what would, at common law, be a jurisdictional error, this is not necessarily the case. That is obvious with respect to the ground of 'error of law' as it need not appear on the face of the record (s 5(1)(f)), but the same point also applies to at least some of the other grounds. For example, in *Jadwan* (ibid) it was doubted that a particular error of taking into account an irrelevant consideration that had been established under the *ADJR Act* would have amounted to a jurisdictional error (had it been necessary to determine that question).

111   See *R v Panel on Take-overs and mergers; Ex parte Datafin Plc* [1987] QB 815, 842. In the *Project Blue Sky* litigation, Davies J, at first instance, held that the impugned decision was invalid but ordered that it be set aside at a date a few months after the date of the court order: *Project Blue Sky Inc v Australian Broadcasting Authority* (1998) 194 CLR 355, 363 (Brennan J). Aronson, Dyer and Groves, n 32 above, 802, cite a number of cases where the operation of certiorari was suspended for a time to 'allow the administration to get its house in order'.

112   *Wattmaster Alco Pty Ltd v Button* (1986) 13 FCR 253, 258.

an order to set aside or quash a decision will operate, it is assumed that the operative date is that of the court's order.[113]

Despite the potential breadth of s 16(1)(d), which allows the court to make any order considered 'necessary to do justice between the parties', the courts have insisted that this power should not normally be used to make a substitute decision as opposed to setting the original decision aside and returning it to the decision-maker for reconsideration. The power to make a substitute decision, it has been said, should 'usually, if not invariably' be limited to situations where the administrative decision-maker has no residual discretion.[114] Nor does the *ADJR Act* enable an applicant to seek an order for damages.[115] As at common law, damages are only available if a private law cause of action is established, such as a breach of contract or a tort (see Chapter 11).[116]

4.5.3 The constitutional remedies

It will be recalled that s 75(v) of the Constitution (which is the basis of the Federal Court's jurisdiction under s 39B of the *Judiciary Act*) entrenches the jurisdiction of the High Court in relation to matters where mandamus, prohibition and injunction are claimed against an officer of the Commonwealth (3.4.1.2).

The 'constitutional writs' of mandamus and prohibition are available only in cases where it can be established that the decision-maker has made a jurisdictional error, or failed to exercise its jurisdiction.[117] Although certiorari is not specifically named in s 75(v) (or s 39B), it is available as an ancillary remedy where it is necessary for the effective exercise of one of the named writs.[118] It appears that certiorari cannot be granted under s 75(v) for non-jurisdictional errors of law because the remedies to which it is ancillary cannot be so granted.[119] The meaning of 'jurisdictional' in this context is considered in 5.4.1. Here we focus on two questions about the nature of High Court's s 75(v) jurisdiction: (1) the extent to which the 'constitutional injunction' expands the scope of review; and (2) the extent to which the principles governing the availability of the constitutional remedies are different from those applicable at common law. Neither question can be given a clear answer.

In *Plaintiff S157/2002 v Commonwealth*,[120] the High Court speculated that injunctive relief under s 75(v) may 'be available on grounds that are wider than those that result in relief by way of prohibition

---

113   Ibid, 256; *Jadwan* (2003) 145 FCR 1, 18.

114   *Minister for Immigration and Ethnic Affairs v Conyngham* (1986) 11 FCR 528, 541.

115   *Park Oh Ho v Minister for Immigration and Ethnic Affairs* (1989) 167 CLR 637. An order for the payment of a statutory entitlement may be made, if that entitlement has been denied in error. The UK Law Commission has proposed the creation of a damages remedy in limited circumstances, including where there is 'serious fault' on the part of the public decision-maker: *Administrative Redress: Public Bodies and the Citizen*, Consultation Paper No 187 (2008).

116   Note, however, that the Commonwealth Scheme for Compensation for Detriment caused by Defective Administration (CDDA) enables discretionary payments to be made to compensate for losses caused by an agency's defective administration. The scheme is non-statutory, based on the executive power of the Commonwealth conferred by s 61 of the Constitution. For discussion, see Senate Legal and Constitutional References Committee, Parliament of Australia, *Review of Government Compensation Payments* (2010).

117   *Re Refugee Review Tribunal; Ex parte Aala* (2000) 204 CLR 82; *Plaintiff S157/2002 v Commonwealth* (2003) 211 CLR 476, 508.

118   *Bodruddaza v Minister for Immigration and Multicultural Affairs* (2007) 228 CLR 651, 673, [62–64].

119   *Re McBain; Ex parte Australian Catholic Bishops Conference* (2002) 209 CLR 372, 393–4, 403, 440–1. There are other sources of jurisdiction for the High Court to issue certiorari: e.g. 75(iii) (3.4.2).

120   (2003) 211 CLR 476.

and mandamus'.[121] If this suggestion were to be accepted, a question would arise about whether it makes sense to confine review under s 75(v) to jurisdictional errors in cases where an applicant seeks mandamus or prohibition, but to allow this restriction to be outflanked by the expedient of seeking injunctive relief. What 'rational foundation' could there be for such a position?[122] Although this question has not received any sustained analysis by the High Court, one interpretation of the comments in *Plaintiff S157/2002* is that, whereas the writs of prohibition, mandamus and (as an ancillary remedy) certiorari are yoked to the idea of retrospective invalidity (via the notion of jurisdictional error), the constitutional injunction is not necessarily so linked. If injunctive relief under s 75(v) is available for non-jurisdictional error, then it may be that this relief will only have prospective operation. Prospective relief may be sufficient where an applicant wishes to prevent an officer of the Commonwealth from giving effect to an unlawful, though not invalid, administrative decision.[123] But it would be of little use where the goal of a judicial review application was to deprive an administrative decision of legal effects it had already had.

This interpretation of the High Court's speculation in *S157* resonates with our interpretation of *Project Blue Sky*. That decision seems to contemplate that, whereas a jurisdictional error makes a decision invalid, a non-jurisdictional breach of a statute or a non-statutory administrative law norm or other legal requirement may either render a decision prospectively unlawful or have no effect on its validity at all. There is no way of knowing whether this trichotomous scheme of remedial consequences will be applied to review under s 75(v) (the claim in *Project Blue Sky* was made under s 75(iii)). But if it is, the constitutional injunction, not being limited (as prohibition, mandamus and ancillary certiorari are) to jurisdictional errors, could provide a remedy for non-jurisdictional error. We must repeat, however, that the precise role of the injunction under s 75(v) is largely a matter for speculation. In this regard, it should also be noted that the court's description of the availability of declarations and injunctions (in the context of s 75(v)) is sometimes linked to the concept of invalidity, which creates further uncertainty. Indeed, in *Futuris*, the suggestion that the principles of jurisdictional error 'which control the constitutional writs ... do not attend the remedy of injunction including that provided in s 75(v), and thus in s 39B of the *Judiciary Act*', was followed by the comment that 'the equitable remedies ... operate to declare invalidity and to restrain the implementation of invalid exercises of power'.[124] Given that invalidity describes the remedial consequence of jurisdictional error, it is unclear how this comment can be reconciled with the availability of injunctions in the absence of a jurisdictional error.[125]

The High Court has emphasised that the principles of judicial review applicable under s 75(v) do not necessarily coincide with the common law.[126] One obvious difference is that the 'constitutional remedies' are available to enforce constitutional limits on the exercise of Commonwealth executive power. It has been suggested, however, that any remaining areas of divergence may be minimised or forgotten

---

121   Ibid, 508.

122   See *Re Minister for Immigration and Multicultural Affairs; Ex parte Miah* (2001) 206 CLR 57, 122 (Kirby J).

123   Cf *Abebe v Commonwealth* (1999) 197 CLR 510, 551–2 (Gaudron J).

124   *Commisioner of Taxation v Futuris* (2008) 237 CLR 146, 162.

125   It is also worth noting that, in *Plaintiff S157* (2003) 211 CLR 476, 508, the only examples given of injunctive relief (after the suggestion that the grounds for such relief are wider than jurisdictional error) were 'fraud, bribery, dishonesty or other improper purpose'. These listed examples of 'improper purposes' grounding injunctive relief also, presumably, constitute implied restrictions on the jurisdiction of a decision-maker exercising statutory powers: see 5.3.2.

126   *Re Refugee Review Tribunal; Ex parte Aala* (2000) 204 CLR 82, 92, 140–1. Nor should it be assumed that general principles developed in the context of the *ADJR Act* are always relevant to s 75(v) jurisprudence: *Re Minister for Immigration and Multicultural Affairs; Ex parte S20/2002* (2003) 198 ALR 59, [53]–[60].

over time.[127] Given the underlying unity of purpose for constitutionalising the review jurisdiction of the High Court and the state Supreme Courts articulated in *Kirk's* case (3.4.3; 7.1) it is at least less likely that principled reasons will be found to justify any differences.[128]

4.6 Discretion to refuse a remedy

Despite the fact that an error has been established for which a remedy is, in principle, available, a court may nevertheless decide in its discretion to refuse a remedy. The existence of this discretion to refuse a remedy indicates that, although there is a general public interest that government agencies stay within the limits of their powers, this does not mean that every attempt to enforce those limits is necessarily in the public interest. Indeed, a contrary public interest in finality is part of the justification for the imposition of time limits for bringing judicial review applications (though normally courts have a discretion to grant extensions of time).

On the other hand, if the exercise of the discretion to refuse a remedy is overused, or if it is not exercised by reference to some guiding principles, the result may be unacceptable uncertainty in application of the law. Although the courts have not attempted to give exhaustive guidance, possible justifications for a refusal to grant a remedy include the existence of a more convenient and satisfactory remedy (such as a statutory right of appeal),[129] the futility of a remedy,[130] unreasonable delay,[131] 'bad faith' on the part of the applicant, and acquiescence or waiver.[132]

The discretion to refuse a remedy is not exercised lightly. Indeed, it is sometimes said that there is an onus on the respondent to demonstrate that the circumstances justify withholding a remedy.[133] While a remedy can be denied on the basis of futility,[134] the courts are unlikely to refuse a remedy merely because it appears that the decision would have been the same even if the error had not been made. Thus, where

---

127   J Spigelman, 'The Centrality of Jurisdictional Error' (2010) 21 *Public Law Review* 77, 81. For an example, see *Public Service Association of South Australia Inc v Industrial Relations Commission of South Australia* [2012] HCA 25.

128   For example, prior to *Kirk*, it appeared to be the case that, although there is a discretionary power to refuse all constitutional remedies (including prohibition), the same may not hold true for prohibition common law because the writ goes 'as of right' for patent excess of jurisdiction (i.e. where the error is apparent on the formal record): *Batterham v QSR Ltd* (2006) 225 CLR 237, 249–50 (Gleeson CJ, Gummow, Hayne, Callinan and Crennan JJ), citing *R v Australian Stevedoring Industry Board; Ex parte Melbourne Stevedoring Co Pty Ltd* (1953) 88 CLR 100, 118–19. This aspect of *Batterham* was accepted recently in *Meriton Apartments Pty Ltd v Industrial Court of New South Wales* (2011) 284 ALR 130, 147, without any reference to whether this difference in approach is appropriate or justified.

129   Though the remedial flexibility of the *ADJR Act* is no reason to refuse certiorari and the constitutional writs: *Lansen v Minister for Environment and Heritage* (2008) 174 FCR 14, 53. '[F]ollowing a decision of an appellate body, judicial review proceedings may not be brought in respect of the original decision'—though whether relief is available against the original decision-maker will depend upon the nature of the error and the statutory scheme: *Vitaz v Westfarm (NSW) Pty Ltd* [2011] NSWCA 254 [24], [53].

130   See, e.g., *SZBYR v Minister for Immigration and Citizenship* [2007] 235 ALR 609, [29]. The prematurity of an application may also be relevant, particularly in relation to prohibition where it is sometimes thought that a court or tribunal should have the opportunity to rule on its own jurisdictional limits before the involvement of the courts.

131   See, e.g., *SZGME v Minister for Immigration and Citizenship* (2008) 168 FCR 487, 502–3.

132   On these factors, see generally *R v Commonwealth Court of Conciliation and Arbitration; Ex parte Ozone Theatres (Aust) Ltd* (1949) 78 CLR 389, 400. Aronson, Dyer and Groves, n 32 above, comprehensively discuss the cases on the exercise of the discretion in relation to each of the remedies: 826–31(certiorari and prohibition); 846–7 (mandamus); 910–3 (declaration); 949–51 (injunction).

133   *Re Minister for Immigration and Multicultural Affairs; Ex parte Miah* (2001) 206 CLR 57, 103.

134   See, e.g., *JJ Richards & Sons Pty Ltd v Fair Work Australia* [2012] FCAFC 53.

the ground of review is breach of procedural fairness, a remedy will be denied only where a fair hearing could not possibly have altered the ultimate decision.[135]

4.7 The idea of invalidity and the importance of context

So far in this chapter the distinctions between jurisdictional and non-jurisdictional errors, ultra vires and intra vires decisions, and voidness and voidability have been discussed primarily in terms of the consequences of the various judicial review remedies—that is, whether the particular remedy retrospectively or prospectively quashes the challenged decision. As we have seen, an ultra vires decision—one affected by jurisdictional error and which is retrospectively invalid—is a nullity, 'in law … no decision at all'.[136] This principle is sometimes referred to as the 'absolute theory of invalidity', because its logical corollary seems to be that a void decision can have no legal effects: how can a legal nothing, a nullity, have any legal effects?

However, it is recognised that the absolute theory of invalidity can have some surprising and unacceptable consequences and, despite judicial rhetoric to the contrary, it is not the case that a void decision can have no legal effects. So, for instance, by and large courts have rejected the ridiculous proposition that, because a void decision never exists, it cannot be the subject of an appeal or even an application for judicial review, because there is nothing to appeal against or review.[137] Nor is it necessarily the case that a void decision can simply be ignored. Until a court decides that a void decision is indeed retrospectively invalid, an affected person will ignore it at their peril.[138]

The basic point is that the legal status and effect of a void decision needs to be considered contextually. As it is sometimes put, invalidity is a relative, not an absolute, concept. We will discuss three contexts in which the legal status and effects of void decisions have been considered. Although the issues discussed are not directly about the availability of particular judicial review remedies (the topic of this chapter), they are conveniently dealt with at this point due to their connection with the idea of retrospective invalidity or nullity—an idea which we have seen is important to the availability of some judicial review remedies (that is, prohibition, mandamus and often certiorari).

4.7.1 Remaking administrative decisions

What happens when an administrative decision-maker believes a decision made is erroneous and should be changed? Can a new decision simply be substituted? Normally, once a decision is made decision-makers are *functus officio*, which means that they have exercised their function and their powers are spent. In that case, there may be a statutory right of appeal to another tribunal allowing the decision to be challenged. Additionally, in the absence of an effective 'privative clause' (Chapter 7) judicial review will be available. The principle of *functus officio* recognises that it is not the function of the original decision-maker

---

135   *Re Refugee Review Tribunal; Ex parte Aala* (2000) 204 CLR 82, 109. See also 5.2.5.1.

136   See *Minister for Immigration and Multicultural Affairs v Bhardwaj* (2002) 209 CLR 597, 615.

137   *Collector of Customs (NSW) v Brian Lawlor Automotive Pty Ltd* (1979) 24 ALR 307.

138   Cf 4.4.3. In *F Hoffmann-La Roche and Co AG v Secretary of State for Trade and Industry* [1975] AC 295 the House of Lords granted an injunction to enforce a prices order against a drug company which it was ignoring on the basis that it was retrospectively invalid.

to effectively usurp any appellate function, nor to undertake the judicial function of determining the legality of the decision. In general, it is wrong for an administrative decision-maker, having already exercised their function, to act as if the slate was clean by making a second decision on the same subject.

This principle, however, requires qualification. In *Bhardwaj*,[139] the Immigration Review Tribunal misplaced a fax advising that the applicant could not attend the hearing due to illness. In the absence of the applicant, the tribunal upheld a decision cancelling his visa. On discovering its administrative oversight, the tribunal scheduled a new hearing and, ultimately, reversed its decision. The minister sought judicial review of this second decision on the basis that the tribunal, having already exercised its statutory functions, lacked the power to make its second decision. The High Court accepted that the tribunal's initial decision denied the applicant a fair hearing and also failed to constitute a 'decision on review' as required by the *Migration Act*, both errors qualifying as jurisdictional errors. In these circumstances, it was held that the tribunal had not erred in remaking its decision because its first attempt had so completely misfired.

Some statements in *Bhardwaj* appear to accept that a void decision that could be retrospectively invalidated in judicial review proceedings can have no legal effects whatsoever. For instance, Gaudron and Gummow JJ say that a 'decision that involves jurisdictional error is a decision that lacks legal foundation and is properly regarded, in law, as no decision at all'. They detected a 'certain illogicality in the notion that, although a decision involves a jurisdictional error, the law requires that, until the decision is set aside, the rights of the individual to whom the decision relates are or, perhaps, are deemed to be other than as recognised by the law that will be applied if and when the decision is challenged'.[140]

Despite such statements, the judgments in *Bhardwaj* all appear to accept that the issue of whether or not a decision affected by error may be remade does not turn only on the question of whether or not a jurisdictional error is established. Even Gaudron and Gummow JJ accept that the legislation under which a decision is made may expressly or impliedly provide that a decision affected by a jurisdictional error can have some legal effect.[141] On this interpretation, the question is whether there is a legislative intention that a decision affected by jurisdictional error is, nonetheless, to be given a particular legal effect. Having said that, the emphatic language invoked in *Bhardwaj* does suggest that 'there is a very strong interpretative presumption of the ineffectiveness of jurisdictionally flawed administrative decisions'.[142]

In *Bhardwaj*, Gaudron and Gummow JJ concluded that where, in law, there was no decision at all, the decision-maker not only may perform their function again, but 'as a matter of strict legal principle, he or she is required to do so'.[143] Understandably, this has left administrative decision-makers wondering about their obligations to reconsider decisions allegedly compromised by jurisdictional error. However, in a case where the decision-maker insists that they have not acted on the basis of a jurisdictional error, the only way to resolve the dispute is through a judicial review application. The duty to reconsider may not, therefore, be of much practical significance. It is also the case that the question of whether there is a jurisdictional error is very often not self-evident. Thus, a decision-maker who remakes a decision on

---

139   *Minister for Immigration and Multicultural Affairs v Bhardwaj* (2002) 209 CLR 597.

140   Ibid, [51]. McHugh J agreed with this aspect of the judgment: [63]. See also *Plaintiff S157/2002 v Commonwealth* (2003) 211 CLR 476, 506.

141   As concluded by the Full Federal Court in *Jadwan Pty Ltd v Secretary, Department of Health and Aged Care* (2003) 145 FCR 1, 15. See also *SZKUO v Minister for Immigration and Citizenship* (2009) 180 FCR 438; *Minister for Immigration and Citizenship v Maman* (2012) 200 FCR 30, 44, [44].

142   Aronson, Dyer and Groves, n 32 above, 716. See also *Jadwan Pty Ltd v Secretary, Department of Health and Aged Care* (2003) 145 FCR 1, 16–7.

143   *Minister for Immigration and Multicultural Affairs v Bhardwaj* (2002) 209 CLR 597 [53].

the basis of a belief they have made such an error runs the risk that a court will find that any subsequent (remade) decision is invalid.[144] There is, we believe, wisdom in the AAT's view that it is appropriate for decisions to be reconsidered only if they are 'obviously wrong' or 'when the cause of error is some administrative or similar mistake'.[145]

4.7.2 'Collateral' challenges

Decisions may be challenged 'directly' or 'collaterally'. Judicial review is a way of challenging decisions directly: a person with standing (Chapter 6) makes an application for review to which the respondent is the decision-maker (or someone responsible for the decision-maker's conduct) and which may result in an order being made against the respondent. But decisions may also be 'challenged in proceedings whose primary object is not the setting aside or modification of that act or decision'.[146] Examples include cases where the liability of an official in a tort action depends upon whether otherwise unlawful conduct (for example, trespass) was authorised by statute; the guilt of a defendant in a criminal case depends upon the validity of the regulation under which they are charged (or on some action taken in pursuance of that regulation); and where the admissibility of evidence in a criminal trial depends in some way upon whether a warrant under which it was obtained was valid.[147] In situations such as these the validity of the administrative decision is incidental to the main issues. Although usage varies, the phrase 'collateral challenge' can be taken to refer to these sorts of cases.[148]

It may be thought that persons affected by government decisions should have the opportunity to challenge them in whatever court, and in whatever legal dispute, they happen to find themselves. If a decision or act is invalid and does not in law exist, then surely no court should act on any other basis. However, this strong 'rule of law' rationale for the availability of collateral challenge obscures policy arguments which pull in the opposite direction. At least where judicial review is readily available, it might be thought that administrative law issues are best dealt with by courts which have developed the relevant expertise rather than courts with little public law experience. This problem may be compounded in cases where the parties most directly affected by the challenged decision are not involved in the litigation.[149] As judicial review remedies are discretionary and their availability is subject to a variety of limitations, one may ask whether these limits should be capable of circumvention where decisions are challenged collaterally. And, finally, the effective operation of a particular statutory scheme might be compromised where affected persons are entitled to wait until being prosecuted before raising any objections to administrative decisions. The extent to which collateral challenges should be available is thus a matter of considerable debate and disagreement.

---

144   *Flaherty v Secretary, Department of Health and Ageing* (2010) 184 FCR 564 illustrates this possibility.

145   *Michael v Secretary, Department of Employment, Science and Training* (2006) 42 AAR 488, [17]. The AAT noted a number of practical problems which would face the tribunal were it to routinely reconsider its decisions when allegations of jurisdictional error were asserted by disappointed applicants: [10].

146   *Ousley v The Queen* (1997) 192 CLR 69, 99 (McHugh J).

147   This is not an exhaustive list. For other examples see A Rubinstein, *Jurisdiction and Illegality: A Study in Public Law* (Clarendon Press: Oxford, 1965), 39–46; M Aronson, 'Criteria for Restricting Collateral Challenge' (1998) 9 *Public Law Review* 237.

148   *Ousley v The Queen* (1997) 192 CLR 69, 99 (McHugh J).

149   For example, *Director of Public Prosecutions v Head* [1958] 1 QB 132 involved a prosecution for a crime of sex with a woman under the care of a mental health institution. The accused avoided prosecution on the basis that the order which committed the woman to the institution was invalid. The determination of the validity of the committal order proceeded in the absence of the woman and the Home Secretary who made the order.

The basic principle in Australia is that all administrative acts are open to collateral challenges in the absence of a legislative indication to the contrary.[150] As the legislature can expressly or impliedly indicate that collateral attack is not allowable, the policy questions concerning its appropriateness may be debated in the context of the interpretation of particular statutes. The grounds of review which may, in a collateral challenge, establish the invalidity of an administrative decision do not extend beyond those grounds which would establish that the decision-maker has exceeded their jurisdiction. This reflects the theory that a decision based upon an error within jurisdiction is valid, that is, not a nullity (4.4.3). In *Ousley*,[151] some members of the High Court appear to have assumed that grounds on which collateral challenges to the validity of a warrant during a criminal trial may succeed are confined to those jurisdictional errors which appear on the face of the warrant. The case has, however, been criticised on the basis that the policy questions relevant to the extent to which collateral challenge should be restricted were not adequately considered.[152]

4.7.3 Invalidity and privative clauses

The idea that invalid decisions are void and, in law, not decisions at all is part of a common judicial strategy to avoid the operation of 'privative clauses' (Chapter 7). Privative clauses typically state that 'decisions' or 'determinations' made under a particular piece of legislation are not to be reviewed or challenged in any court of law. For good measure, many privative clauses are even more specific, and state that each of the judicial review remedies is not available in relation to decisions made under the legislation.[153] In most circumstances, the intention behind a privative clause could not be clearer—the courts are not to review the specified decisions.

The standard judicial response to privative clauses is clearly articulated in *Anisminic Ltd v Foreign Compensation Commission*, where it was argued that it is not 'even reasonable' to think that a privative clause which excludes the review of a 'decision' is intended to exclude the review of a *purported* decision which is beyond the decision-maker's jurisdiction and, therefore, no decision at all.[154] As privative clauses typically exclude only review of 'decisions', they can have no effect where the alleged error goes to jurisdiction. On this approach, it is only judicial review of non-jurisdictional errors (that is, those made within jurisdiction) that is ousted. The irony, of course, is that, subject to the limited exception for certiorari for error of law on the face of the record, the prerogative writs were not available for non-jurisdictional errors in any event.

We return to the courts' interpretation of privative clauses in more detail elsewhere (Chapter 7). Here we merely note that the interpretation of privative clauses is another context in which the concept of retrospective invalidity has played an important role. The fact that a decision affected by a jurisdictional error is treated, in this context, as being 'no decision at all' does not, however, mean that the same logic applies in all contexts. As we have already emphasised, the legal effects of a decision which breaches the principles of administrative law must be assessed contextually.

---

150   *Attorney-General (Cth) v Breckler* (1999) 197 CLR 83, 131.

151   *Ousley v The Queen* (1997) 192 CLR 69.

152   Aronson, n 147 above. In *Gedeon v NSW Crime Commission* the High Court did not suggest any such restriction in relation to the challenge, in committal proceedings, of the validity of an 'authority' to, among other things, obtain evidence of criminal activity. But for the 'authority' the evidence may have been excluded in a criminal trial on the basis it was illegally obtained.

153   See, e.g., *Migration Act 1958* (Cth), s 474.

154   [1969] 2 AC 147, 170. This logic was also invoked in *Plaintiff S157/2002 v Commonwealth* (2003) 211 CLR 476 (see 7.2.2).

5

The Grounds of Judicial Review

5.1 Introduction

This chapter explains the grounds on which the acts or decisions of administrative decision-makers can be held to be unlawful or invalid.[1] Insofar as these grounds are the basis for questioning the lawfulness or legality of an administrative decision they necessarily establish a set of norms (which we will call 'administrative law norms') that apply to the exercise of 'administrative powers'.[2] If a decision-maker breaches an administrative law norm—that is, they make an error which establishes a ground of judicial review—a judicial review remedy may be available.[3]

5.1.1 Values and the grounds of review

It is clear that the overarching rationale of judicial review is to keep administrative decision-makers within the legal boundaries of their powers (3.2.1; 3.2.2). Whatever else the contestable notion of the 'rule of law' means, the Anglo-Australian common law tradition starts from the proposition that 'all claims of governmental power must be justified in law'.[4] When government purports to act or decide anything it must be able to point to some source of legal authority for what is done.

The grounds of judicial review flesh out this basic principle: not only must there be a source of legal authority, but government decisions must not be made in breach of an accepted administrative law norm. In this sense, the grounds of review can also be seen to reflect a number of abstract values, in addition to the basic principle of legality. Further values which are often said to underpin judicial review (and administrative law generally) include accountability, rationality, efficiency and the public interest,

---

1   A decision in breach of a ground of review may be unlawful even though the decision is not (retrospectively) invalid: 4.1.1 and 4.3.

2   In this chapter, 'administrative powers' is used as a short-hand for the exercise of powers which fall within the scope of judicial review.

3   The availability of particular remedies is discussed in Chapter 4.

4   M Elliott, *The Constitutional Foundations of Judicial Review* (Oxford: Hart Publishing, 2001), 100. For an illustration of this principle at work, see *A v Hayden (No 2)* (1984) 156 CLR 532.

fairness, the protection of rights, participation, transparency and impartiality.[5] However, although reference to such values may deepen our understanding of why particular results have been reached, they are too abstract to provide either judges or administrators with meaningful guidance about how to perform their respective decision-making roles. The grounds of review can thus be understood as expressing more concrete principles (which we are calling 'administrative law norms') designed to give substance to the values which ultimately underpin judicial review.

Although the grounds of review are less abstract than the values which ultimately justify judicial review, they nonetheless are best conceptualised as expressing principles or standards rather than clear-cut rules capable of straightforward application. This is to be expected given that the norms expressed by the grounds of judicial review are applicable to the performance of public functions across a wide range of government decision-making contexts. It is unlikely that hard and fast rules would be sufficiently flexible to perform this task. How well the established grounds of review provide norms or standards which are at least capable of guiding administrative conduct is something about which reasonable minds may well disagree. If, however, one concluded that the grounds of review completely failed to establish norms capable of providing some guidance to administrators and judges, then it would make little sense to attempt to write books which focus on the general principles of administrative law at all. We would perhaps be better served by books focusing on particular areas of interaction between the governors and the governed (for example, on immigration law, social security law and so on).

Various High Court judges have stated that judicial review should not allow courts to impose ideas about 'good administration' on the executive branch of government.[6] It is debatable, however, how literally such statements can or should be taken. Although it is clear that the overarching rationale of judicial review is to keep administrators within the legal boundaries of their powers, the contours of these boundaries can be difficult to discern for a number of reasons. First, the question of whether these legal limits have been exceeded is often far from simple. Where administrative powers are conferred by statute, the meaning of the statute may be unclear due to the 'open texture' of the legislation's language, structure and purposes.[7] Judicially developed principles of statutory interpretation can, in some cases, help to clarify statutory meaning. For example, it is accepted that legislation will not be read to allow a government official to encroach upon the liberty of the person, deprive a person of their property rights, or impose a tax, unless a contrary intention is expressed with unmistakeable and unambiguous language.[8]

Where statutory powers are not coercive, the courts are often prepared to imply 'incidental powers' to allow administrators to do anything which is reasonably necessary to make the exercise of their express powers effective. But such principles of interpretation cannot cure the problem of statutory uncertainty as they are also subject to uncertainties of meaning and application (because of their own 'open texture').[9] It should also be noted that the limits of non-statutory (common law) executive powers,

---

5   See, e.g., D Woodhouse, *In Pursuit of Good Administration* (Oxford: Clarendon Press, 1997), Chs 7–8 and P Cane, 'Theory and Values in Public Law' in P Craig and R Rawlings (eds), *Law and Administration in Europe: Essays in Honour of Carol Harlow* (Oxford: Oxford University Press, 2003).

6   See, e.g., *Re Minister for Immigration and Multicultural Affairs; Ex parte Lam* (2003) 214 CLR 1, 13 (Gleeson CJ), *Minister for Immigration and Multicultural Affairs v Bhardwaj* (2002) 209 CLR 597, 603 (Hayne J), *NAIS v Minister for Immigration and Multicultural and Indigenous Affairs* (2005) 228 CLR 470, 175 (Gummow J). Cf *Re Minister for Immigration and Multicultural Affairs; Ex parte S20/2002* (2003) 198 ALR 59, 98 [170] (Kirby J).

7   H L A Hart, *The Concept of Law* (Oxford: Clarendon Press, 1961), 128.

8   See, e.g., *Coco v The Queen* (1994) 179 CLR 427. See also 5.2.2.2 and 5.4.6.

9   They can also conflict with one another: see, e.g., K N Llewellyn, 'Remarks on the Theory of Appellate Decision and the Rules or Canons About How Statutes Are to Be Construed' (1950) 3 *Vanderbilt Law Review* 395.

such as prerogative powers, are arguably subject to even greater uncertainties—there may be disputes about the existence of a particular power, about whether and how such powers can be adapted to novel circumstances, and about how they interact with statutory powers (see 3.6.2.2).

Second, although the administrative law norms expressed by the grounds of review are less abstract than the values which underpin judicial review, they remain sufficiently abstract to be capable of different interpretations and applications. Moreover, the reality is that the legal boundaries of administrative powers are necessarily determined by the complicated interaction between the statutory limitations on the exercise of particular powers and common law doctrine (that is, the grounds of review), as applied to the facts of an individual case. In short, the difficulties of statutory interpretation and the difficulties of applying the 'grounds of review' compound one another.

For these reasons, we should be somewhat sceptical of the claim that the application of the general norms constituted by the grounds of review can be completely divorced from notions of 'good administration'. To be sure, the norms applied in judicial review cases are only a subset of the principles and criteria of good administration. It is certainly true that not all examples of maladministration will also fall within a ground for judicial review. This partly explains why the parliament has created other accountability mechanisms such as merits review tribunals (Chapter 8) and the ombudsman (Chapter 9). But if the law does not always clearly determine the boundaries of administrative powers, then an obvious set of ideas to which judges (consciously or unconsciously) are likely to turn are concepts of good administration.

Perhaps, however, we are getting ahead of ourselves: the extent to which the grounds of review prevent judges from having recourse to norms or assumptions about 'good administration' is a question best considered after the operation of those grounds has been explained. For now, we can conclude that the purpose of the grounds of review is both to give more concrete substance to the very abstract values which underpin judicial review and also to facilitate the application of those more abstract values to particular facts and statutory contexts.

5.1.2 Identifying the grounds of review

As explained in Chapter 4, the identification of the grounds of judicial review depends upon which remedial model is applicable. Under the 'common law remedial model'[10] the key question is whether an error which gives rise to a particular ground of review can be classified as a jurisdictional error because some remedies (prohibition and mandamus) only issue for such errors. If it cannot, the error may still attract a remedy (that is, certiorari) if it is an 'error of law apparent on the face of the record' (see 4.1.1).[11] If the error results in an 'unlawful' but not 'invalid' decision (because it does not amount to a jurisdictional error but nonetheless involves a breach of an administrative law norm or a statutory provision), then declaratory and injunctive relief may be available (4.3).

In contrast, the *ADJR Act* identifies 15 discrete grounds of review which were largely thought to reflect the common law.[12] Although it is often said that the grounds of review in the *ADJR Act* were intended

---

10   This model most obviously applies in the context of the supervisory review jurisdiction of the state Supreme Courts, and review under s 75(v) of the Constitution: 4.3.

11   As certiorari is not a named 'constitutional writ' it is not available for non-jurisdictional error under s 75(v): 4.5.3.

12   This count does not include (1) two listed grounds which allow for the identification of new grounds of review (ss 5(1)(j) and 5(2)(j)); or (2) the ground of improper exercise of power mentioned in s 5(1)(e), as its content is specified by the grounds listed in s 5(2)(a)–(j). To date, the grounds inviting the recognition of new heads of review have not been utilised by the courts.

(subject to a couple of clear exceptions) to 'codify' the common law, the Act had important effects on thinking about the grounds of review. Most significantly, the Act reversed the priority given to the availability of a remedy, placing the availability of a named ground of review at the heart of the legal analysis.

An advantage often attributed to the *ADJR Act* is that the detailed specification of the grounds of review has an educative effect (both for administrators and lawyers), providing 'a much clearer indication than previously of the challenges that can be made to administrative decisions and thus some guidance as to the principles administrators should follow'.[13] On the other hand, the *ADJR Act* has been accused of introducing an unfortunate level of technicality into discussion of the grounds of judicial review.[14] There is no question that the *scope* of application of the *ADJR Act* has become a legal minefield (3.5.1). However, the charge that the *ADJR Act* has produced unwarranted technicality into the doctrinal development of the grounds of review is more difficult to sustain. It is true that the meaning of the 'no evidence' ground of review in the *ADJR Act* (ss 5(1)(h) and s 5(3)) has been the subject of close textual analysis (5.4.3.2). However, in relation to most other grounds—which are defined using less precise and detailed language than is the case in relation to the 'no evidence' ground—there is much less discussion in the cases about the meaning of the terms of the Act itself.[15] One reason why the courts have been able to avoid a greater level of technicality in the interpretation of the grounds is that, although applicants must plead discrete grounds of review, it is often possible to legitimately characterise a particular error in terms of more than one ground. As the courts have not insisted that the grounds cover mutually exclusive territory, it has usually been unnecessary for precise boundaries between the grounds to be drawn.

Another criticism of the *ADJR Act* is that the articulation of the deeper values which underpin judicial review has been stymied by a focus on the particular grounds listed in the legislation. Defenders of the *ADJR Act* have a number of responses. One is to emphasise its educative benefits. We suggested above that overly abstract principles—such as the rule of law, participation, or fairness—have limited capacity to guide administrative (and judicial) decisions-makers. A further response is to question the appropriateness and utility of encouraging judges to embark on the politically charged task of articulating and systematising the bedrock principles which justify judicial review.[16] Judges do not necessarily make good political philosophers.[17]

5.1.3 The legal basis of the grounds of review

It is clear that the *ADJR Act* grounds of review can only be applied in relation to the exercise of statutory powers—more precisely, where the impugned administrative decision or conduct is 'made under an enactment' (3.5.1.4). This means that the non-statutory powers—that is, the common law or prerogative powers of executive government (3.6.2.2)—are not reviewable under the Act. Where the *ADJR Act* does apply, the legal basis for applying its grounds of review to reviewable decisions is the Act itself.

---

13   D Woodhouse, *In Pursuit of Good Administration* (Oxford: Clarendon Press, 1997), 201.

14   T H Jones, 'Judicial Review and Codification' (2000) 20 *Legal Studies* 517.

15   See, e.g., *Kioa v West* (1985) 159 CLR 550, 576 (Mason J). Review on the ground that 'procedures required by law to be observed in connection with the making of the decision were not observed' (*ADJR Act*, s 5(1)(b)) may also invite close textual analysis: 5.2.5.2. It is also worth noting that attempts in the *Migration Act 1958* (Cth) to codify, more prescriptively, the common law rules of procedural fairness have led to a level of unhelpful technicality: see 5.2.2.2.

16   M Aronson, 'Is the ADJR Act Hampering the Development of Australian Administrative Law?' (2004) 15 *Public Law Review* 202, 216–19. It may be that there is more likely to be an 'overlapping consensus' on mid-level principles of review than on their ultimate justification.

17   The reverse is also true!

The legal basis for the grounds of review in the common law and constitutional review regimes is less clear. On one view, the legal authority of the grounds of review is derived from judicial power, which is to say that the obligations imposed on administrators are common law obligations. An alternative view is that the authority of the grounds of review is derived from parliament. As the grounds of review (or even the possibility of review) are rarely stated expressly in the legislation which confers powers on administrators, this approach is based on imputing to parliament an intention to make compliance with administrative law norms a condition of the lawful exercise of power.

Although individual High Court judges have expressed their preference for one or other of these theories, no clear winner has been pronounced. Despite the fact that for some time there have been increasing indications that the implied intention approach may prevail,[18] the High Court has recently indicated that the question may remain 'open'.[19] This uncertainty can persist because both approaches accept that the availability of a ground of review will yield to a sufficiently clear statutory expression to the contrary.[20] Thus, in many cases, nothing will turn on which approach is accepted. However, the difference of approach to the legal foundation of the grounds of review might be of some practical importance for two reasons. First, acceptance of the 'common law' approach might mean that the grounds of review are less likely to be *impliedly* excluded by a statute or, perhaps, that the grounds will be applied in a more rigorous manner.[21] Second, the 'statutory implication' approach does not account for the reviewability (at common law and under s 75(v)) of non-statutory powers (3.6.2.2).[22] Unless the High Court decided that judicial review is never available to examine the exercise of non-statutory powers,[23] 'statutory implication' cannot be a complete theory of the legal foundations of judicial review—even if it is accepted as the appropriate foundation for the review of statutory powers.

Regardless of which approach is preferred, there can be no denying the extensive and creative role that judges have played in developing the grounds of judicial review. And, as noted above, the key question in most cases will be how the grounds of review interact with the statute in the context of particular cases.

5.1.4 Classifying the grounds of review

There are many different ways of classifying the grounds of review. Our discussion of the grounds classifies them into three general categories. First, we consider *procedural* grounds of review. These grounds impose on decision-makers requirements which focus on the conduct of the decision-maker, rather than the decision-maker's reasoning processes or the content of the decision reached. Second, we consider a number of grounds which relate to the reasoning processes of decision-making. These are referred to as *reasoning process* grounds. Finally, we collect together a number of grounds which,

---

18   M Aronson, 'Private Bodies, Public Power and Soft Law in the High Court' (2007) 35 *Federal Law Review* 1, 2; *Saeed v Minister for Immigration and Citizenship* (2010) 241 CLR 252, 258.

19   *Plaintiff M61/2010E v Commonwealth* (2010) 243 CLR 319, 352.

20   Subject to any constitutional limitations applicable in relation to review under s 75(v) of the Constitution. In *Saeed v Minister for Immigration and Citizenship* (2010) 241 CLR 252, the High Court avoided directly responding to this question—the court appeared to assume the correctness of the orthodox view that procedural fairness principles can be excluded by unmistakable and unambiguous language.

21   Cf B Dyer, 'Legitimate Expectations in Procedural Fairness after *Lam*' in M Groves (ed), *Law and Government in Australia* (Annandale NSW: Federation Press, 2005), 197.

22   For an example of the problem, see *Stewart v Ronalds* (2009) 76 NSWLR 99.

23   This would be a surprising result given the trends discussed at 3.6.2.2 and 3.6.2.3.

in one way or another, relate to the decision itself, that is, what was actually decided as opposed to the procedures or reasoning processes through which the decision was reached. We refer to these—somewhat awkwardly, we admit—as *decisional* grounds. No classificatory scheme for the grounds of review is without difficulties, but we hope this classification illuminates the various ways in which different facets of decision-making processes can give rise to unlawful administrative decisions.

5.2 Procedural grounds

Judicial review is often said to be about the procedures by which a decision was made, as opposed to the substance of the decision. Although this generalisation about the grounds of judicial review is misleading (3.2.1), there is no denying the importance the common law has always attached to procedural propriety. In this section, we examine the so-called rules of natural justice or procedural fairness—terms which in modern Australian law are used interchangeably. The *ADJR Act* enables review for breach of the 'rules of natural justice', but does not purport to change the applicable common law principles.[24]

In addition to the common law rules of procedural fairness, the legislature can, and often does, lay down statutory rules of procedure. Such rules raise two broad issues. First, there are complex questions concerning how statutory procedures interact with the common law rules of procedural fairness. Should statutory rules be treated as displacing or modifying the common law procedural obligations? The second issue concerns the consequences of a breach of statutory procedural rules. Subject to a tightly confined exception (5.2.5.1), breach of the common law rules of procedural fairness leads to (retrospective) invalidity. In other words, such a breach constitutes a jurisdictional error. Although breach of statutory rules can also render a decision invalid, we will discover that this is not necessarily the case.

5.2.1 The rules of procedural fairness

There are two basic 'rules'. The 'rule against bias' requires that decision-makers neither be, nor appear to be, biased. Thus a person should neither be, nor appear to be, judge in their own cause. The 'fair hearing rule' requires that a person who may be adversely affected by a decision be given an opportunity to 'put their case' prior to the decision being made.

There are some difficulties in categorising the 'actual' bias rule as a procedural norm. Actual bias is available only if the decision-maker's mind is closed and not open to persuasion.[25] Thus the error involved does not concern the conduct of any hearing, but is directly focused on the decision-maker's reasoning processes. For this reason, it makes better conceptual sense to classify actual bias cases as a 'reasoning process' error (see 5.3), such as failure to consider a relevant consideration, taking account of an irrelevant consideration, acting for an improper purpose, or the inflexible application of policy.[26] In contrast, the rule against 'apparent' bias is broadly about how the proceedings have been conducted—that is, whether anything said or done has given rise to a reasonable apprehension of bias. To the extent

---

24   *Kioa v West* (1985) 159 CLR 550, 576–7 (Mason J).

25   See, e.g., *Minister for Immigration and Multicultural Affairs v Jia Legeng* (2001) 205 CLR 507, 519–20.

26   There may be strategic reasons for framing the argument in terms of actual bias as courts are loathe to remit decisions invalidated for actual bias to the original (i.e. biased) decision-maker.

that it is outward *appearances* that matter, not facts about how the decision-maker reasoned, the rule against apparent bias has a stronger case for categorisation as imposing a procedural norm. A similar issue of categorisation arises in relation to the accepted rule that a fair hearing will be compromised if the decision-maker fails to deal with a significant aspect of a claim, at least where the facts on which it rests are established or are not in dispute.[27] Although the High Court has characterised such an error as a denial of procedural fairness,[28] there is force in the suggestion that a better approach is to treat such an error as compromising the reasoning process of the decision-maker insofar as it involves a failure to take into account a relevant consideration (see 5.3.1).[29]

The right to be heard by a decision-maker who appears to be impartial secures a level of participation in administrative decision-making and is basic to most theories of procedural justice. There are two broad ways to justify the participation secured by the rules of procedural fairness. The first highlights *instrumental* justifications for allowing participation: good procedure promotes good decision-making. For example, the fair hearing rule increases the chance that decision-makers will receive all the relevant information by enabling affected persons to be heard. Because seemingly 'open and shut cases' are not always as they appear, judges normally apply the fair hearing rule even when it *appears* unlikely that a hearing would have changed the outcome. But in theory the instrumental case for fair procedures can cut both ways; it may also indicate that further procedures are not required where they would (probably) not have changed the outcome (see further 5.2.5.1).

'Instrumental' justifications for fair procedures can be contrasted with 'intrinsic' or 'non-instrumental' justifications. Intrinsic justifications argue that the fair procedures ought to be followed regardless of whether they increase the chances of reaching better or correct outcomes.[30] For example, allowing individual participation may be justified as enhancing human dignity and self respect.[31] The rules of fair procedure can thus be understood as serving an expressive purpose—that is, to embody and promote certain values. This expressive purpose can be fulfilled independently of whether the rules contribute to the correct or preferable decisions being reached.

Rules of fair procedure may also be justified on the basis that they are part of a general commitment to keep the governors accountable to the governed, by enabling affected people to participate and be heard on decisions affecting them. Social science research suggests that people are more likely to accept the outcomes of decisions (and to obey legally authorised decisions) if they believe fair processes have been followed.[32] Being able to complain (for example, by way of a judicial review application) about a breach of the rules of procedural fairness may also be considered an aspect of this general commitment to accountable decision-making. Again, whether or not this commitment actually promotes 'better' decisions in individual cases is irrelevant to the persuasiveness of this justification for fair procedures.

---

27   For a recent application of the principle, see *SZQJH v Minister for Immigration and Citizenship* (2012) 126 ALD 488.

28   *Dranichnikov v Minister for Immigration & Multicultural Affairs* (2003) 197 ALR 389, 394; see also *Plaintiff M61/2010E v Commonwealth* (2010) 243 CLR 319, 35 and *Minister for Immigration v SZJSS* (2010 243 CLR 164, 177).

29   Which can be described as 'the essential elements of the applicant's claim': John Basten, 'The Supervisory Jurisdiction of the Supreme Courts' (2011) 85 *Australian Law Journal* 273, 288. A requirement to consider the essential elements of an applicant's claim could be implied into most statutory grants of power.

30   Often the imposition of particular procedures is justified by reference to both rationales: e.g. *John v Rees* [1970] 1 Ch 345, 402.

31   J Mashaw, 'Administrative Due Process: The Quest for a Dignitary Theory' (1981) 61 *Buffalo Law Review* 885.

32   T Tyler, *Why People Obey the Law*, 2nd edn (Princeton, NJ: Princeton University Press, 2006).

5.2.2 The fair hearing rule

In response to concerns that administrative processes may become 'over-judicialised', the courts have looked for ways to limit the reach of the fair hearing rule. For a long period, the rule only applied to decision-makers obliged to 'act judicially', and to decisions which affected legal rights. *Kioa v West*[33] changed the focus of the law. Although the 'threshold question' (that is, whether the rule applies) is of continuing relevance (5.2.2.1), it is equally clear that the 'content question' (5.2.2.3) (that is, what the rule requires in the circumstances of a particular case) is the 'critical question in most cases'.[34]

5.2.2.1 When does the fair hearing rule apply?
The 'threshold' question

Mason J is widely credited with the 'leading judgment' in *Kioa*, though Brennan J's judgment has also been extensively cited. In any event, the judgments can be read in such a way that little of practical importance separates them.

According to Mason J, an administrative decision which affects an individual's 'rights, interests or legitimate expectations' will attract 'a common law duty' to accord procedural fairness. This duty is subject to two clear limitations. The first of these is obvious: as a common law duty it is 'subject ... to the clear manifestation of a contrary statutory intention'. Second, the duty arises *only* if the individual's rights, interests or legitimate expectations are affected in 'a direct and immediate way'.[35]

Mason J's reference to 'legitimate expectation' signalled an intention to adopt an expansive approach to the scope of application of the fair hearing rule. Prior to *Kioa*, the concept of legitimate expectation had been developed as a way to expand the interests protected by procedural fairness beyond a narrow conception of 'legal rights'. Although the phrase 'legitimate expectation' has not been used consistently, the basic idea is that some expectations (in Australia, these are said to be 'reasonable' expectations)[36] should not be disappointed without first giving an affected person a hearing. Understood this way, a legitimate expectation is a particular sort of interest which is protected by the rules of procedural fairness. For example, a legitimate expectation may arise where a representation has been made. Such representations may take a number of forms; for example, specific undertakings,[37] policy statements[38] and a course of consistent conduct[39] have all been held to give rise to a legitimate expectation. A person may have a legitimate expectation where they seek the renewal of some benefit (for example, a licence) in circumstances where they have no right to succeed but something more than a mere hope of success.[40]

In our view it is not necessary to explore the precise meaning of legitimate expectation by examining such examples in further detail. This is because recent cases have indicated that the hearing rule now

---

33   *Kioa v West (1985) 159 CLR 550.*

34   Ibid, 585.

35   Ibid, 584.

36   An applicant need not show that they consciously held the expectation. See, e.g., *Re Minister for Immigration and Multicultural and Indigenous Affairs; Ex parte Lam* (2003) 214 CLR 1, 20, 31.

37   See, e.g., *Attorney-General of Hong Kong v Ng Yue Shiu* [1983] 2 AC 629.

38   See, e.g., *Haoucher v Minister for Immigration and Ethnic Affairs* (1990) 169 CLR 648.

39   See, e.g., *Council of Civil Service Unions v Minister for the Civil Service* [1985] 1 AC 374.

40   See, e.g., *FAI Insurances Ltd v Winneke* (1982) 151 CLR 342.

applies to decisions adversely affecting such a wide variety of 'interests' that the notion of legitimate expectation is redundant.[41] As McHugh and Gummow JJ concluded in *Lam*, 'the rational development of this branch of the law requires acceptance of the view that the rules of procedural fairness are presumptively applicable to administrative decisions'.[42] In essence, this conclusion accepts the logic of Brennan J's approach in *Kioa* to the question of which interests are protected by procedural fairness. Brennan J argued that 'it ill accords with modern legislative intention to restrict the application of the presumption [of procedural fairness] to statutory powers which affect only' the sorts of interests the common law has traditionally protected, such as liberty, property and reputation. For this reason, it is not the kind of interest that matters (that is, whether it can be characterised as a right or legitimate expectation or whatever), but the manner in which an individual's interests are 'apt to be affected that is important'.[43] If an individual is apt to be affected in a way 'substantially different' from the 'public at large', the individual is entitled to a fair hearing.[44]

Though it may be accepted that the concept of legitimate expectation no longer plays a meaningful role in answering the threshold question, it may nonetheless have a continuing role in the determination of 'the practical content of the requirements of fairness in a particular case' (see further 5.2.2.4).[45] It also appears that in cases where there is no obligation even to consider whether a discretionary power should be exercised, the courts may attend more closely to identifying what rights and interests are directly affected.[46]

These developments have led some to question whether the 'threshold question' has become redundant.[47] However, although it is useful to start from the proposition that 'the rules of procedural fairness are presumptively applicable' to administrative actions,[48] it must also be accepted that this general presumption is subject to statutory abrogation (5.2.2.2) and *only* applies in relation to decisions which are apt to affect individual interests in a direct and immediate way.

What does it mean to say that a decision is apt to affect individual interests in a 'direct and immediate' way or (as Brennan J put it) a way 'substantially different' from the manner in which the 'public at large' is affected? Brennan J held that a person is affected in a substantially different way if 'relevant

---

41   For one example of an expansive approach to the nature of the 'interests' protected by procedural fairness, see *Ainsworth v Criminal Justice Commission* (1992) 175 CLR 564 (see 4.5.1.1).

42   *Re Minister for Immigration and Multicultural and Indigenous Affairs; Ex parte Lam* (2003) 214 CLR 1, 27 (McHugh and Gummow J) quoting *Minister for Immigration and Ethnic Affairs v Teoh* (1994) 183 CLR 273, 311–12 (McHugh J). Callinan J also endorses the same passage from *Teoh*: 48–9. Cf 123 (Gleeson CJ) and 37–6 (Hayne J) who are less clear about the redundancy of the notion of legitimate expectation in the context of the threshold test. See also the statement of principle in *Saeed v Minister for Immigration and Citizenship* (2010) 241 CLR 252, 258, which involved an offshore visa applicant.

43   *Kioa v West* (1985) 159 CLR 550, 619.

44   Ibid. Brennan J also held that procedural fairness obligations arise as a matter of statutory implication as opposed to being common law obligations. The differing approaches of Mason J and Brennan J in *Kioa* to the legal basis of procedural fairness obligations have formed the focus, in Australia, of the 'common law' versus 'statutory implication' debate described at 5.1.3.

45   *Re Minister for Immigration and Multicultural and Indigenous Affairs; Ex parte Lam* (2003) 214 CLR 1, 12 (Gleeson CJ). See also 28, 34 (McHugh and Gummow JJ).

46   See e.g. *Plaintiff M61/2010E v Commonwealth* (2010) 243 CLR 319, 353. The court emphasised that a decision to consider the refugee status of the plaintiff had the effect of prolonging their detention and, thus, affected their 'right to liberty'. The extent, if any, that the approach taken in this case undercuts the logic of Brennan J's focus on the manner in which individuals are apt to be affected rather than the nature of the affected interest is unclear.

47   See, e.g., *Haoucher v Minister for Immigration and Ethnic Affairs* (1990) 169 CLR 648, 653 (Deane J). See M Aronson, B Dyer and M Groves, *Judicial Review of Administrative Action*, 4th edn (Pyrmont, NSW: Lawbook Co, 2009), 423–4.

48   *Minister for Immigration and Ethnic Affairs v Teoh* (1995) 183 CLR 273, 311 (McHugh J).

considerations' (see 5.3.1) relate to the individual.[49] Mason J gave the examples of the imposition of a rate or a general charge for services as decisions which would not affect individuals in a direct or immediate way. One reason often given for not imposing procedural fairness obligations in relation to general policy decisions affecting the public or a section of it in an undifferentiated way is that it would not be feasible or practical for all people affected by such legislative decisions to be heard.[50] This is why the hearing rule does not apply to the process of making delegated legislation.[51] A possible response to such pragmatic objections to the imposition of procedural fairness is that the courts could develop a duty to 'consult', inviting participation without requiring individual hearings.

5.2.2.2 Statutory exclusion of the hearing rule

In theory, parliament may exclude procedural fairness obligations. In practice, establishing their exclusion may be difficult.

The fundamental importance attributed to a fair hearing means that 'plain words of necessary intendment' are required to exclude procedural fairness obligations;[52] 'indirect references, uncertain inferences or equivocal considerations' will not be sufficient.[53] This presumption is an instance of the broader principle that courts will not 'impute to the legislature an intention to abrogate or curtail fundamental rights or freedoms unless such an intention is clearly manifested by unmistakable and unambiguous language'.[54] Although the possibility that a statute may impliedly (as opposed to expressly) exclude procedural fairness has not been precluded, the presumption is very difficult to dislodge, especially where important individual interests are affected.[55]

Miah's case provides an interesting case study[56]—in part because it elicited a legislative response which led to further litigation. It was argued that amendments to the Migration Act 1958 (Cth) evinced an intention to exclude the hearing rule. The amendments specified statutory procedures (which were designated as a 'code' of procedure) in considerable detail. The explanatory memorandum left little doubt that the purpose of the Bill introducing the amendments was to replace 'the uncodified principles of natural justice with clear and fixed procedures which are drawn from those principles'.[57] According to the dissent of Gleeson CJ and Hayne J, the cumulative effect of these factors, along with a statutory right of appeal (merits review), manifested a legislative intention to 'prescribe comprehensively' for the fair hearing rule (thus excluding the imposition of additional common law obligations).[58]

---

49 *Kioa v West* (1985) 159 CLR 550, 619. Aronson, Dyer and Groves, n 47 above, 451–65 argue that Brennan J's approach should be slightly modified so that there is an obligation to afford a hearing when (1) an individual's interests must be considered, which is to say that they constitute a mandatory relevant consideration (see 5.3.1); or (2) where the decision-maker does in fact consider an individual's interests, even though they are under no legal duty to do so.

50 See for example *Ozepulse Pty Ltd v Minister for Agriculture Fisheries and Forestry* (2007) 163 FCR 562, 577.

51 See G J Craven, 'Legislative Action by Subordinate Authorities and the Requirement of a Fair Hearing' (1988) 16 *Melbourne University Law Review* 569, 570.

52 *Annetts v McCann* (1990) 170 CLR 596, 598.

53 *Commissioner of Police v Tanos* (1958) 98 CLR 383, 396.

54 *Plaintiff S157 v Commonwealth* (2003) 211 CLR 476, 492; *Saeed v Minister for Immigration and Citizenship* (2010) 241 CLR 252, 271.

55 For a recent example of an 'unequivocal' expression of an intent to exclude procedural fairness obligations being judicially accepted, see *Seiffert v The Prisoners' Review Board* [2011] WASCA 148.

56 *Re Minister for Immigration and Multicultural Affairs; Ex parte Miah* (2001) 206 CLR 57.

57 Explanatory Memorandum, Migration Reform Bill 1992 (Cth), [51].

58 *Re Minister for Immigration and Multicultural Affairs; Ex parte Miah* (2001) 206 CLR 57, 74 (Gleeson CJ and Hayne J).

The majority judges offered a number of counter-arguments. The fact that the statutory procedures were labelled a 'code' was not determinative. The silence of the code on the rule against bias made the conclusion that all aspects of common law procedural fairness were excluded unlikely. Nor, it was argued, should the express inclusion of some procedures in the 'code' indicate that all other procedural rules were excluded[59]—particularly since the statutory procedures included 'permissive or facultative' provisions which allowed the decision-maker to seek further information.[60] Although it was conceded that a statutory right to appeal *may* 'exclude or limit the rules of natural justice',[61] this was highly unlikely if 'an applicant's life or liberty' was put at risk by a decision.[62]

The judicial resistance to statutory attempts to exclude procedural fairness obligations (evidenced in *Miah*) needs to be considered in light of the acceptance that the statutory context is an important determinant of the content of those obligations in particular cases. What obligations are imposed on decision-makers 'depends to a large extent on construction of the statute', and this, in turn, reflects 'the nature of the inquiry, the subject matter, and the rules under which the decision-maker is acting'.[63] Courts can thus ensure that statutory objectives are not frustrated by excessive procedural safeguards without denying the applicability of the rules of procedural fairness.

The decision in *Miah* left unanswered many questions about how the *Migration Act*'s 'highly prescriptive code of procedures'[64] would be applied. An underlying concern has been that the common law's flexibility in determining the content of the hearing rule may be lost where detailed statutory procedures are preferred. This possibility is well illustrated by *SAAP*, where the High Court held that breach of a statutory rule that required disclosure of certain information in writing was a 'jurisdictional error'.[65] This meant that non-compliance with the requirement would invalidate the decision, *regardless* of whether any unfairness could be established.[66] In *SAAP*, the relevant information was not disclosed in writing but it had been orally disclosed. For this reason, the trial judge concluded that there had, in the circumstances of the case, been a fair opportunity to comment on the information. But since *SAAP*, other cases have complicated matters, as it seems not all breaches of the *Migration Act*'s procedural code will result in invalidity. In *SZIZO* a breach of a statutory requirement—which required that correspondence be addressed to the 'authorised recipient' if the applicant had nominated one—did not cause any unfairness because all affected people attended the tribunal hearing.[67] Breach of the requirement was held not to amount to a jurisdictional error. According to the High Court, the requirement related only to 'manner' of giving notice and to that extent was not necessarily of significance. At least in circumstances where the applicant suffered no procedural unfairness it should not therefore be concluded that the legislature would have intended that breach of the requirement invalidate the decision (see further 5.2.5.2).

---

59   Reliance on the *expressio unius* maxim of interpretation (i.e. the expression of one excludes the inclusion of another) 'can seldom, if ever, be enough to exclude the common law rules of natural justice': ibid, 96 quoting *Baba v Parole Board (NSW)* (1986) 5 NSWLR 338, 349.

60   *Re Minister for Immigration and Multicultural Affairs; Ex parte Miah* (2001) 206 CLR 57, 85.

61   A number of factors may indicate that an appeal right excludes or limits procedural fairness. For the list, see ibid, 99–102 (McHugh J).

62   Ibid, 102 (McHugh J), 114–15 (Kirby J).

63   *Kioa v West* (1985) 159 CLR 550, 584–5 (Mason J). See also 5.2.2.3.

64   *SZEEU v Minister for Immigration and Multicultural and Indigenous Affairs* (2006) 150 FCR 214, 254 [174].

65   *SAAP v Minister for Immigration and Multicultural and Indigenous Affairs* (2005) 215 ALR 162.

66   Breach of a statutory procedure does not always constitute a jurisdictional error or undermine the legal effectiveness or 'validity' of a decision: see *Project Blue Sky v Australian Broadcasting Authority* (1998) 194 CLR 355 (see 4.3).

67   *Minister for Immigration and Citizenship v SZIZO* (2009) 238 CLR 627.

How this provision was distinguished from the requirement considered in *SAAP* that notice be communicated in a particular form (that is, writing) is not, however, immediately apparent.[68] Given that the introduction of procedural 'codes' into the *Migration Act* was intended to replace 'the uncodified principles of natural justice with clear and fixed procedures which are drawn from those principles',[69] it is, no doubt, an unexpected result that the statutory procedures may, in some cases, turn out to be more onerous than the common law and, in others, that the common law may be relevant to establishing whether or not a breach of a statutory requirement invalidates a decision.[70]

Our case study would not be complete without mention of further amendments to the *Migration Act* designed to overturn the result of *Miah*. Each of the *Migration Act*'s procedural 'codes' was prefaced with a statement that the code constituted 'an exhaustive statement of the requirements of the natural justice hearing rule in relation to the matters ... dealt with'.[71] Although the Full Federal Court has concluded that 'exhaustive statement' provisions are effective to 'exclude the common law natural justice hearing rule',[72] this position was reached only after a spirited debate.[73] The argument for the conclusion that the common law is *not* completely excluded by the amendment begins by emphasising that the purported exclusion of the hearing rule is qualified by the words 'in relation to the matters [the 'code'] deals with'. Surely, it is argued, these words would be 'otiose' if the hearing rule was excluded in its entirety. Further, the general principle that it takes 'plain words of necessary intendment' to exclude the requirements of procedural fairness is strongly reiterated. In *Saeed*, the High Court held that common law requirements associated with the disclosure of adverse information were applicable despite the fact that the statutory code covered similar ground on the basis that the 'matter' dealt with by the code applied only to onshore, rather than offshore, visa applicants—opening the door to the applicability of common law requirements of procedural fairness.[74] Clearly, the introduction of a statutory procedural code may introduce more uncertainty than it resolves.

5.2.2.3 The content of the hearing rule

The presumptive applicability of the fair hearing rule to administrative decision-makers has sharpened judicial awareness of important differences between administrative and judicial decision-making processes. For example, in contrast to collecting evidence in a continuous hearing, administrative decision-makers often gather information over time and through a variety of methods which are not constrained by the rules of evidence. Administrative decision-makers also face different resource

---

68   Ibid, 639.

69   Explanatory Memorandum, Migration Reform Bill 1992 (Cth), [51].

70   For discussion of further aspects of the thicket of law created by the *Migration Act*'s procedural codes, see A Ashbolt, 'Taming the Beast: Why a Return to Common Law Procedural Fairness Would Help Curb Migration Litigation' (2009) 20 *Public Law Review* 264; M Alderton, M Granziera and M Smith, 'Judicial Review and Jurisdictional Errors: The Recent Migration Jurisprudence of the High Court of Australia' (2011) 18 *Australian Journal of Administrative Law* 138.

71   See, e.g., *Migration Act 1958* (Cth), ss 51A(1), 357A(1) and 422B(1). It is worth noting that *SAAP* was decided before these amendments, whereas *SZIZO* was decided after. Although the point was not developed, the High Court noted in *SZIZO* that 'in light of the introduction of s 422B it would be surprising if [the procedural requirement at issue in *SAAP*], s 434A were interpreted as having an operation going well beyond the requirements of the hearing rule at common law': *SZIZO*, 639.

72   *Minister for Immigration and Multicultural Affairs v Lay Lat* (2006) 151 FCR 214, 225, [66].

73   For example, see *Antipova v Minister for Immigration and Multicultural and Indigenous Affairs* (2006) 151 FCR 480.

74   *Saeed v Minister for Immigration and Citizenship* (2010) 241 CLR 252. The extent to which there may be some 'matters' not covered by the exhaustive statement provisions in relation to onshore visa applicants, and thus some room for the common law to continue to operate, was not clearly resolved by the High Court.

and institutional constraints from those faced by judges.[75] But the classic doctrinal statements of the content of the fair hearing rule have not required modification: they have always emphasised the need for flexibility. 'What is fair in a given situation depends upon the circumstances' and cannot be subject to 'any fixed body of rules'.[76] The overarching inquiry is whether an affected person has had a fair opportunity to 'put their case'. In most circumstances, this opportunity at least requires adequate notice that an adverse decision may be made; disclosure of prejudicial allegations and sufficient details to enable a meaningful hearing on the critical issues arising for decision;[77] the opportunity to make relevant submissions and adduce relevant evidence; and allowance of sufficient time to prepare for the hearing.

In determining what is required to enable an affected person to put their case adequately, the courts have identified a number of relevant factors, which are usually linked to an analysis of the statutory context in which a particular power is exercised.[78] The importance of the nature of the decision-making process can be illustrated by a number of examples. The content of procedural fairness may be reduced because the decision is part of a decision-making process which 'viewed in its entirety entails procedural fairness'.[79] If the process of decision-making is characterised as 'adversarial', it is more likely that fairness will require the sort of procedures typically associated with courts, such as an oral hearing, legal representation, or the right to cross-examine witnesses. In determining the necessity of such procedures, reference is also made to issues such as the seriousness of the matter and the complexity of the legal and factual issues.[80] Where decision-making processes are 'inquisitorial', it may be inappropriate to require premature disclosure of adverse information.[81] In some cases, the nature of the decision-making process has raised issues about whether information provided in confidence should be disclosed. For example, in *VEAL* it was held that, although the substance of allegations contained in a confidential 'dob in' letter must be disclosed, fairness did not require the disclosure of the author's identity. The requirements of fairness were moulded to recognise the importance of decision-makers having access to information supplied by 'informers'.[82] In general, the courts have felt most comfortable imposing procedures where administrative decision-making bears some resemblance to their own *modus operandi*. This explains the reluctance of judges to impose a duty to consult—an obligation often imposed by statute, but foreign to the judicial mode of decision-making.[83]

The nature of the power being exercised (that is, the subject matter of the power, the width of a discretion, the identity of the decision-maker, the likely consequences of a decision and so on) is also often emphasised by courts in determining the content of a fair hearing. For example, the need for

75   For a good, brief overview, see P Bayne, 'The Content of Procedural Fairness in Administrative Decision-making' (1994) 68 *Australian Law Journal* 297.

76   *Mobil Oil Australia Pty Ltd v Federal Commissioner of Taxation* (1963) 113 CLR 475, 504 (Kitto J).

77   See also n 92.

78   See, e.g., *SZBEL v Minister for Immigration and Multicultural and Indigenous Affairs* (2006) 228 CLR 152, 160–1.

79   *South Australia v O'Shea* (1987) 163 CLR 378, 389 (Mason CJ). See also *Ainsworth v Criminal Justice Commission* (1992) 175 CLR 564, 578.

80   See, e.g., *Cains v Jenkins* (1979) 28 ALR 219.

81   See, e.g., *National Companies and Securities Commission v News Corporation Ltd* (1984) 156 CLR 296.

82   *Applicant VEAL of 2002 v Minister for Immigration and Multicultural and Indigenous Affairs* (2005) 225 CLR 88, 98. This ruling necessarily deprived the applicant of the opportunity to challenge the credibility of their accuser. In *Minister for Immigration and Citizenship v Kumar* (2009) 238 CLR 448, the same basic approach was taken in the context of a statutory requirement to disclose certain information.

83   See Aronson, Dyer and Groves, n 47 above, 471–7 for a discussion of the relevant cases.

urgent decision-making may reduce (perhaps, even to 'nothingness') the requirements of procedural fairness.[84] Indeed, in some cases, the specific subject matter of a power may indicate that notice of the case to be met is not required—for example, prior notice of a deportation decision may not be required if a prohibited immigrant is deliberately seeking to evade the authorities.[85] On the other hand, decisions which have serious effects on individual interests are more likely to be rigorously reviewed.[86]

Although the nature of decision-making processes and particular powers are important considerations in determining the requirements of the hearing rule, they do not generate generally applicable rules. This reflects a dilemma faced by the courts in developing procedural fairness doctrine. On the one hand, the sheer diversity of administrative decision-making contexts counsels against attempts to develop general rules. On the other hand, if the only principle is 'fairness in the circumstances', then decision-makers will be left guessing about the content of their legal obligations.

This dilemma has led some commentators to argue that courts should defer to administrators' determinations about what procedures are appropriate, at least where (1) there is evidence that serious thought has been given to the question of fairness; and (2) where the ultimate decision is not unreasonable.[87] One important advantage attributed to this proposal is that administrators are better placed to understand the practical consequences of adopting particular procedures, and also to evaluate the countervailing policy considerations (for example, how to trade off fairness against efficiency). Many things may be demanded in the name of fair procedures, but there must come a point where the costs of additional procedures outweigh the benefits. Indeed, long delays in decision-making may themselves risk unfairness.[88]

Perhaps the most interesting argument for a deferential approach is that it enables the principles of procedural fairness to have a greater normative (or 'educative') effect on public administration. If administrators have incentives to seriously consider the reasonableness of their own determinations about what fairness requires (because their conclusions will then be deferred to), the values which underpin the law are more likely to be internalised and widely adopted. This argument fits in with a regulatory, forward-looking approach to administrative law as it seeks to optimise compliance with principles of good administration (see 1.3). If the law of procedural fairness is conceptualised only as a backward-looking tool of accountability, then its underlying values may not be protected in the vast majority of cases (which, of course, are never litigated).

Deference to administrative determinations of what fairness requires might also be defended on the basis of a commitment to democratic forms of decision-making. After all, determinations about the

---

84   For example, *Marine Hull and Liability Insurance Co Ltd v Hurford* (1985) 10 FCR 234. On the possibility that the content of procedural fairness may in some circumstances be reduced to nothingness see *Kioa v West* (1985) 159 CLR 550, 615 (Brennan J).

85   *Kioa v West* (1985) 159 CLR 550, 586 (Mason J).

86   Though even refugee decision-making processes need not adopt court-like hearings: *Chen Zhen Zi v Minister for Immigration and Ethnic Affairs* (1994) 48 FCR 591. It is probably inevitable that courts also consider the likely efficiencies and costs of particular procedures, even though these considerations are rarely articulated.

87   B Dyer, 'Determining the Content of Procedural Fairness' (1993) 19 *Monash University Law Review* 165. See also Aronson, Dyer and Groves, n 47 above, 522–4.

88   Delays are sometimes justified, but in other circumstances 'justice delayed is justice denied'. Although delay will not normally amount to a denial of procedural fairness, *NAIS v Minister for Immigration and Multicultural and Indigenous Affairs* (2005) 228 CLR 470 held that in extraordinary circumstances, excessive delay may amount to an unfair hearing. In *NAIS* the unexplained delay between an oral hearing and the time of decision created a real and substantial risk that the decision-maker's capacity to assess the applicant's case was impaired. See also *Starkey v South Australia* (2011) 111 SASR 537.

appropriate levels of fairness raise difficult and contestable value judgments, and it may be argued that the fact that courts are not accountable to the electorate is a reason to prefer an approach which enables the executive to take the lead on what may be politically controversial decisions. In evaluating this sort of argument, it should be remembered that the executive branch of government is not monolithic, and that not all of its component parts can claim the same level of democratic legitimacy.[89]

The variety of decisions which are now subject to the hearing rule (see 5.2.2.1) suggests that a level of deference is probably inevitable. However, even proponents of deference acknowledge that the prevailing view is that the question of what procedural fairness requires is ultimately for the reviewing court to determine.[90]

The diversity of statutory contexts makes it difficult to progress beyond generalities without considering particular decision-making processes in detail. *Applicant VEAL of 2002 v Minister for Immigration and Multicultural and Indigenous Affairs*[91] well illustrates the tensions in this area of the law. Interestingly, however, the case is also suggestive of a reluctance to develop a general theory of deference. This is consistent with the notion that under Australian constitutional arrangements it is for the courts to determine what the law requires (see 5.4.3.1.1).

VEAL concerned the extent of obligations to disclose prejudicial allegations or information.[92] The Refugee Review Tribunal received a highly prejudicial 'dob-in' letter but was unable to test its contents as its author had requested it be kept confidential. The tribunal decided not to disclose the letter on the basis that, in reaching its decision, it did not give it any weight. (In its reasons, the tribunal expressly disavowed any reliance.) The tribunal thus made a deliberate and considered judgment about what a fair hearing required in the circumstances of the case. Arguably, this view was not unreasonable.[93]

The High Court had a different view about what fairness required. Prior to *VEAL* it had been established that an adverse allegation must be disclosed only if it is 'credible, relevant and significant'.[94] As procedural fairness is about procedures rather than outcomes, the court held that the 'credibility, relevance and significance' of any adverse information must be judged *before the ultimate decision is*

---

89   Edward L Rubin claims, in 'Getting Past Democracy' (2001) 149 *University of Pennsylvania Law Review* 711, that 'the existence of a massive, appointed, and credentialed bureaucracy that carries out the great bulk of the government's activities represents a challenge to our characterisation of that government as a democracy': 711. On this view, the administration as well as the judiciary may lack democratic legitimacy.

90   See Dyer, n 87 above.

91   (2005) 225 CLR 88.

92   The provision of an opportunity to an affected person to 'put their case' may, in addition to an obligation to disclose adverse allegations, require decision-makers to disclose issues which are critical to the outcome of a decision when those issues would not otherwise be obvious: *Commissioner for Australian Capital Territory Revenue v Alphaone Pty Ltd* (1994) 49 FCR 576, 591; *Re Minister for Immigration and Multicultural Affairs; Ex parte Miah* (2001) 206 CLR 57, 97. Beyond these requirements a decision-maker is not 'obliged to expose his or her mental processes or provisional views to comment before making the decision in question': *Australian Capital Territory Revenue v Alphaone Pty Ltd* (1994) 49 FCR 576, 592. See also *Habib v Director of Security* (2009) 175 FCR 411, 428 ('There may nevertheless be circumstances where fairness requires prior disclosure of such matters, as where they relate to a critical issue or factor, or where they do not follow from an obvious or natural evaluation of the evidence.'). In *SZBEL v Minister for Immigration and Multicultural and Indigenous Affairs* (2006) 228 CLR 152 it was held that where a tribunal undertakes a 'review' of an administrative decision, the applicant is entitled to assume (unless told otherwise) that the reasons for the rejection of the initial application will be the central and determinative questions on review.

93   For a suggestion that non-disclosure of prejudicial statements would not be unreasonable if a decision-maker were to conclude that they 'were not credible or did not need to be relied on', see Dyer, n 87 above, 202.

94   *Kioa v West* (1985) 159 CLR 550 (5.2.2.1). It may not be necessary to disclose particular adverse documents on which the decision-maker has relied if 'the substance of the legal and factual concern is disclosed': *Dunghutti Elders Council (Aboriginal Corporation) RNTBC v Registrar of Aboriginal and Torres Strait Islander Corporations* (2011) 195 FCR 318, [64]; see also *Minister for Immigration and Citizenship v SZQHH* (2012) 200 FCR 223.

reached. Thus, it was beside the point that the tribunal purported to ignore the letter as the allegations were clearly relevant to the veracity of the applicant's claim for asylum and could not be dismissed as completely lacking in credibility. The necessity to disclose adverse allegations 'is not based on answering a causal question as to whether the material did in fact play a part in influencing the decision'.[95] Fairness required that the substance of the allegations be revealed but the applicant was not entitled to know the identity of his accuser, as there was a public interest in allowing the tribunal (an inquisitorial body) to access information provided in confidence.[96]

Isolating the disagreement between the tribunal and the High Court about what fairness required suggests a number of conclusions. First, there is no suggestion of a deferential standard of review. Second, even if the court had limited itself to asking whether the tribunal's view of what fairness required was unreasonable, it is not clear that the decision in *VEAL* would have been upheld. Decisions about refugee status have potentially life-threatening consequences and procedures which pose *any* risk of subconscious prejudice may be considered unreasonable. How reasonable an administrator's conclusions about fair procedures will appear to be may depend upon which of the 'instrumental' or 'intrinsic' justifications for fair procedures is given emphasis. In *VEAL*, the court's insistence that the question of whether the allegations had an impact on the decision was irrelevant may reflect an assumption that procedural fairness is important regardless of any impact on outcomes (see 5.2.1).

Thus, although the general case for deference is a strong one, it may be that deference makes more sense in certain decision-making contexts than others. It may also be that the successive attempts by the legislature to limit judicial involvement in the review of migration decisions has undermined the conditions of mutual respect on which any normative theory of deference must rely.[97]

No question of deference can arise when the procedural unfairness arises through no fault of the decision-maker. Although the courts have shied away from finding procedural unfairness where it arises because an affected person relies on the advice of another (for example, their representative or lawyer),[98] 'unfairness can occur without any personal fault on the part of the decision-maker'.[99] For example, it has been held that unfairness may arise where an oral hearing is compromised because the person being heard is under extreme distress or the influence of drugs, even though the decision-maker is not aware of these circumstances.[100] In *SZFDE*, the High Court held that the fraudulent behaviour of a person purporting to be a migration agent and lawyer, which caused the appellant to decline an invitation to appear before a tribunal, undermined the efficacy of 'critical' statutory provisions intended to provide exhaustively for the common law hearing rule. Because the fraud disabled the tribunal from exercising its mandatory statutory functions, the court concluded that the state of affairs could be described as not merely a fraud on the appellant, but also a fraud 'on' the tribunal.[101] In such a situation, the imposition of procedural fairness cannot possibly affect the behaviour of administrators. The purpose of invalidating

---

95   *Applicant VEAL of 2002 v Minister for Immigration and Multicultural and Indigenous Affairs* (2005) 225 CLR 88, 97.

96   The obligation to disclose prejudicial information which may be claimed to be confidential is considered in *Minister for Immigration and Citizenship v Maman* (2012) 200 FCR 30.

97   To speculate, part of the explanation for the decision in *VEAL* may also be background judicial assumptions about the quality of decision-making in the RRT and its lack of independence: see *NAIS v Minister for Immigration and Multicultural and Indigenous Affairs* (2005) 228 CLR 470, 498, [91]–[92].

98   See, e.g., *Al-Mehdawi v Secretary of State for the Home Department* [1990] 1 AC 876.

99   *Hot Holdings Pty Ltd v Creasy* (2002) 210 CLR 438, 448 (Gleeson CJ).

100   *Minister for Immigration and Multicultural and Indigenous Affairs v SCAR* (2003) 128 FCR 553.

101   *SZFDE v Minister for Immigration and Citizenship* (2007) 232 CLR 189, 206. Fraud is also an independent ground on which administrative decisions can be invalidated: see 5.3.2.

the decision in these sorts of cases is arguably best understood in terms of the 'legal' (as opposed to 'regulatory') approach to administrative law (1.3)—which involves addressing particular grievances and upholding certain values, regardless of whether doing so has some sort of impact or effect on decision-making.

5.2.2.4 Content and legitimate expectations

We noted earlier that the concept of legitimate expectations may sometimes have a role in determining the content of a fair hearing. A controversial example is *Teoh*, where the High Court held that ratification of a treaty grounded a legitimate expectation of government compliance with the treaty, absent statutory or executive indications to the contrary.[102] This legitimate expectation had consequences for what a fair hearing required in cases where the government proposed to depart from its obligations under a ratified treaty. In particular, fairness required that, prior to the making of the decision, an affected person be given a hearing on the issue of whether the legitimate expectation should be honoured. *Teoh* has been the subject of much political and legal debate.[103]

The most substantial criticism of the reasoning in *Teoh* resurfaced in *Lam's* case. McHugh and Gummow JJ questioned the consistency, on the one hand, of denying that international obligations, which are not enacted into domestic law, were relevant considerations which *must* be taken into account (see 5.3.1), while, on the other hand, requiring a hearing before departing from those obligations. To the extent that a hearing on whether international obligations should be honoured is tantamount to a rule that these obligations must be considered, it was also suggested that the effect of *Teoh* is to allow the executive (through the ratification of a treaty) to modify the nature of its statutory powers.[104] Callinan J concluded that this elevates 'the executive above the parliament'.[105] Although *Lam* did not formally overrule the central holding in *Teoh*, it left it teetering on the verge of extinction.[106]

It needs to be emphasised, however, that in *Lam* the High Court did not object to the notion that some 'legitimate expectations' may affect the content of procedural fairness. If, for example, a decision-maker tells an affected person that they will 'hear further argument upon a certain point, and then delivers a decision without doing so it may be easy to demonstrate that unfairness in involved'.[107] But the mere fact that a legitimate expectation is disappointed will not amount to a breach of the hearing rule if no unfairness or 'practical injustice' is occasioned. In *Lam*, the department's failure to keep its promise to the applicant (to contact his children's carers) did not breach the hearing rule because, on the facts of the case, the failure did not deprive the applicant of any opportunity to advance his case.[108]

---

102   *Minister for Immigration and Ethnic Affairs v Teoh* (1995) 183 CLR 273.

103   After *Teoh* the Attorney-General and Minister for Foreign Affairs issued a joint general statement attempting to negate the decision, though there have been doubts about the effectiveness of the statement: see for discussion *Lam v Minister for Immigration and Multicultural Affairs* (2006) 157 FCR 215, [28]–[31]. Legislative efforts to override the decision were introduced into the Commonwealth parliament on a number of occasions but were not passed by the Senate. Cf *Administrative Decisions (Effect of International Instruments) Act 1995* (SA).

104   *Re Minister for Immigration and Multicultural and Indigenous Affairs; Ex parte Lam* (2003) 214 CLR 1, 33–4.

105   Ibid, 48.

106   See generally, M Groves, 'Treaties and Legitimate Expectations—The Rise and Fall of *Teoh* in Australia' (2010) 12 *Judicial Review* 323.

107   *Re Minister for Immigration and Multicultural and Indigenous Affairs; Ex parte Lam* (2003) 214 CLR 1, 12 (Gleeson CJ).

108   Ibid, 35.

Expectations which may affect the requirements of the hearing rule may be procedural (that is, about the procedures to be followed) or substantive (that is, about the substance of the decision to be made). It is very important to understand that the nature of the protection which may be given to either category of expectation is procedural, not substantive. At most, substantive or procedural expectations may be protected by a requirement that an affected person be heard prior to the taking of action inconsistent with the expectation. In the case of an expectation that a particular procedure will be followed, this means that the courts will not 'enforce' the actual expectation; they will require only those procedures that fairness demands in the circumstances.[109] In some cases what fairness requires *may* overlap or coincide with a procedural legitimate expectation. For example, if the legitimate expectation is that a decision-maker will take further submissions prior to making a decision, a fair hearing is likely to require the opportunity to make further submissions. On the other hand, if there is a legitimate expectation that there will be an opportunity to make further *oral* submissions, it *may* be the case that the requirements of fairness could be satisfied if the decision-maker decided only to invite further *written* submissions.[110] The test is 'fairness', not whether a legitimate expectation is disappointed or whether a person was forewarned that a legitimate expectation would not be fulfilled.[111]

More generally, it can be observed that administrators are not bound to exercise their statutory power in accordance with expectations (no matter how 'reasonable' or 'legitimate' they seem). English courts have accepted that there are limited circumstances in which expectations can, in effect, be substantively enforced.[112] In *Lam*, some judges argued that this approach is precluded in Australia by the constitutional separation of powers.[113] Requiring an administrator to fulfil the substance of an expectation would involve the courts in assessing the 'quality of the decision-making and thus the merits of the outcome', this being an executive, not a judicial, function.[114]

5.2.3 The rule against bias

Although it is sometimes assumed that the *Kioa* 'threshold test' also applies to the bias rule, the bias cases have not emphasised the qualification that interests must be affected in a 'direct and immediate way'.[115] Hearings cannot be extended to everyone affected by a general policy decision, but such practical impediments do not prevent decision-makers from complying with the rule against bias by acting and appearing to act with impartiality. There is thus no reason why the rule cannot be taken to apply to 'the decisions of every public office-holder'.[116] This breadth of application has meant that the rule's

---

109   *Attorney-General (NSW) v Quin* (1990) 170 CLR 1, 54 (Dawson J).

110   Cf *SAAP v Minister for Immigration and Multicultural and Indigenous Affairs* (2005) 228 CLR 294.

111   *Re Minister for Immigration and Multicultural and Indigenous Affairs; Ex parte Lam* (2003) 214 CLR 1.

112   *R v North and East Devon Health Authority, ex parte Coughlan* [2001] QB 213. It was held that a disappointment of a legitimate expectation may in some circumstances constitute an 'abuse of power'.

113   See, e.g., McHugh and Gummow JJ in *Re Minister for Immigration and Multicultural and Indigenous Affairs; Ex parte Lam* (2003) 214 CLR 1. See also Brennan J in *Attorney-General (NSW) v Quin* (1990) 170 CLR 1.

114   *Re Minister for Immigration and Multicultural and Indigenous Affairs; Ex parte Lam* (2003) 214 CLR 1, 23, 25. Requiring an administrator to fulfil the substance of a legitimate expectation would also offend the no-fettering principle: see 5.3.4. For a review of differences in approach to the concept of legitimate expectation in English and Australian administrative law, see M Groves, 'Substantive Legitimate Expectations in Australian Administrative Law' (2008) 32 *Melbourne University Law Review* 470.

115   See, e.g., *Hot Holding Pty Ltd v Creasy* (2002) 210 CLR 438, 447, 459.

116   *Minister for Immigration and Multicultural Affairs v Jia Legeng* (2001) 205 CLR 507, 549 (Kirby J).

requirements must be adapted to the circumstances of the case.[117] Like the hearing rule, the bias rule can be excluded by statute.[118]

Most cases concern apparent bias, as opposed to actual bias.[119] This is partly because apparent bias does not require an applicant to establish the actual state of mind or attitude of decision-makers whereas actual bias is established only where the decision-maker can be shown to have had a closed mind and was not open to persuasion.[120] Thus, where a decision-maker is actually biased it is highly likely that some other ground of review, such as improper purpose, failure to consider relevant considerations, or inflexible application of policy, could more easily be established. Not only is actual bias harder to prove than apparent bias, but a finding of actual bias is also more likely to undermine public confidence in the integrity of government decision-making—which is a core justification for the rule against bias. This explains why judges may prefer to uphold bias claims without directly concluding that the decision-maker's mind was not open to persuasion.[121]

The test for apparent bias is whether an informed and 'fair-minded lay observer might reasonably apprehend' that the decision-maker 'might not bring an impartial mind' to the decision to be made. The question to be asked is 'one of possibility (real and not remote), not probability',[122] though the claims which form the basis of any apparent bias must be 'firmly established' and it is not sufficient 'that the reasonable bystander has a vague sense of unease or disquiet'.[123] Clearly, there are many ways in which an impartial mind may appear to be lacking, including the making of derogatory or insulting statements,[124] personal connections or contacts with interested people,[125] and prior involvement with the matter being determined.[126] For a long time, any direct pecuniary (financial) interests in the outcome of a decision automatically disqualified a decision-maker.[127] The basic test for apparent bias now applies even in relation to pecuniary interests. But if a decision-maker holds 'a not insubstantial, direct, pecuniary or proprietary interest in the outcome of litigation' this 'will ordinarily result in disqualification'.[128]

In cases where it is alleged that a fair-minded person would conclude that a decision-maker might have prejudged the outcome of a decision, courts have emphasised that an open mind need not be an empty one.[129] A predisposition or tendency of mind does not of itself indicate that a decision-maker

---

117   *Hot Holding Pty Ltd v Creasy* (2002) 210 CLR 438, 460.

118   Subject to constitutional impediments: see 7.2.3 for a discussion of the minimum entrenched provision of judicial review at the federal level.

119   For a period the *Migration Act* excluded apparent but not actual bias, increasing the number of applications raising allegations of actual bias: see *Minister for Immigration and Multicultural Affairs v Jia Legeng* (2001) 205 CLR 507.

120   *Minister for Immigration and Multicultural Affairs v Jia Legeng* (2001) 205 CLR 507.

121   See *Webb v R* (1994) 181 CLR 41, 71–2 (Deane J).

122   *Ebner v Official Trustee in Bankruptcy* (2000) 205 CLR 337, 344–5.

123   *Minister for Immigration and Multicultural Affairs v Jia Legeng* (2001) 205 CLR 507, 549.

124   See, e.g., *Vakauta v Kelly* (1989) 167 CLR 568.

125   Whether a connection between a decision-maker and a person with an interest in the outcome of a decision will lead to an apprehension of bias is a highly contextualised question, depending on factors such as 'the nature of the association, the frequency of contact, and the nature of the interest of the person associated with the decision-maker': *Hot Holdings Pty Ltd v Creasy* (2002) 210 CLR 438, 461.

126   For a catalogue of the 'main categories' of apprehended bias, see J Griffith 'Apprehended Bias in Australian Administrative Law' (2010) 38 *Federal Law Review* 353, 357–8.

127   *Dimes v Proprietors of the Grand Junction Canal* (1852) 3 HL Cas 759.

128   *Ebner v Official Trustee in Bankruptcy* (2000) 205 CLR 337, 358.

129   *Minister for Immigration and Multicultural Affairs v Jia Legeng* (2001) 205 CLR 507, 531.

is unwilling to genuinely listen to argument.[130] What it takes for a fair-minded observer to conclude that a matter has been prejudged needs to be considered in the context of the statute under which the decision is to be made, an inquiry which includes reference to the general nature of the decision-making processes and the identity of the decision-maker.[131] For example, where an administrator has a 'continuing relationship with a particular issue or particular person during the course of which they necessarily form a view', it will 'generally be impossible for them to bring an open mind to a new decision pertaining to that issue or person'.[132] In *Jia* it was held that it would be wrong to apply standards of judicial 'detachment' to a minister who occupies a political office and who is accountable to the parliament and electorate.[133] A minister is entitled to express, prior to making a decision in a particular case, views consonant with a lawful policy.[134]

In *Jia* the gist of the complaint was that the minister's general remarks about how his powers should be exercised had singled a particular case out for comment. The majority concluded that these comments, properly interpreted, would not have led a fair-minded observer to apprehend that the minister would not impartially decide the case which had been specifically mentioned. In dissent, Kirby J argued that this conclusion was based upon a 'lawyer's fine verbal analysis' to the evidence, rather than the general impressions a reasonable person would bring to the task.[135] This highlights a recurring and difficult question: what levels of knowledge about the circumstances of a particular case should be attributed to the fair-minded observer? By attributing detailed knowledge and analytical capacity to the fair-minded observer, judges are sometimes able to turn an initial apprehension of the real possibility of partiality on its head. For example, in one case, the High Court attributed to the fair-minded observer knowledge of the detailed legal rules of pleading.[136] Of course, in the end, it is judges who must decide whether appearances of impartiality are so imperilled that a decision should be invalidated.[137]

Most government decisions are made in the context of a decision-making hierarchy and many involve various stages of decision-making. It is possible that an ultimate decision may be invalidated for apparent bias, not because the actual decision-maker was compromised, but because some other officer involved in the process of decision-making had an interest in the decision. In such cases, however, it is necessary to show how the alleged bias of an individual involved in the decision-making process can generate a reasonable apprehension of bias in relation to the ultimate decision made. The peripheral or mechanical involvement of an officer with an interest in the outcome of the

---

130   See, e.g., *R v Commonwealth Conciliation and Arbitration Commission; Ex parte Angliss Group* (1969) 122 CLR 546 where the president of the Commonwealth Conciliation and Arbitration Commission had, in an earlier case, expressed the view that reducing the wage differential between men and women was a step in the right direction.

131   The issue of how to deal with apprehended bias attributed to one or more people in a multi-member decision-making body is considered in *McGovern v Ku-ring-gai Council* (2008) 72 NSWLR 504.

132   *Century Metals and Mining NL v Yeomans* (1989) 100 ALR 383, 417; *Reece v Webber* (2011) 192 FCR 254, 272, [52].

133   *Minister for Immigration and Multicultural Affairs v Jia Legeng* (2001) 205 CLR 507, 539. The effectiveness of political accountability has been questioned in other contexts: *R v Toohey; Ex parte Northern Land Council* (1981) 151 CLR 170.

134   See also *Franklin v Minister of Town and Country Planning* [1948] AC 87.

135   *Minister for Immigration and Multicultural Affairs v Jia Legeng* (2001) 205 CLR 507, 552.

136   *Laws v Australian Broadcasting Tribunal* (1990) 170 CLR 70.

137   For example, the different conclusions reached in *Minister for Immigration and Citizenship v SZQHH* (2012) 200 FCR 223 can be explained on the basis of the level of knowledge of the decision-making process attributed to the fair-minded observer. The general issue is discussed in M Groves, 'The Rule Against Bias' (2009) 39 *Hong Kong Law Journal* 485.

decision is unlikely to be sufficient.[138] Again, much will depend upon the level of knowledge about the decision-making process attributed to the 'fair-minded' observer.[139]

Finally, the courts have given a lukewarm recognition to an exception to the bias rule in cases of 'necessity'. This is really an application of the principle that the legislature can exclude the operation of the bias rule where a tribunal or decision-maker would otherwise be 'disabled from performing its statutory functions'.[140] There have been some suggestions that the necessity exception should not apply in cases where it would cause 'substantial injustice' or where it would frustrate the 'principles of fairness'.[141] It may be that such suggestions merely emphasise the general principle that strong indications are required to exclude the common law rules of procedural fairness.

5.2.4 Extending the boundaries of procedural fairness

It is sometimes suggested that the obligations of procedural fairness extend beyond the requirements of a fair, unbiased hearing. Procedural fairness has been said to also require that findings of fact be based on 'probative material and logical grounds'.[142] There is no doubt that the instrumental value (and much of the intrinsic value) attributed to fair, unbiased hearings will be lost if the decision-maker bases the decision on findings which are not rationally or logically supported by the evidence. However, it probably makes more sense to treat any such errors as being related to reasoning processes rather than procedure.

In a few cases, decisions have been invalidated on the ground of a failure to make further inquiries. The legal basis of the duty to inquire has not, however, been clearly identified.[143] Although it has been linked to procedural fairness requirements, it has also been concluded that it is part of a decision-maker's obligation not to act unreasonably in the *Wednesbury* sense (see 5.4.4).[144] The High Court has observed that it 'is difficult to see any basis upon which a failure to inquire could constitute a breach of the requirements of procedural fairness'.[145] However, any error involved in failing to make inquiries does relate to a procedural failing, even if it is thought that a failure to make particular inquiries will have consequences for the rationality or reasonableness of the decision ultimately reached.

---

138   *Hot Holdings Pty Ltd v Creasy* (2002) 210 CLR 438. The majority in *Hot Holdings* also held that the relationship between an officer involved in the process with his son (who had a possible interest in the outcome of the decision) 'provided no sufficient basis for reaching' the conclusion that a fair-minded and informed member of the public would have had a suspicion that the minister, who made the ultimate decision, had not acted impartially: 452 (Gaudron, Gummow and Hayne JJ).

139   See, e.g., Kirby J's dissent in *Hot Holdings Pty Ltd v Creasy* (2002) 210 CLR 438.

140   *Laws v Australian Broadcasting Tribunal* (1990) 170 CLR 70, 88. This explanation for the exception has the consequence that it cannot operate against any aspects of the bias rule which are constitutionally entrenched. In the context of Ch III courts, see Gaudron J in *Ebner v Official Trustee in Bankruptcy* (2000) 205 CLR 337.

141   *Laws v Australian Broadcasting Tribunal* (1990) 170 CLR 70, 96 (Deane J), 102 (Gaudron and McHugh JJ).

142   *Re Minister for Immigration and Multicultural Affairs; Ex parte Applicant S20/2002* (2003) 198 ALR 59, 85 [116] (Kirby J), 62 [9] (Gleeson CJ). See also *Australian Broadcasting Tribunal v Bond* (1990) 170 CLR 321 366–7 (Deane J).

143   For an excellent analysis of the conceptual basis for the imposition of a duty to inquire and a comprehensive review of the case law, see M Smyth, 'Inquisitorial Adjudication: The Duty to Inquire in Merits Review Tribunals' (2010) 34 *Melbourne University Law Review* 230.

144   E.g. *Prasad v Minister for Immigration and Ethnic Affairs* (1985) 6 FCR 155, 169; *Visa International Service Association v Reserve Bank of Australia* (2003) 131 FCR 300, 429–31 [622]–[629].

145   *Minister for Immigration and Citizenship v SZIAI* (2009) 259 ALR 429, 436.

In *SZIAI* the High Court accepted the possibility that 'failure to make an obvious inquiry about a critical fact, the existence of which is easily ascertained', may amount to a jurisdictional error, though the reasons why this may be so were left unclarified.[146] In this context the reference to jurisdictional error is unhelpful as denial of procedural fairness and *Wednesbury* unreasonableness can both be thought of as instances of such errors (5.4.1). What is clear, however, is that any duty of inquiry is exceptional and limited:[147] duties to inquire have been rejected by the courts where the inquiry is not 'obvious', 'centrally relevant' or 'readily ascertainable'.[148]

The traditional view that the common law does not recognise any general duty on administrative decision-makers to give reasons for their decisions was affirmed in *Public Service Board (NSW) v Osmond*.[149] Although the High Court raised the possibility that there may be special cases where procedural fairness might require the provision of reasons for administrative decisions, the clear message was that the imposition of duties to provide reasons for administrative decisions was best left to the legislature. Two developments have ameliorated this position. First, since the enactment of s 28 of the *AAT Act* (which allows those who have a right to appeal to the tribunal to obtain a written statement of reasons setting out the material findings of fact and the reasons for the decision),[150] there has been a proliferation of similar statutory entitlements in most Australian jurisdictions.[151]

Second, the courts have accepted that implied statutory obligations to give reasons in relation to particular statutory powers may arise.[152] Such an implication is more likely to be drawn if there is a right to appeal (which would typically be meaningless without a statement of reasons), and in circumstances where the decision-maker undertakes functions similar to those undertaken by judges.[153] In England, it is well accepted that procedural fairness may impose an obligation to give reasons in special circumstances. For example, a decision may be so counter-intuitive that explanation is required.[154] Although *Osmond* did not foreclose the possibility that procedural fairness may require reasons in special circumstances, the nature of any exceptions remains largely unexplored and Australian courts continue to emphasise the existence of the general rule that administrators are not required to give reasons.[155] Any recognition of a common law obligation to give reasons would raise difficult questions about whether every breach should result in the 'retrospective invalidity' (see 4.2) of the decision (as is normally the case with breaches of procedural fairness—5.2.5.1). The legal consequences of a failure to comply with a statutory obligation to give reasons also raises difficult questions (see 5.2.5.2).

---

146 *Minister for Immigration and Citizenship v SZIAI* (2009) 259 ALR 429, 436. *Minister for Immigration and Citizenship v SZGUR* (2011) 241 CLR 594 also failed to progress the debate.

147 The post-*SZIAI* cases have confirmed the judicial reluctance to impose a duty to inquire on tribunals: see M Smyth 'Tribunal Error and the Duty to Inquire' (2011) 22 *Public Law Review* 163.

148 Picking up on the case law, the High Court's judgment in *SZIAI* appears to indicate that these are threshold requirements, without which no duty could be imposed: (2009) 259 ALR 429, 43.

149 (1986) 159 CLR 656.

150 Section 13 of the *ADJR Act* provides for the same entitlement in relation to reviewable 'decisions', subject to decisions excluded by Schedule 2 of the Act or by regulation.

151 For the details, see Aronson, Dyer and Groves, n 47 above, 629–30.

152 See, e.g., *Campbelltown City Council v Vegan* (2006) 67 NSWLR 672, [106].

153 Ibid. Though the second reason has been doubted *Sherlock v Lloyd* (2010) 27 VR 434, 439.

154 See *R v Civil Service Board, ex parte Cunningham* [1991] 4 All ER 310. It is more likely that reasons will be demanded where the affected person's interests are of great importance: see *R v Secretary of State for the Home Department, ex parte Doody* [1994] 1 AC 531.

155 *L & B Linings Pty Ltd v WorkCover Authority of New South Wales* [2012] NSWCA 15 [52].

The case for a right to reasons for administrative decisions is a strong one. Not only is the formulation of reasons an integral part of rational decision-making (unreasoned decisions are arbitrary), but also the provision of reasons is a necessary condition for securing the accountability and legitimacy of government action. A right to reasons could serve both the instrumental and intrinsic benefits which are often associated with procedural fairness.[156] No doubt the right to reasons can impose significant costs on administrative decision-making processes. However, it can be argued that the importance of reasons is such that the onus should be on the legislature to exclude the right when it concludes that the costs outweigh the benefits in particular decision-making contexts (as is the case with the hearing rule and the rule against bias).

5.2.5 Remedial effect of procedural errors

5.2.5.1 Common law

Breach of the common law rules of procedural fairness is a 'jurisdictional error'[157] which generally means that an affected decision will be (retrospectively) invalid (see 4.1.1; 4.4.1).[158] Where a court can be satisfied that the breach of procedural fairness 'could have made no difference' to the outcome, it may exercise its discretion to decline to award a remedy (see 4.6).[159] In *Aala* it was emphasised that courts should be very reluctant to conclude that a fair hearing could not possibly have altered the ultimate decision.[160] After all, this conclusion requires judges to take a view about the correctness or merits of a decision. As such, Australian courts have declined to qualify the basic rule with an exception for 'trivial' breaches of procedural fairness.

It has, however, been accepted that a concluded appeal may 'cure' any breaches of procedural fairness by the original decision-maker.[161] A more straightforward approach, in general, is to recognise that 'following a decision of an appellate body, judicial review proceedings may not be brought in respect of the original decision'.[162] The right to object to non-compliance with both the hearing and bias rules can be waived. However, the courts are unlikely to accept waiver has occurred unless the breach of fairness was obvious and there was an informed and calculated decision not to object at the time of the breach.[163]

---

156 P P Craig, 'The Common Law, Reasons and Administrative Justice' (1994) 53 *Cambridge Law Journal* 282, 284. It has been suggested that a stronger basis for a duty to give reasons for decisions is that it makes no sense for courts, on the one hand, to review decisions for errors concerning the decision-maker's reasoning processes (5.3) while, on the other hand, not requiring reasons for decision to be disclosed: see Geoff Airo-Farulla, 'Rationality and Judicial Review of Administrative Action' (2000) 24 *Melbourne University Law Review* 543, 553.

157 *Re Refugee Review Tribunal; Ex parte Aala* (2000) 204 CLR 82.

158 *Minister for Immigration and Multicultural Affairs v Bhardwaj* (2002) 209 CLR 597.

159 *Stead v State Government Insurance Commission* (1986) 161 CLR 141, 145; *SZBYR v Minister for Immigration and Citizenship* (2007) 235 ALR 609, [28].

160 *Re Refugee Review Tribunal; Ex parte Aala* (2000) 204 CLR 82, 88–9, 109, 117, 130–1.

161 Assuming, of course, that a fair hearing is provided by the appeal. The confused jurisprudence on this question (in particular, *Calvin v Carr* [1980] AC 574) is examined in Aronson, Dyer and Groves, n 47 above, 501–3.

162 *Vitaz v Wetfarm (NSW) Pty Ltd* [2011] NSWCA 254, [24]. Whether relief will lie against the original decision-maker may depend on the nature of the statutory scheme: ibid, [53].

163 See, e.g., *Vakauta v Kelly* (1989) 167 CLR 568; *Thompson v Ludwig* (1991) 37 IR 437.

5.2.5.2 Statutory procedures

Project Blue Sky v Australian Broadcasting Authority articulated a general approach for determining the legal status of a decision made in breach of a statutory provision, including provisions imposing procedural requirements (see 4.3). It will be recalled that the analysis of the court in *Project Blue Sky* envisaged three possible remedial outcomes where a statutory provision was breached: retrospective invalidity, prospective unlawfulness, and no remedy (in the case of a genuinely 'directory' provision). Which outcome is appropriate is said to be a matter of statutory interpretation.

This general approach does not lay down any precise rules, but the courts have identified a number of factors for consideration.[164] Close attention should be paid to the language and structure of the statute. Where a statutory procedure is intended to replicate or replace the common law requirements of procedural fairness, breach will likely result in invalidity.[165] *Project Blue Sky* also indicated that the more amorphous (that is, less rule-like) a requirement is, the less likely breach will lead to invalidity. The fact that the retrospective invalidation of a decision will affect many individuals or the public generally, thereby causing public inconvenience,[166] may indicate a legislative intention that non-compliance with a statutory requirement should not render the decision legally ineffective.[167] Breaches of procedural provisions may be particularly difficult for those not directly involved in the decision-making process to detect,[168] and members of the public who are inconvenienced will often have no control over whether procedures are complied with.[169]

In *SZIZO* the High Court applied the *Project Blue Sky* approach to determine whether a breach of a statutory requirement that all correspondence relevant to a hearing before the Refugee Review Tribunal be sent to an applicant's 'authorised recipient' (if one had been nominated) resulted in a jurisdictional error and, thus, invalidity.[170] The breach of this procedural requirement had not caused any unfairness as the applicants and their 'authorised recipient' were all members of the same family and resided at the same address. According to the High Court, the question to be answered was whether 'it was a purpose of the legislation that, despite holding a hearing at which all of the applicants for review, including their authorised recipient, appeared before the tribunal to give evidence and to present arguments ... the Tribunal could not validly decide the review'.[171] In concluding that invalidity would not have been intended by the parliament, the court emphasised the fact that the requirement related to the manner of providing notice of a hearing and was not an end in itself. As the purpose of the provision was to facilitate a fair hearing, the legislature would not have intended invalidity where a breach did not amount to a denial of procedural fairness. *SZIZO* suggests that the question of what remedial result is intended may

---

164 *Egglishaw v Australian Crime Commission (No 2)* (2010) 186 FCR 393, 400.

165 *SAAP v Minister for Immigration and Multicultural and Indigenous Affairs* (2005) 228 CLR 294; *Italiano v Carbone* [2005] NSWCA 177 (unreported, Spigelman CJ, Basten JA and Einstein J, 2 June 2005).

166 For a recent example of emphasis being given to this factor, see *Marrickville Metro Shopping Centre Pty Ltd v Marrickville Council* (2010) 174 LGERA 67.

167 *Project Blue Sky v Australian Broadcasting Authority* (1998) 194 CLR 355, 392–3. The court placed great weight on the fact that invalidity would upset the reasonable expectations in an industry where participants were necessarily required to make large-scale investments on the basis of the regulator's decisions.

168 Ibid.

169 *Montreal Street Railway Co v Normandin* [1917] AC 170, 175.

170 *Minister for Immigration and Citizenship v SZIZO* (2009) 238 CLR 627.

171 Ibid, 637.

depend not merely on an analysis of the statutory requirement, but on further intentions relating to the circumstances of a breach.

The *Project Blue Sky* 'test' gives the legislature the option of choosing what, if any, effect a decision made in breach of a procedural requirement shall have—the test, after all, relies on an analysis of statutory purposes. In *Palme*, the High Court considered the remedial effect of a breach of a requirement in the *Migration Act* to provide reasons for a decision to cancel a visa.[172] The statute specifically stated that any failure to comply with the reasons requirement would not 'affect the validity of the decision'. The majority of the court argued that the idea that a requirement to do something *after* a decision had been made (that is, to give reasons) could affect the validity of the decision was, while possible in theory, counter-intuitive.[173] How counter-intuitive the idea is arguably depends upon one's view about the importance to good decision-making of an obligation to give reasons (see 5.2.4). If reasons were thought to be a common law requirement of procedural fairness, then the force of the majority's argument would be diminished.[174] In the end, however, the majority in *Palme* could simply point to the express and very clear legislative instruction that any breach of the reasons requirement would not affect the validity of the decision. The only remedy available to the applicant, in relation to the breach of the reasons requirement, was to seek an order of mandamus requiring the obligation to be fulfilled.[175]

It is apparent that a 'no-invalidity clause' (such as the one discussed in *Palme*) has the potential to seriously reduce the High Court's constitutional judicial review jurisdiction—particularly if such a clause were to be given a wide operation (that is, by declaring that breach of many or all of statutory requirements in a statute did not affect validity). We return to this question in 7.2.3 and 7.2.4.1, where 'no-invalidity' clauses are discussed in the context of the concept of a constitutional minimum provision of judicial review.

One interesting question which arises in a number of different contexts is the legal consequence of a breach of a statutory requirement to give reasons.[176] The Federal Court has claimed that 'it may readily be accepted that a failure to give reasons does not of itself invalidate a decision'.[177] However, in truth, it is difficult to generalise. The consequences of a failure to give adequate reasons, when required to do so by statute, will be determined by a 'process of statutory implication' in the context of particular statutory contexts and requirements.[178] Relevant to this inquiry, as emphasised in *Palme*, is the question of whether the reasons are required after the decision was made or are a 'step in the giving of the decision'.[179] It has

---

172   *Re Minister for Imigration and Multicultural and Indigenous Affairs; Ex parte Palme* (2003) 216 CLR 212.

173   Ibid, 225–6. Cf *Minister for Immigration and Multicultural Affairs v Yusuf* (2001) 206 CLR 323, 337, [30]–[31] (Gaudron J).

174   Cf the dissent of Kirby J, a longtime supporter of a common law right to reasons, in *Re Minister for Immigration and Multicultural and Indigenous Affairs; Ex parte Palme* (2003) 216 CLR 212, 249–50.

175   The court apparently accepted that there was a jurisdictional error in relation to the breach of the reasons requirement (mandamus under s 75(v) only lies for jurisdictional error), but denied that this resulted in any jurisdictional error in the decision to cancel the applicant's visa. The logic of this position rests on the contestable assumption that the decision and the reasons requirement are not part of a single process of decision-making.

176   Where reasons are required interesting questions also arise as to what inferences courts should draw from a failure to provide reasons or from reasons which have been provided in the course of consideration of whether the decision-maker's reasoning process was legally flawed: see e.g. *Minister for Immigration and Citizenship v SZLSP* (2010) 187 FCR 362.

177   *Vanstone v Clark* (2005) 47 FCR 299, 360. In circumstances where failure to provide reasons is not a jurisdictional error, the duty to provide reasons 'may be susceptible to enforcement by an order of mandamus': *O'Donoghue v Honourable Brendan O'Connor (No 2)* (2011) 283 ALR 682701; see also *Palme* (2003) 216 CLR 212.

178   *L & B Linings Pty Ltd v WorkCover Authority of New South Wales* [2012] NSWCA 15, [52].

179   *Sherlock v Lloyd* (2010) 27 VR 434, 444.

also been suggested that it is difficult to construe a requirement to provide adequate reasons as going to validity where it is contained in a generally applicable statute (such as the *ADJR Act* or *AAT Act*).[180]

The *ADJR Act* allows for review on the ground 'that procedures that were required by law to be observed in connection with the making of the decision were not observed' (s 5(1)(b)). There is an emerging consensus that this ground allows for review of procedural errors which would not result in the retrospective invalidity of a decision at common law (see 4.2).

5.3 Reasoning process grounds: the control of administrative choice

Discretion gives administrators a degree of freedom of choice. Although discretion potentially carries with it certain costs, such as the risk of exploitation, arbitrariness and uncertainty, it can also achieve certain benefits, such as flexibility, consistency and responsiveness (see 4.1.2). But no matter how the pros and cons of administrative discretion are assessed in particular contexts, it is impossible to eliminate discretion entirely. As parliament's capacity to generate legal rules is limited by resource and time constraints, it is inevitable that much rule-making will in practice be undertaken by the executive arm of government. To the extent that administrative bureaucracies are called upon to determine which rules (or general policies) to adopt, this inevitably involves the exercise of discretion. Furthermore, even where administrators apply pre-existing rules to make individual decisions, they must (at the very least) determine when particular fact situations come within the rule to be applied. Although rules can confer more or less choice upon an administrator, a rule cannot itself determine how it is to be applied to particular facts.[181]

In any event, the conferral of discretionary powers on government bureaucracies remains a standard response to complexity and uncertainty. The view (most famously held by Dicey) that wide 'arbitrary' powers undermine the rule of law has led to the development of a number of grounds of review which work to 'structure' discretion—that is, by controlling the way in which administrators choose between the options open to them.[182] The law 'structures' discretion through the procedural norms considered above (5.2) and also through a number of grounds of review which can be said to focus on the reasoning processes of decision-makers. For example, by requiring decision-makers to consider certain 'relevant' factors and refrain from considering 'irrelevant' ones, their discretion is structured but not removed or confined (5.3.1).[183] The identification of errors associated with the 'reasoning processes' of administrators

---

180   Ibid; *Seiffert v The Prisoners Review Board* [2011] WASCA 148, [172]. An alternative approach, focusing on the court's discretion to make an appropriate order, has been taken in the context of the AAT's statutory duty under s 43(2) of the *AAT Act* to give adequate reasons. Breach of this obligation is an error of law, and may thus be appealed to the Federal Court, but the appropriate order to be made (by the Federal Court pursuant to s 44 of the *AAT Act*) 'will depend upon the facts and circumstances of each individual case and the exercise of the discretion thereby conferred': *Civil Aviation Safety Authority v Central Aviation Pty Ltd* (2009) 179 FCR 554, [55].

181   See R Goodin, 'Welfare, Rights and Discretion' (1986) 6 *Oxford Journal of Legal Studies* 240, 237–9.

182   K C Davis argued in *Discretionary Justice: A Preliminary Inquiry* (Urbana, Ill: University of Illinois Press, 1971) that discretion should be 'checked' (i.e. subjected to review), 'confined' (i.e. limited by way of rules which rigidly define its area of operation) and 'structured'.

183   Norms of statutory interpretation can effectively operate to remove or confine discretion. For example, unambiguous language is required before a discretionary power is allowed to abrogate fundamental common law rights: e.g. *Coco v The Queen* (1994) 179 CLR 427.

is very difficult when reasons for decisions are not provided. However, if a decision-maker fails to give reasons it may sometimes be inferred that there were no lawful reasons for the decision.[184] And the High Court has indicated that reasons are designed to inform and should not 'be scrutinised by over-zealous judicial review'.[185] What inferences (as a matter of fact) may or may not be drawn from statements of reasons will depend on the circumstances of a particular case.[186]

The law does not require that reasoning processes be perfect. Rather, these grounds of review highlight a number of limited respects in which failures in reasoning processes will invalidate decisions. If perfection were required, the notion that the merits of a decision are off-limits to judges would become meaningless (3.2.2). Thus, while discretion may be structured, the courts have accepted that it should not be removed. The acceptance (consistent with the legality/merits distinction) that it is not for judges to remove discretion points to the law's ambivalence about the value of administrative discretion. On the one hand, the law rebels against the notion of unstructured and uncontrolled discretions.[187] On the other hand, the law does not allow administrators themselves to fetter or transfer discretions conferred upon them and, in this way, preserves the existence of administrative discretion. Thus, a non-binding government policy must not be applied rigidly (5.3.3), an authorised decision-maker must not act under the dictation of another person (5.3.4), and discretion cannot be exercised by an unauthorised delegate (5.3.5).

In theory, the grounds of judicial review apply both to the making of individual decisions and to rule-making (subordinate or delegated legislation) by the executive (see 9.4.3). In practice, however, some grounds of review have no or little application to rule-making. For example, we have seen that because rules typically apply generally or to a class of the public, the fair hearing rule has no application to rule-making (5.2.2.1). Similarly, reasoning process grounds of review, such as the 'considerations' grounds, can be difficult to apply to rule-making powers because such powers are often conferred in very broad terms. The broader a discretionary power appears to be, the less willing courts are to impose implied limits on how that power is exercised.[188]

It is also the case that the reasoning process grounds of review are often difficult to apply to the exercise of non-statutory executive powers. Statutory discretions are 'readily susceptible to judicial review' because, *inter alia*, the statute necessarily provides a reference point for the identification of legitimate or proper purposes and express or implied 'considerations' which may then be used to 'structure' any exercise of the power. Prerogative or common law powers (3.6.2.2) lack this point of reference.[189] This does not mean that judges could not in theory imply analogous common law criteria or purposes to structure such powers,[190] but in practice the courts have been

---

184   *Re Minister for Immigration and Multicultural and Indigenous Affairs; Ex parte Palme* (2003) 216 CLR 212, 224; *Avon Downs Pty Ltd v Federal Commissioner of Taxation* (1949) 78 CLR 353, 360.

185   *Minister for Immigration and Ethnic Affairs v Wu Shang Liang* (1996) 185 CLR 259, 272.

186   *Minister for Immigration and Citizenship v Khadgi* (2010) 190 FCR 248.

187   As many social scientists have emphasised, lawyers often forget that wide discretionary powers can be subject to a host of non-legal norms and influences which confine and structure its exercise and thereby promote the rule of law values of certainty and predictability: see e.g. M P Baumgartner, 'The Myth of Discretion' in K Hawkins (ed), *The Uses of Discretion* (Oxford: Clarendon Press, 1992), 129.

188   For a detailed treatment of judicial review of delegated legislation, see D Pearce and S Argument, *Delegated Legislation in Australia*, 3rd edn (Sydney: LexisNexis Butterworths, 2005), Ch 12.

189   See *R v Toohey; Ex parte Northern Land Council* (1981) 151 CLR 170, 219.

190   'Just as the common law can be a source of public power, so too can it be a source of restraints upon public power': M Aronson, 'Private Bodies, Public Power and Soft Law in the High Court' (2007) 35 *Federal Law Review* 1, 23.

reluctant to do so.[191] This explains why applications for review of non-statutory powers typically involve allegations of breaches of the rules of procedural fairness.

5.3.1 The 'considerations' grounds

A decision which is based on consideration of irrelevant matters or which results from a failure to consider relevant matters is invalid.[192] Stated in the abstract, these grounds of review appear to allow judges a great deal of control over the reasoning processes of administrators. Clearly, what is relevant or irrelevant to a particular decision is a matter about which reasonable minds may disagree. Moreover, the relevance of particular matters is often best judged with the benefit of hindsight.[193] For these reasons, the courts have insisted that the categories of 'relevant considerations' and 'irrelevant considerations' do not cover the field—there are also considerations which *may be* considered but *need not* be considered (that is, permissible considerations). Thus, a party affected by a decision is not 'entitled to make an exhaustive list of all the matters which the decision-maker might conceivably regard as relevant, then attack the decision on the ground that a particular one of them was not specifically taken into account'.[194]

In determining whether a consideration either must or must not be considered, the question to be answered is whether the statute conferring a discretionary power creates an *obligation* on the decision-maker one way or the other. Thus, where a discretion is conferred in broad terms the factors which may be considered are similarly unconfined, unless 'there may be found in the subject matter, scope and purpose of the statute some implied limitation on the factors to which the decision-maker may legitimately have regard'.[195] Only if a consideration is expressly or impliedly 'extraneous' to the statute will it be classified as irrelevant. Courts have rejected the notion that statutory discretions can be completely 'unfettered'.[196] But although some considerations, such as matters of personal or 'whimsical' concern, will always be extraneous to governmental administration, the broader the discretionary power, the more difficult it will be to limit the range of permissible considerations.[197] This is particularly so when the statute empowers administrators to make decisions in the 'public interest',[198] or where the discretion is exercised by a politically accountable minister.[199]

Whether or not a decision-maker may consider the political ramifications of the decision depends upon the statutory context. It is unlikely, however, that a minister's decision would be stigmatised on account of acting in accordance with an election promise.[200] It is also accepted that decision-makers are entitled to consider lawful government policy, but it is not permissible for a decision-maker to consider themselves *bound* to exercise discretionary powers in accordance with a policy or a promise (see 5.3.4).

---

191   This reluctance is sometimes expressed by a finding that a decision is non-justiciable: 3.5.2.

192   These grounds are stated in *ADJR Act*, s 5(2)(a) and (b) and s 6(2)(a) and (b).

193   Aronson, Dyer and Groves, n 47 above, 283.

194   *Sean Investments Pty Ltd v MacKellar* (1981) 38 ALR 363, 375.

195   *Minister for Aboriginal Affairs v Peko-Wallsend Ltd* (1986) 162 CLR 24, 40.

196   *Padfield v Minister of Agriculture, Fisheries and Food* [1968] AC 997; *Goldie v Commonwealth* [2002] FCA 261, [45] ('There is, of course, no such thing as an absolute discretion in the literal sense. A statutory discretion must be exercised by reference to the subject matter, the scope and the purpose of the legislation which creates it.').

197   See, e.g., *Murphyores Inc Pty Ltd v Commonwealth* (1976) 136 CLR 1.

198   *R v Australian Broadcasting Tribunal; Ex parte 2HD Pty Ltd* (1979) 144 CLR 45; *Gbojueh v Minister for Immigration and Citizenship* [2012] FCA 288, [58].

199   *Minister for Aboriginal Affairs v Peko-Wallsend Ltd* (1986) 162 CLR 24, 42.

200   *Botany Bay City Council v Minister for Transport and Regional Development* (1996) 66 FCR 537, 560–1.

Ministers (and presumably other politically accountable decision-makers) may sometimes even have regard to their own political fortunes when making decisions.[201]

Statutes often expressly state that certain matters must be considered. Where a decision-maker is required to 'have regard' to a matter, this may require that they are bound to regard the factor as 'a fundamental matter for consideration' or merely that they must consider the matter.[202] It is possible that an express statutory requirement to consider a matter may be interpreted as not being a condition for the valid exercise of a power. Put differently, the *Project Blue Sky* approach to determining the consequence of breach of a statutory requirement (4.3) may lead to a conclusion that failure to consider a matter which is expressly required does not result in invalidity.[203]

Even when a statute expressly requires the consideration of some matters, further relevant considerations may be held relevant by implication. As already emphasised, it must be concluded that the decision-maker was bound to consider a particular matter. In *Peko-Wallsend*, the minister was bound to consider the detriment third parties would suffer before making a land grant under the Aboriginal land rights legislation. This was not simply because 'detriment' was 'relevant' in a generic sense but because the legislation required the Aboriginal Land Commissioner, who was required to make recommendations to the minister, to specifically 'comment' on the issue.

Where decision-makers are bound to consider a matter, it has been said that 'nearly every statute' posits that this is to be done 'on the basis of the most current material available to the decision-maker'.[204] On the other hand, there is a longstanding principle in administrative law which holds that a mere error of fact does not amount to an error of law. Although this principle requires qualification (see 5.4.3), it is reflected in cases which resist the conclusion that a 'factor' or 'matter' was not considered merely because a particular piece of relevant evidence was ignored.[205] The crux of this issue is the 'level of particularity' with which relevant considerations are to be identified.[206] Where relevant considerations are not expressly stated, there is considerable scope for judges to either allow or deny review by choosing whether to describe a relevant consideration in particular or general terms. If the relevant consideration is stated in very particular terms, it will be easier to conclude that failure to consider a piece of evidence directly related to the consideration and amounted to a failure to consider the matter. If, however, the relevant consideration is described in very general terms (for example, 'the circumstances of an affected individual') it may be easy to conclude that general matter was considered even though a particular piece of evidence relevant to that matter was not. Thus, the more general the description of a relevant matter, the more difficult it may be to conclude that it was not considered. Nevertheless, although 'an error of fact may be so fundamental as to cause the decision-maker to fail to take into account a mandatory

201   See, e.g., *Hot Holdings Ltd v Creasy* (2002) 210 CLR 438, 455. But contrast *Padfield v Minister of Agriculture, Fisheries and Food* [1968] AC 997, 1032 where it was said that potential political embarrassment was an unlawful reason for the decision.

202   The issue will turn on statutory context: *Minister for Immigration and Citizenship v Khadgi* (2010) 190 FCR 248, 270-1, [60–62].

203   An argument to this effect was rejected by a majority of the Full Court of the Federal Court in *Lansen v Minister for Environment and Heritage* (2008) 174 FCR 14. Such a conclusion is probably an alternative way to say that the decision-maker is not *bound* to consider the matter.

204   *Minister for Aboriginal Affairs v Peko-Wallsend Ltd* (1986) 162 CLR 24, 45. This includes material of which the decision-maker should be aware, such as material which is held by a minister's department but is not included in a memorandum briefing the minister. *Minister for Immigration and Multicultural and Indigenous Affairs v Huynh* (2004) 139 FCR 505 held that the presumption that matters will be considered on the basis of the most up-to-date information available to the decision-maker does not apply in relation to matters which the decision-maker may choose to consider (but is not bound to consider).

205   See *Minister for Immigration and Multicultural Affairs v Yusuf* (2001) 206 CLR 323, 347–8.

206   *Foster v Minister for Customs and Justice* (2000) 200 CLR 442, 452.

relevant consideration', such cases will be 'exceptional and the court should remain vigilant to ensure that cases in which the substantial complaint is that of error of fact are not masqueraded as cases seeking judicial review on the grounds of error of law'.[207] While there may be circumstances where a decision-maker may commit an error by failing to respond to a substantial, clearly articulated argument,[208] the weighing of various pieces of evidence is for the decision-maker, not the court.[209]

That the application of the 'considerations' grounds can be influenced by judicial value judgments is illustrated even more vividly by the fact that, although the principles have remained constant, there is no doubt that the results of some of the older cases would now be different. For instance, a 1947 case held that it was permissible to consider the opinion that Italians were not good farmers and the policy that 'further aggregation' of Italians in prime farming districts should not be encouraged.[210]

In addition to establishing that the decision-maker was bound either to ignore or to consider a matter, applicants must also show that this obligation was, as a matter of fact, breached. The application of the considerations grounds of review requires proof that the decision-maker considered an irrelevant matter or failed to consider a relevant one.[211] It has been said that a decision-maker can pick up and discard a red herring 'so long as he does not allow it to affect his decision'.[212] (If, however, the red herring is an allegation which is 'credible, relevant and significant', procedural fairness may require disclosure (5.2.2.3).) In *Tickner v Chapman* it was held that the minister's consideration of a report which included over 400 submissions was not adequate, on the basis of evidence which demonstrated that his consideration could not possibly have involved 'an active intellectual process' directed at the material he was obliged to consider.[213]

Related to the question of whether there is sufficient proof that a relevant matter has been considered are suggestions, in a number of cases, that the decision-maker must give relevant matters 'real, genuine and realistic' consideration.[214] The orthodox approach is to insist that how much weight is given to a relevant consideration is a matter for the decision-maker,[215] and the 'real, genuine and realistic' formula has been criticised on the basis that it invites merits review.[216] The formula may also cut against the general principle that courts should not apply a 'fine appellate tooth-comb' to the reasons of administrators.[217] On the other hand, the requirement to consider relevant matters will ring hollow

---

207 *Seiffert v The Prisoners Review Board* [2011] WASCA 148, [195].

208 *Dranichnikov v Minister for Immigration & Multicultural Affairs* (2003) 197 ALR 389, 394. This error has been styled as a denial of a fair hearing (5.2.1).

209 *Minister for Immigration and Citizenship v SZJSS* (2010) 243 CLR 164, 176. Relatedly, 'a failure to expressly mention particular material is not', as a matter of fact, 'conclusive evidence that it has not been taken into account': *Reece v Webber* (2011) 192 FCR 254, 276, [65].

210 *Water Conservation and Irrigation Commission (NSW) v Browning* (1947) 74 CLR 492. See also *Roberts v Hopwood* [1925] AC 578 where a decision to pay workers above market rates and to pay women equal pay for equal work was held to be based on irrelevant considerations, including 'eccentric principles of socialistic philanthropy' and 'a feminist ambition to secure equality of the sexes'.

211 For a discussion of the issue in the context of multi-member decision-making bodies, see *Kindimindi Investments Pty Ltd v Lane Cove Council* (2006) 143 LGERA 277, [61]–[70].

212 *Australian Conservation Foundation Inc v Forestry Commission of Tasmania* (1988) 19 FCR 127, 135.

213 *Tickner v Chapman* (1995) 57 FCR 451, 464.

214 This formulation was introduced in *Khan v Minister for Immigration and Ethnic Affairs* (1987) 14 ALD 291, 292.

215 Unless the result is reviewable for unreasonableness (5.4.4): *Minister for Aboriginal Affairs v Peko-Wallsend Ltd* (1986) 162 CLR 24, 48. Cf *Re Minister for Immigration and Multicultural Affairs; Ex parte Applicant S20/2002* (2003) 198 ALR 59.

216 This point has been recognised, though not developed, by the High Court in *Minister for Immigration and Citizenship v SZJSS* (2010) 243 CLR 164, 175–6.

217 *Minister for Immigration and Ethnic Affairs v Wu Shan Liang* (1996) 185 CLR 259.

if courts require nothing more than an assertion by decision-makers that relevant considerations were noted, even where it appears that those matters did not figure in the reasoning process at all.[218] Although the High Court has expressed reservations about the formula, it has not been clearly rejected.[219]

A 'considerations' error will not justify a remedy if it is so insignificant that it 'could not have materially affected the decision'.[220] It appears that this 'exception' will not apply in cases where the error deprived an applicant of the possibility of a successful outcome—that is, it will only apply if the error could not have had any bearing on the outcome.[221] It is best viewed as an example of the court's discretionary power to refuse relief (4.6).[222]

5.3.2 Improper or unauthorised purpose

This ground is described in the *ADJR Act* (ss 5(2)(c) and 6(2)(c)) in terms of 'an exercise of a power for a purpose other than a purpose for which the power is conferred'. To make out this ground it must be established that the decision-maker acted for a purpose which is extraneous to (that is, unauthorised by) the statutory scheme. For example, a power to deport a person cannot be exercised for the purpose of 'disguised extradition'.[223] In another example, a power to make rules for town planning purposes could not be used to defeat an Aboriginal land claim.[224] The oft-used word 'improper' does not imply that dishonesty or fraud is required, though decisions or rules will be invalidated if actual bad faith or fraud can be demonstrated.[225]

A decision based on an unauthorised purpose may also be described as a decision which was made after the consideration of an irrelevant matter (that is, the unauthorised purpose)—the test in both cases is whether the purpose or consideration is extraneous to the statute. If, however, the ground of unauthorised purpose is successfully established, it may often be practically difficult for the administrative decision-maker to remake the same decision. This is because unauthorised purpose is available only if the court is satisfied that no attempt would have been made to exercise the power if

---

218   *Hindi v Minister for Immigration and Ethnic Affairs* (1988) 20 FCR 1.

219   *Minister for Immigration and Citizenship v SZJSS* (2010) 243 CLR 164, 175–6.

220   *Minister for Aboriginal Affairs v Peko-Wallsend Ltd* (1986) 162 CLR 24, 40.

221   *VAAD v Minister for Immigration and Multicultural and Indigenous Affairs* [2005] FCAFC 117 (unreported, Hill, Sundberg and Stone JJ, 20 June 2005), [79]–[83]. The same test is applied in the context of breach of the requirements of procedural fairness: 5.2.5.1.

222   The Full Court of the Federal Court has concluded that this requirement goes to the question of whether a decision-maker is bound to consider a relevant matter rather than to the question of whether a remedy should be granted: *Lansen v Minister for Environment and Heritage* (2008) 174 FCR 14.

223   *Schielske v Minister for Immigration and Ethnic Affairs* (1988) 84 ALR 719. In this context it is often hard, on the evidence, to establish that the decision-maker was motivated by the unauthorised purpose because there will usually be valid reasons to deport a person if a foreign country is also seeking their extradition.

224   *R v Toohey; Ex parte Northern Land Council* (1981) 151 CLR 170.

225   In *SZFDE v Minister for Immigration and Citizenship* (2007) 232 CLR 189 it was held that a fraud practised (by a person purporting to be a lawyer) on an appellant in tribunal proceedings also amounted to a fraud 'on' the tribunal and that the tribunal had therefore failed to properly exercise its jurisdiction (i.e. had made a jurisdictional error). Note, however, that the court in *SZFDE* did not purport to resolve the general question of the effect of 'third party fraud' on the validity of administrative decisions, but based its decision on the terms of the legislation under consideration and the facts of the case: see ibid, [28]. Sections 5(2)(d) and 6(2)(d) of the *ADJR Act* allow review on the ground of 'bad faith'; ss 5(2)(j) and 6(2)(j) allow for review on 'any other exercise of power in a way that constitutes abuse of power'.

'it had not been desired to achieve the unauthorised purpose'.[226] Where the irrelevant considerations ground is argued, all that must be shown is that the irrelevant matter was considered.

5.3.3 Inflexible application of a rule or policy

When parliament confers a discretionary power, the courts have insisted that 'such a power must be exercised on each occasion in the light of the circumstances at that time'.[227] The future exercise of a discretionary power cannot be fettered. This no-fetter principle does not preclude administrative decision-makers developing policies (non-statutory rules) to guide the exercise of discretionary powers. The principle does, however, mean these policies must not remove the discretion or be applied inflexibly (that is, in a blanket fashion).[228] Thus in *British Oxygen Co Ltd v Minister of Technology*, it was said that, even where a decision-maker has a large number of similar applications to process, they must always be willing to listen to 'anyone with something new to say', that is, to be ready to make exceptions or waive their policy if that is justified in the circumstances of particular cases.[229]

Of course, any policies must be lawful, in the sense that they must be consistent with the statutory scheme. For example, a policy which, in effect, attempted to add a criterion to a scheme entitling a person to unemployment benefits was held to be inconsistent with the statute.[230] Similarly, a policy would be unlawful if it prevented the consideration of a relevant matter or required the consideration of irrelevant matters.[231] Indeed, this principle, that policy must be consistent with the statute explains why a policy which, on its face, fetters or removes discretion granted by statute is impermissible.[232]

We have already noted that discretion and rules both have benefits and costs (5.3). A helpful way to understand the rule against inflexible policies (or the inflexible application of a policy) is as a compromise which attempts to preserve the benefits of both rules and discretion, while limiting their costs.[233] On the one hand, it seeks to allow administrators to achieve a level of certainty and efficiency while, on the other, it enables a consideration of whether the particular circumstances of a case warrant exceptional treatment. (The extent to which tribunals undertaking merits review should apply applicable government policy is discussed in Chapter 8.) The rule against inflexible application of policy applies to

---

226 *Samrein Pty Ltd v Metropolitan Water, Sewerage and Drainage Board* (1982) 41 ALR 467, 469. Where an unauthorised purpose is one among several purposes, the decision will be invalidated only if that purpose is a 'substantial purpose' in the sense described in the text.

227 *R v Secretary of State for the Home Department, ex parte Venables* [1998] AC 407, 496–7.

228 Sections 5(2)(f) and 6(2)(f) state the ground of review as involving an 'an exercise of a discretionary power in accordance with a rule or policy without regard to the merits of a particular case'.

229 [1971] AC 610.

230 *Green v Daniels* (1977) 13 ALR 1.

231 See *R v Secretary of State for the Home Department, ex parte Venables* [1998] AC 407, 496–7.

232 Whether or not a policy that fetters discretion in a particular way is consistent with the statute may raise difficult questions of construction. In *Seiffert v The Prisoners Review Board* [2011] WASCA 148 ('Seiffert') different views were expressed as to whether a policy not to provide an oral hearing was invalid in the context where the statute allowed the board to conduct an oral hearing before cancelling a parole order but where the rules of procedural fairness in relation to the making of such a decision had been effectively excluded by the statute. *Seiffert* also illustrates the fact that the existence and nature of a policy (including whether it is 'inflexible') may depend on 'sketchy' evidence and what inferences judges are prepared to draw: e.g. ibid, [72].

233 For an excellent discussion, see C Hilson, 'Judicial Review, Policies and the Fettering of Discretion' [2002] *Public Law* 111.

existing policies; it does not require the adoption of a policy, and thus allows administrators to prefer an open-ended discretionary approach to decision-making.[234]

It has been suggested that the compromise struck by the rule against inflexible application of policy (namely, that policy is always allowed if not applied so as to fetter discretion, but is not required) may itself be a one-size-fits-all rule which is not well suited to all circumstances.[235] On the one hand, there may be thought to be decision-making contexts where administrators should be required to adopt policies or to apply their policies strictly. On the other hand, there may be other contexts where any reference to general policies or rules would inappropriately load the dice against affected individuals. In a few cases, the strictures of the rule against the inflexible use of policies have been relaxed on the basis that 'rule-based' decision-making seems appropriate in the circumstances and consistent with statutory purposes.[236]

Although decision-makers must not apply a policy in a way which excludes a consideration of the merits of an individual case, the statutory context of a power will determine what a consideration of the merits of the case entails. Thus, where an applicant claims that the 'merits' of their case were ignored but the substance of the complaint is that matters which were not mandatory, relevant considerations were not considered, it will not be to the point to say that the policy precluded a consideration of these matters.[237]

Questions can arise when an administrator decides not to apply a published policy,[238] or not to adhere to some other form of representation that they will exercise their power in a way favourable to an affected person. Is there any reviewable error involved when administrators go back on their word?[239] The logic of the no-fettering principle entails that decision-makers must be free to depart from previously announced policies or earlier representations about how discretionary powers will be exercised. Where a person has detrimentally relied on a government representation, this general point is sometimes made by saying that the principles of estoppel do not apply in relation to the exercise of public powers. This is just a fancy way of stating that the fact that a person has relied to their detriment on government promises or advice does not prevent the government exercising its statutory powers inconsistently with its earlier representations as to how its powers would be exercised. Some discussions of estoppel in Australia have left open the possibility that it may have a limited operation in public law cases.[240] But these dicta are not easily reconciled with the High Court's obvious disapproval of English cases[241] which appear to enable the substantive protection of some 'legitimate expectations'.[242]

---

234   In some circumstances, however, treating like cases unequally (i.e. inconsistently) may be reviewable on the ground of 'Wednesbury unreasonableness' (5.4.4): see Sunshine Coast Broadcasters Ltd v Duncan (1988) 83 ALR 121. Of course, administrators, and even adjudicative tribunals, are not bound by anything like the doctrine of precedent.

235   See Hilson, n 233 above.

236   For example, Wetzel v District Court of New South Wales (1998) 43 NSWLR 687. It is difficult to reconcile such cases with the blanket applicability of the principle against fettering. For further examples, see Aronson, Dyer and Groves, n 47 above, 252–3. For an interesting example of the strict application of the inflexible application of policy rule, see Rendell v Release on Licence Board (1987) 10 NSWLR 499.

237   See, e.g., the analysis of Gleeson CJ in NEAT Domestic Trading Pty Ltd v AWB Ltd (2003) 216 CLR 277, 288–99.

238   The Freedom of Information Act 1982 (Cth) (ss 8–10) requires government agencies to publish an index of their applicable policies. The agency cannot rely on a policy to the detriment of a person if these disclosure requirements are breached.

239   On the question of the extent to which governments are bound by contractual promises, see 11.3.1.2.

240   Minister for Immigration, Local Government and Ethnic Affairs v Kurtovic (1990) 21 FCR 193; Attorney-General (NSW) v Quin (1990) 170 CLR 1.

241   In particular, R v North and East Devon Health Authority, ex parte Coughlan [2001] QB 213.

242   Re Minister for Immigration, Multicultural Affairs; Ex parte Lam (2003) 214 CLR 1, 21: 5.2.2.4. It has been argued that, despite the inability of Australian courts, on current doctrine, to accept the enforcement of an estoppel or legitimate expectation, equitable compensation may be developed as an alternative equitable remedy where the justice of a case so demands: G Weeks, 'Estoppel and Public Authorities: Examining the Case for an Equitable Remedy' (2010) 4 Journal of Equity 247.

The strict application of the logic of the no-fettering principle can obviously come at the price of unfairness to individuals who, it may be thought, are at least in some circumstances entitled to take the government at its word. However, although non-statutory rules are not legally binding, they are not without legal consequence. Significantly, failure to consider applicable policy may amount to a failure to consider a relevant consideration.[243] It is also the case that a hearing may be required if a decision-maker proposes to depart from previous policy or a prior representation (see 5.2.2.4).

5.3.4 Acting under dictation

The no-fettering principle also has the consequence of preventing decision-makers from exercising their discretionary powers on the say so of someone else. Like an inflexible application of a policy, doing someone else's bidding or adopting a practice of 'rubber stamping'[244] disables decision-makers from considering the merits of a case. The gist of the 'dictation' ground of review is a requirement that the decision-maker ensure that their *own* reasoning processes are not overwhelmed by the views of another person. As it is put in the *ADJR Act* (ss 5(2)(e) and 6(2)(e)), a personal discretionary power must not be exercised at 'the direction or behest of another person'. As the use, in the *ADJR Act*, of the word 'behest' indicates, the key issue is whether the exercise of a power was overwhelmed by the views of someone who is not authorised to exercise the power, not whether the outcome was 'dictated' in some literal sense.[245]

Most difficulties involved in the application of the 'dictation' ground stem from the fact that, although administrative powers are typically conferred on particular people or officers, those people or officers are part of a broader bureaucratic hierarchy. One of the most difficult issues has been the extent to which a minister may influence the discretionary powers of officers for which they are 'responsible' in a political sense. On the one hand, there is the fact that parliament chose (presumably, for good reasons) to give a power to a particular officer. On the other hand, the principle of responsible government arguably rests on the assumption that 'the departments of the executive government', for which the minister takes responsibility, will be administered 'in accordance with the directions and policy of the minister'.[246]

Although these arguments have been raised in a number of High Court cases, the general issue remains unresolved and is subject to conflicting approaches.[247] This is understandable as both considerations noted above are based on valid and important public law principles (namely, parliamentary supremacy and ministerial responsibility). Inevitably, then, which principle is to prevail in a particular case will depend upon 'the particular statutory function, the nature of the question to be decided, the character of the [decision-maker] and the general drift of the statutory provisions in so far as they bear on the relationship between the [decision-maker] and the responsible minister'.[248] As is so often the case, the courts turn to an analysis of the general nature of the power and decision-maker to determine how a particular ground of review is to be applied in a particular case. For example, the more independence

---

243   See, e.g., *Nikac v Minister for Immigration, Local Government and Ethnic Affairs* (1988) 20 FCR 65, 81. However, where a decision-maker is free to 'deliberately depart from his own policy, it is difficult to see that a decision … could be rendered invalid because' the policy is misinterpreted: 78. See also *Black v Minister for Immigration and Citizenship* (2007) 99 ALD 1.

244   *Habib v Minister for Foreign Affairs and Trade* (2010) 192 FCR 148, 167.

245   See *Telstra Corp Ltd v Kendall* (1995) 55 FCR 221, 231.

246   As put by Murphy J in *Ansett Transport Industries (Operations) Pty Ltd v Commonwealth* (1977) 139 CLR 54, 87.

247   Ibid. See also, *R v Anderson; Ex parte Ipec-Air Pty Ltd* (1965) 113 CLR 177.

248   *Bread Manufacturers of New South Wales v Evans* (1981) 180 CLR 404, 411.

from political control a decision-maker is given, the more rigorously the rule against dictation will be applied.

Many modern statutes give ministers express powers to issue 'directions' to administrative decision-makers.[249] Sometimes these powers overcome any suggestion that a decision-maker has 'acted under dictation'. However, the extent to which such powers rebut the common law presumption against dictation is often in dispute. In some cases, powers to give directions have been interpreted as allowing only for general policy guidelines. If the statute allows only for directions of a general nature, then the decision-maker must not apply the 'direction' inflexibly, that is, they must not allow the direction to overwhelm their own exercise of the discretion.[250] Alternatively, a direction will not be authorised by such a statute if it attempts to determine outcomes of particular cases.[251] The language in which a power to give 'directions' is expressed does not always determine whether directions may be specific, or are limited to general matters. For example, in one case, quite specific directions were allowed despite the fact that the statutory power required the making of 'guidelines'.[252]

5.3.5 Unauthorised delegation

The purpose of this ground of review is to ensure that powers legally conferred on a particular decision-maker are exercised personally, and not by some other body or person. It facilitates efforts to hold decision-makers accountable for their actions, and prevents bureaucratic buck-passing. Unauthorised delegation is not specifically mentioned in the *ADJR Act*, though it clearly is an instance of the ground that 'the person who purported to make the decision did not have jurisdiction to make the decision' or simply the ground that the decision was not 'authorised by the enactment'.[253]

The rule against delegation is best understood as a statutory presumption.[254] As such, it can be expressly rebutted by statute. Indeed, modern statutes routinely give decision-makers express power to delegate their powers.[255] Where this is so, powers must be delegated in accordance with any statutory requirements. Express powers to delegate some powers do not necessarily exclude an implied power to delegate others, but the usual presumption is that the powers not expressly delegated must be exercised personally.[256]

The presumption that statutory powers cannot be delegated can sometimes appear unrealistic and out of touch with the realities of public administration. Although many powers are reposed in ministers or high-level bureaucrats, it is unrealistic to believe such decision-makers could give their personal

---

249   Where a statute allows the minister to give formal directions, it is inadvisable to engage in informal communications which may be interpreted as akin to a direction: *Hughes Aircraft Systems International v Airservices Australia* (1997) 76 FCR 151, 231.

250   *Riddell v Secretary, Department of Social Security* (1993) 42 FCR 443.

251   *Aboriginal Legal Service Ltd v Minister for Aboriginal and Torres Strait Islander Affairs* (1996) 69 FCR 565.

252   *Smoker v Pharmacy Restructuring Authority* (1994) 53 FCR 287.

253   Which are recognised in the *ADJR Act*: see s 5(1)(c) and (d); s 6(1)(c) and (d).

254   The prerogative and common law powers of the Crown 'can theoretically be exercised by any officer with actual or ostensible authority to act': R Creyke and J McMillan, *Control of Government Action: Text, Cases and Commentary* (Sydney: LexisNexis, 2005), 430; see also E Campbell, 'Ostensible Authority in Public Law' (1999) 27 *Federal Law Review* 1.

255   Interpretation Acts typically contain provisions relevant to understanding express powers of delegation: see, e.g., *Acts Interpretation Act 1901* (Cth), ss 34AA, 34AB and 34A.

256   *Minister for Aboriginal Affairs v Peko-Wallsend Ltd* (1986) 162 CLR 24, 38. This is subject to the 'agency' principles discussed below.

attention to the plethora of statutory functions conferred on them. The law has (at least partially) responded to this problem in two ways. First, in most circumstances it is permissible for decision-makers to rely on administrative assistance. A minister may thus rely on a memorandum or briefing note which summarises the issues and makes recommendations, even though they have an obligation to make the decision personally. Where a decision-maker does rely on a briefing note, however, the note must accurately identify all mandatory relevant considerations.[257] The line between permissible assistance and assistance which undermines the obligation on the decision-maker to consider matters personally can be controversial. In *Tickner v Chapman*, the minister was required to consider all representations attached to a report. It was accepted that the minister could rely on his staff to sort the representations into categories, to put the representations in a 'common form', and to summarise technical material. However, some representations were incapable of effective summary (for example, photographs) and 'nothing short of personal reading ... would constitute proper consideration' of them.[258]

The second response to the practical problems which may arise if the presumption against delegation is applied strictly is that it is sometimes possible, as a matter of statutory interpretation, to conclude that the 'principal' (that is, the statutory holder of the power) may act through an authorised 'agent'.[259] This sounds like an implied delegation, but the legal position of an 'agent' is subtly different from that of a 'delegate'. Where a person acts as a delegate, the power is exercised in their own name, and independently of the principal; where a person acts as an authorised agent, they act on behalf of the principal, and in law their decision is that of the principal.[260] The notion that an agent's decision may be invalidated for failing to sign-off in the name of the principal has, however, been criticised for elevating form over substance.[261] Although a statute may authorise delegation of power to a non-government decision-maker, it may be thought inappropriate to accept that a person not within the principal's own department or agency can act as an agent.[262]

The principles determining when a decision-maker may be allowed to act through an agent are 'not entirely satisfactory'.[263] The classic justification for implying that a minister may act through an agent, articulated in *Carltona Ltd v Commissioner of Works*, is that it would be impossible for ministers to personally attend to all of their statutory functions and that, in any event, ministers remain accountable to the parliament for any errors in judgment.[264] In Australian law, however, the '*Carltona* principle' has been interpreted so that its application is limited neither to ministers nor to decision-makers who are

---

257   *Sean Investments Pty Ltd v Mackellar* (1981) 38 ALR 363, 371. Similarly, if a briefing paper placed emphasis on an irrelevant matter, this would be strong evidence that it was considered.

258   (1995) 57 FCR 451, 464. It was also held that the male ministers had an obligation to consider a sealed representation which contained references to secret matters that, according to Ngarrindjeri cultural norms, should not be disclosed to women.

259   An authorised agent may rely on administrative assistance but cannot 'consign [the] substantive aspects of the making of the decision to subordinates': *Pattenden v Federal Commissioner of Taxation* (2008) 175 FCR 1, 1.

260   *Re Reference under Section 11 of Ombudsman Act 1976 for an Advisory Opinion; Ex parte Director-General of Social Services* (1979) 2 ALD 86, 93.

261   M Campbell, 'The *Carltona* Doctrine' (2007) 18 *Public Law Review* 251. Paragraph 34AB(c) of the *Acts Interpretation Act 1901* (Cth) provides that 'a function or power so delegated, when performed or exercised by the delegate, shall, for the purposes of the Act, be deemed to have been performed or exercised by the authority [i.e. the principal]'. The extent (if any) the enactment of this provision blurs the common law distinction between delegates and agents is unclear. For a suggested operation of the provision which preserves the distinction, see J McMillan and R Creyke, *Control of Government Action: Text, Cases and Commentary* 2nd edn (Sydney: LexisNexis, 2009), 572.

262   In *Plaintiff M612010E* (2010) 243 CLR 319 the High Court avoided answering the question of whether a contractor might act as the minister's agent.

263   E Campbell, n 254 above, 3.

264   [1943] 2 All ER 560.

directly accountable to the parliament.[265] This suggests that the 'administrative necessity' argument will sometimes be sufficient to justify the implication that parliament could not have intended a decision-maker to exercise all of their powers personally.

In *O'Reilly v Commissioners of State Bank of Victoria*, the High Court decided that the Commissioner of Taxation (or a Deputy Commissioner of Taxation) may act through authorised agents, despite the fact that the commissioner had a formal power to delegate his powers to a wide range of departmental officials. In the circumstances of the case, the commissioner had delegated his powers to issue an investigation notice to his deputy commissioners, but the challenged notice had been issued by an officer authorised to act on the behalf of one of the deputy commissioners. The High Court upheld the validity of the notice, principally to preserve 'administrative order and efficiency'.[266] In a persuasive dissent, Mason J pointed to the fact that the commissioner could have formally delegated the powers (if that was, indeed, necessary) and argued that an implied capacity to act through an agent is not appropriate when the power involves 'a substantial exercise of discretion' and 'may have a great impact on the affairs of individual persons'.[267] The majority judgments in *O'Reilly* give little guidance as to when issues of administrative efficiency should trump these other considerations, but the width of a discretionary power and its capacity to affect individuals adversely have been emphasised in some later cases which have taken a stricter approach to the question of whether decision-makers who have express powers of delegation can act through an agent.[268] Despite the fact that administrative necessity may justify decisions by agents, little consideration has been given to what necessity might mean and what evidence is necessary to prove its existence. However, the fact that express powers of delegation do not inevitably undermine agency arrangements suggests that necessity, strictly speaking, is not required.[269]

Finally, it is worth noting that the idea of agency in administrative law focuses on whether the statute allows a person to act on the decision-maker's behalf, whereas in private law the concept of agency is directed at the issue of when it is 'appropriate to fix civil liabilities on principals for actions they themselves might have taken'.[270] For this reason, although the terminology is now well entrenched, it might have been preferable to avoid use of the term 'agency' in attempts to avoid unrealistic applications of the presumption against delegation.

5.4 Decisional grounds

In this section, we consider grounds related, in some way or another, to the decision itself. These grounds of review may be available even if the decision-maker has assiduously followed all required procedures and has made no reasoning process errors. The most obvious way in which a decision-maker may make an error directly related to the decision itself is by making a mistake about the law to be applied.

---

265   *O'Reilly v Commissioners of State Bank of Victoria* (1983) 153 CLR 1.

266   Ibid, 32.

267   Ibid, 19.

268   See, e.g., *Secretary, Department of Social Security v Alvaro* (1994) 50 FCR 213; *Din v Minister for Immigration and Ethnic Affairs* (1997) 147 ALR 673.

269   The issues are helpfully discussed in Campbell, n 261 above, 254–257, where it is argued that necessity should be thought of as 'a presumption arising from the nature of modern government'. The appropriateness of this approach may be thought to depend on the reach of the *Carltona* doctrine beyond the context of ministerial decision-making.

270   E Campbell, n 254 above, 3.

This idea sounds like a straightforward application of the principle that government decision-makers must be able to justify their acts and decisions on the basis of some source of the legal authority (5.1.1). But what it means to make a legal error is complicated by some of the most elusive concepts and distinctions in administrative law.

5.4.1 Jurisdictional error

Under the common law remedial model the availability of a remedy will, in many cases, depend on whether an identified error is a jurisdictional error (4.1.1). The concept of jurisdictional error can thus be understood as a device which is designed to limit the extent to which judges can correct for legal, factual or policy errors related to the decision itself.

The theory behind the development of the concept of jurisdiction was simple: jurisdictional errors relate to the question of whether the decision-maker has the legal authority to make a decision, whereas a non-jurisdictional error is made in the course of exercising jurisdiction already established. In other words, 'jurisdictional questions ... related to the scope of the decision-maker's power to decide'—not to questions which 'arose in the exercise of an admitted decision-making power'.[271] In this way, the theory of jurisdiction functioned to allocate decision-making powers between particular decision-makers.

On the traditional theory, jurisdiction was understood in a sort of spatial or temporal sense which involved a distinction between conditions of power to decide and the exercise of that power. Some judges thus spoke of jurisdictional errors as those relating to 'preliminary questions'. If a decision-maker's powers depended on the question of whether certain conditions existed or were fulfilled, the courts would ensure that these questions were answered 'correctly' (that is, the judge's opinion about how the question should be answered would trump the administrator's view). The corollary of this was that decision-makers had the legal power to answer any non-jurisdictional question 'wrongly' (that is, the judge's opinion about how the question should be answered would *not* trump the administrator's view)—and such errors did not affect the legal validity of the decision (see 4.4.1).

Although the theory of jurisdiction is, in the abstract, straightforward, it has long been the subject of criticism. The main difficulty with the theory is that it says very little about how a court is to establish the jurisdictional boundaries in particular cases.[272] Consider, for example, a statute which gives an administrative tribunal a power to *reinstate* an *employee* who has been *unfairly dismissed*. Which of these italicised matters go to the tribunal's jurisdiction? Can a court correct any errors made in determining what it means to reinstate; who qualifies as an employee; and the meaning of unfair dismissal? If not, what are the core elements giving the tribunal the power to exercise the power of reinstatement? The reality is that many statutes give little explicit guidance as to whether giving a correct answer to a particular question is a precondition to the very existence of the power to make the decision.

The difficulty inherent in finding stable criteria by which courts can clearly distinguish between preconditions to the existence of a power and the actual exercise of the power was a contributing factor to the ultimate rejection of the distinction between jurisdictional and non-jurisdictional errors of law in England, with the consequence being that a decision may be retrospectively invalidated whenever it is

---

271   G Airo-Farulla, 'Rationality and Judicial Review of Administrative Action' (2000) 24 *Melbourne University Law Review* 543, 551. The *ADJR Act*'s grounds of review include 'that the person who purported to make the decision did not have jurisdiction to make the decision' (s 5(1)(c)) and 'that the decision was not authorised by the enactment in pursuance of which it was purported to be made' (s 5(1)(d)).

272   Jack Beatson, 'The Scope of Judicial Review for Error of Law' (1984) 4 *Oxford Journal of Legal Studies* 22, 25.

affected by an 'error of law'.[273] But the demise of the spatial–temporal approach to jurisdiction in English administrative law should also be understood in the context of a broader trend, namely the increasing willingness of the courts to take a more proactive or 'activist' role in judicial review. Over time, the conclusion was reached that the traditional theory of jurisdiction unduly limited the courts' powers, especially in relation to the control of administrative (as opposed to judicial) decision-makers.[274] In relation to administrative decision-makers, this trend led to an extension of the category of legal errors having the consequence that affected decisions would be invalid.

Despite the urgings of some Australian judges,[275] the High Court has not followed the English lead. The court's refusal to abolish the distinction between jurisdictional and non-jurisdictional errors needs to be understood in the context of three factors. First, the High Court has accepted that the role played by the concept of jurisdictional error in determining the appropriate level of judicial supervision means that the underlying policy question will not be resolved by the development and application of logically water-tight categories or precise tests.[276]

Second, the difficulty in drawing a 'bright line' distinction between jurisdictional and non-jurisdictional error has not been considered a sufficient reason to jettison the underlying concepts. One reason often cited for this is that blurriness at the margins does not necessarily demonstrate that there are no relevant differences to be observed. However, the more fundamental reason for retaining the concept of jurisdictional error is that it has been held to be the basis of judicial review under the Australian Constitution. As we have seen, the High court has held that the Constitution's incorporation of the writ-based common law remedial model of judicial review means that the constitutional writs of mandamus and prohibition are available only for 'jurisdictional error' (4.5.3). As this review is constitutionally entrenched (by s 75(v)), it cannot be removed by the parliament (see 7.1). Moreover, Kirk's case (3.4.2; 7.1) extended the constitutional significance of the distinction between jurisdictional and non-jurisdictional error, by giving it 'the same general effect' in state law 'as had earlier been established for Commonwealth law'.[277] In Australian administrative law, the approach to the articulation of what legality (that is, judicial) review must entail—that is, what may and may not be reviewed under its banner—can be understood through the outcome of determinations about whether errors are, or are not, jurisdictional.

Third, the retention of the distinction between jurisdictional and non-jurisdictional errors has not exempted Australian law from the broader trend towards more intrusive standards of judicial review. Whereas in England the extension of review standards was achieved by the demise of the concept of jurisdiction as the central limiting device for review, in Australia a similar extension has been achieved by the expansion of the concept of jurisdiction so that the category of errors which may qualify as jurisdictional errors has been significantly enlarged. This expansion has been most dramatic in relation to administrative (as opposed to judicial) decision-makers, and it is now clear that jurisdictional error can occur not just in relation to preliminary questions—which would mean the decision itself was not authorised in a relatively straightforward sense—but also in the process of determining the merits of an issue.

---

273   See *Anisminic Ltd v Foreign Compensation Commission* [1969] 2 AC 147; *R v Lord President of the Privy Council, ex parte Page* [1993] AC 682.

274   Recall that 'inferior courts' are also subject to judicial review.

275   *Re Minister for Immigration and Multicultural Affairs; Ex parte Miah* (2001) 206 CLR 57, 123 (Kirby J).

276   *Kirk v Industrial Relations Commissioner* (2010) 239 CLR 531, 570.

277   *Chase Oyster Bar Pty Ltd v Hamop Industries Pty Ltd* (2010) 78 NSWLR 393, 402.

The modern starting point for any discussion of jurisdictional error in Australia is the High Court's decision in *Craig v South Australia*.[278] The High Court rejected the argument that an order to stay a criminal trial involved a jurisdictional error because the 'inferior court' judge had not properly understood the legal test to be applied. Any error was, it said, within jurisdiction.

The High Court's decision in *Craig* placed considerable emphasis on the fact that the decision-maker was an 'inferior court' as opposed to an 'administrative tribunal' (or, presumably, any other administrative official). It was held, as a general rule, that the concept of jurisdictional error should be defined more narrowly in the case of inferior courts than in the case of administrative tribunals and decision-makers. Whereas the ordinary jurisdiction of a court encompasses the 'authority to decide questions of law' (and therefore to answer questions of law wrongly), presumptively at least, the court argued that administrative tribunals lack this authority. In part this presumption was justified because inferior courts are staffed by legally trained officials, whereas administrative tribunals may not be. It was also said that, whereas inferior courts are plugged into the 'ordinary hierarchical judicial structure', tribunals are not.[279] But while both of these factors are true in some cases, they are false in others. Some tribunals, such as the Commonwealth Administrative Appeals Tribunal (8.4), have judges as members; and the decisions of many tribunals are subject to appeals to courts on questions of law. Perhaps for this reason the High Court indicated that its analysis should not be taken as applicable to what it called 'anomalous courts or tribunals' which do not fit the standard profile.[280] Arguably, the court was on firmer ground when it pointed out that the constitutional separation of judicial power prevents Commonwealth tribunals from authoritatively deciding questions of law.[281] Even here, however, the differences between inferior courts and administrative tribunals may be overstated, as tribunals must decide legal questions and the answers given are binding until challenged by appeal or by judicial review.

These sorts of reasons led the court in *Kirk's* case to question the assumptions underpinning inferior court/tribunal distinction, and it is likely that less emphasis will be placed on the distinction in the future.[282] The court's analysis in *Kirk* is consistent with an acceptance that the critical issue in determining whether or not to apply a narrower or broader conception of jurisdictional error is one of 'function and purpose, not nomenclature'.[283] As intimated above, the reason why the court drew a distinction between inferior courts and tribunals in *Craig* was to articulate two different approaches to the determination of jurisdictional error. On a narrow approach (which typically would apply in relation to inferior courts) jurisdictional boundaries were said to be defined by the preconditions for the existence of authority to decide a matter or by any clear limits on functions or powers. For example, a jurisdictional error is involved where an inferior court, the jurisdiction of which is limited to civil matters, purports to hear and determine a criminal charge. An inferior court will also exceed jurisdiction where an essential precondition (such as the existence of a fact or state of satisfaction) has not been fulfilled or where a

---

278   *Craig v State of South Australia* (1995) 184 CLR 163.

279   Ibid, 176, 179.

280   Ibid, 177.

281   Ibid, 179.

282   C Finn, 'Constituionalising Supervisory Review at State Level: The End of *Hickman*?' (2010) 21 *Public Law Review* 92, 103. In *Craig* it was accepted that there would be 'anomalous' tribunals and that distinction's significance was to establish a starting presumption only.

283   *Re Carey; Ex parte Exclude Holdings Pty Ltd* (2006) 32 WAR 501, [104]. This approach may be conceptualised as part of a broader 'functional' approach to review, where the appropriate level of judicial scrutiny in part depends upon the functions performed and powers exercised by a decision-maker: see J Basten, 'The Supervisory Jurisdiction of the Supreme Courts' (2011) 85 *Australian Law Journal* 273.

particular matter must be considered or ignored 'as a pre-condition of the existence of any authority to make a decision'. Finally, the High Court held that an inferior court will 'fall into jurisdictional error' if it misconstrues the statute or other instrument which confers its jurisdiction and 'thereby misconceives the nature of the function which it is performing or the extent of its powers', though it was conceded that in such cases, the line between jurisdictional and non-jurisdictional errors of law 'may be particularly difficult to discern'.[284] This is because it may be argued that a decision-maker misconstruing the law to be applied (thereby considering a wrong question) amounts to misconceiving the nature of its functions or the extent of its powers.

On the broader approach to jurisdictional error (typically appropriate for administrative tribunals and other administrative officials), it was said that jurisdiction will be exceeded where the decision is affected by 'an error of law which causes it to identify a wrong issue, to ask itself a wrong question, to ignore relevant material, to rely on irrelevant material, or, at least in some circumstances, to make an erroneous finding or to reach a mistaken conclusion'.[285] Thus, wherever the law to be applied is misconstrued, jurisdictional error will probably result. Moreover, as amplified by later cases, it is clear that jurisdictional errors may be made by breaching grounds of review related to reasoning processes. Breach of the considerations ground of review can clearly amount to a jurisdictional error,[286] and there is no principled reason for excluding other sorts of reasoning process errors.[287] It is also clear that breach of procedural fairness obligations does, and breach of statutory procedure may, amount to jurisdictional error.[288]

To the extent that the court's approach to determining whether an error goes to jurisdiction in *Craig* is premised on the distinction between inferior courts and administrative tribunals, it needs to be treated with care. More broadly, *Kirk's* case emphasised that the categories of jurisdictional error associated with the narrow approach to jurisdiction in *Craig* were not 'a rigid taxonomy of jurisdictional error'. Rather they were just examples. The move away from an attempt to authoritatively categorise instances of jurisdictional error in *Kirk* can be read as emphasising the contextual nature of the enquiry: it is not possible, the court declared, to 'mark the metes and bounds of jurisdictional error'.[289] One interpretation of this aspect of the decision is that the key issue will be an assessment of the gravity or seriousness of the error.[290] There is an element of welcome realism in this assessment. However, the courts are more likely to rationalise conclusions through accepting the gravity of an error as a relevant factor in assessing, though a process of statutory interpretation, whether a particular ground of review or legal error, should be read as a condition of validity (so breach will amount to a jurisdictional error).

To sum up, in relation to most administrative decision-makers, it can be assumed that jurisdictional errors comprise not only misunderstanding or misapplication of the substantive legal tests to be applied but also breaches of the grounds of review related to procedure and reasoning processes. It may also be accepted that the decisions of inferior courts should normally be subject to less searching judicial review.

---

284   *Craig v State of South Australia* (1995) 184 CLR 163, 177–8.

285   Ibid, 179.

286   *Minister for Immigration and Multicultural Affairs v Yusuf* (2001) 206 CLR 323, 351, 339.

287   As has been recognised in the Federal Court where a wide range of 'reasoning process' grounds have been confirmed as amounting to jurisdictional errors in the context of migration decisions. For discussion of a large number of cases, see C Beaton-Wells, 'Judicial Review of Migration Decisions: Life after *S157*' (2005) 33 *Federal Law Review* 141.

288   See *Re Refugee Review Tribunal; Ex parte Aala* (2000) 204 CLR 82 and *SAAP v Minister for Immigration and Multicultural and Indigenous Affairs* (2005) 228 CLR 294.

289   *Kirk v Industrial Relations Commissioner* (2010) 239 CLR 531, 573.

290   E.g. Finn, n 282 above, 103.

These propositions, however, are subject to the possibility that a particular statute may indicate that a narrower or broader concept of jurisdiction error is applicable. Two observations can be made about this conclusion. First, any emphasis on context and statutory interpretation over the articulation of accepted categories of jurisdictional errors for specified decision-makers may make the law more, rather than less, uncertain. As the High Court itself has emphasised in *Project Blue Sky*, answers to the question of whether or not it is a purpose of the legislation that breach of a statutory provision (or, one might add, an administrative law norm) should go to jurisdiction 'often reflect[s] a contestable judgment'.[291]

Second, the overall Australian position on the identification of jurisdictional errors is a far cry from the traditional theory of jurisdiction. Although many jurisdictional errors relate to the decision itself (because the substance of the decision is beyond the powers conferred), procedural and reasoning process errors also routinely amount to jurisdictional errors. The modern approach to jurisdictional error thus cuts across our division of the grounds of review into procedure, process, and decisional errors. That some remedies are available only for jurisdictional errors is certainly a lesser barrier to review than it once was.

5.4.2 The concept of error of law

The concept of error of law has also proved treacherous. Part of the problem is terminological confusion: 'error of law' can be legitimately used in a number of different ways. In one sense, any breach of an administrative law norm (that is, ground of review) which can potentially justify the award of a remedy can be thought of as an 'error of law'. There is nothing wrong with this usage, but it tells us nothing about the concept of error of law as a distinct ground of judicial review.

In the context of 'error of law on the face of the record' (a ground enabling certiorari to issue (4.1.1)) the focus in most cases has been on errors made in the interpretation of statutory rules.[292] Because the courts have historically defined the 'record' narrowly (so that reasons for decisions are excluded), the question of whether the reasoning process grounds of review qualify as errors of law for the purposes of certiorari has not often arisen. It seems, however, that in jurisdictions where legislation has expanded the 'record' to include reasons, reasoning process grounds of review are included within the concept of error of law.[293]

The error of law concept has also been developed in the context of statutory rights of appeal, which are often limited to 'questions of law'. Despite the prevalence of such appeal rights, the High Court has recently indicated that understand the scope of particular statutory provisions for appeal must be attentive to particular statutory contexts.[294] In this context questions can arise about the extent to

---

291   *Project Blue Sky Inc v Australian Broadcasting Authority* (1998) 194 CLR 355, [91].

292   A misinterpretation of common law rule may also constitute an error of law: see, e.g., *Craig v State of South Australia* (1995) 184 CLR 163.

293   See e.g. *Saville v Health Care Complaints Commission* [2006] NSWCA 298 (unreported, Handley, Tobias and Basten JJA, 2 November 2006), [55]. However, as such errors will also normally constitute jurisdictional errors when made by administrative decision-makers, this is of practical importance only in relation to inferior courts.

294   Appeal rights which are restricted to 'legal' questions come in a variety of statutory formulations and the 'language of the statute must be the relevant starting point, not a taxonomy which seeks to reduce a wide variety of statutory provisions to a few discrete categories'. Moreover, even in relation to particular statutory language, general attempts at definition are dangerous. See *Kostas v HIA Insurance Services Pty Limited* (2010) 241 CLR 390, 417–8, [88–89]. Although this approach gives due regard to the ability of legislatures to confer appeal rights in whatever terms they see fit, it does not place a high value on legal certainty.

which the concept of error of law encompasses the grounds of review generally.[295] For example, it is normally thought that decisions of the Administrative Appeals Tribunal (which can be appealed to the Federal Court on a question of law under s 44 of the *Administrative Appeals Tribunal Act 1975* (Cth)) can be reviewed not only on the basis of a misinterpretation of the legislation, but also on the basis of a 'breach of one of the general grounds on which administrative action is reviewed by the courts'.[296] This conclusion makes practical sense as a narrow construction of 'question of law' could easily be outflanked by an application for review under the *ADJR Act*. Despite this, there have been suggestions that the meaning of question of law should be circumscribed more tightly, so that at least some of the grounds of review arguable in an *ADJR Act* application may not be arguable in a s 44 appeal.[297] If confirmed, such suggestion would have the undesirable result that legal challenges to AAT decisions may fail simply on account of having been pleaded incorrectly in the Federal Court. Further, there would be implications for the debate as to whether the *ADJR Act* applications should be dismissed given the availability of an appeal right under the *AAT Act*.[298]

'Error of law' (even if *not* apparent on the face of the record) is also listed as a discrete ground of review in the *ADJR Act* (ss 5(1)(f); s 6(1)(f)). In most circumstances, it has not been necessary for the courts to consider the relationship between the error of law ground and other grounds of review.[299] The *ADJR Act* states that a decision must involve an error of law, which means that the error must be 'material to the decision in the sense that it contributes to it so that, but for the error, the decision would have been, or might have been different.'[300] (A similar requirement applies to non-jurisdictional errors of law on the face of the record and jurisdictional errors at common law.)[301]

In all contexts in which the concept of error of law applies, the issue which most often arises involves how to distinguish between errors of law, which are reviewable, and errors of fact, which in most cases are not.

5.4.3 Errors of fact

There are a number of reasons why the courts have long resisted reviewing administrative determinations of fact. Theoretically speaking, the basic rule of law rationale which justifies judicial review does not extend to allowing judges to exercise powers given to administrative decision-makers. Such powers necessarily require administrators to make determinations of fact. As Mason J put the point in *Bond*,

---

295   It has been held that the requirement that appeals lie only on questions of law means that success requires an appellant to demonstrate an error of law: see *Waterford v Commonwealth* (1987) 163 CLR 54, 77–8.

296   D Pearce, *Administrative Appeals Tribunal* (Sydney: LexisNexis, 2003), 180. See also *Clements v Independent Indigenous Advisory Committee* (2003) 131 FCR 28.

297   See *Comcare v Etheridge* (2006) 149 FCR 522, 530. In *Kostas v HIA Insurance Services Pty Limited* [2010] HCA 32 the High Court had no difficulty in concluding that the 'no evidence' ground of review raised a question of law enlivening an appeal right on 'a question with respect to a matter of law' decided by the Consumer, Trader and Tenancy Tribunal.

298   For a discussion of the interaction between the *ADJR Act* and *AAT Act*, see *Ugar v Commissioner of Federal Police* [2010] FCA 303; see also *Australian Securities and Investments Commission v Administrative Appeals Tribunal* (2010) 187 FCR 334, 335–6; *Australian Postal Corporation v Sellick* (2008) 245 ALR 561, 582.

299   The exception is the relationship between error of law and no evidence (s 5(1)(h)), considered below at 5.4.3.2.

300   *Australian Broadcasting Tribunal v Bond* (1990) 170 CLR 321, 353.

301   E.g. *House v Defence Force Retirement and Death Benefits Authority* (2011) 193 FCR 112; *Screen Australia v Eme Productions No 1 Pty Ltd* (2012) 200 FCR 282, 294–5, [51–57].

'[t]o expose all findings of fact, or the generality of them, to judicial review would expose the steps in administrative decision-making to comprehensive review by the courts', [302] inevitably involving judges in the merits of administrative decisions.

Additionally, there are a number of practical and policy reasons which counsel against the review of fact-finding. These include resource constraints faced by courts (could courts cope with the caseload if applicants could simply argue an administrator made a factual error?), and the view that administrators are often in a better position, due to their experience and expertise, to interpret relevant facts. Thus, although courts are also expert finders of fact, the orthodox view is that 'there is no error of law simply in making a wrong finding of fact'.[303]

Despite this orthodoxy, judges understandably show unease when faced with clear factual errors, and it is perhaps unsurprising to discover that there are qualifications to the basic rule.[304] We have already seen that errors of fact can sometimes ground an argument that a decision-maker failed to consider a relevant matter or considered an irrelevant one, though the courts often draw a distinction between errors about mere pieces of evidence and the more general concept of 'matters' which must be considered (5.3.1). And it may also be that fact-finding processes can be reviewed on account of serious irrationality or illogicality, though the application of this ground of review beyond the context of establishing jurisdictional facts relating to a decision-maker's state of mind is uncertain (5.4.3.1.2). It has also been long accepted that where the evidence appears inadequate, it may be a short step to the conclusion that the decision-maker has misconceived its jurisdiction or powers (and thereby committed a jurisdictional error)[305]—though courts often emphasise that they should be slow to take such a step.[306] But the assumed line between mere (albeit serious) factual error and jurisdictional error is often easier to state than apply.[307]

In addition to errors of fact being used as part of an argument to make out one of the other grounds of review, there are two general exceptions to the rule that factual error is not reviewable: the review of 'jurisdictional facts' and the 'no evidence' ground of review.

5.4.3.1 Jurisdictional facts

According to a recent High Court statement, the expression 'jurisdictional fact' is generally 'used to identify a criterion the satisfaction of which enlivens the exercise of the statutory power or discretion in question'.[308] In the court's recent jurisprudence on the topic, two important categories of jurisdictional facts have been identified.[309] The nature of the criterion on which jurisdiction depends is quite different in each case. Importantly, the intensity of judicial review differs depending on which class of jurisdictional fact is applicable.

---

302   *Australian Broadcasting Tribunal v Bond* (1990) 170 CLR 321, 341.

303   *Waterford v Commonwealth* (1987) 163 CLR 54, 77.

304   J McMillan, 'Developments Under the *ADJR Act*: The Grounds of Review' (1991) 20 *Federal Law Review* 50, 59.

305   *R v Australian Stevedoring Industry Board; Ex parte Melbourne Stevedoring Co Pty Ltd* (1953) 88 CLR 100, 120.

306   *Re Minister for Immigration and Muilticultural Affairs; Ex parte Cohen* (2001) 177 ALR 473 [35].

307   And can lead to exasperation for students and judges alike: e.g. *SZHFC v Minister for Immigration and Multicultural and Indigenous Affairs* [2006] FCA 1359 (unreported, Allsop J, 19 October 2006), [42].

308   *Gedeon v NSW Crime Commission* (2008) 236 CLR 120, 139.

309   *Perrinepod Pty Ltd v Georgiou Building Pty Ltd* [2011] WASCA 217, [98–111].

5.4.3.1.1 Type 1: the traditional usage

The most straightforward (and traditional) use of the phrase 'jurisdictional fact' refers to situations where a decision-maker's statutory power is conditioned on the existence of a particular fact such that the making of a valid decision depends upon the existence of the fact. In these instances, the crucial point to appreciate about jurisdictional facts is that the court can substitute its opinion, about whether the fact exists, for the opinion of the administrative decision-maker. (Although it is sometimes said that jurisdictional facts are 'objective', the existence of a fact is never self-evident—which, of course, explains why people routinely disagree about questions of fact.) Thus, as with any jurisdictional requirement, a jurisdictional fact must be determined correctly (that is, the court gets to say what is 'correct'). The worry is that if administrators' determinations of jurisdictional facts were reviewable on only the standard grounds of judicial review (which do not generally encompass errors of fact), administrators could widen their own powers.

A useful example of the traditional jurisdictional fact principle in operation is *Enfield v Development Assessment Commission*.[310] The issue was whether or not the commission's conclusion, that a particular development did not relate to a 'special industry' (that is, one which was 'offensive or repugnant' to others in the locality), was a factual finding the correctness of which was a condition of the existence of its powers to approve a development application without the consent of the relevant local council and the minister. Although the finding of fact that the development did not relate to a 'special industry' did not occur at the preliminary stage of the application process, the High Court concluded that it was nonetheless a jurisdictional fact and thus reviewable for correctness. The court emphasised the language of the relevant provision, which was expressed in mandatory and objective terms. That is, the legislation stated that applications relating to special industries 'must not' be granted if further conditions were not fulfilled, and did not suggest that the special industry question was a matter to be resolved according to the subjective 'opinion' of the decision-maker. But perhaps the most important consideration was the pivotal role the factual determination played in the legislative scheme: if an application was classified as relating to a 'special' as opposed to 'general' industry, a different set of procedures (including public consultation) and conditions applied.

The lesson of *Enfield* is that whether a question of fact is jurisdictional is a question of statutory interpretation. A number of additional relevant factors have been identified in the cases. Where a power is conditioned on the existence of a fact, the determination of which involves broad, value-laden judgments, the fact is less likely to be classified as jurisdictional.[311] And, as with any statutory precondition, public inconvenience may lead a court to determine that a factual precondition is of a 'directory', as opposed to 'mandatory', nature (see 5.2.5.2). As was the case in *Enfield*, the most important factor in interpreting the statute is often a consideration of the importance of the factual determination in the overall decision-making scheme.[312] Evidently the interpretive task parallels the approach taken in the context of asking whether compliance with a statutory requirement or administrative law norm is a condition for the making of a valid decision.[313]

---

310   *Corporation of the City of Enfield v Development Assessment Commission* (2000) 199 CLR 135.

311   *Timbarra Protection Coalition Inc v Ross Mining NL* (1999) 46 NSWLR 55, 72; For a review of the authoriites, see *Ilic v City of Adelaide* (2010) 107 SASR 139.

312   See also *Australian Heritage Commission v Mount Isa Mines Ltd* (1997) 187 CLR 297.

313   *Project Blue Sky Inc v Australian Broadcasting Authority* (1998) 194 CLR 355 (see 4.3)

Although the traditional usage of the jurisdictional fact doctrine appears to be a straightforward application of the theory of jurisdiction, its operation is often controversial. If courts too readily classify factual requirements as jurisdictional preconditions, they will regularly become immersed in second-guessing administrative determinations of fact. Moreover, in some cases the jurisdictional fact doctrine can be applied to facts determined at the commencement of or early in a long decision-making process. This outcome will often result in 'regulatory indecision, wastefulness and inefficiency' and may also undermine the respect accorded to administrative decisions.[314] One commentator has concluded that although 'there is nothing inherently illogical about the theory of jurisdictional fact', its 'consequences are so inconvenient and counterproductive that it is rarely an attractive interpretative option'.[315] On the other hand, the High Court has insisted that where a fact is appropriately classified as 'jurisdictional' it would be inappropriate for judges to defer to administrative determinations of the factual issue. Notwithstanding the reality that an administrator's experience and expertise may provide sound reasons for deferring to their judgment as to the existence or non-existence of complex facts, the judicial response in Australia has been that it is the province and function of the courts to enforce the legal limits on administrative powers. Despite the court's insistence that the courts must independently determine whether a tribunal acted within jurisdiction, judges are permitted (though not required) to give weight to factual determinations of administrators where that is appropriate.[316] But this is a far cry from building a notion of deference into the applicable standard of judicial review. If one believes that questions of jurisdictional fact (or indeed questions of law generally (see below 5.4.3.3)) can sometimes be reasonably answered in more than one way (that is, there is no single correct answer), one may also wonder about the strength of the assumption that courts should not (due to their constitutional role) defer to administrative determinations (at least where those determinations are, in some sense or another, reasonable).[317]

5.4.3.1.2 Type 2: A decision-maker's 'state of mind'

Statutes often provide that a decision-maker must or may take certain action if they have a certain 'state of mind', such as being 'satisfied' of a particular matter or holding a particular 'opinion' or 'belief'.[318] For example, the *Migration Act 1958* (Cth) provides that, if the minister (or review tribunal) is satisfied that a person is a refugee, they must grant a protection visa; if the minister (or review tribunal) is not so satisfied, a visa must be refused.

The High Court considers that such state of mind requirements also amount to 'jurisdictional fact' provisions.[319] Be that as it may, conditioning a power on the formation by the decision-maker of a

---

314   M Aronson, 'The Resurgence of Jurisdictional Facts' (2001) 12 *Public Law Review* 17, 27. The fact that judicial review remedies are discretionary and may be refused on account of 'delay' in bringing an application has been emphasised in some jurisdictional fact cases: e.g. *Timbarra Protection Coalition Inc v Ross Mining NL* (1999) 46 NSWLR 55, 72.

315   Ibid, 39.

316   *City of Enfield v Development Assessment Commission* (2000) 199 CLR 135.

317   As is done in the United States of America for review of administrative agencies interpretations of law: see *Chevron USA Inc v Natural Resources Defence Council, Inc*, 467 US 837 (1984) which held that courts should defer to agency interpretations of their empowering statutes unless the statute is clear or the interpretation is unreasonable.

318   *Buck v Bavone* (1976) 135 CLR 110, 118.

319   *Minister for Immigration and Citizenship v SZMDS* (2010) 240 CLR 611; see also *Re Minister for Immigration and Multicultural Affairs; Ex parte Applicant S20/2002* (2003) 198 ALR 59.

particular state of mind is a jurisdictional fact of a 'special kind'.[320] In particular, the courts do not review the formation of a required state of mind for correctness (for example, by requiring the administrator's opinion or belief to coincide with the state of mind the court would itself have formed). Unlike the traditional usage of the jurisdictional fact doctrine, courts will not substitute their own judgments about whether the decision-maker should have reached a particular conclusion.

This raises the question of the basis on which state of mind jurisdictional facts are reviewable. The applicable principles are in a state of flux. Although state-of-mind provisions undoubtedly broaden the scope of a decision-maker's powers,[321] it has long been accepted that they do not confer an 'absolutely uncontrolled and unlimited discretion'.[322] Thus, if the opinion or belief which a decision-maker 'formed was reached by taking into account irrelevant considerations or by otherwise misconstruing the legislation, then it must be held that the opinion has not been formed'.[323] Similarly, if the opinion was formed in the light of an improper purpose, then the reasoning processes of the decision-maker would demonstrate that the law (that is, the nature of the opinion required) had not been understood. It has also been accepted that a decision-maker's state of satisfaction may be reviewed on the basis that 'the decision reached was so unreasonable that no reasonable authority could properly have arrived at it',[324] or where the opinion could not have been 'formed by a reasonable man who correctly understands the meaning of the law under which he acts'.[325] Although there may be subtle differences between these formulations, the applicable standard of review appears to provide, at the very least, a close parallel to the *Wednesbury* unreasonableness standard (see 5.4.4).

Nevertheless, the High Court has more recently indicated that where the existence of a particular state of mind is a statutory precondition to the discharge of a statutory duty (as in the above migration example), the *Wednesbury* unreasonableness ground (5.4.4) has no application. This ground of review only applies to *discretionary* powers, and a statutory obligation to act only if the decision-maker is satisfied that a particular matter is not a discretionary power.[326] The exclusion of *Wednesbury* unreasonableness in this context must be considered in light of the fact that the High Court has developed an alternative ground on which the rationality or logicality of the formation of a state of mind can be reviewed. It should also be noted that the accepted view, that the reasoning process grounds of review are available in this context, has not been challenged.

---

320   J Basten, 'The Supervisory Jurisdiction of the Supreme Courts' (2011) 85 *Australian Law Journal* 273, 289.

321   *Minister for Immigration and Ethnic Affairs v Wu Shan Liang* (1996) 185 CLR 259, 276.

322   *R v Connell; Ex parte The Hetton Bellbird Collieries Ltd (No 2)* (1944) 69 CLR 407, 432.

323   Ibid.

324   *Buck v Bavone* (1976) 135 CLR 110, 118.

325   *R v Connell; Ex parte The Hetton Bellbird Collieries Ltd* (1944) 69 CLR 407, 430. It was also said (at 432) that the opinion will not be lawful if its formation was 'arbitrary, capricious, irrational, or not bona fide'.

326   See *Minister for Immigration and Citizenship v SZMDS* (2010) 240 CLR 611, 624 and 647, though it should be noted that acceptance by Crennan and Bell JJ of restricting *Wednesbury* unreasonableness to the exercise of a discretion is less clear than that in the joint judgment of Gummow and Keifel JJ. Heydon J was silent on the issue. See also *Re Minister for Immigration and Multicultural Affairs; Ex parte Applicant S20/2002* (2003) 198 ALR 59. The basis for so restricting *Wednesbury* unreasonableness implies that a sharp distinction can be drawn between a discretionary power and a duty. These concepts are, however, better situated on a continuum. It is, for example, unrealistic to think that a duty to grant a refugee visa if satisfied that a person has a well-founded fear of persecution (or to deny a visa if not so satisfied) does not give the decision-maker a significant degree of choice. Although the statute expresses the power as a duty, it is an imprecise one and judicial review does not enable the courts to substitute their own opinion about whether the duty arises. Interestingly, in *Coal and Allied Operations Pty Ltd v Australian Industrial Relations Commission* (2000) 203 CLR 194, 205 a majority of the High Court accepted that achieving a state of satisfaction involves a 'degree of subjectivity' and can 'in a broad sense' be 'described as a discretionary decision'.

In *SZMDS*, Gummow ACJ and Kiefel J explained that the critical question in reviewing the formation of a state of mind jurisdictional fact requirement is 'whether the determination was irrational, illogical and not based on findings or inferences of fact supported by logical grounds'.[327] Many questions can be raised about this newly formulated ground for establishing jurisdictional error—including the extent to which rationality and logicality are separate ideas.[328]

The focus of our discussion will, however, be upon whether this ground of review impermissibly encroaches on the merits of administrative decision-making. The High Court's response to this objection is two-pronged. First, the ground does not licence review for alleged deficiencies in 'intra-mural' fact-finding, but is directed at ensuring that a required jurisdictional threshold has been crossed. Put slightly differently, the ground of review will only be available in relation to illogical and irrational reasoning related to factual determinations that are critical to forming the required state of mind.[329] This appears to limit the potential for irrationality in fact-finding processes to become a generally applicable ground of judicial review.[330] Second, it has been emphasised that review on this basis will be successful only in rare cases. In *S20* it was held that there was no illogicality or irrationality in a tribunal disbelieving the applicant's corroborating evidence on the basis that they did not believe what the applicant had already told them.[331] However, although it is clear that *serious* irrationality is required, the nature of the standard of review to be applied was articulated in two distinct ways in *SZMDS*.[332]

In *SZMDS* the Refugee Review Tribunal refused an application because it was not *satisfied* that the applicant was a genuine refugee. The applicant had been working for a number of years in the United Arab Emirates, but was a Pakistani national. He claimed a well-founded fear of persecution, were he to return to Pakistan, on the basis of his homosexuality. The tribunal had rejected the applicant's claim to be a homosexual and, on this basis, rejected his claim that he would face persecution in Pakistan. The tribunal identified two factual matters which were considered to be 'inconsistent' with the applicant's case: (1) he had voluntarily returned to Pakistan, for a brief period, prior to coming to Australia; and (2) he had not sought asylum at his first opportunity (on an earlier visit to the UK).

---

327   *Minister for Immigration and Citizenship v SZMDS* (2010) 240 CLR 611, 625 (Gummow and Kiefel JJ); 643 (Crennan and Bell JJ). The Full Federal Court has concluded that the availability of this basis for establishing a jurisdictional error is 'not in doubt': *MZXSA v Minister for Immigration and Citizenship* (2010) 117 ALD 441. As Crennan and Bell JJ point out in *SZMDS*, the acceptance of this irrationality and illogicality ground of review in relation to state of mind jurisdictional facts 'may well have first emerged in Australia ... as a reaction to the ouster of the review ground of '*Wednesbury* unreasonableness' which applied in relation to the Federal Court's jurisdiction for a period in immigration law: *SZMDS* (2010) 240 CLR 611, 647.

328   Although it makes sense to think about degrees of irrationality (as perfect rationality is unattainable in the real world), inferences are either logical or illogical (i.e. logic is a binary system). However, that which is illogical will also be irrational and how serious the irrationality is in the context of the decision-making process and the interests affected may then be assessed.

329   *Minister for Immigration and Citizenship v SZMDS* (2010) 240 CLR 611, 624, 628 (Gummow and Kiefel JJ), 643 (Crennan and Bell JJ).

330   English courts have gone further in allowing review for errors of fact: see P Craig, 'Judicial Review, Appeal and Factual Error' [2004] *Public Law* 788; M Groves, 'Judicial Review and the Concept of Unfairness in English Public Law' (2007) 18 *Public Law Review* 244.

331   *Re Minister for Immigration and Multicultural Affairs; Ex parte Applicant S20/2002* (2003) 198 ALR 59. The ground has been argued successfully on the basis of acting in defiance of unequivocal and uncontested material (*Ortiz v Minister for Immigration and Citizenship* [2011] FCA 1498) and where a required statement of reasons did not 'disclose any material by reference to which a rational decision-maker' could have based their conclusions (*Minister for Immigration and Citizenship v SZLSP* (2011) 187 FCR 362, 385). Arguably, however, these examples could also be captured by the 'no-evidence' ground of review (see 5.4.3.2).

332   As noted in *MZXSA v Minister for Immigration and Citizenship* (2010) 117 ALD 441, 451, [45]; see also *SZOOR v Minister for Immigration and Citizenship* [2012] FCAFC 58.

Gummow and Kiefel JJ concluded that this aspect of the tribunal's reasoning related to a critical finding (because it determined the existence of the relevant jurisdictional fact) and was reached by an inference 'not supported on logical grounds'.[333] In relation to the first 'inconsistency', their Honours pointed out that the conclusion rested on an assumption that it would be likely that the applicant's sexual identity would be discovered—despite the fact that the tribunal had not made any findings on that issue. For this reason there was no logical connection between the evidence and the conclusion reached.[334] In relation to the second claimed inconsistency, there was no evidence before the tribunal which provided any grounds for rejecting the applicant's explanation as to why he had not earlier claimed asylum in the UK—the explanation related to the fact he was then living in the United Arab Emirates. Because the actual reasoning adopted was said to involve illogical inferences, jurisdictional error was established.

Crennan and Bell JJ more directly addressed the standard of illogicality or irrationality required to establish jurisdictional error. (Gummow and Kiefel JJ merely state that conclusions that a factual determination or inference was irrational or illogical would not be 'lightly' reached.) After noting the 'undeniable semantic overlap' between irrationality, illogicality and unreasonableness, their Honours argued that irrationality review should adopt a review standard which is of the 'same order' as that applied in the context of establishing *Wednesbury* unreasonableness. The test is 'whether logical or rational or reasonable minds might adopt different reasoning or might differ in any decision or finding to be made on the evidence upon which it is based'.[335] This test is very close to asking whether a state of mind decision has been reached on the basis of a reasoning process which is so irrational or illogical that no reasonable person could have so decided.[336] Crucially, however, in applying this test, Crennan and Bell JJ appear to ask whether there was room for a rational tribunal to reach the conclusions reached in 'light of all the evidence' before the decision-maker, rather than focusing more narrowly on the tribunal's actual reasoning processes.[337] If this is what was intended, it has the significant result of requiring only that the evidence can possibly support the finding (in an objective sense) rather than requiring that the decision-maker's actual reasoning be rational or logical.[338] For example, one federal court judge concluded that the approach of Crennan and Bell JJ in *SZMDS* compelled him to uphold a decision despite his own view that the tribunal's use of an anonymous letter that could not be tested was 'irrational, illogical and unreasonable'.[339] This was because it was not possible to conclude that no decision-maker could have reached the decision on the basis of the totality of the evidence.

---

333   *Minister for Immigration and Citizenship v SZMDS* (2010) 240 CLR 611, 627.

334   It was emphasised that the tribunal had been inattentive to the nature of the applicant's case insofar as it related to his sexual identity which is a matter that would not be 'perceived unless disclosed': *Minister for Immigration and Citizenship v SZMDS* (2010) 240 CLR 611, 627.

335   *Minister for Immigration and Citizenship v SZMDS* (2010) 240 CLR 611, 648.

336   If this is the test to be applied then it is unsurprising that Crennan and Bell JJ do not appear completely convinced that illogicality and irrationality are needed as a distinct ground of review, given the availability of *Wednesbury* unreasonableness. See the discussion at 648.

337   *MZXSA v Minister for Immigration and Citizenship* (2010) 117 ALD 441, 450–1, [43–44]. Gummow and Kieffel JJ's approach in *SZMDS* focuses on the logicality of the reasons which were given by the decision-maker.

338   It has been suggested that this general approach to rationality review 'sends the wrong message' to administrators by not legally requiring them to 'think rationally about the evidence that is before them'. G Airo-Farulla, 'Rationality and Judicial Review of Administrative Action' (2000) *Melbourne University Law Review* 534, 568.

339   *SZOOR v Minister for Immigration and Citizenship* [2012] FCAFC 58, [16]. The majority of the court held that the tribunal had reached its adverse conclusion about the appellant's credibility 'quite independently of any comfort which may have been drawn by reference to the anonymous letter': [102], [114]. Relief was withheld for the reason that any possible error could not possibly have made a difference to the result.

The approach to the standard of review in applying the irrationality or illogicality ground of review in relation to jurisdictional facts of the state-of-mind type thus remains uncertain.[340] On the approach of Crennan and Bell JJ, it may be that this newly formulated ground of review does not materially progress beyond the idea that critical factual findings must be made on the basis of some probative evidence (see 5.4.3.2. below).

Although the principles applicable to reviewing state-of-mind jurisdictional facts remain uncertain, it is clear that the role of judicial review is quite different in relation to this species of jurisdictional fact. Sometimes, however, it will not be clear whether or not the methodology of review associated with the traditional usage of jurisdictional fact (type 1 cases) should be applied or whether that associated with state-of-mind jurisdictional facts (type 2 cases) is appropriate. In *Plaintiff M70/2011 v Minister for Immigration and Citizenship*[341] the applicants were asylum seekers who were detained on Christmas Island. The minister wished to transfer them to Malaysia but could only lawfully do so if he had validly declared Malaysia to be a 'specified country'. The minister had a discretionary power to transfer 'offshore entry' people to a country declared to be a 'specified country'. The minister was also empowered to make a written declaration that a specified country 'has' met a number of criteria—principally that the country provides asylum seekers with access to 'effective procedures' for assessing their claims and offers protection for asylum seekers and refugees in line with relevant human rights standards. The plurality judgment in *Plaintiff M70* held that the power to make a declaration was conditioned on the actual existence of the criteria declared to exist by the minister. That is, the criteria were held to be jurisdictional facts (in the traditional sense). In reaching this conclusion emphasis was given to the fact that the power to make a declaration was not framed in terms of what the minister thinks or believes or whether he was satisfied that the criteria existed. The plurality also gave emphasis to the minister's discretion being to 'declare that a specified country *has* the relevant characteristics'.[342]

In contrast, French CJ held that the criteria only amounted to jurisdictional facts in the sense that the minister must be satisfied that the criteria are fulfilled by a specified country. Although the power was not expressly conditioned upon the formation of an opinion or belief on the part of the minister, there were reasons for construing it in this way. Importantly, the minister was required to make evaluative judgments in relation to the criteria. Although the existence of legal obligations was relevant to determining whether the criteria were met in a particular country, so was the question of whether such obligations were fulfilled in practice. The consequence was that the court should not make its own findings as to the existence of the listed criteria and that review was limited to whether the minister formed his opinion about their existence having correctly understood the law.[343]

---

340   Heydon J, the fifth member of the court in *SZMDS*, concluded there was no illogicality and stated that this excused him from determining any of the questions of law at issue in the case. This approach is disappointing in the context of widespread uncertainty surrounding the application of this ground of review prior to *SZMDS*. The Full Federal Court appears to have concluded that Heydon J's judgment should be read in line with Crennan and Bell JJ's approach: *SZOOR v Minister for Immigration and Citizenship* [2012] FCAFC 58.

341   (2011) 244 CLR 144.

342   *Plaintiff M70/2011 v Minister for Immigration and Citizenship* (2011) 244 CLR 144, 193–4. The plurality was able to conclude that the jurisdictional facts did not exist because Malaysia did not provide the required access or protection set out in the criteria 'in accordance with an obligation [i.e. legal obligation] to do so': ibid, 201. The relevant provisions of the *Migration Act* were read as reflecting a legislative intention to adhere to Australia's international obligations in relation to refugees. As such it was held, as a matter of statutory interpretation, that the criteria should be 'understood as a reflex of Australia's obligations': ibid, 196. Kiefel J took a similar approach to the plurality; Heydon J dissented.

343   *Plaintiff M70/2011 v Minister for Immigration and Citizenship* (2011) 244 CLR 144, 180–1. French CJ held that the application of this approach to review also led to invalidity: the minister could not properly consider whether the criteria were met without consideration of the fragility of protection and access offered by the domestic law of Malaysia to asylum seekers and refugees: ibid, 183.

In conclusion three points can be emphasised. First, which type of jurisdictional fact analysis applies (if any) is a question which is answered through the standard techniques of statutory interpretation. Second, finding that the state of mind species of jurisdictional fact applies is one way in which courts can, in practical effect, adopt a more deferential approach to administrative determinations of fact. Nevertheless, the fact that a jurisdictional condition is expressly or impliedly framed in terms of an administrator's state of mind does not prevent review, though the intensity of that review is a matter of continuing controversy.

5.4.3.2 No evidence

Although it is routinely assumed that the common law 'no evidence' (or 'no probative evidence') ground of judicial review is well established, its precise status remains subject to uncertainties.[344] One difficulty is that it is possible to explain the result in at least some of the key 'no evidence' cases on the basis that the non-existence of evidence to support a factual finding justified a conclusion that the decision-maker had misconceived their jurisdiction.[345] Further, although it is often said that the making of findings of fact 'in the absence of evidence is an error of law',[346] the reach of this principle is unclear. Does it apply to any finding of fact, or only to findings that pass a certain threshold of importance or which are central to the decision? The Full Federal Court has said that the ground is made out if there 'is no evidence to support' a finding which is a 'critical step in its ultimate conclusion'.[347] Further, where a judicial review remedy requires that jurisdictional error be established, it has been suggested that the no evidence ground of review can only be established where the factual finding relates to a 'jurisdictional fact'.[348]

Whatever the precise reach of the no evidence ground of review, what is clearer is that Australian judges have generally resisted attempts to convert the ground into review for insufficiency of evidence.[349] One reason for this is the view that 'the "no evidence" ground of judicial review depends not on the reasoning of the decision-maker, but on a comparison between the material available to the decision-maker and the conclusion reached'.[350] It is also clear that acting on the basis of no evidence is an instance of the potentially broader idea that jurisdictional facts must not be found on the basis of illogical and irrational factual findings.[351]

---

344   'Evidence' includes material which 'would not count as evidence in a judicial context': *L & B Linings Pty Ltd v WorkCover Authority of New South Wales* [2012] NSWCA 15, [34].

345   See T H Jones and R Thomas, 'The 'No Evidence' Doctrine and the Limits to Judicial Review' (1999) 8 *Griffith Law Review* 102, 107–12. See also *NAIZ v Minister for Immigration & Multicultural and Indigenous Affairs* [2005] FCAFC 37 (unreported, Branson, RD Nicholson and North JJ, 11 March 2005), [22] where, despite the existence of some probative evidence on an critical issue, it was held that the summary way in which that issue was dealt with indicated that the decision-maker did not 'apply the right test'.

346   *Australian Broadcasting Tribunal v Bond* (1990) 170 CLR 321, 356; *Kostas v HIA Insurance Services Pty Limited* (2010) 241 CLR 390.

347   *SFGB v Minister for Immigration and Multicultural and Indigenous Affairs* (2003) 77 ALD 402, 407; *SZMWQ v Minister for Immigration and Citizenship* (2010) 187 FCR 109, 144. In the context of the *ADJR Act* 'no evidence' ground, judges have used similar formulations: see below.

348   *Minister for Immigration and Multicultural and Indigenous Affairs v SGLB* (2004) 207 ALR 12, 21, [39]; *Minister for Immigration and Citizenship v SZMDS* (2010) 240 CLR 611, 622.

349   See, e.g., *Bruce v Cole* (1998) 45 NSWLR 163, 188–9. Difficult questions may arise when there may have been evidence but it has not been adequately described in a required statement of reasons: see *Minister for Immigration and Citizenship v SZLSP* (2010) 187 FCR 362.

350   *L & B Linings Pty Ltd v WorkCover Authority of New South Wales* [2012] NSWCA 15, [34].

351   See *Brennan v New South Wales Land and Housing Corporation* [2011] NSWCA 298, [93].

The *ADJR Act* (s 5(1)(h)) allows review on the ground that 'there was no evidence or other material to justify the making of the decision'. The Act further provides (s 5(3)) that this ground:

shall not be taken to be made out unless—

a   The person who made the decision was required by law to reach that decision only if a particular matter was established, and there was no evidence or other material (including facts of which he was entitled to take notice) from which he could reasonably be satisfied that the matter was established; or

b   The person who made the decision based the decision on the existence of a particular fact, and that fact did not exist.

This is one of the few instances where the drafters of the *ADJR Act* intentionally departed from the common law. Unfortunately, however, the detailed description of the no evidence ground in s 5(3) has not resulted in a clearer understanding of the statutory form of the no evidence ground. Indeed, perhaps there are more uncertainties about its meaning than that of the common law version.

On one view, the requirements of ss 5(3)(a) and (b) are necessary but not sufficient elements of the no evidence ground of review. That is, even after an applicant establishes that their case falls within one of those paragraphs, there is an additional question as to whether it can be concluded that 'there was no evidence or other material to justify the making of the decision'. The alternative view is that ss 5(3)(a) and (b) articulate the precise content of the *ADJR Act*'s version of the no evidence ground, that is, all an applicant need do is bring their case within either paragraph. In *Rajamanikkam*, two High Court judges adopted the first view; two adopted the second; and there is a dispute as to which view was adopted by the fifth member of the court in that case.[352] In *S20*, McHugh and Gummow JJ were content to note (not very helpfully) that the scope of review for facts under the *ADJR Act* 'may give rise to differences of opinion' in the High Court.[353]

Many of the details of the meaning of paragraphs (a) and (b) of s 5(3) also remain to be worked out. For example, the reasonableness standard in paragraph (a)—that there must be no evidence from which the decision-maker could be reasonably satisfied of a matter—has been noted but not subjected to extensive analysis. And while it seems that a matter 'required by law' is appropriately described as a 'critical' finding, the High Court has cast little light on what this means and whether or how it differs from the common law position.[354] It has also been concluded that a fact is only 'required by law' where 'the legislation prescribes it be established as 'an objective fact'—that is, as a traditionally conceived jurisdictional fact.[355]

With respect to paragraph 5(3)(b), it appears that an applicant must positively establish that a fact on which the decision was based does not exist.[356] And while the weight of authority appears to accept that the reference in paragraph (b) to a 'particular fact' means a fact which was 'critical' (in logic or law)

---

352   *Minister for Immigration and Multicultural Affairs v Rajamanikkam* (2002) 210 CLR 222. Aronson, Dyer and Groves, 4th ed, 262 argue a majority position rejecting the first ('cumulative') interpretation can be discerned from the judgments in *Rajamanikkam*. Cf *Sunchen v Pty Ltd v Commissioner of Taxation* (2010) 264 ALR 447 (Perram J concluding that *Rajamanikkam* does not formally overturn the decision of the Full Court of the Federal Court in *Curragh Queensland Mining Ltd v Davies (1992)* 34 FCR 212, 220–1 which adopted the 'cumulative' interpretation).

353   *Re Minister for Immigration and Multicultural Affairs; Ex parte Applicant S20/2002* (2003) 198 ALR 59, 72.

354   See *Minister for Immigration and Multicultural Affairs v Rajamanikkam* (2002) 210 CLR 222, 233–4, 240.

355   *Watson v Australian Community Pharmacy Authority* (2011) 284 ALR 293, 304.

356   *Australian Retailers Assoication v Reserve Bank of Australia* (2005) 148 FCR 446 [580]; *Watson v Australian Community Pharmacy Authority* (2011) 284 ALR 293, 306.

to the making of the decision,[357] the High Court has applied this standard in a very strict way. While it is normally said that a remedy should not be denied if there is any possibility that the decision-maker would have reached an alternative conclusion,[358] it seems that a decision based on a finding of fact (even if the fact does not exist) will not be 'critical' to the decision if the same decision could have been made in any event. Thus, in *Rajamanikkam*, the fact that only two of the eight reasons given for disbelieving the applicant were based on facts which did not exist meant that it could not be concluded that the decision was based on those (non-existent) facts. It was not possible to say that the decision-maker would not have reached the same decision in any event.[359] Thus, though many details remain unclear, it does seem that the majority of the High Court is not minded to interpret the no evidence ground of review in the *ADJR Act* expansively.

5.4.3.3 Distinguishing law from fact

The jurisdictional fact and no evidence grounds of review are exceptions to the general principle that an error of fact is not, of itself, a ground of judicial review. However, in any context where a court may review a decision or hear an appeal on the basis of an error of law (see 5.4.2), it is notoriously difficult to determine whether a particular error is properly characterised as one of law or fact. The identification of questions of law has been described as 'an esoteric and highly technical matter'.[360] If a question is classified as one of law, the consequence is that the review or appeal court can determine the correct answer for itself. On the other hand, courts cannot correct errors of fact. Thus, what is at stake is the distribution of decision-making power as between administrators (and inferior courts) on the one hand, and reviewing and appeal courts on the other.

The analysis of whether a particular error is one of law or fact is normally broken down into three stages: fact-finding, law-stating and law-applying (that is, application of law to the facts as found).[361] It is very difficult for an error committed in finding primary facts to amount to an error of law—even findings which are perverse or clearly against the weight of the evidence will not suffice.[362] Having said that, the line between acting completely without evidence and acting 'perversely' will often be a matter of judgment, as what it means to say that a finding was reached on the basis of no evidence inevitably raises questions of whether the evidence which was before the decision-maker was relevant to any factual conclusions which bear legal consequences.

One might assume that the law-stating phase of decision-making—where the decision-maker identifies and interprets the legal norm or rule to be applied—should also be capable of a relatively simple treatment. Surely any error made in stating the *legal* norm to be applied is necessarily an error of *law*. The trouble with this assumption is that the courts have devised a number of strategies to qualify this basic proposition. Matters are further complicated because the qualifications are built on the

---

357   E.g. *Sunchen v Pty Ltd v Commissioner of Taxation* (2010) 264 ALR 447, 457.

358   See 5.2.5.1; 5.3.1.

359   *Minister for Immigration and Multicultural Affairs v Rajamanikkam* (2002) 210 CLR 222, 243. Gleeson CJ further argued that even if paragraph (b) was made out, it could not be concluded that there was 'no evidence or other material to justify the decision': 236

360   *OV v Members of the Board of the Wesley Mission Council* (2010) 270 ALR 542, 550, [28].

361   There are no bright lines between these stages of decision-making. For instance, fact-finding necessarily occurs in the shadow of the rule to be applied: see Aronson, Dyer and Groves, n 47 above, 203.

362   See, e.g., *Azzopardi v Tasman UEB Industries Ltd* (1985) 4 NSWLR 139.

introduction of distinctions which are easily manipulable. Perhaps the most popular way to qualify the idea that the identification and interpretation of the law to be applied involves a question of law is the notion that where a statute uses an 'ordinary' term[363] or a non-legal 'technical' term,[364] the meaning of the term is a question of fact (though its original classification, as an ordinary, technical or legal term is a question of law).[365] These categories are premised on the existence of a further distinction between the *meaning* of a term and the *construction* or effect given to a statutory term, because the meaning of a term (even if used in a 'non-legal' sense and thus a question of fact) can always be qualified by asking how the term is to be construed in the wider context of the statute (and this raises a question of law).[366]

The incoherence of this elaborate analytical scheme was laid bare by the High Court in *Collector of Customs v Agfa-Gevaert Ltd*,[367] and its influence appears to be diminishing.[368] The court labelled the distinction between the *meaning* of a term and the *construction* or effect given to a statutory term 'artificial, if not illusory'.[369] As the court argued, meaning and construction go hand in hand: it is not as if one precedes the other.[370] This means that whenever a decision-maker identifies and interprets the law as incorporating an ordinary or technical term, this analysis necessarily involves a question of construction which raises an issue of law. The problems of applying the above distinctions are compounded where the statute uses a complex amalgam of ordinary, specialised and legal language. Thus, the Full Federal Court has concluded that '[w]here there is uncertainty as to the meaning of a statutory word or expression … the process of construction raises a question of law'.[371] It is little wonder that commentators—even those who believe a defensible distinction between questions of law and fact can be maintained—have argued that the distinctions between ordinary, technical and legal terms are unhelpful.[372]

This brings us to the most problematic stage of the analysis: the question of whether the application of the law to the facts raises a question of fact or law. One common approach relies on the distinction between ordinary and legal meanings (discussed above): although the question of whether the facts as found fall within the provision of a statutory enactment properly construed is generally a question of law, when a statute uses words according to their ordinary meaning it will—unless the conclusion is not reasonably open—be a question of fact.[373] Such judicial attempts to have one's cake and eat it too are understandable. On the one hand, the application of vague statutory language will often raise questions of 'fact and degree'.[374] For example, reasonable people may disagree about whether particular activities

---

363 That is, one whose meaning is to be ascertained by reference to ordinary English usage.

364 That is, one whose meaning is to be ascertained by reference to expert technical evidence or appropriate specialised reference works.

365 See, e.g., *Collector of Customs v Pozzolanic Enterprises Pty Ltd* (1993) 43 FCR 280.

366 Ibid.

367 (1996) 186 CLR 389.

368 The Full Court of the Federal Court and the New South Wales Court of Appeal have accepted the logic of the High Court's critique: *Screen Australia v Eme Productions No 1 Pty Ltd* (2012) 200 FCR 282, 292, [41]; *OV v Members of the Board of the Wesley Mission Council* (2010) 270 ALR 542, 550–1, [29–32].

369 *Collector of Customs v Agfa-Gevaert Ltd* (1996) 186 CLR 389, 396.

370 A good example of an error of law arising from the application of a statutory term used in its 'ordinary' sense on the basis that the term must be construed in light of the broader statutory phrase is *Hope v Bathurst City Council* (1980) 144 CLR 1.

371 *Screen Australia v Eme Productions No 1 Pty Ltd* (2012) 200 FCR 282, 292, [42].

372 Aronson, Dyer and Groves, n 47 above, 213.

373 See e.g. *Blacktown Workers' Club Ltd v O'Shannessy* (2011) 183 LGERA 184, [44].

374 See *Edwards (Inspector of Taxes) v Bairstow* [1956] AC 14, 33.

involve the 'carrying on' of a 'business',[375] or whether a particular trip constitutes a 'journey' home from work.[376] On the other hand, conclusions about such questions clearly have legal consequences and thus may also appear as a question of law. Of the courts' attempts to determine when applying the law to facts gives rise to a question of law, the best that can be said is that (1) where the court concludes that there is more than one reasonable answer to the question of whether the facts as found fall within or outside of a legal term, it will intervene only if an unreasonable answer is given[377] and (2) where, alternatively, the court concludes that only one conclusion is open (that is, that the facts necessarily fall within or outside a statutory or legal terms), it will correct any wrong answer given.[378] What remains unexplained is when and why a court will conclude that only one answer is open or that there is more than one reasonable answer which may be given to the application question.

Given the Janus-faced nature of the courts' approach to applying the law to facts, many commentators have concluded that an 'analytical' approach to the problem—which tries to determine in advance whether an issue raises a question of law or fact and which is inevitably accompanied by more detailed definitions of each category[379]—cannot solve the problem. If, in the abstract, a question can be equally thought of as raising a question of fact and law, the only way forward is to ask why the classification must be made.[380] This requires a court to determine whether or not it ought to hear an appeal (on a question of law) or engage in judicial review (for error of law). Very few scholars or judges think that this question is to be answered in a 'cynical' way, that is, based on a judge's gut feeling as to which of the parties should win the particular case. Rather, the question is to be answered by an analysis of what level of legal supervision of administrative decision-makers (and inferior courts) is appropriate. The question is by no means an easy one: it may involve difficult trade-offs between achieving consistency (which may come with more judicial intervention) against benefits associated with allowing some autonomy for administrative determinations, based on their more particular experience and expertise (which favours less intervention). How such trade-offs are to be made will depend on the particular decision-making and statutory context. Some label this approach 'pragmatic' because it clearly rests on value judgments rather than supposedly neutral analytical categories.[381]

5.4.3.4 The twin pillars of Australian administrative law

One judge has argued that Australian judicial review is built upon two fundamental 'pillars': (1) that the courts must not encroach on the merits of administrative decision-making; and (2) that the courts bear the responsibility for interpreting and applying the law which constrains administrative decision-makers.[382] The result of the application of these principles is that, although Australian judges, in effect,

---

375   *Hope v Bathurst City Council* (1980) 144 CLR 1.

376   See *Vetter v Lake Macquarie City Council* (2001) 202 CLR 439.

377   This conclusion may be expressed by holding that a statutory term is used in its ordinary sense: *Hope v Bathurst City Council* (1980) 144 CLR 1, 7. For a recent example, see *Australian Securities and Investments Commission v Administrative Appeals Tribunal* (2011) 195 FCR 485, 495–6, [89–91].

378   In an often cited formulation of this point, an error of law will arise if 'the true and only reasonable conclusion contradicts the determination': *Edwards v Bairstow* [1956] AC 14, 36.

379   For example, the definitions of ordinary, technical and legal terms.

380   T Endicott, 'Questions of Law' (1998) 114 *LQR* 292.

381   On how best to describe this approach compare Endicott, ibid, and P Cane, *Administrative Law*, 5th edn (Oxford: Clarendon Press, 2011), 62.

382   See R Sackville, 'The Limits of Judicial Review: Australia and the United States' (2000) 28 *Federal Law Review* 107.

show great deference to administrative determinations of fact, they do not defer to administrative determinations of law—once an issue is characterised as raising a legal question, the judges insist that it is for them to give the appropriate answer. According to the High Court, 'an essential characteristic of the judicature is that it declares and enforces the law which determines the limits of the power conferred by statute upon administrative decision-makers'.[383]

Given the strength of the assertion that legal interpretation is the exclusive function of the courts (in the sense that their interpretations will always prevail), it is worth noting that other views are possible. Although judges often write as if every legal question admits of only one right answer, the fact that the individual justices of the High Court so often come to different conclusions casts serious doubt on this thesis. Indeed, most legal theorists accept that, at least by the time a case gets to an appellate court, it will be necessary to choose between one of a number of reasonable answers to the question of law posed. This means that appellate court judges routinely look beyond 'doctrine' to make their decisions. The recognition that the law may, sometimes at least, 'under-determine' the outcome of cases (in the sense that there may be more than one legally permissible outcome)[384] raises an important issue: why should judges always get to second-guess administrative interpretations of the law?

Interestingly, in the USA, the court's role in reviewing administrative interpretations of the statutes is more limited: judicial review courts are required to defer to an administrative agency's construction of the statute which it administers, unless that interpretation conflicts with the clear meaning of the statute or is unreasonable. This so-called *Chevron* doctrine has its own detractors (as the High court noted in *Enfield*), but the US experience at least shows that it is not the case that 'the twin pillars of Australian administrative law can never be challenged', even though the immediate prospects of any such challenge appear unlikely.[385]

5.4.4 *Wednesbury* unreasonableness

In 1948 in *Associated Provincial Picture Houses Ltd v Wednesbury Corporation*,[386] the English Court of Appeal rejected an argument that a condition (on a licence to operate a cinema) prohibiting the admittance of children under the age of 15 years on Sundays was invalid. Although the validity of the condition was upheld, the court accepted that administrative determinations could be ultra vires if they were unreasonable in the sense that the decision was 'so unreasonable that no reasonable authority could ever have come to it'. The *ADJR Act* (ss 5(2)(g) and 6(2)(g)) test for unreasonableness adopts this same standard: decisions or conduct may be reviewed on the ground that 'an exercise of power' was 'so unreasonable that no reasonable person could have so exercised the power'.

It has been concluded in a number of Australian cases that a decision-maker acted unreasonably in the *Wednesbury* sense (although often the affected decisions are also invalidated on the basis of some other, less controversial, ground of review). In one example, it was held that a decision to require

---

383   *Corporation of the City of Enfield v Development Assessment Commission* (2000) 199 CLR 135, 153.

384   A stronger thesis would be to say that the law is indeterminate, meaning that all possible outcomes are legally acceptable: see L Solum, 'On the Indeterminacy Crisis: Critiquing Critical Dogma' (1987) 54 *University of Chicago Law Review* 462.

385   Sackville, n 382 above, 329. Justice Sackville also emphasises that the US courts are much more likely than Australian courts to conduct in-depth reviews of administrative judgments of policy, which are often intermingled with conclusions of fact.

386   [1948] 1 KB 223. For an discussion of this case which places it in the political and social context of its time, see M Taggart, 'Reinventing Administrative Law' in N Bamforth and P Leyland (eds), *Public Law in a Multi-Layered Constitution* (Oxford: Hart Publishing, 2003), 311.

a doctor to pay his entire medical income in satisfaction of a tax debt was unreasonable.[387] Although the discretionary power was delegated in broad terms, the court argued that this 'extraordinary power' carried with it a 'special obligation' to have sufficient regard to the justice of particular cases. If emphasis had been given to the difficult policy questions which arise in attempts by tax officials to combat tax avoidance by well-resourced tax payers adequately, a different conclusion about whether no reasonable decision-maker could have made the decision may have been open. In another case, a plan allocating quotas was invalidated because it was formulated on the basis of a statistical fallacy.[388] That case also demonstrated that delegated legislation may be invalidated on the basis of unreasonableness, though the courts are normally reluctant to do so given the broad range of policy considerations which arise in the context of making general rules.[389]

Two features of the *Wednesbury* unreasonableness ground of review immediately stand out. First, the ground clearly requires the court to make judgments about the substantive correctness or merits of the decision. Although the test does not enable the court to substitute its view of what a reasonable authority should do, a determination about what no reasonable authority could do must be based on an assessment of arguments for and against the authority's decision. Further, the test for unreasonableness does not refer to any independent criteria to guide the making of these judgments (that is, unreasonableness is defined in a circular way by reference to how a reasonable person would act or decide).[390] As such, the 'test' invites judges to measure the reasonableness of decisions against their values.

Second, the court in *Wednesbury* attempted to make it plain that the unreasonableness ground should be applied in a restrained or deferential manner.[391] This is reflected, first and foremost, in the stringency with which the test is stated—decisions cannot be challenged on this ground unless *no* reasonable person *could* have so decided. If the unreasonableness ground is made out, the direct implication appears to be that the decision-maker was not a reasonable person. Understandably, judges may be reluctant to tag some decision-makers (for example, ministers) with this label. Further, Lord Greene chose an example of an unreasonable decision which reinforced the idea that the ground will be made out only in very extreme circumstances—the dismissal of a teacher on account of their hair colour is clearly absurd. Indeed, this example may be taken to suggest that a separate ground of review for unreasonableness is not really necessary, as other grounds of review would invariably be available to invalidate such extreme decisions (for example, consideration of an irrelevant matter). On the other hand, Lord Greene clearly envisaged some situations where a decision-maker who stayed 'within the four corners of the matters which they ought to consider' may nonetheless come to an unreasonable conclusion.[392] As an independent ground of review, *Wednesbury* unreasonableness thus allows for the review of what are considered to be egregious errors or clearly wrong decisions in circumstances where no other ground of review is available. For this reason, *Wednesbury* unreasonableness has been said to operate as a 'safety net'.[393]

The above two features of *Wednesbury* unreasonableness inevitably lead to disputes over the intensity of review which is appropriate in particular cases: how serious must errors be before they

387   *Edelsten v Wilcox* (1988) 83 ALR 99.

388   *Minister for Primary Industries and Energy v Austral Fisheries Pty Ltd* (1993) 40 FCR 381.

389   See D Pearce and S Argument, *Delegated Legislation in Australia*, 3rd edn (Sydney: LexisNexis Butterworths, 2005), 254.

390   *Minister for Immigration and Citizenship v SZMDS* (2010) 240 CLR 611, 647.

391   See *Attorney-General (NSW) v Quin* (1990) 170 CLR 1, 36.

392   See also *Williams v Minister for Justice and Customs* (2007) 157 FCR 286.

393   Aronson, Dyer and Groves, n 47 above, 370.

will be caught in the unreasonableness safety net? The answer to this question will depend on at least two considerations. First, there is understandable pressure on judges to undertake a more searching analysis of the reasonableness of decisions which have a significant impact on important individual interests, or which undermine fundamental common law rights.[394] As with all grounds of review, the subject matter and nature of the decision, the sort of interests affected and the seriousness of those effects will be important. Although not an 'easy' decision, the fifth straight rejection of a parole board's well-considered recommendation to release a prisoner was not held to be unreasonable. Important individual interests were obviously involved, but the decision-maker was entitled to have regard to their own understanding of the public interest.[395] Second, and more generally, it can be observed that the intensity of unreasonableness review is likely to wax and wane in accordance with background judicial beliefs about the appropriateness and legitimacy of the application of any review grounds which necessarily involve a degree of merits review.

The contemporary consensus among commentators is that the unreasonableness safety net is catching less than it once did.[396] The evidence for this proposition includes increasing judicial comments which emphasise that unreasonableness must be 'manifest' and the ground is 'extremely confined',[397] and requires something exceptional.[398] Perram J has gone so far as suggesting that review on this basis will only succeed 'when a level of unreasonableness is reached which, in essence, permits of no contrary view'.[399] The restrictive mood can also be gauged by the conclusion in *SZMDS* (see 5.4.3.1.2) that *Wednesbury* unreasonableness applies only to 'discretionary' decisions, and thus has no application in cases where the alleged unreasonableness is based on fact-finding errors or where the decision-maker is under a 'duty' to exercise a power. If the rationale of *Wednesbury* unreasonableness is to act as a safety net to catch egregious errors in administrative decision-making, this restriction makes little sense.

One possible reason for thinking that a decision could not have been reached by a reasonable decision-maker is that it imposes burdens which are out of all proportion to the objectives which are legitimately pursued by the exercise of the power. It is clear that gross disproportionality 'often lies behind a conclusion that a decision is unreasonable'.[400] It is also 'tolerably clear' that delegated legislation may be invalidated (as being ultra vires) if it is not reasonably proportional to the authorised purposes.[401] Nonetheless, Australian courts have been reluctant to adopt the language of proportionality in relation to the review of administrative discretions generally—that is, to conceptualise proportionality as an independent ground of review (see further below, 5.4.6).[402]

---

394 This consideration has been more explicitly recognised in England: e.g. *R v Ministry of Defence, ex parte Smith* [1996] QB 517.

395 *Watson v South* Australia (2010) 278 ALR 168, 190.

396 Aronson, Dyer and Groves, n 47 above, 367–8; R Panetta, '*Wednesbury* Unreasonableness: Judicial or Merits Review?' (2002) 9 *Australian Journal of Administrative Law* 191.

397 *Attorney-General (NSW) v Quin* (1990) 170 CLR 1, 36.

398 *Whisprun Pty Ltd v Dixon* (2003) 200 ALR 447, 473 [100].

399 *Griffiths v Rose* (2011) 192 FCR 130, 146, [50].

400 Sir Anthony Mason, 'The Scope of Judicial Review' (2001) 31 *Australian Institute of Administrative Law Forum* 21, 38. For example, *R v Barnsley Metropolitan Borough Council, ex parte Hook* [1976] 1 WLR 1052 (a penalty was held to be excessive given the nature of the offence); see also *Edelsten v Wilcox* (1988) 83 ALR 99.

401 See *Vanstone v Clark* (2005) 147 FCR 299, 337–8 for a helpful review of the cases. Sometimes it is argued that the reasonable proportionality test only applies in relation to delegated law-making powers which are 'purposive' as opposed non-purposive limits (i.e. powers granted to make rules or regulations with respect to particular subject matters or areas). Given that judicial review routinely involves courts implying statutory powers which may then be used to structure the exercise of discretion (5.3.2), the importance of this distinction in this context is unclear.

402 See, e.g., *James v Military Rehabilitation and Compensation Commission* (2010) 186 FCR 134, 143–4, [37–41].

5.4.5 Uncertainty

Finally, it is necessary to mention briefly a ground of review which is expressed in the *ADJR Act* as involving 'an exercise of a power in such a way that the result of the exercise of the power is uncertain'. There is some uncertainty over whether this basis for review is also recognised at common law. But even if it is not, it is accepted that particular statutes may give rise to an implication that a degree of certainty in decision-making is required. The ground of review is not made out merely because delegated legislation, a licence or the effect of a determination is unclear or not immediately obvious; courts will in most cases be able to construe such words in a way which will avoid ambiguity. However, in some circumstances, a determination may be so vague or unclear that it fails to give the level of guidance demanded by the legislation. For example, a prices order which is intended to 'fix' prices will be invalid if it fails to provide an objective standard by which prices are to be determined.[403]

5.4.6 The potential impact of human rights

Judicial review has long played a role in the protection of individual rights, in particular rights to liberty, property, and natural justice. In theory, such 'common law rights and freedoms' can be overridden by parliaments (acting within their constitutional powers), but statutory and non-statutory administrative powers are assumed to be granted (respectively, by the legislature or the common law) subject to these fundamental rights. Thus, in the famous case of *Entick v Carrington*, property rights were protected by requiring that any trespass by government officers, however 'minute', must be clearly authorised by law; as no statutory or common law source of power which authorised an invasion of property rights, the plaintiff could sue for trespass could be found.[404] In *Cooper v Wandsworth Board of Works*,[405] it was held that government officers who were clearly empowered by statute to demolish a building built in non-compliance with statutory requirements were not empowered to act before first affording natural justice. The statute authorising government action was read subject to fundamental rights; as Byles J put it, 'the justice of the common law will supply the omission of the legislature'.[406] In this way, judicial review protects rights which are thought to have attained the status of fundamental common law rights or principles.[407] The idea that legislation should not be read as reflecting an intention to 'abrogate or curtail fundamental rights or freedoms unless such an intention is clearly manifested by unmistakable and unambiguous language'[408] has come to be known as the 'principle of legality'.

The nature of the common law means that the rights and principles protected by the principle of legality are not canonically stated and may change over time. Given this, applications of the principle of legality which lead to outcomes that appear inconsistent with legislative policy sometimes attract

---

403   *King Gee Clothing Co Pty Ltd v Commonwealth* (1945) 71 CLR 184. For a fuller discussion of uncertainty, see Aronson, Dyer and Groves, n 47 above, 364–7.

404   (1765) 19 St Tr 1030; 95 ER 807. The 'silence of the books' on the existence of a power authorising the violation the common law right was 'an authority against the defendant': 1065.

405   (1863) 143 ER 414.

406   For a more modern example, see *Coco v The Queen* (1994) 179 CLR 427.

407   These principles have been called a 'common law bill of rights': for discussion, see K Roach, 'Common Law Bills of Rights as Dialogue Between Courts and Legislatures' (2005) 55 *University of Toronto Law Journal* 734.

408   *Plaintiff S157* (2003) 211 CLR 476, 492 (Gleeson CJ). See also the plurality in *Saeed v Minister for Immigration and Citizenship* (2010) 241 CLR 252, 259.

criticism. Nevertheless the courts have argued that legislative drafters can and should be aware of the operation of the principle of legality. Indeed, in recent years, the principle of legality has been strongly reasserted on the basis that it forms a 'working hypothesis', known to parliament and the courts.[409] On this basis, judges have argued that they are justified in insisting that if parliament proposes to undercut fundamental rights it 'must squarely confront what it is doing and accept the political cost'.[410]

Judicial review can protect a wider category of rights in further ways. Clearly it has an important role to play in protecting statutory rights conferred on individuals or groups. For example, if a person is denied a welfare benefit to which they have a statutory entitlement, they can seek judicial review of the decision.[411] Where the meaning of legislation is ambiguous, courts will favour a construction of legislation which accords with Australia's obligations under relevant international treaties.[412]

It is often observed, however, that Australia is now unique among its common law cousins (countries like Canada, the UK, and New Zealand) in lacking a statutory or constitutional bill or charter of rights. This observation still applies at the federal level, but two Australian jurisdictions (the Australian Capital Territory and Victoria) have enacted statutory bills of rights which were modelled (to varying degrees) on the United Kingdom *Human Rights Act 1998*. Given that the enactment of the UK *Human Rights Act* has had dramatic effects on English administrative law, it is worth briefly considering the potential impact that the Australian Capital Territory *Human Rights Act 2004* (*HRA*) and the Victorian *Charter of Rights and Responsibilities Act 2006* (*Charter*) may have on judicial review in those jurisdictions.

The Australian Capital Territory *HRA* and the Victorian *Charter* require legislative provisions to be interpreted compatibly with listed human rights 'so far as it is possible to do so' consistently with the terms and purposes of the statute.[413] Both Acts also empower judges to issue a declaration of 'incompatibility' (in the Australian Capital Territory) or of 'inconsistent interpretation' (in Victoria),[414] if it is concluded that it is not possible to interpret a legislative provision as being consistent with one of the listed human rights. These declarations have no impact on the validity of impugned statutory provisions. In this way, such statutory bills of rights are said by their proponents to promote a 'dialogue' between the various branches of government. They enable courts to express conclusions about whether legislation violates rights but leave the final word on how rights should be interpreted and limited to elected parliaments.[415]

These two central elements Victoria's and the Australian Capital Territory's statutory bill of rights (that is, the interpretive and declaration provisions) were considered by the High Court in

---

409   Gleeson CJ considered the principle to be 'an aspect of the rule of law': *Electrolux Home Pty Ltd v Australian Workers Union* (2004) 221 CLR 309, 329.

410   *R v Secretary of State for the Home Department; Ex parte Simms* [200] 2 AC 115, 131; quoted with approval in *Evans v New South Wales* (2008) 168 FCR 576, 594.

411   See, e.g., *Green v Daniels* (1977) 13 ALR 1. Where legislation confers benefits on individuals, it is often given a 'beneficial construction'; and 'the principle that particular statutory provisions must be read in light of their purpose … [has] particular significance in the case of legislation which protects or enforces human rights': *AB v Western Australia* (2011) 281 ALR 694, 700, [24].

412   E.g. *Chu Kheng Lim v Minister for Immigration, Local Government and Ethnic Affairs* (1992) 176 CLR 1, 38; *Minister for Immigration and Ethnic Affairs v Teoh* (1995) 183 CLR 273, 287. See also the discussion of *Teoh* at 5.2.2.4.

413   See s 32(1) of the Victorian *Charter* and s 30(1) and (2) of the Australian Capital Territory *HRA*.

414   See s 36 of the Victorian *Charter* and s 32 of the Australian Capital Territory *HRA*. The Victorian formulation expressly flags the reality that there are typically multiple ways in which human rights can be reasonably interpreted.

415   The literature on 'dialogue' models of human rights protection is large. One issue which has been raised is the extent to which 'dialogue' is an appropriate metaphor to describe the interaction between the courts and the other branches of government under such legislation: see, L McDonald, 'New Directions in the Australian Bill of Rights Debate' [2004] *Public Law* 21.

Momcilovic v R.[416] Much of the High Court's attention in its lengthy judgment concerned questions of constitutionality—in particular, the consistency of the provisions with principles flowing from Chapter III of the Constitution. The judgment in *Momcilovic* is very complex, but two general conclusions on the main constitutional issue, the validity of the declaration of inconsistency provision, can be extracted.[417] First, the court held that the power to issue declarations of inconsistency was a non-judicial power and, thus, could not be conferred on federal ('Ch III') courts. Under the Australian conception of the separation of powers the federal judicature can, as a rule, only exercise judicial power.[418] Second, by a slim majority it was held that the declaration power did not violate the *Kable* principle,[419] which prevents the conferral of powers on state courts which undermine the institutional integrity of a state court, are incompatible with the exercise by a state court of federal judicial power or deprive a state court of an essential characteristic. This means that such a power can be validly exercised by a state court when it exercises state jurisdiction.[420] Both of these conclusions have left the future efficacy of the dialogue model of statutory human rights protection in doubt. Certainly, such a model (at least as currently configured) could not be established at the Commonwealth level. Furthermore, when it comes to the limits imposed by Ch III principles on state and territory Supreme Courts to issue declarations of inconsistency, it has been fairly concluded that '[b]ecause of its multiple levels of complexity across six judgments, *Momcilovic* presents serious difficulties for lower courts looking for majority statements of how the key judicial provisions in the *Charter* are to be applied'.[421] The unstable constitutional foundations for statutory charters of rights in Australia make it less likely the 'dialogue' model of rights protection will play a significant role in reorienting administrative law doctrine in Australia.[422]

The interpretive requirement, contained in both the Australian Capital Territory and Victorian legislation, will influence how the courts interpret statutory provisions conferring powers on administrators in those jurisdictions. For example, legislation authorising delegated legislation (which is often framed in very wide terms) may be read more narrowly than would otherwise be the case. More generally, statutory powers will not be read as authorising a breach of human rights unless the law clearly (in light of its terms or statutory purposes) must be interpreted as requiring that conclusion. There are, however, uncertainties about the sort of interpretations that are authorised by the interpretive provision.

Two issues arose in *Momcilovic* concerning the interpretation of s 32 of the Victorian *Charter* (the interpretive provision). The first was the extent to which the interpretive provision should be interpreted as conferring a power on a court to change the meaning of legislation to bring it into conformity with a human right. UK decisions have read a similar interpretive principle in the *Human Rights Act* (UK)

---

416   *Momcilovic v R* (2011) 280 ALR 221.

417   For a sophisticated and illuminating dissection of the six judgments in *Momcilovic*, see W Bateman and J Stellios, 'Chapter III of the Constitution, Federtal Jurisdiction and Dialogue Charters of Human Rights' (2012) 36 *Melbourne University Law Review* (forthcoming).

418   Crennan and Kiefel JJ held that the declaration power was valid insofar as it was incidental to an exercise of judicial power, but this was a dissenting view: *Momcilovic v R* (2011) 280 ALR 22, 392–4, [600].

419   *Kable v Director of Public Prosecutions (NSW)* (1996) 189 CLR 51.

420   The issues arising when state courts are exercising federal jurisdiction are intricate: see Bateman and Stellios, n 417 above.

421   Bateman and Stellios, n 417 above. Note also that the Victorian Scrutiny of Acts and Regulations Committee's, *Review of the Charter of Human Rights and Responsibilities Act 2006* (September 2011) makes numerous recommendations for amendments *if* the *Charter* is retained in that jurisdiction. Recommendation 31 is that consideration be given to conferring the power to make an inconsistent interpretation to a non-judicial body.

422   Cf, on the impact of rights adjudication on English administrative law, T Poole, 'The Reformation of English Administrative Law' (2009) 68 *Cambridge Law Journal* 142.

as enabling judges to 'read in words which change the meaning of the enacted legislation'.[423] That interpretation of the interpretive provision was rejected for two main reasons by the majority of the court in *Momcilovic*. First, as a matter of statutory interpretation, emphasis was placed on the text of the *Charter*. Section 32 authorises judges to 'interpret' laws, thereby indicating that their task remains bounded by the process of construction as 'ordinarily applied by courts'.[424] Further, s 32 expressly requires interpretations to be consistent with statutory purpose, thereby confirming that legislative intention is to be 'revealed by consideration of the subject and scope of the legislation in accordance with principles of statutory construction and interpretation'.[425] Second, it is clear that a broader reading of s 32 would have raised constitutional problems as it would involve judges in a law-making function and would, for that reason, 'be repugnant to the exercise of judicial power'.[426]

The second issue that arose in *Momcilovic* was whether the process of interpretation required by the s 32 interpretive provision should include reference to s 7 of the *Charter*, which provides that the specified human rights can only be subject to 'such reasonable limits as can be demonstrably justified in a free and democratic society based on human dignity, equality and freedom'.[427] This provision is commonly thought to allow for limitations on rights so long as the limits are proportionate to the legitimate ends being pursued. Unfortunately, the judgments in *Momcilovic* do not yield a clear answer to whether this 'proportionality provision' is relevant to the application of the interpretive principle (s 32).[428] Although four judges held that s 7 of the *Charter* was relevant to the application of the interpretive principle, one of the four concluded that this spelt invalidity for s 32. The other three judges concluded that the s 7 (that is, the proportionality provision) is not relevant to considering whether it is possible to interpret a provision consistently with human rights. For this reason, it is difficult to state with confidence whether an interpretation which accepts proportionality as part of the analysis required to determine whether an interpretation of a statutory provision is consistent with human rights would be accepted by a majority of the High Court as constitutionally valid. As has been observed, this has placed lower courts required to apply the interpretive rule in an 'invidious position'.[429]

In reviewing decisions for alleged infringement of human rights, UK courts have concluded that proportionality review involves a greater level of judicial scrutiny of the merits of the decision than allowed under the *Wednesbury* unreasonableness standard.[430] In determining whether human rights violations can be justified as a proportionate response to achieve a legitimate purpose the court must ask: (1) whether the decision was suitable or rationally connected to achieving a legitimate purpose;

---

423   *Ghaidan v Godin-Mendoza* [2004] 2 AC 557, 571–2.

424   *Momcilovic v R* (2011) 280 ALR 221, 356, [454].

425   Ibid, 280, [170].

426   Ibid, 280, [171]. Reading an interpretive provision to enable judges to rewrite legislation has also been criticised on the basis that it undermines a meaningful 'dialogue' about human rights. To the extent the questions of what rights mean and the reasonableness of limitations are approached through questions about the possible meaning of words, the substantive issues may be occluded: e.g. A Butler, 'The Bill of Rights Debate: Why the New Zealand Bill of Rights Act 1990 is a Bad Model for Britain' (1997) 17 *Oxford Journal of Legal Studies* 323, 336.

427   The Australian Capital Territory *HRA* contains a similar provision (s 28).

428   Bateman and Stellios, n 417 above.

429   Bateman and Stellios, n 417 above.

430   *R (on the application of Daly) v Secretary of State for the Home Department* [2001] 2 AC 532. It is difficult to understand why this is necessarily so (because both proportionality and *Wednesbury* unreasonableness can in theory be applied with different levels of intensity). In *Daly* it was said that proportionality analysis may require the courts to assess the balance struck between competing interests and the relative weight accorded to particular interests and considerations. But the same is true of *Wednesbury* unreasonableness: see e.g. *Minister for Aboriginal Affairs v Peko-Wallsend Ltd* (1986) 162 CLR 24, 41.

(2) whether it was reasonably necessary to achieve that purpose; and (3) whether it nonetheless imposed excessive burdens on affected individuals (that is, the impact on individuals was out of all proportion to the purpose).[431] The adoption of this analysis in the human rights context has led to debates about whether or not the more intrusive standards of proportionality review should replace *Wednesbury* unreasonableness across the board.[432] Although similar arguments and debates may arise in the Australian Capital Territory and Victoria about whether that the standard of review applicable to establish a breach of human rights should seep through into administrative law more generally, there are reasons to be cautious about the prospect of any significant reorientation of administrative law principle.

One difficulty, as we have already observed, is that *Momcilovic* has not resolved the question of whether or not a proportionality analysis should be incorporated into the interpretive task set for the courts. The application of the principle of legality by Australian courts has not been attended by any structured approach to the question of whether statutory limits on a fundamental right or principle are proportionate to a legitimate legislative objective. As French CJ observed in *Momcilovic*, if the interpretive principle does not incorporate an express requirement to undertake a proportionality analysis, the effect of the Victorian *Charter* is to require 'statutes to be construed against the background of human rights and freedoms set out in the *Charter* in the same way as the principle of legality requires the same statutes to be construed against the background of common law rights and freedoms'. In short, the *Charter* gives the principle of legality a 'wider field of application'[433] but does not change the standard or methodology statutory interpretation undertaken by a judicial review court.

Another reason to doubt whether the statutory bills of rights in the Australian Capital Territory and Victoria will encourage Australian courts to apply more intensive standards of review is that Australian courts have, in general, been made wary of proportionality review because of the perceived concern that it will lead the courts further down the path towards 'merits review'.[434] In large part, this reflects the idea that, at the federal level, such review is thought to be a non-judicial function and thus is precluded by the separation of judicial power (see 3.2.2). But this general approach has seeped through to state law[435] and the conclusion reached is that the concept of proportionality lies 'at the boundaries of accepted administrative law' in Australia.[436] Further, as emphasised by a number of judges in *Momcilovic*, UK developments cannot be confidently relied on as the constitutional and legal context which has shaped them is very different from that applicable in Australia. Clearly, there is a tension between the logic driving the adoption in the states of statutory bills of rights, indicating more intrusive judicial review, and the conception of the separation of powers that has so far underpinned the Australian law of judicial review.

Under the Victorian *Charter* (s 38(1)) and Australian Capital Territory *HRA* (s 40B) it is unlawful for a public authority to act incompatibly with a human right or, in making a decision, to fail to give proper

---

431   See P Bayne, 'The Human Rights Act 2004 (ACT) and Administrative Law: A Preliminary View' (2007) 52 *Australian Institute of Administrative Law Forum* 3, 8.

432   See, e.g., Taggart, n 386 above, 334.

433   *Momcilovic v R* (2011) 280 ALR 221, 245, [51].

434   It has also been observed that Australia's single common law 'makes it difficult' for the courts of the Australian Capital Territory or Victoria 'unilaterally to attempt to develop the common law standard of review in response' to the legislation in either jurisdiction: C Evans and S Evans, 'Legal Redress under the Victorian Charter of Human Rights and Responsibilities' (2006) 17 *Public Law Review* 264, 278.

435   Perhaps the most quoted passage on the need for judges to respect the legality merits distinction was written in the context of a state case: *Attorney-General (NSW) v Quin* (1990) 170 CLR 1, 36 (Brennan J).

436   *Bruce v Cole* (1998) 45 NSWLR 163, 185 (Spigelman CJ).

consideration to a relevant human right.[437] Moreover, both Acts provide for people to seek remedies on the basis of breaches of these obligations in other court proceedings—though any right to damages is expressly excluded.[438] The practical effect of these provisions is to introduce breach of human rights as a ground of judicial review (as has occurred in the UK).[439] There may be a question as to whether *Charter*-based 'unlawfulness' (referred to in the Victorian *Charter*) amounts to a jurisdictional error, but declarations and injunctions are clearly available where a breach of a human right is established.[440] The obligation on public authorities to comply with human rights and, also, to give them proper consideration applies to both statutory and non-statutory powers (which obviously are unaffected by the interpretive principle).

An obvious question about the obligations placed on public authorities is why a requirement to give proper consideration to a relevant human right is necessary given there is also an obligation to comply with the specified human rights. If a decision-maker has acted consistently with human rights, should their decision be impugned on the basis that the decision-making process does not reveal adequate consideration of the human rights issues involved? Arguably, the obligation to give proper consideration is overly attentive to procedure rather than outcomes. Such a focus might also encourage the 'juridification' of the administrative process, to the extent administrative decision-makers feel it necessary to undertake sophisticated legal analysis.[441] On the other hand, it might be thought a process-based obligation is necessary to encourage normative change in the administration, that is, to change the way that human rights issues are approached. Wherever the merits of this debate lie, Victorian and Australian Capital Territory courts will be required to examine the meaning of 'proper' consideration, which presumably means something more substantive than the normal obligation on decision-makers to consider relevant considerations.[442]

Although the Commonwealth government has recently rejected the latest proposal to introduce a national statutory bill of rights,[443] a new 'human rights framework' has been introduced. The most significant part of this framework for Australian administrative lawyers flows from the enactment of the *Human Rights (Parliamentary Scrutiny) Act 2011* (Cth).[444] This Act defines 'human rights' to mean the rights included in seven core United Nations human rights treaties[445] and establishes a Parliamentary

---

437 'Public authority' is defined in both Acts by reference to institutional *and* functional criteria. Compare with 3.6.1.

438 The opaque remedies provision of the *Charter* has been the subject of well-directed critique: J Gans, 'The *Charter's* Irremediable Remedies Provision' (2009) 33 *Melbourne University Law Review* 105.

439 Section 38(2) of the *Charter* states that 'if, as a result of a statutory provision or a provision made by or under any Act of the Commonwealth or otherwise under law, the public authority could not reasonably have acted differently or made a different decision', s 38(1) does not apply.

440 See e.g. s 39(2)(b) of the *Charter*.

441 See T Poole, 'Of Headscarves and Heresies: The Denbigh High School Case and Public Authority Decision-making under the Human Rights Act' [2005] *Public Law* 685.

442 For discussion, see M Schleiger, 'One Size Fits All: The Obligation of Public Authorities to Consider Human Rights Under the Victorian *Charter*' (2011) 19 *Australian Journal of Administrative Law* 17.

443 National Human Rights Consultation Report (2009), recommendation 18. Any future proposals for a statutory bill of rights will, of course, need to be attentive to the constitutional issues agitated in *Momcilovic*. See generally, Bateman and Stellios, n 417 above.

444 For a helpful overview, see J Stellios and M Palfrey, 'A New Federal Scheme for the Protection of Human Rights' (2012) 69 *AIAL Forum* 13.

445 The following treaties are listed: the International Covenant on Civil and political rights; the International Covenant on Economic, Social and Cultural Rights; the Convention on the Elimination of All Forms of Racial Discrimination; the Convention on the Elimination of All Forms of Discrimination Against Women; the Convention against Torture and Other Cruel, Inhuman and Degrading Treatment or Punishment; the Convention on the Rights of the Child; and the Convention on the Rights of Persons with Disabilities.

Joint Committee on Human Rights (PJCHR). The PJCHR is required to examine Bills and legislative instruments that come before either house of the parliament (and existing legislation) for compatibility with human rights, and to report to the parliament on this issue. The PJCHR can also conduct inquiries into human rights issues referred to it by the Attorney-General.

The scrutiny function to be performed by the PJCHR is facilitated by ss 8 and 9 of the Act, which provide that all Bills and legislative instruments must be accompanied by a statement of compatibility which includes an assessment of whether the Bill or instrument is compatible with human rights.[446] Little can be said about how the PJCHR will perform its scrutiny function, as it has not yet commenced issuing reports. Clearly, however, the committee's capacity to undertake its broad and wide-ranging functions will be affected by the resources made available. It is also the case that it may be necessary for the committee to report quickly to enable parliamentary debate to benefit from its views. Further issues to be confronted by the committee include the level of detail it will expect in statements of compatibility and, in particular, whether assessments of human rights compliance will be made on the basis of legal analysis[447] or political judgement about how human rights can legitimately be limited;[448] the nature of any overlap and interaction between the PJCHR and other parliamentary committees, such as the Senate Standing Committee for the Scrutiny of Bills and the Senate Standing Committee on Regulations and Ordinances (see 9.4.3); and whether or not the committee will take strong positions on particular human rights issues or focus on alerting the parliament to the relevant arguments, so that human rights issues are exposed for debate.

The *Human Rights (Parliamentary Scrutiny) Act* does not make human rights enforceable in the courts. Nor does it empower judges to make declarations of incompatibility or include an interpretive principle requiring rights-respecting interpretations where possible. Nevertheless, statements of compatibility and the reports of the PJCHR may be relevant to the interpretation of Commonwealth legislation and legislative instruments passed after the introduction of the new scheme. Although the High Court has clearly held that statements indicative of legislative intention gleaned from the historical records associated with parliamentary processes do not override parliamentary intention as manifested in the text of the legislation, such material may be of assistance to the courts in the event of ambiguity. Thus, after the commencement of the Act courts may, in cases of ambiguity, look to the 'historical record for context, and that context will include executive and legislative assessments of compatibility with the human rights set out in the seven core UN treaties'.[449] For example, it is possible that a broad discretionary power, which does not unambiguously authorise the infringement of a human right, could be interpreted in a manner which does not authorise such an infringement on the basis of a statement of compatibility which indicates that the power is considered to be compatible with human rights.

---

446   Failure to comply with this requirement does not affect the validity or operation of a law: subss 8(5) and 9(4).

447   Although the Act does not contain a general proportionality clause, the committee will also have to confront the issue, which arose in *Momcilovic*, concerning whether statements of compatibility should incorporate a consideration of a proportionality analysis as most rights are generally thought to be legitimately subject to reasonable limitations.

448   Given that Australian domestic courts have not developed a well-established human rights jurisprudence it is likely that legal analysis will look principally to international human rights law. What may be expected of statements of compatibility should also be considered in the context that the responsibility for drafting them has been decentralised to individual departments, though the Attorney-General's Department has responsibility for providing training and advice.

449   Stellios and Palfrey, n 444 above.

6

Access to Judicial Review

6.1 Two approaches to standing

To be entitled to make a judicial review application, an applicant[1] must establish that they have standing (*locus standi*). In other words, the rules of standing are about who may initiate judicial review proceedings.

There are at least two ways of thinking about the law of standing and the functions of standing rules. The first approach can be called the interest-based grievance model of standing (the 'interest model' for short). In this model the question of whether or not a particular applicant may initiate judicial review is determined by asking whether they personally have a legal right or an interest which has been adversely affected by the impugned administrative decision. In short, the question of standing is answered by reference to the interests of the applicant. This focus on the applicant's interests reflects the view that the primary purpose of judicial review is the protection of individuals against the abuse of government power.[2]

The second approach to the question of standing can be described as the 'enforcement model'. On this approach, the applicant's standing is determined by asking whether they are an appropriate person to enforce administrative law norms. In answering this question, the court may have regard to the identity and qualifications of the applicant.[3] Of course, one possible answer (or part of an answer) to the question of who should be allowed to initiate judicial review proceedings to enforce administrative law norms is 'those whose interests are affected by a decision'. For this reason, the answer, in the enforcement model, to the question of who may appropriately enforce the law cannot merely be based on the nature of the applicant's interests in the subject matter of the decision. Unless (on the enforcement model) some applicants may be granted standing for reasons unrelated to their individual interests in the subject matter of the impugned decision, the distinction between the enforcement and interest models would collapse. Thus, the enforcement model recognises that an applicant's identity or qualifications may, in at least some cases, be sufficient reason to grant standing even if their personal interests are not affected by the decision.

---

1 We use the term 'applicant' in this chapter to cover any person who seeks a judicial review remedy.

2 Thus the interest-based grievance model of standing resonates with what we described (in 1.3) as the 'legal' approach to administrative law, insofar as its focus is on holding decision-makers legally accountable by providing redress or remedies to those adversely affected by the abuse of government power.

3 The enforcement model of standing resonates with what we described (in 1.3) as the 'regulatory approach' to administrative law.

Both models of standing can be discerned in the law, as can be illustrated by reference to comments made by the High Court in *Bodruddaza v Minister for Immigration and Multicultural Affairs*.[4] The court tracked changing understandings of judicial review by reference to three distinct phases in the historical development of the prerogative writs—in particular, the writ of prohibition (see also 2.1.4). According to the High Court, the writs were originally developed as a means by which more powerful officials (the 'Crown') could control inferior government bodies by ensuring that they complied with the law.[5] In this phase of its development, judicial review was conceived of primarily in terms of enforcement of compliance with the law by a particular class of administrative or government decision-makers.

But, the court continued, 'by the end of the nineteenth century,' prohibition 'was seen as protective of the rights of the subject rather than as a safeguard of the prerogative'.[6] Arguably, this change in the way prohibition was understood was part of a more general reconceptualisation of the purpose of judicial review in terms of the protection of individual interests against the abuse of administrative power. It is not surprising, therefore, that in this second phase of historical development we find standing being defined in terms of whether the applicant had suffered 'special damage peculiar to himself'.[7] In the third phase of development, the purposes of judicial review were again reconceptualised—this time in the context of the Australian Constitution. In this context, judicial review cannot be understood only by reference to its role in protecting individual rights and interest. This is because the purposes of s 75(v) also include policing the federal compact and ensuring that the courts are able to restrain officers of the Commonwealth from exceeding their jurisdiction.[8] This broader 'rule of law' purpose of judicial review explains the change in nomenclature from 'prerogative' to 'constitutional' writs (3.4.1.1). The court's constitutional role in protecting the 'rule of law' (by ensuring that decision-makers respect the jurisdictional limits of their powers) also helps explain why at least some High Court justices have recently indicated (6.2) their amenability to 'open standing' (that is, a regime under which *any* person may enforce administrative law norms by making an application for judicial review: 6.4). Finally, the constitutional overlay on the purposes of judicial review in Australia may also be part of the explanation of why the High Court has held that the requirement of a 'matter' under s 75 (3.4.1.3) does not necessitate adoption of interest-based standing rules or prevent the legislature enacting an open standing regime.[9]

Traces of both the interest and enforcement models of standing can also be seen in the rule that the Attorney-General may bring proceedings for declarations and injunctions to enforce administrative law norms: the Attorney-General always has standing to enforce public law norms. Clearly, this right is not based on the Attorney-General's personal interest, but on the Attorney-General's identity (as representative of the government) and qualifications (as 'principal law officer of the Crown'). The right of the Attorney-General to enforce administrative law norms is premised on the view that, where no personal interests are interfered with, the 'enforcement of the public law of a community is part of

---

4   *Bodruddaza v Minister for Immigration and Multicultural Affairs* (2007) 228 CLR 651.

5   Ibid, 665.

6   Ibid, 665.

7   *Boyce v Paddington Borough Council* [1903] 1 Ch 109, 114 (concerning who may claim standing to seek an injunction).

8   *Bodruddaza v Minister for Immigration and Multicultural Affairs* (2007) 228 CLR 651, 666. See also *Bank of New South Wales v Commonwealth* (1948) 76 CLR 1, 363 (Dixon J); *Pape v Federal Commissioner of Taxation* (2009) 238 CLR 1, 69.

9   See *Truth About Motorways v Macquarie* (2000) 200 CLR 591.

the political process'.[10] The Attorney-General's right to bring an action to enforce administrative law norms can thus be understood in terms of the enforcement model of standing: the right is recognised in answer to the question of who should be allowed to initiate proceedings to enforce administrative law norms.

The Attorney-General can also give permission ('fiat') to another person to apply for judicial review in the Attorney-General's name by way of a 'relator action'. (If permission is granted to bring a relator action, the 'relator' (that is, the real applicant) is usually responsible for the conduct of the proceedings and bears the costs, even though in theory the 'Attorney-General has complete charge of the litigation at all times'.[11]) By this procedure, an individual who lacks a sufficient interest (standing) to apply for judicial review in their own name and right may nevertheless be able to initiate such proceedings. However, as the High Court has recently pointed out, citizens are unlikely to place much faith in the relator action given that the Attorney-General is a minister of the government and, for that reason, is unlikely to authorise legal actions which will cause the government embarrassment.[12] Moreover, it is generally accepted that the Attorney-General's decision to grant or withhold their permission is not reviewable because of the political (or 'non-justiciable') nature of such a decision. It is probably for such reasons that the relator action has atrophied as a means of enforcing administrative law norms. These facts may also partly explain why the law of standing has moved and is still moving in the direction of widening access to judicial review. The starting point of the modern Australian law of standing is the case of *Australian Conservation Foundation v Commonwealth* (*ACF*),[13] to which we now turn.

6.2 *Australian Conservation Foundation* and the special interest test

Because the relator action plays very little role in the contemporary Australian law of standing, the central question is: what amounts to a sufficient interest to give a person standing to apply for judicial review in their own name? The core holding in *ACF* was that an applicant must show either that the decision interferes with their private law rights (such as property or contractual rights), or that they have a 'special interest' in the subject matter of the application.

In *ACF* the challenged decision had given the go ahead to a project to develop a tourist resort. No private law right of the Australian Conservation Foundation was affected by the decision; and so it needed to establish that it had a special interest in the subject matter of the decision. The High Court did not articulate a positive test to determine when a person will be recognised as having such an interest, but rather elaborated the concept of 'special interest' negatively: a special interest is more than a 'mere

---

10   *Bateman's Bay Local Aboriginal Land Council v Aboriginal Community Benefit Fund Pty Ltd* (1998) 194 CLR 247, 276 (McHugh J). McHugh J, who was responding to comments by the majority indicating their amenability to 'open standing', went on to argue (at 278): 'The decision when and in what circumstances to enforce public law frequently calls for a fine judgment as to what the public interest truly requires. It is a decision that is arguably best made by the Attorney-General who must answer to the people, rather than by unelected judges expanding the doctrine of standing to overcome what they see as a failure of the political process to ensure that the law is enforced.'

11   *Bateman's Bay Local Aboriginal Land Council v Aboriginal Community Benefit Fund Pty Ltd* (1998) 194 CLR 247, 262–3.

12   *Re McBain; Ex parte Australian Catholic Bishops Conference* (2002) 209 CLR 372, 473. Whatever the historical role played by the Attorney-General, in contemporary Australia there is little doubt that the role has become politicised.

13   *Australian Conservation Foundation Incorporated v Commonwealth* (1980) 146 CLR 493.

intellectual or emotional concern', no matter how intense or strong that concern may be.[14] The applicant must be seeking more than 'the satisfaction of righting a wrong, upholding a principle or winning a contest'.[15] Although a special interest need not be unique to the applicant, interests shared with the public at large (or perhaps a significant section of it) are insufficient to establish standing. Applying these principles, the court held that the ACF's clear commitment to conservation did not give it a special interest in the preservation of the environment of the particular site slated for development.[16] Its interest was essentially ideological.

The articulation of the law in *ACF*, and its application to the facts of the case, reflect the interest model of standing we outlined above (6.1). The basic reason for the refusal of standing was that the applicant was not seeking to remedy a personal grievance. Rather it was concerned to enforce the law so as to promote the cause of environmental protection, which provided its *raison d'etre*. This approach to standing is related to a view that the primary purpose of judicial review is the protection of individual interests against government abuse. According to this view, the courts do not have a more general role of enforcing administrative law norms (unless the Attorney-General effectively invites them to undertake that task by giving permission for a relator action). The implication of *ACF* is that ideological, intellectual and emotional interests and concerns should be vindicated through political, not legal, mechanisms of accountability.

The special interest test is a vague standard and capable of more or less expansive application. A common judicial strategy to justify outcomes which appear difficult to reconcile with the idea that an intellectual or emotional concern is insufficient to establish standing is to emphasise that whether an applicant has a special interest cannot be answered by reference to hard and fast rules but depends on contextual analysis of the facts of each case.[17] For this reason, it is often observed that post-*ACF* cases demonstrate that the application of the special interest test involves a large degree of judicial discretion.[18]

This is most clearly evidenced by the history of environmental litigation. Although standing was refused in the *ACF* case, this has not prevented environmental organisations with objectives similar to those of the Australian Conservation Foundation from successfully establishing standing in other cases. In concluding that environmental groups do sometimes have a special interest in the circumstances of particular cases, judges have emphasised factors such as the prior involvement of the organisation in the particular matter to which the application for review relates, the fact that the group is recognised and/ or funded by the government, whether the group 'represents' a significant strand of public opinion, and the expertise of the organisation.[19] The conceptual framework established by *ACF* forces such applicants

---

14   Though there are some cases which are difficult to reconcile with the notion that intensity of belief is irrelevant. For example, in
       Ogle v Strickland (1987) 71 ALR 41, three clergymen were given standing to challenge a censorship decision. McHugh
       J doubted the correctness of this case in *Re McBain; Ex parte Australian Catholic Bishops Conference* (2002) 209 CLR 372,
       423–4.

15   *Australian Conservation Foundation Incorporated v Commonwealth* (1980) 146 CLR 493, 530.

16   The court did not foreclose the possibility that in some instances a person might have a special interest in the preservation of a
       particular environment even in the absence of a private legal right.

17   See, e.g., *Onus v Alcoa of Australia Ltd* (1981) 149 CLR 27.

18   For a more detailed discussion of the 'inconsistencies and incoherence' demonstrated by the case law, see E C Fisher and
       J Kirk, 'Still Standing: An Argument for Open Standing in Australia and England' (1997) 71 *Australian Law Journal* 370.

19   See *Tasmanian Conservation Trust Inc v Minister for Resources* (1995) 55 FCR 516; *Northcoast Environmental Council
       Inc v Minister for Resources* (1994) 55 FCR 492. For further discussion, see Fisher and Kirk, n 18 above, 375–80. In other
       contexts, groups (such as trade unions) have been granted standing on the basis of interests their membership have 'as a
       particular class': e.g. *Shop Distributive and Allied Employees Association v Minister for Industrial Affairs (SA)* (1995) 183 CLR 552.

to frame their case for access to the court in terms of the interest model. But typically, such groups are unable to show that they have a special personal interest of the sort contemplated by the interest model as traditionally understood. Factors such as an applicant's commitment to a particular issue, their expertise in the subject matter of the decision and whether they have been recognised in some way by government simply lack salience in that model.[20] On the other hand, they can easily be understood as relevant to the enforcement model, which directly raises the question of whether or not an applicant's qualifications and identity should entitle them to enforce administrative law norms.

It is arguable that in cases such as these the law has reached a tipping point:[21] although the special interest test is purportedly applied, it is reinterpreted consistently with the enforcement model rather than the interest model of standing. Assessing an applicant's interest in terms of their identity and qualifications does not involve applying the special interest test, but replaces it with criteria of a different sort. The courts, we might say, have shifted from thinking about standing in terms of protecting rights and interests to understanding it as defining who may enforce administrative law norms.

Of course, even in the enforcement model, individuals whose private law rights or special interests have been affected may initiate judicial review. But this model poses the further question of whether these are the only appropriate criteria for allowing someone to enforce administrative law norms or whether other characteristics may make a person a suitable enforcer of the law. The answers that courts have given to this question in terms of the identity and qualifications of applicants may not seem inappropriate, but they are likely to be controversial. For example, it might be argued that giving weight to whether or not an applicant has an established a track record of involvement in a particular subject matter, is acknowledged as an expert body, or has been recognised by government (for example, through receiving funding), tends to entrench the status quo by privileging well-established groups who are already part of the relevant decision-making loop (or 'policy network').[22] It might also be argued that 'expert' opinion relevant to the resolution of many contentious issues of social policy reflects not merely technical knowledge but also normative or political judgments. Arguments such as these alert us to the difficulty of the issues likely to confront courts in developing widely acceptable criteria to identify suitable enforcers of administrative law norms other than people whose rights or personal interests are affected, or politically accountable decision-makers.

The very complexity of the task suggests that once the interest model is left behind and replaced by the enforcement model, it may be difficult to resist calls for a regime of open standing, that is, the rule that *any* person (subject, perhaps, to limited exceptions) may bring proceedings to enforce administrative law norms regardless of their identity or qualifications. In *Bateman's Bay Local Aboriginal Land Council v Aboriginal Community Benefit Fund Pty Ltd*, three members of the High Court suggested that the special interest test, despite its flexibility, results in 'an unsatisfactory weighting of the scales in favour of defendant public bodies', by requiring a plaintiff to do more than show 'the abuse or threatened

---

20 Indeed some of them are perverse judged from the perspective of the interest model: why, for instance, should the receipt of government funding be relevant to a person or group's right to challenge a government decision?

21 Note, however, that in some cases environmental or public interest groups continue to be denied standing under the special interest test: see, e.g., *Animal Liberation Ltd v Department of Environment and Conservation* [2007] NSWSC 221; *Friends of Elliston—Environment & Conservation Inc v South Australia* (2007) 96 SASR 246, 269–70. Standing requirements have been liberalised by the legislature under some Australian environmental legislation: see, e.g., the discussion of standing in the context of the *Environment Protection and Biodiversity Conservation Act 1999* (Cth) by A Edgar, 'Extended Standing—Enhanced Accountability? Judicial Review of Commonwealth Environmental Decision' (2011) 39 *Federal Law Review* 436.

22 G Airo-Farulla, 'Administrative Law and Governance', in C Finn (ed), *Administrative Law for the New Millennium: Sunrise or Sunset* (Canberra: Australian Institute of Administrative Law, 2000), 278.

abuse of public administration'.[23] Although these comments do not explicitly jettison the special interest test, it was concluded that the test should be 'construed as an enabling, not a restrictive' requirement. Thus, although the special interest test continues to apply, some members of the court appear to have sanctioned the sort of expansive applications witnessed in some post-*ACF* cases.[24] These comments in *Bateman's Bay* may also indicate willingness to embrace 'open standing' if and when the opportunity presents itself. Interestingly, the judges noted that any move to open standing would affect neither the court's power to strike out vexatious and frivolous claims nor its obligation to hear only justiciable controversies.[25] Thus, in enforcing the rule of law under an open standing regime, it was emphasised that the courts (1) would have available the ordinary means to prevent abuse of court processes; and (2) could rely on the principles of non-justiciability to avoid being drawn into disputes over 'political' or 'polycentric' issues.[26]

Despite the fact that the 'special interest' test has been applied expansively in some contexts, there remain instances where a more restrictive approach has been taken. In cases where standing has been denied, emphasis has sometimes been placed on whether or not the applicant's interest in the challenged decision is within the 'zone of interests' which the legislation was intended to protect. On this basis, an anti-abortion group was denied standing to challenge a decision made under legislation which was primarily concerned to ensure the provision of safe, high-quality drugs.[27] In other cases, applicants have been said to lack a special interest in decisions which benefit their commercial rivals, though the decisions on this question 'exhibit mixed results'.[28] Notably, in *Bateman's Bay*, the High Court accepted that a business competitor could seek review of a decision favourable to a rival operating in the 'same limited market'.[29]

6.3 Standing and specific remedies

In *Bateman's Bay*, the High Court emphasised that the special interest test was stated and applied in *ACF* in the context of applications for injunctions and declarations and is distinct from the standing requirements in applications for (orders in the nature of) the prerogative writs. As McHugh J put it, 'the doctrine of standing is a house of many rooms'.[30] However, it is unclear how important remedy-specific

---

23   *Bateman's Bay Local Aboriginal Land Council v Aboriginal Community Benefit Fund Pty Ltd* (1998) 194 CLR 247, 258, 261. See also n 10 above.

24   It is worth noting that one argument in favour of the adoption of open standing is the failure of the courts to produce a coherent body of jurisprudence in their efforts to apply the special interest test. See Fisher and Kirk, n 18 above.

25   *Bateman's Bay Local Aboriginal Land Council v Aboriginal Community Benefit Fund Pty Ltd* (1998) 194 CLR 247, 263–4.

26   In the context of judicial review cases concerning the *Environment Protection and Biodiversity Conservation Act 1999* (Cth), it has been argued that the statutory liberalisation of standing requirements has not led to a greater focus on alternative filtering mechanisms such as the non-justiciability and 'matter' concepts: Edgar, n 21 above.

27   *Right to Life Association (NSW) Inc v Secretary, Department of Human Services and Health* (1995) 56 FCR 50; see also *Alphapharm Pty Ltd v SmithKline Beecham (Australia) Pty Ltd* (1994) 49 FCR 250.

28   The cases are discussed in M Aronson, B Dyer and M Groves, *Judicial Review of Administrative Action* 4th edn (Pyrmont, NSW: Lawbook Co, 2009), 763–7.

29   *Bateman's Bay Local Aboriginal Land Council v Aboriginal Community Benefit Fund Pty Ltd* (1998) 194 CLR 247. The actual holding in the case was framed cautiously: the question to be determined was said to be 'standing in a case where the plaintiff seeks injunctive relief to prevent apprehended economic loss as a consequence of ultra vires activities by a statutory body using or enjoying recourse to public monies'.

30   *Bateman's Bay Local Aboriginal Land Council v Aboriginal Community Benefit Fund Pty Ltd* (1998) 194 CLR 247, 280, [92].

differences in standing requirements will be in practice. On the one hand, the High Court insists that so-called 'strangers' may have standing to seek prohibition and certiorari even though they lack 'a relevant legal interest'.[31] But on the other hand, it seems clear that the discretion to refuse such relief may be 'greater' or will be exercised more 'frequently' in cases where the applicant lacks such an interest.[32]

It is difficult to think of good reasons why standing rules should differ according to the remedy sought. In this respect it should be emphasised that the *ADJR Act*'s formula—that only 'persons aggrieved' can bring applications—has to all intents and purposes been applied consistently with the 'special interest' test.[33] The requirement that a person be 'aggrieved' fits well within the interest model of standing as we have described it.

6.4 Towards open standing?

Although Australian courts remain bound by the special interest test, the above discussion shows that (1) in some cases the test has been extended to the point of virtual abandonment; and (2) there is a significant level of judicial support in the High Court for replacing the test with a regime of open standing. We suggested above (6.1) that the High Court's tentative support for open standing may reflect its understanding of the high constitutional purpose of judicial review in the context of s 75(v), that is, to ensure that constitutional, statutory and common law limits on administrative powers are not exceeded.

Support for open standing has also come from the Australian Law Reform Commission (ALRC) which, in 1996, recommended legislative reform of the law. The ALRC concluded that:[34]

Any person should be able to commence and maintain public law proceedings unless,

a   The relevant legislation clearly indicates an intention that the decision or conduct sought to be litigated should not be the subject of challenge by a person such as the applicant; or

b   In all the circumstances it would not be in the public interest to proceed because to do so would unreasonably interfere with the ability of a person having a private interest in the matter to deal with it differently or not at all.

Although the government rejected these recommendations, open standing continues to attract a high level of academic support.[35] According to its advocates, the reasons in favour of open standing include that it would (1) recognise the failure of the courts to produce a coherent jurisprudence fleshing out the special interest test; (2) allow increased citizen and group participation consistently with (some)

---

31   See *Re Refugee Review Tribunal; Ex parte Aala* (2000) 204 CLR 82, [48]. For a critique, see Aronson, Dyer and Groves, n 28 above, 781–5. It is not clear whether (or the extent to which) mandamus might be subject to a different standing requirement than the other writs: see S Evans and S Donaghue, 'Standing to Raise Constitutional Issues in Australia', in G Moens and R Biffot (eds), *Convergence of Legal Systems in the 21st Century: An Australian Approach* (Brisbane: The Australian Institute of Foreign and Comparative Law and contributors, 2002), 74–5.

32   See, e.g., *Bateman's Bay Local Aboriginal Land Council v Aboriginal Community Benefit Fund Pty Ltd* (1998) 194 CLR 247, 263; *Re McBain; Ex parte Australian Catholic Bishops Conference* (2002) 209 CLR 372, 422.

33   Aronson, Dyer and Groves, n 28 above, 790–2, discuss the relevant cases. Statutory standing rules use a number of different formulae. Although it is often asserted that 'the specific statutory test differs from the general law test', this 'is difficult to demonstrate in practice': ibid, 680.

34   ALRC, *Beyond the Door-keeper: Standing to Sue for Public Remedies* (Report No 78 1996), 57. See also the earlier report by the ALRC: *Standing in Public Interest Litigation* (Report No 27, 1985).

35   Note also that open standing rules have been adopted in a number of particular decision-making contexts: see e.g. *Protection of the Environment Operation Act 1997* (NSW); *Environmental Planning and Assessment Act 1979* (NSW).

theories of democracy; and (3) not preclude the use of alternative mechanisms designed to protect the courts from vexatious or inappropriate applications for review (for example, strike out powers and non-justiciability principles).[36] Given the level of judicial and scholarly support for open standing, it is worth considering some of the broader implications and possible effects that such a regime may have.

First, acceptance of open standing marks a decisive move from the traditional interest model to the enforcement model of standing. Moreover, the basic rule that *any* person may initiate proceedings indicates a more substantial role for courts in enforcing administrative law norms. While the Attorney-General's standing to enforce the law and the mechanism of the relator action has traditionally recognised the role of the executive branch of government in enforcing administrative law norms, open standing seriously undercuts any idea that 'enforcement of the public law of a community is part of the political process'.[37] Open standing gives effect to the view, clearly expressed by Gaudron J, that the rule of law requires that 'the courts should provide whatever remedies are available and appropriate to ensure that those possessed of executive and administrative powers exercised them only in accordance with the laws which govern their exercise'.[38] Open standing rules reflect a preference for legal accountability over political modes of holding government decision-makers to account for their decisions.[39] One suggested reason for giving the courts an expanded role (beyond that envisaged by the interest model of standing) is that some areas of modern government (for example, matters of environmental, cultural, economic and international concern) would otherwise be effectively beyond any form of legal accountability because such areas typically raise matters of general, not individual, concern. On the other hand, if the substance of the decision being made about 'public' interests is based on a number of considerations which must be weighed in the balance, it may be that many of the grounds of judicial review provide little traction. Although open standing may facilitate review applications other factors may work to restrict its effectiveness.[40] Second, any open standing regime will need to confront a number of obvious problems. One is that although the 'any person' rule would continue to allow people with personal grievances to challenge decisions which interfered with their private rights or personal interests, it would also allow others to challenge such decisions. However, there are various reasons why a person who is personally affected by a decision may wish to accept the decision without challenge. For example, they may be satisfied with the decision, they may not wish to incur the trouble and expense of challenging it, they may not wish to expose themselves to publicity or criticism, it may be in their long-term interests to stay on good terms with the decision-maker, or they may accept that a fair outcome has been reached even if the decision-maker made an error which would establish a ground of judicial review. In private law, we normally allow people to choose whether or not to waive or enforce their legal rights so as to vindicate their personal interests. The question that open standing raises is whether there are any circumstances in which those with a personal interest in a decision should have priority (or even the exclusive voice) in determining whether or not the decision should be challenged by way of judicial review proceedings. Once open standing has been adopted there is no easy or obvious answer to

---

36   See generally Fisher and Kirk, n 18 above.

37   *Bateman's Bay Local Aboriginal Land Council v Aboriginal Community Benefit Fund Pty Ltd* (1998) 194 CLR 247, 276 (McHugh J); see 6.1. As Hanna Wilberg has suggested to us, McHugh J's equation of political accountability with executive discretion whether to enforce the law arguably rests on an unduly narrow conception of political accountability—an idea which may also incorporate the mobilisation of parliamentary and public opposition to government decisions.

38   *Corporation of the City of Enfield v Development Assessment Commission* (2000) 1999 CLR 135, 157; see also *Re Refugee Review Tribunal; Ex parte Aala* (2000) 204 CLR 82, [55].

39   See J Miles, 'Standing in a Multi-Layered Constitution' in N Bamforth and P Leyland (eds), *Public Law in a Multi-Layered Constitution* (Oxford: Hart Publishing, 2003), 391, 407–8.

40   Edgar, n 21 above, argues that this is what has occurred in the context of the 'extended standing' provisions under the *EPBC Act*.

this question if only because decisions affecting individuals may often also have broader implications of concern to others in the community.

Consider, for example, individual tax determinations. Although such determinations affect the rights and obligations of particular individuals, others may have a more general interest in ensuring that all tax payers pay their fair share. Inevitably, there will be controversy about when decisions indirectly affecting third parties raise genuine matters of public concern and when they do not. The ALRC's second exception to its proposed 'any person rule' addresses this issue. However, the fact the exception is expressed in very vague terms (such as 'public interest' and 'unreasonable interference') may illustrate the difficulties of articulating a clear principle to resolve this question. The criteria suggested by the ALRC would in practice amount to little more than an instruction to courts to make discretionary judgments about the circumstances in which individuals personally affected by a decision should be allowed to decide how, if at all, to challenge decisions that affect their personal interests but also raise wider issues.

Third, it is sometimes argued that open standing would lead to a flood of (unmeritorious) judicial review applications. However, the strength of this argument may be doubted. For one thing, courts have general powers to strike out frivolous or vexatious claims. More importantly, the formidable cost of litigation (particularly for losing parties) is likely to deter most applicants who have weak or insubstantial cases.[41] Here, as elsewhere, the 'floodgates' argument is not very persuasive.

Fourth, the introduction of an open standing regime may affect the development of other administrative law principles. Consider first the relationship between standing and the doctrine of non-justiciability (3.6.2). Whereas standing rules concern the appropriateness of hearing an application brought by a particular applicant, the idea that some decisions are non-justiciable concerns whether the review of a particular decision raises issues that are not appropriately brought before the courts by anyone. Although the general distinction between standing and non-justiciability is clear in theory, both mechanisms operate to mark the limits of judicial control of administrative decision-making, and address similar concerns about the appropriate role of courts in a constitutional democracy.[42] Interestingly, the trend in both areas of the law is towards the expansion of the reach of judicial review (see 3.6.2.2; 3.6.2.3). To the extent, however, that open standing encourages citizens or 'interest groups' to turn to the courts to achieve their political objectives, it may require the courts to clarify the principles of non-justiciability. Some commentators have expressed concern that broad standing rules may encourage interest groups to use applications for judicial review as a political tactic. The worry is that courts may be drawn into politically charged debates about the public interest, placing the idea of the courts as impartial arbiters under strain.[43]

It is also worth noting that, in the context of federal administrative law, assessment of the extent to which either the legislature or courts can move further down the path of open standing must take account of the constitutional limitation that judicial power may only be exercised over 'matters'.

---

41   Although it is possible that trial judges *may* depart from the normal rule that costs should follow the cause (i.e. the loser in litigation must pay the legal costs of the winner) in 'public interest' litigation the normal rule remains entrenched. See generally *Oshlack v Richmond River Council* (1998) 193 CLR 72 and the Full Federal Court decision in *Bat Advocacy NSW Inc v Minister for Environment Protection, Heritage and the Arts (No 2)* (2011) 280 ALR 91, 93–6.

42   Cf *Re McBain; Ex parte Australian Catholic Bishops Conference* (2002) 209 CLR 372, 458 (Hayne J): 'Questions of standing ... are not arid technical questions but are to be understood as rooted in fundamental conceptions about judicial power just as much as are questions of what is meant by a "matter". Similarly, questions about the availability of remedies like prohibition, mandamus and certiorari cannot be considered without identifying the place which they have in the judicial system and, in this case, in the federal judicature.'

43   See, e.g., C Harlow, 'Public Law and Popular Justice' (2002) 65 *Modern Law Review* 1.

The connection between standing rules and the 'matter' requirement has been the subject of a number of dark judicial pronouncements, and the precise relationship remains uncertain. Some judges have commented that the issue of standing is 'subsumed' within the constitutional requirement of matter, which might be taken to suggest that the Constitution imposes a minimum standing requirement for invoking Commonwealth judicial power.[44] On the other hand, the High Court has clearly expressed the opinion that it would be constitutionally permissible for the legislature to adopt an open standing rule, indicating that a 'matter' may exist even though a case is brought by a person who is not connected in any special way to the challenged decision.[45]

More generally, moves away from the interest model of standing raise the question of whether developments in the law of standing may outstrip the development of the grounds of review. For example, it is clear that applicants, such as environmental groups, may in some cases be granted standing even though the decision-maker would not be under an obligation to afford them a prior hearing precisely because the interests of such groups are not specifically affected.[46] As we have seen (5.2.2.1), there is no general principle of administrative law requiring consultation with concerned individuals or groups. Two points can be made here.

First, if an applicant's complaint is that they were not consulted, broad standing rules may not assist them unless the rules of procedural fairness are further developed to impose a general duty to consult.[47] Second, to the extent that one thinks that public interest groups or concerned citizens should be allowed to participate in government decision-making, it may be argued that the proper place for the expression of their points of view is in administrative and political processes, not in the courts. At the same time, however, to the extent that such applicants are allowed to participate in the legal processes of judicial review, it may appear anomalous to exclude them from participation in primary decision-making processes. More generally, it can be concluded that wide access to judicial review may not yield much benefit if the grounds of judicial review are not also developed in a way which recognises that administrators should be open to and consider the points of view of individuals and groups other than those whose legal rights or personal interests are affected.

Finally, proposals for the adoption of an open standing regime should be assessed in light of the fact that the law also recognises ways, besides initiating proceedings, in which people or groups may seek to participate in litigation. There are two ways in which third parties may participate in litigation commenced by others: as interveners and as *amici curiae* ('friends of the court'). When a person is granted leave to intervene, they are joined as a party to the proceedings. Interveners enjoy the procedural rights of a party (so, for example, they can appeal)[48] and will be bound by the judgment. Costs orders may be made against or for interveners, though normally an intervener is only ordered to pay additional costs occasioned by their intervention.[49] *Amici curiae* do not become parties to the proceedings; they

---

44   See *Croome v Tasmania* (1997) 191 CLR 119, 132–3. See also *Edwards v Santos Ltd* (2011) 242 CLR 421, 435.

45   *Truth About Motorways v Macquarie* (2000) 200 CLR 591. One judge suggested that there may be some cases where 'absent standing, there is no justiciable controversy': ibid, [46] (Gaudron J).

46   For discussion, see *Botany Bay City Council v Minister of State and Transport and Regional Development* (1996) 66 FCR 537, 568; *Griffith University v Tang* (2005) 221 CLR 89, 102–3.

47   See Edgar, n 21 above, for a helpful discussion of the issues raised in this paragraph in the context of environmental cases. Edgar concludes that commonly argued grounds of review have not been developed after the introduction of an extended standing rule under the *EPBC Act* and that the reality is that the grounds of review typically cannot reach the issues of concern to environmental groups.

48   See *Re McBain; Ex parte Australian Catholic Bishops Conference* (2002) 209 CLR 372.

49   See Evans and Donaghue, n 31 above, 94.

cannot 'file pleadings adduce evidence, examine witnesses or bring an appeal'.[50] Their role is merely to make submissions to assist the court, and the court has a broad discretion whether or not to accept what, in the US, are called 'amicus briefs'.

Relative to standing, there is little case law or scholarly literature in Australia dealing with rights of participation (as opposed to initiation). Although the High Court has given some consideration to the issues, clear legal principles have not emerged.[51] The best that can be said is that, in practice, Australian courts have adopted a restrictive approach to allowing third parties to intervene or participate as intervenors and *amici curiae*.[52] This reflects the traditional model of adjudication, which sees litigation as a two-sided affair in which the parties to the dispute are, in general, 'entitled to carry on their litigation free from the interference of persons who are strangers to the litigation'.[53] The attitude of the courts to intervenors and *amici curiae* seems to resonate with the interest model of standing. This conclusion poses a more general question: what relationship ought there to be between the right to initiate, and the right to participate in proceedings as an intervener or *amicus curiae*? Should initiation rules and participation rules reflect one and the same model of the judicial role and one and the same understanding of the purpose of judicial review? Or might there be good reasons why participation rules should be different from initiation rules? It might be argued that adoption of an open standing regime under which *any* person may initiate judicial review proceedings would make it 'much more difficult to justify limiting participation in public law litigation to the initiating parties and others directly involved'.[54] As one commentator has noted 'it may be difficult for a court to deny' a person who would have standing on that person's own account 'leave to intervene in the proceedings'.[55]

There are, however, reasons why a more relaxed approach to intervention might be resisted. Broad participation rules might increase the cost, in time and resources, of litigation. It has also been suggested that an 'open participation' regime might so change the nature of the judicial process that courts would begin to look more like executive decision-makers, formulating public policy on the basis of consultations with interested parties.[56] On the other hand, it might be argued that the abstractness of administrative law norms (5.1.1) and the fact that their proper application may be a matter of reasonable disagreement may indicate that judicial review will enjoy greater legitimacy to the extent that participation by a wide range of parties is permitted. What does seem clear is that if a rule of open standing were adopted, more attention would need to be paid to the development of clearer principles regulating other modes of involvement in litigation.

We can conclude this chapter by observing that the trend towards the liberalisation of standing law, and the possibility of adopting an open standing regime and even an open participation regime, need to be assessed in the light of views about what judicial review is for, and what role courts ought to play in ensuring compliance with administrative law norms.

---

50   S Kenny, 'Interveners and Amici Curiae in the High Court' (1998) 20 *Adelaide Law Review* 159, 160.

51   See *Levy v Victoria* (1997) 189 CLR 579; George Williams, 'The Amicus Curiae and Intervener in the High Court of Australia: A Comparative Analysis' (2000) 28 *Federal Law Review* 365.

52   For some statistics on the participation of third parties in the High Court, see Williams, ibid.

53   *United States Tobacco Co v Minister for Consumer Affairs* (1988) 20 FCR 520, 536.

54   P Cane, 'Open Standing and the Role of Courts in a Democratic Society' (1999) 20 *Singapore Law Review* 23, 44.

55   E Campbell, 'Intervention in Constitutional Cases' (1998) 9 *Public Law Review* 255, 262.

56   Cane, n 54 above, 44–5.

7

Restricting Judicial Review

When the legislature chooses to delegate decision-making powers to particular administrative tribunals or officers, judges have accepted that their judicial review role should not allow them to usurp those powers; their role, as we have seen, is limited to 'legality review' (3.2.2; Chapter 5). In part, this reflects judgments about the competence and legitimacy of the decision-makers on whom the legislature has chosen to confer particular powers. Sometimes, however, the legislature may have reasons for thinking that the role of judges should be reduced even further. For example, there is a long history of attempts to protect the decisions of industrial tribunals from judicial review, reflecting a judgment about the importance of the prompt and final resolution of industrial matters. In other cases, attempts to restrict the courts' normal review function may be based on a legislative judgment that the grounds of judicial review are being applied in a way which frustrates the capacity of the government to make what are considered to be legitimate policy choices. Here an apt example is migration decision-making, which has been the focus of various legislative strategies to limit judicial intervention (see 7.3).

Statutory clauses which purport to exclude the courts' judicial review jurisdiction normally go by the name of 'privative' or 'ouster' clauses. (Given that merits review jurisdiction (see 8.5.1.2) is entirely a creature of statute—that is, there is no inherent or constitutional source for jurisdiction to undertake review on the merits—the legislature can simply remove or fail to grant jurisdiction in relation to decisions it does not wish to be subject to merits review.) Such clauses can be worded in a variety of ways, but are targeted directly at the courts' jurisdiction to engage in judicial review.[1] Out of an abundance of caution, legislatures often not only state that an administrator's decision is final and not to be called into question in any court, but also specifically preclude the granting of the judicial review remedies. By its terms, a privative clause does not alter any applicable legal limitations on the exercise of a power but, rather, purports to remove the legal mechanism (judicial review) for enforcing those limits.[2] The language of such clauses is typically emphatic, but the courts have various resources at their disposal to combat attempts to diminish their judicial review jurisdiction. A simple example of the courts' interpretive resources to evade a privative clause is the limited effect given to so-called 'no certiorari' clauses: clauses which have commanded courts not to issue certiorari have been read as only excluding the availability of certiorari for non-jurisdictional, as opposed to jurisdictional, errors. However, the most powerful judicial resource is the

---

1   Although there are 'standard' forms of words used in privative clauses, judicial decisions on the validity and effect of particular clauses are, of course, determinative only in relation to the precise wording of a particular clause, interpreted in the context of particular legislation.

2   W Bateman, 'The Constitution and the Substantive Principles of Judicial Review: The Full Scope of the Entrenched Minimum Provision of Judicial Review' (2011) 39 *Federal Law Review* 463, 464.

Constitution which has been interpreted as providing for an 'entrenched minimum provision of judicial review' that must be respected by Commonwealth and state parliaments. Although the boundaries of this minimum provision of judicial review are uncertain, its existence will continue to legitimate creative interpretive responses to attempts to limit judicial review and may require the invalidation of laws which cannot be read consistently with constitutional requirements.

This chapter considers how the courts have responded to legislative attempts to protect 'administrative decisions'[3] from judicial review. Our consideration examines clauses which are ostensibly designed to oust judicial review jurisdiction (privative clauses) and, also, other statutory devices or techniques which may result in limiting the effective exercise of judicial review.

7.1 The constitutional foundations of judicial review

Before considering how Australian courts have interpreted privative clauses (7.2), it is helpful to set out the basis of the entrenched minimum provision of judicial review in Australia.

On the face of it, the Constitution provides a different level of protection against federal privative clauses than is provided in relation to state clauses. Section 75(v) of the Constitution entrenches the High Court's jurisdiction to issue prohibition, mandamus and injunctions. If read literally, this provision would render any statutory attempt to prevent the issue of these named remedies against an 'officer of the Commonwealth' invalid. Surprisingly, however, the High Court has not invalidated provisions which do purport to oust judicial review in terms which include express reference to the named constitutional remedies. We will explain how the High Court has read such clauses to avoid this result below (7.2). The important point, for now, is to emphasise that the Constitution expressly provides for an entrenched judicial review jurisdiction for High Court which is defined by the terms of s 75(v). In *Plaintiff S157* (discussed in detail below) the High Court explained that s 75(v) preserved to it an entrenched minimum provision of judicial review jurisdiction to ensure that officers of the Commonwealth neither exceeded nor neglected 'any jurisdiction which the law confers on them';[4] that is, parliament cannot deprive the court of its jurisdiction to issue the constitutional remedies on the basis of jurisdictional error.

In marked contrast, there is no constitutional provision analogous to s 75(v) to protect the supervisory jurisdiction of the Supreme Courts of the states. Although in practice the courts have often evaded the application of strongly worded state privative clauses—by relying, for example, on the basic presumption that legislatures do 'not intend to deprive the citizen of access to the courts, other than to the extent expressly stated or necessarily to be implied'[5]—the orthodox position has been that an insistent state parliament may, by a well-drafted privative clause, exclude judicial review.[6] Sometimes

---

3   For the purposes of this chapter, the phrase 'administrative decisions' is used to refer to all decisions which, in the absence of a privative clause, would be subject to judicial review. 'Administrative decision-maker' is shorthand for those decision-makers subject to judicial review.

4   *Plaintiff S157/2002 v Commonwealth* (2003) 211 CLR 476, 513–4.

5   *Public Service Association (SA) v Federated Clerks' Union* (1991) 173 CLR 132, 160. For a recent application of this presumption, see *Perrinepod Pty Ltd v Georgiou Building Pty Ltd* [2011] WASCA 217. As a rule statutory time limits for bringing a judicial review claim are a more effective way of excluding review than are privative clauses, but see below 7.2.4.3.

6   State parliaments, subject to the Commonwealth Constitution and any applicable 'manner and form' requirements (2.3.1, 2.4.2.1), enjoy plenary legislative power.

this orthodoxy has been occluded within confusing formulations;[7] but until recently there have been few doubters.

In *Kirk* the orthodox position in relation to state privative clauses was dramatically rejected.[8] The High Court held that state legislation cannot deprive a state Supreme Court of its jurisdiction to review administrative decisions on the basis that an administrative decision-maker has made a jurisdictional error. According to the High Court, the distinction between jurisdictional and non-jurisdictional error marks the relevant limit on state legislative powers to exclude judicial review. The effect of this ruling is that there is also an 'entrenched minimum provision of judicial review' at the state level, to be understood in the same basic way as is the review jurisdiction of the High Court under s 75(v). The obvious question is how the High Court reached this conclusion.

The argument establishing that the Constitution entrenches judicial review at the state level proceeded in three basic steps.[9] First, the court began from the assumption that Chapter III of the Constitution—in particular s 73(ii) which provides that the High Court shall have appellate jurisdiction from 'the Supreme Court of any State'—requires the continuing existence of a judicial institution which answers the constitutional description of 'the Supreme Court of a State'. Second, the legislature could not deprive such an institution of its character as Supreme Court.[10] Third, it was argued that the power to ensure that inferior courts and tribunals stayed within the limits of their authority to decide (that is, to review for jurisdictional error) was an essential or defining characteristic of a Supreme Court of a state. In justification of this claim the court asserted that, at federation, the Supreme Courts of the colonies had this jurisdiction, *notwithstanding* the existence of any privative clause. More generally, the court claimed that this jurisdiction operates to prevent the creation of 'islands of power' and 'distorted positions'[11]— though this policy reason for entrenching judicial review was not tightly linked to the Constitution's text or structure.

The harmonisation of state and Commonwealth administrative law achieved by *Kirk* certainly has the virtue of simplifying the law. Further, some commentators have applauded the decision on the basis that it enhances the rule of law by securing a level of judicial enforcement of the legal limits on administrative decision-making at both levels of government.[12] Nevertheless, the constitutional foundations of the

---

7   E.g. *Darling Casino* (1997) 191 CLR 602, 634, where Gaudron and Gummow JJ stated that 'provided the intention is clear, a privative clause in a valid State enactment may preclude review of errors of any kind. And if it does, the decision is entirely beyond review so long as it satisfies the *Hickman* principle'. *Kirk v Industrial Court of New South Wales* (2010) 239 CLR 531 removes any need to consider how these comments are best interpreted.

8   *Kirk v Industrial Court of New South Wales* (2010) 239 CLR 531.

9   *Kirk v Industrial Court of New South Wales* (2010) 239 CLR 531, 578–81. *Kirk* held that all state Supreme Courts must maintain a supervisory jurisdiction to review for jurisdictional error. However, the precise basis on which such a jurisdiction is maintained has given rise to complications in Queensland, where the *Judicial Review Act 1991* (Qld) has abolished the Supreme Court's power to issue the prerogative writs. The issue was discussed, though not resolved, in *Northbuild Constructions Pty Ltd v Central Interior Lining Pty Ltd* [2011] QCA 22.

10   These two stages of the analysis had been accepted in the court's previous Chapter III jurisprudence. In *Forge v Australian Securities & Investments Commission* (2006) 228 CLR 45, 76, Gummow, Hayne and Crennan JJ stated that '[i]t is beyond the legislative power of a State so to alter the constitutional character of its Supreme Court that it ceases to meet the constitutional description'. See also Gleeson CJ at 67–8.

11   *Kirk v Industrial Court of New South Wales* (2010) 239 CLR 531, 581. The court explained that 'distorted positions' may develop if 'tribunals of limited jurisdiction' are not subjected 'to the control of the courts of more general jurisdiction': ibid, 570. The point appears to be an assertion of a judicially enforced conception of the rule of law. The causes of so-called 'distorted positions' are not elaborated. See further 7.4.

12   E.g. C Finn, 'Constitutionalising Supervisory Review at State Level: The End of *Hickman*?' (2010) 21 *Public Law Review* 92.

decision have been fairly described as 'fragile'.[13] In particular, the claim that an essential or defining characteristic of a Supreme Court is the power to grant relief on the basis of jurisdictional error has been questioned. One influential judge has noted that 'the mere use of the expression "Supreme Court" does not indicate why the failure to permit [judicial] review ... prevented the Supreme Court of New South Wales satisfying the constitutional descriptor of "Supreme Court of the State"'.[14] And although the High Court cited a pre-federation case to justify the conclusion that the Supreme Courts of the colonies had an entrenched judicial review jurisdiction at the time of federation, it has been rightly doubted whether the case is indeed authority for the proposition that the Supreme Court of a colony 'could grant relief for what is now described as 'jurisdictional error'', regardless of the width of a privative clause'.[15] However, regardless of the strength or weakness of the constitutional argument, the result of *Kirk* has been to synchronise the basic principles relevant to the interpretation and validity of federal and state privative clauses.[16]

7.2 The interpretation of privative clauses: the general approach

As we have noted, the fact that it has always been clear that a minimum of judicial review is constitutionally protected in relation to Commonwealth administrative decision-making has not resulted in the automatic invalidation of clauses which are seemingly in direct conflict with the terms of s 75(v). Rather, privative clauses (even when purporting to oust the High Court's power to issue mandamus, prohibition or injunction) have been interpreted creatively so as to preserve their validity. This raises the question of why the High Court has not chosen simply to invalidate privative clauses when their terms are directly inconsistent with the terms of s 75(v). One reason may be judicial sympathy with the policy reasons leading legislatures to enact privative clauses. Creative interpretation of privative clauses that preserve their validity is arguably one way in which judges can defer to administrative determinations of law in some circumstances.[17] Another historically important reason for not relying on s 75(v) to invalidate federal privative clauses is that an interpretive approach—which may preserve a role for judicial review even if in a diminished form—could also be deployed in the context of state privative clauses, prior to the court's holding in *Kirk* that state Supreme Courts also have entrenched judicial review jurisdiction.[18] We are returned, then, to the question of how privative clauses have been read as being consistent with the Constitution despite their terms.

---

13   R Sackville, 'The Constitutionalisation of State Administrative Law' (2012) 19 *Australian Journal of Administrative Law* 127, 130.

14   J Basten, 'The Supervisory Jurisdiction of the Supreme Courts' (2011) 85 *Australian Law Journal* 273, 279.

15   Sackville, n 13 above, 130. The case cited was *Colonial Bank of Australiasia v Willan* (1874) LR 5 PC 417.

16   Bateman, n 2 above, 476. Although it is clear that jurisdictional error is the central organising principle for judicial review in the context of s 75(v) and the supervisory jurisdiction of state Supreme Courts, there remain questions about what, if any, doctrinal differences in the availability of particular remedies may persist after *Kirk*. This issue is considered at 3.4.3 and 4.5.3.

17   See P Bayne, 'Fuzzy Drafting and the Interpretation of Statutes in the Administrative State' (1992) 66 *Australian Law Journal* 523.

18   See e.g. *Darling Casino Ltd v NSW Casino Control Authority* (1997) 191 CLR 602. As Bateman has noted, a theme of the High Court's doctrine concerning privative clauses has been an attempt to maintain parity in respect of state and federal privative clauses. Prior to *Kirk*, this was achieved primarily through interpretive means; post-*Kirk* parity is required by operation of Ch III of the Constitution: see Bateman, n 2 above, 476.

7.2.1 The *Hickman* 'reconciliation' approach

The High Court's general preference for interpretive rather than constitutional responses to privative clause is well illustrated by reference to *R v Hickman; Ex parte Fox and Clinton*.[19] Although the so-called *Hickman* principle was styled as *a* principle of statutory interpretation, for many years it was the *main* interpretive lens through which privative clauses were read. Our discussion of *Plaintiff S157* and *Kirk* below will indicate that the accepted interpretation of the *Hickman* principle has fallen into disfavour. Nevertheless, it is useful to briefly describe the interpretive approach for two reasons. First, it is difficult to understand the arguments made in *Plaintiff S157* (the most significant general discussion of the entrenched s 75(v) jurisdiction) without understanding why the Commonwealth had assumed that the High Court would not invalidate a clause which was patently in conflict with the Constitution. Second, it is possible that the basic interpretive strategy adopted in *Hickman* may resurface in the context of developing responses to alternative statutory devices to limit the efficacy of judicial review (7.2.4.1).

In *R v Hickman; Ex parte Fox and Clinton*,[20] the High Court held that a privative clause which stated that the decisions of an industrial relations board 'shall not be challenged, appealed against, quashed or called into question, or be subject to prohibition, mandamus or injunction, in any court on any account whatever' was not constitutionally invalid, despite the fact that its terms were in direct conflict with the Constitution. To achieve this outcome it was necessary to interpret the privative clause so that it meant something quite different from what it said. Dixon J's 'classic' analysis began from the premise that parliament had, in effect, spoken with a forked tongue. In one breath it had delegated limited powers to the board, yet in the next breath the privative clause appeared to license breaches of those limitations, insofar as it provided that decisions that breached them could not be judicially reviewed. Viewed this way, the statute contained 'provisions which would contradict one another' if no attempt was made to 'reconcile' them.[21] The task for the court was therefore to undertake a process of reconciliation.

Prior to *Plaintiff S157*, the outcome of the application of this reconciliation process in *Hickman* was routinely understood in this way: the privative clause worked to expand the jurisdiction or authority of the decision-maker beyond the express or implied limitations contained in the statute, so that the only enforceable limitations on the decision-maker's powers were constituted by the so-called '*Hickman* provisos'. Accordingly, the privative clause did not mean that judicial review was ousted but that decisions would be treated as valid provided only that the decision-maker had made a 'bona fide attempt to exercise its power, that [the decision] relate[d] to the subject matter of the legislation, and that [the decision was] reasonably capable of reference to the power given to the body'.[22] It should also be noted that the actual result in *Hickman* indicated that the privative clause could not prevent review for breach of a fundamental jurisdictional requirement. As explained in later cases, the 'reconciliation' of some jurisdictional requirements with the privative clause may result in the conclusion that a particular requirement is 'inviolable', 'essential' or 'indispensable'.[23] That is, in relation to some jurisdictional

---

19   *R v Hickman; Ex parte Fox and Clinton* (1945) 70 CLR 598. For an brief but insightful doctrinal history of privative clauses, see Bateman, n 2 above, 470–9.

20   *R v Hickman; Ex parte Fox and Clinton* (1945) 70 CLR 598.

21   Ibid, 616.

22   Ibid, 615, 617 (the third proviso is formulated differently in a different passage as the requirement that no decision can 'on its face' exceed the decision-maker's authority).

23   See, e.g., *R v Murray; Ex parte Proctor* (1949) 77 CLR 387. These adjectives are used interchangeably in the case law considering *Hickman*.

limitations, the privative clause may have no operation at all. Nevertheless, 'the assumption underlying the *Hickman* principle is that the enactment of a privative clause loosens the jurisdictional fetters contained in a statute, thus expanding the jurisdiction of the decision-maker'.[24]

The judicial creativity inherent in the application of the *Hickman* principle may be questioned on at least two bases. First, although a privative clause may be read as loosening the jurisdictional shackles placed on an administrative decision-maker, the terms of the privative clause provide no clues about the extent to which those shackles are loosened. Unless the principle is applied in a mechanistic way, such that the jurisdictional limits are the same in all statutes that include a privative clause,[25] it must be accepted that the principle licenses a large measure of judicial discretion.[26] More fundamentally, the soundness of the premise on which the whole argument is based can be questioned: is there really an internal contradiction in statutes which impose limitations on administrative powers but which also contain a privative clause? An alternative view might be that there is no necessary contradiction involved because those provisions of a statute which expressly or impliedly limit an administrator's powers are 'logically distinct' from the privative clause, which is directed to the jurisdiction of the courts (not the powers of the administrator).[27] Arguably, then, although it *may* be that a privative clause evidences a legislative intention to expand jurisdictional limits,[28] there is a necessary contradiction only if 'one assumes that it is the essence of there being legal limits that these limits are enforceable by judges'.[29] (We will come back to this assumption in 7.4).

7.2.2 The contemporary position: *Plaintiff S157* and *Kirk*

The *Hickman* 'reconciliation approach' has been accepted in many cases. Although it was not expressly disavowed by the High Court in *Plaintiff S157*, the High Court reconceived it in a way which clearly limits its effectiveness in diminishing the efficacy of the High Court's s 75(v) judicial review jurisdiction. *Plaintiff S157* considered the *Migration Act* privative clause, which had been drafted in similar terms to the clause considered in *Hickman* (in the hope that it would be interpreted in line with the *Hickman* principle).[30] Although the privative clause survived a challenge to its constitutional validity, the court's analysis reinterpreted the '*Hickman* principle', largely by placing considerably more emphasis on the constitutional significance of s 75(v).

---

24   Bateman, n 2 above, 472–3.

25   And this would sit uneasily with the status of the principle as one of statutory interpretation.

26   J Kirk, 'The Entrenched Minimum Provision of Judicial Review' (2004) 12 *AJ Admin L* 64, 70.

27   See ibid, 65–6.

28   Bateman, n 2 above, 479.

29   D Dyzenhaus, *The Constitution of Law: Legality in a Time of Emergency* (New York and Cambridge: Cambridge University Press, 2006), 104. Mark Aronson has argued that any contradiction is not internal to the Act in question but 'is a contradiction between such Acts and Dicey's version of the rule of law', which places the ordinary courts at the 'apex of every claim that government has broken the law' and is also premised on 'respect for what Parliament enacted': M Aronson, 'Commentary on "The Entrenched Minimum Provision of Judicial Review and the rule of law" by Leighton McDonald' (2010) 21 *Public Law Review* 35, 37.

30   An interpretation of the clause which expanded decision-maker's jurisdictional limits up to the *Hickman* provisos would have drastically limited the grounds on which relief could be granted: not many decisions made under the *Migration Act* would fail to be bona fide, relate to migration matters or not be reasonably capable of reference to the power given to the decision-maker.

The plurality judgment (joined in by five members of the court) rejected an argument that the privative clause operated to expand the jurisdiction of the decision-makers under the *Migration Act* up to the limits of the *Hickman* provisos. (We explain this conclusion below.) If the privative clause does not expand the scope of the decision-maker's power, the obvious alternative reading of the clause is that it addresses the power of the court. But if that is so, how could it be concluded that the privative clause was not directly inconsistent with s 75(v)? The plurality began by arguing that, before any issue of reconciling 'inconsistent' statutory provision needs to be confronted, it is first necessary to determine the protection a privative clause 'purports to afford'. As the *Migration Act* privative clause applied only in relation to decisions made 'under the Act', it was concluded that a decision infected by jurisdictional error was not such a decision for the reason that a jurisdictionally flawed decision is 'regarded, in law, as no decision at all'.[31] This interpretation of the scope of the privative clause was warranted both as a matter of 'general principle'[32] and because a broader interpretation of the privative clause according to which it would also apply to decisions infected by jurisdictional error (that is, 'purported decisions') would generate a direct conflict with s 75(v) and, therefore, render the privative clause constitutionally invalid.[33] Properly interpreted, the privative clause did not purport to oust review in cases where 'decisions' were infected by a jurisdictional error. Thus, there was no constitutional problem as the constitutional writs of prohibition and mandamus are available only for jurisdictional error (4.5.3). (The court clearly accepted that a privative clause could prevent the issue of certiorari for non-jurisdictional errors, though the position in relation to the 'constitutional injunction' remains uncertain; see 4.5.3.) And as the alleged error in *Plaintiff S157* was a denial of procedural fairness—a well-established species of jurisdictional error—the privative clause did not protect the challenged decision from review.

Although this analysis saved the provision from constitutional invalidity, without more it also appears to deprive the privative clause of any meaningful role.[34] Where, if anywhere, does the *Hickman* reconciliation approach fit into this analysis of the *Migration Act* privative clause? This is not an easy question to answer. To begin with what is clear: as noted above, the joint judgment rejected the suggestion that the reconciliation approach meant that the privative clause could, in effect, impliedly repeal detailed provisions of the *Migration Act* limiting the decision-maker's powers, so that 'decisions are protected so

---

31   *Plaintiff S157/2002 v Commonwealth* (2003) 211 CLR 476, 506 [76], quoting *Bhardwaj* (2002) 209 CLR 597, 614–5 (see also 4.7.1).

32   Here the joint judgment deployed the same basic logic used in *Animinic Ltd v Foreign Compensation Commission* [1969] 2 AC 147. In this case, the House of Lords read a clause which stated that decisions could not be 'called into question in any court of law' as having virtually no effect on the courts' judicial review jurisdiction. The court (1) held that the privative clause was ineffective to protect against the review of decisions infected by a jurisdictional error—because a jurisdictionally flawed decision is merely a 'purported' decision, and the review of purported decisions was not excluded by the clause—see 4.7.3; and (2) took a very broad approach to what qualifies as a jurisdictional error.

33   The court relied on the general principle of statutory interpretation, which holds that statutes should be construed conformably with the Constitution, where that interpretation is fairly open.

34   Dyzenhaus interprets the approach in the joint judgment as effectively reading the privative clause out of the statute. He argues that Gleeson CJ's concurring judgment prefers the 'reconciliation approach', articulated in *Hickman*, to the 'evisceration approach', characterised by *Anisminic* and accepted by the joint judgment in *Plaintiff S157*. See Dyzenhaus, n 29 above, 108–17. Gleeson CJ argued that the *Hickman* principle must, as a principle of statutory interpretation, be understood in the context of other principles of statutory interpretation. These principles included: that courts should construe legislation in accordance with international obligations in cases of ambiguity; that unmistakable clarity is required to abrogate fundamental common law rights (such as procedural fairness rights and the right to access the courts); that the Constitution should be understood as being premised on the assumption of the rule of law (an assumption which favours maintaining citizens' access to the courts); and that legislation should be interpreted as a 'whole', which sometimes involves the reconciliation of conflicting provisions. Gleeson CJ concluded, by reference to these principles, that the legislature had not 'evinced an intention that a decision' under the *Migration Act* could be made in contravention of the requirements of natural justice, so long as it conformed to the *Hickman* provisos (i.e. was a decision that related to migration, was bona fide, and was reasonably capable of reference to the powers conferred by the migration legislation).

long as there has been a bona fide attempt to exercise the power in question, that they relate to the subject matter of the legislation and are reasonably capable of reference to the power'.[35] Rather, and less clearly, it was said that, properly understood, the *Hickman* provisos are conditions which must be satisfied before the 'protection' which the privative clause 'purports to afford' will be applicable.[36] This appears to mean that the provisos are not the result of a reconciliation process which (re)defines the jurisdiction of the administrative decision-maker, but rather constitute threshold requirements of some sort which must be met before any reliance can be placed on a privative clause. Why this might be so is left unexplained.

Matters are even more complicated, however. At the conclusion of the analysis of the *Hickman* line of cases, the plurality emphasised that 'it may be that, by reference to the words of [the privative clause], some procedural or other requirements laid down by the Act are to be construed as not essential to the validity of a decision'. That is, the 'process of reconciliation' of 'an apparent conflict between the provisions which impose those requirements and the privative clause in question'[37] may turn what at first blush appears to be a 'mandatory' requirement into a 'directory' provision.[38] But if the existence of a privative clause is relevant to categorising a statutory requirement as not being essential to the validity of a decision, it seems that the powers of the administrative decision-maker *can* be expanded by the privative clause.[39] Thus, the reconciliation approach (as explained in the *Plaintiff S157* plurality judgment) may expand the powers of the decision-maker, but not necessarily so that the *Hickman* provisos become the only jurisdictional limits.

This analysis suffers from an obvious difficulty: the terms of the privative clause, which are directed to the issue of limiting the court's judicial review jurisdiction and the availability of judicial review remedies, do not themselves provide any meaningful guidance for the task of determining which statutory limits on the administrative decision-maker's powers are 'mandatory'[40] and which are not.[41] The judges are simply left to make these judgments based on their own opinions of how the statutory scheme in question will best function; the privative clause may tip the balance, but it may not. Later migration cases have proceeded on the basis that the privative clause will have very little or no impact on the analysis of whether the decision-maker has made a jurisdictional error.[42] It thus seems clear enough that the privative clause has effectively been read out of the *Migration Act*.[43]

It is possible that not all privative clauses will be read into oblivion when it comes to the availability of review for jurisdictional error. In *Plaintiff S157* the High Court emphasised that there is 'no general

---

35   That is, so long as the *Hickman* provisos are satisfied: *Plaintiff S157/2002 v Commonwealth* (2003) 211 CLR 476, 502.

36   Ibid, 502.

37   Ibid, 504.

38   On the distinction between mandatory and directory provisions, see 4.3. Although the court has said that the distinction does not assist in determining whether breach of a statutory provision has the remedial consequence of invalidity (*Project Blue Sky Inc v Australian Broadcasting Authority* (1998) 194 CLR 355, 389–90), the terminology can (usefully) be used to record the outcome of the process of statutory construction directed to that question: cf Gleeson CJ in *Plaintiff S157* (2003) 211 CLR 476, 489.

39   Put another way, the privative clause is relevant to the *Project Blue Sky* analysis of whether breach of a particular provision or administrative law norm affects the validity of a decision: see 4.3.

40   Such provisions can also be described as 'essential', 'indispensable', or 'inviolable'.

41   Kirk, n 26 above, 71.

42   See *Minister for Immigration and Multicultural and Indigenous Affairs v SGLB* (2004) 207 ALR 12; in *Minister for Immigration and Citizenship v SZIZO* (2009) 238 CLR 627, where it was held that failure to strictly comply with a statutory requirement did not, in the circumstances, affect the validity of the tribunal's decision, no emphasis was placed upon the Act's privative clause.

43   One commentator has reasonably concluded that the course of litigation since *Plaintiff S157* 'must be seen as sounding the death knell for the privative clause': C Beaton-Wells, 'Judicial Review of Migration Decisions: Life After *S157*' (2005) 33 *Federal Law Review* 141, 160.

rule of the meaning or effect of privative clauses'.[44] Notably, however, the High Court's analysis of whether there was a jurisdictional error in *Kirk* made no reference to the existence of the privative clause. Thus, it appears somewhat doubtful that any continuing reliance will be placed on a traditionally worded privative clause in determining the scope of an administrative decision-maker's jurisdictional limits.

It can be concluded that the contemporary doctrinal approach of the High Court to the interpretation of traditional privative clauses indicates judges have ample room to effectively ignore them, even if they are not constitutionally invalidated.[45] Indeed, in *Kirk* it was concluded, on the basis of the constitutional considerations that underpinned the entrenchment of state judicial review jurisdiction, that a privative clause which referred to both decisions and *purported* decisions of the Industrial Court should not be read as purporting to protect a decision 'that was attended by jurisdictional error'.[46] In this context it is unsurprising that attention is turning to alternative legislative devices to reduce the efficacy of judicial review. Before considering such strategies, however, it is useful to better understand the notion of an entrenched minimum provision of judicial review. In *Plaintiff S157* the court emphasised the constitutional significance of this concept and, thus, the underlying principles are likely to be of relevance to statutory attempts to limit judicial review whether they be by way of a traditional privative clause or some other legislative technique.

7.2.3 The 'entrenched minimum provision of judicial review'

The notion of 'jurisdictional error' can play two roles in the law of judicial review. The established usage, as we have seen (see 4.1.1), regulates the relationship between the courts and administrative decision-makers: judicial review remedies normally issue only if a decision-maker has made a jurisdictional error. In *Plaintiff S157* and *Kirk*, jurisdictional error was also invoked as the key concept to regulate the relationship between the High Court and the Commonwealth and state parliaments.

The plurality judgment in *Plaintiff S157* included a coda on 'general principles' which emphasised that the interpretation of the *Migration Act* privative clause had proceeded on the basis that s 75(v) introduced into the Constitution an 'entrenched minimum provision of judicial review', something which no privative clause could erode. The important purpose of s 75(v) is to secure the 'rule of law' by 'assuring to all people affected that officers of the Commonwealth obey the law and neither exceed nor neglect any jurisdiction which the law confers on them'.[47] And parliament cannot deprive the court of this 'constitutional function'. Although the rule of law is not referred to in *Kirk*, the court's emphasis on judicial review's role in avoiding 'distorted positions' and 'islands of power' reflects similar concerns. Two points can be noted about these references to the rule of law. First, the court identifies the rule of law ideal as the foundational value underpinning the entrenched minimum provision of judicial review at the Commonwealth and state levels. Judicial review may incidentally protect other values, but its minimum content is understood in terms of a conception of the rule of law which includes a requirement

---

44   *Plaintiff S157/2002 v Commonwealth* (2003) 211 CLR 476, 501.

45   As noted above, federal privative clauses can, subject to uncertainties about the 'constitutional injunction', protect against review for non-jurisdictional error, i.e. errors not having the consequence of retrospective invalidity. The same is true in relation to state clauses: *Kirk v Industrial Court of New South Wales* (2010) 239 CLR 531, 581.

46   Ibid, 582. See also *Batterham v QSR Ltd* (2006) 225 CLR 237.

47   *Plaintiff S157/2002 v Commonwealth* (2003) 211 CLR 476, 513–4.

that judges play a role in ensuring legal accountability (see further 12.1.3.1). Second, what is meant by the rule of law is not further elaborated. All we are offered is the conclusion that the rule of law, in the context of s 75(v) and the supervisory jurisdiction of state Supreme Courts, requires judicial review for jurisdictional errors; that is, the High Court's role in maintaining the rule of law is to ensure that decision-makers subject to judicial review do not act in excess of their legal powers.

There are at least two possible difficulties with conceptualising the minimum entrenched provision of judicial review in terms of jurisdictional error. First, the extent to which the concept of jurisdictional error used to protect the court's supervisory review jurisdiction coincides with the content of jurisdictional error as it is conceptualised in the context of determining the boundaries of administrator's powers is unclear. As explained earlier (5.4.1), jurisdictional error is an omnibus concept, which potentially encompasses all or most of the grounds of judicial review (in the sense that if an error establishes one or other of the grounds of review it may also amount to a jurisdictional error). The conclusion that none of the standard grounds (including breach of a statutory requirement) are entrenched would enable parliament to evade the courts' constitutional review jurisdiction. Yet the idea that all grounds of review are constitutionally entrenched seems equally implausible. For one thing, there are many statements that affirm that even a ground of review as important as breach of the rules of procedural fairness can be excluded by statute (5.2.2.2).[48] More generally, it may be thought that there are objections to entrenching judicial interpretations of the values served by the grounds of review in the absence of clearer guidance from the constitutional text, particularly given that the abstractness of many grounds of review (see 5.1.1) means that this result would set up the courts as the ultimate arbiters of the balance between the interests of individuals and the public interest.[49]

If the courts were to accept that particular substantive principles could not be ousted by even unmistakeably clear legislation, then it is likely that any entrenched grounds of review would be narrowly identified. For example, the *Hickman* provisos might be accepted as constitutional requirements. Another suggestion is that legislation authorising administrative decision-makers to act 'arbitrarily, capriciously, irrationally, or in bad faith'[50] would be inconsistent with the minimum provision of judicial review. In *Bodruddaza v Minister for Immigration and Multicultural Affairs* six members of the High Court warned that '[i]t would be a bold exercise of legislative choice for the Parliament to enact that ministers and their delegates were authorised to exercise fraudulently any of the powers of decision conferred upon them by statute ... [I]n such an unlikely eventuality questions of validity might well arise'.[51]

The second difficulty with the court's conclusion that the minimum provision of judicial review is to be understood in terms of the concept of jurisdictional error is that the characterisation of an error as being jurisdictional ultimately depends upon questions of statutory interpretation (at least for statutory powers) (see 5.4.1; 4.3). If the categorisation of an error as one which goes to jurisdiction is ultimately a matter of statutory interpretation, then parliament might attempt to evade meaningful judicial review by simply expanding the powers (that is, widening the jurisdiction) given to administrators such that there are no, or no meaningful, limits on power. This raises the prospect that other legislative techniques

---

48   A recent example is *Sieffert v Prisoners Review Board* [2011] WASCA 148, which held *Kirk* had not changed the accepted position that, although parliament could not oust the courts' jurisdiction, it could define the duties placed on an administrative decision-maker.

49   For discussion, see J Kirk, 'Administrative Justice and the Australian *Constitution*' in R Creyke and J McMillan (eds), *Administrative Justice—the Core and the Fringe* (Australian Institute of Administrative Law, 2000).

50   J Basten, 'Constitutional Elements of Judicial Review' (2004) 15 *Public Law Review* 187, 201.

51   (2007) 228 CLR 651, 663.

may be invoked to achieve precisely this outcome. Before turning to consider some such techniques it is worth noting that this problem was acknowledged in *Plaintiff S157*, in response to the suggestion (put in argument by the Commonwealth) that parliament may drastically diminish the effect of judicial review (even if it continues, in theory, to be available) by conferring 'totally open-ended' discretionary powers on administrators. Although judicial review's grounds of review resist the acceptance of unfettered powers, the resistance is achieved by means of statutory interpretation. If, however, parliament indicated (with unmistakeable clarity) that a power was intended to give unfettered power, for example by indicating that the detailed provisions of a statute amounted to no more than 'non-binding guidelines', judicial review on the basis of jurisdictional error would be rendered largely illusory.

In *Plaintiff S157* the High Court offered some brief comments about this problem, indicating that the parliament's ability to diminish judicial review by purporting to give decision-makers extremely wide or 'open-ended' jurisdiction or powers is not unlimited. One explanation, contemplated by the plurality, is that a statute which confers an extremely broad discretion may not really be a 'law', because it would not exemplify the concept of a law 'as a rule of conduct or a declaration as to power, right or duty'.[52] Another constitutional principle emphasised in the *Plaintiff S157* joint judgment is that a Commonwealth law could not operate so as to allow a non-judicial decision-maker to determine conclusively the limits of its own jurisdiction, as this would be an exercise of the judicial power of the Commonwealth.[53] It may therefore be that an entirely open-ended discretion, not subject to any meaningful limits, would violate this aspect of the Australian approach to the separation of powers (see 2.4.1.4; 2.4.2.4) Both of the court's constitutional objections have been subjected to persuasive criticism;[54] and both await further clarification. What the court's objections do clearly indicate, however, is that strong resistance will be offered in the event a parliament adopts drastic measures to disable the High Court from performing its constitutional function as the court understands it.

7.2.4 Alternatives to privative clauses

As already noted, traditional privative clauses—which purport to oust the jurisdiction of the courts to engage in judicial review or to issue named judicial review remedies—are not the only way in which a legislature may seek to restrict judicial review. In this section we examine a number of alternative techniques which are likely to be increasingly explored in light of the fate suffered by the privative clauses in *Plaintiff S157* and *Kirk*. We will consider, in turn, 'no-invalidity clauses', 'no-consideration clauses' and 'time-limit clauses'.[55] Our discussion considers these techniques for limiting judicial review in the context of the entrenched minimum provision of judicial review.

---

52   *Plaintiff S157/2002 v Commonwealth* (2003) 211 CLR 476, 513. The court also stated that such a law may not, as it must, identify a factual connection between a given state of affairs and a constitutional head of power.

53   Ibid, 505.

54   Bateman, n 2 above, 492–500.

55   It is also worth noting that the availability of judicial review in certain contexts may be more theoretical than real on account of forensic or evidentiary difficulties in making out a claim. In *South Australia v Totani* (2010) 242 CLR 1, the High Court held that, although a declaration made by the Attorney-General (SA) that an organisation put public health and safety at risk was not protected by a privative clause from judicial review, the fact that there were real difficulties in successfully challenging a declaration based on criminal intelligence was not held to be inconsistent with the constitutional principles outlined in *Kirk's* case. See Sackville, n 13 above, 136–7. A similar point can be made in the context of the non-justiciability doctrine: although a matter may be justiciable in principle, demonstrating an error in relation to a subject matter such as national security may be a 'formidable task': *Church of Scientology v Woodward* (1982) 154 CLR 25, 61.

7.2.4.1 No-invalidity clauses[56]

A distinction may be drawn between statutory attempts to diminish judicial review which are aimed at depriving the courts of their review or remedial powers and those which change the powers of administrators by removing the substantive basis upon which a judicial review remedy may be issued. There are a number of ways in which the substantive basis for granting a judicial remedy may be removed. One obvious option is simply to confer broad discretionary powers on administrators, for example by conferring powers which may be exercised on the basis of subjective state-of-mind criteria (see 5.4.3.1.2). In general, the broader a discretion is, the more difficult it will normally be to argue that the reasoning process grounds of review have been breached, or that a decision is *Wednesbury* unreasonable. However, as we have seen in Chapter 5, such discretionary powers are not unlimited and are in principle subject to review. A no-invalidity clause is another alternative, though it focuses on the consequences of breaching legal requirements rather than the terms in which those requirements are drafted or defined.

A no-invalidity clause does not purport to deprive the courts of their review jurisdiction but indicates that an act done or decision made in breach of a particular statutory requirement or other administrative law norm does not result in the invalidity of that act or decision. The conclusion that a decision is not invalid means that the decision-maker had the power (that is, jurisdiction) to make it. Thus, to the extent that, in general, judicial review remedies are issued only on the basis of jurisdictional errors, no-invalidity clauses may be read as converting errors that would otherwise be jurisdictional in nature into errors which are made within the decision-maker's powers and will not justify a remedy. In this way, no-invalidity clauses expand the decision-maker's powers to make legally valid decisions.

No-invalidity clauses may be narrowly or broadly framed. Whereas a narrow clause will be directed at a particular statutory or other administrative law requirement, a broadly framed clause might be directed to all or most of the jurisdictional requirements that would otherwise be applicable. An 'all-encompassing' no-invalidity clause might be drafted in something like the following terms: 'breach of any statutory provision in the Act or any administrative law requirement does not result in the invalidity of a decision'. It is helpful to consider the question of how courts have and should interpret such provisions by reference to two case examples, one involving a narrow no-invalidity clause and the second involving a clause having much broader application.

Administrative law principles indicate that narrowly framed no-invalidity clauses should, at least generally, be given effect according to their terms. In *Project Blue Sky Inc v Australian Broadcasting Authority* (4.3), the High Court held that whether or not a breach of statute amounts to a jurisdictional error, and therefore results in retrospective invalidity, is to be determined by ordinary methods of statutory interpretation: was it 'a purpose of the legislation that an act done in breach of the provision should be invalid'?[57] Thus, in *Re Minister for Immigration and Multicultural and Indigenous Affairs; Ex parte Palme* the High Court gave effect to a 'no-invalidity clause' which expressly stated that non—compliance with a statutory requirement to give reasons did not invalidate the decision.[58] Although the outcome in *Palme* is defensible, the problem raised above with conceptualising the minimum

---

56   This section draws on L McDonald 'The Entrenched Minimum Provision of Judicial Review and the Rule of Law' (2010) 21 *Public Law Review* 14.

57   *Project Blue Sky Inc v Australian Broadcasting Authority* (1998) 194 CLR 355 at 392–3.

58   *Re Minister for Immigration and Multicultural and Indigenous Affairs; Ex parte Palme* (2003) 216 CLR 212. The court also emphasised the idea that the breach of a requirement to do something after a decision had been made could invalidate the decision was counter-intuitive (though possible in theory).

entrenched provision of judicial review by reference to 'jurisdictional error' can now be framed with more precision: what is to stop parliament expressly indicating that breaches of a particular provision (or, indeed, of all provisions) are not to have the remedial result of invalidity (that is, that statutory requirements are not mandatory requirements on which jurisdiction depends)? In the case of a narrow no-invalidity clause (relating to a particular or a restricted number of statutory provisions), *Palme* and the logic of *Project Blue Sky* indicate that the breach of such provisions would not amount to jurisdictional error, and therefore that there would be no inconsistency between such a clause and the continuing availability of the writs named in s 75(v) (which are available only where jurisdictional error can be demonstrated).[59] However, this approach seems less attractive in relation to no-invalidity clauses which have broader application. Certainly, if the logic is applied to an 'all-encompassing' no-invalidity clause, it would have the practical effect of evading the High Court's s 75(v) jurisdiction. Why? Because breaches of the statute or of administrative law norms (norms accepted by the common law or as routinely implied statutory requirements) would not amount to jurisdictional errors. Could the constitutional purposes of judicial review emphasised in *Plaintiff S157* and *Kirk* be so easily outflanked by the parliament?[60]

The question of how a broadly framed federal no-invalidity clause should be interpreted arose in *Futuris*.[61] Futuris Corp Ltd objected to a tax assessment which purported to apply difficult anti-avoidance provisions concerning capital gains tax. Although it originally sought to appeal the assessment to the Federal Court through the process provided for under Pt IVC of the *Taxation Administration Act 1953* (Cth), that appeal was left in abeyance while Futuris's later application for judicial review under s 39B(1) of the *Judiciary Act 1903* (Cth) was determined. To succeed in its judicial review claim, Futuris thus needed to show that the errors it alleged occurred were jurisdictional in nature. Here, however, the legislation presented it with a serious problem. Section 175 of the *Income Tax Assessment Act 1936* (Cth) (*Tax Act*) provides that: 'The validity of any assessment shall not be affected by reason that any of the provisions of this Act have not been complied with.' Perhaps this is not an *all*-encompassing no-invalidity clause (insofar as it makes no mention of 'common law' administrative law principles or requirements which are readily implied from the statute), but its terms are nonetheless very broad. Taken literally, it indicates that any statutory provision which may (in its absence) be thought to be a mandatory requirement is to be treated as directory; put differently, non-compliance with such provisions would not affect the decision-maker's jurisdiction to make a legally valid decision. As the constitutional writs are available only for jurisdictional error, the clause appears to render review on the basis of an error in applying the provisions of the *Tax Act* a theoretical possibility with little practical bite.

The unavailability of judicial review of taxation assessments on the basis of a failure to correctly apply the legislation may appear to be an alarming result. This result is, however, ameliorated by the fact the tax legislation provides for merits review by the Administrative Appeals Tribunal, and also for appeals to the Federal Court. The *Tax Act* states (in s 175A) that: 'a taxpayer who is dissatisfied with an assessment made in relation to the taxpayer may object against it in the manner set out in Part IVC of the *Taxation Administration Act*.'[62]

---

59   On the constitutional injunction, see 4.5.3.

60   Cf *Bank of New South Wales v Commonwealth* (1948) 76 CLR 1 at 367.

61   *Commissioner of Taxation v Futuris Corp Ltd* (2008) 237 CLR 146.

62   As the joint judgment (ibid, 153) points out, Pt IVC 'meets the requirement of the Constitution that a tax may not be made incontestable because to do so would place beyond examination the limits upon legislative power', citing *MacCormick v Federal Commissioner of Taxation* (1984) 158 CLR 622 at 639–40.

How, then, did the court interpret the s 175 no-invalidity clause in the *Tax Act*? The joint judgment stated that:

> The significance of s 175 for the operation of the Act and for the scope of judicial review outside Pt IVC is to be assessed in the manner indicated in *Project Blue Sky* ... Section 175 must be read with ss 175A and 177(1). If that be done, the result is that the validity of an assessment is not affected by failure to comply with any provision of the Act, but a dissatisfied taxpayer may object to the assessment in the manner set out in Pt IVC of the *Administration Act* ... Where s 175 applies, errors in the process of assessment do not go to jurisdiction and so do not attract the remedy of a constitutional writ under s 75(v) of the *Constitution* or under s 39B of the *Judiciary Act*.[63]

A number of comments can be made about this passage. First, it is clear that the court was prepared to give effect to s 175 according to its terms—despite the potential for broadly worded no-invalidity clauses to significantly limit the extent of review under the constitutional scheme of judicial review and the High Court's clear doubts in *Plaintiff S157* about any such legislative attempts at evasion. The plurality in *Futuris* held that 'no-invalidity clause' would not apply to (that is, reach) an error where the commissioner had knowingly misapplied the Act (because in those cases there would be no 'assessment'). Nevertheless, due to the s 175 no-invalidity clause, errors made in applying the terms of the *Tax Act* were held to occur 'within, not beyond, the exercise of the powers of assessment given by the Act to the Commissioner'. The result was that such errors could be challenged only in Pt IVC proceedings.[64] Second, the court states that this conclusion is the result of applying the *Project Blue Sky* method of considering the 'purposes of the legislation' when determining whether the consequence of a particular error is the invalidity of the decision made. Clearly, importance is placed on s 175A and the statutory appeal process, but the import of these provisions is not fully explained. Last, it is noteworthy that no mention is made of the role of s 75(v) of the Constitution in preserving the entrenched minimum provision of review or ideal of the rule of law, despite the reality that s 175 drastically limits the capacity for meaningful judicial review of taxation assessments under s 75(v).

The *Futuris* case raises the question of whether broad no-invalidity will always be read according to their terms, thereby being a much more effective technique to limit review than traditional privative clauses. If they were then it would be hard to reconcile this result with the emphasis given in *Plaintiff S157* and *Kirk* to the rule of law purposes served by the entrenched minimum provision of judicial review.[65] Certainly if all-encompassing no-invalidity clauses are read literally, then the strictures protecting review set up by *Plaintiff S157* and *Kirk* could be evaded.

There are two reasons why care should be taken before extrapolating too far from the result and analysis in *Futuris*. First, *Futuris* can be read as placing weight on the existence of appeal rights to the AAT and the Federal Court for decisions made under the tax legislation (though the point is submerged in the court's reasoning). The existence of appeal rights may mean that 'the rationale underlying the constitutional requirement for maintenance of the supervisory jurisdiction' of the courts is not 'self-evidently engaged'.[66] Put differently, there is an argument that the preservation of the entrenched

---

63   *Commissioner of Taxation v Futuris Corp Ltd* (2008) 237 CLR 146 (2008) 237 CLR 146, 156–7.

64   Ibid, 161–2.

65   Kirby J's dissent in *Futuris* reflected a view that no-invalidity clauses can be at least as threatening to the entrenched provision of judicial review as traditional privative clauses: see McDonald, n 56 above, 23–24.

66   *Simpson Design Associates Pty Ltd v Industrial Court of New South Wales* [2011] NSWCA 316, [17]. See also Basten, n 14 above, 294–5.

minimum provision of judicial review was, in effect, considered in a broader institutional context of legal accountability. On this basis, it might be thought that it was appropriate to read the no-invalidity clause in *Futuris* as limiting the role played by judicial review in the protection of the rule of law because the legislature had provided (more than) adequate alternative processes of legal accountability through which the commitment to the rule of law could be served.[67] Second, the broader a no-invalidity clause, the more likely it is that it will run into the potential constitutional problems which were discussed in *Plaintiff S157*. As we have noted, the High Court has clearly indicated that a clause which attempts to confer entirely open-ended discretionary powers will run into the potential constitutional problems which it identified.

For this reason we agree that it would be surprising if the High Court did not hold invalid a no-invalidity clause which 'purported to characterise any breach whatsoever by a decision-maker as non-jurisdictional'.[68] The difficulty is that the criteria for determining when a no-invalidity clause goes too far have not been articulated. In our view, there are reasons to suspect that the boundaries of the minimum provision of judicial review will remain imprecise. The reason is that, analogously to the doctrinal history of privative clauses, the primary approach of the courts may be to focus on techniques of statutory interpretation to protect values associated with the rule of law.

Thus, if legislation containing a broad no-invalidity clause does not also include adequate alternative accountability mechanisms overseen by appropriate judicial institutions, it may be that such a no-invalidity clause would receive a more restrictive interpretation than was adopted in *Futuris*. For example, it is at least possible to argue that a no-invalidity clause gives rise to an 'internal contradiction' within the statute which a court would be entitled to resolve. A no-invalidity clause (unlike a traditional privative clause) has the same subject matter as the statutory provisions the effect of which it purports to specify—namely, the powers of the administrative decision-maker. That is, unlike the supposed contradiction which underpinned the *Hickman* principle—between a privative clause (relating to the jurisdiction of the courts) and statutory limitations on a decision-maker's power—a no-invalidity clause and the provisions limiting the administrative decision-maker's powers relate to the same issue. On this basis, it might be concluded that at least some limitations on power should not give way to the general intention indicated by a no-invalidity clause which applies to most or all of the statute.[69] Whether or not there is thought to be a 'logical' contradiction here, it can be argued that a conclusion that there is such a contradiction is no more surprising than the similar conclusion which has been drawn in the context of the interpretation of privative clauses. It is also possible that no-invalidity clauses could only be read as reaching or applying to valid decisions—an argument which in essence mirrors the key part of the reasoning in *Plaintiff S157* establishing that the privative clause did not purport to apply to jurisdictionally flawed decisions. Finally, it might be argued that the so-called 'principle of legality' (5.4.6) could be invoked to provide normative justification for attempts by the courts to read no-invalidity and like clauses in a way which preserves a meaningful role for judicial review.

Two comments can be noted in conclusion. First, interpretive responses to no-invalidity clauses will not lead to general rules concerning the interpretation of no-invalidity clauses; each clause will be interpreted in its particular statutory context. Nevertheless, an interpretive approach does give courts

---

67 An argument along these lines is considered in detail in McDonald. See also J Spigelman, 'The Centrality of Jurisdictional Error' (2010) 21 *Public Law Review* 77, 91; Sackville, n 13 above, 135–6.

68 Sackville, n 13 above, 136.

69 The point is considered in more detail in McDonald, n 56 above, 30–31. Cf *Seiffert* [2011] WASCA 148, [102]–[104].

the capacity to attempt to creatively calibrate the appropriate level of judicial review in the context of particular legislative contexts in a way which pays regard to values which have often been associated with the rule of law idea. Second, it must be acknowledged that it is always open to parliament to attempt to clarify an unsuccessful attempt it has made to provide that particular administrative law norms of statutory requirements do not result in the invalidity of administrative decisions. And these attempts may reach a point where they cannot plausibly be resisted by the rigorous application of the techniques of statutory interpretation. The point may therefore be reached where the High Court will be forced to articulate more precisely some of the boundaries which constitute the entrenched minimum provision of judicial review.[70]

7.2.4.2 No-consideration clauses

A no-consideration clause provides something like the following: 'a decision-maker "does not have a duty to consider whether to exercise" a particular power, whether the decision-maker is requested to do so "or in any other circumstances".[71] Very often statutory powers are read as including a legally enforceable obligation to consider whether the power should be exercised. A no-consideration clause explicitly denies the operation of this assumption. There may be circumstances where such a clause appears perfectly justifiable—where for instance the power is exercisable by a minister on the basis of policy considerations. However, where such a clause is applied in relation to the exercise of powers which directly (and routinely) affect individuals, if read literally they may deny review in circumstances where review is thought appropriate.

Although the terms of a no-consideration clause do not purport to oust judicial review, if it is accepted that there is no obligation (or 'public duty') even to consider the exercise of a power, then mandamus will not be available (4.5.1.3). And if mandamus will not be available, then issuing certiorari to quash any decision which has been made in an exercise of the power may have no utility (4.6). Thus, although a no-consideration clause does not purport to oust judicial review or the availability of particular remedies, it may have a similar effect.

In *Plaintiff M61* the High Court considered no-consideration clauses in the *Migration Act* which related to the minister's powers to (1) allow an 'offshore entry person' to make a valid application for a visa; and (2) grant a visa to such a person. According to the High Court, these no-consideration clauses involved the minister in two distinct stages of decision-making: there is, first, a decision to *consider* exercising the power in question and, second, the decision whether to exercise the power.[72] On the facts in *Plaintiff M61*, the court concluded that the minister had decided to consider exercising his powers in all cases where an offshore entry person had claimed to be a refugee. Having made a decision to consider the exercise of the relevant powers, the legality of the decision whether or not to exercise those powers was then capable of being reviewed, despite the fact that the minister was not under any statutory obligation to commence any consideration about whether to exercise the powers. The court went on to hold that the process of considering whether to exercise the powers was indeed compromised by

---

70   See generally Bateman, n 2 above, where it is argued that the constitutional objections to broad discretionary powers (including no-invalidity clauses) raised in *Plaintiff S157* are problematic. Bateman proposes that the entrenched minimum provision of review be elaborated by reference to a 'non-arbitrariness principle', though it is acknowledged that this principle would only 'invalidate the most extreme statutory powers': ibid, 506.

71   C Tran, 'The "Fatal Conundrum" of 'No-Consideration' Clauses After *Plaintiff M61*' (2011) 39 *Federal Law Review* 303, 304.

72   *Plaintiff M61/2010E v Commonwealth* (2010) 243 CLR 319, 350.

a denial of procedural fairness and an error of law. However, although the court did examine the legality of the decision-making process as it unfolded after the minister had decided to consider the exercise of his powers, if it is clear that a decision-maker has refused to even consider whether to exercise a power, it is possible that a no-consideration clause may well be more effective in precluding the grant of any meaningful remedy.[73]

Although, in *Plaintiff M61*, the High Court held that it could examine the legality of the minister's refusal to exercise his powers given that a decision had been taken to consider whether those powers should be exercised, the court nevertheless accepted that '[b]ecause the Minister is not bound to consider exercising either of the relevant powers, mandamus will not issue to compel consideration, and certiorari would have no practical utility'.[74] In the absence of the availability of these remedies, it can fairly be asked: what is the point of any review of the legality of the decision made to refuse to exercise the powers? The court's answer to this question was to hold that the no-consideration clauses did not prevent the making of a declaration. A declaration was appropriate in the circumstances given that it would be directed to a legal controversy (as opposed to a hypothetical question); each plaintiff had a 'real interest' in the questions being determined; the matters determined bore upon 'informing the Minister' of matters of direct relevance to compliance with Australia's international obligations; and 'there is a considerable public interest in the observance of the requirements of procedural fairness in the exercise of the relevant powers'.[75] Although a role for judicial review was preserved in *Plaintiff M61*, insofar as declarations were available despite the no-consideration clauses, the efficacy of declarations may be questionable in some contexts. The government responded to *Plaintiff M61* by accepting that there would be a continuing role for the courts in reviewing the legality of decisions in relation to offshore entry persons. It has been suggested that, even if declaratory relief is available in other legislative contexts which include no-consideration clauses, this relief may 'be symbolic at best'.[76]

It can also be asked whether the availability of declaratory relief is sufficient to preserve the entrenched minimum provision of judicial review. An argument that *Migration Act's* no-consideration clauses were inconsistent with s 75(v)—being an attempt to grant power without any enforceable limit—was dismissed in *Plaintiff M61*. This argument was rejected on the basis that the capacity to enforce limits on power 'does not entail that consideration of the exercise of a power must always be amenable to enforcement, whether by mandamus or otherwise'.[77] The court concluded that the no-consideration clause did 'not prevent any exercise of jurisdiction under s 75(v)' because, if the minister chooses to embark on a consideration of the case, 's 75(v) can be engaged to enforce' the limits on these powers. For this reason, the no-consideration clause was not inconsistent with place of judicial review in the constitutional structure.

It has been observed, however, that '[r]eliance on declaratory relief to support a conclusion that s 75(v) remains intact' requires 'further elaboration as to how declaratory relief can do so, given that it is not expressly a constitutional remedy'.[78] The extent to which there may be limits on the capacity of

---

73   Tran, n 71 above, 314 rightly notes that if 'even a modicum of consideration' by a decision-maker establishes that they have commenced the process of considering whether to exercise a power, then the conclusion in *Plaintiff M61*—that the legality of the consideration of whether to exercise the power could be examined—would be applicable in most cases.

74   *Plaintiff M61/2010E v Commonwealth* (2010) 243 CLR 319, 335.

75   Ibid, 359–60.

76   Tran, above n 71, 326.

77   *Plaintiff M61/2010E v Commonwealth* (2010) 243 CLR 319–47.

78   Tran, above n 71, 322.

the Australian parliaments to enact no-consideration clauses is thus unclear. The High Court recently considered an argument that the entrenched provision of judicial review at state level applies only in relation to jurisidictional errors that can be classified as an 'excess or want of jurisdiction' but not to jurisdictional error arising from a failure or refusal to exercise jurisdiction.[79] The argument was invoked in support of a state legislature's power to allow judicial review for errors of the first but not second variety. It might be thought that ousting review for a refusal or failure or refusal to exercise a power is little different from enacting a no-consideration clause that provides there is no duty to consider whether a power or jurisdiction should be exercised. Nevertheless, the court gave some persuasive reasons for its emphatic rejection of the argument.[80] For one thing, the reasoning in *Kirk* does not emphasise a distinction between excess of jurisdiction and failure to exercise jurisdiction; the fundamental distinction identified as the foundation of the Supreme Courts' entrenched review jurisdiction is that between jurisdictional error and non-jurisdictional error. It was also noted that failure to exercise jurisdiction has long been accepted as a jurisdictional error and the basis for mandamus. Further, the introduction of distinction between different variteies of jurisdictional error would have the result that mandamus for wrongful refusal of jurisdiction is outside the constitutionally protected boundaries of judicial review at the state level but not at Commonwealth level where mandamus is expressly referred to in s 75(v).[81]

To the extent that decisions not to consider exercising powers subject to a no-consideration clause may be made arbitrarily, such clauses may operate to limit the effectiveness of the constitutionally protected judicial review jurisdiction.

7.2.4.3 Time-limit clauses

A common way to attempt to limit the availability of judicial review is through statutory provisions limiting the time in which a judicial review application may be brought. There is, of course, nothing intrinsically objectionable about time limits for bringing legal action: it is reasonable to expect that at some point there will be an end of litigation. The only real issues concern the date on which the 'limitation period' begins, and the length of the period in which an application may be made. The former issue arose in *Bodruddaza v Minister for Immigration and Multicultural Affairs*,[82] which involved a challenge to the constitutional validity of a time-limit provision in the *Migration Act*. The challenged section provided that the limitation period would begin to run on the 'date of actual (as opposed to deemed) date of notification of the decision' to the applicant. The High Court unanimously held the provision inconsistent with s 75(v) of the Constitution because, the justices said, 'it subverts the constitutional purpose of the remedy provided by s 75(v)'.[83] It had this effect because it did not allow the court to take account of various circumstances in which the date of actual accrual rule might cause unfairness to an applicant.[84] The issue of the length of the period did not arise, and indeed, in this respect,

---

79   *Public Service Association of South Australia Inc v Industrial Relations Commission of South Australia* [2012] HCA 25.

80   *Public Service Association of South Australia Inc v Industrial Relations Commission of South Australia* [2012] HCA 25. The majority of the court was able to read the privative clause in a way which it did not distinguish between the two categories of jurisdictional error and, as such, were able to uphold its validity. Heydon J would have invalidated the clause as he concluded its terms did prohibit review for jurisdictional errors which were based on a failure to exercise jurisdiction.

81   As explained in 4.5.1.3 mandamus is available for a failure to exercise a jurisdiction.

82   *Bodruddaza v Minister for Immigration and Multicultural Affairs* (2007) 228 CLR 651.

83   Ibid, 672.

84   Ibid.

the challenged provision was by no means ungenerous to applicants. The court did warn, however, that 'a rule precluding what is considered by the legislature to be an untimely application' is a path that is 'bound to encounter constitutional difficulties'.[85] In *Plaintiff S157* Callinan J had taken the view that the validity of a time-limit provision depended, in part, on the length of the specified period and on whether the court was given a discretion to extend it.[86]

After *Kirk*, the validity of state time-limit clauses will be considered according to the constitutional purposes underpinning the entrenched review jurisdiction of state Supreme Courts.[87]

7.3 Privative clauses and politics

By now it will be clear that privative clauses and other attempts to limit the efficacy of judicial review have the potential to bring parliaments and the courts into political conflict. Australian parliaments may, through a number of legislative techniques, attempt to keep the courts out of a particular decision-making domain. But Australian courts have ample resources with which they can respond, including their power to interpret legislation authoritatively and the existence of a constitutionally entrenched minimum provision of review which may be invoked to repel both Commonwealth and state legislation.

For this reason, the case law on privative clauses is, in our view, best understood as a site of power struggles between courts and legislatures. Consider, for example, the now familiar example of the *Migration Act* privative clause at issue in *Plaintiff S157*. The Federal Court had been publicly and strongly criticised by the government on the basis that some of the court's decisions undermined the implementation of legitimate government policy choices.[88] The privative clause was enacted in 2001 after the failure of successive legislative attempts to limit judicial review of migration decisions, in the context of an ever-rising number of applications,[89] and in the political wake of the arrival the *MV Tampa*, a ship carrying a large number of asylum-seekers who, in controversial circumstances, had not been allowed to set foot on Australian soil.

In this context, the High Court's decision in *Plaintiff S157* can be understood not only as an exercise in legal interpretation but also as a political compromise. On the one hand, the court upheld the constitutional validity of the clause. Striking the clause down as invalid may have elicited further attacks against the judiciary which may ultimately have adversely affected the High Court's political legitimacy. On the other hand, the clause was restrictively interpreted, enabling the court to maintain its declared commitment to the rule of law. Further, the court's reasons left some (ultimately misplaced) hope that the privative clause may have a minor role to play in limiting judicial review. An interpretation of the *Plaintiff S157* judgment as having political concerns is also consistent with the fact that the High Court took the opportunity to fire warning shots over the government's bow, in relation to any future

---

85   Ibid.

86   The other justices expressed no opinion on these matters in *S157*, and they were not considered in *Bodruddazza: see Plaintiff S157/2002 v Commonwealth* (2003) 211 CLR 476, 537–8.

87   Sackville, n 13 above, 136. In *Woolworths v Pallas Newco Pty Ltd* (2004) 61 NSWLR 707 it was held that a time-limit clause requiring judicial review applications to be lodged within three months was intended to insulate decisions based on jurisdictional errors. A former Chief Justice of the Court of Appeal of the Supreme Court of NSW has expressed the view that provision considered in that case is likely to be constitutionally permissible: Spigelman, n 67 above, 90.

88   See J McMillan, 'Judicial Restraint and Activism in Administrative Law' (2002) 30 *Federal Law Review* 335, 338.

89   For a concise and clear overview of the history, see J McMillan, 'Controlling Immigration Litigation—A Legislative Challenge' (2002) 10 *People and Place* 16.

attempt to find alternative legislative means to dramatically diminish its constitutionally entrenched review function. As explained above, the court raised a number of constitutional objections to legislative attempts to confer open-ended discretions on Commonwealth administrators.

These brief comments do not purport to be a comprehensive analysis of the background political context of the decision in *Plaintiff S157*, but they are sufficient to show that there is more to the privative clause cases than meets the doctrinally focused eye.

7.4 Privative clauses and institutional design

In Australian law, thinking about privative clauses tends to be framed by 'rule of law' ideas. Within this framework privative clauses are almost inevitably characterised as problematic. This framework has been clearest in the context of s 75(v) of the Constitution—which the High Court sees as reinforcing the constitutional significance of the rule of law by entrenching a minimum level of judicial review of Commonwealth decisions—but now is also apparent in the context of the supervisory jurisdiction of state Supreme Courts. More generally, the rule of law framework places courts at the centre of the project of enforcing limits on administrative power.

Within the rule of law framework, privative clauses are easily characterised as attempts to prevent individuals from having their legal claims against the government heard by courts and as obstructing access to law's protective function as a shield against the abuse of power. As Wade stridently put the point: to 'exempt a public authority from the jurisdiction of the courts of law is, to that extent, to grant dictatorial power … in violation of the rule of law'.[90] To the extent that the rule of law is also thought to include fundamental common law principles,[91] the tension between privative clauses and the rule of law may be exacerbated as citizens are denied access to the very institution (that is, courts and judges) by which those values are developed and are (presumably) best understood.[92] The clear assumption underpinning much rule of law discourse (at least understood by judges and lawyers) is that access to the courts is crucial to the maintenance of the rule of law. Indeed, it is only on the basis of this assumption that Australian courts have been able to conclude that privative clauses are inconsistent with the conferral of limited powers (7.2.1). This conclusion, as we observed earlier, is *only* justified if it is also assumed that the essence of a legal limit is that it can be enforced by judges. In sum, if we think about privative clauses purely in terms of their effect on judicial review, and if judicial review is considered to be the means for maintaining the rule of law, privative clauses will almost inevitably be viewed with hostility. On this approach, to be in favour of a privative clause implies indifference to the rule of law.

In reality, however, judicial review is one of various ways of keeping government officials within the boundaries of their legal powers. Not only are there political forms of accountability (see 12.1.3.2), but modern administrative law has developed a number of other modes of legal accountability, such as merits review, ombudsmen and so on. We discuss this broader administrative law framework in chapters 8–11.

---

90   H R W Wade, *Constitutional Fundamentals* (Hamlyn Lectures, 32nd series, 1980), 66.

91   This is a controversial interpretation of the rule of law in legal theory: see B Tamanaha, *On the Rule of Law: History, Politics, Theory* (Cambridge: Cambridge University Press, 2004), Chs 7 and 8.

92   See the discussion of 'common law constitutionalism' in 12.1.3.1.

If our frame of reference for thinking about privative clauses is expanded to include such modes of accountability, a very different light is cast on them. It may be possible to characterise a privative clause as part of an overall strategy to secure effective and appropriate accountability in a particular area of decision-making. Of course, such a characterisation is not possible in the absence of other applicable accountability mechanisms. But on this approach, it no longer appears contradictory to delegate limited powers while at the same time exempting the exercise of those powers from one particular mode of enforcing those limits (that is, judicial review). If privative clauses are part of the design of an overall accountability system, the appropriateness of excluding judicial review is not pre-emptively decided by a commitment to the rule of law, but will rather depend on the existence, adequacy and costs of alternative forms of accountability considered in the context of the nature and subject matter of the powers being exercised. Considered in an institutional-design framework, a privative clause may be part of an overall accountability system designed to promote good decision-making without compromising the ideal of legality.

It should be stressed that thinking about privative clauses in terms of principles of institutional design does not mean that such clauses should always be given support or that judges should always apply them according to their terms. Rather, it encourages us to think about judicial review as one accountability mechanism among others. It also encourages us to think more deeply about what meaning we should give to the ideal of the rule of law. Such lines of inquiry open up the possibility that the costs of judicial review may sometimes outweigh its benefits. On the other hand, it may be considered that judicial review can do some things that other accountability mechanisms cannot do, or that it can do them better. If that is accepted, there may be circumstances where it will be right to conclude that its exclusion, even considered from the perspective of overall institutional design, does compromise a commitment to keeping administrative decision-makers legally accountable. On this approach the analysis of the relationship between privative clauses and the rule of law is much more complicated.

The basic point to be made is merely that the threat posed by privative clauses to the rule of law cannot be assessed in isolation from the broader administrative law context or without reference to more particular legislative attempts to ensure accountability in relation to particular areas of decision-making. Indeed, this is a lesson which can be generalised: any overall assessment of judicial review needs to be undertaken within the broader context of administrative law. We cannot, for example, properly evaluate the appropriateness of judicial review standards (that is, the grounds of review) or the adequacy of judicial review remedies in isolation from the role played by the other public and private law accountability mechanisms which may be used to keep government decisions accountable. This lesson should be kept in mind as we now turn to consider this wider context of administrative law.

8

Tribunals and Merits Review

8.1 Introduction

The distinction between judicial review and merits review was introduced into Australian law by the Commonwealth Administrative Review ('Kerr') Committee. Its 1971 report formed the basis of a new Commonwealth administrative law system, the main components of which were the *ADJR Act*, the Ombudsman, freedom of information (FOI), the Administrative Appeals Tribunal (AAT) and the Administrative Review Council (ARC).[1] The committee's recommendation for the establishment of a general 'administrative review tribunal' rested on several propositions:

- First, the committee said, 'it has been universally accepted that judicial review by courts … must be supplemented by provision for review … on the merits of administrative decisions affecting the rights and property of the citizen'.[2]

- Second, the committee argued that, as a matter of constitutional law, federal courts could not be invested with jurisdiction to review the 'merits' of decisions that raised 'non-justiciable' issues because such jurisdiction involved the exercise of non-judicial power.[3] In 1956, in the famous *Boilermakers'* case,[4] the High Court held not only that federal judicial power could not be conferred on non-judicial bodies,[5] but also non-judicial power could not be conferred on federal courts.

- Third, the committee expressed the opinion that 'the vast majority of administrative decisions involve the exercise of a discretion by reference to criteria that do not give rise to a justiciable issue'.[6]

---

1 The ARC was established under Part V of the *AAT Act*. Its job is to oversee and advise the government about the operation of the system as a whole. For more extensive discussion of the subject matter of this chapter see P Cane, *Administrative Tribunals and Adjudication* (Oxford: Hart Publshing, 2009).

2 Commonwealth Administrative Review Committee, *Commonwealth Administrative Review Committee Report*, Parliament of the Commonwealth of Australia Paper No 144 (1971) ('Kerr Committee Report'), para 5.

3 In federal constitutional law, there are three types of power: judicial, non-judicial and innominate. Innominate powers may be conferred on either judicial or non-judicial bodies. The power to make findings of fact is an example of an innominate power.

4 *R v Kirby; Ex parte Boilermakers' Society of Australia* (1956) 94 CLR 254.

5 In fact, this proposition was first stated by Griffith CJ in 1909 in *Huddart Parker Pty Ltd v Moorehead* (1909) 8 CLR 330, 335.

6 Kerr Committee Report, n 2 above, para 68.

LIVERPOOL JOHN MOORES UNIVERSITY
LEARNING SERVICES

It followed that the proposed general 'merits review' body could not be set up as a 'court' under Chapter III of the Constitution. Nevertheless, the committee recommended that the chair of the tribunal should be a federal judge, and it noted the view of the English Franks Committee on Administrative Tribunals and Inquiries (which reported in 1957) that 'tribunals should be regarded as machinery for adjudication rather than as part of the machinery of administration'. It seems that although the proposed review body had to be technically non-judicial, the committee envisaged that it would operate, in effect, as a court substitute.

This, indeed, is the way things turned out. Section 7 of the *AAT Act* provides that the President of the AAT must be a judge of the Federal Court,[7] and a substantial proportion of the members of the AAT are either judges or qualified lawyers. In early important decisions Sir Gerard Brennan, the first president, exercised and counselled caution in questioning ('non-justiciable') government policy;[8] throughout the life of the AAT, the issue of the 'independence' of its members has been much debated against a background assumption that, whatever the constitutional niceties, merits review tribunals should operate as an external check on the administration, free from the influence and control of those being checked.

Although it was the Kerr Committee that first made explicit the distinction between merits review and judicial review, by 1971 merits review tribunals had been in existence for almost 50 years. A series of cases in the 1920s was concerned with provisions in tax legislation that allowed taxpayers to challenge tax assessments first by lodging a formal objection with the Commissioner of Taxation and then by appealing to the High Court, a state Supreme Court (exercising federal jurisdiction) or the Taxation Board of Appeal. The High Court held that the provisions relating to the board of appeal were unconstitutional because they conferred judicial power on a body not established under Chapter III of the Constitution.[9] The legislation was amended, turning the board of appeal into the board of review, giving it 'all the powers and functions of the commissioner' and providing that its decisions 'shall ... be deemed to be assessments, determinations or decisions of the commissioner'. Both the High Court[10] and the Privy Council[11] subsequently held that the new provisions validly conferred non-judicial power on the board. The board had been transformed, in modern parlance, into a merits review tribunal. A limited survey by the Kerr Committee found various instances in which tribunals had statutory power to review administrative decisions on the merits;[12] but the committee concluded that 'in the vast majority of cases' Commonwealth legislation made no provision for review of administrative decisions on the merits.[13] Its aim was to remedy that situation.

Although the prime focus in this chapter will be on the AAT, much of what is said applies to federal merits review tribunals generally, and to tribunals in the states that perform similar functions. First we need to say something more about tribunals.

---

7   In *Drake v Minister for Immigration and Ethnic Affairs* (1978) 2 ALD 60 ('*Drake No 1*') it was held that the appointment of federal judges to membership of the AAT was not unconstitutional; and the significant role of judges in the AAT has, no doubt, influenced the way its powers have been understood and developed. However, it would be unconstitutional to require a judge, acting as a member of the AAT, to perform functions incompatible with the office of judge: *Hussain v Minister for Foreign Affairs* (2008) 103 ALD 66.

8   Similar caution is found in the Kerr Committee Report (n 2 above, paras 297, 299). The ('Bland') Committee on Administrative Discretions recommended that the proposed tribunal should have no power to question government policy: Final Report (Parliamentary Paper 316, 1973), para 172(g)(iii).

9   *British Imperial Oil Co Ltd v Federal Commissioner of Taxation* (1925) 35 CLR 422.

10   *Federal Commissioner of Taxation v Munro* (1926) 38 CLR 153.

11   *Shell v Federal Commissioner of Taxation* (1930) 44 CLR 530.

12   Kerr Committee Report, n 2 above, para 18.

13   Ibid, para 17.

8.2 Tribunals

8.2.1 What are tribunals?

The term 'tribunal' is used in many different senses. For present purposes, a tribunal is a body with two defining characteristics, one positive and one negative. Positively, a tribunal resolves disputes, primarily by adjudication.[14] Applications to federal tribunals involve disputes between citizen and government, whereas some state tribunals have jurisdiction over significant categories of disputes between citizen and citizen. Adjudication is traditionally understood to involve the finding of facts, the ascertainment of law, and the application of the law as ascertained to the facts as found.

Negatively, a tribunal is not a court. In the federal context, a precise meaning can be given to this statement. Federal courts are institutions established under Chapter III of the Constitution and staffed by judges ('justices') who hold office in accordance with the terms of s 72. Under this section, federal judges have 'security of tenure' in the sense that they must be appointed for a term expiring on their 70th birthday, they can be removed only by parliament for 'proved misbehaviour or incapacity', and their remuneration cannot be reduced during their term of office. Such constitutionally protected security of tenure represents a sort of gold-standard guarantee of 'judicial independence'.

In a federation, independence of the federal judiciary from the other branches of the federal government is considered particularly important in relation to the adjudication of disputes between the federal and state governments about their respective powers under the Constitution. It is also seen as providing an important protection for citizens, especially in relation to disputes with the federal government (notably those involving judicial review of legislative and administrative action), and prosecutions under federal criminal laws. We have already seen that s 75(v) has been interpreted as guaranteeing a minimum of judicial review (of decisions and actions of officers of the Commonwealth) which cannot be removed by parliament.[15] Similarly, it is sometimes said that Chapter III guarantees a minimum of 'due process', thus limiting the power of the legislature to modify the procedures followed by courts exercising federal judicial power.[16]

Whether a federal adjudicatory body is a tribunal or a court depends partly on what it is called ('tribunal' or 'court'), and on what its adjudicators are called ('judges' or 'members'). Also important is the nature of its functions. For instance, in the *Boilermakers'* case,[17] it was held that, despite its name, the Arbitration Court was not a court because its predominant functions were non-judicial. It followed that it could not exercise judicial functions. So far as security of tenure is concerned, it is only judges of federal courts who enjoy constitutionally protected security of tenure. The terms and conditions of appointment of members of tribunals are a matter for parliament,[18] whereas the power of parliament to specify the terms and conditions of appointment of judges is subject to the provisions of s 72. Similarly, the power of parliament to specify the procedures to be followed by courts is limited by any guarantee of due process contained in Chapter III of the Constitution; but parliament's power to specify procedures to be followed by tribunals is not so limited.

---

14   'Primarily' because alternatives to adjudication (under the general description of 'alternative dispute resolution' (ADR)) are increasingly available in tribunals.

15   *Plaintiff S157 v Commonwealth* (2003) 211 CLR 476; see further 7.2.2.

16   F Wheeler, 'Due Process, Judicial Power and Chapter III in the New High Court' (2004) 32 *Federal Law Review* 205.

17   *R v Kirby; Ex parte Boilermakers' Society of Australia* (1956) 94 CLR 254, especially 288–9.

18   But see text before n 23 below.

This precise account of the distinction between tribunals and courts, which is a feature of federal law, is a function of the strict version of separation of powers that the High Court has held to be embodied in Chapters I, II and (especially) III of the Commonwealth Constitution. In the states,[19] separation of powers is not constitutionally entrenched in this way, and is understood less strictly. As a result, the distinction between courts and tribunals is less clear-cut. The significance of this difference does not reside primarily in the issue of independence. Although the terms and conditions of service of state judges may not be as well protected as those of federal judges,[20] they are on the whole similar to those required by s 72. Conversely, the terms and conditions of service of members of state tribunals, like those of members of federal tribunals, are generally less 'secure' than those of judges. What the looser concept of separation of powers enables state legislatures to do (and what the Commonwealth parliament cannot do) is to confer *both* judicial and non-judicial power on *both* tribunals and courts. So, for example, we find tribunals (such as the Victorian Civil and Administrative Appeals Tribunal) and courts (such as the New South Wales Land and Environment Court) which exercise a mixture of what, in federal law, would be understood as judicial and non-judicial powers. This is not to say that the strict federal version of separation of powers has no impact on the freedom of state legislatures to create multi-functional adjudicatory bodies. Under s 71 of the Commonwealth Constitution the parliament may confer federal judicial power on state 'courts'.[21] Although this does not have the effect that state courts exercising federal jurisdiction must possess all the characteristics of federal courts, the High Court has held that it does impose a limit on the power of state legislatures to confer on courts functions 'incompatible' with the exercise of federal judicial power.[22] It would also limit the power of state legislatures to depart too far from the s 72 model of judicial independence.[23]

In federal law, there are certain 'non-judicial' adjudicatory functions that only tribunals (non-courts) can perform—notably merits review of administrative decisions;[24] and there are certain 'judicial' adjudicatory functions that tribunals cannot, and only courts can, perform.[25] In state law, it seems, both tribunals and courts can perform any and all adjudicatory functions, while in federal law there are certain ('innominate') adjudicatory functions that both courts and tribunals can perform. The concept of innominate adjudicatory functions was invented in the 1920s, primarily in order to facilitate the use of non-courts to supplement adjudicatory resources available at a time when federal judicial power was invested mainly in the High Court and state Supreme Courts and before the establishment of the Federal

---

19   The position in the territories is less clear: G Carney, *The Constitutional Systems of the Australian States and Territories* (Melbourne: Cambridge University Press, 2006), 380–92.

20   Concerning financial security in New South Wales, for instance, see A Twomey, *The Constitution of New South Wales* (Sydney: Federation Press, 2004), 722–4.

21   The New South Wales Administrative Decisions Tribunal is not a court for the purposes of the Commonwealth Constitution because, although it has many of the characteristics of a court, it is not composed predominantly of judges: *Trust Company of Australia Ltd v Skiwing Pty Ltd* (2006) 66 NSWLR 185; *Attorney-General (NSW) v 2UE Sydney Pty Ltd* (2006) 236 ALR 385. See generally G Hill, 'State Administrative Tribunals and the Constitutional Definition of "Court"' (2006) 13 *Australian Journal of Administrative Law* 103; G Kennett, 'Fault Lines in the Autochthonous Expedient: The Problem of State Tribunals' (2009) *Public Law Review* 152.

22   *Kable v Director of Public Prosecutions (NSW)* (1996) 189 CLR 51; *International Finance Trust Co Ltd v New South Wales Crime Commission* (2009) 240 CLR 319. See generally Carney, n 19 above, Ch 10.

23   *North Australian Aboriginal Legal Aid Service Inc v Bradley* (2004) 218 CLR 146; *Forge v Australian Securities and Investments Commission* (2006) 229 ALR 223.

24   The power to give an advisory opinion, conferred by *AAT Act*, s 59, is also a non-judicial power.

25   There are two noteworthy exceptions to the latter principle. First, military tribunals can decide issues of criminal liability; and, second, parliament has the power to 'convict' and punish for contempt of parliament.

Court and the Federal Magistrates Court. By contrast, the Kerr Committee considered tribunals to be necessary for the performance of non-judicial adjudicatory functions that courts constitutionally cannot perform. Part of the explanation of this change of emphasis is the decision of the High Court in the *Boilermakers'* case in 1956 to the effect that federal courts cannot be invested with non-judicial functions.

8.2.2 Tribunals and courts

In fact, outside the context of Australian federal administrative law, the idea that tribunals provide a pragmatically desirable supplement (as opposed to a legally necessary alternative) to courts was the predominant approach to the design of adjudicatory institutions throughout the twentieth century. There are various respects in which the typical tribunal differs from the typical court, and it is these differences that account for the fact that in many jurisdictions—since the beginning of the twentieth century, anyway—many more tribunals than new courts have been established. In the first place, reference can be made to the qualifications for membership of courts and tribunals respectively. While the typical qualification for becoming a judge of a court is expertise as a lawyer, the expertise of tribunal members may lie in the subject matter of the tribunal's jurisdiction—for instance, taxation as opposed to taxation *law*, immigration as opposed to immigration *law*. The basic idea is that a person who has knowledge and experience of immigrants and immigration (for instance) is likely, at least in the first instance, to do a better job of resolving immigration disputes consistently, coherently and in a way that makes good practical sense than a person who has been trained and has practised as a lawyer—perhaps even if their expertise and experience is in immigration law. It is often said that the advantages of expertise are greatest in relation to the finding of facts and the application of law to facts. Ascertaining the law is more likely to be thought of as a job for law specialists. This explains why provision is often made for appeals 'on points of law' from tribunals to a court; and why, in federal law, only Chapter III courts can resolve disputes about the law 'conclusively'. In this light, too, the fact that the president and the most senior members of the AAT are not only trained lawyers, but actually judges, is noteworthy and reflects its court-like status.

The validity of the expertise argument is perhaps open to doubt, but it is certainly useful for governments wishing to reduce the involvement of lawyers in the resolution of disputes, especially disputes between citizen and government. Law and lawyers tend to be associated with certain values—often loosely and compendiously described by the vague phrase 'rule of law'—which are often contrasted with governance goals, such as efficiency and effectiveness in the implementation of social and economic policy and programs. Related to the issue of the expertise of the members of an adjudicatory body is the nature of its jurisdiction. Classically, tribunals have tended to be identified as 'specialist' and courts as 'generalist'. The Migration Review Tribunal and Refugee Review Tribunal are good examples of specialist tribunals with jurisdiction over a quite narrowly defined range of disputes. By contrast, the High Court is an extreme example of a generalist court, with jurisdiction (of one sort or another) over the full range of disputes that can arise under federal and state law. The development of tribunals in England throughout the twentieth century was characterised by piecemeal creation of a very large number of such bodies, many with narrow jurisdiction and very small caseloads. In Australia, by contrast, the Kerr Committee favoured a generalist approach. As a result, the AAT has jurisdiction under more than 400 statutes covering a wide range of government activities. Several states have now established generalist tribunals with jurisdiction even wider, in terms of types of dispute, than the AAT.

Other characteristics that are frequently touted as 'advantages' of tribunals over courts are 'speed', 'low cost' and 'informality'. The problem with all of these superficially attractive qualities is that none is desirable in itself. Delay, it is true, may result in a denial of justice, but so may excessive haste in investigating and adjudicating a complex dispute, especially if much is at stake for one or both of the parties. In the case of a generalist tribunal with very diverse jurisdiction, informality may be more desirable in some types of case (social security, for example), than in others (high-value taxation and customs matters, for instance).

So far as cost is concerned, a distinction needs to be drawn between cost to the state and cost to the disputing parties—especially, in the case of disputes between citizen and government, cost to the citizen. If we assume that quicker and more 'informal' procedures cost less than slower and more 'formal' ones, we may conclude that tribunals would be relatively cheaper for governments to run than courts. On the whole, too, it costs relatively less to staff tribunals than courts, if only because judicial salaries are higher than the amounts paid to tribunal members. From the government's point of view, tribunals probably provide good value for money relative to traditional courts. From the point of view of applicants, the main costs of litigation are court fees and lawyers' expenses and charges. The financial risks of litigation in courts are increased by the normal rule that the loser must pay the winner's costs. Fees for applying to tribunals are generally lower than for claiming in courts and, as a rule, each party is responsible only for their own costs. It is normally assumed, too, that, because of the 'informality' of their procedures and the relatively minor nature of many of the types of dispute with which tribunals deal, applicants before tribunals will often not need (paid) representation, and will certainly not need to be represented by a lawyer. On the other hand, research has shown that applicants who are represented, but not necessarily by a lawyer, fare better as a group than unrepresented applicants.[26] Such findings are particularly troubling in circumstances where representation before tribunals is limited by statute or publicly funded legal aid is unavailable for applications to tribunals. Even so, litigation in court is widely considered to be very expensive, and tribunals are generally thought to provide a valuable lower-cost alternative forum for adjudication.

The concept of 'formality' in adjudication refers to various factors, including the design of hearing rooms, the way the adjudicators dress and interact with the parties, the extent to which the procedure followed is generally 'adversarial', what rules of evidence (if any) are followed, and so on. Courts vary in terms of informality. So do tribunals. It is widely assumed that the less formality the better. On the other hand, one English commentator has observed that informality of procedure may be positively disadvantageous to claimants because 'cases ... may not be properly ventilated, the law may not be accurately applied, and ultimately justice may not be done'.[27] From this perspective, procedure should be as formal as is reasonably necessary to maximise the chance that a sound decision will be reached and that the legitimate interests of the parties will be respected and their legitimate concerns met.

Whether tribunals actually provide quicker, less costly and more informal adjudication are matters that, in theory at least, could be tested empirically. However, little rigorous research has been done. There are significant differences between courts and tribunals, and we might wonder whether attempts

---

26   T Mullen, 'Representation at Tribunals' (1990) 53 *Modern Law Review* 230; Australian Law Reform Commission, *Review of the Federal Justice System*, DP 62 (1999), paras 12.218–12.224. The ALRC found that the median total legal costs for represented applicants in the Federal Court were $15 820, and in the AAT $2585: ALRC DP 62, para 4.56. We do not know what factors account for the difference.

27   H Genn, 'Tribunal Review of Administrative Decision-Making' in G Richardson and H Genn (eds), *Administrative Law and Government Action* (Oxford: Oxford University Press, 1994), 263.

to measure their relative advantages and disadvantages would end up comparing apples and oranges. This caveat is particularly relevant to the study of federal courts and tribunals, precisely because there are certain adjudicatory functions that only tribunals can perform, and others that only courts can perform. There is simply no point in asking whether a federal court or, by contrast, a federal tribunal would provide quicker, less costly and more informal merits review.

Set against the supposed advantages of tribunals over courts are worries about their independence.[28] Such concerns are particularly relevant to adjudication of disputes between citizen and government.[29] The concept of 'independence' is not clear-cut. For instance, although federal judges have security of tenure once appointed, the qualifications for appointment to the federal judiciary are (it seems) entirely a matter for parliament; and federal judges are effectively appointed by the executive branch of government following procedures that are far from transparent. By contrast, debates about the independence of tribunals have been concerned not only with security of tenure, but also with matters such as qualifications of appointees; procedures for appointment, reappointment and dismissal; mechanisms and formulae for funding tribunals; and relations between tribunals and the departments whose work they review.[30] Moreover, independence is not merely a function of institutional design but also a matter of cultural practices and expectations. There is no reason to think that the sorts of protections embodied in s 72 will, by themselves, guarantee independence or, conversely, that only such protections can foster high levels of independence.

Underlying debates about the independence of tribunals are two important distinctions: one between the making and the review of administrative decisions, and the other between internal and external review of administrative decision-making. It obviously makes no sense to say that officials in government departments who make administrative decisions in the first instance should be 'independent' of the executive: they *are* the executive. While we might expect a senior official in the department who conducts an 'internal' review of the decision to exercise 'independent' judgment, we would not expect that judgment to be unaffected by governmental policies or goals. But when it comes to 'external review', we certainly do expect that the reviewer will be 'independent' of the department and the government in somewhat the same way we expect courts to be independent. In the states, this expectation can be expressed by aligning tribunals with the judicial branch of government. At the federal level, however, the constitutionally driven distinction between courts and (non-judicial) tribunals prevents this alignment. So, for example, although the AAT is thought of as an external review body, it is also said (freely paraphrasing the AAT Act) to 'stand in the shoes of the decision-maker'. The AAT appears to be in the acutely uncomfortable position of being at one and the same time part, but not part, of the executive. Perhaps what we should say is that while federal tribunals are clearly not part of the judicial branch of government, neither are they straightforwardly part of the executive. Instead, we might think of tribunals and courts together as forming a federal system of (independent) adjudication made possible by the combination of parliament's power under s 71 to create courts, and its (incidental) power, under the heads of s 51, to create tribunals to deal with disputes about matters falling within its legislative competence.

---

28   This is not to say that there may not be worries about the independence of judicial officers. See, e.g., K Mack and S R Anleu, 'The Security of Tenure of Australian Magistrates' (2006) 30 *Melbourne University Law Review* 370.

29   Indeed, one of the ironies of the federal administrative law system is that merits review—which, by definition, involves a dispute between a citizen and the government—is a function that cannot be invested in the only sort of adjudicator whose independence is protected by the Commonwealth Constitution, namely a federal court.

30   Concerning the last of these, see, e.g., C Bostock, 'The Effect of Ministerial Directions on Tribunal Independence' (2011) 66 *AIAL Forum* 33.

8.3 The merits review 'system'

The AAT stands at the apex of the federal merits review system. In the areas of taxation and Commonwealth workers' compensation, the AAT provides first-tier review. In the social security area, the Social Security Appeals Tribunal (SSAT) and the Veterans' Review Board (VRB) provide a first tier of review on the merits, and the AAT a second tier. In the immigration area, the AAT plays only a small second-tier role, review on the merits being provided mainly by the Refugee Review Tribunal (RRT) and the Migration Review Tribunal (MRT). The specialised first-tier tribunals are aligned with the relevant government department and are, in this way, more closely integrated than the AAT with the executive branch of government. In the words of one commentator, the government has 'greater control of appointments, resources and procedures' in the case of the MRT and RRT than in the case of the AAT.[31] Nevertheless, review of decisions by such tribunals can be distinguished from what is called 'internal review' by administrative officers of the department (9.2.4).

The various federal merits review tribunals can be said to be part of a 'system' in several respects. First, they are arranged in tiers. For instance, the AAT has appellate jurisdiction in relation to decisions of the SSAT, which, in turn, has appellate jurisdiction in relation to internal reviews by departmental officials. Second, it may be possible to appeal to a court from a decision of a tribunal. For example, in relation to decisions of the AAT, there is a general right of appeal on a question of law to the Federal Court.[32] Third, decisions of federal merits review tribunals may be subject to judicial review under the *ADJR Act* or s 75(v) of the Constitution. As we have seen, constitutional judicial review has become particularly significant in relation to decisions of the MRT and RRT as a result of legislation limiting statutory judicial review (2.4.2.5, 3.4.1.1).

In recent years, tribunals with wide and varied merits review jurisdiction have been established in several states: notably the Victorian Civil and Administrative Tribunal (VCAT), the New South Wales Administrative Decisions Tribunal (ADT) and the Western Australian State Administrative Tribunal (SAT). Each of these tribunals has significant jurisdiction over citizen–citizen disputes, as well as over disputes between citizen and government. In other words, the state tribunals exercise a mix of 'original' jurisdiction (over contractual disputes between businesses and consumers, for instance), and '(merits) review' jurisdiction (in relation to decisions of state government officials and bodies); the federal tribunals with which we are concerned exercise only merits review jurisdiction. Because of the variety of their jurisdiction, these state tribunals have some sort of divisional structure, each division specialising in disputes of a particular type. Concerning appeals, the ADT, for instance, has an appeal panel that hears appeals from divisions of the ADT and also from decisions of some other tribunals; and decisions of the VCAT can be appealed to the Victorian Supreme Court on points of law. The state tribunals would also be subject to judicial review under state law.

Although it would be wrong to think of the federal and state tribunals as part of a single integrated tribunal system, it is important to understand the place of these state tribunals in the Australian legal system as a whole. An obvious connection between the state and federal legal systems is that the High Court of Australia has ultimate appellate jurisdiction in all matters of both state and federal law. Under s 73(ii) of the Constitution, the High Court has jurisdiction to hear appeals (*inter alia*) from state

---

31   D Pearce, *Administrative Appeals Tribunal*, 2nd edn (Australia: LexisNexis Butterworths, 2007), 263.

32   *AAT Act*, s 44.

Supreme Courts. To the extent that state Supreme Courts have appellate and supervisory (judicial review) jurisdiction over decisions of state tribunals, matters arising out of decisions of such tribunals may be the subject of appeals to the High Court. Under s 73(ii) the High Court also has jurisdiction to hear appeals from 'courts' exercising federal jurisdiction; and under s 39 of the federal *Judiciary Act* state 'courts' have wide jurisdiction to decide matters of federal law.[33] It is possible, in theory at least, that a state 'tribunal' might be a 'court' for the purposes of s 73(ii) and the *Judiciary Act*.[34] If it were, it would have power to decide matters of federal law that arose in cases falling within its jurisdiction even if this would involve an exercise of judicial power—something federal tribunals cannot do.

We can see, therefore, that, although an appreciation of the distinction between state and federal law is essential for a proper understanding of administrative law in general and the role of tribunals in particular, it is also necessary to give due weight to the pivotal role of the High Court at the apex of an integrated Australian system of law and legal institutions.

8.4 The Administrative Appeals Tribunal

The AAT commenced operation in 1976. The president must be a federal court judge. A deputy president must be a legal practitioner of at least five years' standing. Senior members and non-presidential members may, but need not, be lawyers. Instead, they may be appointed for their expertise in areas such as accountancy, the environment, engineering and social welfare. The term 'presidential member' refers to the president, a deputy president and a member who is a judge. The AAT has around 90 members, including some 18 judges.

The AAT exercises merits review jurisdiction under more than 400 Commonwealth statutes and in relation to thousands of types of decisions.[35] It operates in six divisions including, for instance the Taxation Appeals Division and the Veterans' Appeals Division. In 2010–11, 5437 applications for review were made to the AAT, 6177 were finalised, and there was a backlog of 3858 awaiting finalisation. Of the applications made in 2010–11, 1176 related to taxation, 1649 to social security, 1158 to workers' compensation and 479 to veterans' benefits. These four areas represent about 81% of the AAT's caseload. In 2010–11, in 72% of cases a decision was delivered within 12 months of receipt of the application for review.

The basic rule is that an application for review must be made within 28 days after notification of the decision,[36] but various statutes that confer jurisdiction on the AAT specify different periods. In 2010–11, the standard fee for making an application to the AAT was $777 (but this fee is waived in a significant proportion of cases, and in certain cases is not payable). In some types of case, the AAT has power to 'award costs' (that is, to order one party, typically the loser, to pay the other's costs); otherwise, each party bears their own costs.[37] In some areas of the AAT's jurisdiction, lawyers are prepared to take

---

33 This feature of the Australian legal system—namely, the use of state courts effectively as federal courts—goes by the curious name of the 'autochthonous expedient'.

34 See n 21 above. Section 77(iii) of the Constitution expressly empowers the parliament to invest non-federal courts with federal jurisdiction (i.e. judicial power).

35 See <www.aat.gov.au/LegislationAndJurisdiction/JurisdictionList.htm>.

36 *AAT Act*, s 29(2).

37 Pearce, n 31 above, 218–225.

cases on a no-win, no-fee basis. Indeed, a majority of applicants to the AAT are represented by lawyers.[38] In a few areas, legal aid may be available to an applicant.[39] The AAT conducts an 'outreach' program under which officers provide information to and answer questions from unrepresented applicants, usually by telephone. In some states, the AAT runs a legal advice scheme, in cooperation with the local legal aid commission, under which unrepresented applicants can make an appointment with a legal aid commission solicitor at an AAT registry.

So far as procedure is concerned, the AAT Act (s 33) provides that this is a matter for the tribunal; but also that the AAT is not bound by rules of evidence[40] and that 'the proceeding shall be conducted with as little formality and technicality, and with as much expedition as [statutory requirements] and a proper consideration of the matters before the tribunal permit'.[41] Section 39 requires the AAT to ensure that parties are given a reasonable opportunity to present their case, and to inspect, and make submissions in relation to, relevant documents. The AAT is also, of course, subject to the rules of procedural fairness, breach of which by the AAT could be challenged as an error of law.[42] For example, it has been said that 'the ability of review tribunals to assist unrepresented applicants is limited by the requirements of procedural fairness'.[43] More generally, to the extent that rules of fairness reflect an essentially judicial and adversarial model of decision-making, they may prevent the AAT diverging significantly from the sorts of procedures followed by ordinary courts. On the other hand, first-tier federal merits review tribunals (notably the MRT, RRT and SSAT) play a much more active ('inquisitorial') role than the AAT in investigating the case and gathering relevant material, and there is ongoing debate about the extent to which the AAT can and should adopt a more inquisitorial mode of procedure.[44] Another noteworthy difference between AAT procedure and that followed by first-tier tribunals is that the appropriate government body is always a party to, and participates in, proceedings in the AAT, whereas in the MRT and RRT the department is not a party to the proceedings, and in the SSAT the department is a party but may only make written submissions.[45] These differences emphasise the court-like characteristics of the AAT as compared with the other tribunals.

In practice, most applications are resolved without the delivery of a decision by the AAT following a hearing (79% in 2010–11). One explanation for this high rate of pre-hearing resolution may be the use of 'conferences'[46]—informal meetings conducted by a member or officer of the AAT, designed to define

---

38   ALRC DP 62, paras 12.11–12.15. But the proportion of represented applicants varies greatly from one area to another.

39   *Managing Justice: A Review of the Federal Civil Justice System* (ALRC 89, 2000), paras 5.132–46.

40   Such as rules about burden of proof: *McDonald v Director-General of Social Security* (1984) 6 ALD 6.

41   See also s 2A: the AAT must pursue an objective of providing a mechanism of review that is fair, just, economical, informal and quick.

42   *Kowalski v Military Rehabilitation and Compensation Commission* (2010) 114 ALD 8, [57]. However, the operation of the rules of procedural fairness is significantly modified by statute in relation to hearings in the Security Appeals Division of the AAT: G Downes, 'Procedural Fairness, Hearings and Decision-Making in the Security Context of the Administrative Appeals Tribunal', <www.aat.gov.au/Publications/SpeechesAndPapers/Downes/pdf/SecurityAppealsDivisionMarc%202010.pdf>.

43   ALRC 89, para 9109. See also D O'Connor, 'Is There Too Much Natural Justice?' (1994) 1 *Australian Institute of Administrative Law Forum* 82, 83–4.

44   Important issues concern who bears the cost of information-gathering (the AAT or the parties) (on which see *Minister for Immigration and Citizenship v SZIAI* (2009) 259 ALR 429), who can control the flow of information (the AAT or the parties) and whether the AAT is properly resourced for active information-gathering. For helpful discussion see G Osborne, 'Inquisitorial Procedure in the Administrative Appeals Tribunal—A Comparative Perspective' (1982–83) 13 *Federal Law Review* 150.

45   Some people argue that lack of agency participation in review proceedings lessens the possible impact of review on the quality of administrative decision-making: e.g. M Adler, 'Tribunal Reform: Proportionate Dispute Resolution and the Pursuit of Administrative Justice' (2006) 69 *Modern Law Review* 958, 974.

46   *AAT Act*, s 34.

and refine the issues between the parties and to explore possibilities for settlement, perhaps by some form of alternative dispute resolution (ADR).[47] In a large majority of cases before the AAT at least one conference is held.[48] The fact that most applications to the AAT are resolved by agreement between the parties and without a tribunal decision raises an important issue about its function.

On the one hand, the AAT may be seen as designed primarily to ensure that citizens' reasonable grievances are resolved. In this view, it would not matter much how any particular application was finalised so long as the outcome was fair. On the other hand, in addition to addressing individual grievances, the AAT may be seen as designed to develop and enunciate principles of sound administration and in this way affect administrative practices and procedures. In this view, that fact that most cases are settled without a tribunal decision could be cause for concern because it is only by making and publishing decisions that the AAT could have what is sometimes called a 'normative' effect on the ways of the administration (8.8.1).[49] In theory, it seems reasonable to ascribe both functions to the AAT, and in practice the AAT probably lacks the resources formally to decide all the applications it receives. Also, although in theory these two views are in some tension, in practice it may be that relatively few of the applications to the AAT raise general issues of decision-making policy, practice and procedure on which it would be desirable for the AAT to pronounce formally. On the other hand, of course, there is no guarantee that the cases that are formally decided by the AAT fall into this category and that the cases that are settled do not. High rates of settlement might seem more troublesome in those areas where the AAT conducts a second-tier review than in cases where it operates as a first-tier reviewer on the basis that either cases raising important questions of principle are being settled, or the first-tier review is failing to resolve cases that raise no question of principle and which should not be coming to the AAT.[50]

8.5 Access to merits review in the AAT

Two issues need to be considered under this heading: (1) what can the AAT review? and (2) who can (that is, has 'standing' to) make an application for review to the AAT?

8.5.1 What can the AAT review?

Under s 25(1)(a) of the *AAT Act* 'an enactment may provide that applications may be made to the [AAT] for review of decisions made in exercise of powers conferred by the enactment'. So in determining whether the AAT has jurisdiction to hear an application it is necessary first to ask: does the application

---

47   Pre-hearing conferences are much more used in the AAT than in first-tier merits review tribunals such as the SSAT. This probably reflects the more adversarial nature of proceedings in the AAT as compared with the SSAT. The ALRC reported that represented applicants in the AAT are more likely than unrepresented applicants to settle their claim by agreement in the pre-hearing phase: ALRC 89, paras 5.9, 9.100. In some cases, settlement may be promoted by use of alternative dispute resolution (ADR) techniques such as mediation and conciliation. Such methods are typically designed to help the parties reach a compromise solution. Some question their appropriateness to disputes between citizen and government, at least in cases where the issue is a black-and-white one of whether or not the citizen is entitled to some benefit rather than one about whether and how a discretion should be exercised in the citizen's favour.

48   ALRC DP 62, para 12.53; G Downes, 'Practice, Procedure and Evidence in the Administrative Appeals Tribunal, <www.aat. gov.au/Publications/SpeechesAndPapers/Downes/pdf/PracticeProcedureEvidenceMay2011.pdf>.

49   See, e.g., G Fleming, 'Administrative Review and the "Normative" Goal—Is Anybody Out There?' (2000) 28 *Federal Law Review* 61.

50   See D F O'Connor, 'Effective Administrative Review: An Analysis of Two-Tier Review' (1993) 1 *Australian Journal of Administrative Law* 4, 6–8.

relate to a 'decision'? Second, was the decision made in exercise of a power conferred by an enactment that confers jurisdiction on the AAT to review that decision?

8.5.1.1 Decision

The word 'decision' has been held to include 'purported decision'. This point is fundamental to the concept of merits review. For present purposes, the phrase 'purported decision' is synonymous with 'illegal ("ultra vires") decision'. Typically, a decision-maker who makes an illegal decision will be attempting ('purporting') to decide legally. But if the decision is in fact illegal, then no question of its merits—of whether it is 'right or wrong'—will arise. So does a merits review tribunal have jurisdiction to review an illegal (purported) decision and to set it aside on the ground that it is contrary to law (regardless of its merits)? The decision (in the *Brian Lawlor* cases)[51] that the AAT does have such power established that, although merits review tribunals (unlike courts) can review administrative decisions 'on the merits', this is not all they can do. In addition to the non-judicial power of merits review, merits review tribunals can also exercise innominate functions. One of these functions is to decide questions of law.[52] However, what a merits review tribunal cannot do (but a court can) is to decide questions of law 'conclusively': this is a judicial function.

The precise meaning of 'conclusively' is a matter of some debate. It may be related to the distinction between appeal and judicial review. According to this approach, a conclusive decision could be challenged only by way of an appeal, whereas a non-conclusive decision could be challenged by way of judicial review or in 'collateral proceedings' (4.7.2)—for instance, proceedings to enforce the decision. However, this approach is hard to reconcile with the fact that the Federal Court—which can exercise the judicial power of deciding questions of law conclusively—is subject to judicial review under s 75(v) of the Constitution. So it may be that the distinction between a conclusive and a non-conclusive decision turns entirely on whether the decision can be challenged 'collaterally'.[53] Be that as it may, (non-conclusive) decisions of the AAT on points of law can be challenged either by way of an 'appeal' to the Federal Court,[54] or by way of judicial review.[55]

Whatever the theoretical or practical significance of the distinction between conclusive and non-conclusive decisions, it relates to their effects and not to the nature of the decision-making process: when a merits review tribunal decides (or, more accurately, expresses an opinion about) a question of law, it performs a juristic task essentially similar to that performed by a court in deciding a question of law. On the other hand, the fact that merits review tribunals in general, and the AAT in particular, cannot conclusively decide questions of law reflects their second-class status as adjudicators.

The definition of 'decision' in s 3(3) of the *AAT Act* is similar to that in the *ADJR Act* (3.5.1.1). However, several differences are noteworthy. First, while the *AAT Act* definition refers to a 'decision',

---

51   *Re Brian Lawlor Automotive Pty Ltd and Collector of Customs (NSW)* (1978) 1 ALD 167; affirmed *Collector of Customs (NSW) v Brian Lawlor Automotive Pty Ltd* (1979) 2 ALD 1.

52   Including questions about the proper interpretation of the provisions of the *AAT Act* conferring jurisdiction on the AAT: e.g. *Re Adams and Tax Agents Board* (1976) 1 ALD 251. However, the prevailing view is that the AAT has no power to set aside a decision on the ground that the provision under which it was made was unconstitutional or invalid: Pearce, n 31 above, 18–21.

53   Disconcertingly, however, the Federal Court has held that decisions of the AAT cannot be challenged collaterally: *Coffey v Secretary, Department of Social Security* (1999) 56 ALD 338, 347.

54   There is a 'right of appeal' on questions of law from the AAT to the Federal Court. Despite the word 'appeal', this is effectively judicial review. But see 5.4.2.

55   But perhaps only in exceptional circumstances: Pearce, n 31 above, 253–5.

the *ADJR Act* definition refers to the 'making of' and 'failure to make' a decision.[56] One commentator concludes from this difference that the AAT has no general power to review failure to make a decision.[57] However, where a time limit is laid down for the making of a decision, s 25(5) of the *AAT Act* provides that failure to make a decision within the specified time 'shall be deemed to constitute the making of a decision'. Furthermore, where no time limit is specified, a person may seek a certificate from the Ombudsman (under s 10 of the *Ombudsman Act 1976*) that there has been unreasonable delay in making the decision, in which case it will be deemed that a decision has been made. In any case where a failure to make a decision is deemed to be a decision, the AAT could set aside the (failure to make a) decision, and remit the matter to the decision-maker with a direction or recommendation to make a decision.

A second noteworthy feature of the *AAT Act* is that it contains no equivalent of s 6 of the *ADJR Act*, which makes reviewable 'conduct [engaged in] for the purpose of making a decision'. The distinction between decisions and conduct played an important part in the reasoning, in the leading case of *Australian Broadcasting Tribunal v Bond*,[58] about the meaning of 'decision' under the *ADJR Act*. In *Bond*, the existence of s 6 was used to justify giving a narrower rather than a broader meaning to the word 'decision', on the basis that giving it a relatively narrow meaning (referring to something that is 'ultimate' or 'final' or 'determinative' or 'operative') was consistent with the limited nature of judicial review and would reduce the risk that decision-making processes would be unduly fragmented and delayed. In a series of AAT decisions[59] *Bond* has been used to justify refusal of merits reviews. However, one commentator concludes that 'the impact of *Bond's* case ... is still unclear as far as AAT applications are concerned'.[60]

This conclusion leads to a third point. In *Bond*, the particular question at issue was whether certain findings of fact constituted 'decisions' for the purposes of the *ADJR Act*. Mason CJ held that 'in ordinary circumstances, a finding of fact ... will not constitute a ... decision' under the *ADJR Act*.[61] This was because, in interpreting the *ADJR Act*, account had to be taken of the existence of the AAT and the merits review system. Judicial review (as opposed to merits review) 'ordinarily does not extend to findings of fact as such'.[62] An implication of this reasoning is that the word 'decision' has a broader meaning under the *AAT Act* than it has under the *ADJR Act* in that it is more likely to cover decisions on questions of fact. However, Mason CJ's exposition begs a more general question about the extent to which administrative decisions on questions of fact should be subject to external review, whether by a tribunal or a court.

Fourth, we should note another argument used by Mason CJ in *Bond* in favour of a narrow interpretation of 'decision', namely that a broad interpretation would create the risk of 'fragmentation of the processes of administrative decision-making' and of adversely affecting 'the efficiency of the administrative process'.[63] The worry here is that allowing elements of the decision-making process other than the final 'decision' to be challenged by way of judicial review would allow the processes of

---

56   Curiously, however, s 5 of the *ADJR Act* (which sets out the grounds of judicial review) is couched in terms of applications for review of a 'decision', not in terms of 'the making of or failure to make a decision'.

57   Pearce, n 31 above, 25.

58   (1990) 170 CLR 321.

59   See Pearce, n 31 above, 30.

60   Ibid.

61   (1990) 170 CLR 321, 340.

62   Ibid, 341.

63   Ibid, 337.

administration to be interrupted and delayed for illegitimate purposes (whatever they might be).[64] Assuming there is a significant risk of such disruption, and that it is important to prevent it materialising, would the same reasoning count against giving a broad interpretation to 'decision' in the *AAT Act*? One commentator thinks not, on the ground that the 'AAT is part of the administrative process'.[65] But while the AAT is, in theory, part of the administration, in reality it provides an external check on the administrative process. Others have pointed out that the definition of 'decision' may be relevant not only to whether an application for review should be allowed before the decision-making process is complete. An administrative process may involve the making of various 'decisions' over a period of time, culminating in the 'final' 'decision'. Once the process is complete and the final decision has been made, review may be sought of earlier stages of the process. In such a case, the definition of 'decision' will be relevant to whether any particular element of the process can be reviewed. In that context, it is argued, the AAT has defined 'decision' broadly in order to make up for the fact that the *AAT Act* does not refer to 'conduct leading to a decision'.[66]

8.5.1.2 Made in exercise of powers conferred by an enactment that confers jurisdiction on the AAT

The equivalent phrase in the *ADJR Act* is 'made under an enactment'. The *ADJR Act* confers on the Federal Court jurisdiction to review decisions made under Commonwealth statutes subject to any express provision to the contrary. By contrast, the AAT has jurisdiction to review a decision only if a Commonwealth statute expressly confers jurisdiction to review a decision of *that* class.[67] Why this difference? A possible explanation is that while the *ADJR Act* merely purported to codify the law relating to the courts' already existing general power of judicial review, the merits review system was proposed in answer to the open question of how much more external review was needed in addition to that already provided by judicial review and the various tribunals in existence in the early 1970s. We might further speculate that because the Kerr Committee had to persuade the government of the need for more external review, it was seen as politically wise to give the parliament as much power as possible over the expansion.

The Final Report (1973) of the (Bland) Committee on Administrative Discretions (which was set up in the wake of the Kerr Committee) contained a list of decision-making powers, conferred by existing statutes, which the committee recommended should be subject to review by the proposed AAT. One of the functions of the Administrative Review Council (ARC), established under Part V of the *AAT Act*, is to advise the government about whether particular 'classes of decisions' should be subject to merits review.[68] In performance of this function, the ARC has developed a set of principles about the scope of merits review.[69] These principles are in no sense binding, and ultimately the scope of merits

---

64   Note, too, that the *ADJR Act* definition of 'decision' (unlike that in the *AAT Act*) refers to decisions 'proposed to be made' as well as decisions 'made'.

65   Pearce, n 31 above, 31.

66   R Creyke and G Hill, 'A Wavy Line in the Sand: *Bond* and Jurisdictional Issues in Judicial and Administrative Review' (1998) 26 *Federal Law Review* 15, 49–51.

67   *Re Woods and Secretary, Department of Education, Science and Training* (2007) 94 ALD 265.

68   *AAT Act*, s 51(a) and (b).

69   Administrative Review Council, *What Decisions Should be Subject to Merits Review?* (1999).

review is a political issue.[70] There is no constitutionally guaranteed minimum of merits review analogous to the constitutional minimum of judicial review identified in S157 (7.2.2). The factors which may, according to the ARC, justify 'excluding' (more accurately, 'not providing for') merits review are a mixed bag. For instance, the ARC suggests that 'decisions to institute proceedings' should not be subject to review because they are, in fact, not 'decisions'.[71] On the other hand, the suggestion that decisions 'of a high political content' should not be subject to merits review[72] seems to rest on some concept of 'non-justiciability' or unsuitability for external review. It will be recalled that the Kerr Committee considered that the non-justiciability of many administrative decisions was precisely the reason why a non-judicial review body was needed. The ARC's position reinforces the point that, although the AAT is technically part of the executive, it is in reality an external, court-substitute reviewer of the executive. The ARC's proposal that 'legislation-like decisions of broad application' are unsuitable for merits review[73] perhaps echoes the provision, contained in the *ADJR Act* but absent from the *AAT Act*, that only decisions that are of an 'administrative character' are reviewable (see further 3.5.1.3).[74]

One commentator has suggested a quite different approach to the scope of merits review based on a distinction between primary administrative decision-making and merits review of administrative decision-making.[75] The idea is that, whereas ensuring justice to individuals is the central function of merits review, administrators tend to focus on the characteristics that individuals share with members of some relevant group, rather than those that set them apart from other members of the group.[76] This is particularly so in 'high volume' decision-making contexts such as immigration and social security. Based on this distinction, it is argued that merits review is most appropriate, and most likely to be acceptable to government in areas where an added element of individualisation is desirable. This argument is based on a concept sometimes referred to in terms of 'comparative institutional competence'. Administrators—especially those working in high-volume areas—lack the time and resources to investigate every case in great detail, and so it is to be expected that a certain (probably quite small) proportion of decisions will be unfair because they take insufficient account of the personal situation of the affected individual. Viewed in this light, merits review may be understood not so much as a mechanism for correcting 'mistakes', but as an efficient means of injecting an element of individualised justice into the administrative decision-making process. This approach focuses on the role of the AAT as an integral component of the administrative decision-making process, and emphasises the distinction between merits review and judicial review—the latter being basically concerned negatively with identifying errors in decision-making while the former plays a more positive part in the 'administrative justice' system.

Although the *ADJR Act* refers to decisions made 'under an enactment' while the *AAT Act* refers to decisions made 'in exercise of powers conferred by an enactment', this difference of wording seems merely to reflect the fact that the Federal Court has general review jurisdiction under the *ADJR Act*

---

70   This conclusion is perhaps supported by the view of one writer that, tested against the ARC principles, the current jurisdiction of the AAT is riddled with inconsistencies: V Thackeray, 'Inconsistencies in Commonwealth Merits Review' (2004) 40 *Australian Institute of Administrative Law Forum* 54.

71   ARC Report, n 69 above, 13.

72   Ibid, 16–18.

73   Ibid, 7.

74   The Federal Court's judicial review jurisdiction under the *Judiciary Act*, s 39B (like the High Court's jurisdiction under the Constitution, s 75(v)) is not subject to this limitation.

75   J Sharpe, *The Administrative Appeals Tribunal and Policy Review* (Sydney: Law Book Company, 1986), 198.

76   See also P Bailey, 'Is Administrative Review Possible Without Legalism?' (2001) 8 *Australian Journal of Administrative Law* 163.

whereas the AAT only has jurisdiction to review such decisions as are expressed to be reviewable by some statute other than the *AAT Act*. Whereas an applicant for review under the ADJR may (in theory, anyway) trawl the whole statute book to find a provision that supports the decision, a limited number of statutory provisions is available to the applicant for review under the *AAT Act*. This explains why the issue of the alleged nexus between decision and enactment is much more problematic under the *ADJR Act* (see 3.5.1.4) than it is under the *AAT Act*. Consider, for instance, *NEAT Domestic Trading Pty Ltd v AWB Ltd*.[77] Under a statutory provision, the Wheat Export Authority had power to consent to the export of wheat, but only with the written approval of a non-statutory corporation owned by wheat growers. Was a decision of the corporation, whether or not to give approval, made under the statutory provision? Such a question would be unlikely to arise in an application to the AAT, because typically it could not convincingly be argued that a decision, such as that of the corporation whether or not to give approval, was reviewable by the AAT unless such a decision was expressed to be reviewable.[78] Of course, this conclusion raises the underlying question of the appropriate scope of merits review in an environment where functions formerly performed by government are privatised or contracted out.

8.5.2 Applicants

Under s 27 of the *AAT Act*, an application for review of a decision may be made by or on behalf of any person whose interests are affected by the decision. The term 'person' includes a Commonwealth agency. The phrase 'a person whose interests are affected by the decision' includes a corporation or an unincorporated association, provided the decision relates to a matter included in its objects or purposes, unless the association was formed, or the relevant matter was included in its object or purposes, only after the decision was made. 'Interests' is understood broadly, but it is not enough for a person to have an interest in a decision—the interest must be affected by the decision.[79] However, if the effect is too slight or indirect, the person affected may lack standing. Beyond this, not much more can usefully be said about standing in general terms, because whether a person has an interest in a decision and whether that interest has been sufficiently affected depends on an exercise of judgment in the light of the facts of the case and the provisions of the statute under which the challenged decision was made. Similarly, although there may be grounds for thinking that the standing rules under the *AAT Act* are more generous to applicants than the rules applicable to applications for judicial review under the *ADJR Act* (in which the equivalent terminology refers to a 'person aggrieved' by a decision), or at common law, so much depends on context and circumstance that any dogmatic conclusion on the point would be hard to substantiate. Nor is it easy to think of any general reasons why the standing requirements applicable to applications for merits review should be systematically different from those applicable to applications for judicial review.

Supplementary to standing rules—which regulate applications for review—are rules about who may become a party to or intervene in an application made by another person or persons. The person who made the decision under review is a party to the proceedings before the AAT. In addition, the Attorney-General may intervene on behalf of the Commonwealth in any application before the AAT.

---

77   (2003) 216 CLR 277 (3.5.1.4.2).

78   *Re Qantas Airways Ltd and Deputy Commissioner of Taxation (Western Australia)* (1979) 2 ALD 291. See also Administrative Review Council, *The Contracting Out of Government Services*, Report No 42 (1998), Ch 6.

79   *Re Gay Solidarity Group and Minister for Immigration and Ethnic Affairs* (1983) 5 ALD 289; *Re Rudd and Minister for Transport and Regional Services* (2001) 65 ALD 296.

Any other 'person whose interests are affected' may, with the consent of the AAT, become a party either to support[80] or oppose the decision under review. This last provision makes no express mention of unincorporated associations, but a member of such an association could be given consent to become a party on behalf of (all the members of) the association.[81] In the abstract, it is hard to say whether the 'affected interests' test has been applied more or less generously in the case of persons seeking to become parties as compared with persons seeking to make an application for review. However, there may be good reasons why the requirements for becoming a party should be more demanding than those for making an application: the more parties to an application, the more time-consuming and expensive the proceedings are likely to become for everyone involved and the more wide-ranging in terms of the issues raised.[82] Relevant, too, are the nature and function of merits review. Generous intervention rules (even more than generous standing rules for applications) would tend to support a view that the role of the AAT is not limited to resolving individual grievances, but extends to promoting the public interest in good administrative decision-making. They would, in other words, be more consistent with viewing the AAT as an administrative body than as a court substitute.

8.6 The basis of merits review

8.6.1 The general nature of merits review

Section 43 of the *AAT Act* is central to an understanding of the nature of merits review and its relationship to judicial review. The provisions of this section encapsulate the split nature of the AAT, at one and the same time part of the administrative process and an external reviewer of the executive. For present purposes, we can say that s 43 does three things. First, it sets out the powers of the AAT in relation to a reviewed decision: it can affirm or vary the decision, or set it aside and either make a substitute decision or remit the decision for reconsideration by the decision-maker with directions (binding) or recommendations (non-binding). Second, it provides that when the AAT varies a decision or makes a substitute decision, the AAT's decision is deemed to be a decision of the original decision-maker as from the date of coming into effect of the original decision.[83] Third, it provides that in reviewing the decision, the AAT 'may exercise all [and only] the powers and discretions' conferred on the original decision-maker: as it is often put, the AAT 'stands in the shoes' of the original decision-maker.[84] Whereas the task of a court exercising judicial review jurisdiction is to police the limits of decision-making power, the task of the AAT is to reconsider decisions.[85] Despite this, however, the AAT is not an original decision-maker. It is a reviewer of decisions made by others, and it may exercise the powers of the original decision-maker only 'for the purpose of reviewing a decision'. The power of the AAT (we might say) is not to make a

---

80   *Re Sew Eurodrive Pty Ltd and Collector of Customs* (1994) 35 ALD 790.

81   *Arnold (on behalf of Australians for Animals) v State of Queensland* (1987) 13 ALD 195.

82   See, e.g., *Re Control Investment Pty Ltd and Australian Broadcasting Tribunal (No 1)* (1980) 3 ALD 74, 80–1.

83   In the terms used in 4.4.3, the original decision is treated as void and a nullity.

84   *Minister for Immigration and Ethnic Affairs v Pochi* (1980) 4 ALD 139, 143 *per* Smithers J.

85   There are exceptions to this general principle. For instance, under s 58(5) of the *Freedom of Information Act 1982* (Cth) the task of the tribunal is to decide whether there were reasonable grounds for the issue of a ministerial certificate: *McKinnon v Secretary, Department of Treasury* (2006) 228 CLR 423. This function is closer to judicial review than merits review.

decision of the type under review, but to make a decision about the decision under review, which may or may not be a decision to *remake* (or vary) that decision. In doing so, it is not limited to considering the material available to or the reasons given by the original decision-maker.[86] Furthermore, if the AAT decides to vary or remake the decision, it is not restricted to exercising the power that the original decision-maker purported to exercise, but may exercise any of the powers of the decision-maker relevant to varying or remaking the decision.[87]

By providing, in effect, that the AAT stands in the shoes of the decision-maker, the *AAT Act* supplies essential legal underpinning for the AAT's powers to vary a decision and to make a substitute decision. The conferral on the AAT of the powers of the decision-maker, in support of its remedial powers to vary, and make substitute, decisions is what fundamentally distinguishes merits review from judicial review. On the other hand, when the AAT affirms a decision,[88] or sets it aside and remits it for reconsideration,[89] it exercises power conferred by the *AAT Act*, not any power of the original decision-maker. In such cases, the AAT performs a function similar in nature to that performed by a court exercising judicial review jurisdiction.

Expressed in the terminology of the *AAT Act*, the characteristic judicial review remedy is setting aside accompanied by remission for reconsideration. Although this remedy is available to the AAT, the characteristic merits review remedies are to vary the decision under review, and to set it aside and make a substitute decision. The grounds of judicial review discussed in Chapter 5 encapsulate the bases on which the characteristic judicial review remedy may be awarded. Surprisingly, perhaps, the *AAT Act* says nothing about the basis on which the AAT may exercise its various remedial powers. It was left to the AAT to develop the law in this respect. Thus, one of the first questions the AAT had to answer (as we saw in 8.5.1.1) was whether it had power to set aside a decision on the ground of illegality ('error of law'). The decision that it did established that illegality provides a basis for the exercise of the AAT's remedial powers.

In an early general statement, 'the question for the determination of the [AAT]' was said to be whether the decision under review was 'the correct or preferable one'.[90] 'Correct' is taken to refer to situations in which the AAT considers that there is only one acceptable decision, and 'preferable' refers to situations where it considers there to be more than one acceptable decision. The correct-or-preferable standard tells us not only what can trigger an exercise of the AAT's remedial powers—namely, an application for review of a decision which the AAT considers not to be the correct or preferable one. It also tells us the purpose of the AAT's remedial powers, namely to bring it about that the correct or preferable decision is made. Thus, if the AAT decides to vary a decision or make a substitute decision, it assumes responsibility for producing the correct or preferable outcome. If it decides to remit a decision for reconsideration, it imposes responsibility on the original decision-maker to produce the correct or preferable outcome. In principle, this latter course would seem appropriate in cases where the AAT concludes that the original decision-maker (guided by the AAT's directions or recommendations) is in a better position than the AAT to make the correct or preferable decision because, for instance, 'substantial amounts of new documentation would be required to enable the tribunal to decide the matter on the facts as they stood at the time of the hearing'.[91]

---

86   *Re Greenham and Minister for Capital Territory* (1979) 2 ALD 137.

87   Pearce, n 31 above, 176–8.

88   *Powell v Department of Immigration and Multicultural Affairs* (1998) 53 ALD 228.

89   *Re Brian Lawlor Automotive Pty Ltd and Collector of Customs (NSW)* (1978) 1 ALD 167, 175.

90   *Drake (No 1)* (1979) 2 ALD 60, 68 *per* Bowen CJ and Deane J.

91   *Re SRRRRR v Commissioner of Taxation* (2008) 100 ALD 690. This decision concerned the power to remit under s 42D of the *AAT Act*, not under s 43. However, one would expect the relevant principles to be the same in both contexts.

By contrast, when a court exercising judicial review jurisdiction remits a decision to the original decision-maker for reconsideration, it does so not because it has concluded that the original decision-maker is better placed to produce the best outcome, but because it has no power to make a substitute decision. While the grounds of judicial review embody the sorts of defects in decision-making that are considered to justify sending the decision back to the original decision-maker for reconsideration, the 'correct or preferable' standard of merits review refers, in abstract terms, to norms of good decision-making, departure from which triggers the remedial jurisdiction of the AAT and application of which underpins exercise by the AAT of its various remedial powers—in particular, the powers to vary a decision and to make a substitute decision. It is by enunciating such norms and applying them in individual cases that the AAT may be able to perform what is called its 'normative' function of improving the quality of primary decision-making (8.8.1).

What are the norms of good decision-making to which the 'correct or preferable' standard refers? A good place to start in answering this question is with the three broad categories into which (in Chapter 5) we divided the grounds of judicial review—namely procedural grounds, reasoning process grounds and decisional grounds.

8.6.2 Procedure

Breach of the rules of procedural fairness (the bias rule and the fair hearing rule) and of statutory procedural requirements is, perhaps, the archetypal ground of judicial review. Judicial review, it is often said, is primarily concerned with the procedure by which decisions are made, not their substance. Although it is sometimes said that a court will not quash a decision on the ground of procedural impropriety if the procedural defect 'could have made no difference' (see 5.2.5.1), a decision may be quashed on procedural grounds regardless of its merits. In judicial review law, we might say, procedural error is of 'independent' significance. Moreover, whereas an 'appeal' against a decision may 'cure' procedural defects in the original decision-making process,[92] judicial review of the decision cannot.

In these respects, merits review is quite different from judicial review. The basic question for the AAT is whether the decision under review was the correct or preferable one. Although procedural defects may result in a decision that is not the correct or preferable one, the AAT's prime task is not to identify such defects and require the decision-maker to repair them, but rather to reach the correct or preferable decision, and to repair ('cure') procedural defects if this is necessary to enable it to do that.[93] In this sense, procedural error lacks the independent significance in merits review law that it has in judicial review law. Of course, proceedings before the AAT will cure procedural defects only if the AAT itself complies with the requirements of procedural fairness; and procedural unfairness on the part of the AAT may constitute a ground of appeal to the Federal Court[94] or provide a basis for seeking judicial review of the AAT's decision. The principles of procedural fairness provide a normative framework within which provisions of the AAT Act dealing with procedure must be interpreted and put into effect. It is at this level that the rules of procedural fairness assume independent importance in the merits review system.

---

92   M Aronson, B Dyer and M Groves, *Judicial Review of Administrative Action*, 4th edn (Sydney: Lawbook Co, 2009), 496–503.

93   E.g. *Re Murdaca and Australian Securities and Investments Commission* (2010) 118 ALD 202.

94   *Sullivan v Department of Transport* (1978) 1 ALD 383.

8.6.3 Reasoning process

The main grounds of judicial review in this category are failure to take account of a relevant consideration, taking account of an irrelevant consideration, exercising a power for an improper purpose (that is, a purpose other than that for which it was conferred), and various forms of impermissible fettering and transferring of discretion. Just as procedural defects may result in a decision that is not the correct or preferable one, so may defects of reasoning. And just as the prime function of the AAT in relation to procedural defects is to cure them by acting in a procedurally proper way, so its prime function in relation to reasoning defects is to cure them by reconsidering the decision under review in accordance with norms of sound reasoning.[95]

In this context, the fact that the AAT is a reviewer of decisions rather than a primary decision-maker has given rise to some of the most difficult issues in the law of merits review. Here is one. Considerations relevant to the exercise of a decision-making power may be exhaustively and exclusively spelled out in the statute that confers the power. In that case, both the decision-maker in making the decision, and the reviewer in affirming or varying the decision or in making a substitute decision, would be bound to take account of all and only the stated considerations. Typically, however, relevant considerations are not fully specified by statute and may be expressed, more or less formally, as 'policy', which (in this context) means a sort of general[96] guideline establishing considerations relevant to the exercise of decision-making powers in individual cases. In *Drake (No 1)* Bowen CJ and Deane J said that 'the consistent exercise of discretionary administrative power in the absence of legislative guidelines will, in itself, almost inevitably lead to the formulation of some general policy or rules relating to the exercise of the relevant power'.[97] In the absence of explicit legislative or non-legislative policies, consistency may be facilitated by, and may demand, the formulation of policies by the decision-maker as part of the decision-making process. Is the same true of the AAT?

The answer to this question is clear: the demands of consistency apply to the AAT as much as to the decision-makers over whom it exercises jurisdiction. As Brennan J famously said: 'Inconsistency is not merely inelegant: it … [suggests] an arbitrariness which is incompatible with commonly accepted notions of justice.'[98] It follows that, although the AAT is not 'bound' by its own previous decisions,[99] it should aim to be consistent in its decision-making, and consistency may often be most effectively realised by the formulation of general norms (in the nature of policies)[100] to structure not only the AAT's own decision-making, but also that of decision-makers subject to its jurisdiction.[101] Of course, such norms must themselves be consistent with relevant legal rules, and the AAT must not treat them as if they were

---

95   For example, *Minister for Human Services and Health v Haddad* (1995) 38 ALD 204.

96   *Leppington Pastoral Co Pty Ltd v Department of Administrative Services* (1990) 20 ALD 607; *Re Malincevski and Minister for Immigration, Local Government and Ethnic Affairs* (1991) 24 ALD 331.

97   (1979) 2 ALD 60, 69.

98   *Drake No 2* (1979) 2 ALD 634, 639. Of course, consistency is not of unqualified value. There is no virtue in being consistently unjust.

99   Pearce, n 31 above, 200–2. Some decisions may carry more weight than others: *Re Littlejohn and Department of Social Security* (1989) 17 ALD 482, 486.

100   Remember that the AAT cannot conclusively decide questions of law. It follows that any general norms it articulates will not have the same force as rules of common law made by courts.

101   L Pearson, 'Policy, Principles and Guidance: Tribunal Rule-Making' (2012) 23 *Public Law Review* 16.

legally binding. Moreover, just as when courts make law they do so 'incrementally' or 'interstitially', as an incidental by-product of resolving individual disputes, and not 'legislatively' as a parliament does, so the AAT has always shied away from laying down general norms unrelated to the facts of particular cases.[102] The tribunal understands its prime function in terms of doing justice in individual cases, not establishing general norms of good decision-making.[103]

A second issue concerning the AAT's role in relation to 'policy' arises as follows. The crucial legal distinction between a statutory provision and a policy is that the former is binding in a strict way that the latter is not.[104] Policies, it is often said, are relevant considerations to be taken into account along with other relevant matters, not binding rules to be followed to the exclusion of other considerations. The central question in the present context is whether policies developed by the government (as opposed to the AAT itself) have the same force in relation to decision-making by the AAT as they do in relation to primary decision-making by public administrators. This question arises precisely because the AAT is a reviewer of decisions, not a primary decision-maker. It seems clear that primary administrative decision-makers are typically under a prima facie obligation (perhaps based on the constitutional principle of ministerial responsibility) to give effect to government policy. Standing as it does in the shoes of the original decision-maker, is the AAT under a similar prima facie obligation? Suppose that, in a particular case, the AAT considers that a primary decision is not the correct or preferable one precisely because it applies or is consistent with some government policy. Can it vary the decision or make a substitute decision in a way that is inconsistent with the policy? In other words, may the AAT consider the *merits* of government policy?[105]

The first point to make in answering this question is that if government policy conflicts with some legal rule (whether constitutional, statutory or common law) it is illegal, and the AAT[106] (as well as a primary decision-maker)[107] would be bound not to act in conformity with it. Second, it is illegal for a primary administrative decision-maker to 'fetter' its discretion by treating a policy as if it were legally binding and exclusive of other considerations;[108] and it would also be illegal for the AAT to do this. However, this conclusion is consistent with saying that the AAT is under an obligation to take account of the policy and to apply it in appropriate circumstances. The crucial question is whether the AAT is entitled to refuse to apply a lawful policy, not because it is inapplicable in the circumstances but because

---

102   For example, *Re Australian Metal Holdings Pty Ltd and Australian Securities Commission and Others* (1995) 37 ALD 131, 144. See also P Cane, 'Merits Review and Judicial Review—the AAT as Trojan Horse' (2000) 28 *Federal Law Review* 213, 237–8; Sharpe, *The Administrative Appeals Tribunal and Policy Review*, Ch VI.

103   For example, *Re Presmint Pty Ltd and Australian Fisheries Management Authority* (1995) 39 ALD 625.

104   In practice, the distinction between policies and binding rules is not always clear or easy to apply: R Creyke and J McMillan, *Control of Government Action: Text, Cases and Commentary* (Sydney: LexisNexis Butterworths, 2005), 628–33.

105   Statute may expressly provide that it shall not do so: *Leppington Pastoral Co Pty Ltd v Department of Administrative Services* (1990) 20 ALD 607.

106   *Australian Fisheries Management Authority v PW Adams Pty Ltd* (1995) 39 ALD 481; *Bateman v Health Insurance Commission* (1998) 54 ALD 408.

107   *Green v Daniels* (1977) 13 ALR 1. See, e.g., *Re Lanham and Secretary, Department of Family and Community Services* (2002) 67 ALD 173. But suppose that a minister gives an undertaking to parliament that a statutory provision will be applied, contrary to its express terms, in such a way as to benefit some citizens: *Re Sharpe and Department of Social Security* (1988) 14 ALD 681, 693–4. See also *Re Witheford and Department of Foreign Affairs* (1983) 5 ALD 534.

108   For example, *Re Goodson and Secretary, Department of Employment, Education, Training and Youth Affairs* (1996) 42 ALD 651, 655.

it is not, in the AAT's opinion, a sound or wise policy.[109] A further question is whether the AAT is entitled to enunciate a new policy, inconsistent with an existing policy, as the basis for varying or making a substitute decision.

We saw earlier (5.4.4) that one of the grounds of judicial review is '*Wednesbury* unreasonableness'. Among other things, it allows a court to quash an administrative decision that the court considers to be unreasonable from a policy point of view. Merits review, as its name implies, is more concerned than judicial review with whether administrative decisions are 'correct or preferable' as opposed to 'legal'. It seems to follow that merits review must be at least as concerned as judicial review with the soundness of policies. And since, unlike a court, the AAT can vary and make substitute decisions, it must have the power to act inconsistently with government policy.[110] So the difficult question is not whether the AAT can act inconsistently with government policy, but when it can act inconsistently.

A distinction is drawn between policies according to the 'political level' at which they are formulated.[111] For instance, the AAT is less likely to be justified in departing from a policy adopted by Cabinet and approved by parliament than from an internal departmental guideline developed by officials, perhaps in consultation with the minister. In one case, the AAT said, in relation to a policy developed 'at the highest level', that the policy should be applied by the tribunal unless 'evidence showed that it was entirely misconceived or proceeded on a wholly erroneous basis'.[112] This test seems similar to the judicial review standard of *Wednesbury* unreasonableness. There are various statements in the cases that relate to policies apparently developed at 'lower levels',[113] but they do not address the question of whether the relevant policy was sound or wise; rather the issue is whether the decision-maker paid due attention to the facts of the individual case in deciding whether or not to apply the policy, regardless of its desirability—in other words, whether application of the policy had fettered the decision-maker's discretion. Indeed, in one case Deane J reasoned in this way despite describing the policy as 'draconian and, indeed, callous'.[114]

It would seem, therefore, that, although the AAT is entitled to act inconsistently with government policy, it is very reluctant to do so, and perhaps even more reluctant than courts to reject government policy as 'unreasonable'. Instead of addressing the merits of government policy, the AAT is more likely, if it can, to hold a policy of which it does not approve to be illegal on the basis of a proper interpretation of the empowering statute.[115] If it feels unable to do this, it will typically go no further than asking whether

---

109   However, the clear theoretical distinction between 'lawful' on the one hand and 'sound or wise' on the other is, in practice, not so clear-cut. For instance, the AAT might reject government policy on the basis that its application involves unlawfully taking into account a consideration which is not relevant on a proper interpretation of the statutory provision conferring the power to make the decision (see the discussion in Sharpe, *The Administrative Appeals Tribunal and Policy Review*, Ch VII). In this way the AAT can reject government policy that it considers unsound or unwise on the ground that it is illegal. In *Re Drake and Minister for Immigration and Ethnic Affairs* (1979) 2 ALD 634 ('*Drake No 2*') Brennan J recommended that the AAT should normally apply lawful policies in the interests of 'consistency'; but this, of course, does not resolve the question we are currently considering.

110   For an early statement by the Federal Court to this effect see *Drake No 1* (1979) 2 ALD 60, 69–70. See also E Morrow, 'Merit Review in WA: The Cost of Applying Government Policy in the Course of Review' (2006) 49 *Australian Institute of Administrative Law Forum* 48.

111   *Re Becker and Minister for Immigration and Ethnic Affairs* (1977) 1 ALD 158. See generally Pearce, n 31 above, 194–8.

112   *Re Aston and Department of Primary Industries* (1985) 8 ALD 366, 380.

113   For example, *Re Evans and Secretary, Department of Primary Industry* (1985) ALD 627; *Re Jetopay Pty Ltd and Australian Fisheries Management Authority* (1993) 32 ALD 209, 231–2; *Stoljarev v Australian Fisheries Management Authority* (1995) 39 ALD 517.

114   *Nevistic v Minister for Immigration and Ethnic Affairs* (1981) 34 ALR 639, 647.

115   See further n 109 above.

the decision-maker, in applying the policy, took proper account of the interests of the applicant and, if it did not, making good the deficiency.

8.6.4 The decision

8.6.4.1 Law

The main substantive grounds of judicial review are error of law, error of fact and *Wednesbury* unreasonableness (which was mentioned in 8.6.3). Most errors of law are, in essence, the result of misinterpretation or misapplication by the decision-maker of a statutory provision.[116] A decision may be illegal because, for instance, it fell outside the power the decision-maker was purporting to exercise, or because the particular decision-maker had no power to make the decision.[117]

In Australian judicial review law, questions of law are generally treated as having only one correct answer. On the other hand, it is widely acknowledged that there is often room for reasonable disagreement about the meaning of particular statutory provisions. In effect, therefore, the idea that questions of law have a single correct answer reduces to the proposition that the correct answer to a question of law is the answer preferred by the body with the final say about what the answer is to any particular question of law. The task of the AAT is to review decisions that are not 'correct or preferable', and to identify the decision that *is* correct or preferable. In theory, the AAT's task in relation to questions of law is to identify the 'correct' answer.[118] However, in cases where reasonable minds could differ about which interpretation is correct, the 'correct' answer may be equivalent to the 'preferable' answer; but it is probably not open to the AAT explicitly to apply the 'preferable' standard when reviewing decisions on questions of law.

In some cases—where, for instance, the decision-maker simply had no power to make the decision under review—the appropriate course of action for the AAT would be to set the decision aside and direct the decision-maker to take no action to give it effect.[119] In other cases,[120] the AAT may be able to correct the legal error by varying the decision, making a substitute decision, or remitting the decision to the decision-maker with appropriate directions.

8.6.4.2 Fact

As we have seen, there are two varieties of factual error. One—taking account of an irrelevant fact or failing to take account of a relevant fact—is a reasoning error (8.6.3). Here, we are concerned with factual errors that consist in making factual findings on the basis of inadequate evidence. It will be recalled (from 8.5.1.1) that in *Bond* Mason CJ stressed that normally error of fact of this sort—which is a function of the weight given to available evidence—will not provide a ground of judicial review either at common law or under the *ADJR Act* (5.4.3), partly because review of decisions on questions of fact has been committed to merits review tribunals such as the AAT.

---

116 For an example of error in interpreting a policy see *Minister for Immigration, Local Government and Ethnic Affairs v Gray* (1994) 33 ALD 13.

117 For example, *Re Baran and Department of Primary Industries and Energy* (1988) 18 ALD 379.

118 Subject to the proviso that the AAT cannot decide questions of law 'conclusively' (8.5.1.1).

119 As in *Re Brian Lawlor Automotive Pty Ltd and Collector of Customs (NSW)* (1978) 1 ALD 167. The order made in this case does not fit neatly into any of the remedial categories in *AAT Act*, s 43. See the explanation at (1978) 1 ALD 167, 176.

120 For instance, where the decision-maker acts in bad faith: see *Re Mika Engineering Holdings Pty Ltd and Commissioner of Taxation* (2006) 92 ALD 688, 692–3.

It appears that the AAT can review any and every relevant question of fact. If it concludes that a relevant question of fact admits of only one acceptable answer, which is different from that given by the decision-maker, it can intervene on the basis that the decision was not 'correct'. If it concludes that the question of fact admits of more than one acceptable answer, and that the answer given by the decision-maker was not the best of the available options, it can intervene on the basis that the decision was not the 'preferable' one. In determining the relevant facts, the AAT is not, as a general rule, limited to evidence that was available to the decision-maker.[121] The AAT conducts reviews on the basis of the relevant facts as they are at the date of the review, and it has various powers to enable it to gather fresh evidence relating to factual findings made by the decision-maker, as well as evidence of changes in relevant factual circumstances.[122] In this respect, the AAT can exercise even more control over fact-finding than appellate courts, which normally do not have power to admit new evidence. As a result, the AAT will typically be in a position to correct errors of fact by varying the decision under review or making a substitute decision. Rarely would it seem be appropriate for the AAT to set aside a decision for error of fact and remit it to the decision-maker for reconsideration.[123]

It is in this area of factual review that we find the greatest and most practically significant difference between merits review and judicial review. Not only does the AAT have much wider power to review decisions on questions of fact, but also, in theory at least, the correct or preferable standard of review allows the AAT to exercise more control over the fact-finding process than courts can by way of judicial review.

Moreover, while decisions of the AAT are subject to appeal to the Federal Court on questions of law, they are not subject to appeal on questions of fact (although an error on a factual matter may constitute an error of law).[124] Whether it is desirable for an external reviewer to have such extensive powers in relation to fact-finding is another matter. After all, the sorts of arguments used to justify judicial restraint in reviewing factual decisions of administrators, tribunals and inferior courts are not obviously inapplicable to the AAT, viewed as an external reviewer. Even if we think of the AAT as a part of the administrative process, there may be arguments against allowing the fact-finding and decision-making process to be reopened quite so comprehensively as the current regime allows.

8.6.4.3 Weighing relevant considerations

The third main substantive ground of judicial review is *Wednesbury* unreasonableness. In 8.6.3, we were mainly concerned with the question of whether the decision-maker, in reaching the decision,

---

121   *Shi v Migration Agents Registration Authority* (2008) 235 CLR 286. The general rule was originally established in *Re Greenham and Minister for Capital Territory* (1979) 2 ALD 137. Legislation may indicate a contrary intention: Creyke and McMillan, *Control of Government Action*, 144–7.

122   However, in practice these powers are apparently little used. See generally J Dwyer, 'Overcoming the Adversarial Bias in Tribunal Procedures' (1991) 20 *Federal Law Review* 252.

123   By contrast, if the Federal Court sets aside an AAT decision for an error of law related to fact-finding, the proper course is for it to remit the matter to the AAT for reconsideration: *Harris v Director General of Social Security* (1985) 7 ALD 277, 284; *Osland v Secretary to the Department of Justice* (2010) 241 CLR 320, [19]–[20]. This is partly because fresh evidence is rarely admissible in an appeal under the *AAT Act*, s 44: *Committee of Direction of Fruit Marketing v Delegate of Australian Postal Commission* (1979) 2 ALD 561. However, the Federal Court may in certain circumstances make findings of fact: *AAT Act*, s 44(7).

124   It may be possible to challenge a decision of the AAT on a question of fact by way of judicial review or (perhaps) in collateral proceedings. This suggests that the AAT cannot decide questions of fact conclusively any more than it can decide questions of law conclusively. See L Zines, *The High Court and the Constitution*, 5th edn (Sydney: Federation Press, 2008), 247.

took account of matters that ought to have been ignored, or vice versa. Here we are concerned with the respective weights the decision-maker assigned to the various matters (facts, policies, statutory purposes and so on) that were rightly taken into account or, in other words, how the various relevant considerations were balanced against one another to produce and justify the final decision. In judicial review law, a court will quash a decision only if the balance struck by the decision-maker can be described as so unreasonable that no reasonable decision-maker could have considered the decision reasonable. The AAT's task in this respect is, by contrast, to reconsider the decision and to ask whether it is the correct or preferable one. While judicial review courts have often said that it is not for them to quash a decision merely because they do not consider it to be the best of the available options, it is precisely the job of the AAT to decide which of the possible outcomes is, in its view, the correct or preferable one.[125] The fact that some other outcome could be considered reasonable is of no moment. Here, then, we seem to find another stark contrast between judicial review and merits review. However, in practice, much may depend on how willing particular reviewers are, in particular contexts, to interfere with administrative decision-making. This may be especially true of merits review: different tribunal members may reasonably disagree in particular cases about which decision is the correct or preferable one and in general, or in particular contexts, some tribunal members may be more or less willing than others to set aside or vary administrative decisions. But even in relation to judicial review, judges may reasonably disagree about whether particular decisions are *Wednesbury*-unreasonable or not.

Nevertheless in theory, the difference between saying that a decision is extremely unreasonable and saying that it is not the preferable one is clear enough—and it prompts us to ask why a body such as the AAT should be empowered to set aside an administrative decision merely on the ground that if it had been the original decision-maker, it would have struck a different balance between the various relevant considerations. This question leads to another point: suppose that, in a series of similar cases, the AAT repeatedly decides that too much or too little weight was given to a particular relevant consideration.[126] Should the AAT have power, in this way, effectively to create new policies about the way the various considerations, relevant to a particular type of decision, should be balanced? As we saw in 8.6.3, the AAT has generally been wary of departing from government policy, and a certain willingness to do so in relation to immigration decision-making in the early days of the AAT was, no doubt, one reason why specialist tribunals, more closely integrated into the relevant government department, were established in this area. This is also why the AAT now has very little power in immigration matters. Once again, we can detect tension between the AAT's two roles—part of the administrative process on the one hand, but external checker of that process on the other. Whatever the theory, caution in questioning and departing from government policy is, no doubt, a strategy essential for the survival of the AAT.

---

125   English courts have developed certain grounds of judicial review—such as 'material error of fact', (lack of) proportionality and substantive legitimate expectation—which Australian courts might consider unsuitable as grounds of judicial review because they go to the merits: J Spigelman, *AIAL National Lecture Series on Administrative Law No 2* (Australian Institute of Administrative Law, 2004), especially 9–13, 26–8. But even if (lack of) proportionality, for instance, is not a ground of judicial review, it may be a norm of good decision-making, departure from which could provide the basis for a successful application for merits review. For contrasting judicial views of the relationship between merits review and judicial review see *Re Brian Lawlor Automotive Pty Ltd and Collector of Customs* (1978) 1 ALD 167, 177 (Brennan J) and *Drake (No 1)* (1979) 2 ALD 60, 77–85 (Smithers J).

126   For an example see Sharpe, *The Administrative Appeals Tribunal and Policy Review*, 76–94, 168–75.

8.7 Outcomes of merits review

As we saw in 8.6.1, the AAT may affirm or vary the decision under review, or set it aside and either make a substitute decision or remit it for reconsideration to the original decision-maker. Because federal merits review tribunals are not courts, they cannot be given power to enforce their decisions,[127] this being a judicial function.[128] Moreover, the *AAT Act* establishes no mechanism for the enforcement of decisions of the AAT. Of course, some decisions of merits review tribunals may be 'self-executing'—for example, a decision affirming the decision under appeal. If the decision is not self-executing, and the decision-maker fails to comply with the tribunal's order (for instance, to reconsider the decision), proceedings of some sort before a court would be necessary to secure enforcement of the decision.[129] Similarly, if the effect of the tribunal's decision is (for instance) that the applicant owes a debt to the government (perhaps the applicant received pension payments to which they were not entitled), the decision-maker would need to bring proceedings in a court of law to recover the debt if the applicant refused to pay. It is clear that in such proceedings it must be open to the enforcing court to 'review' the decision,[130] but it is unclear what such a review must entail. For instance, would it be necessary for the reviewer to have the same powers to review the AAT's findings of fact as the AAT has to review findings of fact by the primary decision-maker? Note that it is not enough that there be the possibility of review—the decision must actually be reviewed before being enforced.[131]

That decisions of the AAT cannot be enforced unless they are actually reviewed by a court is a clear signal of the AAT's inferior status in the adjudicatory hierarchy. It is questionable whether the respects in which the AAT differs from a Chapter III court are sufficient to justify such distrust of its decisions. While the unenforceability of decisions of the AAT is of no great practical significance,[132] perhaps the centrality of the AAT (and of merits review tribunals more generally) in the federal administrative justice system justifies a reassessment of the relationship between courts and tribunals and between merits review and judicial review.

Whatever we can say about the 1970s when the merits review system was being established, it no longer seems satisfactory or even realistic to think of merits review as accessory to judicial review and of tribunals as inferior to courts. By reason of its breadth and depth, it can be argued that merits review is a more significant mechanism than judicial review for holding government accountable. In this light, it seems odd that the merits-review job should (and constitutionally must) be entrusted to bodies— tribunals—that have lower legal (and social) status than the courts that conduct judicial review. In practice, perhaps the most significant ground of the relationship of inferiority and superiority between

---

127　Or 'issue process requiring execution': *Re Ward and Department of Industry and Commerce* (1983) 8 ALD 324.

128　*Brandy v Human Rights and Equal Opportunity Commission* (1995) 183 CLR 245. See generally E Campbell and M Groves, 'Enforcement of Administrative Determinations' (2006) 13 *AJ Admin L* 121. For application of *Brandy* to a state tribunal see *Attorney-General (NSW) v 2UE Sydney Pty Ltd* (2006) 236 ALR 385.

129　Where the AAT makes a substitute decision, that decision will become the decision of the decision-maker. This does not, of course, guarantee that the decision-maker will implement it, but it does presumably make it more likely than if (as in the case of judicial review) the tribunal's only power were to order the decision-maker (not) to act.

130　*Brandy*, n 128 above.

131　Ibid. For a different interpretation of *Brandy* from that presented in the text see M Allars, 'Theory and Administrative Law: Law as Form and Theory as Substance' (1996) 7 *Canberra Bulletin of Public Administration* 20, 20–24.

132　Because (1) most applications are resolved without a decision by the AAT; (2) some of its decisions may be self-executing; and (3) the government can normally be expected to comply with AAT decisions.

federal tribunals and courts is not that the 'independence' of courts is constitutionally guaranteed while that of tribunals is not, but that the (non-constitutional) qualifications for being a judge focus on legal expertise.[133] At the same time, however, even courts recognise that legal expertise is not the only, or perhaps even the most useful, qualification for those whose job is holding government formally to account. In this light, systemic subordination of tribunals to courts looks rather like a restrictive trade practice on the part of courts! The twentieth century witnessed exponential growth in the 'subjudicial' sector of the administrative justice system. Perhaps it is time to think through seriously and comprehensively the implications of this development for the structure of that system and the relationship between its various parts.

8.8 Two topics for further reflection

We round off this chapter with two general observations, one about the so-called 'normative' function of the AAT, and the other about review of policy (8.6.3 and 8.6.4.3). Both points address issues raised by taking a regulatory approach to administrative law (1.3).

8.8.1 The 'normative' function of the AAT

The Kerr Committee's vision for the AAT focused on strengthening the accountability of the executive branch of government. Yet from the start, debate about the AAT was as much about improving the quality of administrative decision-making as about accountability and the resolution of disputes. In terms of the distinction between the legal and regulatory approaches (1.3), viewing the AAT as an agent for improving the quality of decision-making involves taking a regulatory approach. In the literature about the AAT, the term 'normative' is used to refer to this function of merits review.

Judicial review has not (explicitly at least) been understood in this normative way. Two explanations of this difference suggest themselves. First, whereas the focus of judicial review is on identification by the court of bad decision-making, the emphasis in merits review is on the making by the AAT of the 'correct or preferable' decision. In so doing, we might say, the AAT was to lead by example. Second, merits review is concerned with all aspects of the decision under review whereas judicial review is limited to its 'legality'.

There is a widespread view that merits review and the AAT have had a beneficial effect on the quality of administrative decision-making. Three recurrent general themes can be found in the literature. One is that the very existence of the AAT and the very possibility of merits review impressed upon managers in the public service the need to train decision-makers and to regulate and monitor decision-making processes. A second theme concerns the impact of the requirement to give reasons, imposed on decision-makers by *AAT Act*, s 28. Third, it is said that in some cases, at least, the AAT has

---

133   The subordination of tribunals to courts underpins the decision in *Craig v South Australia* (1995) 184 CLR 163, where the High Court distinguished between 'inferior courts … constituted by persons with either formal legal qualifications or practical legal training' and 'tribunals … constituted, wholly or partly, by persons without legal qualifications or legal training' (176–7). For a particularly disparaging comment on the capacities of tribunal members who lack legal training see *NAIS v Minister for Immigration and Multicultural and Indigenous Affairs* (2005) 223 ALR 171 at [91]–[92] per Kirby J. The tribunal in question in this case was the RRT. Ironically, about two-thirds of the members of the RRT listed in its 2004–05 Annual Report were trained, or practised, as lawyers, or both.

improved decision-making by elaborating the meaning of statutory provisions that had not previously been 'authoritatively'[134] interpreted by an external reviewer—indicating, for instance, the considerations relevant to the exercise of a statutory discretion, or elucidating the requirements of a statutory procedural regime.

A striking aspect of debates about the normative function of the AAT is the implicit assumption that establishing an accountability mechanism is a good way—perhaps even the best way—to improve the quality of administrative decision-making.[135] This assumption reflects the dominance of lawyers and legal ways of thinking in the reform processes of the 1970s, and the continuing lack of interaction between lawyers and public administrators. For instance, from a public administration perspective, adequate resources, good recruitment practices, careful training, effective personnel management and systematic performance-monitoring by agencies themselves (perhaps reinforced by an external inspection, audit and quality assurance body) might be much more likely to produce significant improvements in the quality of decision-making than an inevitably sporadic external review or appeal process.[136]

Be that as it may, it is commonly said that by the late 1980s the reforms of the 1970s had produced a sea change in public administration, and the 'administrative law package' was counted a 'success'. By this time, the 'new administrative law' had been joined by the 'new public management', which put increased emphasis on financial efficiency and cost-cutting in government. Another important development of the 1980s was increasing use of internal merits review mechanisms (9.2.4) within government departments. Some started to question whether the AAT continued to represent value for money,[137] given its assumed regulatory success, and its small caseload relative to the many millions of potentially reviewable decisions made every year.

The AAT is, of course, still with us,[138] and the place of external merits review in the governmental system seems secure. However, it may be that the AAT is now seen as having a lesser role to play in transforming public administration, and it has settled into the sedate middle age of a court-substitute, dispute-resolution and accountability mechanism—no longer a scourge of the public service but, like judicial review, a minor irritant.

8.8.2 Policy review

The basic function of 'policy' in the administrative decision-making process is to supplement the legal instructions given to the executive by the legislature (in statutes). Making and implementing policy is one of the main functions of the executive branch of government. This helps to explain why the role of government policy in merits review has always been such a debated and contested topic.

---

134   Remember that the AAT cannot decide questions of law conclusively, but in practice its interpretations of statutory provisions are typically treated as authoritative.

135   For some questioning see N Wikeley, 'Decision Making and the New Tribunals' (2006) 13 *Journal of Social Security Law* 86, 88–92.

136   A classic exposition of this point of view is J Mashaw, *Bureaucratic Justice: Managing Social Security Disability Claims* (New Haven: Yale University Press, 1983). See also J Mashaw, 'The Management Side of Due Process' (1973–4) 59 *Cornell Law Review* 772.

137   For a contemporary discussion see R Balmford, 'The Life of the Administrative Appeals Tribunal—Logic or Experience?' in R Creyke (ed), *Administrative Tribunals: Taking Stock* (Canberra: CIPL, ANU, 1992), 79–82.

138   In *Better Decisions: Review of Commonwealth Merits Review Tribunals* (Report No 39, 1995) the ARC recommended an overhaul of the federal merits review system and the replacement of the AAT by an Administrative Review Tribunal (ART). The report generated much controversy, and legislation to establish the ART eventually lapsed.

Policy-making is a type of rule-making. A distinction can be drawn between two sorts of rule-making, which we might respectively call 'legislative' and 'adjudicative'. As its name suggests, adjudicative rule-making is a by-product of the adjudication of disputes. It is often called 'common law'. By contrast, legislative rule-making is typically unrelated to consideration of individuals and their circumstances. Policy-making by the executive is predominantly legislative in nature, whereas policy-making by the AAT is adjudicative. This point enables us to see that the debate about the role of policy in merits review is concerned not only with who should make policy (the executive or the merits reviewer), but also with how best to make policy—legislatively or adjudicatively. The fact that merits review, unlike judicial review, is concerned with all aspects of the decision under review gives the latter question a salience in relation to merits review that it lacks in relation to judicial review.

The 'founders' and the 'founding documents' of the administrative law system did not address this question about the best way to make policy, partly because they seem to have thought that the AAT would simply apply government policy, and partly because they focused on accountability and dispute resolution. As we noted in 8.8.1, it is widely accepted that merits review by the AAT does affect policy-making by the executive. For instance, if the AAT holds that a particular government policy is inconsistent with a relevant statutory provision, the policy should be changed; interpretations of statutory provisions by the AAT may be incorporated into policy guidelines; and the AAT may itself contribute to policy-making by deciding that particular matters are, or are not, relevant to particular types of decisions. However, being adjudicative in nature, the AAT's contributions to policy-making are inevitably marginal. External review of government policy-making by the AAT does not address larger questions about how legislative policy is made. As we will see in 9.4.3, the making of delegated legislation is subject to a certain amount of formal external review. By contrast, there is very little legal regulation of informal legislative policy-making by the executive. Debates about the appropriate role of the AAT in reviewing policy have tended to divert attention from larger questions about external review and scrutiny of legislative policy-making by the executive.

Putting the point bluntly, if the aim were to monitor and regulate policy-making by the executive, empowering an external adjudicatory merits review body such as the AAT to review the policy aspects of decisions in addition to their legal and factual aspects would not be an obvious strategy. Debates about the role of the AAT in reviewing government policy are tangential to much more important issues about the way governments informally supplement the statutory instructions under which they operate.

9

Beyond Courts and Tribunals

9.1 Introduction

In one sense, judicial review by courts and merits review by tribunals form the core of administrative law as traditionally understood in terms of accountability. This is why they occupy such a large proportion of this book, and why they form such a large component of most administrative law courses. However, one of the things the regulatory approach (outlined in 1.3) teaches us is the value and importance of casting our gaze beyond these core mechanisms of legal accountability, and of comparing and contrasting them with various other avenues and techniques of accountability with a view to understanding their respective strengths and weaknesses, and their place in the broader accountability landscape in which they operate. Such issues of 'institutional design' are the main business of this chapter.

Judicial review and merits review basically involve the use of adjudication as a technique for reviewing decisions. Adjudication is a three-party or 'tripolar' affair in which a neutral (or 'independent') third party resolves a dispute, between a decision-maker and person affected by or interested in the decision, about the legality or merits of the decision. Adjudication is tripolar regardless of whether the procedure followed by the adjudicator is 'adversarial' or 'inquisitorial'. In adversarial adjudication, the prime responsibility for adducing relevant facts and information rests on the disputing parties, while in inquisitorial adjudication the adjudicator takes the initiative, either by specifying information which the parties must provide or by gathering information independently of the parties. Either way, the ultimate task of the adjudicator is to resolve the dispute in favour of one party or the other. In practice, the distinction between these two procedural paradigms is not as clear-cut as this analysis implies. For instance, although a party to proceedings before the AAT, the decision-maker's role is to assist the AAT to identify the correct or preferable decision, not to argue that the decision under review should be affirmed.

Adjudicative decision-making may be contrasted with 'administrative' (or 'bureaucratic') decision-making, the latter being understood as a two-party or 'bipolar' process in which an official, agency or organisation makes a decision affecting some other person. In terms of the distinction between adversarial and inquisitorial procedures, administration is necessarily inquisitorial. The distinction between two-party and three-party decision-making helps to explain why the rules of procedural fairness (5.2.1), which are based on a three-party model of decision-making, may need to be modified when applied to two-party decision-making. For present purposes, however, the most important point to make is that tripolar adjudication is one possible mechanism for *reviewing* bipolar administrative decisions.

This chapter focuses on mechanisms and processes that depart to a greater or lesser extent from the adjudicative model. Closest to the adjudicative model is the institution of the ombudsman (9.3). Like adjudication, investigations by an ombudsman are typically (but not universally) triggered by receipt of a complaint made by a person affected by or interested in an administrative decision. Ombudsmen follow inquisitorial, investigatory procedures with the aim of deciding whether or not the complaint against the decision-maker is justified, and may recommend that some action be taken to remedy the grievance. Ombudsmen, like courts and tribunals, provide a form of 'external' scrutiny. Independence and neutrality are generally considered essential characteristics of the office of ombudsman as of other external monitors of government. Despite these similarities, the basic function of ombudsmen is very different from that of courts and tribunals: whereas the latter review decisions, ombudsmen (and internal complaint-handlers (9.2.3)) investigate complaints.

Closest to the bureaucratic model is internal review (9.2.4). As its name implies, internal review is conducted 'within' the organisation in which the decision under review was made—although the distinction between internal and external review may become blurred when an 'external' review body, such as the RRT, has close connections with the organisation whose decisions it reviews. Internal review is distinguishable from 'reconsideration' of a decision, the latter being conducted personally by the original decision-maker, but the former by some other (typically more senior) decision-maker within the organisation. Typically, internal review is triggered by a request for review by a person affected by the decision, and the review is conducted in essentially the same way as the original decision was made (that is, inquisitorially). The aim of the review is not to resolve a disagreement between the original decision-maker and the complainant, but solely to identify the correct or preferable decision. The internal reviewer 'stands in the shoes of the decision-maker' in a stronger sense than the AAT does (see 8.6.1). Nevertheless, internal reviewers resemble courts and tribunals in that, unlike ombudsmen, they review decisions.

When we turn our attention to mechanisms that focus not on individual grievances and complaints but more broadly on the operation of administrative *systems*—on the 'macro' as opposed to the 'micro' level, we might say—the language of 'review' may give way to that of 'accountability'. To be accountable is to be answerable. An accountability mechanism requires an official or organisation to 'give an account' of decisions or actions for which they are in some sense 'responsible'. Whereas review and complaint mechanisms are typically triggered by an application from a person interested in or adversely affected by events (including decisions), accountability mechanisms are often triggered by events themselves. Some accountability mechanisms, such as public inquiries and royal commissions, are temporary and ad hoc in nature. Others have a continuing existence. The archetypal continuing accountability mechanisms are parliaments (9.4). Parliaments perform various functions in relation to administrative decision-making, not all of which are aptly described in terms of 'accountability'. For instance, the term 'scrutiny' perhaps better describes the parliamentary oversight of delegated legislation (9.4.3).

The distinction between what we might call 'grievance handling' and 'system monitoring' can be understood in terms of the distinction drawn in 1.3 between the traditional backward-looking approach to administrative law and the forward-looking regulatory approach. Although, by virtue of being an accountability mechanism, system monitoring has a backward-looking element, the typical reason to focus more broadly on a system rather than on individual complaints and grievances is to find ways of improving the system for the future. Once again, however, this distinction is not as sharp in practice as it is in theory. Not only may review of individual decisions have the *effect* of bringing about improvements in the decision-making system more broadly, but improvement may also be considered to be one of its *aims*. As we saw in Chapter 8, for instance, merits review by the AAT has always been seen, in part, as a means of improving the quality of original decision-making, as has investigation of complaints. On the other hand, both grievance-handling and system monitoring, being 'reactive' accountability mechanisms, may be distinguished from 'proactive', prophylactic management techniques for improving administrative performance (such as recruitment policies, education and training of decision-makers and the provision of manuals for their guidance) and the use of 'expert (IT) systems' to support or even replace human decision-making.

The past 30 years have witnessed uncoordinated proliferation of review and accountability mechanisms: merits review tribunals, human rights commissions (such as the federal Human Rights and Equal Opportunities Commission (HREOC)), anti-corruption bodies (such as the New South Wales Independent Commission Against Corruption (ICAC)), privacy watchdogs, complaints procedures, private sector ombudsmen (such as the Telecommunications Ombudsman) and so on. This chapter focuses only on internal complaint-handling and review, ombudsmen and parliaments. One reaction to rapid growth of the accountability industry has been to suggest that we should now recognise the existence of an 'integrity branch of government'.[1] This phrase refers to the concept of separation of powers according to which the institutions of government are of three distinct types—legislative, executive and judicial. The suggestion is that this threefold classification no longer reflects reality, and that we should recognise a fourth branch of government consisting of non-judicial bodies that are independent of, and therefore not identifiable with, either the legislature or the executive, and the main function of which is to ensure, by various procedures and mechanisms, that the executive (in particular) acts with integrity. The term 'integrity' may be understood broadly to cover errors and misconduct as diverse as corruption, 'illegality' in the administrative law sense, making decisions that are not correct or preferable, incompetence and inefficiency.[2] In Chapter 8 we noted that the AAT does not fit neatly into either the executive or the judicial branch; it might be thought of as an archetypal fourth-branch institution.

It has been argued that the whole concept of separation of powers (not only its tripartite version) provides an outmoded, although still legally and politically central, account of governmental institutions and functions.[3] It is not clear that extending the metaphor adds greatly to our understanding of governance. For one thing, in the US the idea of a fourth branch of government has been used quite differently to accommodate quasi-autonomous agencies charged with economic and social regulation ('regulatory agencies'), as opposed to institutions of accountability. For another, in Australian law the distinction between judicial and non-judicial bodies (and hence the pressure to recognise a fourth branch of government) is much less significant in its application to the states than to the federal system. Third, going as far as constructing a fourth branch to accommodate institutions that are 'independent' of ('external' to) the executive may make it more difficult to imagine and design an integrated system of internal and external review and accountability mechanisms. In the long term, it may be better to co-opt the overseen into the 'integrity project' than drive an even thicker wedge between the overseers and the overseen.

---

1   For example, J McMillan: 'The Ombudsman and the Rule of Law' (2005) 44 *Australian Institute of Administrative Law Forum* 1.

2   However, the person credited with first suggesting the idea of an integrity branch, Chief Justice Spigelman of the New South Wales Court of Appeal, understands 'integrity' more narrowly in terms of legality, plus fidelity to public purpose and adherence to public values (such as due process): 'The Integrity Branch of Government' (2004) *Australian Institute of Administrative Law National Lecture Series on Administrative Law No 2*, 2. One report defines integrity basically in terms of absence of corruption: National Integrity Systems Assessment, *Chaos or Coherence? Strengths, Opportunities and Challenges for Australia's Integrity Systems* (Griffith University and Transparency International, 2005).

3   E L Rubin, *Beyond Camelot: Rethinking Politics and Law for the Modern State* (Princeton: Princeton University Press, 2005), Ch 2.

9.2 Internal processes

9.2.1 Reconsideration and review of decisions

In 9.1 we noted the distinction between reconsideration and review of decisions. Under what circumstances a decision-maker can reconsider a decision is a complex and difficult question. First, it is necessary to distinguish between the decision and things done (including, perhaps, provisional or preliminary decisions made) in the process of making the (final) decision. Second, the point at which the decision becomes final has to be identified. Third, a distinction must be drawn between cases in which a decision-maker is asked to reconsider a decision *adverse* to the applicant and cases in which the decision-maker reconsiders a decision *favourable* to the applicant. Fourth, it is necessary to distinguish between illegal (ultra vires) and legal (intra vires) decisions.

The default principle is that, once a final decision has been made, it stands unless and until it is reversed on appeal, or quashed by a judicial reviewer, or a merits reviewer sets it aside, varies it or replaces it with a substitute decision. This principle is based on an idea of 'legal certainty', which is explicitly recognised (for instance) in European Community administrative law,[4] and finds implicit expression in the principle of Australian law that non-statutory policies are 'relevant considerations' to be taken into account in making decisions (5.3.3). However, this finality principle applies only to intra vires decisions. An ultra vires decision is not really a decision at all, but only a 'purported' decision. If a decision-maker is asked to reconsider an adverse ultra vires decision, the finality principle will not, in theory at least,[5] prevent such reconsideration.[6] Conversely, an agency may, in principle at least, refuse to give effect to a favourable decision which, on examination, is found to be illegal (and, therefore, not a decision at all), subject only, perhaps, to a narrow doctrine of 'estoppel'.[7]

Suppose that the decision to be reconsidered is intra vires. In relation to courts and tribunals, the finality principle is expressed in the doctrine of *res judicata*, which prevents resolved cases being reopened. So far as administrative decision-makers are concerned, the finality principle can, of course, be overridden by statutory provision expressly or impliedly allowing reconsideration. In the absence of such provision, however, there are very few circumstances in which an intra vires decision may be reconsidered.[8] On the other hand, a decision-maker who reconsiders a decision and makes a decision is unlikely to refuse to give effect to the substitute decision and, unless some third party has sufficient interest to seek judicial or merits review of the substitute decision, there may be no practical barrier to reconsideration, however problematic this may be in principle.

If a decision-maker refuses to reconsider an intra vires decision, the adversely affected person may be able to apply for merits review of the decision. Alternatively, a complaint to an ombudsman may

---

4   T Hartley, *The Foundations of European Community Law*, 7th edn (Oxford: Oxford University Press, 2010), 160–5.

5   In practice, it will often not be clear whether a decision is ultra vires or not, and an application for judicial review or merits review may be the only way to have it reconsidered.

6   *Minister for Immigration and Multicultural and Indigenous Affairs v Bhardwaj* (2002) 209 CLR 597. See also 4.7.1.

7   For the English position see P Cane, *Administrative Law*, 5th edn (Oxford: Oxford University Press, 2011), 144–52. The position in Australia is unclear: M Aronson, B Dyer and M Groves, *Judicial Review of Administrative Action*, 4th edn (Sydney: Lawbook Co, 2009), 392–4.

8   On the English position see Cane, *Administrative Law* 152–3. See also E Campbell, 'Revocation and Variation of Administrative Decisions (1966) 22 *Monash Law Review* 30, 49–54.

be possible. However, as we will see (in 9.3), ombudsmen have no power to set aside, vary or make substitute decisions. It follows that the capacity of an ombudsman to help a person affected by an adverse intra vires decision is (in principle) limited by the binding status of the decision.[9] In such circumstances, the ombudsman may, for instance, recommend that compensation be paid for loss suffered as a result of the adverse decision.

9.2.2 Reviews and complaints

As indicated in 9.1, there is an important distinction between applications for review and complaints. While the subject of a review is a decision (including conduct leading up to a decision), any action (including a decision) may be the subject of a complaint. Review is of two types: judicial and merits. Review may result in a decision being affirmed, set aside, varied, or replaced by a substitute decision. If a complaint relates to a decision, the complaint-handler may be able to achieve a similar result by recommending that the decision-maker reconsider the decision. But as we will see (in 9.3), public sector complaint-handlers (ombudsmen) typically cannot *require* decision-makers to reconsider decisions, and a recommendation that a decision be reconsidered will operate subject to the principles discussed in 9.2.1. Alternatively, the ombudsman may decide not to investigate the complaint on the ground that an application for judicial or merits review would be a more suitable course of action.

9.2.3 Internal complaint procedures

Another ground on which public sector ombudsmen very frequently decide not to investigate complaints is that the complainant has not utilised a complaint-handling mechanism operated by the agency against which the complaint is made. The establishment within agencies of machinery for handling complaints was an aspect of reforms of the public service that went under the broad title of 'managerialism'. Managerialism brought an increased emphasis on efficiency and the use of (quasi-) contractual and market-like techniques to create incentives for better performance. One such technique involved the reconceptualisation of 'citizens' as 'customers' or 'clients', and the adoption of customer service charters that provided, among other things, for complaint-handling machinery.

Managerialism was a phenomenon of the 1980s and 1990s, whereas the office of public ombudsman—the basic function of which is to investigate citizens' complaints against government— was established in the 1970s. As originally conceived, this office was understood, in terms of the constitutional doctrine of individual ministerial responsibility, as a means of supplementing government accountability to parliament. However, managerialism provoked a reinterpretation of the office of ombudsman so that, for the job of investigating individual complaints, ombudsmen are now seen as a last resort—an external, second tier only to be engaged when internal, first-tier complaints procedures have failed to give satisfaction. In this managerialist interpretation, the ombudsman assumes the role of intermediary between complainant and agency, and the ultimate aim is to benefit both parties by providing satisfaction to the complainant in the form of either some action to remedy defective administration or (much more often) an explanation of the agency's action. Consistent with the 'last-resort' approach, public ombudsmen encourage agencies to establish effective internal complaints procedures, and provide guidance and assistance to this end.

---

9   McMillan, n 1 above, 9.

The creation of two-tier systems, in which both tiers perform an essentially similar function, inevitably raises the question of why two rather than one. This is a large topic that cannot be fully explored here. In relation to complaints, part of the answer probably lies in the fact of limited resources. Ombudsmen's offices have a financial incentive to encourage the creation of first-tier mechanisms and to divert to them as many complaints as possible, thus allowing the ombudsman to concentrate on more difficult cases and functions other than the handling of individual complaints (9.3.7).

It might be argued that a two-tier system made up of an internal and an external tier is better than a single internal tier because of the greater distance of the second tier from the decision-maker, and because of the opportunity the external tier would provide to check the output of the first tier and correct its mistakes. On the other hand, we might counter that a single external tier would be even better. The traditional arguments against this conclusion are to the effect that an internal complaint procedure is likely to be more accessible, less formal, and cheaper to operate than an external counterpart. In the absence of empirical evidence, such arguments are difficult to assess.

Not much can be said about the operation of internal complaint procedures within government agencies. Given the role of public ombudsmen in advising about and designing such mechanisms, it is perhaps safe to assume that the state of the art is represented by the *modus operandi* of ombudsmen's offices (9.3.5).

9.2.4 Internal review

In this context, 'review' means 'merits review'. Functionally, reconsideration is also a form of merits review even though conducted by the decision-maker, not a third party. The concept of merits review was explored in detail in Chapter 8 in relation to the AAT. It provides the basic model for review at all levels, including the internal.[10]

The sorts of issues about the design of complaint-handling systems discussed in 9.2.3 also arise in relation to systems for reviewing decisions. Here, however, the situation is even more complex. Internal complaint procedures are typically not required by statute, whereas internal review procedures are typically authorised by statute. Indeed, in the absence of statutory support, the finality principle would, in theory if not in practice, fatally undermine the efficacy of internal review. Not only is internal review typically statutory, but recourse to statutory internal review is typically a precondition of application for external review. Moreover, in some cases there are two tiers of external review, thus creating a three-tiered system. A fourth tier will be added if the decision is subject to reconsideration before internal review. Moreover, determinations by the second-tier, external reviewer may be subject to appeal or judicial (as opposed to merits) review by a court at the bottom of a three-tier hierarchy of courts. In theory, then, a decision could be subject to some form of reconsideration, review or appeal seven times![11] In practice, very few, if any, decisions would be so repeatedly scrutinised (although a significant number are, no doubt, considered three or four times). Nevertheless, the very existence of such a review skyscraper raises serious questions of institutional design that are rarely addressed except in areas of high political sensitivity, such as immigration. No particular tier deserves to exist unless it adds value to the review process.

---

10 But concerning the involvement of the applicant in internal reviews, see Administrative Review Council, *Internal Review of Agency Decision Making* (Report 44, 2000), paras 5.2–13.

11 Or even more if there are several tiers of internal review: ARC Report n 10 above, paras 3.37–49.

The relationship between internal and external review can be analysed by reference to the common statutory formula[12] that merits review should be 'fair, just, economical, informal and quick'.[13] This formula establishes two types of criteria, which we might dub 'legal' (the first two) and 'managerial' (the last three). The two sets of criteria are potentially in tension with one another: satisfaction of one set may compromise or jeopardise satisfaction of the other. It is generally assumed[14] that because external review is conducted at a greater distance from the original decision-maker than internal review, it is more likely than internal review to satisfy the legal criteria. Similarly, it is usually assumed that reviewers higher up the ladder are more likely to satisfy the legal criteria than the managerial, and that reviewers at lower levels are more likely to satisfy the managerial than the legal.

This approach suffers from a serious problem. While degrees of satisfaction of the managerial criteria (cost and speed, anyway) may be quantified reasonably easily, satisfaction of the legal criteria is much more difficult to measure in this way (and perhaps even to define). Moreover, while justice and fairness are not literally priceless or invaluable, it is not unreasonable to think (contrary to what this approach might suggest) that they are worth more than their purely financial cost. By setting more easily measured managerial criteria in competition with less easily measured legal criteria, the statutory formula arguably encourages establishment of (relatively informal, economical and quick) internal review mechanisms primarily as a filter to limit the caseload of (relatively formal, expensive and slow) external reviewers. It also encourages the creation of multi-tier systems of external (and internal) review so that (relatively informal, economical and quick) lower tiers can operate as filters to limit the caseload of (relatively formal, expensive and slow) higher tiers. Setting managerial criteria in competition with legal criteria encourages proliferation of complex, multi-tier systems of review primarily for financial reasons and regardless of whether the additional tiers add value or only save money.[15]

In its report on internal review,[16] the ARC identified various suggested disadvantages of internal review—which are disadvantages of multi-tier systems of review more generally. These include 'appeal fatigue': if an application for internal review is made a precondition (either formally or in effect) of applying for external review, a person who is unsuccessful internally may give up without making an application for external review. This is a bad thing if—as is commonly assumed—external review is more likely than internal review to produce the correct or preferable result. Some suggest that compulsory internal review may encourage primary decision-makers to decide in the applicant's favour in cases of doubt in order to avoid an internal review.[17] However, others argue that internal review gives decision-makers an incentive, in cases of doubt, to decide adversely to the applicant and in that way offload the problem onto the internal reviewer. Perhaps both effects occur. Either way, internal review provides decision-makers with an incentive to prefer the 'soft option', and this is seen to cast doubt on the idea that internal review can contribute[18] to improving the quality of primary decision-making (the 'normative effect'), especially in situations where primary decision-makers are inadequately trained and supported to perform an inherently difficult task.[19]

---

12   For example, *AAT Act*, s 2A.

13   Informality also implies easy accessibility. Concerning accessibility see ARC Report, n 10 above, Ch 4.

14   For instance, this assumption is the implicit approach of the ARC Report, n 10 above.

15   On the tension between value and cost see ARC Report n 10 above, paras 5.14–19.

16   See n 10 above. See also D Cowan and S Halliday, *The Appeal of Internal Review* (Oxford: Hart Publishing, 2003), 207–9.

17   ARC Report, n 10 above, paras 7.3–10.

18   More than external review: ARC Report, n 10 above, paras 3.34–6.

19   ARC Report, n 10 above, paras 7.11–13.

9.3 Ombudsmen

9.3.1 Introduction

The origins of the ombudsman are usually traced to an office created in Sweden in 1809. The idea did not take off in the English-speaking world until the mid-twentieth century. New Zealand (1962) and England (1967) led the way. Western Australia was the first local jurisdiction to create the office (in 1971). The office of the Commonwealth Ombudsman (CO) was established by the *Ombudsman Act 1976*.[20] Now there are ombudsmen everywhere. There is no standard model to which all conform. The following discussion emphasises distinctive characteristics of the office of ombudsman by analysing some key issues and themes in its development and operation. The CO will be used to illustrate some of the points to be made.

9.3.2 Constitutional and institutional location

The Kerr Committee recommended the creation of the office of 'General Counsel for Grievances' as an integral component of a set of institutions for controlling government activity.[21] As a 'grievance man', the counsel would complement courts and merits review tribunals by dealing with legitimate 'complaints against administration' regardless of whether the complaint would fall within the jurisdiction of a court or tribunal. The counsel was to be located 'within the system of administrative review rather than in the parliament-executive context'. In addition to recommending to an agency that remedial action be taken, the counsel (who would be a 'highly qualified member of the Bar') would also be empowered to assist complainants, in appropriate cases, to pursue the complaint in a court or tribunal.

On the advice of the Bland Committee,[22] the Kerr model, casting the counsel in the role of a sort of citizen's champion, was rejected in favour of one in which the ombudsman would act neutrally between complainant and agency. In other respects, however, the Kerr vision came to pass. Although ombudsmen are not required to have legal qualifications, many are lawyers, and promoting 'administrative law values' (such as legality and due process) is commonly considered to be an important role of ombudsmen.

Institutionally, ombudsmen are positioned somewhere between the executive and the legislature. Some ombudsmen are officers of parliament and their role is understood (like that of a public financial auditor) in terms of assisting and supplementing parliamentary oversight of the government. In this model (followed in England and New South Wales, for instance), parliament has a role in the appointment and funding of the ombudsman, and a parliamentary committee is charged with regularly supporting and overseeing the ombudsman's work. By contrast, in the Kerr/Bland model (which has been followed at the Commonwealth level), the ombudsman is an officer of a department of state (the Prime Minister's Department in the case of the CO). This is not to say that such an ombudsman has no links with parliament. The CO, for instance, appears as a witness before parliamentary committees, is

---

20   Referred to from here on as *Ombudsman Act*. 'Ombudsman' is a Swedish, gender-neutral word, and it is very difficult to use felicitously in English. A widely accepted plural form is 'ombudsmen' and, although this usage treats the word as masculine in gender, it will be adopted for convenience here.

21   Commonwealth Administrative Review Committee, *Commonwealth Administrative Review Committee Report*, Parliament of the Commonwealth of Australia Paper No 144 (1971) (Kerr Committee Report), Ch 15.

22   Interim Report of Committee on Administrative Discretions, 1973.

required to make an annual report to parliament, and receives some complaints indirectly via a member of parliament rather than directly from the complainant. But the CO lacks the protection and support that being an officer of the parliament could provide, especially (it is often said) in respect of the funding of the CO's office and in dealing with recalcitrant agencies.[23]

A parliamentary committee with responsibility for the ombudsman can also play a role in holding the ombudsman accountable for the way the office exercises its powers. It is sometimes suggested that because ombudsmen can only make recommendations, and have no determinative or coercive powers (9.3.8), there is less need (and it may be undesirable) for them to be subject to formal external accountability mechanisms.[24] Most investigations by ombudsmen are not publicly reported; ombudsmen typically cannot be sued unless they act in bad faith; ombudsmen's recommendations are not subject to merits review; and in some jurisdictions ombudsman are even protected from judicial review. Regardless of whether this situation is considered good or bad, it does represent a very significant point of distinction between ombudsmen and other public agencies.

Ombudsmen were originally established to deal with complaints against government agencies. Shifts of service delivery from governmental to non-governmental organisations have, to some extent, removed complaints about delivery of public services from the jurisdiction of ombudsmen.[25] At the same time, however, they have led to the creation of 'private ombudsmen' to handle complaints about services, such as telecommunications[26] and banking, the supply of which has been privatised. Unlike public ombudsmen, who hold statutory offices, private ombudsmen typically operate under contractual arrangements entered into by service deliverers among themselves. Unlike public ombudsmen, they often have coercive powers and may be empowered to resolve disputes about legal rights and obligations. However, because private ombudsmen frequently apply and enforce principles of good administration (such as due process and reason-giving) similar to those developed and applied by public ombudsmen, they can be understood as representing an extension of public law ideas, about proper relations between governors and the governed, to relations between private organisations and their customers or clients.

The ombudsman institution has spread even more widely to industries and activities that were never part of the public sector, being seen as an efficient and beneficial way of dealing with customers' complaints and of promoting and maintaining good customer relations.[27] As in the public sector, a significant advantage of an ombudsman over an internal complaints department is an element of distance and independence from the organisation. The following discussion focuses on public ombudsmen.

---

23   D Pearce, 'The Commonwealth Ombudsman: The Right Office in the Wrong Place' in R Creyke and J McMillan (eds), *The Kerr Vision of Australian Administrative Law—At the Twenty-Five Year Mark* (Canberra, Australian Institute of Administrative Law, 1998).

24   B Barbour, 'The Ombudsman and the Rule of Law' (2005) 44 *Australian Institute of Administrative Law Forum* 17, 24–5.

25   The jurisdiction of a public ombudsman may be extended to private organisations that deliver public services under contract to a governmental agency by (for instance) deeming delivery of the service by the contractor to be delivery by the agency. A public ombudsman may also be given jurisdiction directly over non-governmental organisations. For example, in New South Wales certain non-government organisations have an obligation to report to the ombudsman allegations of child abuse made against their employees.

26   A Stuhmcke, 'Privatising Administrative Law: the Telecommunications Industry Ombudsman Scheme' (1998) 6 *Australian Journal of Administrative Law* 15.

27   It has been argued that the term 'ombudsman' is overused and that its deployment should be regulated: J McMillan, 'What's in a Name? Use of the Term "Ombudsman"', <www.ombudsman.gov.au/files/22_April_2008_Whats_in_a_name_use_of_the_term_Ombuds an.pdf>.

9.3.3 Who can complain to an ombudsman?

The office of ombudsman was conceived in part as a way of improving 'access to administrative justice' for the ordinary citizen, especially the disadvantaged.[28] The typical user of ombudsman services is an individual, and a distinctive feature of ombudsman regimes is that the service is free to the complainant. Access is further facilitated by the absence of limitations equivalent to rules of standing (Chapter 6). However, ombudsmen have loosely structured[29] discretion not to investigate, or not to continue investigating, complaints that fall within their remit; and this discretion can be used to decline to investigate matters in which the complainant lacks sufficient interest.[30] It also allows ombudsmen to reject complaints on the ground that the complainant could and should have recourse to a more suitable avenue of redress, such as an internal complaints procedure or a tribunal;[31] or because too much time has elapsed since the complainant became aware of the action which is the subject of the complaint.[32] The discretion not to investigate (further) is one of the most distinctive characteristics of the institution of ombudsman. It gives ombudsmen a much greater degree of personal control over which cases they deal with than courts and tribunals typically enjoy.

9.3.4 What complaints can ombudsmen entertain?

Typically, public ombudsmen (like the Federal Court in its judicial review jurisdiction) may investigate complaints made against government agencies generally, subject to specific exceptions. Some exceptions (such as that protecting judges and courts) are common; but beyond a common core, the exceptions vary considerably from one jurisdiction to another, and not much more can be said than that they identify areas that particular governments want to immunise from the prying eyes of the ombudsman. Perhaps the most significant exception covers actions taken by ministers.[33] The make-up of the workload of particular ombudsmen will obviously depend on the powers of the relevant government. For instance, the bulk of complaints investigated by the CO relates to pensions and social welfare benefits, child support payments, taxation and immigration.

The standard phrase that defines the jurisdiction of public ombudsmen is 'action that relates to a matter of administration'.[34] The first thing to note is the word 'action', as opposed to 'decision' (as in the *AAT Act*) or 'decision' plus 'conduct' (in the *ADJR Act*). The use of this word forecloses many of the arguments about jurisdiction that plague judicial review in particular. In some jurisdictions, 'action' is

---

28   See, e.g., R Fitzgerald, 'ACOSS on the 20th Anniversary of the Commonwealth Ombudsman' in *Twenty Years of the Commonwealth Ombudsman, 1977–1997* (Canberra: Commonwealth Ombudsman's Office, 1997), 53.

29   The CO has a residual discretion not to investigate (further) if satisfied that (further) investigation is 'not warranted having regard to all the circumstances': *Ombudsman Act*, s 6(1)(b)(iii).

30   For example, *Ombudsman Act*, s 6(1)(b)(ii).

31   For example, *Ombudsman Act*, s 6(2), (3). In practice, failure by the complainant to raise the issue first with the relevant agency is the most important ground of refusal to investigate. Exercise by the CO of the discretion has increased greatly in recent years: A Stuhmcke, '"Each for Themselves" or "One for All"? The Changing Emphasis of the Commonwealth Ombudsman' (2010) 38 *Federal Law Review* 143.

32   Ibid, s 6(1)(a).

33   But this would not prevent investigation of actions of public servants in giving advice on which the minister acted: in the Commonwealth context see *Ombudsman Act*, s 5(3A).

34   D Pearce, 'The Jurisdiction of the Australian Government Ombudsman' in M Groves (ed), *Law and Government in Australia* (Sydney: Federation Press, 2005).

defined to include the making of a decision or recommendation, the formulation of a proposal, and failure or refusal to act. It is not clear whether the absence of such a provision leads in practice to a narrower interpretation of the ombudsman's powers.

Second, it should be noted that the action need not have been done 'under an enactment' (as in the *AAT Act* and the *ADJR Act*), but may have been an exercise of non-statutory power, or an action merely incidental to the exercise of a statutory or non-statutory power. This, too, forecloses many of the most problematic jurisdictional issues in the law of judicial and merits review. For instance, it brings within the jurisdiction of ombudsmen certain aspects of the contracting out of provision of public services—such as the contracting process itself—that courts typically cannot examine. The CO has express power to investigate complaints against entities that provide (outsourced) services to the public under a contract with a government agency.[35] Ombudsmen can also investigate the administration of what have become known as 'executive schemes'. This term refers to programs involving, for instance, the making of grants or payment of compensation in exercise not of statutory powers but of 'common law' or 'inherent' executive power.[36]

Third, it should be noted that the phrase 'relates to a matter of administration' has much broader connotations than the phrase 'of an administrative character' used in the *ADJR Act*.

The only phrase that has generated any real difficulty is 'a matter of administration'. An obvious point to make is that 'matter' as used here does not have the technical meaning that term bears in Chapter III of the Australian Constitution (3.4.1.3). 'Administration' implies a contrast with legislation and activities of legislatures on the one hand, and the exercise of judicial power by courts and (in the state context) tribunals on the other.[37] There are various statutory provisions and a small body of case law dealing with these boundaries,[38] but it is unclear how much difficulty they present in practice. There are several possible explanations for the relative dearth of reported litigation about the jurisdiction of ombudsmen. For one thing, when in doubt, an ombudsman may be inclined to exercise the discretion not to investigate, such a decision perhaps being less likely to be challenged than a decision to investigate. For another, because ombudsmen typically deal with complaints in a cooperative and consultative way (9.3.5), agencies may be less likely to take jurisdictional points than they would be if the process were more confrontational.

'Administration' may also be contrasted with 'policy'. Here it is necessary to distinguish between two senses of the word 'policy': it may refer to a general non-statutory norm or, alternatively, to an issue so politically controversial or sensitive that an official, such as an ombudsman, who is meant to be 'apolitical', should avoid 'taking sides' in relation to it.[39] The idea that ombudsmen should avoid investigating complaints that raise 'issues of policy' and should stick to 'matters of administration' must be referring to 'policy' in the second sense. It is widely accepted that ombudsmen legitimately investigate complaints about the application, and even the making and formulation, of general non-statutory norms. Indeed, an ombudsman may be explicitly empowered to recommend that such a norm be altered[40] if the

---

35   *Ombudsman Act*, s 3BA.

36   See, e.g., Commonwealth Ombudsman, *Executive Schemes*, Report 12/2009 (2009); *Putting Things Right: Compensating for Defective Administration*, Report 11/2009 (2009).

37   Concerning the administrative/judicial borderline see Commonwealth Ombudsman, *Commonwealth Courts and Tribunals: Complaint-Handling Processes and the Ombudsman's Jurisdiction*, Report No 12, 2007, especially paras 2.16–2.27.

38   See ibid, 114–21.

39   In this latter sense, a 'policy' is analogous to a 'non-justiciable' issue (3.5.2).

40   For example, *Ombudsman Act*, s 15(2)(d).

ombudsman considers it to be 'unreasonable, unjust, oppressive or improperly discriminatory'.[41] On the other hand, ombudsmen generally avoid making recommendations on matters thought to lie properly within the province of parliament's scrutiny of the executive. In this respect, ombudsmen march to the same beat as courts and tribunals. It is not only constitutionally proper but also pragmatically sensible for such bodies to avoid political controversy as far as possible.

Finally, we may contrast 'administrative' with 'commercial' matters. The jurisdiction of an ombudsman may extend to agencies (sometimes called 'government business enterprises' (GBEs)) that operate in market or quasi-market contexts, and such entities may seek to avoid investigation by the ombudsman by arguing that their activities are commercial, not administrative.[42] On the whole, ombudsmen have resisted such attempts to limit their jurisdiction, and have been prepared to investigate many of the activities of such agencies. As far back as 1991, a Senate review of the CO concluded that the ombudsman could play a useful role in relation to GBEs, and that this was recognised by GBEs themselves.[43]

9.3.5 How do ombudsmen handle complaints?

Ombudsmen typically have wide discretion as to the procedure for handling complaints.[44] Five procedural characteristics of ombudsmen's investigations of individual complaints[45] deserve mention. First, while courts and tribunals typically operate in public, ombudsmen conduct their investigations 'in private'.[46] The CO, for instance, is not required to give a hearing[47] to anyone except a person whom the CO proposes to criticise in a report.[48] The privacy of the CO's investigations is bolstered by general obligations of confidentiality imposed on the CO and other investigatory officers,[49] subject to specific exceptions.[50] Only relatively rarely do ombudsmen publish reports of investigations of individual complaints.[51] The confidentiality of ombudsmen's investigations seems designed primarily to shield activities of agencies, against which complaints are made, not only from public gaze but also from that of the complainant.

That 'justice' should be done openly is a cardinal legal value, and the fact that ombudsmen are required to operate privately suggests that they are better viewed as part of the administration than as part of the administrative justice system. It is true that hearings of the RRT, for instance, are held in private. It is also true that although the AAT holds most of its oral hearings in public, only a small proportion of reviews involve an oral hearing, and many applications are resolved as a result of private

---

41   Ibid, s 15(1)(a)(iii).

42   The CO, for instance, may decline to investigate a complaint about a 'commercial activity': *Ombudsman Act*, s 6(12).

43   Senate Standing Committee on Finance and Public Administration, *Review of the Office of the Commonwealth Ombudsman* (Canberra: AGPS, 1991).

44   For example, *Ombudsman Act*, s 8(2).

45   The following discussion does not concern conduct of own-motion investigations or inspectorial and auditing functions, although some of the points made are likely to be relevant in those contexts.

46   For a discussion of the meaning of this phrase in relation to the RRT see *SZAYW v Minister for Immigration and Multicultural and Indigenous Affairs* (2006) 229 ALR 423.

47   *Ombudsman Act*, s 8(4).

48   Ibid, s 8(5).

49   *Ombudsman Act*, s 35.

50   For example, *Ombudsman Act*, s 35A.

51   For various criticisms of the lack of reporting see H Selby, 'Ombudsman Inc: A Bullish Stock with a Bare Performance' (1989) 58 *Canberra Bulletin of Public Administration* 174, 176.

meetings and without a formal determination of the AAT. Nevertheless, the privacy principle that governs the operations of ombudsmen gives to this institution a very different complexion from that of more open mechanisms of accountability and review. It also raises questions about the accountability of ombudsmen because openness itself is an important aspect of accountability.

The second noteworthy characteristic of ombudsmen's procedure is that they investigate complaints inquisitorially. For this purpose, ombudsmen have strong powers at their disposal (the same as those of a royal commission) to compel the giving of evidence and the production of documents. Inquisitorial methods do not, as such, distinguish ombudsmen from courts and tribunals, some of which (can) operate more or less inquisitorially. More significant is the fact that ombudsmen typically have unrestricted access to relevant agency files. As a result, a complaint to an ombudsman is much more likely to uncover defects in administration than proceedings before a court or tribunal, in which access to government documents may be limited by rules of evidence (such as public interest immunity) and exclusions from freedom of information regimes (10.6.6). Access to agency files is undoubtedly a valuable dividend of privacy and confidentiality, without which much information and many documents would be unavailable to ombudsmen. Whether the dividend is worth the price must be a matter of judgment.

A third distinctive feature of the *modus operandi* of ombudsmen is its informality. Typically, complaints can be made by telephone or on the internet as an alternative to hard copy. Formal investigation occurs in only a relatively small proportion of complaints. Many are resolved orally by discussion between the ombudsman and the relevant agency without formal reports or recommendations for remedial action. One result is that many complaints can be resolved quickly.[52] Related to such informality is a fourth characteristic of ombudsmen's investigations, namely that complaints are often resolved by negotiation and compromise. In some cases, the ombudsman may act as a mediator between the complainant and the agency or refer the parties to an independent mediator.[53] More typically, where an ombudsman's investigation reveals that a complaint is justified, the process of resolution will involve identifying some remedial action that the ombudsman considers reasonable and the agency finds acceptable. Although ombudsmen operate within a framework of legal rules (see 9.3.6), they do not perform the judicial function of enforcing legal rights and obligations, but the non-judicial function of recommending and securing administratively workable remedies for legitimate grievances. This characteristic of ombudsmen is a practical corollary of their lack of coercive powers, which inevitably requires them to secure the cooperation of agencies in remedying justified complaints.

A risk inherent in the negotiatory style of complaint handling is 'capture' of the monitor by those required to give an account of themselves—'capture' in the sense of an undesirably close identification of the monitor with the ethos, concerns and values of those under scrutiny.[54] The possibility of capture does not, of course, demonstrate its realisation, but it does throw a great deal of weight on the personal capacity of the monitor to resist capture. This is especially troubling in the situation where the ombudsman is effectively chosen by an official of an agency subject to the appointee's oversight (the Prime Minister in the case of the CO).

---

52   In 2009–10, the CO resolved 77% of complaints and other matters within a month of receipt: *Annual Report 2009–10*, 23.

53   J R Taylor, 'The Role of Mediation in Complaints Handling: The Experience of the Office of the Commonwealth Ombudsman' in C Finn (ed), *Administrative Law for the New Millennium* (Canberra: Australian Institute of Administrative Law, 2000). Mediation is a form of alternative dispute resolution (ADR)—'alternative', that is, to (tripolar) adjudication.

54   A former CO has described ombudsmen's investigations as 'unthreatening': Pearce, n 34 above, 129. Some people think that the risk of capture is greater in the case of private-sector, as opposed to public, ombudsmen. Some even seek to restrict the use of the name 'ombudsman' to schemes that meet minimum criteria of independence, accessibility and so on.

A fifth characteristic is also related to the third and fourth. We might refer to it as the 'asymmetry' of ombudsmen's investigations. Court proceedings are symmetrical in that each of the disputing parties has an equally active part to play. In this respect, the AAT operates like a court. By contrast, proceedings before the SSAT and the RRT (for instance) are asymmetrical in that the agency plays a less active part than the applicant. Ombudsmen's investigations are also asymmetrical in that the centre of gravity of the process is in dealings between the ombudsman and the agency that marginalise the complainant. Crudely described, the ombudsman receives the complaint, talks to the agency about it and reports back to the complainant.[55] The ombudsman must inform the complainant of a decision not to investigate the complaint or to terminate the investigation, and give reasons for the decision. When an investigation is completed, the ombudsman must furnish the complainant with particulars of the investigation. But throughout, the complainant is passive except to the extent that the ombudsman chooses to involve them in the investigation.[56] In some cases, the ombudsman may bring the complainant and the agency into direct contact; but in most cases, it seems, the fate of the complaint depends primarily on negotiations between the ombudsman and the agency.[57] Unsurprisingly, perhaps, a significant majority of complaints is resolved favourably to the agency.[58] Because the ombudsman has a greater incentive to maintain good relations with agencies than with complainants, the process appears weighted against the latter.

9.3.6 The basis of ombudsmen's recommendations

The basis of judicial review is 'illegality'. Merits review is concerned not only with legality but also with ensuring that the correct or preferable decision is made (8.6). The basis on which ombudsmen can find a complaint to be justified and recommend remedial action is wider still. The principles applied by ombudsmen begin with, but are not exhausted by, the principles of judicial review and merits review.[59] In some jurisdictions, the ombudsman's particular concern is described as 'maladministration'. Making decisions that are illegal, or not correct or preferable, obviously amounts to maladministration. But this term may also encompass delay, rudeness, inefficiency, incompetence, and so on, regardless of whether they lead or are related to decisions that are illegal, or not correct or preferable. Indeed, the CO (for instance) has a residual power to recommend remedial action where of the opinion that the agency's action 'was otherwise, in all the circumstances, wrong'.[60] While the remedial powers of courts and tribunals are limited to enforcing the existing law, the CO can intervene, even when the conduct

---

55 This picture is reflected in complaint-handling guides for government agencies published by ombudsmen (which tend to be much more detailed than statements about how the ombudsman handles complaints): e.g. the section entitled 'How to Investigate a Complaint' in Ombudsman Victoria's *Good Practice Guide to Complaint Handling for Victorian Public Sector Agencies* (Nov 2007). Ombudsman Victoria's website describes the ombudsman's own procedures similarly, but much more briefly.

56 The CO, for instance, is subject to the *Freedom of Information Act 1982* (Cth), and receives a number of applications each year from complainants seeing information about the handling of their complaints. See CO, *Annual Report 2009–10*, 149.

57 This may help to explain why only 65% of a sample of complainants whose complaints were investigated by the CO expressed satisfaction with the service provided: CO, *Annual Report 2004–05*, 14.

58 For instance, in 2009–10, the CO identified 'some agency error or deficiency' in only 10% of cases: *CO, Annual Report 2009–10*, 20.

59 See, e.g., *Ombudsman Act*, s 15(1). For a general discussion see Administrative Review Council, *The Relationship between the Ombudsman and the Administrative Appeals Tribunal* (Report No 22, 1985), Ch 2.

60 *Ombudsman Act*, s 15(1)(a)(v).

complained of was in accordance with law, on the basis that the relevant law 'is or may be unreasonable, unjust, oppressive or improperly discriminatory' and should be altered.[61]

A good example of the scope of ombudsmen's remit is that they frequently secure remedies for false or misleading advice in cases where the law would not require the agency to act in accordance with its advice. Again, a former CO has expressed the view that, despite the fact that Australia lacks a bill of rights and that international human rights instruments have no direct legal force in Australia, ombudsmen can play an important role in promoting compliance by government agencies with human rights standards.[62]

It does not follow that a complaint would be found justified merely because the ombudsman thinks the agency should have behaved differently, any more than a merits review tribunal will find a decision not to be the preferable one merely because it disagrees with the decision-maker (8.6.4.3). A former CO has said that an ombudsman would recommend remedial action only if the decision was 'unsupportable'.[63] Moreover, a corollary of the negotiatory *modus operandi* of ombudsmen is a loosening of the relationship between grounds of justified complaint and exercise of the recommendatory power. While in the case of courts and tribunals, justified grievances will, in principle at least, attract a remedy and unjustified grievances will not, it is difficult to be confident of such a link, even in principle, between complaints to ombudsmen and remedial recommendations. A former CO once said that his office gave 'comparatively more emphasis to finding a practical solution and remedy to a problem than to passing judgment on whether the complaint arose from the fault of the agency or the misapprehension of the complainant'.[64]

9.3.7 What else can ombudsmen do?

The basic function of ombudsmen is to investigate and resolve individual complaints. Ombudsmen perform various other functions as well. These include 'own-motion' investigations—investigations, initiated by an ombudsman actively rather than in reaction to complaints, into matters the relevance of which extends beyond any one individual complaint and which, in that sense, raise 'systemic' issues. Own-motion investigations are the prime medium[65] through which ombudsmen can have a 'normative impact' on administrative practice. They typically generate formal reports, recommendations and guidelines that are of general relevance to dealings of government agencies with the public. In this way, ombudsman can (in theory at least) have much greater influence on the conduct of government business than courts or tribunals; and even, it is said, perform the role of educator, and management and

---

61   *Ombudsman Act*, s 15(1)(a)(iii) and 15(2)(d).

62   McMillan, n 1 above, 10–11; 'The Ombudsman's Role in Human Rights Protection—An Australian Perspective' <www.ombudsman.gov.au/files/2-5_November_2009_The_Ombudsmans_role_in_human_rights_protection_ an_Australian_perspective.pdf>. Under the *Charter of Human Rights and Responsibilities Act 2008* (Vic) the Victorian Ombudsman's remit expressly covers compliance of administrative action with human rights: A Stuhmcke, 'Australian Ombudsmen and Human Rights' (2011) 66 *AIAL Forum* 43.

63   D Pearce, 'The Commonwealh Ombudsman: Present Operation and Future Developments' (1990) 7 *Papers on Parliament* at p 6 (pages un-numbered).

64   CO, *Annual Report 2004–5*, 11. In 2004–05, the CO resolved 43% of complaints that were investigated without determining whether or not there had been defective administration: ibid, 19. In some cases this was because the problem was not in the service provided by the agency but in the law under which it operated. The emphasis on 'finding solutions and fixing problems, rather than laying blame or simply identifying error' seems set to continue: CO, *Annual Report* 2009–10, viii.

65   Investigation of complaints may also have normative relevance if they reveal problems that extend beyond the cases that generated the complaints.

risk consultant,[66] to the public service. Unlike courts and tribunals, ombudsmen can cultivate ongoing interactive relationships with government agencies, enabling them to monitor implementation of their recommendations in a way that courts and tribunals cannot.

Besides conducting investigations, ombudsmen may also be given power to supervise investigations of complaints by other bodies, such as internal police complaints units.[67] Controversy surrounds the role of ombudsmen in the investigation of complaints against police and security agencies, partly because they may involve allegations of corruption and criminal wrongdoing.

In principle, the investigatory functions of ombudsmen can be distinguished from the functions of auditing and inspecting the conduct of government business. In practice, however, this boundary has become blurred. Traditionally, auditors focused on financial accounting and probity, but increasingly in recent years have become involved in 'performance auditing',[68] which is effectively analogous to an ombudsman's own-motion investigation. Conversely, some ombudsmen have been given power to perform 'compliance audits', a sort of inspection function designed to monitor adherence by decision-makers to statutory requirements.

Opinions differ about the desirability of extending the role of ombudsmen beyond their core investigatory functions. Some see it as a sign of the success of the institution and a vote of confidence of sorts. A few even seem to favour the transformation of the ombudsman into a general auditor of government activity, complementary to the public financial auditor. Others worry that, without adequate resources, assumption of new tasks may be at the expense of the ombudsman's main business of investigating complaints,[69] or that some of the new functions may bring ombudsmen into dangerously political waters.

Because ombudsmen have a relatively high public profile, their offices tend to receive a significant number of inquiries about government and government services that are not specifically related to the ombudsman's official functions.[70] In this way, ombudsmen's offices may operate as a sort of citizens' advice bureau. It is sometimes suggested that the review and accountability system has become so complex that there needs to be a single point of entry for those wishing to make a complaint or seek review of a government decision, and that ombudsmen's offices might provide such a point. Without some advice, it is perhaps unlikely that the ordinary citizen will be able to find their way around the increasingly complex administrative justice system.

Finally, it is worth mentioning a point sometimes made in discussions of ombudsmen, namely that they play an important role not only in obtaining redress for complainants but also—and relatively much more often—in finding that the complaint is not justified and, in this way, 'legitimising' government processes.[71] This point is also sometimes made in the literature about judicial and merits review but more often, it seems, about ombudsmen. This may suggest that, on the spectrum between internal and external

---

66   D Pearce, 'The Ombudsman: Neglected Aid to Better Management' (1989) 48 *Australian Journal of Public Administration* 359.

67   See generally P Boyce, 'The Role of the Ombudsman in Oversighting Police Services' in M Barker (ed), *Appraising the Performance of Regulatory Agencies* (Canberra, Australian Institute of Administrative Law, 2004).

68   See, e.g., Auditor-General, *Centrelink's Review and Appeals System* (Audit Report No 35, 2004–05).

69   Stuhmcke, n 31 above; 'Changing Relations between Government and Citizen: Administrative Law and the Work of the Australian Commonwealth Ombudsman' (2008) 67 *Australian Journal of Public Administration* 321.

70   In 2009–10, 51% of the complaints and 'approaches' received by the CO were 'out of jurisdiction': CO, *Annual Report 2009–10*, 2.

71   'The rule of law is as much concerned with explaining to a person why an adverse decision was made and is unimpeachable as it is with examining whether a decision was legally proper. A chief responsibility of the Ombudsman's office is to discharge that mixture of functions in an integrated fashion': McMillan, n 1 above, 5.

accountability mechanisms, the ombudsman is perceived as being closer to the former than the latter pole. If this is right, it raises the issue of the independence of ombudsmen. Typically, ombudsmen are appointed for a (renewable) fixed term and can be removed from office only if the houses of parliament so resolve; and the ombudsman's salary is set by a body independent of government. But formal arrangements are only part of the story. Ombudsmen who are not officers of parliament often complain that the funding of their activities is unduly subject to the 'whim' of the government. Commentators often stress the heavy dependence of the success of the office on the willingness and ability of individual incumbents to deal robustly with government agencies, while ombudsmen stress the importance of cultivating the trust and cooperation of senior public servants. The emergent picture is of an institution kept on quite short leash, its continued flourishing perhaps unduly dependent on the good opinion of the very agencies it oversees.

9.3.8 The outcome of ombudsmen's investigations

Typically, courts have power to make coercive orders in support of conclusive determinations of legal rights and obligations. Merits review tribunals have power to determine legal rights and obligations, but not conclusively; nor can they make enforceable orders to give effect to such determinations. Ombudsmen have no power to make determinations of legal rights and obligations. All they can do is 'report' and make 'recommendations' to the agency against which the complaint was made. On the other hand, the power to make recommendations is typically very wide. For instance, the CO may recommend that some action should be reconsidered, or cancelled or varied; that something should be done to remedy the effects of some action; that reasons should have been (and should be) given for some action; that some statutory provision, legal rule or government practice, on which some action was based, should be altered; and that 'any other thing should be done in relation to a decision, recommendation, act or omission'.[72] If the ombudsman formally recommends that some action be taken but the recommendation is not implemented, the next step may be to make a special report to the minister under whose aegis the ombudsman operates (the Prime Minister in the case of the CO), or to parliament (in the first instance if the ombudsman is an officer of parliament), or both. Special reports are very rarely made. Informally, publicity is an important means by which an ombudsman can put pressure on a recalcitrant agency. However, the potential of publicity is limited by the confidentiality of the investigatory process and the importance to ombudsmen's success of maintaining ongoing relationships of trust and cooperation with the administration. On the other hand, a countervailing advantage of such relationships is that ombudsmen can monitor compliance over the longer term in a way not open to a court or tribunal.

An advantage of the very wide powers that ombudsmen have to make recommendations is that they may be able to craft remedies and achieve positive outcomes for complainants that a court or tribunal could not. This is partly because, although ombudsmen operate in a legal framework, their powers are not subject to the sorts of rule-based limitations that apply to courts and tribunals.[73] Ombudsmen can recommend actions that courts could not order—for example, an explanation or apology. Ombudsmen have proved particularly effective in securing the payment of monetary compensation for loss and damage caused by defective administration in circumstances where a court or tribunal could not. Ombudsmen can also recommend systemic change—such as the establishment

---

72   *Ombudsman Act*, s 15(2).

73   See McMillan n 1, 8–9.

or reform of a complaint-handling mechanism—of a sort that no court or tribunal could order. There seems little doubt that the non-coercive nature of ombudsmen's remedial powers partly explains why, in practice, they can secure systemic change, as well as remedial action for individual complainants, that other institutions of accountability cannot.

There is an ongoing debate about whether ombudsmen should be given power to make formal determinations, as opposed to recommendations, and to enforce those determinations, as opposed to reporting failure to comply to a higher authority. This is a pointless proposal because the nature of ombudsmen's remedial powers is integral to the institution. It would not be possible to alter this aspect of its operation successfully without redesigning the institution as a whole. To think of the ombudsman as a court or tribunal minus powers of determination and coercion is to misunderstand the nature of the office.

9.3.9 Conclusion

There are two different ways of understanding the role of the ombudsman as an accountability mechanism. The first involves viewing ombudsmen within a legal framework: just as merits review extends the boundaries of legal accountability beyond the sorts of errors and mistakes that principles of judicial review catch, so ombudsman review extends the limits of accountability even further to defects in administration that fall outside the remit of both courts and tribunals. From this perspective, we might think of ombudsmen, partly at least, as guardians and enforcers of essentially traditional 'legal' values of reasonableness, fairness and due process. So viewed, however, the location of the ombudsman firmly within the executive branch, and the ongoing, interactive relationships of trust and cooperation that underpin ombudsmen's success, seem antithetical to concepts of the rule of law on which legal accountability of government is traditionally based.

Ombudsmen may alternatively be understood as part of a system of political accountability centred on parliament. However, the nature of the relationships that ombudsmen (need to) cultivate with government agencies may seem problematic from this perspective as well. Successful parliamentary scrutiny of the executive depends on the maintenance of a degree of adversariness in the relationship between overseer and overseen, whereas the structure of the institution of the ombudsman seems designed to make it more or less difficult for such a relationship to develop and be maintained between ombudsman and government.

Perhaps the best way to understand and assess the ombudsman is not by comparison with other institutions of accountability, but in its own terms as a general government complaints department. So viewed, the role of the ombudsman is to satisfy complainants by convincing agencies of the value of satisfying their 'customers'. This approach makes sense of much of the rhetoric that surrounds the activities of ombudsmen, no matter how alien it may be to the vision of the founders of the ombudsman institution (9.3.2). We might construct a sort of balance sheet of the main structural features of the ombudsman institution that are likely to promote, on the one hand, complainant satisfaction and, on the other, agency cooperation. Features on the one side might include service free of charge; ombudsmen's more-or-less unfettered access to departmental files; remedial flexibility; wide grounds of investigation extending beyond legality and merits of decisions; and reasonable security of tenure and salary for office-holders. Features on the other side might include privacy and confidentiality of investigations; passivity of complainant and ombudsmen's control over the investigation; negotiatory style of investigations; and ombudsmen's lack of determinative and coercive power, and relative lack of accountability to bodies outside the government.

Such an approach provides a nuanced and realistic understanding of the office of public ombudsman, while at the same time suggesting that the ombudsman's role is less constitutionally (although not less practically) significant than that of bodies, such as courts and tribunals, that maintain greater distance from government and are better equipped to 'keep it honest'. However, not everyone agrees with this assessment. In a comment on the last paragraph of 9.3.7 above and this paragraph (as they appeared in the first edition), the then-CO, Professor John McMillan, said that the views there expressed fail to 'comprehend the way that Ombudsman offices … relate to government and impact upon it … Many Ombudsmen in Australia have a relatively high public profile that derives from their forthright criticism of agency maladministration … and … many have encountered direct agency displeasure at the stance they have taken.'[74]

9.4 Parliaments

As a crude generalisation, we can say that the centre of gravity of all the review and complaint mechanisms we have discussed so far is the individual grievance. By contrast, the centre of gravity of oversight of government by parliament is, we might say, the public interest or, at least, the interests of groups rather than individuals. For this reason, it focuses more on improving administrative systems and practices than rectifying mistakes—on large-scale rather than small-scale issues.

The same point is sometimes made by saying that whereas courts, tribunals and so on are concerned with 'justice to the individual', parliaments are concerned with 'distributive justice'. Related distinctions—between 'law' and 'policy', 'administrative functions' and 'legislative functions', 'matters of administration' and 'matters of policy', and so on—have run through this book and are recurring themes. However problematic such contrasts may be, they deeply colour all thinking about administrative law and justice.

9.4.1 Constitutional background

As we saw in Chapter 2, a key event in the history of Australian administrative law was the development of 'responsible government' in the various colonies. The phrase 'responsible government' refers to what is alternatively called 'Westminster-style' or 'parliamentary' government. It can be contrasted with 'presidential' government, of which the US system provides the most pertinent example. By the time the founders of Australian federation met to draft a constitution in the 1890s, responsible government was firmly established in Australia. Despite the significant influence of US constitutional theory and practice on the formulation of the Australian Constitution (especially in relation to separation of powers), the High Court has formally affirmed that the Australian Commonwealth is built on a system of responsible government.[75]

The key conceptual feature of responsible government is integration (as opposed to separation) of the legislative and executive branches of government. Such integration is a corollary of fact that elected ('political') members of the executive branch[76] are elected not as members of that branch

---

74   J McMillan, 'Ten Challenges for Administrative Justice' (2010) *61 AIAL Forum* 23, 32.

75   *Victorian Stevedoring and General Contracting Co Ltd v Dignan* (1941) 46 CLR 73.

76   As opposed to appointed members of the Australian Public Service (APS)—'public servants'.

but as members of the legislature (that is, 'parliament'). They become members of the executive by appointment according to constitutional conventions regulating their selection. Being members of the legislature, they are (collectively and individually) 'responsible' to the legislature for the performance of their functions as members of the executive, both personally and through the agency of members of the 'bureaucratic' executive (public servants).[77] It is by virtue of its function of scrutinising the executive in accordance with the logic of responsible government that parliament finds its place among the institutions of accountability and review with which this book is concerned. The other main function of parliaments (acting in concert with an official such as the Governor-General of Australia) is to confer the technical imprimatur of 'Act of Parliament' on Bills for legislation, most of which are promoted by the executive. It does this in accordance (typically) with the principle of majority voting and, in jurisdictions with a bicameral parliament, rules about the respective powers of, and relations between, the two houses.

In very broad terms, the executive performs three functions: making proposals for and formulating 'primary' legislation, formulating and making 'delegated' (or 'secondary') legislation and conducting the administration of government ('running the country'). We will say something in turn about parliamentary scrutiny of each of these broad functions.

9.4.2 Legislation

Primary legislation is legislation made by the legislature—'Acts of Parliament' or, less formally, 'statutes'. Proposals for legislation (Bills) are typically developed by Cabinet, ministers of state and public servants in consultation with the government's political party, with members of the public—most often through the medium of interest groups and other community representatives and organisations—and with other relevant organisations (such as foreign governments). Bills are typically drafted by a specialist section within the public service, in consultation with the relevant government department. The process of developing and drafting proposals for primary legislation is more or less unregulated by law. It is under the control of the government and much of it takes place out of sight of the public and of parliament.

Parliament as such normally enters the picture only when a draft Bill is presented. Bills may be considered in some detail by a parliamentary committee and may be the subject of more or less extensive discussion on the floor of the parliament. Members of the public may seek to influence members of parliament (MPs) in their consideration of the Bill, and MPs may make informal representations to the government about the content of the Bill. As a result of all this, the draft Bill may be amended or even, in truly exceptional circumstances, withdrawn for reconsideration. The ability of parliament and MPs to exert influence and secure amendments at this late stage depends crucially on the balance of the political parties in the legislature: the greater the risk that a legislative proposal may not be approved by one or other of the houses (typically the upper house),[78] the greater the government's incentive to agree to amendments perceived to be necessary to secure passage of the legislation in a form acceptable to the government.

---

77   A live issue in recent times has been the accountability of, and of the responsibility of ministers for, so-called 'ministerial advisers'. See M Keating, 'In the Wake of "A Certain Maritime Incident": Ministerial Advisers, Departments and Accountability' (2003) 62(3) *Australian Journal of Public Administration* 92.

78   For a useful account of the importance of upper houses in the Australian version of responsible government see B Stone, 'Bicameralism and Democracy: The Transformation of Australian Upper Houses' (2002) 37 *Australian Journal of Political Science* 267.

On the whole, the ability of parliaments to affect the content of primary legislation is very limited. In constitutional terms, we can say that, although, in theory, our system of government is both 'responsible' and 'representative', the practices by which primary legislation is made are predominantly bureaucratic and consultative. Parliament does not play a central role in the system of accountability for the making of primary legislation. Nor do courts, tribunals or ombudsmen. Public opinion, expressed formally through elections and informally through the media and in other ways, provides the main forum in which a government's legislative program is judged. Once on the statute book, primary legislation may be subject to legal scrutiny to enforce constitutional limitations on the powers of the legislature; but such *ex post facto* scrutiny takes place, as it were, only at the tip of the iceberg. It is of much less importance in Australia than in many other countries because we have no constitutionally entrenched bill of rights.

9.4.3 Delegated legislation

Primary legislation is legislation made by the legislative branch of government. Delegated legislation is legislation made in the exercise of powers to make legislation delegated by statute to an elected member of the executive branch of government, to a local government authority or to some other government (or, occasionally, non-government) agency.[79] In the phrase 'delegated legislation', 'legislation' refers to instruments that go under a bewildering variety of names, including 'regulations', 'orders', 'ordinances', 'by-laws' and 'rules'.

Delegated legislation should be distinguished from what may be called 'quasi-legislation'[80] or 'soft law'—commonly also referred to as 'policy' in the sense of non-statutory general rules (discussed in 5.3.3, 8.6.3 and 9.3.4). The crucial distinction between these two categories is that soft law, unlike delegated legislation, is not made in exercise of a statutory power *to make legislation*. The italicised words are very important. Much soft law is an incidental by-product of the exercise of statutory powers to make decisions (as opposed to legislation). Just as courts may make law in the process of adjudicating disputes, so officials may make general rules (very often called 'policies') in the process of making individual decisions. Such rules do not count as delegated legislation, so they are not binding in the way delegated legislation is: whereas delegated legislation, like primary legislation, must be 'applied', soft law need and must only be 'taken into account'. Nor are they subject to controls that apply only to delegated legislation.

Delegated legislation may be the product of consultative processes similar to those by which primary legislation is produced.[81] By contrast, the processes by which soft law is produced are typically

---

79   As a general rule, a power to make delegated legislation may not be 'subdelegated' by the delegate. This does not mean, of course, that other people may not assist the delegate in formulating and drafting delegated legislation; but the delegate must 'sign off' the process. Whether the delegate must personally do any more than this is unclear. Despite the adjective 'delegated', it is more accurate to say that the legislature confers on administrators power to make legislation than that it delegates its own power to administrators.

80   But note that this term is sometimes used in the sense of delegated legislation that is not subject to parliamentary scrutiny: e.g. D Pearce and S Argument, *Delegated Legislation in Australia*, 3rd edn (Sydney: LexisNexis Butterworths, 2005), paras [1.12]–[1.17].

81   However, in the case of delegated legislation there is no equivalent to the Bill stage. On the other hand, a delegated legislator may be required by law to consult. For instance, the *Legislative Instruments Act 2003* (Cth) (hereafter '*LI Act*') imposes a general obligation to undertake 'appropriate' and 'reasonably practicable' consultation (s 17). Failure to do so does not affect the validity or enforceability of the legislation (s 19). Where the relevant legislation does not specify the effect of failure to comply with an obligation to consult this will be for a court to decide: *Delegated Legislation in Australia*, [13.20]. The SSCRO (see text to note 84 below) has expressed various concerns about the operation of the consultation provisions of the *LI*: SSCRO, *Consultation under the* Legislative Instruments Act 2003, Interim Report (113th Report, 2007).

less consultative and less public than this. Like primary legislation, delegated legislation (and soft law) may be subject to judicial scrutiny to test its compatibility with constitutional limitations on the powers of its authors. Unlike primary legislation, delegated legislation (and soft law) may be subject to judicial review for consistency with principles of administrative law.[82] However, judicial review under the *ADJR Act* (unlike judicial review at common law, and under Constitution s 75(v) and *Judiciary Act*, s 39B) is limited to 'decisions of an administrative character', and this phrase has been read as implying a contrast with conduct of a legislative nature (3.5.1.4). The prevailing view is that merits reviewers have no power to set aside a decision on the ground that the provision (whether in primary or delegated legislation) on which it was based was unconstitutional or unlawful (8.5.1.1, n 52). The extent to which merits review can reach soft law is a difficult and complex issue (8.6.3). The jurisdiction of ombudsmen is defined in terms of 'matters of administration' (9.3.4); but this must be read subject to the power to recommend that a rule of law, a provision of an enactment or a practice on which the complained of action was based be altered on the ground that it is 'unreasonable, unjust, oppressive or improperly discriminatory'.[83]

It would seem to follow from the principle of responsible government that parliament should play an active part in scrutinising the making of *delegated* legislation on the basis that the delegate is exercising power conferred by the legislature. However, this raises a serious problem because there is much more delegated than primary legislation. Moreover, one of the main justifications for delegation of legislative powers is to supplement the law-making resources of parliament. So how can parliament realistically be expected to exercise a reasonable level of scrutiny over delegated legislation? The typical solution is to allocate this task to a committee, such as the Standing Committee on Regulations and Ordinances of the Australian Senate (SSCRO).[84]

Even so, there is significant room for doubt about the efficacy of the 'solution'. Membership of such committees is, of course, only a part-time job (MPs have many other tasks besides committee membership); and the SSCRO, for instance, considers more than 1500 pieces of delegated legislation each year. Scrutiny committees typically consider delegated legislative instruments that are required by statute to be tabled in parliament and which parliament must expressly approve or which it may 'disallow'.[85] At the Commonwealth level, the *LI Act* provides that all 'legislative instruments' as defined in the Act must be registered in a public register, then laid before parliament. Notice of a motion to disallow an instrument[86] may be given within 15 sitting days of tabling.

There are basically two ways of defining the class of instruments to which such requirements apply. The traditional method is by reference to what the instrument is called (for example, 'regulations'). The advantage of this method is clarity. Its disadvantage is that, unless the relevant power to make legislation is expressed to be exercisable only by making an instrument of the specified type, the maker can determine whether or not the requirements for tabling, and so on, apply to the instrument simply by choice of name. The *LI Act* adopts a different basic approach. It applies to 'legislative instruments'.

---

82   For detailed consideration see *Delegated Legislation in Australia*, Chs 12–32.

83   For example, *Ombudsman Act*, ss 15(1)(a)(iii) and 15(2)(d).

84   See generally *Delegated Legislation in Australia*, Chs 1–11. A scrutiny of bills committee may play a part by identifying proposed provisions of primary legislation that are considered to delegate excessively wide powers to legislate. Upper houses of parliament tend to take the lead in scrutinising delegated legislation.

85   The former—and much less common—approval option obviously gives parliament a greater role and responsibility than the latter, typical, disallowance option. Moreover, because delegated legislation typically comes into force before being scrutinised by parliament, individuals may be adversely affected by the implementation of provisions that are later disapproved or disallowed.

86   Except an exempt instrument: *LI Act*, s 44.

A legislative instrument (LI) is defined as an instrument 'in writing' that is 'of a legislative character' and 'made in exercise of a power delegated by Parliament'. However, the Act (in s 6) also 'declares' certain instruments to be LIs (for example, instruments described as 'regulations' by the enabling legislation); and (in s 7) declares certain other instruments not to be LIs. The effect of s 6 is to dispense with the requirement that the instrument be of a legislative character. An instrument is of a legislative character if it 'determines the law or alters the content of the law rather than applying law in a particular case' and 'it has the … effect of affecting a privilege or interest, imposing an obligation, creating a right, or varying or removing a right or obligation'. The leading Australian text on delegated legislation describes this test (perhaps with an element of understatement) as 'not necessarily simple [to apply] or logical'.[87] This is a matter of no little importance, since failure to comply with the requirements of the Act may render an instrument unenforceable (*LI Act*, ss 31, 32). It is said that the test will 'greatly increase the workload' of the SSCRO by bringing many more instruments than formerly within its jurisdiction.[88] The Act came into force only in 2005, and the SSCRO has not (as at July 2012) reported generally on its activities since then; so we do not know whether this prediction will be proven true.

The function of a scrutiny committee is to identify instruments that, by reason of falling foul of one or more criteria, seem suitable candidates for non-approval or disallowance. These criteria vary from one jurisdiction to another. A common core includes the following: that the instrument interferes unduly with rights or liberties;[89] that it is not within the powers or objects of the enabling legislation; and that it deals with matters more appropriately dealt with by primary legislation.[90] The SSCRO applies an additional criterion requiring adequate provision for merits review of decision-making powers conferred by the instrument.[91] It is said that these criteria are concerned with 'technical' matters rather than the policy or merits of the instrument. However, this distinction is not easy to draw. In what sense, for instance, is 'undue interference with rights or liberties' a technical matter? The distinction is made because it is said that the proper place for matters of policy to be raised is on the floor of the parliament, not in committee. However, unless a scrutiny committee questions a piece of delegated legislation, it is extremely unlikely that any other MP will.[92]

In practice, no doubt, it is strategically sensible for scrutiny committees to operate on a bipartisan basis and avoid party political controversy. The distinction between technical and policy matters provides a convenient rationale for such a strategy. At all events, relatively very few delegated legislative instruments fail to pass muster. For instance, in 2003–04 the SSCRO considered 1561 instruments and identified only 121 that raised 'concerns'.[93] Only 18 notices of motion to disallow were given: most concerns are resolved informally as a result, for example, of a minister 'undertaking' to act to meet the

---

87   *Delegated Legislation in Australia*, [2.5]. In 2008 a review committee recommended that the definition of 'legislative instrument' be amended in various respects: Legislative Instruments Act Review Committee, *2008 Review of the Legislative Instruments Act 2003* (2009), Ch 1.

88   *Delegated Legislation in Australia*, [2.28].

89   Concerning scrutiny for compliance with human rights see above 5.4.6, n 40 and text.

90   Ibid, [11.6]. The first criterion is of particular significance in jurisdictions—Victoria and the Australian Capital Territory—that have statutory bills of rights.

91   Ibid, [2.17].

92   The size of this problem is unclear. On the one hand, it is often said that governments have a tendency to seek to avoid parliamentary scrutiny of policy by omitting potentially contentious matters from primary legislation and leaving them to be dealt with by delegated legislation. On the other hand, it is also said that relatively little delegated legislation is politically contentious. For detailed discussion see S Argument, 'Legislative Scrutiny in Australia: Wisdom to Export?' (2011) 32 *Statute Law Review* 116.

93   SSCRO, *40th Parliament Report* (PP 141 of 2005), p 15.

concern. An incentive to pursue this latter course is that the notice of motion process typically does not permit an instrument or a provision in an instrument to be amended—the instrument can only be disallowed *in toto*.

9.4.4 Administration

This is a residual category covering all government conduct that does not fall within the description of legislation or delegated legislation. Administration is the field of parliamentary scrutiny that overlaps most with the domain of the other institutions we have considered. Four mechanisms deserve brief mention: debates, questions, committee inquiries and representations by MPs.

9.4.4.1 Debates and motions

Control of the business of parliament is dominated by the government. However, there are various opportunities within the framework of the parliamentary timetable—such as adjournment debates and debates on matters of public interest—for the opposition to raise matters in the hope, perhaps, of embarrassing the government into providing information and explanation and even taking appropriate action.

In extreme situations, notice may be given of a motion to censure the government or a minister, or even to express 'no confidence' in the government. A censure motion by itself is unlikely to lead to the resignation of a minister (let alone a government), but may play a part, along with other pressures, to inflict considerable, if not fatal, political damage. A motion of no confidence in a government, if passed, should lead to the resignation of the whole government. Such a motion is unlikely to be passed if the government has a majority in the so-called 'house of government' (the house the support of which is needed to form a government—the lower house in a bicameral parliament, as opposed to the upper, so-called 'house of review'). Motions of censure against ministers are similarly unlikely to be passed if the government has a majority. If the government does not control the house of review (as was the case at the federal level throughout the 1980s and 1990s) a minister who sits in that house may be the subject of a successful censure motion; but its impact is likely to be slight.

9.4.4.2 Questions

Questions (and answers) are of two types: with notice (written) and without notice (oral). Questions play a more important role in the house of government than in the house of review simply because most ministers (to whom questions are normally addressed) will be members of the former, not the latter. The stated purposes of questions are to elicit information and to influence government conduct. In practice, oral questions—which are asked at question time—are often used for political point-scoring. A study of question time in the House of Representatives argued that oral questions are relatively ineffective as an accountability mechanism and suggested three explanations: evasive answers; partiality in the management of question time by the Speaker of the house (who is a member of the majority party and chairs question time); and planted questions from government back-benchers.[94]

---

94   P Rasiah, 'Does Question Time Fulfil its Role of Ensuring Accountability?' (2006), <http://democratic.audit.anu.edu.au>, accessed October 2006.

A problem that afflicts both types of question is that ministers are required to answer only questions that relate to matters for which they are 'responsible'. The vagueness of this term provides ample opportunity to find reasons not to answer questions. Changes in the way public services are delivered have had an impact on this as on other accountability mechanisms. Privatisation obviously removes activities from the scope of formal ministerial responsibility, and contracting out will at least limit its scope.[95] Moreover, many public functions are performed by quasi-autonomous agencies (for example, service providers such as Centrelink, and regulators such as the Australian Competition and Consumer Commission) that operate outside the traditional departmental structure of government by reference to which ideas of responsibility have traditionally been elaborated.

Ministers may also try to avoid answering questions about conduct of public servants working within the departmental structure by arguing that their responsibility extends only to what they personally do, and not what is done on their behalf. Taken too far, this argument has the potential to reshape the traditional relationship between parliament and government radically. It perhaps rests on a legalistic understanding of the concept of 'responsibility' as being analogous to 'liability'. If so, it is not surprising that ministers want to minimise its scope and reject any idea that they can be vicariously responsible for the shortcomings of their public servants. But political responsibility is not only, or even primarily, about blame. It is also about openness and explanation and a willingness to eliminate bad practices and improve inefficient systems. It would not be reasonable to hold a minister personally to blame for everything done in their department, let alone by non-departmental bodies operating in the same policy area. It does not follow, however, that the scope of responsibility in this narrow sense should also mark the boundary of the obligation to answer questions and to provide information and explanations reasonably available to the minister about the conduct of public business related to their portfolio, or of the obligation to take remedial measures—which may include securing the resignation of someone who is personally responsible.

It may be that developments in administrative law in the past four decades have encouraged changed attitudes to the responsibility of ministers for the activities of their departments. For instance, a senior judge has argued that the 'new administrative law' (judicial review, merits review, ombudsmen, freedom of information and so on) has led to the creation of a system of 'administrative responsibility' of the bureaucratic executive parallel to the 'political responsibility' of the political executive.[96] The basic idea seems to be that while it is the job of parliament and other political institutions to hold ministers personally and publicly accountable, courts, tribunals and so on can and do hold individual bureaucrats personally and publicly accountable.

This approach compounds the mistake involved in thinking about individual ministerial responsibility primarily in terms of personal fault. Government is best understood not as a collection of individuals, but as a complex corporate entity separate from its members and employees.[97] The remedies for individual grievances that are provided by courts, tribunals, ombudsmen and so on typically do not target individuals within the corporation, but the corporation itself. It is the role of those who manage

---

95   For an excellent discussion see R Mulgan, 'Government Accountability for Outsourced Services' (2006) 65(2) *Australian Journal of Public Administration* 48 arguing that, although outsourcing and privatisation may enable individual ministers to evade formal responsibility, political pressures may operate informally to force the government as a whole to accept 'corporate responsibility' for the way privatised industries are regulated and outsourced services delivered.

96   J J Spigelman, 'Foundations of Administrative Law: Toward General Principles of Institutional Law' (1999) 58(1) *Australian Journal of Public Administration* 3, 7–8.

97   R Mulgan, 'On Ministerial Resignations (and the Lack Thereof)' (2002) 61(1) *Australian Journal of Public Administration* 121.

the corporation to take appropriate measures to determine and enforce the personal responsibility of its agents. The main role of ministers is to manage the affairs of the government corporation, not personally to conduct them. Far from devaluing ministerial responsibility, this corporate model makes very clear its continuing significance by realistically clarifying the tasks for which ministers must take responsibility, and by showing that the administrative law system in no way relieves ministers of their managerial responsibilities.

9.4.4.3 Committee inquiries

The main effective function of lower houses is to provide a forum for political contestation, and to maintain and support the government and legitimise its legislative program. The use of parliamentary committees to scrutinise government activity is primarily associated with upper houses. For instance, since 1970[98] the Australian Senate has had a system of scrutiny committees that perform three main functions: inquiries directed at the policy of Bills;[99] examination of budget 'estimates'—proposals for government expenditure—and departmental reports;[100] and investigations of aspects of government administration.[101] A fourth, and increasingly significant, function of committees is to oversee the work of independent accountability institutions, such as auditors, ombudsmen and anti-corruption investigators.[102]

The ability of committees to turn a spotlight on government activity depends to a considerable extent on whether the government controls the upper house. For example, after gaining control of the Senate in 2005 the Howard federal government changed the committee system from one in which the opposition parties formed the majority on certain committees, which were also chaired by a member of an opposition party, to one in which the government has a majority on, and chairs, all committees. But even when the government does not control the upper house, the effectiveness of committees in scrutinising government depends to a significant extent on the government's cooperation in providing information and allowing ministers and public servants to appear before committees to be questioned.

9.4.4.4 Grievance-handling by members of parliament (MPs)

Although most complaints to ombudsmen are made directly by the complainant, ombudsmen also receive some complaints indirectly via MPs rather than directly from the complainant. Handling of constituents' grievances is a traditional role of MPs. Indeed, one of the arguments against the establishment of the office of ombudsman was that it would interfere with the performance of this function. We are surprised, therefore, that we have been unable to find in the Australian literature any significant discussion of, or research into, this topic.[103]

---

98   But the original predecessor of the SSCRO was established in 1932.

99   To be distinguished from 'technical' scrutiny of bills by a scrutiny of bills committee. For an excellent discussion of the role of such scrutiny committees in relation to human rights see C Evans and S Evans, 'Legislative Scrutiny Committees and Parliamentary Conceptions of Human Rights' [2006] *Public Law* 785.

100   For discussion of this process in the Australian Senate see PG Thomas, 'Parliament Scrutiny of Government Performance in Australia' (2009) 68 *Australian Journal of Public Administration* 373. See also J Halligan, R Miller and J Power, *Parliament in the Twenty-First Century: Institutional Reform and Emerging Roles* (Melbourne: Melbourne University Press, 2007).

101   Mention should also be made of accounts committees, the role of which is to monitor the work of public financial auditors.

102   See, e.g., G Griffith, *Parliament and Accountability: The Role of Parliamentary Oversight Committees* (NSW Parliamentary Library Research Service, Briefing Paper 12/05).

103   For some English research see R Rawlings, 'The MP's Complaints Service' (1990) 53 *Modern Law Review* 149.

9.4.4.5 Sanctions

Sanctions and, in particular, ministerial resignation loom large in discussions of responsible government and the role of parliament as an accountability institution. It is often implied that there was a golden age in which ministers regularly resigned not only for personal wrongdoing (such as financial impropriety and lying to parliament), but also for policy failures and administrative inefficiency. Just as frequent are denials that there was any such golden age.[104]

Part of the problem here is that ministerial responsibility is a matter of conventional practice, not formulated rules. More fundamentally, however, to judge parliamentary accountability in these terms is to treat it as a legal rather than a political mechanism. Legal institutions can impose sanctions because they have a certain sort of authority. The language of politics and political accountability is power and persuasion, not authority and coercion. To the extent that parliaments can secure ministerial resignations (and typically parliamentary pressure will be only one of several contributory factors), they can do so only by deploying political power—they have no authority over governments. Here lies the most fundamental difference between legal and political accountability.[105] Lack of formal sanctions is not a contingent defect of political accountability, but an inherent characteristic.

9.4.5 The relationship between parliament and other accountability mechanisms

How does parliament interact with other accountability institutions? By virtue of the doctrine of separation of powers, courts and tribunals operate quite independently of parliaments. This is true even of federal merits tribunals, despite their association with the executive branch of government. Members of courts and tribunals are typically appointed by or on the advice of the executive, not by parliament; and typically they do not report to parliament. The main link between courts and parliaments is found in procedures for the removal of judges from office, which typically requires parliament's consent.

We have seen that the relationship between public ombudsmen and parliament is a central issue in the design of the ombudsman institution (9.3.2). A theme of writings by Australian ombudsmen is the general and regrettable lack of interest in and support for their work on the part of MPs. Although Australian public ombudsmen report to parliament, most are not 'officers' of parliament, and in most jurisdictions, there is no parliamentary committee with responsibility to oversee the work of the ombudsman. A contrast can be drawn with the office of public auditor, a role to which ombudsmen increasingly aspire. At the Commonwealth level, for instance, the Auditor-General is an 'independent officer of parliament'[106] and reports to parliament. Parliament plays a role in appointing the auditor, and the Joint Committee of Public Accounts and Audit oversees and supports the work of the auditor. Funding for the audit office is guaranteed by statute.[107] The strengthening of the link between the Auditor-General and parliament by the enactment of the *Auditor-General Act* in 1997 was a response to

---

104 A useful discussion is E Thompson and G Tillotson, 'Caught in the Act: the Smoking Gun View of Ministerial Responsibility' (1999) 58(1) *Australian Journal of Public Administration* 48.

105 And, incidentally, an explanation of why ombudsmen are not best understood as institutions of legal accountability.

106 *Auditor-General Act 1997* (Cth), s 8.

107 Ibid, s 50.

a report by the Joint Committee of Public Accounts (as it then was), which in turn was triggered by an annual report of the Auditor-General criticising the inadequate funding of his office.[108]

These events suggest that, although in some respects parliaments may appear to be relatively ineffectual overseers of government activity, they are not impotent. Indeed, a former Clerk of the Commonwealth Senate has argued that 'accountability relies ultimately on the political process' of which parliament is the 'principal forum'.[109] Even if you think that this argument exaggerates the centrality of parliament, it usefully emphasises the value of political support—of a sort that parliaments may provide—to supposedly apolitical accountability mechanisms. The Clerk cites the case of the Auditor-General to illustrate the point. It is true even of courts: witness the concern of judges when it is suggested that they must defend themselves against public criticism and should not rely on an Attorney-General to stand up for the courts. The unease of ombudsmen about their relationship with parliament reflects the relatively weak political support that their offices typically receive. Parliament is a high-profile player in the political process, the general value of which exceeds the efficacy of its specific procedures for holding governments accountable.

---

108   P Nicoll, *Audit in a Democracy: The Australian Model of Public Sector Audit and its Application in Emerging Markets* (Aldershot: Ashgate, 2005), 13. Auditing of public expenditure and the use of public money is obviously an extremely important aspect of the arrangements for overseeing government activity. Its significance is sometimes signalled by identifying 'financial accountability' as a particular aspect of parliamentary control of the government ('political accountability').

109   H Evans, 'Parliament and Extra-Parliamentary Accountability Institutions' (1999) 58 *Australian Journal of Public Administration* 87, 89.

10

Freedom of Information

10.1 What is freedom of information?

This chapter is about 'freedom of information' (FOI), a phrase used to refer to legal regimes under which individuals have a right to seek access to information held by public agencies and which, subject to specified exemptions, create a presumption in favour of disclosure of such information. FOI is related to but distinguishable from 'transparency' and 'open government'. A good example of transparency is the giving of reasons for decisions. Open government, or 'government in the sunshine' as it is sometimes called, refers to legal provisions requiring, for instance, that formal meetings of public agencies be open to the public and that members of the public have a right to participate in some way in public decision-making processes. The relationship between FOI and open government is explicitly acknowledged in the 'objects clause' of the Commonwealth *Freedom of Information Act 1982* (*FOI Act*), which expresses parliament's intention of 'increasing public participation in Government processes, with a view to promoting better-informed decision-making' (s 3(2)(a)).

10.2 The value of information

Control of information is a potent form of power. This is why governments value secrecy. The traditional 'corridors of power' are not only long and cold, but also inaccessible and shrouded in mystery. It is often said that the parliamentary (or 'Westminster') system of government that we have in Australia particularly discourages FOI because it rests on the basic constitutional principle of ministerial responsibility. As we have seen (2.1.2, 2.3.3 and 2.4.1.3), ministerial responsibility has two aspects: collective and individual. Collective ministerial responsibility (CMR) provides one of the justifications for the confidentiality of Cabinet proceedings and more generally encourages in senior politicians and bureaucrats an aversion to openness, transparency and publicity about government decision-making. At least in its traditional form, individual ministerial responsibility (IMR) is designed—negatively—to protect bureaucrats from being personally answerable for the conduct of government lest (it is often said) public servants might be discouraged from giving candid and fearless policy advice to their political masters.[1] Positively, IMR empowers parliament to demand information and explanations from ministers, but effectively leaves to the government the power to decide how much information and what explanations to provide. Missing from this constitutional scheme is a formal mechanism by which information can flow directly from government to citizens.

We may doubt that there is a special link between secrecy and the parliamentary system of government if only because, in modern times, Australia was one of the first national governments (and the first in a parliamentary system) to enact an FOI regime giving citizens a right to seek access to 'public sector information' (PSI).[2] It is because the powerful typically value secrecy so highly that this right is so valuable. However, unlike freedom of speech and privacy, FOI is not widely recognised as a 'fundamental human right'.[3] Typically, FOI regimes are statutory, although in a few legal systems FOI has constitutional status.

In 1979, a committee of the Australian Senate identified three reasons for promoting citizens' access to PSI:[4] first, so that individuals can discover what government knows about them personally and have such 'personal information' corrected if it is inaccurate; second, so that government can be more effectively held accountable for what it does (or fails to do);[5] and third, so that citizens can more effectively participate in 'the processes of policy-making and government itself'.[6]

Nevertheless, despite the value of access to PSI, no one suggests that all information held or controlled by public agencies should be publicly available. In areas such as national security and defence, it is generally accepted that effective government, community safety and 'the public interest' may justify confidentiality and a degree of secrecy in public administration. The trick is to find the optimum balance between openness and secrecy. Historically, the balance rested heavily in favour of secrecy. Legally enforceable obligations were imposed on public officials not to disclose information of certain types.[7] As for the rest, the government was free to decide whether or not to make information available to the public and what information to release. FOI legislation fundamentally readjusts this balance by creating a presumption in favour of disclosure and giving citizens a right to request information held by public agencies. In an FOI regime, certain classes of information are protected—as before—by legally enforceable obligations of secrecy;[8] but also by 'exemptions' from the general obligation to disclose. Initially, decisions about whether or not specific requests for information must be met are made by the government agency

---

1   Recall that the price of access by ombudsmen to departmental files is a secretive investigation process. The CO is subject to the *FOI Act* (see e.g. *Kavvadias v Commonwealth Ombudsman* (1984) 54 ALR 285). As we will see later (10.8), documents relating to 'deliberative processes' involving the performance of government functions are conditionally exempt from disclosure under the *Freedom of Information Act 1982* (Cth) ('*FOI Act*'), s 47C.

2   J M Ackerman and I E Sandoval-Ballesteros, 'The Global Explosion of Freedom of Information Laws' (2006) 58 *Administrative Law Review* 85, 97–8.

3   For an argument that FOI should be recognised as a fundamental human right see P Birkinshaw, 'Freedom of Information and Openness: Fundamental Human Rights?' (2006) 58 *Administrative Law Review* 177.

4   For a discussion of the objectives of the UK FOI regime in particular and of FOI regimes more generally see R Hazell, B Worthy and M Glover, *The Impact of the Freedom of Information Act on Central Government in the UK: Does FOI Work?* (Houndsmills, Hants: Palgrave Macmillan, 2010), Ch 2.

5   For an empirically informed conclusion that the UK FOI regime has improved accountability only to a small extent see Hazell et al., n 4 above, especially Chs 8 and 10.

6   Senate Standing Committee on Constitutional and Legal Affairs, *Freedom of Information* (1979), paras 3.3–3.5. See Hazell et al., n 4 above, Ch 15 for the conclusion that the UK FOI regime has 'not increased public participation to a significant extent'.

7   For a thorough review of such provisions see Australian Law Reform Commission, Report 112, *Secrecy Laws and Open Government in Australia* (2009).

8   E.g. *FOI Act*, s 38.

that holds the information. Therefore, also central to an FOI regime are robust controls over such decision-making to ensure that government does not withhold information without good reason.

In short, FOI is a legal regime that strikes a balance between the values of secrecy and confidentiality in public affairs on the one hand, and the free flow of PSI from government to citizens on the other.

10.3 A very short history of FOI in Australia

The chief architects of the new administrative law regime put in place in Australia in the 1970s—the Kerr Committee and the Bland Committee—were not invited to (and did not) consider the possibility of freedom of information legislation. The initial proposal, made contemporaneously in 1972 by the Whitlam Labor government, was prompted by the enactment of FOI legislation at the federal level in the US in 1966. Whereas the Kerr/Bland package of reforms was relatively uncontroversial and quickly enacted, FOI was much more contentious, and the *FOI Act* did not become law until 1982. Strong resistance to FOI came from within the public service, and this resistance did not cease when the *FOI Act* was passed. As a result, it is generally agreed that the first two decades of FOI in Australia did not produce the 'cultural shift' towards a regime of public access to PSI that the most committed proponents of the regime had hoped for. Various features of the *FOI Act* itself also militated against such change, including the financial cost of making FOI requests, the content and width of various exemptions from disclosure of specified categories of information, and the power of ministers, in justification of refusals to disclose information, to issue 'conclusive certificates' (certificates that were binding on a court or tribunal) that disclosure of particular information would harm the public interest. In addition, it was widely perceived that when reviewing refusals to disclose, tribunals and courts tended to interpret the legislation narrowly against disclosure rather than broadly in its favour.[9]

In something of a repeat of earlier history, and in response partly to a 1995 report by the Australian Law Reform Commission,[10] and partly to certain high-profile instances of informational parsimony by the Howard Liberal government and associated public pressure, especially from a media lobby group (Australia's Right to Know Coalition),[11] the Rudd Labor government initiated a major overhaul of the FOI regime that culminated in the enactment in 2010 of the *Freedom of Information Amendment (Reform) Act* and the *Australian Information Commissioner Act* (*AIC Act*). As we will see later, the new FOI regime differs from the 1982 regime in various significant respects. Following the enactment of the *FOI Act* in 1982, the states and territories each introduced FOI regimes that differ among themselves and from the federal regime in various ways. Since our concern in this chapter is with general FOI principles rather than fine details,[12] we will focus on the federal regime, which provides a suitable illustration of those principles.

---

9   See e.g. R Stubbs, 'Freedom of Information and Democracy in Australia and Beyond' (2008) 43 *Australian Journal of Political Science* 667; R Snell, 'The Torchlight Starts to Glow a Little Brighter: Interpretation of Freedom of Information Legislation Revisited' (1995) 2 *Australian Journal of Administrative Law* 197. For a general account of the history from 1960 to 2000 see G Terrill, *Secrecy and Openness: The Federal Government from Menzies to Whitlam and Beyond* (Melbourne University Press, 2000).

10   Australian Law Reform Commission and Administrative Review Council, Report 77, *Open Government: A Review of the Federal Freedom of Information Act 1982* (1995).

11

12   For detail see M Paterson, *Freedom of Information and Privacy in Australia* (Australia: LexisNexis Butterworths, 2005). But note that this book pre-dates the major changes made to the federal FOI regime in 2009 and 2010. The best up-to-date account of federal FOI law can be found in Office of the Australian Information Commissioner (OAIC), *Guidelines Issued by the Australian Information Commissioner under s 93A of the* Freedom of Information Act 1982 ('*Guidelines*') (available on the OAIC website).

10.4 The main functions of FOI regimes

The original and, perhaps, still the basic function of an FOI regime is to enable individuals to gain access by request to certain types of information held or controlled by agencies and entities subject to the regime (see *FOI Act*, s 3(1)(b) and 3(4)). Individuals may seek access to information about themselves in order to discover what government knows about them and to have the information corrected or annotated if it is inaccurate. Under the federal FOI regime, the large majority of requests (82.6% in 2010–11) relate to personal information about the requester.[13] Other requests are for information about third parties and government processes.

A second main function of FOI regimes is to require agencies to publish information about certain aspects of the agency's operations, including information relevant to FOI concerning, for instance, types of information held by the agency. In the federal FOI regime,[14] this requirement finds expression in the Information Publication Scheme (IPS). The IPS requires agencies to publish an 'agency plan' showing how they will implement the IPS, to publish certain specified categories of information, and to consider voluntarily publishing other PSI that is not required to be published. Under s 10 of the *FOI Act*, an agency cannot rely to the citizen's detriment on 'any rule, guidance or practice' contained in 'operational information' that should have been, but was not, published under the IPS. 'Operational information' is defined (in s 8A) as 'information … to assist the agency to perform or exercise the agency's functions or powers in making decisions or recommendations affecting members of the public'. An aim of the IPS provisions is to promote proactive as opposed to reactive provision of information.

A third function of FOI regimes is 'to increase recognition that information held by government is to be managed for public purposes, and is a national resource'.[15] This statement of purpose, introduced into the *FOI Act* in 2010, represents potentially the most significant difference between the old and the new federal FOI regimes. It figures prominently in official publications about the new regime and it informs the account of the role of the Information Commissioner (IC)[16] provided in those publications by Professor John McMillan, formerly Commonwealth Ombudsman and now the first IC. The OAIC's *Principles on Open PSI*[17] give the information-management function pride of place: the community should be engaged in designing information policy (Principle 2), which should aim at 'effective information governance' (Principle 3); 'robust information asset management' (Principle 4); the provision of 'discoverable and useable information' (Principle 5) and 'clear reuse rights' through open licences (Principle 6). This focus on information as a public asset and resource goes well beyond facilitating individuals' access to PSI and encouraging voluntary publication of information to embrace a third goal of actively managing and regulating the use and reuse of PSI, whether or not it is publicly available.

This upgrading of the aspirations of the FOI regime may be understood as an adaptation to the IT revolution that has taken place since the *FOI Act* was first passed in 1982. Technology now facilitates

---

13   Three agencies receive the majority of such requests (71% in 2010–11): Centrelink, the Department of Immigration and Citizenship and the Department of Veterans' Affairs. The most common issue in applications for merits review of FOI decisions is the personal privacy exemption (see 10.7.1): OAIC, *Annual Report 2010–11*, 2–3, 12.

14   *FOI Act*, Part II.

15   *FOI Act*, s 3(3).

16   As defined in s 7 of the *AIC Act 2010*.

17   Office of the Australian Information Commissioner, *Principles on Open Public Sector Information: Report on Review and Development of Principles (May 2011)*. See also OAIC, *Understanding the Value of Public Sector Information in Australia* (November 2011). Unlike the *Guidelines* (n 12 above), to which 'regard must be had' in FOI decision-making (*FOI Act*, s 93A(2)), the principles are not binding on agencies.

the collection, storage, use and dissemination by governments[18] of vast amounts of information, the efficient and productive management of which presents ever more complex challenges.[19] It has created an 'open market in information'.[20] Against this background, the image implicit in the 1982 FOI regime— of the individual approaching an agency to request access to specified 'documents' for which the agency conducts a physical search—seems quaintly anachronistic. Now the emphasis is on maximising the social and economic value of PSI, to which facilitating access in response to requests by individuals is only one, and not the most important, contributor. There is, perhaps, a danger in this development that pursuing regulatory and managerial goals will divert attention and resources away from more specific constitutional and political purposes, such as those identified in 10.2 above, of protecting personal information, holding governments accountable and promoting citizen participation in public decision-making; and even from the overarching purpose of striking an appropriate balance between secrecy and openness in government.

10.5 What is information?

This question is more complex than it may at first appear. To begin, it is helpful to distinguish between information that governments collect from myriad outside sources on a wide range of topics (which we may call 'external information') and information generated within government, most notably information about the conduct of government (which we may call 'internal information').[21] The contemporary rhetoric of FOI does not make this distinction. However, it might be thought relevant to the issue raised at the end of the last section: the goal of managing and regulating the use of information is arguably more important in relation to external information, while internal information is arguably more important to achieving the goals of holding government accountable and striking an appropriate balance between government secrecy and confidentiality on the one hand, and openness and transparency on the other. It may be important to distinguish between internal and external information when formulating and implementing FOI policy.

The potential value of FOI is tied up with a crucial ambiguity in the word 'information'. Australian FOI legislation (as opposed, for instance, to the FOI legislation in New Zealand), is primarily concerned not with access to information as such, but with access to documents. The *FOI Act* imposes no obligation on agencies to reduce information to documentary form, except to the extent that information is stored electronically and can, for instance, be easily printed. This also marks a basic difference between FOI and certain other informational mechanisms. For instance, requirements that agencies report about their activities to parliament or to a minister, obligations to give written reasons for decisions, processes for collecting evidence in court and tribunal proceedings, and ombudsman investigations, may all require agencies to generate documents that embody information. By contrast, a right of access to documents can only bring to light information that has already been embodied in documentary form—even though the term 'document' is broadly defined.[22]

---

18   And others, e.g. Wikileaks.

19   See e.g. J Lye, 'Have Recent Changes to FOI Caused a Shift in Agencies' Practices?' (2011) 66 *AIAL Forum* 61; J McMillan, 'Information Law and Policy: The Reform Agenda' (2011) 66 *AIAL Forum* 51, 58–60.

20   McMillan, n 19 above, 60.

21   This category includes 'operational information' as defined in s 8A of the *FOI Act*.

22   See, for instance, *FOI Act*, s 4(1).

10.6 The federal FOI regime

10.6.1 The recent reforms

As noted earlier, the federal FOI regime, which was first enacted in 1982, was overhauled in 2009 and 2010. The new federal FOI regime differs from the 1982 regime in various significant ways:

- Ministers can no longer issue conclusive certificates, binding on a court or tribunal, that a document is exempt from disclosure (see 10.6.6).[23] All claims of exemption are now reviewable.

- The objects clause in the *FOI Act* (s 3) has been redrafted to reinforce the aim of actively promoting disclosure.

- The coverage of the *FOI Act* has been extended to certain information held by contractors providing public services on behalf of the government (see 10.6.5).

- Certain exemptions from disclosure have been repealed, the exemption for Cabinet documents has been narrowed and certain exemptions have been made conditional on establishing that disclosure would harm the public interest (see 10.6.6).

- Fees and charges for obtaining information have been reduced and in some cases abolished (see 10.6.4).

- The Office of the Australian Information Commissioner (OAIC) has been established (see 10.6.2).

- The Information Publication Scheme (IPS), under which public agencies publish PSI independently of requests, has been expanded and strengthened. In addition, subject to certain qualifications, agencies are now required to maintain a 'disclosure log', which means that agencies must publish information provided in response to individual requests for information.

This last feature of the new regime deserves some explanation. As we will see later (10.7), FOI regimes are part of a larger network of legal regimes concerned with publication of information, both private information and PSI. FOI operates against a background in which public agencies are free to publish PSI provided there is no legal requirement of non-publication (secrecy). An FOI regime imposes an obligation on public agencies, subject to exemptions, to publish certain types of information; but it does not prevent the voluntary publication either of information that is required to be published under the FOI regime or of information that is not required to be published under the regime[24] provided, in the latter case, that there is no legal prohibition of publication of the information in question. The IPS imposes certain obligations to publish, but is also designed to encourage and maximise voluntary (or 'discretionary') publication. The task of working with public agencies to develop their IPSs may be considered one of the most important of the OAIC's functions because of its potential for promoting 'cultural change' in bureaucratic attitudes to FOI.

---

23   This was the first reform of the package, achieved by the *Freedom of Information (Removal of Conclusive Certificates and Other Measures) Act 2009* (Cth).

24   In other words, which falls within one of the exemptions from the obligation to publish.

10.6.2 Institutions

One of the most significant of the 2010 changes to the federal FOI regime was the creation of the offices of Information Commissioner (IC) and Freedom of Information Commissioner (FOIC). Together with the Privacy Commissioner (PC), these two officers constitute the Office of the Australian Information Commissioner (OAIC). Under the 1982 FOI regime, an application for external merits review of a decision by an agency to refuse or grant access to documents or about charges for access (10.6.4) could be made to the AAT. But unlike the federal privacy regime, into which the office of Privacy Commissioner was built from the start, the 1982 FOI regime did not include a statutory official responsible for the administration and development of FOI policy, practice and compliance across government generally: each agency was responsible for its own FOI program.

The OAIC has three groups of functions: the information commissioner functions, the FOI functions and the privacy functions. All three commissioners can exercise the FOI and privacy functions, but only the IC can exercise the information commissioner functions. The FOI functions include merits review of FOI decisions by agencies, investigation of complaints about FOI administration, promoting good FOI practice and monitoring agencies' compliance with the *FOI Act*.[25] The main information commissioner function (*AIC Act*, s 7) is

> to report to the Minister on any matter that relates to the Commonwealth Government's policy and practice with respect to: (i) the collection, use, disclosure, management, administration or storage of, or accessibility to, information held by the Government; and (ii) the systems used, or proposed to be used, for the activities covered by subparagraph (i).

The effect of this somewhat oddly worded provision is to give the IC the job of 'giving strategic advice to the Australian Government on information management generally'.[26] This function is central to the fundamental goal of the new FOI regime, namely a 'cultural change' from reactive to proactive disclosure of PSI. Besides the Commonwealth IC, there are now offices with that name in New South Wales, the Northern Territory, Queensland and Western Australia. The ombudsman in Tasmania has functions similar to those of an information commissioner.[27]

Because it goes well beyond enforcing legal obligations to disclose and is framed in extremely wide and vague terms, it seems likely that success in achieving the goal implicit in the *FOI Act*'s definition of the information commissioner function will depend to a significant extent on the personality and determination of the holder of the office of IC from time to time. The first IC is Professor John McMillan. In the light of his career-long commitment to FOI and his track record as Commonwealth Ombudsman, it is fair to say that if anyone can make significant progress towards realising the objectives of the new regime, it is Professor McMillan.

10.6.3 Access

FOI regimes differ in terms of who may make a request for information. Under some schemes, only citizens may seek access; but under the *FOI Act* (s 11) 'every person' has such a right. A person's right of

---

25   It is worth noting that the OAIC has a mix of legislative, administrative and adjudicative functions. It issues guidelines, monitors compliance with those guidelines and adjudicates disputes about their application. This arrangement may not breach constitutional separation of powers principles, but it may create an appearance of conflict of interest.

26   OAIC, Issues Paper 1, *Towards an Australian Information Policy* (November 2010), 22.

27   Ibid, 31–3.

access is not affected by their reasons for seeking access or by the agency's belief as to what those reasons might be (*FOI Act*, s 11(2)). This means that an agency may not refuse access on the basis of what the information may be used for; and it implies that information obtained may be used for any (lawful) purpose.

A request under the *FOI Act* has to be made in a certain form and in a certain way (*FOI Act*, s 15). This means that an agency is under no obligation to disclose information except in response to a formal request that meets the statutory requirements. However, it does not prevent agencies voluntarily providing information in response to informal requests or, of course, under its IPS independently of any request. Unless it seeks an extension of time, the agency must make a decision within 30 days whether or not to meet a formal request.

An important feature of the new federal FOI regime is that the IC has power (under *FOI Act*, s 89K) to declare a person to be a 'vexatious applicant'. The effect of such a declaration is that a request for information or for review of an FOI decision made by such a person need not be considered.

10.6.4 Cost

One of the most common complaints about FOI regimes is the high cost to the requester of obtaining information. This concern has been addressed in the new federal FOI regime, under which no fees are payable for making an FOI request or an FOI complaint, or for seeking review by the OAIC of an FOI decision. A fee (of $777 from 1 July 2011) is payable for an application to the AAT for (second-tier) review of a decision by the OAIC reviewing an FOI decision of an agency. Agencies may not charge for providing access to an individual's own personal information or the first five hours spent in making an access decision (as opposed to time spent searching for and retrieving documents). An agency that fails to deal with a formal request within 30 days without seeking an extension of time from the OAIC may not make any charge.[28] Charges have not been increased since 1986.

Agencies have discretion whether or not to levy (and, therefore, whether or not to waive) charges that they are entitled to make and whether or not to charge less than they are entitled to charge. According to the *Guidelines* (see n 12 above), under the old federal FOI regime, general government policy was that agencies should levy the charges they were entitled to make. However, 'the Information Commissioner takes the view that this policy is not reflected in the Act as amended in 2010 and that agencies are not expected to exercise the discretion … to impose a charge, unless in the agency's view it is appropriate to do so'.[29] The *FOI Act* and the *Guidelines* say quite a lot about how the discretion (not) to charge should be exercised; and, of course, in exercising the discretion, decision-makers must comply with the general principles of administrative law.

The other side of the charging coin (as it were) is that the lower the fees and charges paid by requesters, the greater the proportion of the cost of the FOI regime that must be met out of public funds. In the last year of operation of the old federal regime (2009–10), fees and charges represented only 1.9% of the total cost of the FOI regime, while in 2010–11 (for the last eight months of which the new regime was in operation) this fell to 1.7%. In 2010–11, the total cost of the regime was more than $36 million. This may increase if the abolition of fees and the reduction of charges encourage greater use of the system and the average cost per request continues to rise (it rose from $1208 in 2008–09 to

---

28   For more detail see OAIC, *Review of Charges under the* Freedom of Information Act 1982 (October 2011).

29   *Guidelines*, n 12 above, para 4.5.

$1403 in 2009–10 and to $1799 in 2010–11). Under certain circumstances an agency may refuse to deal with a request if doing so would 'substantially and unreasonably divert the resources of the agency from its other operations' (*FOI Act*, s 24AA(1)(a)(i)).[30] This provision is likely to be of greatest significance for smaller agencies that may not be able to dedicate to FOI resources equivalent to those utilised by their larger counterparts. It must also be read in the light of the general goal of the new FOI regime of promoting efficient handling and storage of information by agencies: it is not intended to provide a cover for bad information practice.

10.6.5 Scope

A factor that significantly affects the potential value of FOI legislation is its institutional scope. For instance, the scope of the UK FOI legislation is defined by a very long list of agencies to which it applies.[31] By contrast, the *FOI Act* applies generally to 'agencies'. 'Agency' is defined broadly to include departments and prescribed authorities. A prescribed authority (subject to certain exclusions, including royal commissions) is an incorporated or unincorporated body established for a public purpose by statute or Order in Council. Other bodies may be declared to be prescribed agencies, while certain persons and bodies (such and the Auditor-General and the Australian Security Intelligence Organisation (ASIO)) are expressly stated not to be agencies for the purposes of the *FOI Act*. So far as federal courts are concerned, the *FOI Act* applies only in relation to 'matters of an administrative nature' as opposed to judicial functions. With a few exceptions, this qualification does not apply to tribunals. The *FOI Act* applies to 'official documents of a minister' (s 11(1)(b)), but not to personal documents.

A recurring complaint about the old FOI regime was that it did not apply to private providers of services (such as utilities) that had once been provided by government-owned business entities but had been 'privatised'. Nor did it apply to private entities to which the provision of services to the public had been outsourced by government agencies. The position in relation to privatisation remains the same under the new regime. By contrast, a request may now be made to an agency that has outsourced the provision of public services for access to documents held by the entity to which provision of the service has been contracted out. The agency is required (under s 6C of the *FOI Act*) to include in the contract with the service-provider provisions that enable the agency to fulfil its obligations under the *FOI Act*.

10.6.6 Exemptions

Central to an FOI regime are the exemptions that specify types of documents to which access may be refused. The nature and scope of such exemptions fundamentally affect the value of the regime, and their interpretation and application tend to be highly contested. The *FOI Act* specifies many classes of exempt documents. They fall into two categories: 'exempt' and 'conditionally exempt'. Categories of exempt documents include documents affecting national security, defence or international relations, Cabinet documents, documents affecting law enforcement and documents to which secrecy provisions apply. An agency may refuse to disclose a document that falls within an exempt category;

---

30   In the case of a minister, the test is whether the request would 'substantially and unreasonably interfere with the performance of the Minister's functions' (*FOI Act*, s 24AA(1)(a)(ii)).

31   Estimated as being between 100 000 and 115 000: P Birkinshaw in J Jowell and D Oliver (eds), *The Changing Constitution*, 7th edn (Oxford: Oxford University Press, 2011), Ch 14.

but with the exception of documents that it would be unlawful to disclose, agencies have discretion to disclose documents that fall within an exempt category.

Access must be given to a conditionally exempt document unless, in the circumstances at the time access is requested, it would be contrary to the public interest to disclose the document. In this respect, the new federal regime differs from the old in three important ways. First, some categories that were exempt under the old regime are only conditionally exempt under the new regime. Second, under the old regime, there were several different public interest tests, while under the new regime there is only one. Third, under the new regime it is stated that certain factors weigh in favour of disclosure, but also that certain other factors must be ignored in applying the public interest test.[32] Conditionally exempt documents include those relating to Commonwealth–state relations, deliberative processes (see further 10.8) and personal privacy.

The public interest test is framed in terms that favour disclosure, and the express factors favouring disclosure include that disclosure would promote the objects of the *FOI Act* and inform public debate. Factors that must be ignored include that granting access might embarrass the government, or cause unnecessary debate or confusion or loss of confidence in the government; that the document might be misunderstood or misinterpreted; and that the author of the document was a senior bureaucrat.

In general, the exemptions under the new regime are considerably narrower than those under the old. However, whether or not an exemption applies is a question to be decided in relation to each document requested and the circumstances at the time of the request. In other words, exemption decisions are highly fact-sensitive. As a result, agencies have considerable scope for using the exemptions to refuse access, despite the pro-disclosure bias of the new regime in general and of the new public interest test in particular. This is why abolition of the power of ministers under the old regime to issue binding certificates that a particular document was exempt, in conjunction with the new arrangements for review of FOI decisions (including exemption decisions) (10.6.7), is so important. Major complaints about the old regime were that agencies tended to interpret the exemptions as widely as possible and that tribunals and courts were unduly reluctant to overturn such interpretations. Only time will tell whether the new regime can bring about a cultural shift in the interpretation and application of the exemptions by decision-makers at all levels of the FOI institutional structure.

10.6.7 Complaints and reviews

The old federal regime made provision for internal review of FOI decisions within agencies. FOI decisions were also subject to merits review by the AAT and, in theory at least, to judicial review. Complaints about the administration of the FOI regime could be made to the Commonwealth Ombudsman. Under the new regime, unlike the old, applying for internal review is not a precondition of applying for external merits review. However, 'the Information Commissioner is of the view that it is usually better for a person to seek internal review of an agency decision before applying for IC review'.[33] First-tier external merits review is an FOI function that can be performed by the IC, the FOIC and the PC. Most OAIC reviews are conducted on the papers, and the IC encourages resolution by agreement between the parties. The AAT provides a second-tier of external merits review. There is no fee for applying for internal review or for first-tier external merits review.

---

32 The latter provision is designed, in part, to reverse the decision in *Re Howard and the Treasurer* (1985) 7 ALD 645, and provides a clear illustration of the pro-disclosure bias of the new regime.

33 *Guidelines*, n 12 above, para 9.4.

Investigating complaints about the FOI administration is also an FOI function of the OAIC, and the service is free to the complainant. Formerly, FOI complaints were investigated by the ombudsman. Under the new regime, the ombudsman still has jurisdiction over FOI complaints, and the IC has power to refer an FOI complaint to the ombudsman in appropriate cases (as where, for instance, the FOI complaint is only one element of a larger grievance against an agency). However, it is anticipated that most FOI complaints will be investigated by the OAIC and that the ombudsman will refer to the OAIC most FOI complaints received by that office.[34]

10.7 The relationship between FOI and cognate bodies of law

This section examines the general relationship between a freedom of information regime and other related legal regimes.

10.7.1 Privacy

As we have seen, as well as the FOIC, the OAIC also houses the Privacy Commissioner, who is primarily responsible for administration of the federal regime of personal privacy protection law. Although privacy law is as much concerned with the private sector as with PSI, this arrangement signals the important relationship between FOI and privacy. Under the *FOI Act*, 'a document is conditionally exempt if its disclosure would involve the unreasonable disclosure of personal information about any person (including a deceased person)' (s 47F). This exemption is designed to protect third parties and does not, of course, apply to information about the person requesting access to the document (*FOI Act*, s 47F(3)). In certain circumstances, an agency must consult an affected third party before deciding whether or not to give access to a document; and a third party can apply for review of a decision to give access. According to the IC, a 'unifying theme' of the contrasting values of FOI and privacy is that they are 'both concerned with responsible information management by government agencies, premised on a recognition of the information rights that belong to members of the public.'[35]

The FOI and privacy regimes are also related in that they both allow individuals to seek access to their personal information held by public agencies and to have it corrected or annotated if it is inaccurate. The ALRC has made a recommendation, which the government has accepted, that there be only one mechanism for access to personal information (whether held by public or private entities) and that it be part of the privacy regime.[36] In the light of this recommendation, the combining of FOI functions and privacy functions in the OAIC seems particularly apt.

10.7.2 Secrecy

As noted earlier, FOI and secrecy are two sides of the one coin. Documents the disclosure of which is prohibited by statute are exempt from disclosure under the *FOI Act* (s 38). Also exempt are documents

---

34   *Guidelines*, n 12 above, paras 11.13–11.15.

35   J McMillan, 'Freedom of `Information Reform—The Australian Government' (2011) 65 *AIAL Forum* 31.

36   *Guidelines*, n 12 above, para 7.1–7.2.

the disclosure of which would, or could reasonably be expected to, cause damage to security, defence or international relations (s 33), or to prejudicially affect public safety or law enforcement (s 37). These are all areas in which secrecy and confidentiality have always been considered more or less legitimate. Remember, however, that agencies have discretion to disclose exempt documents unless disclosure would be unlawful. In other words, secrecy is a legal obligation only if disclosure is prohibited by law.

10.7.3 Archives

The National Archives of Australia play an important role in the management of PSI. Retention and disposal of and access to archival (older) records is governed by the *Archives Act 1983*, which was developed alongside the *FOI Act*. Certain records, including Cabinet notebooks and census information, exempt under the *FOI* Act, are made available for public access after a specified period. The FOI regime does not apply to documents that are publicly available under the *Archives Act*.[37]

10.7.4 Whistleblower protection

A whistleblower has been defined as:

a concerned citizen, totally or predominantly motivated by notions of public interest, who initiates of his or her own free will, an open disclosure about significant wrongdoing directly perceived in a particular occupational role, to a person or agency capable of investigating the complaint and facilitating the correction of wrongdoing.[38]

Statutory provisions prohibiting disclosure of PSI ('secrecy laws') may, by way of exception, allow disclosure for the purposes of legal proceedings or law enforcement, for instance, or to avert threats to life or health, or in the course of the performance of statutory duties or functions. Such exceptions may facilitate exposure of wrongdoing in the public sector. But as the above definition implies, whistle-blowing that involves breach of a prohibition on disclosure may be motivated only by some concept of 'public interest' and may not fall within any more specific exception. Without express statutory protection, a whistleblower who makes an unauthorised disclosure may risk criminal prosecution, civil liability or other legal or disciplinary action, such as dismissal.

In 2009 a House of Representatives Committee recommended the enactment of a general Public Interest Disclosure statute to provide significant protection for whistleblowers.[39] In March 2010 the federal government announced that it accepted most of the committee's recommendations and would introduce legislation to provide significant protection for whistleblowers. At the time of writing, this had not been done.

Because the FOI regime operates subject to secrecy laws (*FOI Act*, s 38) and because many of the exemptions from disclosure relate to types of information covered by secrecy laws, there is no direct

---

37 For more detail see Paterson, n 12 above, 1.52–1.63; Australian Law Reform Commission, Report 77, *Open Government: A Review of the Federal* Freedom of Information Act 1982 (1995), Ch 5.

38 W De Maria, 'Quarantining Dissent: The Queensland Public Sector Ethics Movement' (1995) 54 *Australian Journal of Public Administration* 442, 447 cited House of Representatives Standing Committee on Legal and Constitutional Affairs, *Whistleblower Protection: A Comprehensive Scheme for the Commonwealth Public Sector* (2008), para 2.20. For useful research about whistleblowing in Australia see AJ Brown (ed), *Whistleblowing in the Australian Public Sector: Enhancing the Theory and Practice of Internal Witness Management in Public Sector Organisations* (ANU E Press, 2008).

39 See n 37 above; see also ALRC Report, n 7 above, paras 2.61–2.79, 7.109–7.130, 10.131–10.141; M Dreyfus, 'Whistleblower Protection for the Commonwealth Public Service' (2010) 59 *Admin Review* 14.

connection between FOI and whistleblower protection, the latter relating, as it does, to unauthorised disclosure. However, the two regimes share goals such as transparency, openness and accountability.

10.7.5 Public interest immunity in the law of evidence

At the time the federal FOI regime was created in 1982 there was already a principle of the law of evidence to the effect that a party to litigation cannot be ordered to disclose evidence to another party if doing so would harm the public interest. This principle was originally referred to as 'Crown privilege', but later came to be known as 'public interest immunity' (PII).[40] In the adversarial procedural system, the prime responsibility for adducing relevant information rests on the disputing parties. Rules of evidence specify what types of information a party must supply in response to a request by the other. The PII principle allows government agencies (and other entities) to refuse to supply information (whether in the form of documentary or oral evidence) if doing so would be contrary to the public interest. For much of the twentieth century, courts were prepared to accept as binding (that is, 'conclusive') a certificate of a government minister stating that production of particular documents or the supply of particular information would be contrary to the public interest. It was not until 1968 that the UK House of Lords gave courts the power to question such certificates and to decide whether the public interest in non-disclosure outweighed the 'public interest in the due administration of justice', which was how the interest in disclosure was described.[41] Australian courts soon followed suit.[42]

The main public interest grounds developed by courts for refusing to order parties to litigation to disclose evidence are similar to grounds of exemption in FOI regimes: national security and law enforcement, for instance. However, the relationship between FOI law and evidence law has not been worked out systematically. In principle, the obligation to disclose imposed by the law of evidence should track the analogous obligation imposed by FOI law; and, in practice, one would not expect a public agency to claim PII or a court to accept a PII claim in respect of information that would have to be disclosed in response to an FOI request. Conversely, a court could not order an agency to disclose information that the agency could refuse to disclose in response to an FOI request even though, as we have seen, agencies have a discretion to disclose such information unless disclosure would be unlawful.

10.8 Coda: FOI and accountability

This book is mainly concerned with government accountability. FOI is not itself a mechanism of accountability; but adequate and accurate information about the conduct of government is an essential precondition of the successful operation of such machinery. Indeed, information is the lifeblood of accountability and providing information is central to the concept of giving an account. As we have seen, one of the objects of the *FOI Act*, as of FOI regimes more generally, is to increase 'scrutiny, discussion,

---

40   For more detail see Australian Law Reform Commission, Report 102, *Uniform Evidence Law* (2005), paras 15.152–15.166.

41   *Conway v Rimmer* [1968] AC 910.

42   *Sankey v Whitlam* (1978) 142 CLR 1. PII also applies to proceedings before merits review tribunals. The basic principle, which PII qualifies, is that all relevant evidence must be disclosed. Ironically, the IC foresees problems in applying this principle to merits reviews of FOI decisions: McMillan, n 35 above, 33.

comment and review of the Government's activities' (s 3(2)(b)). But this is only one of the objects of the federal FOI regime; and, as we have also seen, contemporary FOI rhetoric puts at least as much emphasis on management and regulation of the use and reuse of the 'national resource' of PSI as on accountability. It should also be remembered that the large majority of requests for access under the federal FOI regime (82.6% in 2010–11) relate to personal information about the requester rather than 'the Government's activities'. As for the rest, there is no way of knowing to what extent FOI requests for other information are made in support of appeals against or claims for judicial review of public decisions or complaints about the conduct of public agencies. However, we may speculate that transparency—especially in the form of the giving of reasons for decisions—is more important than FOI, as such, in facilitating use of the main accountability mechanisms dealt with in this book.

In this context, it is worth noting two of the exemptions from disclosure under the *FOI Act* that are, at least potentially, in considerable tension with the object of increasing scrutiny, discussion, comment and review of the government's activities: that protecting Cabinet documents (s 34) and that protecting documents relating to deliberative processes (s 47C). The former is designed 'to protect the confidentiality of the Cabinet process and to ensure that the principle of collective ministerial responsibility ... is not undermined'.[43] The latter, a conditional exemption, is designed to preserve the confidentiality of internal government policy-making, which is necessary, it is said, to promote efficient provision of candid and frank advice by bureaucrats to ministers. The precise formulation of both exemptions is complex, and the details need not concern us here. The general point to make is that both exemptions are open to wider, anti-disclosure and narrower, pro-disclosure interpretation and application.

In this respect, it is worth observing that the *FOI Guidance Notes* issued by the Department of Prime Minister and Cabinet in July 2011 strike an anti-disclosure note. Regarding the exemption for Cabinet documents, the *FOI Guidance Notes* observe that '[m]aintaining the confidentiality of Cabinet deliberations is the foundation for the proper functioning of the Cabinet process' (para 5), and that there is 'an overriding need for protection of Cabinet confidentiality' (para 14). Therefore '[g]iven the importance of Cabinet confidentiality FOI decision-makers should make use of the Cabinet exemption whenever it is properly available' (para 6). (Remember that agencies have discretion to disclose PSI even if it would be exempt under the *FOI Act*.)

The *FOI Guidance Notes* adopt a similar tone in relation to the deliberative documents exemption. 'Where a document has a close connection with Cabinet but may not necessarily be covered by the Cabinet exemption, the potential application of [the deliberative documents exemption] should be considered' (para 29). Referring to the IC's *Guidelines*, the *FOI Guidance Notes* comment that, although they 'do not currently list factors that might be relevant in deciding against release ... [t]here are nevertheless factors relevant to non-disclosure that are available' (para 36).[44] They include allowing ministers and agencies 'the scope to explore and develop sensitive policy issues' (para 37), maintaining the 'quality, clarity and frankness of written advice' (para 38), encouraging the use of 'innovative processes for policy development' (para 40), 'the importance of the Government having "thinking space" in the development of policy' (para 41), and preserving 'the Government's negotiating position' with third parties (para 43). The potential gap between the approach in the *FOI Guidance Notes*, and that of the

---

43   *Guidelines*, n 12 above, para 5.48.

44   This statement is misleading. The *Guidelines* do not list public interest factors against release of deliberative documents in particular; on the contrary, in this context they stress that certain factors are to be ignored in assessing the public interest (para 6.77). However, in a general discussion of the public interest test there is a long list of factors weighing against disclosure (paras 6.26–9), and these are referred to in the discussion of the deliberative documents exemption.

FOI Act itself and the *Guidelines*, is shamelessly acknowledged in the *FOI Guidance Notes*, which draw a meaningless distinction between using 'inhibition of frankness and candour'[45] as a ground for refusing to disclose a particular document on public interest grounds (which the *FOI Guidance Notes* accept as being inconsistent with the *FOI Act* as interpreted in the *Guidelines*)[46] and citing the danger of inhibiting frankness and candour 'in future advice', which the *FOI Guidance Notes* claim is legitimate (para 45).

The *FOI Guidance Notes* hammer the final nail into FOI's coffin by pointing out that the public interest test has to be applied to the circumstances at the time the request is made (para 42). One implication of this principle is that it may not be against the public interest to disclose a document at time T2 even though disclosure of a similar document was rightly refused on public interest grounds at an earlier time T1. However, the *FOI Guidance Notes* draw out the converse implication, namely that a decision at time T1 that disclosure would not be against the public interest 'does not establish any binding precedent or guide to release [of similar documents] in future cases' (para 42). Although both implications arise, expressing the latter but not the former reinforces the anti-disclosure message of the *FOI Guidance Notes*.

In the light of the attitudes displayed in the DPM&C *Guidance Notes*, we may legitimately wonder whether genuine and fundamental cultural change is likely any time soon. As the IC recognises, a great deal will depend on the effectiveness of the OAIC in persuading public agencies to sign up to the broad pro-disclosure agenda of the *FOI Act*.[47] Perhaps the best sign of success would be replacement of disclosure in response to requests and enforcement of IPS obligations by voluntary, prospective disclosure of all significant public information for which a strong case against disclosure could not be made. Access to personal information will always be request-based; but in information heaven, all other significant information about the workings of government would be freely available to citizens in reasonably accessible form. Of course, whether this state can be achieved in this world will depend on the capabilities of technology and the quality of government record-keeping. This is why the extension of the FOI regime to management of PSI as a national resource, which has placed such issues within the remit of the IC, is a highly significant development.

---

45   As noted in 10.2, this is one of the classic arguments against freedom of information. It was established as a factor weighing against access in *Re Howard and the Treasurer* (1985) 7 ALD 645.

46   Inhibition of frankness and candour is not among the factors that the *FOI Act* expressly requires to be ignored (s 11B(4)), but the *Guidelines* say that it is inconsistent with the objects clause (s 3) and the list of factors favouring access in s 11(3).

47   McMillan, n 19 above, 55.

11

Private Law in a Public Context: Contract and Tort

11.1 Introduction

In terms of the public/private distinction introduced in Chapter 1, the previous chapters of this book have been concerned with public law rules and mechanisms. In this chapter we turn to private law. One reason to do this is to alert the reader to the fact that, in some contexts, private law has for centuries played, and still plays, a significant role in controlling the performance of functions of governance. For instance, the tort of trespass to the person, goods and land can be used to provide remedies for abuse of policing powers of arresting persons, searching premises and seizing property.

A second reason is that the nineteenth-century jurist, A V Dicey, whose ideas greatly influenced the development of (thinking about) Anglo-Australian constitutional and administrative law, strongly believed that private law provided the best vehicle for controlling the exercise of governmental power. He espoused an 'equality principle', according to which governors as well as the governed were subject to private law. Perhaps his prime motivation in adopting the principle was to resist the idea (which he identified with French law) that government was entitled to special protections and immunities from private law liability.[1] He seems to have ignored the fact that an important catalyst for the development of the prerogative writs in the seventeenth century was that 'the suit for civil damages had … serious defects as a means of controlling official actions';[2] and the fact that, in England at the time he was writing, certain organs of government—the 'Crown' (a term that referred basically to the executive branch of central government)—enjoyed immunity from tort liability[3] and protection from contract liability.

---

1   In the process, he underestimated the importance of public law controls on government—but that is a different story.

2   E G Henderson, *Foundations of English Administrative Law: Certiorari and Mandamus in the Seventeenth Century* (Cambridge, Mass: Harvard University Press, 1963), 25.

3   According to F H Lawson, however, the immunity of the Crown would not have worried Dicey because he considered the value of government liability to lie primarily in its deterrent potential rather than in compensation; and for this purpose it was more important that the individual officer who committed the wrong should be personally liable than that the officer's employer should be vicariously liable: 'Dicey Revisited I' (1959) 7 *Political Studies* 109. Lawson also argues that at the time Dicey was writing 'the Crown hardly ever came into contact with the ordinary citizen', and that agencies which did were not immune from liability: 'Dicey Revisited II' (1959) 7 *Political Studies* 207, 211–12.

As we saw in 2.3.5, Australian jurisdictions led the way in passing legislation to abolish such immunity and protection, thus exposing all governmental agencies to the risk of incurring liability for their torts, breaches of contract and other private law wrongs.[4] However, the equality principle thus recognised was subject to a qualification—government was to be 'as nearly as possible' subject to the same rules and principles of private law as applied to private citizens. This qualification leaves open the possibility that bodies of laws (such as tort law and contract law) that were developed to regulate relations between private citizens may justifiably be modified in their application to relations between governors and the governed. An important aim of this chapter is to explore the implications of the qualification in brief discussions of tort and contract law.

A third reason for discussing private law is that the typical remedy for breaches of private law is monetary, most commonly in the form of compensatory damages. By contrast, monetary remedies are normally not available for breaches of public law rules as such.[5] This can be confirmed by revisiting our earlier discussions of judicial review remedies (Chapter 4), the outcomes of merits review (8.7) and the various accountability mechanisms dealt with in Chapter 9. The only accountability mechanism through which monetary recompense can regularly be obtained is a (technically non-binding) recommendation of an ombudsman. The basic position is that a monetary remedy for breach of a public law rule will be available from a court only if that breach also amounts to a private law wrong. As a result, a discussion of public accountability that ignored private law actions for damages would be misleading and incomplete.

A fourth reason for paying some attention to private law in a book on public law is because the private law (concept) of contract has played a central role in recent fundamental changes to the institutions of governance and modes of delivery of public services, such as managerialism, privatisation and outsourcing. These are discussed in 11.3.2.

11.2 Tort

There are, of course, many torts. However, what follows focuses on the tort of negligence, partly because of limitations of space and partly because that tort well illustrates the points that most need to be made. It is also necessary to say something about the tort of misfeasance in a public office, which is unique in being available only against public authorities.

---

4   Concerning the effect of the Australian Constitution on government immunity see *British American Tobacco Australia Ltd v State of Western Australia* (2003) 217 CLR 30. In Australia, 'the Crown' is commonly used to refer to the executive branch of the various governments (although the term is not used in the Australian Constitution). The Crown still enjoys certain immunities and possesses certain rights and powers simply by virtue of being the Crown—as a matter of common law (as opposed to statute). Some of these immunities affect the conduct of litigation against the Crown. Perhaps the most important surviving immunity is encapsulated in a presumption that statutory provisions imposing burdens or obligations do not apply to the Crown: *Bropho v Western Australia* (1990) 171 CLR 1. See D Barnett, 'Statutory Corporations and the Crown' (2005) 28(1) *University of New South Wales Law Journal* 186; G Hill, 'Private Law Actions against the Government— (Part 2) Two Unresolved Questions About Section 64 of the *Judiciary Act*' (2006) 29(3) *University of New South Wales Law Journal* 1, 1–22. Whether or not a particular entity is part of the executive branch of government for these purposes can be a difficult question to answer. See, e.g., *NT Power Generation Pty Ltd v Power and Water Authority* (2004) 219 CLR 90. See more generally N Seddon, *Government Contracts: Federal, State and Local*, 4th edn (Annandale, NSW: Federation Press, 2009), Ch 4.

5   See further n 55 below.

11.2.1 Tort of negligence

11.2.1.1 Negligence law and the functional turn

In Chapter 1 we noted that the English law of judicial review has taken a 'functional turn'. The functional turn was designed to subject the performance of certain ('public') functions to judicial control regardless of whether the decision or action under review had been made or done by a governmental or a non-governmental agency. It represents a change of focus from institutions to functions in defining the scope of application of public law. Australian judicial review law, as we have also explained (1.1 and Ch 3), has taken a less sharp functional turn.

The abolition of governmental immunities and protections from private law liability can be seen to represent a similar change of focus from institutions to functions. The equality principle says that private law applies to both governmental and non-governmental actors—and in its unqualified form it potentially applies to everything they do. However, the qualification to the equality principle suggests that private law may justifiably be modified in its application to some of the functions and activities of government. Both the equality principle and the qualification focus not on the identity of the actor, but on what the actor did. In this area, unlike that of judicial review law, Australian law, like English law, has (necessarily) taken a sharp functional turn.

In general terms, the qualification to the equality principle can be understood as resting on a distinction between private activities and public functions. Private law regulates relationships and interactions between private individuals. Private individuals are generally permitted to conduct their affairs in a self-interested way, provided they respect the right of others to do the same. By contrast, those charged with the performance of public functions are required, in performing those functions, to promote not their own interests or those of any particular individual or group, but the public interest. Public functions, we might say, are functions to be performed in the public interest, even if promoting the public interest inflicts injury or damage on particular individuals or groups. In recognition of the responsibility of repositories of public functions to promote the public interest, the qualification to the equality principle justifies and requires that things done in performance of public functions, in the public interest, be protected from attracting tort liability for harm done to individuals as a result.

We can observe the process of distinguishing between conduct that does and conduct that does not deserve protection from tort liability in cases concerning the interpretation and application of statutory provisions that limit the common law liability of statutory functionaries for things done 'under' the statute.[6] It has been held, for instance, that such a provision would not apply to negligent driving of a fire engine on its way to the scene of a fire,[7] or to failure by a statutory employer properly to maintain its premises and to provide a safe system of work,[8] or to supply of water by a statutory water authority under a commercial contract.[9] On the other hand, if a fire officer decides to interfere with property in order to fight a fire, such a provision would protect the decision to do the act, the decision how to do it, and the doing of it, from action in negligence. Also protected are decisions that it is safe to leave the

---

6   Careful readers will detect resonances with judicial review (3.5.1.4) and merits review (8.5.1.2).

7   *Board of Fire Commissioners of NSW v Ardouin* (1952) 109 CLR 105; see also *Hudson v Venderheld* (1968) 118 CLR 171.

8   *Australian National Airlines Commission v Newman* (1987) 162 CLR 466.

9   *Puntoriero v Water Administration Ministerial Corporation* (1999) 199 CLR 575.

scene of a fire because the fire has been extinguished.[10] More broadly, English courts have, on the one hand, been unwilling to allow decisions by emergency services[11] about whether and how to respond to emergency situations to be the subject of negligence claims. On the other hand, if an emergency service intervenes in a way that creates new danger or makes matters worse, courts may be willing to judge the reasonableness of the conduct.[12]

There are numerous cases in which governmental authorities have been held liable for negligent misstatements,[13] and for negligence in performing building-supervision functions.[14] Prison authorities can be liable for negligent failure to supervise prisoners properly so as to prevent injury or damage to third parties;[15] and for failing to protect vulnerable prisoners from other inmates.[16] A social welfare authority may be liable for failure to warn the person in charge of an open prison of the dangerous propensities of a child put into their charge;[17] and police may be liable for failure to tell prison authorities of the suicidal tendencies of a person committed to their custody.[18] In none of these cases was the relevant conduct considered worthy of protection from the application of ordinary principles of tort law.

11.2.1.2 Negligence liability for performance of public functions

In conceptual terms, protection from liability in the tort of negligence can be provided either by modifying the rules about standard of care or modifying the approach to duty of care. The standard of care technique (and the distinction between the two techniques) can be illustrated by reference to the English case of *Page Motors Ltd v Epsom and Ewell BC*[19] in which a local council delayed for some years in executing an eviction order against gypsies who were camping on a field near the plaintiff's automotive garage and deterring customers. When sued, the council argued (in effect) that its decision to delay in enforcing the eviction order had been taken for reasons of public policy, and that it should not be liable because it had acted within its statutory powers—in effect, a duty of care approach. The court rejected this argument and said that the question was whether, in the terms of ordinary principles of tort law, the council had behaved unreasonably—in effect, a standard of care approach. In answering this question, the court took into account in favour of the defendant the very matters of policy the defendant referred to in its argument.

The relevant Australian cases adopt a duty of care approach. One proposition is clearly established: a duty of care can be imposed only if it would be compatible (would not conflict) with other powers and responsibilities of the alleged tortfeasor (whether statutory or not). For instance, it has been held that a duty to take care not to cause harm to a criminal suspect would potentially conflict with the public responsibilities

---

10   *R & W Vincent Pty Ltd v Board of Fire Commissioners of NSW* (1977) 1 NSWLR 15.

11   With the exception of the ambulance service: *Kent v Griffiths* [2001] QB 36.

12   *Capital & Counties Plc v Hampshire County Council* [1997] QB 1004.

13   For example, *Hull v Canterbury MC* [1974] 1 NSWLR 300; *GJ Knight Holdings Pty Ltd v. Warringah SC* [1975] 2 NSWLR 795; *State of South Australia v Johnson* (1982) 42 ALR 161.

14   For example, *Wollongong C.C. v Fregnan* [1982] 1 NSWLR 244; *Carosella v Ginos & Gilbert Pty Ltd* (1981) 27 SASR 515; *Voli v Inglewood S.C.* (1962) 110 CLR 74.

15   *Dorset Yacht Co. Ltd v Home Office* [1970] AC 1004.

16   *NSW v Bujdoso* (2005) 222 ALR 663.

17   *Vicar of Writtle v Essex County Council* (1979) 77 LGR 656.

18   *Kirkham v Chief Constable of Manchester* [1990] 2 QB 283.

19   *(1982) 80 LGR 337.*

of the police in the investigation of crime and the prosecution of alleged criminals.[20] In *Sullivan v Moody*[21] the High Court used this 'conflict of duties' principle to explain decisions in which it was held that:

- a banking regulator owed no duty of care to depositors;[22]

- the police owed no duty of care to members of the public who might be injured as a result of their negligence in investigating crime or failing to apprehend a dangerous criminal;[23]

- a welfare agency owed no duty of care in respect of decisions whether or not children should be taken into care.[24]

On a similar basis, it has also been held that:

- a parole board owes no duty of care to members of the public in deciding whether or not to allow a prisoner to remain in the community, because such a duty would conflict with its prime responsibility for the rehabilitation of offenders;[25]

- adoption authorities owe no duty of care in relation to the conduct of the adoption process.[26]

Although not explicitly spelled out, the underlying question seems to be whether imposing a duty to take care not to harm the (private) interests of a particular individual would potentially hinder the alleged tortfeasor's capacity to protect and promote societal or public interests, the protection and promotion of which are its responsibility. If so, no duty of care will be owed regardless of whether or not, in all the circumstances of the individual case, imposing a duty would in fact interfere with the protection or promotion of public interests. A slightly different way of asking essentially the same question is in terms of whether the purpose of the powers of the alleged tortfeasor is to protect and promote public interests or, on the contrary, to protect and promote the interests of individuals—and thereby, perhaps, public interests as well. Thus, for example, in *Pyrenees SC v Day*,[27] a purpose of the powers of the council to 'carry out or cause to be carried out ... works ... for the prevention of fires' was to protect neighbours of buildings that presented a fire risk, but not the occupants of such buildings. By contrast, for instance, in the first case listed above, protection of depositors was not the purpose of the powers of the banking regulator. Even if the purpose of statutory powers is to protect individuals, that protection may, for instance, extend only to physical harm and not to economic loss.[28]

The concept of 'control' has emerged as particularly important in cases where the alleged tortfeasor has 'public' responsibilities and powers. This may be because allegations of negligence in such cases

20   *Tame v New South Wales* (2002) 211 CLR 317 (mental harm); *Wilson v State of New South Wales* (2001) 53 NSWLR 407.

21   (2001) 207 CLR 562.

22   *Yuen Kun Yeu v Attorney-General of Hong Kong* [1988] AC 175.

23   *Hill v Chief Constable of West Yorkshire* [1989] AC 53. See also *Brooks v Metropolitan Police Commissioner* [2005] 1 WLR 1495. The result might be different if, as in *Dorset Yacht Co Ltd v Home Office* [1970] AC 1004, injury or damage was caused by a criminal who had negligently been allowed to escape from custody, or if the risk of injury or damage to the plaintiff was significantly greater than that to other members of the public.

24   *X v Bedfordshire CC* [1995] 2 AC 633; by contrast, in *Barrett v Enfield LBC* [2001] 2 AC 550, the House of Lords held that welfare agencies do owe a duty of care in making decisions about the welfare of a child already in care. This distinction was rejected by the Court of Appeal in *D v East Berkshire Community Health NHS Trust* [2004] QB 558, holding that a duty was owed both to the child and its parents. The House of Lords reversed the decision in relation to the parents: *J D v East Berkshire Community Health NHS Trust* [2005] 2 AC 373.

25   *X v South Australia* (No 2) (2005) 91 SASR 258.

26   *Attorney-General v Prince and Gardner* [1998] 1 NZLR 262.

27   (1998) 192 CLR 330.

28   *Governors of Peabody Foundation Fund v Sir Lindsay Parkinson & Co Ltd* [1985] AC 210; *Attorney-General v Carter* [2003] 2 NZLR 160.

typically involve failure to exercise powers in such a way as to protect against or prevent harm, rather than direct infliction of harm. Thus, one reason for a decision that football rule-making bodies owed no duty to players was that their control over the risks in playing the game was too 'remote'.[29] Lack of control was also a factor in a decision that a state government owed no duty of care to oyster growers and consumers in respect of harm resulting from water pollution.[30] By contrast, the high degree of control exercised by a stevedoring authority over the working conditions of waterside workers (and, conversely, the workers' vulnerability) led to the imposition on the authority of a duty to take care to protect workers from exposure to asbestos.[31] Similarly, road authorities owe a duty of care to road users because of the physical control they have over the condition of roads.[32]

Largely missing from the Australian cases is the idea that certain types of function are unsuitable for 'judicial review' in the form of a negligence action (and are in this sense 'non-justiciable'). In the English cases, this idea found expression in a distinction between 'operational' and 'policy' (or 'planning') decisions. The basic principle was that a risky operational decision could form the basis of a negligence claim, but a policy decision could not, unless the policy decision was illegal (ultra vires). The distinction between policy and operational decisions created (what might be called) a 'policy immunity' for intra vires decisions.

The policy immunity received its first important modern consideration in the judgment of Lord Diplock in *Dorset Yacht Co Ltd v Home Office*,[33] and was expounded in greater and more authoritative detail by Lord Wilberforce in *Anns v Merton LBC*.[34] The idea of a policy immunity was not an entirely novel one. For instance, in an early New South Wales case it was held that no action would lie for negligence in respect of the choice of site and method of construction of a lock-up, the noise from which disturbed neighbours. The government, it was said, had to possess a large degree of immunity from liability in respect of the exercise of its important executive functions.[35] In another case it was held that, provided a local board honestly and in good faith exercised its discretionary power to build such drains as it thought necessary, a private individual would have no right to complain if the drainage system inflicted damage on him. The board had to consider the interests of all and keep within a budget.[36]

The policy/operational distinction was accepted as a useful one by Gibbs CJ and Mason J in *Sutherland SC v Heyman*;[37] and something like it played an important part in the reasoning of Brennan J in the *San Sebastian* case.[38] On the other hand, Gummow J has described it as 'not useful in this area';[39] and even if some idea of non-justiciability (3.6.2), to which it gives effect, is still accepted in this context, the distinction itself has gone out of fashion.[40] This may be partly because the distinction is impossible

29   *Agar v Hyde* (2000) 201 CLR 552. Contrast *British Boxing Board of Control v Watson* [2001] 2 WLR 1256 in which the control of the rule-making body over the provision of medical facilities at boxing matches was direct and significant.

30   *Graham Barclay Oysters Pty Ltd v Ryan* (2002) 211 CLR 540.

31   *Crimmins v Stevedoring Industry Financing Committee* (1999) 200 CLR 1.

32   *Brodie v Singleton SC* (2001) 206 CLR 512 as interpreted in *Graham Barclay Oysters v Ryan* (2002) 211 CLR 540 at [151] *per* Gummow and Hayne JJ.

33   [1970] AC 1004, 1067–8.

34   [1978] AC 728. For more detailed discussion of the English cases see Cane, *Administrative Law*, Ch 11.

35   *Davidson v Walker* (1901) 1 SR (NSW) 196.

36   *Local Board of Health of City of Perth v Maley* (1904) 1 CLR 702.

37   (1985) 157 CLR 424, 442, 458, 469.

38   *San Sebastian Pty Ltd v Minister Administering the Environmental, Planning and Assessment Act 1979* (1986) 162 CLR 340, 373–4.

39   *Pyrenees SC v Day* (1998) 192 CLR 330 at [182].

40   For example, *Graham Barclay Oysters Pty Ltd v Ryan* (2002) 211 CLR 540 at [6]–[15] *per* Gleeson CJ.

to draw in the abstract: it depends on the court's view in each particular case about whether the decision in question raises policy issues which it is not prepared to adjudicate upon according to the ordinary rules of negligence.

On the other hand, some judges have taken the view that the exercise of 'legislative' and 'quasi-legislative' functions cannot form the basis of a negligence claim.[41] The basic idea seems to be that because legislation is, by definition, general in application, legislators and quasi-legislators necessarily have public responsibilities, and that a duty of care owed to individuals adversely affected by legislation would be incompatible with the proper discharge of those responsibilities. Although, in its original form, the policy immunity was available only in relation to intra vires decisions, in the form currently being considered, it applies to the exercise of legislative functions (for instance), regardless of whether the allegedly negligent conduct was intra vires or ultra vires.

Another idea from the English cases that has appealed to some Australian courts is that a duty of care will not be owed if a suitable alternative avenue of redress, such as judicial review or a statutory complaint procedure, was available to the victim of the alleged tort.[42] English courts have also expressed unwillingness to impose tort liability on public functionaries on the ground that fear of incurring liability (or even of being sued, whether successfully or not) might lead them to be over-cautious in exercising their powers or unhelpful to citizens who seek their advice or assistance.[43] However, in the absence of substantial evidence of such a 'chilling' effect, this is a weak argument,[44] and Australian courts do not seem attracted to it, at least in this context.

11.2.1.3 Highway authorities

The tort liability of highway authorities used to be limited by a rule that bodies responsible for highways were only liable for misfeasance and not for nonfeasance.[45] One argument for this rule was that highway authorities had to be free to decide for themselves how much to spend on road repair as opposed to road construction, and that authorities whose area of responsibility was large and served by a widespread road system needed special consideration because of the administrative and financial difficulties of their position, the possibility of a flood of claims, and the desirability of encouraging a high degree of self-help among road users.[46] However, these factors could not justify blanket immunity from liability for non-repair, but only a rule that they should be taken into account in deciding what the authority ought reasonably to have done.

At all events, there were several qualifications to the basic rule that limited the scope of its operation. The effect and complexity of these various qualifications—coupled with a feeling that there was no good reason why highway authorities should be treated differently from any other public authority so far as liability in tort is concerned—led the High Court in 2001 to abolish the nonfeasance rule. In future, no

---

41   For example, Gummow J in *Pyrenees* (n 39 above); Gleeson CJ in *Graham Barclay Oysters* (n 40 above).

42   *Jones v Department of Employment* [1989] QB 1.

43   For example, *Calveley v Chief Constable of Merseyside* [1989] AC 1228; *Hill v Chief Constable of West Yorkshire* [1989] AC 53.

44   For a contrasting point of view, see D Nolan, 'Suing the State: Governmental Liability in Comparative Perspective' (2004) 67 *Modern Law Review* 844, 860. For a subtle argument about the relationship between the conflict of responsibilities approach and the 'defensive practice' argument being considered here see H Wilberg, 'Defensive Practice or Conflict of Duties? Policy Concerns in Public Authority Negligence Claims' (2010) 126 *Law Quarterly Review* 420.

45   For more detail, see K Barker, P Cane, M Lunney and F Trindade, *The Law of Torts in Australia*, 5th edn (Melbourne: Oxford University Press, 2006), 594–5.

46   G Sawer, 'Non-Feasance Revisited' (1955) 18 *Modern Law Review* 541.

rigid distinction would be drawn between misfeasance and nonfeasance in applying rules of negligence law to accidents arising from the state of a highway.[47] However, the effect of this decision has been reversed by legislation in most jurisdictions. The provisions are complex, and are likely to generate considerable litigation and to reintroduce many of the distinctions that led to the abolition of the nonfeasance rule.

11.2.1.4 Statute

In recent years, most jurisdictions have enacted legislation to regulate the negligence liability of 'public authorities' (or 'bodies' or 'officers'). The details of the legislation vary considerably from one jurisdiction to another. The definitions of the entities to which the provisions apply contain various elements: institutional (for example, 'the Crown', 'local councils'), functional (for example, 'persons exercising public functions', or 'persons exercising functions prescribed by regulation'), and source-of-power-related (for example, 'statutory authorities').

The various statutes contain four main types of provision. First, in most jurisdictions, there is a provision listing factors to be taken into account in deciding whether a public authority 'has a duty of care or has breached a duty of care'.[48] This provision addresses the extremely difficult issue of the relevance, to the legal liability of public authorities, of the fact that they have limited financial (and other) resources, and are typically responsible for various functions and activities that are in competition for such resources. It appears to have two specific aims. One is to prevent actions against public authorities turning into general audits of the authority's financial management, or provoking a general assessment of the way the authority has allocated its resources among various functions and activities (such as road building and maintenance versus sanitation). The other is to rule out the possibility that an authority might be held to have acted negligently *merely* because a risk of harm could have been reduced or eliminated by the expenditure of more resources. Although this is not made explicit, it may be that the provision applies only in cases where the alleged negligence arose out of the performance of a public function. It may not, for instance, apply to an ordinary occupier's liability claim against a public authority.

Second, in most jurisdictions, there is a complex provision dealing with the liability of public authorities for the tort of breach of statutory duty.[49]

Third, in some jurisdictions, there is a provision dealing with failure to exercise or to consider exercising a 'regulatory function'. The effect of this provision is that an authority cannot be liable in tort for failure to perform or to consider performing such a function unless an order could have been made, at the suit of the plaintiff, requiring the authority to perform or consider performing the power. This means that it is a precondition of such liability that the failure to perform or to consider performing the power was ultra vires, and that the plaintiff could have made a successful judicial review application for an order of mandamus against the authority. There is tension between this provision and the argument, considered earlier, that the availability of alternative remedies provides a reason for limiting the exposure of public authorities to tort liability. Putting the point bluntly, if the plaintiff could have obtained an order of mandamus requiring the authority to exercise or consider exercising its regulatory power, why should the plaintiff now be allowed to make a claim for damages in respect of that failure?

47   *Brodie v Singleton Shire Council* (2001) 206 CLR 512.

48   It is not clear why this provision is expressed to be relevant both to duty of care and to breach of duty, or how the listed considerations might apply differently in the two contexts.

49   For discussion, see Barker, Cane, Lunney and Trindade, *The Law of Torts in Australia*, 5th edn, (South Melbourne: Oxford University Press, 2012) 596–7.

There might be an acceptable answer to this question in cases where although, at some time, the plaintiff could in theory have made a successful claim for a mandatory order against the alleged tortfeasor, there is some good reason or explanation of why no such claim was made before harm was suffered.

Fourth, in most jurisdictions, there is a provision to the effect that the fact that an authority exercises or decides to exercise a 'function' does not 'of itself indicate' that the authority had a duty to exercise the function, or that the function should be exercised in particular circumstances or in a particular way. The meaning and intended effect of this provision are unclear, but the heading of the section may give a clue: 'Exercise of function or decision in exercise does not create duty.' Courts are more willing to impose tort liability for misfeasance than for nonfeasance—for acts than for omissions. The section may be designed to make the point that the mere fact that a public authority has acted rather than failed to act does not justify the conclusion that it owed the plaintiff a duty of care.

11.2.2 Misfeasance in a public office

The equality principle and its qualification regulate the potential liability of public authorities for torts that can be committed by private individuals. By contrast, the tort of misfeasance in a public office can be committed only by public authorities or, more precisely, holders of a 'public office'.[50] Although the concept of a 'public officer' is institutionally focused, the scope of the tort is defined functionally. Thus, in *Cannon v Tahche*,[51] it was held that a public officer is one who has duties or responsibilities to the public, the discharge of which involves the exercise of public power. Misfeasance in a public office involves the wrongful exercise of public power.

Some torts are actionable *per se*—without proof of 'special' or 'material' damage such as personal injury or economic loss. But as in the case of the tort of negligence, such damage is 'the gist' of—a precondition of liability for—misfeasance in a public office.[52] The requirement of damage means that the misfeasance tort cannot be used to provide a remedy for interferences with rights—such as breaches of fundamental human rights—that result in no material harm. The rationale for this approach appears to be that other remedies and forms of accountability, such as judicial review, provide more appropriate responses to such wrongs.

Liability for misfeasance[53] can arise where an official exercises a public power with the intention of harming an individual, regardless of whether the power was exercised legally (intra vires) or illegally (ultra vires). Alternatively, liability may arise where an official acts illegally, knowing that the action is or might be illegal and knowing that the illegal action will or might injure some individual. These requirements clearly distinguish this tort from negligence: it is never enough to establish liability for misfeasance that the officer ought to have known that their action was illegal and might injure someone. *A fortiori*, it would never be enough merely to establish a causal link between illegal exercise of a public power and harm to an individual. The alternative 'mental element' requirements of intention to harm, and knowledge of unlawfulness and the possibility of harm, establish misfeasance as a tort designed to provide a monetary remedy for *abuse* of public power. They address the qualms that underpin the qualification to the equality principle: inflicting harm by abusing public power can never be in the public

---

50   For more detailed examination of this tort see Barker, Cane, Lunney and Trindade, *The Law of Torts in Australia*, 5th edn, 297–302.

51   (2002) 5 VR 317.

52   *Watkins v Secretary of State for the Home Department* [2006] 2 AC 395.

53   Despite the name of the tort, inaction (nonfeasance) as well as action (misfeasance) can attract liability.

interest, but inflicting harm by negligent (or, *a fortiori*, non-negligent) exercise of public power may be, especially if the power is exercised lawfully and, in some circumstances, even though it is exercised illegally. The focus of the misfeasance tort on abuse of power is reflected in the English rule (the status of which is unclear in Australia) that liability for misfeasance may attract punitive damages.[54]

As noted earlier (11.1), there is a long-standing and deeply entrenched bias in the common law against awarding damages for public law illegality as such.[55] This bias is consistent with the implication of Dicey's equality principle that commission of some private law wrong—such as a tort or a breach of contract—is a precondition of recovering damages in respect of the exercise of public powers. The misfeasance tort represents a relatively recent departure from the traditional common law position: although the origins of the tort can be traced back several centuries, it remained largely undeveloped and unexploited until the later part of the twentieth century. As long as the required mental element for the tort is defined quite narrowly and the requirement of material damage is firmly maintained, it will remain an exceptional remedy. But it is perhaps inevitable that courts will come under increasing pressure to relax those requirements in order further to strengthen judicial control of the exercise of public power. Also relevant to the tort's potential is the issue—yet to be resolved in Australia—of whether the employer of the holder of a public office can be held vicariously liable for the official's misfeasance.

11.3 Contract

In order to understand the relevance of the law of contract and the legal concept of contract to issues discussed in this book, it is helpful to distinguish between contract as a medium of exchange and contract as a technique or tool of governance. In relation to the former, the main topics to be addressed are 'public procurement'—acquisition of goods and services for public purposes—and the application of the private law rules of contractual liability to public contracting parties.

Phenomena that can be understood (to some extent at least) in terms of contract as a technique of governance include privatisation of public assets; outsourcing (or 'contracting out') of the provision of public services such as prisons and detention centres, health and education; 'public/private partnerships'; delivery of public services through 'government business enterprises' (GBEs)—corporations wholly or partly owned or controlled by the government;[56] and arrangements under which recipients of welfare

---

54   *Kuddus v Chief Constable of Leicestershire Constabulary* [2002] AC 122.

55   P Cane, 'Damages in Public Law' (1999) 9 *Otago Law Review* 489; *Administrative Law*, 5th edn (Oxford: Oxford University Press, 2011), 310–15. This does not mean that monetary compensation is never available for harm inflicted by governors on the governed. See, e.g., *Jarratt v Commissioner of Police for New South Wales* (2005) 224 CLR 44 (compensation for wrongful dismissal in breach of rules of natural justice). Compensation schemes may be established by statute, and such schemes may cover lawful as well as unlawful action. Statutes may create civil rights of action ('statutory torts'), e.g. *Telecommunications (Interception and Access) Act 1979* (Cth), Part 2-10. Ombudsmen have a good record of success in making recommendations for the payment of compensation in certain contexts (9.3.8). Governments also run non-statutory, discretionary compensation schemes. For an overview of the various Commonwealth schemes see Department of Finance and Administration, *Discretionary Compensation and Waiver of Debt Mechanisms* (Finance Circular 2009/9). See also Commonwealth Ombudsman, *To Compensate or not to Compensate?* (Own-motion Investigation of Commonwealth Arrangements for Providing Financial Redress for Maladministration, 1999); Australian National Audit Office, *Compensation Payments and Debt Relief in Special Circumstances* (Report No 35, 2003–04). In the UK, compensation may be recoverable for breaches of the European Convention on Human Rights, and member states of the European Union may be liable in damages for breaches of EC law. This catalogue emphasises one of the themes of this book—namely, the importance of considering the various mechanisms and arrangements for controlling governance as part of a complex web rather than in isolation.

56   This phenomenon is sometimes referred to as 'corporatisation'. For a useful historical and terminological introduction see R Wettenhall, 'Corporations and Corporatisation: An Administrative History Perspective' (1995) 6 *Public Law Review* 7.

benefits and services undertake obligations in return for the assistance they receive.[57] The issues raised by these various topics (which are sometimes collectively referred to as the 'New Public Management') are many and complex, and limitations of space allow only a very brief introduction to the area. Unsurprisingly, the discussion will focus on the relationship between contract and accountability.

11.3.1 Contract as a medium of exchange

The private law of contract deals with two main topics—the creation of legally enforceable rights and obligations (the rules of offer and acceptance, intention to create legal relations, consideration, mistake and so on are relevant here), and breach of such obligations.[58]

11.3.1.1 Creation of contractual obligations

Governments are significant consumers of goods and services.[59] They employ large numbers of people and buy items as diverse as battleships and paper clips, motor vehicles and legal services. Public procurement represents a very significant proportion of public expenditure. The traditional assumption has been that the executive branches of the various Australian governments, as manifestations of the Crown (see n 4 above), enjoy the same basic (non-statutory or 'common law') power to make contracts as private citizens. However, as was noted in Chapter 3 (3.6.2.2), the High Court held in *Williams* that the Commonwealth does not have the same common law contracting power as a private person. A contract made by the Commonwealth in exercise of non-statutory power may be unlawful if it exceeds the limits on Commonwealth executive power contained in s 61 of the Constitution, which are defined by reference to considerations such as responsible government and federal distribution of powers. The precise nature of these limits remains unclear,[60] as does the impact of *Williams* on the non-statutory contracting powers of state governments.

Many of the contracts entered into by public authorities are made in exercise of statutory contract-making powers. Such powers are typically drafted in broad terms; but if a public body exceeds its statutory contract-making power, the contract will be ultra vires and void. The practical consequences of voidness and unlawfulness may be inconvenient and undesirable, and in the UK some of the problems have been addressed by legislation.[61]

An important limitation on government contracting powers that does not apply to private contractors is the principle that it is illegal for a public body to 'fetter' its exercise of a statutory discretion by giving a contractual undertaking that it will exercise the discretion[62] in a particular way or not exercise it at all.[63]

---

57   Space limitation prevents further discussion of such arrangements. For some discussion see T Carney, 'Contractualism, Managerialism and Welfare: The Australian Experiment with a Marketised Employment Services Network' (2000) 29 *Policy and Politics* 59; *Social Security Law and Policy* (Sydney: Federation Press, 2006), 86–90.

58   The major Australian book on government contracting is N Seddon, *Government Contracts* (n 4 above). See also N Seddon, 'The Interaction of Contract and Executive Power' (2003) 31 *Federal Law Review* 541.

59   Of course, governments also sell goods and services. Sale of public assets and utilities (privatisation) is an obvious example. But many public services for which payment is made are not delivered under contracts but by exercise of statutory powers.

60   Seddon, *Government Contracts*, n 4 above, 54–66; see also L Zines, 'The Inherent Executive Power of the Commonwealth' (2005) 16 *Public Law Review* 279, 283–6.

61   See A C L Davies, 'Ultra Vires Problems in Government Contracts' (2006) 122 *Law Quarterly Review* 98, 113–22. See also S H Bailey, 'Judicial Review of Contracting Decisions' [2007] *Public Law* 444.

62   Concerning the non-statutory power to propose legislation see *West Lakes Ltd v State of South Australia* (1980) 25 SASR 389.

63   See also 5.3.4; Seddon, *Government Contracts*, n 4 above, Ch 5.

Underlying this rule is the contrast between choice (which is inherent in discretion) and restriction of choice (which is of the essence of contractual obligations). In *Stringer v Minister of Housing and Local Government*[64] a local authority agreed with Manchester University that it would discourage development in a particular area so as to protect Jodrell Bank telescope from interference. In pursuance of this agreement, it rejected a development application. This refusal was held to be ultra vires because in honouring the agreement the authority had ignored considerations which, under the statute, were relevant to the fate of the planning application.

Two points are worth noting about this decision. First, the agreement between the authority and the university related expressly and directly to the way a particular discretion would be exercised in the future.[65] The relevance of this point will be explained in a moment. Second, the attack by the plaintiff (who was not a party to the agreement) was on the exercise of the discretion. Sometimes, in cases such as this, the attack might be on the contract itself by one of the parties to it. For example, a successor of the original contracting authority might want to get out of the contract, as happened in *Ayr Harbour Trustees v Oswald*,[66] where the trustees wanted to be free of a covenant, given by their predecessors, not to build on Oswald's land.

A mirror image of such a case (where it is the private contracting party who objects to the contract) is *William Cory & Son Ltd v London Corporation*.[67] Cory contracted with the corporation to remove garbage in its barges; later the corporation passed new health regulations making it more expensive for Cory to perform its contract. Cory argued that a term ought to be implied into the contract to the effect that the corporation would not exercise its power to make by-laws in such a way that the contract became more expensive for Cory to perform. The English Court of Appeal held that since such a clause, if put expressly into the contract, would be void as a fetter on the council's power to make health regulations, it could not be implied into the contract so as to protect Cory. Indeed, in one case it was held that a term should be implied into a lease to the effect that, in making the lease, the Crown (the lessor) was not giving an undertaking that it would not exercise its power to requisition the premises should they be needed in case of war emergency.[68] It might be thought that the willingness of courts to enforce (or imply) discretion-constraining undertakings might vary according to the identity of the party seeking to constrain the agency's freedom of action. It is one thing for the beneficiary of an undertaking to seek to enforce it against the agency that made it, but quite another for the agency to seek to rely on it against a third party who argues that it is a void fetter on the agency's powers.

It is clear that not all contracts that in some way limit the exercise of statutory discretionary powers are, for that reason, void as fetters on the discretion. If that were so, it would be extremely difficult, if not impossible, for public bodies to make binding contracts. The difficult task is to identify those that are void. In the first place, it might be useful to draw a distinction between contracts which are specifically intended[69] to regulate the exercise of a discretion, as in *Stringer*, and those which aim not to limit an authority's action but, on the contrary, to exercise one of its powers. At first sight it might be thought that contracts of the first type would be more likely to be void, and in some cases such contracts have indeed

---

64   [1979] 1 WLR 1281.

65   See also, e.g., *Watson's Bay & South Shore Ferry Co Ltd v Whitfield* (1919) 27 CLR 268.

66   (1883) 8 App Cas 323.

67   [1951] 2 KB 476.

68   *Commissioners of Crown Lands v Page* [1960] 2 QB 274.

69   Intention is judged objectively.

been held void. For example, in the *Ayr Harbour* case (above), the covenant not to build on Oswald's land was held to be a void fetter on the powers of the trustees to build. Contrast *Birkdale District Electric Supply Co Ltd v Southport Corporation.*[70] In this case the company agreed not to raise the price of its electricity above the price charged for power supplied by the corporation. When the company tried to raise its prices and the corporation attempted to stop it doing so, the company argued that the agreement was a void fetter on its power to fix prices. The House of Lords rejected this argument on the ground that the agreement did not run counter to the intention of the legislature in setting up the company. It was not intended that it should make a profit, and there was no reason to think that any of the statutory functions of the company had been or would be adversely affected by compliance with the agreement.

So it would appear that the question of incompatibility of a contract (or a provision in a contract) with a discretionary power is a question of statutory interpretation—has the contract already seriously limited, or is it reasonably likely in the future seriously to limit, the authority in the exercise of its statutory powers or the performance of its statutory functions?

Ultimately the court has to make a choice: what is more important in this case, the interest of the other party to the contract and the principle that contracts should be kept, or the public interest in the exercise of the statutory power? There can be no general answer to such a question; it all depends on the facts of the particular case. And although the terms of the statute provide the basic material for answering this question, the terms of statutes often leave considerable choice to courts in interpreting them. Seen in this light the question gives the court a heavy responsibility to make policy choices between public and private interests. No analytical formula will solve the problem; the court must make a value judgment.

An illustration of the type of case in which the contract is intended primarily as an exercise of discretion rather than a limitation of it is provided by the case of *Dowty Boulton Paul Ltd v Wolverhampton Corporation,*[71] in which the corporation (a local council) conveyed to the plaintiff for 99 years certain land for use as an aerodrome. Some years later, when use of the aerodrome had somewhat dropped off, the council sought to exercise a power to reacquire the land for development on the ground that it was no longer required for use as an airfield. It was held that the company was entitled to keep the airfield and that the contract was not a void fetter.

The crucial difference between the contract in this case and that in *Stringer*, for example, is that it was made as part of a genuine exercise of a statutory power other than the one which the contract adversely affected, namely the power to dispose of land. The contract was an unexceptionable way of exercising the former power. It might have been different if the statutory power to reacquire had related only to the specific piece of land involved, because then it might have been said that the contract was a specific attempt to fetter that power. But since the power related to land generally, to hold such contracts to be void fetters on the powers would be to put an excessive limitation on the contract-making power. When two powers impinge on each other in this way some compromise adjustment has to be found. Should the contract-making power prevail to the benefit of the citizen, or should the public interest in the exercise of the conflicting power be protected? In all these cases, at the end of the day, the court is called upon to balance the public and private interests involved and to decide which deserves more weight.

Subject to any constitutional, statutory and common law limitations on the contracting powers of government bodies, the basic principle underlying the rules regulating the creation of legally enforceable obligations is 'freedom of contract': parties are entitled to make what contracts they want, with

70   [1926] AC 355.
71   [1971] 1 WLR 204. See also *L'Huillier v State of Victoria* [1996] 2 VR 465.

whomever they choose, on whatever terms they agree, or not to contract at all. This principle applies as much to public contracting parties as to private individuals; and it applies as much to the statutory contracting powers of public bodies as to the common law contracting power of the Crown. This laissez-faire approach has some very important consequences. First, it limits the scope for judicial control of the conduct of government bodies when inviting tenders for, negotiating the terms of, and making contracts.[72] This relative lack of judicial control over government contracting is matched by a lack of parliamentary control. While governments must obtain parliamentary approval for primary legislation, and much secondary legislation is subject to parliamentary scrutiny (9.4.3), governments do not require parliamentary approval for contracts.[73]

Second, although the basic aim of the government in making contracts for the procurement of goods and services will be to obtain good value for money, the power to contract (whether statutory or common law), may be used for any purpose that is not prohibited by law.[74] Indeed, it has been said that 'whatever the Crown may lawfully do it may do by means of contract',[75] and the same is essentially true of other public bodies. As a result, governments may be able to use their freedom of contract to achieve 'secondary' or 'collateral' social or policy objectives, such as supporting small business, or providing jobs in areas of high unemployment, or encouraging good employment practices and safe workplace conditions.[76] Such objectives may be pursued either by the inclusion of express terms in contracts imposing obligations on providers of goods or services, or by accepting tenders only from potential providers of goods and services who meet certain criteria. Such practices may be understood in terms of the use of contract as a form of regulation.[77] In the UK and the EU, such regulatory use of contract to pursue collateral objectives is itself regulated by statute and EU legislation. The procurement practices of governments—including Australian governments—may also be affected by international trade agreements, most notably the Australia-US Free Trade Agreement (AUSFTA), which greatly limits the government's freedom to protect Australian industries from foreign competition.[78] The AUSFTA may also necessitate changes to Australian law to meet its requirements for review of procurement decisions.[79]

A third important consequence of freedom of contract is that the common law never developed any general principle allowing parties to a contract to obtain relief from unfair consequences of inequality of bargaining power. Governments have very considerable bargaining power both by reason of their

---

72   For full discussion see Seddon, *Government Contracts*, Chs 7 and 8. The leading Australian case is *Hughes Aircraft Systems International v Airservices Australia* (1997) 76 FCR 151, discussed ibid, 274–8.

73   *New South Wales v Bardolph* (1934) 52 CLR 455. To the extent that there is parliamentary scrutiny of government contracting it tends to be 'concerned principally with the efficiency in which government funds have been used to procure goods and services': C Saunders and K K F Yam, 'Government Regulation by Contract: Implications for the Rule of Law' (2004) 15 *Public Law Review* 51, 62.

74   Concerning the extent to which governments are bound by trade practices and fair trading legislation see Seddon, *Government Contracts*, n 4 above, Ch 6.

75   C Turpin, *Government Procurement and Contracts* (London: Longman, 1989), 84.

76   Concerning the last of these see, e.g. J Howe and I Landau, 'Using Public Procurement to Promote Better Labour Standards: A Case Study of the Victorian Schools Contract Cleaning Program. <www.celrl.law.unimelb.edu.au/files/Case_Study_-_Howe_and_Landau1.pdf>. For general discussion in the British context see A C L Davies, *The Public Law of Government Contracts* (Oxford: Oxford University Press, 2008), Ch 9.

77   In this respect, there is an overlap between the categories of contract as a medium of exchange and contract as a technique of governance.

78   Seddon, *Government Contracts*, n 4 above, 42–5.

79   E Carroll, 'Review Mechanisms for Commonwealth Procurement Decisions and Article 15.11 of the Australia-US Free Trade Agreement' (2006) 14 *Australian Journal of Administrative Law* 7.

constitutional position and their economic strength,[80] and because many government contracts are extremely valuable and of long duration. The bargaining power of a government may enable it to secure more favourable terms and conditions than any private contractor could obtain (although, of course, large private corporations can also wield great bargaining power).

In practice, most government contracts are made in standard form. They typically contain a number of special terms (which may be seen as being designed to protect the public interest): for example, giving the government more control over performance than is usual in contracts between private parties, and giving the government certain powers of unilateral variation and termination. However, it should not be thought that the balance of contracting power is always in favour of the government. The problem of excess profits illustrates the point. A common clause in government contracts makes provision for recovery of excess profits made by the contractor. This type of clause is designed to protect the government in areas, such as defence procurement, where there may be very little choice of contractor and where, because of the highly advanced and innovatory nature of the work being done, it may be difficult to assess tenders and to monitor performance. However, the mechanisms for preventing and detecting fraud and the making of 'excess' profits have often proved, in practice, to be ineffectual. Skill on the part of purchasing officers and sound management within purchasing units is crucial in ensuring that the government gets a good deal. Also important is the willingness of individuals (especially employees of contractors) to notify government of fraud, waste and mismanagement on the part of contractors, especially in the defence industry.

The brief discussion in this section can reasonably be summarised by saying that while government contracting power is of great political, economic and social significance, its exercise is, in general, subject to considerably less legal control than the exercise of statutory powers.

11.3.1.2 Enforcing contractual obligations

It is extremely rare for disputes arising out of the performance of government contracts to be the subject of litigation. Such disputes are usually resolved by informal negotiation between the government and the contractor or, if this does not succeed, by arbitration. In general, the law governing the liability of public bodies for breach of contract is the same as that governing the liability of private individuals and corporations. However, a qualification must be added to this general position, which is easy to state but not so easy to apply. Because public bodies have to consider the wider public interest in fulfilling their obligations under contracts, there may be circumstances in which the demands of public policy provide good grounds for a public body to refuse to perform its obligations to the other contracting party. In such cases, the interests and rights of the individual contractor are subordinated to the demands of public policy. In other words, the law recognises a defence of 'executive necessity', which a public body can sometimes plead in answer to a claim against it for breach of contract. The difficulty is to define the scope of this defence and to specify when it will be available.

The question facing a court confronted with a plea of executive necessity in defence to an action for breach of contract is essentially similar to that involved in deciding whether a contract is a void fetter on the exercise of a statutory power. The difference lies in the way the question is typically raised in practice. The fettering principle is usually relevant when a party seeks to force the public body to exercise

---

80   A distinction is sometimes drawn between two types of government power: *imperium* and *dominium*. The former refers to the government's political and legal authority, while the latter refers to its economic resources. The fact that the governors have both types of power, and that the governed lack the former, lies at the bottom of the public/private distinction.

its discretion, or seeks to challenge the exercise of a discretion which has been exercised in accordance with, or contrary to, the demands of a contract. A plea of executive necessity is typically made in a case in which the contractor seeks to enforce the contract or to recover damages for breach of contract. It is important to realise that the same basic issue ties the two areas together, because it serves to show that any sharp division between the public law obligation not to fetter the exercise of discretion and the private law contractual obligations of public bodies is unwarranted. The law of public contracts is basically an application of public law principles to the ordinary law of contract leading to certain modifications of private law principles in their application to public functions.

In the case to which the doctrine of executive necessity is usually traced—*The Amphitrite*[81] (in which the owners of a foreign ship unsuccessfully sued the government for failure to honour a promise, made during wartime, to allow the ship to leave British waters after discharging its cargo)—Rowlatt J seems to have thought that the defence would apply only to 'non-commercial contracts'. But this limitation would make it irrelevant to most cases. The case can be read as supporting the extreme proposition that a defence of executive necessity can be established merely on the public body's word that the demands of public policy justify non-performance of its undertakings. However, it seems clear that the courts retain for themselves the final power to judge the validity of a plea of executive necessity. In some areas, such as the conduct of war, the courts will no doubt exercise their power in a very restrained way and will usually accept official certificates as to the demands of public policy on the ground that the exercise of the power to wage war is unreviewable in the courts (this explains the result in *The Amphitrite*).

In *Commissioners of Crown Lands v Page*[82] it was held that the requisitioning of premises in 1945 could not be held to be in breach of the implied covenant of quiet enjoyment in the lease. Devlin LJ was clearly not prepared to allow decisions about the demands of the conduct of the war to become the subject of judicial inquiry, but denied that this created a general privilege to escape from any contract, which a public body happened to find disadvantageous, by pleading executive necessity. The court will scrutinise the plea and, if it feels competent to do so, will judge its merits. In one sense there is always a legitimate public interest in public functionaries not being bound to disadvantageous contracts, but against that interest must be weighed the contractual rights of the contractor. A contract is a technique by which parties can restrict their freedom of action in the future, and a party to a contract cannot be free to ignore that restriction as it wishes.

What is the effect of a plea of executive necessity? There are three main possibilities. First, the contract may simply be unenforceable against the government, thus denying the contractor any remedy for loss suffered as a result of the government's failure to perform. This would certainly seem to be the logical result of implying into the contract a term entitling the government to refuse to perform on public policy grounds. Second, it may be argued that failure to perform on the ground of executive necessity frustrates the contract. If that analysis were adopted, the contractor might be entitled to restitution of amounts spent in performing the contract, but would not be entitled to damages for other losses (notably, loss of profit). These two options involve application of basic principles of the private law of contract.

A third possibility would be to develop special 'public law' rules to deal with cases of executive necessity. In French law, there are several doctrines dealing with the termination and variation of public contracts, and it is sometimes suggested that common law would do well to adopt something similar.[83]

---

81   *Rederiaktiebolaget 'Amphitrite' v* R [1921] B 500.

82   [1960] 2 QB 274.

83   L N Brown and J Bell, *French Administrative Law*, 5th edn (Oxford: Oxford University Press, 1998), 206–10.

Restitution of benefits received by the public body under the contract would be fair and reasonable to the extent that this is possible. If the contractor has incurred irrecoverable expenses in performance of the contract, it should be entitled to compensation for such reliance losses. If (as in the *Cory* case mentioned earlier (11.3.1.1)), the effect of the government's action has been to increase the cost to the contractor of performing the contract, it would seem fair to award the contractor compensation for the additional cost.[84] Should the contractor ever be entitled to damages for profits that were expected from performance of the contract? There might be an argument for saying that although a contractor should never have to bear actual losses for the sake of the public interest, the contractor should not be allowed to make a profit at its expense.

Finally, it should be said that the defence of executive necessity will frequently be of little relevance in practice because government contracts often contain express provisions conferring on the government a right to withdraw from the contract which would entitle it to give effect to the legitimate demands of public policy.[85]

11.3.2 Contract as a technique of governance

As a technique of governance, contract can be understood as a mode of organising activities and achieving goals that utilises agreement and mutual obligation between counterparts, as opposed to the sort of hierarchical and unilateral control of agents by principals that characterises traditional government bureaucracies.[86] Contract is the basic legal form of competitive market activity, and an important aspect of phenomena, such as those mentioned in 11.3, which exemplify the use of contract as a technique of governance is the subjection of providers of public services to (quasi-) competitive pressures[87] (applied by granting their managers more or less operational independence). This can be either in the open market (as a result of privatisation, for instance) or within the institutional framework of government. For instance, the Australian Government Solicitor, a government business enterprise, competes with private law firms for government legal business;[88] and Centrelink, a non-departmental statutory agency, delivers services to the public under quasi-contractual arrangements[89] with various government departments.[90]

Another important aspect of the use of contract as a technique of governance is the opportunity it provides to achieve policy objectives without the use of legislation. We have already noted that governments may pursue collateral purposes in the procurement process by limiting the opportunity to

---

84   Davies, n 61 above, 111–13.

85   Seddon, *Government Contracts*, n 4 above, 197–200.

86   For a detailed English examination of this topic, see P Vincent-Jones, *The New Public Contracting: Regulation, Responsiveness, Rationality* (Oxford: Oxford University Press, 2006).

87   By 'quasi-competitive pressures' we refer to situations where a service provider has no actual competitors, but is given performance and output targets that operate as the sort of benchmark that competition generates.

88   D O'Brien, 'Outsourcing Legal Services—the Role of the Informed Purchaser' (2007) 52 *Australian Institute of Administrative Law Forum* 40; I Govey, 'Challenges when Outsourcing Legal Services' ibid, 44; R de Gruchy, 'Outsourcing Legal Services— Boon or Bane?' ibid, 50. Allowing or requiring public service providers to compete with the private sector is sometimes called 'market testing'. It can be contrasted with outsourcing, which is a process in which only private sector providers can compete.

89   'Quasi-contractual' in the sense that the arrangement may not be legally enforceable in the courts as a contract. Some would argue that it is a misuse of the term 'contract' to apply it to such arrangements: e.g. Seddon, *Government Contracts*, n 4 above, 31–6.

90   R Mulgan, 'Public Accountability of Provider Agencies: The Case of the Australian "Centrelink"' (2002) 68 *International Review of Administrative Sciences* 45. A term sometimes used to describe governmental bodies that operate outside departments is 'non-departmental public body': R Wettenhall, 'Non-Departmental Public Bodies Under the Howard Governments' (2007) 66(1) *Australian Journal of Public Administration* 62.

tender for government contracts to entities that meet certain conditions, and by inserting into procurement contracts terms that require contractors to meet certain conditions when performing the contract. But this is only one example of a more general phenomenon, other instances of which can easily be found in the context of outsourcing and public/private partnerships, for instance. Through contract, governments can deploy their economic resources and political influence, as opposed to their legal authority, to promote their goals.

The attraction of contract as an alternative to legislation derives from the fact, already noted, that governments do not need parliamentary approval to contract. As a result, parliaments have difficulty in exercising meaningful control over government contracting.[91] In addition, it may be more difficult in practice (although not in theory),[92] for successor governments to terminate unwanted contracts inherited from their predecessors than to amend or repeal inherited legislation. The major limitation of contract as compared with legislation (in theory, at least) is that(as we have also seen) a contractual provision that purports to stipulate the way in which the government will exercise some statutory or common law power may fall foul of the rule against fettering of discretions. As a result, it may be difficult or impossible for the government to use such a provision against the contractor or in the face of opposition from a third party.

From an administrative law perspective, the most important aspect of the use of contract as a technique of governance is its effect on accountability. The point can be illustrated by reference to privatisation. Suppose that a particular service, which was formerly provided to members of the public under statute by an organisation subject to ministerial control, is now provided under contract as the result of the sale of the 'business' to a private corporation. One result of this change will be that modes of 'public accountability' that we have considered so far in this book will cease to be available in respect of delivery of the service in question. Most obviously, ministerial responsibility to parliament will no longer apply. Judicial review under the *ADJR Act* is available only in relation to decisions made under statutory provisions, and not decisions made under contracts;[93] and it is unclear to what extent judicial review is available at common law in relation to contractual decision-making by private entities.[94] Public sector ombudsmen have no jurisdiction over private sector service providers (unless they are providing services under an outsourcing arrangement). FOI legislation does not apply to private entities. And so on.

This does not mean, of course, that customers have no avenues of recourse against private service providers. For instance, there may be an industry-specific, private-sector ombudsman to whom customers can complain. The service provider will also, of course, have certain obligations, and its customers will have certain rights, under the contract for delivery of the service; and these will, in principle at least, be enforceable in contract law. If the service provider has competitors, it will be subject to the 'discipline of the market'. In short, even if the service provider is not subject to public modes of accountability, it may be subject to 'private' modes of accountability, such as liability for breach of contract or in tort, or

---

91   M McGregor Lowndes and A McBratney, 'Government Community Service Contracts:Restraining the Abuse of Power (2011) 22 *Public Law Review* 279.

92   Seddon, *Government Contracts*, n 4 above, 208–11.

93   A good example of the potential effect of privatisation is provided by *NEAT Domestic Trading Pty Ltd v AWB Ltd* (2003) 216 CLR 177, involving regulation of wheat exports. See further 3.5.1.4.2.

94   Seddon, *Government Contracts*, n 4 above, 348–9; H Schoombee, 'The Judicial Review of Contractual Powers' in L Pearson (ed), *Administrative Law: Setting the Pace or Being Left Behind?* (Sydney, Australian Institute of Administrative Law, 1997).

complaint to an industry ombudsman. In addition, the service provider may be subject to government regulation, especially if it is operating in a non-competitive environment; and the regulator may be subject to public modes of accountability.

In some respects, outsourcing (or 'contracting out') the provision of public services to private sector contractors creates greater complications.[95] Typically, there will be a contractual relationship between the government and the service provider, and a contractual relationship between the service provider and the customer; but no contractual relationship between the government and the customer. The former contract may spell out in great detail the obligations of the service provider, but these obligations will be owed to, and will be enforceable by, the government,[96] not the customer.[97] In contrast to the situation in the case of privatisation, the government contracting entity will continue to have obligations in relation to provision of the service, and performance of those obligations will, in theory at least, remain subject to public modes of accountability. However, the effect of the contract between the service provider and the customer may render the delivery of the service to the consumer unamenable to various public modes of accountability.[98]

A similar situation may arise in the case of public–private partnerships. For instance, a private contractor who builds a public road may be given the contractual right—under a contract with the government—to recoup its investment over a period of years by charging tolls. During that period, the relationship between the contractor and road users will be regulated by contract. Again, although the relationship between the government and a GBE may not be contractual (because the government owns, and in that sense is, the GBE), the relationship between the GBE and its customers typically will be. As in the case of outsourcing, under arrangements of these types, the government will play a continuing role in the delivery of the service, and its performance of that role may be subject to public modes of accountability.[99] On the other hand, the introduction of contractual elements into arrangements for the delivery of public services will typically limit the availability and potential efficacy of public modes of accountability.

This general phenomenon can be interpreted in two quite different ways. According to one approach, changes in the mode of delivery of 'public services' (however defined) that limit the availability of avenues of public accountability (such as judicial and merits review, and investigations by ombudsmen) are to be deplored because public modes of accountability protect values different from those protected by private modes. In the UK, this line of thought has led the courts to contemplate, in principle at least, extension of the scope of judicial review, so that in certain cases it may available against contractual

---

95   The Administrative Review Council has made various recommendations about regulation of outsourcing, but few have so far been acted upon: ARC Report No 42, *The Contracting Out of Government Services* (August, 1998). See also R Mulgan, 'Government Accountability for Outsourced Services' (2006) 65(2) *Australian Journal of Public Administration* 48.

96   Perhaps in the guise of a regulator.

97   Seddon, *Government Contracts*, n 4 above, 39–42. Concerning the possibility that the service recipient may have a claim in tort against the government see M Groves, 'Outsourcing and Non-Delegable Duties' (2005) 16 *Public Law Review* 265.

98   Note, however, that the Commonwealth Ombudsman, for instance, can hear complaints against providers of contracted out services: *Ombudsman Act 1976* (Cth), ss 3BA and 3(4B). In *Plaintiff M61/2010E v Commonwealth of Australia* (2011) 272 ALR 14, [51] the High Court left open the question of whether a provider of contracted-out services might fall within the expression 'officer of the Commonwealth' in s 75(v) of the Constitution.

99   GBEs may also be subject to public forms of accountability: M Allars, 'Private Law but Public Power: Removing Administrative Law Review From Government Business Enterprises' (1995) 6 *Public Law Review* 44; N Dixon, 'Is There a Place for Administrative Law in Government Business Enterprises?' in L Pearson (ed), *Administrative Law: Setting the Pace or Being Left Behind?* (Sydney: Australian Institute of Administrative Law, 1997).

providers of public services if they can be said to be performing a 'public function'.[100] As we noted in 1.1, Australian law has not so far taken so sharp a functional turn as English law, and this apparent lack of concern on the part of courts about the impact of 'contractualisation' tends to aggravate worries about the 'accountability gap' it is seen to generate.

At one level, the normative assumption underlying this approach—namely, that providers of public services ought to be amenable to public modes of accountability—is hard to attack. However, there is a problem with the very concept of a 'public service'. Services do not come with a mark of publicness attached, and reasonable people may disagree about whether a particular service is public or not. Such disagreements typically arise from differences of opinion, not about the nature of the service, but about the proper role of government as service provider. In other words, people disagree about which services ought to be provided publicly as a matter of governance, as opposed to privately as a matter of commerce. Moreover, views about whether particular services are public or not may change over time,[101] and particular services may be provided both privately and publicly at the same time (education, for instance). In this light, the assumption that providers of public services ought to be amenable to public modes of accountability looks circular or tautologous.

Another related problem with this first approach lies in a second underpinning assumption to the effect that a public service retains its character as such, however it is delivered; that is, a public service remains a public service even if it is delivered under contract by a private entity. However, unless it is supplemented by the implausible assertion that publicness is an inherent characteristic of certain services, this argument is just another way of saying that the delivery of a particular service ought to be treated as a matter of governance, not of commerce. The basic point is that the first approach is convincing only if we begin by assuming what it sets out to prove, namely that providers of a particular service ought to be subject to public modes of accountability.

According to the second, quite different approach, the distinction—which is central to the first approach—between public and private services, and public and private modes of accountability, is not important. What matters is not whether service providers are subject to public as opposed to private modes of accountability, but only that adequate modes of accountability, of any type, should be available.[102] A common argument in favour of privatisation and contractualisation is that they subject service providers to 'market accountability' (or 'the discipline of the market') and to other forms of private accountability (such as liability for breach of contract), and that these provide at least as much protection to consumers of services as the modes of public accountability which they replace. According to some understandings of the concept of accountability, having to compete in a market is not a form of accountability at all. But accepting, for the sake of the argument, that it is, it might still be suggested that the various modes of accountability are not comparable and interchangeable in the way the second approach seems to assume;[103] and that the quality of accountability is just as important as the quantity. Putting

---

100   The leading case is *R v Panel on Takeovers and Mergers, ex parte Datafin plc* [1987] QB 815 in which the 'service' being provided was regulation of an aspect of the financial services industry (3.6.1). For further discussion of the English law (which really has no Australian counterpart) see P Cane, *Administrative Law*, 5th edn (Oxford: Oxford University Press, 2011), 266–72. For a brief discussion of the position in New Zealand see J McLean, 'New Public Management New Zealand Style' in P Craig and A Tomkins (eds), *The Executive and Public Law: Power and Accountability in Comparative Perspective* (Oxford: Oxford University Press, 2006), 135–6. Even if judicial review is available in principle, it may be more difficult to establish a ground of judicial review in this context than in relation to delivery of the service by a government organisation.

101   The welfare state was, after all, largely a phenomenon of the twentieth century.

102   C Scott, 'Accountability in the Regulatory State' (2000) 27 *Journal of Law and Society* 38.

103   For example, J McLean, 'The Ordinary Law of Tort and Contract and the New Public Management' (2001) 30 *Common Law World Review* 387.

the point crudely, it may be that public modes of accountability protect values and perform functions that private modes of accountability do not, and vice versa.[104] For instance, it may be suggested, in very general terms, that public modes of accountability are concerned with decision-making procedures and inputs much more than private modes, which focus on the outcomes of decision-making.[105]

It should be noted, however, that acceptance of this line of argument need not lead to the conclusion that traditional public modes of accountability should be available under contractual arrangements for the delivery of public services. Instead, some people would argue for a modification of contract law in particular and private modes of accountability in general to take account of the nature of the services being provided under such arrangements. So modified, the law of contract (for instance) would provide a public mode of accountability.

At this point in the argument, we are inevitably brought back to the question of which modes of accountability ought to be available against the providers of particular services. Privatisation and contractualisation are commonly promoted on grounds of economic efficiency. However, a preference for market-based and private modes of accountability over public modes is also frequently at least implicit in such support. Indeed, there is a sense in which public modes of accountability are ideologically incompatible (or at least in tension) with commitment to privatisation, corporatisation and contractualisation, and in which changed accountability arrangements are part and parcel of such developments.[106] This suggests that arguments for the inclusion of public modes of accountability in arrangements for privatisation, corporatisation and contractualisation of the delivery of public services may be based on opposition to these developments as such, and to the values and objectives that motivate them, and not merely on objections to changes in accountability arrangements.

11.4 Private law and the regulatory approach

Consistently with our general approach in this book, the discussion in this chapter has treated the private law of contract and tort as a mechanism for holding governors accountable to the governed.[107] However, it is possible to take a regulatory approach and to understand imposition of liability in contract and tort (for instance) as a means of influencing human behaviour in the future. Earlier (11.2.1.2, at n 43) we noted that English courts have sometimes justified refusal to impose a duty of care on public functionaries on the basis that doing so would cause them to be over-cautious in their dealings with citizens in that they might be led to act, or to refrain from acting, in certain ways, not in order to promote the public interest (however defined), but merely in order to reduce the risk of being held legally liable. This is often referred to as the 'overkill' argument, and it is deployed not only in relation to public authorities, but also, for instance, in relation to medical practitioners.

---

104   Concerning the values promoted by administrative law see 12.1. For a general comparison of accountability in the public and private sectors see R Mulgan, *Holding Power to Account: Accountability in Modern Democracies* (Basingstoke: Palgrave Macmillan, 2003), Ch 4.

105   Mulgan, n 104 above, 166–171.

106   See generally Mulgan, n 104 above, Ch 5.

107   In this context, tort law was once memorably and influentially described as an ombudsman: A Linden, 'Tort Law as Ombudsman' (1973) 51 *Canadian Bar Review* 155.

The overkill argument appeals directly to the anticipated effects of (the fear or risk of) legal liability on human behaviour. It is based on a particular 'economic' version of the regulatory approach, the foundation of which is the proposition that the prime purpose of tort law (for instance) is to provide incentives to behave in socially productive and efficient ways. From this perspective, for example, the concept of negligence is understood in terms of an equation that compares the cost of avoiding harm with the costs inflicted by the harm: a person is negligent if they fail to take precautions against harm that could have been prevented at a cost no greater than the cost of the harm multiplied by its probability. From this perspective, the point of imposing liability for negligence is to provide an incentive for efficient harm-prevention or, in other words, to deter inefficiently harmful behaviour.

According to this approach, liability to compensate for harm should not be imposed if the cost of doing so would exceed the benefit, because this would 'over-deter' the causing of harm and provide incentives for inefficient harm prevention. The overkill argument justifies refusal to impose a duty of care precisely on this ground—namely, that the cost of imposing liability (in terms of its adverse impact on the relationship between governors and the governed) would, in the particular circumstances, outweigh the benefit in terms of compensating the victim of negligence.

In principle, this particular application of the regulatory approach (which could obviously be applied more widely to liability in private law for performance of public functions) is sensible and in no way inconsistent with the accountability perspective. Accountability is valuable, but it also has costs. If the costs of an accountability mechanism, assessed in terms of its impact on the behaviour of those held accountable, are found to outweigh its benefits in terms of the promotion of other values, we should at least question its desirability. In practice, however, we lack agreed criteria against which to assess the costs and benefits of legal liability and other accountability mechanisms, as well as empirical evidence about the impact of liability law on the behaviour of public authorities. There is a large body of research about the deterrent effects of tort law (in particular) in contexts such as road accidents and medical negligence, but almost none in the context of public authority liability. In the absence of agreed criteria and reliable empirical evidence, arguments for or against the use of liability law to regulate performance of tasks of governance operate as make-weights designed to bolster conclusions based on value judgments about how the costs and benefits of governance ought to be distributed between the governors and the governed. The regulatory approach alerts us to an important set of questions, but questions to which we currently lack answers.

12

Values and Effects of Administrative Law

This final chapter addresses two questions: what is administrative law for, and what does it achieve? The aim is not to answer these questions, if only because, as framed, they are impossible to answer simply, straightforwardly or in a way that would be likely to command widespread, let alone universal, assent. Rather, our aim is to examine the sorts of issues that would need to be tackled in order to formulate answers, to suggest ways of addressing such issues, and to survey some of the answers that have been given to the two questions.

12.1 What is administrative law for?

12.1.1 Two views about the purpose of administrative law

It is a widely (albeit not universally)[1] held opinion that law is best understood as a purposive phenomenon. A good starting point for consideration of administrative law is the plausible view that one of its purposes is to promote certain values (or 'ideals') about the way governors should perform their functions and behave in dealings with the governed. We may distinguish between two ways of thinking about how administrative law promotes such values, which we might call non-instrumental and instrumental respectively. From a non-instrumental perspective, administrative law can be said to promote values by embodying and expressing them. From an instrumental perspective, administrative law can be said to promote values by influencing human behaviour and its outcomes.

According to the instrumentalist, the worth of administrative law and the measure of its success (or failure) would lie in its impact on behaviour and outcomes. According to the non-instrumentalist, the worth of law and the measure of its success (or failure) would lie in its rules and practices. For the

---

1 There is a brand of 'formalism' in legal theory according to which law is properly and fully understood in terms of its internal structure and normative logic. The leading example of this approach is E Weinrib, *The Idea of Private Law* (Cambridge, Mass: Harvard University Press, 1995). Weinrib is famous for saying that to the extent private law has a purpose, it is to be private law! A somewhat similar approach to constitutional and administrative law is adopted in M Loughlin, *The Idea of Public Law* (Oxford: Hart Publishing, 2003). But be warned: this is a very difficult book.

instrumentalist, law could be counted a success only to the extent that its effect was to bring behaviour and outcomes into conformity with specified values. By contrast, for the non-instrumentalist, law could be counted a success if it clearly, consistently and coherently expressed specified values. Of course, a non-instrumentalist might judge law to be a greater success to the extent that it also had a positive impact on behaviour and outcomes, but would still think it worthwhile even if it could not be shown to have such impact. On the other hand, although we might speculate that law is unlikely to bring behaviour and outcomes into conformity with specified values unless it expresses those values clearly, consistently and coherently, the instrumentalist would not give law any credit merely for such expression of values if it did not also have a positive impact on behaviour and outcomes.

It should be noted that this distinction between instrumentalist and non-instrumentalist ways of understanding the purpose of administrative law cuts across the distinction, drawn in 1.3 and referred to at various points in the book, between the legal and regulatory approaches to administrative law. Those who take the regulatory approach to administrative law are obviously (indeed, by definition) instrumentalists. On the other hand, people who think that administrative law has an expressive purpose are obviously (indeed, by definition) non-instrumentalists. However, someone who thinks, for instance, that the prime purpose of administrative law is to promote the value of accountability might hold that view either instrumentally or non-instrumentally. Another way of putting this is to say that instrumentalism and non-instrumentalism are ways of thinking about how administrative law promotes values, not ways of thinking about what values administrative law promotes. Instrumentalism and non-instrumentalism alike need to be supplemented with an account (or 'theory') of the values that administrative law promotes.

So what can we say about the values promoted by administrative law?

12.1.2 Discovering administrative law values

We may begin by drawing a distinction between immanent and critical values. Immanent values are, in some sense, 'in' the law. They are the values that administrative law can be said actually to promote, as opposed to values which it is thought administrative law should promote, regardless of whether it actually does or not. These latter are critical values. Immanent values are 'discovered' by analysing legal rules and practices. This is very far from being a straightforward process. For one thing, administrative law as understood in this book is a complex set of individually complex institutional arrangements. Discerning the values immanent in such arrangements, let alone a diverse set of such arrangements, is bound to be a tricky task. For instance, does it really make sense to ask about the values immanent in this set of institutions as a whole? Or to ask about the immanent values of judicial review without distinguishing between the rules and principles of judicial review on the one hand and the mechanisms and procedures by which those rules and principles are given practical effect on the other?

To some extent, the answer to such questions depends on how abstractly or, by contrast, how concretely we talk about values. For instance, 'accountability' is an extremely abstract idea, and it seems plausible to explain all the arrangements discussed in this book as promoting this value. On the other hand, precisely because it is so abstract, accountability can do no more than provide a framework within which to compare and contrast the various arrangements we have surveyed. It is only when we descend to a lower level of abstraction that we can, for instance, distinguish between judicial review and merits review on the basis of the legality/merits distinction. We referred to this issue of levels of abstraction in 5.1.1 where we argued that the grounds of judicial review can be understood as more concrete embodiments of abstract values. For instance, just as we might think of the legality/merits distinction as a more concrete embodiment of the value of accountability, we might think of the grounds of judicial review collectively as a more concrete embodiment of the value of legality.

A further difficulty in uncovering immanent values arises from the very nature of administrative law. Many of its rules and principles, and even some of its institutions, are products not so much of deliberate creation as of organic growth. This is obviously true, for instance, of the grounds of judicial review, which have been developed over hundreds of years (and are still developing) as the result of the more or less uncoordinated activities of numerous courts and judges. As rules and institutions develop and change over time, so might the values they promote. In the case of an institution such as the AAT, or of rules and principles such as those contained in s 5 of the *ADJR Act*, it may be possible, by examining policy documents and parliamentary debates, to discern the values promoted by the relevant statutory provision. By contrast, in the case of judge-made rules and of judicial review and the principles of merits review (for instance), or indeed in the case of the mechanism of judicial review itself, it may be much more difficult to make confident statements about what values they actually promote, as opposed to what values the speaker thinks they ought to promote. And, of course, even statutory regimes and institutions may develop over time, and their immanent values may change.

A third complexity affecting the discovery of immanent values is that precisely the same features of the law may be interpreted in accordance with various different and more abstract values. For instance, the value promoted by the fair hearing rule might be said variously to be that of maximising the chance that the decision made will comply with relevant legal requirements, respecting the dignity and autonomy of individuals, promoting efficiency in decision-making by improving the supply of information to the decision-maker, promoting dialogue, and so on. To the extent that the various values said to be immanent in the rule are in tension or conflict with one another, there may be no way of choosing between them except, perhaps, in terms of some concept of 'fit' (which explanation is most consistent with the details of the relevant law?), or in terms of a preference for one value over the others, or a combination of these two.

A fourth difficulty about discovering the values immanent in administrative law can be explained in terms of a distinction between monistic and pluralistic accounts (or 'theories') of values. As the name implies, a monistic account of administrative law or judicial review (for instance) would suggest that it promotes only one or perhaps one dominant value, such as accountability. By contrast, a pluralistic account would suggest that administrative law or judicial review promotes various different values. For instance, in 8.8.1 we saw that merits review is said by many to have the dual purposes of redressing grievances and improving standards of primary decision-making. Again, thinking about the grounds of judicial review as more concrete expressions of more abstract values may generate a pluralistic account of the values that underpin judicial review: procedural fairness, legality, (bounded) rationality, and so on. The choice between a monistic and a pluralistic approach might depend to some extent on what the theory seeks to explain. For instance, it might seem plausible to suggest that the procedure of judicial review promotes the single (dominant) value of redressing grievances. But if we think of judicial review in terms of the combination of a set of rules and principles, and a set of procedures, it might seem more plausible to give a pluralistic account of the immanent values of judicial review, so understood.

Monistic and pluralistic theories have contrasting strengths and weaknesses. Monistic accounts tend to be couched in terms of more abstract values than pluralistic accounts, and they are typically broader in scope covering, for instance, administrative law rather than judicial review. For such reasons, a monistic account may not provide as convincing or illuminating an explanation of its subject matter as an account that is less broad in coverage and which gives an account of purposes at a lower level of abstraction: there may be particular aspects of the subject matter which a monistic abstract theory has difficulty explaining. If so, the theorist may categorise the inexplicable detail as a 'mistake' and perhaps suggest some change in the law to bring it into harmony with its alleged purpose.

On the other hand, a problem with pluralistic theories is that they may attribute to an area of the law the promotion of values that potentially conflict with one another or at least coexist in unstable tension. One example is provided by freedom of information provisions. Because such provisions seek to strike a balance between open government and public interest confidentiality, it is plausible to say that this area of the law expresses two values—openness and secrecy. But this conclusion is not very helpful unless the theory goes on to explain how these two values are balanced against one another and what (more concrete) values the balancing exercise promotes. Another example can be found in the relationship between the values of 'administrative efficiency' and 'protecting the rights and interests of individuals'. The former justifies the use of general 'policies', especially in high-volume decision-making contexts, whereas the latter requires that decision-makers be prepared to make exceptions to such policies to accommodate individual cases. Once again, without principles suggesting how these two contrasting values are to be accommodated, merely saying that the law promotes both is not very helpful.

A third example is provided by the idea that merits review promotes the two values of addressing grievances and improving primary decision-making. Although these two values may not be in direct conflict, it is plausible to say that the goal of redressing grievances constrains promotion of the improvement goal because there may be much better and more effective ways of improving decision-making than by redressing instances of bad decision-making. A recurring theme of empirical research to be surveyed in 12.2 is that judicial review appears to have relatively little impact on bureaucratic behaviour. One explanation may be that it focuses on accountability, and that this focus limits its regulatory efficacy. The same may be true of merits review.

The existence of these various problems need not force us to the conclusion that we should abandon the language of or the search for values immanent in administrative law, but the complexity of the task alerts us to the fact that it is unlikely to be a simple, descriptive one. Understandings of the values promoted by a set of complex human institutions such as administrative law inevitably have a significant aspirational or ideological component, designed as much to justify and mould those institutions as to describe them. Another way of putting this is to say that, although the distinction between immanent and critical values is clear in principle, it may be much less clear in application. This is a result not only of the inherent difficulties of the task of discovering immanent values, but also of the contested nature of critical values, especially when framed at a high level of abstraction.

The more abstractly a value is stated, the more options there are for giving it more concrete expression, and the more room for disagreement about how it ought to be expressed. For instance, people who agree that accountability is an important value underpinning administrative law might disagree about how that value ought to be given concrete expression. People who agree that legality (or 'the rule of law') is an important value underpinning judicial review might disagree about what legality means. People who agree that procedural fairness is an important aspect of legality might disagree about what procedural fairness requires. And so on. Although expressing critical values abstractly might help us to see what various legal arrangements have in common and to achieve some sort of agreement about what they are for, it may conceal important differences between the various arrangements without helping to resolve disagreements about how those values should be implemented in particular contexts.

With these various caveats in mind, the next section will survey some of the abstract values that have been attributed to administrative law (or some part of it, such as judicial review) immanently or critically or without much regard for that distinction.

12.1.3 Suggested values of administrative law

12.1.3.1 Rule of law

We may begin with the rule of law (or 'legality') if only because the idea that judicial review promotes this value is deeply entrenched in the jurisprudence of the High Court. As deployed by the High Court, the concept of legality rests on a restricted understanding of 'law', which is to be contrasted both with 'merits' and 'policy'. Legality has two aspects: one, that power should be subject to legally enforceable limits; and the other, that the courts should not exceed their appropriate constitutional role of enforcing those limits. The rhetoric of the rule of law, as it is used in this context, displays a common feature of accounts of legal values, namely that values are deployed not only to explain, and justify or criticise, the law, but also to inform its development. For instance, rule of law ideology has played a significant part in reasoning and decisions about the scope of judicial review under s 75(v) of the Constitution (7.4).

The rule of law (in combination with the doctrine of the supremacy of parliament, which is the most important source of the 'ruling law')[2] is undoubtedly the dominant ideology (or foundational value) of Australian administrative law. This is not to say, of course, that administrative law in general (as opposed to judicial review in particular) is concerned only with enforcing the rule of law, as this concept is interpreted by the High Court. For instance, merits review tribunals go beyond the law to the merits, and the function of ombudsmen is not limited to enforcing the law. However, the rule of law provides the background against which these other functions are understood, explained and assessed. To this extent, the legacy of Dicey (2.1.3.2) lives on.

In the UK in recent years, there has been a vigorous debate among public lawyers about the meaning of 'law' in the phrase 'the rule of law'.[3] The essence of the disagreement between the two sides concerns whether the very concept of 'law' imposes certain limitations on the exercise of power by governors that cannot be reduced or removed by the governors themselves.[4] Those who argue that it does disagree among themselves about what those limitations might be, but they agree that the task of specifying and enforcing such limitations properly belongs to the courts. For that reason, this broad line of argument has been dubbed 'common law constitutionalism'.

The idea that courts have a special role in defining and enforcing limitations on powers of governors obviously underpins the proposition that s 75(v) of the Constitution guarantees a minimum of judicial review that the legislature cannot remove (7.2.3). This is the ultimate foundation of the rule of

---

2   There are some complex issues lurking here. The scope of administrative law is not limited to decisions made in exercise of statutory powers. Nor, of course, are the grounds of judicial review statutory in origin, although in some contexts (e.g. *ADJR Act*, but not, for instance, s 75(v) of the Constitution) they now rest on a statutory foundation. To a certain extent, therefore, the 'law' enforced in the name of the rule of law is common law, not statute law.

3   The literature is large. Most of it is written for a specialist audience and much is quite inaccessible. A possible introduction is T Poole, 'Back to the Future? Unearthing the Theory of Common Law Constitutionalism' (2003) 23 *Oxford Journal of Legal Studies* 435. See also M Allars, 'Of Cocoons and Small "c" Constitutionalism: The Principle of Legality and an Australian Perspective on *Baker*' in D Dyzenhaus (ed), *The Unity of Public Law* (Oxford: Hart Publishing, 2004).

4   In theoretical debates about the rule of law, this question is framed in terms of a distinction between formal and substantive versions of the concept. See generally B Z Tamanaha, *On the Rule of Law: History, Politics, Theory* (Cambridge: Cambridge University Press, 2004), especially Chs 7 and 8.

law ideology in Australian administrative law. The important difference between this approach and common law constitutionalism is that, in theory at least, the source of the minimum guarantee of judicial review is the Constitution, not the courts that enforce it. However, because s 75(v) says nothing explicitly about grounds of judicial review, it is unclear whether s 75(v) merely confers jurisdiction to entertain judicial review applications, or whether it also entrenches certain grounds of judicial review.

The latter interpretation is preferable because otherwise the legislature could effectively exclude the judicial review jurisdiction. Historically, the grounds of review available under s 75(v) were developed by the courts in the context of applications for the prerogative writs; and the concept of 'jurisdictional error', which summarises those grounds of review, has been developed by the High Court in recent years mainly in the context of immigration decision-making. This means that if the preferable interpretation of s 75(v) is adopted by the court, it will effectively have read into the Constitution a form of common law constitutionalism: in theory the source of the guaranteed grounds of review will be the Constitution, but in reality their author will be the High Court.

12.1.3.2 Accountability

The value that has framed the analysis in this book is 'accountability', which is, of course, an extremely abstract concept. Perhaps its main theoretical advantage—and a product of its abstract nature—is that all the institutions and arrangements we have surveyed in this book can plausibly be understood as modes of accountability (however else they may be understood). Richard Mulgan provides a helpful exposition of the concept in terms of four 'dimensions': (1) who is accountable? (2) to whom? (3) for what? and (4) how?[5] Jerry Mashaw expands the 'for what?' dimension into three distinct inquiries: (3a) about what? (3b) through what processes? and (3c) according to what standards?[6] The various mechanisms and institutions we have surveyed in this book can be analysed in terms of these factors. For instance, the discussions in chapters 1 and 3 of the scope of administrative law and judicial review address question (1) (who is accountable?) and, perhaps, question (3a) (about what?). In 8.5.1.2 we saw that the scope of judicial review under the *ADJR Act* is defined differently from the scope of merits review under the *AAT Act*; and in 9.3.4 that the jurisdiction of the Commonwealth Ombudsman is defined in yet a different way. And so on.

Answering question (2) (to whom?)[7] provides the subject matter of the discussion in Chapter 6 of access to judicial review, in 8.5.2 of who may apply for merits review, in 9.3.3 of who may complain to an ombudsman, and so on. Question (3) (for what?) is discussed, for instance, in Chapter 5 on the grounds of judicial review, 8.6 on the basis of merits review, and 9.3.6 on the basis of ombudsmen's recommendations. Question (4) (how?) is addressed in Chapter 4 on judicial review remedies, 8.7 on the outcomes of merits review, 9.3.8 on the outcome of ombudsmen's recommendations, and so on. Cutting the material in this way enables us to compare and contrast the various modes of accountability and gain some appreciation of how they might interact in complementary or conflicting ways. It might also help us to understand whether the various mechanisms and arrangements, though all modes of

---

5 R Mulgan, *Holding Power to Account: Accountability in Modern Democracies* (Houndsmill, Basingstoke: Palgrave Macmillan, 2003).

6 J L Mashaw, 'Accountability and Institutional Design: Some Thoughts on the Grammar of Governance' in M Dowdle (ed), *Public Accountability: Designs, Dilemmas and Experiences* (Cambridge: Cambridge University Press, 2006), 117–18.

7 In one sense, the obvious answer to this question is 'to courts, tribunals, ombudsmen and so on'. But to the extent that administrative law redresses grievances, it also makes sense to answer this question by defining who may use administrative law for this purpose.

accountability, could be thought to fulfil different purposes. For instance, we might conclude that, because of the distinctive characteristics of the ombudsman mechanism, it is more plausible to think of its purpose in terms of establishing and promoting standards of good administration than of redressing individual grievances. Generally, we should be alert to the possibility that the differences between various accountability mechanisms are just as significant as their similarities.

Helpful as Mulgan's and Mashaw's structural analysis of accountability may be, it arguably has one notable disadvantage. Mulgan includes the fourth 'how' dimension in his analysis because he thinks that 'rectification and sanctions'[8] are an integral part of the concept of accountability. This is an unnecessarily narrow view. For instance, in Chapter 9 we argued that the obligations of ministers to account to parliament provide a significant avenue of accountability in the form of provision of information, explanations and undertakings to take remedial action regardless of whether individuals secure redress or are sanctioned. There is no good reason to exclude mechanisms that display the first three dimensions, but not the fourth dimension, from our understanding of accountability. Indeed, we might not even consider an accountability mechanism deficient because it 'lacks teeth'. For instance, there is a common view that lack of coercive power is (ironically, perhaps) one of the strengths of the ombudsman institution.

It is helpful to distinguish between various modes of accountability. In this book, we have focused on what is commonly called 'legal accountability'. We have also paid some attention to 'political accountability' through parliaments (9.4) and 'market-based' (or 'competitive') accountability (in 11.3). Another commonly identified mode of accountability may be called 'bureaucratic'. This can be understood in terms of hierarchical lines of responsibility and answerability between managers and officers or workers within organisations such as government agencies.[9] Yet another mode is often referred to as 'social' or 'community' accountability. Characteristic of this mode are relationships of mutual interaction between members of closed groups. Professional organisations that regulate their members' activities provide an example. These various modes of accountability may be roughly categorised according to whether they are 'vertical', 'formal' and 'public' (legal, political, bureaucratic) or 'horizontal', 'informal' and 'private' (competitive and social). Some people would question whether horizontal, informal, private modes of interaction should be classified as modes of accountability;[10] but this largely terminological dispute need not concern us here.

Developments in the past 25 years or so—such as privatisation, corporatisation, contracting out and public/private partnerships—have generated a very high level of interest in and focus on accountability, especially but not exclusively in the academic literature of administrative law. A major concern, especially among lawyers, is that changes such as these in the 'nature of governance'— sometimes referred to as 'the hollowing out of the state'—produce an accountability 'deficit' to the extent that they have the (intended) effect of reducing legal and political accountability for the delivery of 'public services'. In some instances—as is often the case when public utilities are privatised—such developments are accompanied by increased regulation of the provision of services, and the regulators may be subject to public forms of accountability even if the service providers are not. Fears about an accountability deficit are characteristic of those who take a legal approach to administrative law and view

8   Mulgan, n 5 above, 9.

9   The rule against delegation (5.3.5) is a form of legal control over the operation of bureaucratic accountability.

10   For example, E Rubin, 'The Myth of Non-Bureaucratic Accountability and the Anti-Administrative Impulse' in Dowdle, n 6 above.

accountability primarily in terms of the relationship between governors and the governed. By contrast, those who take a more regulatory approach and view accountability primarily in terms of institutional design (see below) tend to argue that the removal of certain modes of accountability need not be a cause for concern because other modes can be substituted, or will spontaneously spring up to take their place.[11]

12.1.3.3 Institutional design values

The rule of law approach (12.1.3.1), which is characteristic of English and Australian thinking about administrative law, focuses on the relationship between governors and governed. Its main concern is that dealings between governors and the governed should be controlled by law. In the USA, by contrast, ideas of separation of powers are more influential and concerns about institutional design more prominent. In a famous article published in 1975,[12] Richard Stewart argued that in American administrative law the rule of law ideology (which he dubbed the 'transmission belt' theory of judicial review) had been replaced by an 'interest representation' model. This model is rooted in a political theory called 'pluralism', the basic idea of which is that the political process can best be understood as a forum in which competing groups vie for influence, power and resources. Viewed from this perspective, the ideal that is or ought to be promoted by administrative law is that all groups affected by government decision-making should be adequately represented in the decision-making process ('procedural fairness for groups' we might say).

Stewart's path-breaking article stimulated others to propose different accounts of the ideology that did, or in their opinion should, underpin administrative law. Two deserve brief mention. Republican theory is based on an ideal of participatory democracy in which citizens and groups engage in dialogue about the public interest, rather than compete to promote their own interests.[13] According to republican theory, the basic value of judicial review and administrative law is that of public dialogue and active participation of citizens and groups in decision-making processes.

Public choice theory rests on the assumption (which it shares with economic analyses of private law (11.4), and which also underpins political pluralism), that individuals are motivated by self-interest.[14] While promotion of personal or partisan interests is both acceptable and desirable in the 'private' sphere of life (to which, in this view, competitive markets belong), it is not acceptable in the public sphere. On the contrary, we expect our governors and governing institutions to serve and promote the 'public interest' rather than their own personal or partisan interests. According to public choice theory, the basic value of administrative law, and public law more generally, is that governors should serve the public interest; and the purpose of administrative law is to give governors incentives to serve the public interest rather than their own personal or partisan interests. One version of this approach is known as principal/agent theory.[15] In this theory, statutory bodies (for instance) are understood as agents of the legislature (the principal), and the legislature is understood as the agent of 'the people' (the principal). According to principal/agent theory, the basic function of administrative law is to express and (thereby) promote the principle that agents should serve the interests of their principals, not their own interests.

---

11   For example, C Scott, 'Spontaneous Accountability' in Dowdle, n 6 above. See also 11.3.2.

12   R B Stewart, 'The Reformation of American Administrative Law' (1975) 88 *Harvard Law Review* 1669.

13   For a useful discussion see M Seidenfeld, 'A Civic Republican Justification for the Bureaucratic State' (1992) 105 *Harvard Law Review* 1511, especially 1562–76.

14   A helpful account will be found in J Mashaw, *Greed, Chaos and Governance: Using Public Choice to Improve Public Law* (New Haven: Yale University Press, 1997).

15   W Bishop, 'A Theory of Administrative Law' (1990) 19 *Journal of Legal Studies* 489.

This very brief account can give no more than a flavour of an extensive literature that interprets public law (both constitutional and administrative law) as an aspect of political activity and explores the relationship between public law and various theories of the nature and role of politics. Conceptualising public law as a form of politics naturally produces analyses that focus on institutions rather than individuals and on issues of institutional design rather than the relationship between political institutions and the individual.

That completes our all-too-brief discussion of the question, what is administrative law for? Next we turn our attention to the second question addressed in this chapter: what does administrative law achieve?

12.2 What does administrative law achieve?

12.2.1 Impact and values

As explained in 12.1.1, according to the instrumentalist approach the purpose of administrative law is to promote specified values (such as those discussed in 12.1.3) by influencing behaviour and outcomes. By contrast, according to the non-instrumentalist approach, the purpose of administrative law is to promote specified values by embodying and expressing them. For the non-instrumentalist, the question of what administrative law achieves can be answered 'analytically' by specifying the values that it does, or should, promote and then examining legal 'doctrine' (the rules and principles of administrative law) and practices to determine whether and to what extent they embody and express those values clearly, consistently and coherently. Such an analytical approach (which sits easily with a rule of law ideology (12.1.3.1)) informs much administrative law scholarship and can plausibly be said to characterise judicial reasoning and methodology, as well as much 'dialogue' between scholars and judges. A conclusion that law does not promote the 'right values', or that it promotes the right values unclearly, inconsistently or incoherently, may lead scholars to make suggestions for changing the law, and judges to do just that.

Discussion of the values that are or should be promoted by administrative law is central to the analytical approach that characterises non-instrumentalism. By contrast, instrumentalists tend to focus on the effects of administrative law on behaviour and outcomes, and give relatively little attention to the values being promoted. In principle, it might be possible to study impact independently of and without making any assumptions about values. In that case, the research questions would be whether the object of study had any discernible effects and, if so, what they were. In practice, however, impact researchers, with little or no discussion, typically begin with some understanding of the values that administrative law does or should promote, and they set out to record its achievements (or failures) in terms of those values.[16] Most of the available research is concerned with judicial review and, to the extent that values are mentioned, they tend to be framed in abstract terms such as 'good decision-making',[17] 'bureaucratic

---

16   A noteworthy exception is an English study of the impact of the UK FOI regime. It carefully analyses the objectives of the regime and uses a mixture of research methodologies to examine the extent to which they have been achieved: R Hazell, B Worthy and M Golder, *The Impact of the Freedom of Information Act on Central Government in the UK: Does FOI Work?* (Houndsmills, Hants: Palgrave Macmillan, 2010).

17   For example, M Sunkin and K Pick, 'The Changing Impact of Judicial Review: The Independent Review Service of the Social Fund' [2001] *Public Law* 736, 745; G Richardson and M Sunkin, 'Judicial Review: Questions of Impact' [1996] *Public Law* 79, 100.

justice',[18] and 'openness and participation in public decision-making'.[19] Such relative lack of attention to values is clearly a weakness in research of this type, and it needs to be borne in mind when assessing its conclusions.[20] An answer to the question of what administrative law achieves can only be properly assessed in the light of an answer to the question of what it is for—and, as we saw in 12.1.2, there are many difficulties in answering the latter question that ideally need to be tackled before addressing the former.

The body of reported research into the impact of administrative law is small and, as already noted, most of it concerns judicial review. Such research is typically quite narrow in focus and is neither designed nor apt to generate conclusions of general application. For these reasons, not much would be gained by examining reports of the research in detail. A better approach is to treat such research as the basis for developing hypotheses about impact that could be further tested by future research in various contexts. Later in the chapter we will examine some of the hypotheses that are supported by the available research. Before doing that, however, some preliminary points should be made.

12.2.2 Research methodology and aims

First, a few words about methodology. Investigations of the impact of administrative law can be sorted into four broad methodological categories. First, there is a considerable body of literature based on unstructured and unsystematic participant observation of the impact of administrative law. The authors are typically public servants, especially managers in posts that have brought them into contact with accountability mechanisms and the administrative law system. Judicial review, merits review, the ombudsman and the federal administrative law system are typical objects of observation. The evidence provided by such observations is largely anecdotal and impressionistic; and although insider accounts of this sort are often fascinating, they probably tell us as much about their authors' attitudes and values as about impact.

In the second category are studies that use quantitative methods. Some impact research is concerned with how (in)effectively administrative law addresses non-compliance with legal rules and principles; other research is concerned with how (in)effective the law is in securing compliance. Quantitative research methods tend to be used more, and to be of more use, in studying non-compliance than compliance. A good example is the research of Robin Creyke and John McMillan into the 'outcomes' of judicial review applications.[21] The typical outcome of a successful judicial review claim is that the decision is remitted (or 'referred back') to the decision-maker for reconsideration. In some cases, the basis on which the reviewing court finds in favour of the applicant effectively leaves the decision-maker no option but to revise the decision in the applicant's favour. But very commonly, the court's reason for remitting the decision will leave the decision-maker free to make the same decision again. It was widely believed that success in judicial review claims was very often Pyrrhic, because bureaucrats had at their disposal various techniques to 'neutralise' the impact of adverse court decisions. Indeed, one of the

---

18   S Halliday, 'The Influence of Judicial Review on Bureaucratic Decision-Making' [2000] *Public Law* 110, 111–2.

19   Richardson and Sunkin, n 16 above, 101.

20   Work that adopts the non-instrumental analytical method may suffer from an analogous weakness. Sometimes branded 'black letter', such analysis is more concerned with the internal coherence and consistency of legal doctrine than with the values it promotes. These tend to be assumed rather than discussed or justified.

21   R Creyke and J McMillan, 'The Operation of Judicial Review in Australia' in M Hertogh and S Halliday (eds), *Judicial Review and Bureaucratic Impact: International and Interdisciplinary Perspectives* (Cambridge: Cambridge University Press, 2004); 'Judicial Review Outcomes—An Empirical Study' (2004) 11 *Australian Journal of Administrative Law* 82.

earliest and most influential articles about the impact of judicial review made precisely this point and identified three such techniques: delaying tactics, making the same decision again but in accordance with the court's decision, and the promotion of legislation to reverse the decision's effect.[22]

To the contrary, Creyke and McMillan discovered that, in a sample of judicial review claims decided by the Federal Court, the applicant eventually achieved a favourable outcome in about 60% of cases. Research in other countries suggests both somewhat higher (75%) and somewhat lower (40%/47%) rates of ultimate success.[23] It is impossible to know what to make of these differences because the various research projects are incomparable in various respects. For the same reason, it is very difficult to know how generalisable the results are. Indeed, this is a problem that afflicts all impact research: each project is inevitably quite limited in focus, and it is difficult or impossible to know whether the results of any particular project would be valid in a different context. This is one reason why impact research is better used to generate testable hypotheses than as a basis for making firm general statements about impact. Creyke and Macmillan conclude that their research establishes the success of judicial review as a mechanism for redressing grievances. But whether a 60% (or a 40% or a 75%) success rate is a cause for celebration is to some extent a question of judgment.

The third methodological category covers impact studies that use qualitative research techniques. The main purpose of such studies is typically to discover whether, to what extent and why decision-makers comply with administrative law. Techniques include inspection of documents such as agency files, interviews with decision-makers and structured, systematic personal observation by researchers. This last technique is often called 'ethnographic'. It involves the researcher being located in the agency under observation—often for significant periods of time—to see first-hand how decisions are made and to interact with decision-makers on a day-to-day basis.[24]

The fourth methodological category comprises case studies. This involves a focus on an individual court decision (or a set of related decisions) to discover its (or their) impact on bureaucratic behaviour. In the US, there is a long history of this sort of study, mainly conducted by political scientists primarily interested in courts as agents of social change. Some of the earliest impact research in the UK followed this model.[25] Although this type of research, like that in the third category, uses qualitative techniques, its focus on individual decisions is distinctive.

Impact research raises various general methodological issues. We have already mentioned the issue of generalisability of the findings of particular research projects, and the distinction between hypotheses for further testing and firm general propositions about impact. Another important methodological issue concerns causation. Consider, for instance, research into the impact of judicial review. Decision-makers are subject to various influences and demands from both within and without their organisations. The notion of impact assumes some sort of causal relationship between legal rules and court decisions on the one hand, and bureaucratic behaviour on the other. Researchers distinguish between two different approaches to this issue: positivist and interpretivist.[26] Positivists, it is said, conceptualise impact on the

---

22   C Harlow, 'Administrative Reaction to Judicial Review' [1976] *Public Law* 116.

23   See Creyke and McMillan, 'The Operation of Judicial Review in Australia', 170, n 21 above.

24   Such research has been described by a wit as involving 'hanging out'. Needless to say, it is very time consuming and expensive even when researchers overcome the initial hurdle of persuading the agency to allow them in.

25   For example, T Prosser, 'Politics and Judicial Review: The Atkinson Case and Its Aftermath' [1979] *Public Law* 59; *Test Cases for the Poor* (London: Child Poverty Action Group, 1983).

26   M Sunkin, 'Conceptual Issues in Researching the Impact of Judicial Review on Government Bureaucracies' in Hertogh and Halliday, n 21 above, 65–9; M Hertogh and S Halliday, 'Judicial Review and Bureaucratic Impact in Future Research' in Hertogh and Halliday, n 21 above, 274–6.

analogy of an interaction between physical objects, one active (the law and the courts) and the other passive (the decision-maker). Interpretivists, by contrast, understand impact as a process in which both the agent and the target of influence play an active part. The concept of causation underpinning the interpretivist approach is obviously more complex than that underpinning the positivist approach. But both approaches necessarily assume that the impact of judicial review can be separated out from the impact of the various other influences to which decision-makers are subject. Under either approach, identifying the particular causal contribution of judicial review is bound to be difficult, and this problem represents one of the most important limitations of impact research.

A final methodological point concerns the aim of impact research. Reports of impact research are often presented as essentially descriptive. However, to the extent that the researcher begins with an assumption about the purpose of the arrangement being studied, and the aim of the research is not to test the validity of that assumption, the results of the research will not be purely descriptive. Sometimes the researcher's aim may be more explicitly prescriptive. For instance, if the researcher assumes that the purpose of judicial review is to promote good decision-making and the research suggests that it does not have this effect, this conclusion may be used as the basis for proposals for reform of the law in some way. In fact, impact researchers are not always as clear as they might be about the aim of the research.

12.2.3 The concept of impact

Another important preliminary point concerns the concept of impact, which is much more complex than might at first appear. There are various dimensions of this complexity:

- *The agent of impact*: Here we can distinguish between courts, tribunals, ombudsmen, internal review and complaint mechanisms, auditors, parliaments and so on. We could further distinguish between courts exercising judicial review jurisdiction and courts exercising appellate jurisdiction. So far as appeals are concerned, we can distinguish between appeals to courts and appeals to tribunals (that is, merits review). The distinction between judicial review and appeals is important because, for instance, the typical result of a successful judicial review application is remission of the decision to the decision-maker for reconsideration, but the typical outcome of an appeal is substitution of a new decision. As already noted, most of the available impact research focuses on judicial review.[27]

- *The 'target' of impact*: We can distinguish, for instance, between legislators (primary and delegated),[28] ministers of state, policy-makers and managers, 'front line' decision-makers, and tribunals.[29] It is easy to see how differences between the various types of target might affect impact. For instance, most front-line decision-makers are subject to the jurisdiction of the ombudsman,

---

27   For a report of a study of the impact of ombudsmen investigations in the Netherlands, see M Hertogh, 'Coercion, Cooperation and Control: Understanding the Policy Impact of Administrative Courts and the Ombudsman in the Netherlands' (2001) 23 *Law and Policy* 47. Concerning UK Social Security Appeal Tribunals see N Wikeley and R Young, 'The Administration of Benefits in Britain: Adjudication Officers and the Influence of Social Security Appeal Tribunals' [1992] *Public Law* 238, 250–62.

28   Recall that one of the techniques identified by Harlow (n 22 above) for neutralising the impact of adverse court decisions was changing the law.

29   For a study of a tribunal see G Richardson and D Machin, 'Judicial Review and Tribunal Decision-Making: A Study of the Mental Health Review Tribunal' [2000] *Public Law* 494. For a study of the impact of judicial review on an internal review mechanism see Sunkin and Pick, n 17 above.

but tribunals are not. Distinguishing between policy-makers and front line decision-makers is important because the impact of law on bureaucratic behaviour is often mediated through materials and training programs prepared by senior bureaucrats for the guidance of those at the coalface.[30] At the Commonwealth level, superior courts, such as the Federal Court, are subject to judicial review. One would intuitively expect the impact of judicial review on senior judges to be very different from its impact on junior bureaucrats with no legal training. The impact of 'appeals' to the Federal Court from the AAT (which are a form of judicial review) might be different again. And so on.

- *The medium of impact*: Here we can distinguish[31] the impact of an agent of review, such as judicial review by a court, from the standards which the various agents enforce (such as the rules and principles of judicial review). For instance, the research conducted by Creyke and McMillan[32] is primarily concerned with the mechanism and outcomes of judicial review, while other researchers have given more attention to the rules and principles of judicial review.[33] Yet other research, as we have noted, focuses on the impact of individual court decisions.

- *The path of impact*: Some research focuses on what might be called 'direct' impacts, such as changes to the decision being reviewed (for example, Creyke and McMillan) or to the law.[34] Other research is more concerned with indirect impact, for instance on the decision-making 'culture', or on 'styles' of decision-making. Another concern is with impact on attitudes towards administrative law and agencies of review. This theme is common in the sort of anecdotal accounts referred to in 12.2.2, and there has been at least one more systematic study in which public servants were asked what they thought about various agencies of impact. The opinions expressed were surprisingly favourable and supportive.[35] However, the significance of such results is unclear, if only because words are so much cheaper than deeds.

- *The context of impact*: Two points deserve to be made about context. The first is that impact is dynamic, not static. For instance, it may vary over time. Research into the impact of judicial review on an internal review mechanism within the UK social security system showed that its influence was greatest soon after the mechanism was established, and waned later.[36] Conversely, we might expect the impact of an agent (such as judicial review) to change as the agent itself changes. Recall (from Chapter 2) the significant changes in judicial review law and institutions in Australia since the mid-twentieth century. Impact might also vary according to the nature, size and functions of the target.

The second point picks up on one of the most persistent themes in the empirical literature about judicial review, namely the interaction between various influences and pressures to which decision-makers are subject. Researchers characterise judicial review as a legal influence and

---

30   For a discussion (based on case studies) of the role of 'soft law' in this context see L Sossin, 'How Judicial Decisions Influence Bureaucracy in Canada' in Hertogh and Halliday, n 21 above. See also M Loughlin and P M Quinn, 'Prisons, Rules and Courts: A Study of Administrative Law' (1993) 56 *Modern Law Review* 497.

31   In principle at least: doing so in practice may be more difficult.

32   See n 21 above.

33   For example, G Richardson and D Machin, n 29 above; S Halliday, *Judicial Review and Compliance with Administrative Law* (Oxford: Hart Publishing, 2004). (discussed in more detail in 12.2.4.).

34   For example, see the research cited in n 21 above.

35   R Creyke and J McMillan, 'Executive Perceptions of Administrative Law—An Empirical Study' (2002) 9 *Australian Journal of Administrative Law* 163.

36   Sunkin and Pick, n 17 above.

contrast it with various non-legal influences and pressures with which it may compete or at least be in tension. For example, in their research on decision-making by mental health tribunals, Richardson and Machin discuss the interaction of legal requirements and medical considerations.[37] In that context, medical considerations are a formal component of the decision-making process, but other influences (such as time pressure, budgetary constraints and productivity demands) may be informal. The basic point is that the impact of judicial review will necessarily be affected (either positively or negatively) by the operation of other influences on decision-makers. When a decision-maker is subjected to conflicting pressures, they may react by yielding to one rather than the other, or by trying to accommodate them in some way. Because of their superior authoritative status, legal requirements will, in principle at least, trump most other influences. In practice, however, non-legal influences may prove stronger.

This way of thinking about impact illuminates at least two important aspects of administrative law. An argument sometimes used to justify limitations on the tort liability of public authorities is the fear of 'overkill'. The idea is that, in reaction to the possibility of incurring legal liability, authorities may engage in 'defensive' behaviour, the prime purpose and motivation of which is (negatively) to reduce the risk of liability rather than (positively) to promote the purposes for which their powers were conferred. This idea recognises the potential conflict between various pressures on decision-makers—in this context, two legally derived pressures, rather than one legal and the other non-legal. Another aspect of administrative law illuminated by noting the various pressures on decision-makers is captured in the idea of 'deference'. Throughout this book we have discussed various rules and principles designed to limit the control exercisable by reviewing bodies over decision-makers. For instance, courts are relatively unwilling to review decisions on questions of fact; and the concept of '*Wednesbury* unreasonableness' signals the caution courts exercise in reviewing policy decisions. One way of understanding the concept of deference is in terms of recognition that decision-makers are subject to various influences, and that they need to be given a certain amount of freedom to decide how to balance the demands of those various influences off against one another.

- *The nature of impact*: A final complexity we will note relates to the decision-maker's reaction to the impact. This may take various forms, such as enactment or amendment of primary or delegated legislation, creation of or changes to 'soft law', initiation of or changes to decision-making procedures or practices, 'cultural change' or changes to attitudes, and so on.

Enough has been said to indicate the difficulty both of conducting impact research and the need for care in drawing firm conclusions from it.

12.2.4 Hypotheses about the impact of judicial review

As we have already suggested, because of the methodological and conceptual complexities of impact research, and the fact that the available body of such research is small and likely to remain so for the foreseeable future, the best way of using it is as a source of testable hypotheses about impact.

---

37   See n 29 above.

This is the approach taken by Halliday in his study of the impact of judicial review on homelessness decision-making by various local authorities in the UK.[38] According to Halliday, his research supports the following hypotheses:

1   The more public decision-makers know about administrative law, the greater its impact will be. This hypothesis raises the issue of how knowledge of administrative law is communicated to and disseminated among decision-makers and agencies. This was one of themes investigated by Creyke and McMillan in their research into executive perceptions of judicial review,[39] but the results leave many questions unanswered.

2   The more conscientious decision-makers are about applying their legal knowledge to the performance of their functions, the greater will be the law's impact. To be legally conscientious is to be motivated to obey the law. Competing demands on decision-makers—such as the need to keep within a budget—may weaken this motivation if those demands conflict with the requirements of the law.

3   The greater the 'legal competence' of decision-makers, the greater will be the law's impact. 'Legal competence' is a complex concept. Essentially, it refers to the ability to apply legal knowledge in such a way as to produce legally compliant outcomes. This may not merely involve mechanical application of legal rules to the facts of individual cases. Much decision-making requires the exercise of discretion, and applying the rules and principles of administrative law properly typically demands a degree of interpretation of the law and individual judgment about its application to the particular case.

4   The less competition there is between law and other influences on the behaviour of public functionaries, and the stronger the law's relative influence, the greater will be its impact. Halliday relates the law's strength to the ability of courts to enforce administrative law. He concludes that law is relatively weak because there is little that courts can do to ensure that decision-makers comply with orders made and rules laid down in judicial review proceedings.[40]

5   The clearer and more consistent the law is, the greater will be its influence on behaviour. Halliday argues that administrative law is 'riven by competing priorities'[41] and sends out mixed messages to public decision-makers. This partly explains why its influence is often weak relative to other demands on decision-makers.

6   The more 'authoritative' the agent of impact, the greater its likely impact.

7   The more publicity the agent of impact and its activities receive, the greater its likely impact.

We have stated these hypotheses in simplified form, and readers are encouraged to refer to Halliday's book for a fuller account of the research and of these hypotheses. Notice that the hypotheses make

---

38   See n 33 above.

39   See n 35 above, 174–80.

40   The importance of this factor is illustrated by a study of the major role played by US federal courts in 'reforming' the prison system (M M Feeley and E L Rubin, *Judicial Policy-Making and the Modern State* (Cambridge: Cambridge University Press, 1999). A significant part of the story is that courts not only laid down standards for the running of prisons, but were also actively involved in ensuring that the standards were implemented. In effect, the courts in these cases operated as multi-functional regulatory agencies, setting standards for the performance of public functions, and monitoring and enforcing compliance with them.

41   'Values' in the terms of the discussion in 12.1.

relative rather than absolute statements about the impact of administrative law. Notice, too, that they are relevant not only to understanding the role of institutions (such as courts and tribunals), but also to that of rules and principles of administrative law as such.

Furthermore, they are relevant to understanding not only why decision-makers fail to comply with administrative law, but also conditions that are likely to promote compliance. In terms of law's impact, understanding compliance is at least as important as understanding non-compliance. In any well-functioning legal system, most people comply with the law most of the time. Judicial review (like other forms of enforcement) is a mark of non-compliance—of the pathology of the legal system, if you like. Whatever the impact of judicial review and other enforcement mechanisms on the decision-making process, it is perhaps unlikely that they hold the key to explaining whether and why most decision-makers comply with administrative law most of the time or to promoting legality in decision-making. Studying what decision-makers do is likely to provide much more illumination than studying what enforcement institutions do. The role of such institutions in promoting compliance with the law is likely to be quite small.

Although other impact researchers have not, explicitly at least, followed the same methodology as Halliday, various other hypotheses can be extracted from their work. These include:

1   The impact of administrative law may vary as between different types of rules. For instance, it has been suggested that procedural rules are likely to have more impact than rules concerning the substance of decisions.[42] Other issues that have been identified concern the relative impact of 'bright line' rules as opposed to more abstract 'principles', and the effect on impact of the clarity of the pronouncements of courts, tribunals and other agents of impact.[43]

2   The more personal experience a decision-maker has had of judicial review, the greater its likely impact on that decision-maker's behaviour. This hypothesis indirectly raises a general issue about the frequency of use of the various accountability mechanisms we have surveyed in this book, including judicial review. In general terms, the impact of any particular mechanism is likely to be related to the frequency of its use—both absolute and relative to potential. This matter has not been the focus of much rigorous investigation. In the 1990s, path-breaking research in England provided the first systematic analysis of numbers of judicial review claims and their distribution across various areas of government activity.[44] In Australia, publicly available statistics provide some useful information. For instance, annual reports of the AAT tell us the total number of applications and their distribution across various areas of government activity (8.4). From a report by the Australian National Audit Office (ANAO) we know that in 2009–10 'customers requested reviews of, or appealed, 194 000 decisions' made by Centrelink officers.[45] A significant proportion of these decisions would have been formally reconsidered by the original decision-maker at the request of the customer. More than 60 000 were internally reviewed by an authorised review officer; and more than 11 000 went on appeal to the Social Security Appeals Tribunal, of

42   Sunkin, n 26 above, 54–6. But see Richardson and Machin, n 29 above, 506–8, 514.

43   We might say that this hypothesis concerns the ideal 'form of law'. Instrumentalist discussions of this issue include R Baldwin, 'Why Rules Don't Work' (1990) 53 *Modern Law Review* 321 and *Rules and Government* (Oxford: Clarendon Press, 1995), Ch 6; J. Black, '"Which Arrow"? Rule Type and Policy' [1995] *Public Law* 94.

44   L Bridges, G Meszaros and M Sunkin, *Judicial Review in Perspective*, 2nd edn (London: Cavendish, 1995).

45   Auditor-General, *Centrelink's Role in the Process of Appeal to the Social Security Appeals Tribunal and to the Administrative Appeals Tribunal* (Audit Report No 16, 2009–10).

which 54% were affirmed. About 2300 proceeded to the AAT and 18% of these were affirmed; 27 were further appealed to the Federal Court, which found in favour of the applicant in three cases. By themselves, however, such statistics tell us little.

We may reasonably speculate that relatively few of the decisions that could, in principle, be challenged result in activation by the affected person of one or other of the mechanisms we have discussed. For instance, the number of formal reconsiderations and internal reviews of Centrelink decisions may seem large, but has to be viewed in light of the fact that Centrelink delivers services to about 6.5 million people a year, and makes many millions of decisions. On this basis, we might further speculate that, in any one year, most Centrelink decision-makers will have relatively little experience of the reconsideration and review processes. There is some careful and valuable empirical research that explores the reasons why relatively few people adversely affected by decisions about housing the homeless, made by two English local authorities, took advantage of the possibility of an internal review.[46] Possible explanations include ignorance of the existence of the internal review mechanism, scepticism about its integrity, a perception that it is too 'rule bound', 'applicant fatigue', and 'satisfaction' with the decision even though adverse. However, the authors of this research scrupulously explain its limitations, and many questions remain unanswered about the extent to which accountability mechanisms realise their potential in terms of frequency of use, let alone in terms of impact.

3   Negotiatory and investigatory complaints procedures are likely to have more impact than adjudicatory procedures.[47] The underlying idea here is that decision-makers are more likely to understand what the law requires of them if they are involved in some sort of dialogue with the complainant and the complaint-handler about resolving the complaint. It is hypothesised that the impersonal and adversarial nature of judicial review militates against such dialogue.

The important point for present purposes is not whether these hypotheses will be shown to be true, either generally or in relation to particular public functions or functionaries. Rather it is that because they are themselves derived from careful empirical observation of public decision-making processes they provide valuable and reliable starting points for thinking about when administrative law is likely to have greatest impact and about how its impact might be increased, if this is thought desirable.

So, by way of conclusion to this section and to the book, how should we answer the second question posed at the beginning of this chapter: what does administrative law achieve? From an instrumental perspective, the best answer would appear to be that we know too little about its impact to do more than venture provisional hypotheses. One such hypothesis about judicial review, which finds some support in the available evidence, is that it is more effective as an accountability mechanism than as a regulatory tool. If correct, this would provide further justification for our decision to use accountability and the legal approach as the main framework for this book. In any event, the distinction between the legal and the regulatory approaches to administrative law has proved to be a fruitful basis for exploring administrative law.

---

46   D Cowan and S Halliday, *The Appeal of Internal Review* (Oxford: Hart Publishing, 2003). The authors also provide some information about the motivations of people who sought internal review, and about the role of lawyers in the process.

47   M Hertogh, n 27 above.

Index